Raccoon John Smith

Religion in the South

John B. Boles, editor

All According to God's Plan: Southern Baptist Missions and Race, 1945–1970
Alan Scot Willis

Can Somebody Shout Amen! Inside the Tents and Tabernacles of American Revivalists
Patsy Sims

Episcopalians and Race: Civil War to Civil Rights
Gardiner H. Shattuck Jr.

A Genealogy of Dissent: Southern Baptist Protest in the Twentieth Century
David Stricklin

God's Rascal: J. Frank Norris and the Beginnings of Southern Fundamentalism
Barry Hankins

The Great Revival: Beginnings of the Bible Belt
John B. Boles

Politics and Religion in the White South
Edited by Glenn Feldman

The Roots of Appalachian Christianity: The Life and Legacy of Elder Shubal Stearns
Elder John Sparks

Serving Two Masters: Moravian Brethren in Germany and North Carolina
Elisabeth W. Sommer

When Slavery Was Called Freedom: Evangelicalism, Proslavery, and the Causes of the Civil War
John Patrick Daly

William Louis Poteat: A Leader in the Progressive-Era South
Randal L. Hall

Raccoon John Smith

Frontier Kentucky's Most Famous Preacher

Elder John Sparks

THE UNIVERSITY PRESS OF KENTUCKY

Publication of this volume was made possible in part by a grant from the National Endowment for the Humanities.

Scholarly publisher for the Commonwealth,
serving Bellarmine University, Berea College, Centre College of Kentucky, Eastern Kentucky University, The Filson Historical Society, Georgetown College, Kentucky Historical Society, Kentucky State University, Morehead State University, Murray State University, Northern Kentucky University, Transylvania University, University of Kentucky, University of Louisville, and Western Kentucky University.

Editorial and Sales Offices: The University Press of Kentucky
663 South Limestone Street, Lexington, Kentucky 40508-4008
www.kentuckypress.com

Frontispiece: Portrait of Raccoon John Smith engraved by John Sartain, taken from John Augustus Williams's *The Life of Elder John Smith* (1870).

Maps by Dick Gilbreath

09 08 07 06 05 5 4 3 2 1

Library of Congress Cataloging-in-Publication Data

Sparks, John, 1961-
Raccoon John Smith : frontier Kentucky's most famous preacher / John Sparks.
p. cm. — (Religion in the South)
Includes bibliographical references and index.
ISBN-13: 978-0-8131-2370-7 (hardcover : alk. paper)
ISBN-10: 0-8131-2370-4 (hardcover : alk. paper)
1. Smith, John, 1784-1868.
2. Disciples of Christ—Clergy—Biography. I. Title. II. Series.
BX7343.S78S63 2006
286.6'092—dc22 2005022924

This book is printed on acid-free recycled paper meeting the requirements of the American National Standard for Permanence in Paper for Printed Library Materials.

Manufactured in the United States of America.

Member of the Association of American University Presses

To
J. D. and Rosie Rice, for Kristi
Claude and Eveline Johnson, for Joshua
Roger and Kathy Blair, for Matthew
Lon and Dusti Meek, for Austin
Roger and Dareatha Murphy, for Rhonda
Chuck and Kim Castle, for Danielle
Tony and Jackie Fitch, for Lauryn
Butch and Ann Conn, for Kelly
Willard and Lynn Collins, for Amber
Sheila, for the small one we never even had the chance to name
And to all who have ever known a similar loss—

Take heed that ye despise not one of these little ones; for I say unto you, that in Heaven their angels do always behold the face of my Father which is in Heaven.

—Matthew 18:10, King James Version

Training myself in stoical fortitude, I might accept the prospect of my own death with a measure of equanimity. It is the death of my neighbor's child which I refuse to accept.

—Peter Berger,
Questions of Faith: A Skeptical Affirmation of Christianity (2004)

As I in hoary winter's night stood shivering in the snow,
Surprised I was with sudden heat which made my heart to glow;
And lifting up a fearful eye to view what fire was near,
A pretty babe all burning bright did in the air appear;
Who, scorchèd with excessive heat, such floods of tears did shed
As though his floods should quench his flames which with his tears were fed.
Alas, quoth he, but newly born in fiery heats I fry,
Yet none approach to warm their hearts or feel my fire but I!
My faultless breast the furnace is, the fuel wounding thorns,
Love is the fire, and sighs the smoke, the ashes shame and scorns;
The fuel justice layeth on, and mercy blows the coals,
The metal in this furnace wrought are men's defilèd souls,
For which, as now on fire I am to work them to their good,
So will I melt into a bath to wash them in my blood.
With this he vanished out of sight and swiftly shrunk away,
And straight I callèd into mind that it was Christmas day.

—Fr. Robert Southwell, S.J.,
written in the Tower of London, 1595,
while awaiting execution

Contents

Acknowledgments

I would like to express my appreciation to the following individuals, whose advice and/or assistance I found invaluable in bringing this work to completion: James Tramel of the Words'n'Stuff Book Store of Van Lear, Kentucky; Karen Daniels, Patricia Patton, Esther Titlow, Lee Pack, Mary Ann Runyon, Gail Spradlin, and the rest of the staff at the Johnson County Public Library at Paintsville, Kentucky; Doris Nolan and Jessie Boyd and their coworkers at the Mount Sterling–Montgomery County Library, Mount Sterling, Kentucky; Brenda Vance and her staff at the Bath County Memorial Library, Owingsville, Kentucky; Charles Heaberlin and Philip Dare of the Bosworth Library at Lexington Theological Seminary, Lexington, Kentucky; Sharman Hartson and her coworkers at the Disciples of Christ Historical Society, Nashville, Tennessee; Sondra Roberts and Nancy Bormes along with the rest of the staff at the Prestonsburg Community College Library, Prestonsburg, Kentucky; Brandon Cowles of Brownsville, Kentucky, Garry Watkins of Leitchfield, Kentucky, and Mark Hogan of Lindseyville, Kentucky, of the Green River Association United Baptist "family"; the succession of librarians and archivists with whom I have corresponded over the years at the American Baptist Historical Society, Rochester, New York; the staff of the Kentucky Historical Society, Frankfort, Kentucky; and fellow medical technologist and Kierkegaard reader Janet L. Johnson of Endicott, Kentucky, for aid in acquiring periodicals, volumes, "minute" pamphlets, documents, and photographs vital to my research, by purchase, borrowing, gift, and interlibrary loan. Many thanks to Rev. E. K. and Phyllis Parker of the Disciples of Christ and Dr. James Stephen Wolfgang, religious scholar and member of the Church of Christ, all of Lexington, Kentucky; Mrs. Anne Frye Caudill, widow of the respected Harry M. Caudill, formerly of Whitesburg, Kentucky, and now of New Albany, Indiana; John and Kim Price Short of Waco, Kentucky; and the many members of Christian Churches and Churches of Christ with whom I have been acquainted over the last twenty-odd years in Johnson, Martin, Floyd, and Pike counties, Kentucky, for their input (in several cases asked for, in many more over the course of my ministry volunteered quite vigorously) on doctrinal and practical issues within the Stone-Campbell movement.

Also, thanks to Dr. Lanier Smythe of Suffolk University, Boston, Massachusetts, and Dr. George Schweitzer of the University of Tennessee at Knoxville for their personal perspectives on the life and work of the late Dr. Richard Marius, an honest historian and the most godly, religious, and inspirational unbeliever that I have ever read. To Dr. John B. Boles of Rice University, Houston, Texas, and Dr. Douglas Foster of Abilene Christian University, Abilene, Texas, for reading the primary draft of this manuscript and offering valuable criticisms and suggestions for its improvement. Likewise to Carol Jones, able successor to Micah Taul in the office of Court Clerk of Wayne County, Monticello, Kentucky; Dr. Glen Taul of Georgetown College, Georgetown, Kentucky; regional historian Edward R. Hazelett of Paintsville, Kentucky; Durbin D. Feeling, Cherokee scholar and linguist of the University of Oklahoma, and Sky Campbell, webmaster of the Cherokee online community *Cherokee-Online.com*; the members of the Yahoo.com Eastern Kentucky Williams Genealogy Message Board; Carl and Hester Murphy Bowling of Van Lear, Kentucky; Jeanne Cobb, of Bethany College, Bethany, West Virginia; B. J. Gooch of Transylvania University, Lexington, Kentucky; the Appalachian scholar Krista M. Loyd of Prospect, Kentucky; Dr. S. Brian Stratton of Alma College, Alma, Michigan; Judges James Trimble, William B. Mains, and Beth Lewis Maze, and Courthouse Security Officer Melinda Melkulcok, of the Menifee County Courthouse, Frenchburg, Kentucky; Jennifer Patton of the First Christian Church, Monticello, Kentucky; B. K. Allen of Central, Kentucky; Bob Sloan, of Morehead, Kentucky; and cartographer Dick Gilbreath of Lexington, Kentucky.

Preachers are often fond of both politics and swooping declarative pronouncements, even while denying an affection for either. Mea culpa. However, my tendency toward the latter vice at least has been curbed herein by the skillful copy editing of Derik Shelor of Shelor & Son Publishing, Greenville, South Carolina. Many thanks to Derik both for his honing and pruning of my grammar and his challenges to me for the clarification of my thoughts. I must also extend my warmest gratitude and best wishes to the staff and staff emeriti of the University Press of Kentucky, who have borne with me for the past several years: Joyce Harrison, Gena Henry, Ann Malcolm, Nichole Lainhart, Leila Salisbury, Allison Webster, Wyn Morris, Mack McCormick, Stephen Wrinn, Teresa Collins, Robert Brandon, Melinda Wirkus, Richard Farkas, Danielle Dove, Jim Russo, John F. Ziegler, Jennifer Peckinpaugh, and Holly Goddard Jones.

And finally, my most sincere gratitude goes, once more, to my wife, Sheila, and to my daughters, Sarah of Morehead, Kentucky, and Amie at home, for their tolerance toward my efforts to complete a second book after I swore I'd never undertake such a daunting project again. I'll not make any such promises in the future. I reckon you can't really trust a preacher at all.

Introduction

FROM THE PAPERS OF ONE STILL LIVING

In frightful inner suffering I became an author.
—Søren Kierkegaard

Elder John Smith, early nineteenth-century minister of the United Baptists and the Disciples of Christ in Wayne, Montgomery, Bath, and Scott counties, Kentucky, and Audrain County, Missouri, is said to have hated his popular nickname "Raccoon John" almost as badly as Lincoln despised being called Honest Abe. All historical figures seem to be surrounded by their own set of myths, though—some created for them by others but many created by their own actions—and neither man could truly be separated from his title however much disdain either entertained for his distinctive appellation. Both men received their nicknames from popular reactions to their own words and characteristics and both used their monikers as political tools to promote their images. And even as the words "Honest Abe" today conjure up visions to nearly all Americans of a stovepipe hat, chin whiskers, homespun wit, and a tall, lanky, self-made fatherly figure whose leadership and martyrdom won the Civil War for the North and abolished slavery, so does the name of Raccoon John Smith—to those acquainted with his life and work—evoke images of a coonskin cap, a rapier sense of humor, a fierce ultra-American backwoods independence, and an utter commitment to "primitive," "non-creedal," "pure" Christianity.

Needless to say, though, Raccoon John was and is no national figure on par with Lincoln. Until Louis Cochran published the historical novel *Raccoon John Smith: A Novel Based on the Life of the Famous Pioneer Kentucky Preacher* in 1963, the preacher's name had become largely unknown outside Kentucky, except within that branch of Protestantism known originally as the Campbell or "Current" Reformation and which exists now in three fairly distinct entities: the Christian Church (Disciples of Christ), the Christian Churches/Churches of Christ (Independent), and the "a cappella" Churches of Christ (these latter in half a dozen or so factions distinguishable from one another by only very small points). Of course, each major faction in which the Campbell movement presently exists always has claimed Raccoon John for its own, but despite these groups' little wars which have led to their separations, and their present differences with one another, they have managed to maintain something of a union on an entity that many other major American religious denominations have lost: a picture of one of their early fathers, as it were, not just as a name in a dusty textbook whose life and mindset are now mere anachronisms, but as a man they want to emulate, whose spirit and ideals still embody their own self-perceptions, the backwoods bulldog of Alexander Campbell's reformation of Christianity who braved personal tragedy and harsh persecutions from bigoted, creed-bound denominationalists to proclaim and promote the pure Gospel of the New Testament. In the writings of the descendants of the original "Current" Reformers this image of Raccoon John Smith has thus endured, with the side benefits of making him the most celebrated preacher in Kentucky during its frontier era and one of the most famous of all American ministers.

This perpetuation of Raccoon John's name and fame—from James Mason's early contemporary reports of his activities in Alexander Campbell's *Christian Baptist* newspaper, the writings of succeeding periodical reporters and editors in the subsequently established Campbell media tradition, and the intriguing biography (or more accurately, hagiography) penned within two years of his death by his friend and coworker John Augustus Williams, to the Fess Parker/Davy Crockett/Daniel Boone image of him conjured up by Louis Cochran in the 1960s and the later and more scholarly but still subjective biographical/religious studies of Everett Donaldson—presents both a great advantage and a great disadvantage to readers of Kentucky, American, and Appalachian history. On one hand, the memory of one of Kentucky's great native sons, or, as Louis Cochran wrote, one who had at least the elements of greatness, has been preserved and perpetuated, and the mere effort at preservation is of itself worthy of notice and honor. On the other, not a single one of the extant accounts of Raccoon John's life and work, with the possible exception of a small article by one Albert Allen that appeared in 1857 in *The Christian Baptist*'s successor, *The Millennial Harbinger,* and which has been all but forgotten since, were written primarily either as history or biography. They were penned, as has been noted, by authors in the media tradition of the Campbell Reformation, and however honest these men tried to be, their main purpose was never the objective recounting of history. They wrote primarily to reaffirm their own faith and that of their targeted audiences within the Campbell media circle, always with an eye to the prospect of using Raccoon John's story to gain proselytes from other Christian groups. Though they may never have realized it, accurate history was actually a secondary consideration to them, and thus they would sweeten or even omit altogether any data they discovered which might cast doubt on the cause they espoused, in the misguided but quite sincere notion that they were doing the right thing. Of course, as religious writers they cannot be singled out for any special blame in this regard. A great many denominational advocates of every stamp have been guilty of no better and no worse, and those brave enough to become exceptions to the rule often suffer for it. One example is the case of Mormon Fawn Brodie, whose carefully researched, well-written exposé of the life and career of Mormon founder

Joseph Smith, *No Man Knows My History,* earned her quick excommunication and much vitriolic criticism from her church. But to return: while these writers give us a mighty picture of Raccoon John the Reform Crusader, and in one form or another pay fair lip service to Raccoon John the American, Raccoon John the Kentuckian, and Raccoon John the Frontiersman, to a great extent Raccoon John the Man remains in the shadows, unexamined.

It must be admitted, a part of our lack of knowledge about Raccoon John may be blamed on the old preacher's own doing. Nearly all the accounts of his life both in biographical and historical-fictional form were based more or less on his own recollections, which, along with some additional information from two of his daughters and only a few other sources, were compiled, organized, and published in *The Life of Elder John Smith, with Some Account of the Rise and Progress of the Current Reformation.* In the last decade or so of his life, Raccoon John had been asked numerous times to pen his own autobiography, much as early Kentucky/Illinois Methodist worthy Peter Cartwright had done in 1856, but he had always demurred, and in the end Williams spearheaded the Smith biography project with Raccoon John's ostensible full approval and cooperation. One difficulty occurred, as it nearly always does in similar situations, because of Raccoon John's quite human propensity to reinterpret those early events of his life which he was able or chose to remember, in the context of later occurrences and influences. The corpus of historical/biographical studies of the life of Harry Truman, for example, amply demonstrates the fallacy of basing historical works on one individual's subjective recollections, however honest and candid he or she may attempt to be. In his own writings and those prepared under his direct supervision, Truman ignored or denied some events that actually happened and, most particularly in his old age, even recalled a few that *didn't* happen. His history was thus left for biographer David McCullough to tidy up, and he did so in the monumental, definitive *Truman* while diminishing neither Truman's character nor greatness as a man or president. Likewise, had John Augustus Williams intended to write an objective, critical biography of Raccoon John Smith, there were other sources against which he could have checked many aspects of the old preacher's story. Although researching many of them would have incurred him much more time, travel, and proportionate expense than would a similar endeavor in modern times, one of the easiest for him to examine, and certainly to quote directly, was the Allen article, with which, as a *Harbinger* subscriber, he must have been familiar. But of course Williams never really intended his story to be objective, and thus his interpretations of Raccoon John's recollections have come down to us as the sole, unqualified account of How Things Happened.

Too, not surprisingly, Williams appears to have added to the confusion by sweetening and editing, in the true style of a denominational advocate, even those recollections about which Raccoon John may have spoken candidly. Several times within *The Life of Elder John Smith* but especially in the earlier chapters Williams words certain events very unusually and apparently very carefully, and when the circumstances in question are checked against other sources—again for only one example, the Allen article, which exhibits enough small inconsistencies and shifts of emphasis between it and the Williams account of the same events to make even a novice historian notice the differences—it begins to appear as if Williams was trying not to lie but at the same time not telling the complete truth, and this had to have been a conscious effort on his part. In addition, he omitted more than one crucial event from the latter part of his story altogether. Notwithstanding, Williams is indeed candid in certain places where one would least expect it, certainly in many instances more so than succeeding denominational authors of the same tradition; he preserved an immense body of recollections from a pioneer preacher which, although subjective, allow many of the definitive aspects of Raccoon John's character to shine through. And a good number of his criticisms of non-Campbell denominations, particularly the Baptists with whom Raccoon John grew up and later continually quarrelled, hit nearer the mark than any of the most popular spokesmen of these religious bodies will ever admit. These attributes in and of themselves make *The Life of Elder John Smith* both a religious and a Kentucky classic.

Unfortunately, Williams's carefully sweetened truths and half-truths became the outright misunderstandings and then the misrepresentations of not only some, but all, Campbell Reform historians and biographers to follow. That which Williams delicately implied often evolved into their own bold statements, resulting only in further obfuscation of many of the most essential events in Raccoon John's life. Within a decade of his death at age eighty-three in 1868, Raccoon John the Man was already well on his way to being lost in Raccoon John the Image, and the old preacher seemed to become more and more two-dimensional with each retelling of his story. Thus it happened that, in the days when Fess Parker represented frontier American male virility to moviegoers and television watchers nationwide, Raccoon John was finally given his coonskin cap—and in great measure his current folk status—by Disciples of Christ historical novelist Louis Cochran. So far as historical fiction goes, Cochran's *Raccoon John Smith: A Novel Based on the Life of the Famous Pioneer Kentucky Preacher* is no better and no worse than most examples of the genre. Claiming to be "essentially a true story" with an extensively researched background, it mixes a very rough outline of a few mostly garbled historical facts with a bit of popular romance and passes itself off as an accurate portrayal of the past. In *Raccoon John Smith,* the Good Guys are good (Raccoon John perhaps should have been sporting a white hat rather than the coonskin cap which, by the way, neither he nor the real Daniel Boone were in the habit of wearing),[1] the Bad Guys are truly, mindlessly evil and pleasantly easy to hate, right and wrong are presented as obvious, clear-cut choices, and the protagonist triumphs, well, triumphantly. And there's nothing wrong with historical romances as such either, so long as their fans are able to maintain a degree of perspective. We can all do with a bit of brain candy now and again, in moderate helpings. What's truly unsettling about this book and its popularity is the degree to which it has been accepted both in the Campbell media circle and beyond as a record of actual facts. Raccoon John Smith history and genealogy webpages can be found all across the Internet, dotted with quotations from the book and references to it. Authors of independently published local histories from the regions where Raccoon John grew up and lived, particularly Wayne, Clinton, and Montgomery counties in Kentucky, often accept its claims implicitly and draw on it liberally; although Everett Donaldson hesitated to quote Cochran directly in his own Smith biographical writings and always admitted the novelist's fictionalizations when he did so, Cochran still managed to color the Donaldson biographies by way of Donaldson's references to these local works. Even Dr. Leroy Garrett, without question one of the most competent and knowledgeable historians of the Campbell Reformation and whose sketch of Smith in his excellent *The Stone-Campbell Movement* pinpoints the one definitive factor of Raccoon John's life more accurately than even he could have known, worked up a Hal Holbrook–style one-man dramatic characterization of Raccoon John based largely on it. He played Raccoon John for churches, Sunday and Bible schools, and other denominational functions, perhaps unconsciously borrowing anecdotes from Cochran for use in *The Stone-Campbell Movement* in the process, and the novel wound up being reprinted by the same publisher as that of Garrett's legitimate history. Strangest of all, Cochran could in fact write seriously and fairly objectively when he wished, as he and his wife, Bess, aptly proved with their own subsequent legitimate account of the Stone and Campbell heritage, *Captives of the Word.* But Raccoon John's nonexistent coonskin cap, his horses "Zebulon" and "Saul," his sister "Fancy Mae," his daughter "Eliza Blaze," both his supposed positions and those of the mindless Bad Guys (i.e., his doctrinal opponents), and many other of Cochran's Fess Parker–influenced speculations, are now more real in the public consciousness than John Augustus Williams's more accurate biography. In essence, what the recent writings of N. Brent Kennedy have done for popular perceptions of the southeastern American mixed-blood group known as Melungeons—and perhaps similarly to what Kentucky writer Chris Offutt did for himself at the expense of his hometown with his recent memoir *No Heroes*—Louis Cochran effected for the Kentucky Disciples and Churches of Christ a generation ago with the writing and publication of *Raccoon John Smith.*

Most warped of all, though, is the hyperbole given the romance angle of the story in the novel's Popular Library version. Picturing a youthful and valiant Raccoon John on its front cover, once in a Patrick Henry–style give-me-liberty-or-give-me-death pose with fashionable colonial-era clubbed hair against a backdrop of burning houses, and once with a voluptuous southern belle, his left arm around her waist and his right hand positioned suggestively on her right upper thigh, the paperback lets that second portrait serve as the perfect complement to the promotional blurb on the reverse side:

> **A powerful man thrust his way into the vast, unknown wilderness**
> Carving his way through the savage wilderness of the American frontier, John Smith, a lanky young preacher in a coonskin cap, comes face to face with hatred, hardship and eternal damnation.
> A man who knows no earthly fear, Raccoon John Smith finds he must stand alone against the horror of savage Indians, the bitterness of beaten pioneers, and the greed of men who have come to wreak havoc in an untamed land.[2]

And so on, ad nauseam. Even if Raccoon John Smith was worthy of all the hate heaped upon him by Cochran's Bad Guys, if that piece of bombast and the supporting artwork, which would have been considered pornographic in the rural South of Raccoon John's time, do not expiate him for at least some of his sins, there is no justice in the universe. Seriously, though, one cannot help but imagine that Cochran was embarrassed by the book's paperback treatment, and that Raccoon John himself would turn over in his grave if he could know that his story had been thus served up to the public. Of course, this eventual romantic fiction/paperback fate has been shared by nearly all American frontier historical figures with any degree of notoriety (and who have the reputation of being anywhere near handsome or beautiful), but in most other cases the influences of the historical fiction are counterbalanced by serious, objective, and even critical historical studies fairly easily accessible to the interested reader. Parson Mason Weems's stories of George Washington are entertaining and a few of them have become popular American folktales, but no one takes them seriously and perhaps no one ever did. Better historical accounts of Washington's life were available both before and after Weems's publication, and his accuracy and integrity were called into question from the first. Even Daniel Boone, whose character has probably figured in as many or more historical novels, television dramas, and movies as all other American historical personages put together, has had his critics among objective historians. So far as we have examined the extant literature, Raccoon John, as can be seen, has had no critics at all, objective or otherwise.

Which brings us to another extremely important point. Since Raccoon John's ministry involved so much verbal sparring with other, non-Campbell religious denominations, should not alternate, critical viewpoints of his life have been left behind by representatives of those faiths? The answer, with two exceptions which will be noted soon, is a decided, and surprising, no. *Everybody* who knew him apparently had something good to say about Raccoon John, even those who believed personally that he was in error. The Baptists as a denomination were given a hard ride in the early writings of Alexander Campbell and many of the scribes who followed in his footsteps, including John Augustus Williams, Louis Cochran, and Everett Donaldson; of modern writers in the tradition Leroy Garrett and Richard T. Hughes, to name only two, are much more inclined to be objective. Baptist apologists, prominent among them the Kentuckians John Henderson Spencer and Thomas M. Vaughan and in more recent years Harold G. Sanders, James E. Taulman, and Chester Raymond Young, have often exhibited a great deal of antipathy toward Campbell in return. Other than the late James E. Tull, whose essay on Campbell in his *Shapers of Baptist Thought* actually appears to be more charitable toward the reformer than the historical writings of some modern scholars in the Campbell tradition such as Hughes, and Jesse Fletcher, whose recent paper "The Separation of the Campbells from the Baptists" points out the faults and failures of both Campbell and his Baptist opponents in roughly equal measure, few Southern Baptists have managed to write about Campbell even with John Augustus Williams's degree of objectivity and introspection, much less Leroy Garrett's. Sanders's blustering declaration that "Baptists trained all the guns in their arsenal on Alexander Campbell. They blew him out of the saddle,"[3] is, in and of itself, worthy of publication right alongside *Raccoon John Smith*'s paperback cover blurb. However, so far as I can tell, only one of these men, James E. Taulman, ever penned an ill word against Raccoon John Smith personally. In his essay "Baptists and Disciples of Christ" in the Kentucky (Southern) Baptist Convention's bicentennial historical collection, *Baptists in Kentucky 1776–1976,* Taulman speculated that "although [Smith] had a keen wit, it at times [*sic*] was consumed by his own brashness."[4] This is indeed an understandable charge, but somehow the verbal picture (found in the same volume) of a Christian minister being blown out of the saddle possesses a kind of consuming brashness all its own.

Of the older Baptist historians, J. H. Spencer, though observing that Raccoon John was instrumental in building up the churches of east-central Kentucky's North District Association "until about 1830, when having fully imbibed Campbellism, he set about perverting them," noted otherwise merely that Raccoon John was a man "whose education was very limited, but [that] he possessed a strong intellect, was a keen wit, and was a vivid humorist," and that he "soon became a leader among the Campbellites of Kentucky . . . lived to a ripe old age, and maintained an excellent character among his people" (ellipsis added).[5] Thomas M. Vaughan, whose father, William, was a preaching colleague of Raccoon John and was given especially harsh treatment by both Alexander Campbell in *The Christian Baptist* and John Augustus Williams in *The Life of Elder John Smith,* had only slightly more to say, and that with nowhere near the vitriol one would expect from a man whose parent had been so ridiculed by Smith's own biographer:

> Conspicuous among the propagators of Campbellism in northern and central Kentucky was John Smith, familiarly known as "Raccoon" John Smith. He was very active in visiting various associations and whenever any proposition was made to withdraw from the Campbellites he opposed it with might and main. His object, we have no doubt, was

> to hold the churches together as long as possible to increase the number of their proselytes, for he and his colleagues knew that when the lines were distinctly drawn, it would be a difficult matter to break the ranks. Smith was a good man, we have no doubt, and we cannot say aught against his moral character; but he had gone over completely to Alexander Campbell, and he was a most zealous champion of the new order of things. He was very successful, too, and it is a great pity that he ever imbibed his heresies.
>
> [William] Vaughan and he ever since their first acquaintance had been on terms of personal friendship. Although they were now as wide apart as the poles on various points of doctrine, there was nevertheless the best state of feeling between them. In fact they were a good deal alike in some respects. They both possessed strong native intellects, with a good share of wit that sometimes seemed to border on roughness. They would occasionally indulge in passages of wit at each other's expense; sometimes one would have the advantage and then the other.[6]

Thus stands the body of available information about Kentucky's most famous frontier preacher. The Leroy Garretts are few and of few words; the Louis Cochran fans are many and vocal; much of what John Augustus Williams, and especially Albert Allen, recorded lies buried under hyperbole and has been only partially excavated by Everett Donaldson; and J. H. Spencer, Thomas Vaughan, and many of their disciples are curiously reticent. Paul Tillich once noted that great historical figures inevitably appear to us not as they actually lived, but rather in the light of their impact on those around them, and this has certainly been the case with Raccoon John. The problem now, of course, is that Raccoon John's life is remembered as a near-epic frontier myth, almost exactly as the Hatfield and McCoy feud came to be recalled and understood by nearly everyone, even its participant families, before Altina L. Waller's 1980s research brought the conflict and its causes back into the realms of reason, logic, and, most importantly, accuracy.

This is not to say that myths, as such, are entirely bad either. As Richard Hughes has pointed out in his most recent scholarly work, *Myths America Lives By,* myths are not necessarily stories that are patently untrue. They are rather tales that speak of meaning and purpose, and for that reason they speak truth to those who take them seriously. But as writer, scholar, Reformation historian, and onetime eastern Tennessee Baptist pastor Richard Marius once remarked, to use history to buttress some present idealism is often to sanitize the past, to convert it to romance, and to grant to it also a stifling power over the present; and Hughes makes a strong case for the idea that the historical mythology of the United States, treated after this fashion, has been a wellspring both of great good and great evil to American citizens. The mythic figure of Raccoon John Smith is certainly no more than a minor individual reflection of these larger American myths addressed by Hughes, but it nonetheless carries within it just as much power to stifle thought when believers absolutize it as religious truth. To paraphrase Marius once more, to make such a man as Raccoon John Smith speak to our times is often to fail to hear him speaking in his own.

At any rate, I should note that there does exist at least one more partial exception to the litany of consistent praise for Raccoon John, and with a certain degree of chagrin I must admit that I wrote it myself. In tracing the ancestry of rural Appalachian and especially eastern Kentucky Churches of Christ back through the United Baptists to the early North Carolina Separate Baptists in my previous work, *The Roots of Appalachian Christianity: The Life and Legacy of Elder Shubal Stearns,* I penned a brief, and, as I frankly stated in the writing itself, inadequate, biographical sketch of Raccoon John that looks at the old preacher with a more critical eye than either Spencer, Vaughan, or any subsequent historian of the Baptist persuasion has ever given him. While my primary theories and arguments concerning Smith's character, his life-shaping experiences, and his work remain essentially unchanged, the Smith biographical sketch's necessary brevity makes it come off much harsher than I would have liked—especially since, as I hope I made clear in the work, my own respect for Raccoon John, though necessarily qualified, is and will always remain firm. Though I am a Baptist preacher and possessed of all the faults and foibles associated with that status, including a rabid and well-nigh irrepressible argumentative and exhortatory streak that glares even through my prose, this esteem is not that of a sectarian advocate intent on using, or misusing, Raccoon John's story to gain proselytes for or lead converts out of any particular religious sect in either the Baptist or Reform tradition. I'd like to think it is objective, but none of us can be truly and completely nonbiased about our subjects of interest; as Marius again wrote in the preface of his highly controversial and provocative mid-1970s biography of Martin Luther, history is, inevitably, partly autobiography. And so to paraphrase Bret Harte's Truthful James, I would rise to explain my earlier remarks about Raccoon John, and state my case for adding another biography to the corpus of Smith research and literature—in plain language.

My first interest in Raccoon John Smith was by no means intellectual, but very personal and well-nigh intuitive as faith itself. I can't remember exactly at what date I first became acquainted with his story, but I know that it was sometime after I was converted as a teenager to Christianity and not long before I began preaching (or trying to), and at this writing that's been more than a quarter century ago. I was introduced to the old preacher in perhaps the usual fashion, the Cochran novel, and to an adolescent who had cut his teeth on television images of Fess Parker and John Wayne and at the time was heavily influenced by the great spate of historical movies and miniseries produced in the wake of the U.S. Bicentennial celebrations, the book was an exciting read that only confirmed a teenage bookworm's opinion that there were giants in the earth (and especially in Kentucky) in the old days. In spite of the novel's pronounced anti-Baptist and pro-Campbell stance, it struck a chord with me, not only from the fact that Raccoon John had come originally from the same Baptist religious tradition I had known all my life, but because he had proven himself willing to stand on the ideal of a pure Christianity that superseded denominational boundaries and was based on the New Testament alone. But the glorious pioneer America that had produced men like Raccoon John Smith was long gone; we were now living in degenerate times and the Lord was sure to come back in the year 2000 (or before, since the calendar was off by a few years), so I suppose I felt that they just didn't make 'em like tough old Raccoon John anymore.

In other words, my attitudes about life and God were roughly typical of a young Christian in just about any southern conservative evangelical or fundamentalist Protestant group, including those numbered within both the Baptist and Campbell traditions, then and now (with, of course, the exception of the outdated obsession with the year 2000). In those days, the brand-new reality into which my conversion experience—the New Birth in Christ of the many generations of my Appalachian ancestors—had grounded me had made the King James Bible inerrant, the worship services at the little church up the left fork of the creek a taste of heaven on earth, and the pretty young sisters across the aisle no longer objects of youthful lust but sanctified and delicious prospects for holy and vigorous matrimony a year or two down the road (that is, if there was any actual difference between the two latter perspectives). Armed with that indescribable feeling of security and promise and that sweet sense of reality, I thought I could tackle anything. When I first read Cochran I knew literally nothing beyond my own tradition, but perhaps it was just as well. Had I been exposed to any book that disagreed with or even questioned my sense of reality at that point, I would have accused its author, with all the pathetic confidence of adolescent backcountry fundamentalism, of not living right, and of having too much education for his (or her) own good.

In keeping with my religious roots, I chose a trade (in my case, in the healthcare industry) rather than opting for the schooling and the career of, as Sinclair Lewis once playfully phrased it, a Professional Good Man. I was raised, so to speak, to disdain both educated and paid ministers, and one of the old preachers I heard frequently when I was growing up always insisted on pronouncing the word "seminary" as "cemetery." Though my attitudes about the efficacy of ministerial education have changed much over the years, I can honestly say I've never regretted my decision; but still, I have a feeling that it's put me into a context that a conventional paid pastor or hospital chaplain might find unfamiliar at times. As an unpaid cleric, I've served churches as pastor and assistant pastor, officiated at baptisms, weddings, diaconal and ministerial ordinations, and funerals, and steered congregations through internal difficulties as well as "trouble in the association," all in circumstances normative for most of my preaching colleagues. I've sensed the presence of the divine mirrored in the joyous born-again experiences of others, and on occasion have been very nearly drowned during baptismal services by new converts who became physically and quite zealously happy in the wake of the event. But I've also had my idealism pierced, as every pastor must, by finding out that Christians are often capable of blaming a great deal of nonsense on their perceptions of both the Deity and the direct impressions of the Holy Ghost, and learning that the mundane wisdom of experience must often prevail over the otherworldly sort in dealing successfully with either a congregation or an association.

At a small, rural hospital a night-duty laboratory technician, especially one with a strong back and the mind generally believed to accompany it, sometimes gets to wear several different hats during the course of a shift at work, and consequently I've also experienced a good many things that perhaps even hospital chaplains rarely get to see from such a close vantage point. I've watched a sweet, genuinely pious old lady suffer for weeks and finally die with a gangrenous limb because her simple mountain Holiness principles required that she keep her body intact for the Glorious Resurrection, and then thought of both God and Guy de Maupassant as I subsequently red-bagged her viscera for the incinerator; it turned out that the pathologist had neglected to put them back in her abdominal cavity after the autopsy, and the mortician who came to get her refused to take them. I've steeled myself to draw blood from the webbed hand of a wailing child predestined to a brief life with a misshapen mind in a misshapen body simply because it had the ill luck to be the product of a depraved, incestuous coupling. I've stood by, as helpless as Camus's Father Paneloux, as an eight-month-old baby died of a rare heart defect that precipitated a cardiac arrest and was diagnosed only in the morgue after the code team finally gave up and managed to coax its grief-shattered mother into surrendering its little gray body from her arms. Later on, after I learned the autopsy results, I realized with the deepest chill I have ever known that the cause of its fierce, heartrending cries before slipping inexorably into respiratory failure was a crushing pain in its tiny chest, neck, and arms that it never deserved, could not comprehend, and was unable to communicate any other way than with a baby's tears and wails. I've mourned silently, like Job's three friends, with a distraught grandfather actually attempting to follow the advice of Job's wife (to curse God and be struck dead that he might be spared the pain of his bereavement), for some reason just not feeling up to trying to answer his question, *"Why?* Why didn't the son of a bitch take *me* instead?" And I've participated with other elders and deacons in the ritual anointing[7] of a lovely young woman undergoing intensive chemotherapy for an inoperable brain tumor, rejoiced with her and her family at the news that the malignant growth had disappeared between sequential CT scans taken before and after the ceremony, and a few years later wept with her parents and loved ones as I officiated at another rite after complications from the chronic leukopenia and thrombocytopenia that she had developed from the chemotherapy killed her.

Many years ago my great-grandfather, who had lost several of his own children due to diphtheria and pneumonia before the days of antitoxins and antibiotics, enjoyed a scandalous notoriety locally for having uttered the blasphemy, "Well, I say *damn* a God that'd take a child!" and then somehow having escaped being struck down immediately by a Divine thunderbolt. Many years before that, and a continent away, Søren Kierkegaard wrote that, to a child, it seems that man and God can play together; to a youth, it seems that an emotional passion for God could bring perfect union with him; but to an adult, God is infinitely vast, and the distance between man and God infinitely great. I can't say that I agree entirely with religion and political science scholar Alan Wolfe's recently stated opinion that Kierkegaard is largely missing in American religion, though. I think he is certainly correct in stating that there ought to be more brooding going on. But be that as it may, after twenty-odd years of crash divinity courses during the daytime in church and associational business meetings, and past midnight, not in any ivory tower but in one of concrete and steel within which a great deal of laughing and crying, loving and hating, and living and dying are going on simultaneously, I've come to understand not only how and why my great-grandfather felt as he did, but that, at least in terms of the concepts of God that I'd been taught in my youth, Kierkegaard was right. Now when I try to look back at my own faith, my reality, and my world when I first cracked the pages of Cochran's *Raccoon John Smith,* they appear almost as shallow as the lack of conviction that preceded my belief, as circumscribed as the binding over the novel itself, and as innocent of knowledge as that eight-month-old child was to the cause of the terrible hurt in its little chest that it couldn't get Mommy and Daddy to make go away. But that memory of reading Cochran's novel simply sticks in my mind with a touch of bittersweet, an enjoyable adventure tale lapped up once a long time ago by a naive, green-as-a-gourd kid who started trying to preach with all the dignity that eighteen years of age could give him and whose bright, eager eyes I wonder if I'll ever see in the mirror again.

Over the years of trying to process what I'd been taught with what I could see daily, align seemingly disparate elements of my life and faith both inside and outside the church, and get a handle once again on my perspectives, I sought comfort in trying to learn a little of the theology and philosophy that I'd bypassed for biology and chemistry in college, as well as attempting to search out the history of my people's particular expression of Christianity. Perhaps needless to say, in the former pursuits I concentrated on theodicy, the branch of theology that defends belief in the goodness of a personal God in the face of the existence of evil and suffering. While my realization was reinforced that many if not most of us depend, perhaps even *must* depend, on faith in God to withstand our tragedies and bereavements, as I pondered the problem over and over again I came to understand finally that any theodicy in and of itself stands or falls only subjectively, on the level of the individual; our very best objective human rationalizations of the Divine involvement in evil and suffering often might as well be categorized as *theidiocy* instead.

Out of the latter endeavor, though, was born *The Roots of Appalachian Christianity,* and here my interest in Raccoon John Smith, as the best-documented nineteenth-century minister who had been raised in the tradition I studied, was rekindled in an objective way. I used both the Williams and the Donaldson biographies as references to cross-check other data dealing with the same events, that is, certain details of the evolution of the religious movement that Shubal Stearns initiated in backcountry colonial North Carolina into one of its (at least) seven modern manifestations in central and southern Appalachia. In this context I had the opportunity to compare Cochran with both Williams and Donaldson, then all three with Baptist histories and documents, lesser known period writers such as James Mason, Albert Allen, and James Challen, and finally with Leroy Garrett's comprehensive history of the Reform movement and Richard Hughes's analysis of that movement's perhaps most vocal and certainly most reactionary modern manifestation. In this work I've already given their studies of Raccoon John Smith what I hope is a qualified and objective, if brief, critical analysis. But this research taught me two things, neither of which I would have accepted completely without having become involved with them personally as a healthcare professional, a minister, and a writer. The first of these was that Raccoon John Smith's life choices were, to a greater extent than any biographer has heretofore examined (other than as validations of the writers' own doctrinal claims), visceral responses to soul-shattering tragedies of the type many Christians prefer to dismiss in fretful complacency and uneasy confusion until such events come home to them. Second, and as a consequence, I learned that, regardless of what theologians or denominational apologists of any breed might claim, our search for truth and our perceptions of any figure of the past are only improved and made fuller by the competent use of historical and textual criticism. It's only natural that the Campbell Reform movement should commandeer Raccoon John's story to further its own ends, and the old preacher definitely set the precedent himself when he submitted his oral memoirs for John Augustus Williams's editing and embellishment. But no historian, especially one working backward only to prove a preconceived supposition, can truly understand Raccoon John as a Reformer without being familiar both with the griefs that dogged him all his life and with the type of Baptist that he was before he ever aligned himself with Alexander Campbell.

Although Smith had a more or less successful high-rank ministry with the Kentucky Baptists of his early years, he and his preaching colleagues represented neither the Williams characters of John's own hindsight nor the Cochran creations based on them, or for that matter any conventional modern Baptist stereotype recognizable except perhaps by "Old Time" Baptists and active preachers in the varied Baptist denominations and subdenominations themselves. But when historical criticism, based on detailed study of both Baptist and Reform chronicles, plus a time line of the occurrences of Smith's personal tragedies and careful consideration of the doctrinal and practical mindset that was normative in the early nineteenth century for most Kentucky Baptists, is applied to Raccoon John's story, the reasons for both Williams's inconsistencies, from which history has only been further misinterpreted by all the writers who have used him as a guide, and the Baptists' curious reticence toward their famous and formidable old adversary suddenly become clear. The key can be found only in the political context shared by both early Kentucky Baptists and early Reformers, to which neither side dared admit; now extant in its old form, so far as I know, only in the Old Time Baptist subgroups of the central and southern Appalachian mountains and perhaps in the most conservative modern elements of the Campbell movement as well, it has nonetheless remained almost as much a Baptist staple as immersion, and it carries overtones that are often surprisingly similar to those of the political environment generated by Southern Baptist fundamentalists in the late twentieth century to wrest control of the Southern Baptist Convention. In addition to providing a compelling political explanation of how and why Baptists are Baptists and Disciples are Disciples, Raccoon John's real-life adventures reveal his own previously unexamined but crucial role as the unintentional negative catalyst for the organization and self-definition of central Appalachia's best known traditionalist Old Time Baptist subgroups.

In short, when an attempt is made to tell the Raccoon John Smith story objectively, a much more comprehensive picture of the life of the old Reform warrior and his well-deserved place in Kentucky, Appalachian, and American history comes to light. The Williams biography, taken at face value, is good and effective denominational propaganda, but when it is viewed critically along with the other extant data of Raccoon John's life, the sum total may prove to be the most telling account, for both better and worse, of what it is like to be a popular rural southeastern American preacher.

Thus I hope that this book may serve readers of the present era, not only in the Campbell Reform tradition but in that of the Baptists as well as Christians generally, as food for thought. Opponents of historical and form biblical criticism in either group might profit by examining the evolution of Raccoon John's own fairly recent life story from fact to myth and recognize that humans, even deeply religious ones, are indeed prone to mythmaking despite their best intentions; if a story such as Raccoon John's can be mythologized even while its main character was still living, and that by men and women genuinely committed to maintaining that which they perceived to be Christian truth, it might follow that academic biblical scholarship may not be, after all, a tool of Satan designed to lead unwary souls to hell, but a discipline to draw on, grow by, and utilize for the benefit of the Christian faith. Both liberal and conservative adherents in the modern variants of the original Campbell Reform movement should remember the price that one individual paid in order to help establish their faith traditions in Kentucky, and ponder the eventual mellowing and hardening of their faith itself into varying liberal, conservative, and ultraconservative expressions. Each modern Stone-Campbell group has appropriated its own variant of the often contradictory teachings of Barton Stone and Alexander Campbell, as well as the developed Raccoon John myth, for its own benefit. Modern Baptists and other evangelicals might like—or not—to reconsider the current moderate-fundamentalist Southern Baptist feud in light of one of its historical precedents, the battle between the Regular and Separate Baptist factions of the Kentucky General Union back in a day when *both* warring factions were unquestionably biblical literalists and inerrantists, and ponder how much, really, organized evangelical Christianity as a whole has progressed since that time. Further, any contemporary Christian group imbued with a reforming zeal of its own, be it of a fundamentalist, conservative, moderate, or liberal cast, should be reminded that there has been a dark side to each and every religious reformation attempted thus far, and should consider that its own actions could make the principles it advocates, whether they are closer to absolute truth than any other doctrinal stance or not, fare no better and no worse than did the Campbell movement of one hundred seventy-odd years ago. But in the midst of all the contention and the violent rush of ideas that the late twentieth and early twenty-first centuries have brought us, Christians, or simply believers in God, of any sort might do well simply to pause for a moment in their brief sojourn between two eternities, remember an era of long ago and yet not so far back, take a look at the causes that drove one poorly educated but well-read, contemplative but ambitious, joke-loving but grief-wracked Kentucky Christian to embrace a new religious movement so thoroughly as to find his deepest fulfillment in being its veritable poster figure, and meditate upon the paths through which their own beliefs, whatever they are, could be and are leading them.

And so finally, to provide a completely honest explanation for why I've written this retelling of Raccoon John Smith's life, I must admit the correctness of Tillich's maxim about historical figures and confess to a certain kinship with Louis Cochran, disappointing as his storytelling accuracy has proven. In the afterword to his novel, Cochran stated that in his youth, "Due probably to the influence of Christian parents who reveled in the stories of [Smith's] mighty feats and witticisms, the name of the great pioneer was as familiar to me as the names of my own playmates."[8] But if Cochran thus in a sense grew up under Raccoon John's impact, so did I. Not in the same way, of course; Cochran simply may never have gotten over the image of Raccoon John as the tall-tale hero of his childhood, which could account for his novel's construction more than any other factor. Perhaps the human psyche needs figures like that, and I'm placing myself in the role of arch-villain in bursting the bubble. I might even burst others, and be considered even more of a villain, by concentrating on the subjective elements that make Scripture real to individual believers rather than the defense of the propositional doctrinal statements of any denomination, including my own. But that risk notwithstanding, the fact remains that learning about the difficulties and the griefs of Raccoon John Smith's life, the frequently extremely hard choices he was forced to make, and especially his courage have compelled me to grow both as man and minister; and I marvel at the relevance of his story to the study even of modern southern religion and indeed to my own ministry and that of the men and women with whom I work most closely. I honor Raccoon John's memory and his rightful place in Kentucky, Appalachian, and American history.

In so doing, I hope to prove myself worthy of a title that the aged Raccoon John himself, as a guest of honor at a Missouri public doctrinal debate between his younger colleague Moses Easterly Lard and Methodist minister W. G. Caples, gave to Caples on the first day of the debate. John Augustus Williams describes the events as follows:

> It was, perhaps, just after the close of . . . morning discussion, that [Smith] remarked to the brethren who were standing around the rostrum, that he had concluded to start home the next day. Mr. Caples, who was nearby at the time, gathering up his books and papers, and who was himself a reputed wit, reached over and touched the venerable man, saying:
>
> "Mr. Smith, don't leave until this debate is over, for I want to take a 'coon hunt with you."
>
> "That would just suit me," replied Smith, putting his palsied hand on Caples's shoulder, "for when I go a 'coon hunting, I always like to have a good dog along."[9]

I'm not a bit too proud to borrow the imagery, and thus in his own words, it would just suit me to be Raccoon John Smith's coon hound. The reader is cordially invited to follow the track with me, but be warned: this coon run goes over steep mountains and through dark, forbidding valleys, and it doubles back many times through a forgotten, brush-covered cemetery dotted with some pitifully small graves. To those who can't stand up to that kind of terrain I apologize, and remind them that Cochran's book is still available at their local bookstores or libraries as a more easily digestible, if sweetened, alternative; but outside the pleasant perspectives of denominational and sectarian worldviews, hagiographies, and historical novels, for better or worse, this is just the way the trail runs.

CHAPTER 1

The Fatherland

If Climacus' character must have seemed odd to anybody not knowing him well, it was by no means inexplicable to someone with a little knowledge of his earlier life. . . .

—Søren Kierkegaard

The headwaters of Virginia's historic James River lie to the central west of the state near its border with present West Virginia, in the county of Botetourt. In the latter days of British colonial rule in America and the early years of the United States, Botetourt County, Virginia, comprised not only its own present territory but that of several later counties created from it both in Virginia and West Virginia, and in this mountainous region we must begin our story of the life of Raccoon John Smith with the little information we have available on the early lives of his parents. Like so many of our forefathers, both Raccoon John and his first biographer, John Augustus Williams, are simultaneously the bane of and inspiration to genealogy researchers; either Raccoon John himself didn't consider information about his ancestry sufficiently important to pass along in any great detail to Williams, or Williams didn't think any further information Smith might have given was significant enough to save for his readers. Nonetheless, the facts are relevant, as all aspects of the context into which an individual is born usually are.

John's father, George Smith, originally Schmidt, was the only son (though perhaps not the only child) of German immigrants who had come to the territory of the upper James about 1735 and who had died when George was a young boy. This is the sum total of the information found in Williams's *Life of Elder John Smith* about George's parentage, although some modern family researchers have augmented and embellished the details with their own speculations. Some claim that George himself was born somewhere in the German states about 1732 and made the sea voyage to America with his parents; others, that he was born in Pennsylvania or Virginia, and that he was the son of one Johann (or Johannes) Schmidt. Either of these claims could be true, or false. The most likely probability is that George Smith was born in America sometime between 1735 and 1740 of immigrant parents who had come to live in one of the new backcountry German settlements, such as Strasburg on the lower Shenandoah River in Virginia, or others in the upper Shenandoah and

Greenbrier valleys which lie in fairly close proximity to the headwaters of the James. When his parents died—whether from some contagious disease or as a result of one of the sporadic but bloody attacks by Indians that were a fact of life in the area until the early 1790s, we can never know because Williams does not tell us—George became a ward of one of the several Buchanan families living on the upper James, and who eventually gave the small Botetourt County community of Buchanan, a few miles back from the river, its name.

In the days George Smith grew up and for all too many generations afterward, an orphan "bound" by a county court to a family willing to pay for his or her upkeep in exchange for unpaid labor had no easy lot. Most colonial parents took "spare the rod and spoil the child" brutally literally even for their own offspring, and the old Appalachian comparative expression of an individual's bad luck, "about like a bound-boy at an ass-kicking," was too painfully true a comparison in most cases of indentured servitude. Nonetheless, in later life George seems to have had nothing but good to say about his former master, whom we know now only as Colonel Buchanan. Writing in the stilted prose of the post–Civil War era, John Augustus Williams recorded that this Colonel Buchanan was both "a master and friend" to the orphan boy, and that he "faithfully brought [George] up to usefulness and virtue."[1]

But if indeed Colonel Buchanan was the kindest and therefore the most unusual of masters, George Smith is recorded to have grown up to be the most unusual of frontier mountain men. He lived and died in a raw, rough, bloody land where epidemics as well as Indian attacks could and did wipe out entire settlements in almost an instant and where a belief in predestination—the idea that something or some One was in control over and above all the dread and uncertainty that made up daily life on the frontier beyond the Blue Ridge—was a virtual necessity for a settler to enjoy any small peace of mind whatsoever. The men and women who comprised the sparse population of the mountain settlements were a contradiction in terms. Their very lives on the danger-ridden frontier instilled in them a nervousness to the point of paranoia, but the coiled springs of tension within were concealed most of the time by an imperturbable mask of nearly phlegmatic calmness. Both these personae, inward and outward, were crucial to these pioneers' survival; weaker men and women either moved back to the eastern settlements with their tails tucked between their legs, if they had the opportunity, or cracked under the strain, died, or got careless and got killed, their scalps decorating the lodges of the natives they were trying to supplant. Perhaps no one historical recollection is as descriptive of the harsh lives of the settlers west of the Blue Ridge in colonial and Revolutionary days as the poignant tale that survives of the one sensual indulgence older married women of the frontier mountain settlements allowed themselves: they loved nothing better than preparing the corpse of a young man dead of natural causes and with no disfiguring wounds for burial, sitting up with the body all hours with rude beef and buffalo tallow lamps and gazing at its unscalped head and figure, shrouded in its linen or muslin "winding sheet" unstained by oozing gore, as the epitome of beauty.[2]

George Smith lived his entire life in the Virginia, Tennessee, and Kentucky backwoods, and he must have had most or all the physical and mental skills necessary for survival in that time and place. He fought Indians when it was obligatory and served one or more hitches in the Revolutionary War, at least as a frontier scout and militiaman if not as a regular infantryman. And if his son John's memories are to be trusted, through all this he remained the mildest, gentlest, and kindest man his children ever knew, a total opposite of the stereotypical frontiersman whose only visible emotion was violent anger. His sons, and daughters too for that matter, were never obligated to call him "Sir," bow to him, or be on their guard in his presence, because his presence was never forbidding. With him they could be, and were, themselves, and they all loved his company. George Smith didn't even use a switch to discipline his children, not because he disagreed with either the injunctions in the book of Proverbs on the subject or frontier mores. It simply hurt him too much to hurt them, and the quiet scoldings he gave his young ones instead often provoked tears simply because they sensed his essential tenderness toward them and felt terribly guilty that they had distressed his mind. Of course, neither John nor any of the other sons were ever perfect angels, and the boys all got into varying degrees of mischief and trouble as they grew up, and after. But they nearly always took pains to hide both misdemeanors and felonies from their good old father, because they regarded hurting him as the most heinous crime of all.

More is known about the family of John's mother, Rebecca Bowen Smith, and in fact more about Rebecca herself. She was born either in Pennsylvania or Virginia about 1747 and spent at least part of her childhood south of the territories of the upper James, on Glade Creek, where her parents cleared and maintained a farm before her father John's death in 1760. Born about 1696, John Bowen was a Pennsylvania native of full-blooded Welsh ancestry. His parents, Moses Bowen and Rebecca Reece, had both come from the Old Country and changed their Welsh patronymics *ap Owen* and *verch Rhys* to the closest English equivalents (any brothers of Rebecca Reece Bowen would have used the masculine form *ap Rhys* and assumed the surname of "Preece" or "Price," but oddly, *verch Rhys* has survived as a given name—*"Vertrice"*—in many rural southern localities). John married Lily or Lillian McIlhaney, daughter of Irish immigrants Henry McIlhaney and Jane McGeehan, in Chester County, Pennsylvania, about 1730. They moved south to the Virginia frontier and raised a family of thirteen tough sons and daughters whose descendants long maintained the Bowen reputation of skill and prowess in frontier survival. Of the branch of the family that ultimately wound up in eastern Kentucky it was often said—sometimes by family members themselves, with a touch of pride—that "All a Bowen ever needed was a dog, a skinning knife and a rifle gun. With [those], he could make it."[3] Many of the Bowen men likewise enjoyed the reputation of being great storytellers, tall tales of hunting and humorous yarns being their specialties, and in his own way Raccoon John Smith would carry on this tradition of his mother's people all his life.

Two of the older daughters of John and Lily Bowen, Nancy and Agnes, married into the Buchanan family in Augusta County, Virginia, from which Botetourt County was formed in 1770. Two younger daughters, Jean (Jennie) and Mary, married Joseph Looney and William Porter, respectively, scions of other families renowned for their pioneering abilities. Two of John and Lily's sons, Reece and Henry, married Smith girls, Levissa or Louisa and Lily, respectively, who appear to have been sisters of George Smith. After his father's death, Reece Bowen moved southwestward and in 1772 became a pioneer settler at Maiden Springs in what was to become Russell County, Virginia, joining other Virginians, including some of the Looneys and Porters, and perhaps more numerous North Carolinans who were escaping the ravages of the Regulators' War in that province, constructing the rude combination cabin-forts that were the only dwellings remotely safe in western and southwestern Virginia at the time. The respect that Reece Bowen gained in the trailblazing of the Russell County area was high; even after the family branched, many members in later generations christened sons after him, and his name is still revered by southwestern Virginia historians and genealogists.

John and Lily's daughter Rebecca, who was among the youngest in this large family, was thus half Welsh, half Irish, and all Celt, and her hardiness through a life of nearly ninety years more than matched the toughness of her brothers. Raccoon John remembered her as having a quick and nervous temper, and thus was more ready to discipline her children by corporal punishment than George Smith ever was, but he also recalled that her anger dissipated quickly and, more often than not, with a touch or two of characteristic Bowen humor. That hard-bitten Celtic sense of humor, and her aggressive temper as well, had both been absolute essentials to her survival in the days of her own youth and young womanhood, though not in ways that John cared to discuss with John Augustus Williams or anyone else. In fact, if, during much of his life, any historian or biographer had penned the paragraph following, the antebellum southern society in which Raccoon John, his brothers, and even his sons lived would have considered it appropriate for any of them to challenge the troublesome scribbler to a duel.

When Rebecca was about fourteen years old, her father having died only recently beforehand and perhaps in some measure because of that tragedy, she married one Jonathan Whitely. He is supposed by family historians to have been either a native Englishman or Ulster Irishman, and perhaps a former British soldier who had been stationed at a frontier outpost somewhere in the Augusta/Botetourt area. The marriage was extremely brief and evidently very unhappy. Whitely left her, moved to York County, South Carolina, and remarried in 1764 to one Katherine Brush who in turn divorced him in 1767 on the grounds of "cruelty." Rebecca's first groom is said by some to have gone home to the British Isles after this second failed marriage, but other records have him returning to Virginia and marrying a third time, to Sarah Cunningham in 1773. A divorce for Jonathan Whitely and Rebecca Bowen has never been discovered in any Virginia court records. Apparently the couple had at least one son, Moses,[4] who may have lived with one of his Bowen uncles in southwestern Virginia, and a daughter, Rebecca, though we cannot say with certainty whether this younger Rebecca belonged to Jonathan Whitely or George Smith. If this whole affair and its eventual resolution appears to us as sufficiently sordid only to have occurred in our own degenerate modern times, we must remember that early backwoods American individuals, couples, and communities often had to exercise their own kind of commonsense law and justice without the benefits of either formal clergy, court niceties, or record keeping. Moreover, if Jonathan Whitely's second wife obtained a legal divorce from him on the grounds of "cruelty," we can hardly expect that Rebecca had fared any better at his hands, although if she had that quick, nervous, and aggressive temperament that the aged Raccoon John remembered it's not that likely that Rebecca ever really let Jonathan Whitely get the best of her. One wonders if he may have departed Virginia for South Carolina with a black eye or two and minus a few of his teeth. It is a testimony to Rebecca's resilience that she could bounce back from an extremely bad marriage and take control of her own life once again. Much the same could be said of a young Philadelphia girl of a generation earlier named Deborah Read, whose own first marriage to a potter named Rogers ended with his departure to the West Indies before she exchanged vows with her better-known second husband, Benjamin Franklin.

But at any rate, by the age of nineteen or so Rebecca found herself completely content to settle down with a mild-mannered, gentle husband rather than a wild and unpredictable one. She seems to have suffered no persecutions whatsoever from either family, community, Church, or State when she remarried to George Smith (whether in legal or common-law fashion, we can't really say for sure) about 1766. Her father had been dead some six years, though her mother and her grandmother McIlhaney were apparently still living, and so many of her brothers and sisters were already married into both the Buchanan and Smith, or Schmidt, families that they may all have served actively as matchmakers for a shy, slow-spoken suitor to a tough, outspoken, and even formidable young Welsh-Irish heiress to the traditions and spirit of princess Eva de Clare. Perhaps most surprisingly of all, Rebecca even named one of her younger sons by George Smith as Jonathan. No more eloquent testimony survives either of Rebecca's grit and backbone, or of George's essential mildness; few women either then or now would dare to name a son by a second husband after a first one, whether he was wild, risky, and just a bit cruel or not, and fewer second husbands would acquiesce to such a christening with anything close to good humor.

However, Jonathan Smith (a preacher like his next-oldest brother John, and incidentally the unknowing victim of a gratuitous, extremely unfair character assassination by historical novelist Louis Cochran that must wait to be explained) was the tenth child of his parents' thirteen, and he was not born until approximately the twenty-second year of their marriage and three years after they had removed from Virginia permanently. All the couple's children older than John were Virginians, and it can be argued that, in a significant sense, much of the entire Smith family's outlook on life was shaped by its collective religious experience in the Old Dominion. This experience was by no means typical for all Virginians or even only those living on the colony's frontiers, but in the Smith family's case it was decisive.

Like the Puritan provinces of New England, Virginia maintained a state-sponsored religious establishment, with its inhabited districts laid off into parishes under the care of formally educated, licensed, and government-approved ministers. Unlike them, Virginia's state faith was the mainline, conventional Church of England, with the reigning British monarch as its titular head and the Archbishop of Canterbury and his subordinate bishops (in the case of all such churches in the colonies, the Bishop of London) as its overseers. Although nonconformist ministers and congregations in various districts enjoyed legal toleration status under Great Britain's 1689 Parliamentary Act for Protestant Dissenters, all Virginia freeholders paid taxes to support the state faith and its rectors, county courts carefully scrutinized nonconformist clergy before granting licenses to preach, and law officers more or less suspiciously monitored all activities at nonconformist meetinghouses. Such was the rule in the coastal lowland or "Tidewater" region of the province, but in outlying areas such as the Shenandoah Valley to the northwest, the New, upper Roanoke, and Dan River valleys to the southwest on the border with North Carolina, and George and Rebecca Smith's home on the headwaters of the James in the Botetourt County wilderness, great latitude was allowed for exceptions. Many settlers there, like the Buchanans and the McIlhaneys, were Scots-Irish; like the Bowens, Welsh; or like George Smith, German, and a great majority had migrated into the western mountains of the Old Dominion from religiously tolerant Pennsylvania. The Virginia colonial authorities accepted the fact that they couldn't make good loyal Anglicans out of all their backwoodsmen, and so as long as the Tidewater could remain under their political/religious domination they were quite content to let dissenters have free rein, within reason, in the backcountry. With the approval of the government, Scots-Irish Presbyterians living beyond the Blue Ridge thus got sporadic visits from itinerant preachers of their persuasion; a group known as Regular, or Particular, Baptists was allowed to spread south from Pennsylvania and worship and proselytize on the lower Shenandoah near its confluence with the Potomac; and in the settled area furthest from Tidewater civilization another group of Baptists, known as Separates, came up from North Carolina and established a strong base in the Dan and New River valleys and at the head of the Roanoke River. There were a few other active groups as well, of course, based on the various old-country faiths of the immigrants.

Of the three groups named, though, the Presbyterians and the Regular Baptists had the most in common. They were both offshoots of the Puritan/Calvinist tradition of the Protestant Reformation (although in the following century some Baptists would begin vociferously to deny this heritage),[5] and as such they shared a common theology in spite of the practical differences that occasionally brought them to harsh words with one another. This theology, which they likewise held in common with the established churches of the New England provinces, was originally part of the first generation of attempts led by men such as Martin Luther, Huldreich Zwingli, and John Calvin to purify or reform Christianity and the institutional Church by emphasizing the direct study of Scripture over the teachings of Roman Catholic tradition. With the passage of time, though, all these initial Reformation thrusts had developed orthodoxies all their own, and the belief shared by the backcountry Presbyterians and Regular Baptists of George and Rebecca Smith's youth, Calvinism, is now perhaps best known in the form of its so-called five points and their famous (or infamous) "tulip" acronym: the total depravity of the human race due to sin, with man's complete inability to save himself; the unconditional election by God of a certain but unknown number of individuals to salvation by grace through his son, Jesus Christ, and the rest of the human race to damnation; the extent of the atonement offered by Jesus's death on the cross limited to that same number of elect individuals; an irresistible calling by the Holy Spirit to repentance and salvation, to these same elect; and the perseverance of the elect in their status of salvation by grace, through earthly life to eternity. None of the five points of Calvinism were understood by John Calvin or his earliest followers except within a theology much broader than a brief listing of the postulates themselves, and this still holds true today for most of their denominational descendants. But the five points did become the hallmarks of Calvinism in all the forms it took, whether articulated in the English Presbyterians' 1644 Westminster Confession or others copied (mostly nearly verbatim) from this document, which included the Congregationalists' or Independent Puritans' 1658 Savoy Declaration and the Particular or Regular Baptists' 1689 Second London and 1742 Philadelphia Confessions.

The main differences between Presbyterian and Regular Baptist Calvinists were in methods of church administration, church-state relationships, and mode and qualification of subjects for the rite of baptism. As bespoke their name, Presbyterians believed that churches should be governed by elected or appointed councils of elders whose authority superseded that of local congregations. Regular Baptists, on the other hand, believed that much, in some cases complete, power should rest in the hands of local churches themselves, as did also the Congregationalists or Independents. But both Presbyterian and Congregational variants of Puritanism accommodated themselves well to become state-established faiths in America, the British Isles, and on the Continent, whereas the Regular/Particular Baptist church had never enjoyed such an opportunity. At least until recently, most Baptist historians have argued that all

Baptists have always believed in the complete separation of church and state, and of course Baptists even as early as the beginning of the seventeenth century advocated this position as a minority dissenting party in Great Britain. But in that day and age, church and state were regarded by many as virtually inseparable, with even most dissenters believing that their own nonconformist positions *should* be state doctrine; and the fact is that several respected Baptist ministers and laymen were involved in the Long Parliament every bit as deeply as the Presbyterian and Congregational parties that supported the English Civil War and the Protectorate of Oliver Cromwell.

As to the questions of baptism and church membership, Congregationalists, Presbyterians, and Regular Baptists all accepted members on their individual professions of faith, but the Presbyterians and Congregationalists carried out the baptismal rite in Lutheran/Calvinist Reformed tradition by sprinkling infants who were under the sponsorship of their parents and godparents. The Regular Baptists insisted on total body immersion, following an individual's own profession of faith, as the only Scripturally valid form of the ordinance. This baptismal position, which in fact had created the Regular/Particular sect when some English Congregationalists borrowed the rite from another, earlier Baptist group that will be mentioned subsequently, probably made for more hard feelings between them and their Puritan brethren than any other. Baptists would not allow unimmersed individuals to participate with them in communion services or any other sacraments; they considered infant baptism a vestige of Roman Catholicism that their Presbyterian/Congregational counterparts had for some indefensible reason allowed to endure, and they held that their own particular view of the rite was entirely Scripture-based. In turn, advocates of infant sprinkling often criticized the Regular Baptists for "cruelty," the reason being that the Presbyterian/Congregational position on the rite softened the most heartless deduced proposition of the five points of Calvinism—one, for reasons alluded to in this work's introduction and which will become even more apparent later, we must now briefly examine: infant damnation.

The Westminster, Savoy, Second London, and Philadelphia Confessions all attempted to soften or at least counterbalance the thrust of the blunt harshness of Calvinism's five points, and John Calvin himself made an extensive endeavor to explain all his propositions both philosophically and practically in his *Institutes of the Christian Religion.* Even so, election, foreknowledge, and predestination were part and parcel of the belief, and in spite of the symbolism of the Bible's Garden of Eden account and the command of Jesus to "suffer the little children to come unto me; for of such is the Kingdom of Heaven," as well as numerous other statements found in the four Gospels, sooner or later Calvinist adherents ran up against the difficulty of explaining the fates of deceased infants in Calvinistic terms as well. If indeed salvation was reserved by grace alone and exclusively for God's predestined elect, under Calvin's principles it stood to reason that some dying before the age of maturity were in this elect family and that some, perhaps many more, were not. And although the "real-life" proof that seems to have been cited by Calvinist ministers for the validity of the doctrine—"that as we saw infants, from their birth, as subjects of pain, anguish, and death, it was unreasonable to suppose [that] a being, infinitely good, would inflict this great penalty on beings perfectly innocent, pure, and blameless; neither was there any way to hope for the salvation of them after death, but through God's electing grace in Christ"[6]—may have been good enough for sermon rhetoric, for most lay Christians this brutal idea was no more digestible or acceptable in that day than it is now. Among other evidence, accused Salem "witch" Rebecca Nurse's forlorn declaration in 1692 Massachusetts that she was as guilty of the crimes for which she had been accused "as the child unborn"[7] makes us wonder to what extent the belief was really held by the general Puritan/Calvinistic laity apart from the times they had to recite their creeds and catechisms.

In fact, even the aforementioned creedal statements used by most eighteenth-century Calvinists in both the British Isles and America all left the issue just a little vague, as if they were paying lip service to those who wanted to take Jesus's pronouncements about children at face value and believe that all persons dying before maturity were de facto in the elect family and thus bound for heaven. Witness the relevant excerpt taken from Chapter X of the 1742 Philadelphia Baptist Confession, which reads virtually identically in the Second London, Savoy, and Westminster Confessions all:

> 3. Elect infants dying in infancy, are (John iii. 3,5,6) regenerated and saved by Christ through the Spirit; who worketh when, and where, and (John iii. 8) how he pleaseth; so also are all other elect persons, who are incapable of being outwardly called by the ministry of the word.
>
> 4. Others not elected, although they may be called by the ministry of the word (Matt. xxii. 14; xiii. 20, 21; Heb. vi. 4, 5) and may have some common operations of the Spirit, yet not being effectually drawn by the Father, they neither will nor can truly (John vi. 44, 45, 65; I John ii. 24, 25) come to Christ, and therefore cannot be saved: much less can men that receive not the Christian religion (Acts iv. 12; John iv. 22; John xvii. 3) be saved; be they never so diligent to frame their lives according to the light of nature and the law of that religion they do profess.[8]

Thus if one wanted to read into these early predestinarian creeds the notion that all persons not surviving infancy were foreordained to be of the elect, they very well could; certainly the only context into which the word "infant" is placed in the four Calvinist confessions named involves election, with "*others not elected*" being decidedly, and very probably purposely, nonspecific. Still, the doctrine in all its ruthless, self-righteous viciousness lay just under the surface even of the most eloquent and philosophical Calvinist statements of faith, and the majority "pedobaptist" branches of Calvinism allowed their laity to cope with the dogma's harshness simply by allowing them this one mental throwback to medieval Roman Catholicism: if parents could get their babies sprinkled, their grief at the loss of a child could be blunted at least a little by the thought that the baby's "original sin" had been somehow washed away by the mediation of a representative of God, the cleric at the baptismal font. No matter that it made no sense in the paradigms of their Reformed faith, or that medieval Roman doctrine on infant baptism, which in the minds of many of its interpreters gave little if any more hope for an *un*baptized baby than nonelection did,[9] seems now to us to be as inhumane in its own way as Calvinism; it was what they and countless generations of their ancestors had been used to, and in a day when most couples lost at least one or two offspring and sometimes more, it was one of the few small, cold comforts for grieving parents in the event of a child's death. But this comfort, such as it was, the Calvinistic Regular Baptist immersionists denied their adherents, and except for the deliberate vagueness about the doctrine of infant election written into the Second London and Philadelphia Confessions, they supplied nothing in its place.

For all that, though, the fatalism of John Calvin's creed was indeed suited to the stark realities of living on the precarious American colonial frontier of George and Rebecca Smith's early married life, both for those who believed themselves to be of the elect and for those who were not so assured. Paradoxically, the idea of existence within a framework where all conclusions were already known and in which any occurrence, no matter how horrible, could be accepted as part of a broader plan that made sense to a higher power may have given the northwestern Virginia frontiersmen a freedom of sorts in and of itself. But there were differing viewpoints. Later on, one of the most notable of these was that of the Methodists, an evangelical minority party within the Church of England who broke with their parent denomination at about the time the American Revolution ended and quickly established themselves as a strong and viable presence on the frontier under the direction of their ultra-autocratic but dedicated first American bishop, Francis Asbury. The Methodists, following the theology of their British founders, John and Charles Wesley, were Arminians (from the name of Dutch Reformed bishop Jacobus Arminius, the doctrinal system's most noted early champion against Calvinism) who believed salvation was a free gift offered to all and conditional only on the individual's acceptance of it. Like their own parent Anglicans as well as the Presbyterians, they too were "pedobaptists," but they had nothing for the proposition of infant damnation from either Catholic or Calvinist perspectives and they often ripped Presbyterian and Regular Baptist preachers to shreds verbally for endorsing it whether their specific Calvinist rivals actually upheld it vocally or not. But on the Virginia frontier of George and Rebecca Smith's early days as a married couple, Methodism, whose tough young "circuit riders" were to play their own part finally in the destruction of the state-sponsored religious establishment in Virginia as well as other former colonies, had not even appeared yet. Nonetheless, in George's and Rebecca's youth there did exist in Virginia a somewhat similar group, of both Baptist and embryonic Methodist heritage and if not outright Arminian very nearly so: the rustic and noisy Baptists known as Separates, operating in the Dan, New, and upper Roanoke River valleys to the southwest of Botetourt County.

Originally a New England entity, the Separate Baptist Church represented a patchwork of influences tacked together during a dramatic religious revival movement, rather than a single Reformation tradition. Its Methodist element came from the emotional, dramatic preaching of the Wesley brothers' colleague George Whitefield, who had turned the state Puritan churches of Connecticut and Massachusetts literally inside out in the 1740s with his outdoor revival preaching stressing a metaphysical, euphoric "New Birth in Christ" as the true sign of an individual's salvation. Like the Wesleys, Whitefield was an ordained Anglican priest, his own particular vocation or "living" consisting in supervising a Church of England–sponsored orphanage in the Georgia colony. All his evangelistic tours were, in fact, taken ostensibly to raise money for this institution. Unlike them, he had definite Calvinistic leanings, which made him acceptable at least initially as a guest speaker in Presbyterian and Congregational pulpits. Still, Whitefield must be described truthfully as being at most a three-point or four-point Calvinist in practice even if he was a five-point Calvinist in belief, one who never completely accepted for practical purposes the doctrines of unconditional election or irresistible calling. Although the great revivalist never really tried, much less succeeded in, supplanting Puritanism with out-and-out Methodism in New England, he did manage to split the state churches in both Massacusetts and Connecticut, causing the formation of "Separate" congregations in both provinces, led mostly by unschooled and unsalaried "farmer-preachers" who more or less aped his dramatic pulpit stylings with a rhythmic, musical, and often nasal "New England Holy Tone" preaching cant of their own.

The Baptist element of this Separate movement originated with a small group in religiously tolerant Rhode Island known as General Baptists, who began to proselytize among the Connecticut and Massachusetts Separates as early as 1742 or 1743. The General Baptists, so called because they also were Arminians who preached a redemption through Christ available to all, having picked up the doctrinal outlook from the Dutch Mennonites who were their own spiritual ancestors, were actually an older presence in both Old and New England than their Regular/Particular cousins. Their first American association, the Rhode Island Yearly Meeting, was organized in 1670, thirty-seven years before the Regular Baptists gathered their own first such body at Philadelphia. The General Baptists gave the Separates the rites of immersion and footwashing and a reinforcement of their favor toward uneducated, unsalaried ministers, but for the most part they failed to draw their proselytes fully into their own associational organization, which maintained a tight, almost Presbyterian-like centralized control over individual congregations. Ironically, most New England Separate Baptist churches eventually united with the Regular Baptists in new associational bodies sponsored by the Philadelphia group and which guaranteed their congregations more autonomy than the General Baptists allowed. Fragments of the Separate Baptist movement later resurfaced in New England, though, in such groups as Benjamin Randall's Free Will Baptists and Elias Smith's and Abner Jones's Christian Churches.[10]

So much has been said here about the birth, growth, and final extinction of the New England Separate Baptists to introduce the fact that the denomination, as it existed in the early 1750s and with most of both its original Separate Congregational and General Baptist influences still completely intact, was transplanted to the backwoods settlements of western North Carolina, South Carolina, and southwestern Virginia beginning in 1755, and was presented not as a religious amalgam but as a unified whole to the settlers there. The primary catalyst for this process was a short, spare, bright-eyed, and passionate little Connecticut Separate Baptist preacher named Shubal Stearns, who got the idea in 1754 that God had laid a "great and extensive work in the west" on his shoulders, and who brought a small following (mostly family members) to the Piedmont area of upland North Carolina in late 1755 to carry it out. It is not our purpose here to rehash historical data that has already been discussed in greater detail elsewhere[11]; suffice it to say for the present that, due to time and chance and some amazingly fortuitous albeit transitory circumstances, Stearns's "great work in the west" proved to be exactly that. Preaching in a loud and extremely melodious variant of the New England Holy Tone, at first with his lieutenant and brother-in-law Daniel Marshall (as well as with Marshall's wife, his baby sister Martha, who was a great singer, prayer leader, and exhorter in her own right) and later with his converts Philip Mulkey, James Read, Samuel Harris, the Lane brothers Tidence and Dutton, the Murphy brothers Joseph and William, and others, Shubal Stearns baptized literally thousands of joyfully born-again Christians on the southern frontier, and within ten years he had made mid-eighteenth century New England Separate Baptist theology and practice a permanent part, and in many areas virtually the standard, of southeastern American Christianity. Even Stearns's own pulpit address was imitated by his followers, and its variants can yet be heard in rural southeastern American churches; indeed, even more than 230 years after Stearns's death, it is still regarded by many southern Appalachian Christians as the only "real preaching" that is done.

Shubal Stearns took his work seriously and tried to give his best, or at least the best he knew, to his new southern converts. Besides bestowing upon them a solid disdain for written creeds, theological systems, and "educated" ministers who dared take "filthy lucre" for their preaching, he gave them footwashing as an essential part of the communion service, his own musical New England Holy Tone, a sense of fervent affection between themselves expressed in frequent handshakes and embraces, and a definite concept of the New Birth in

Christ as the foundation of their lives. He even dealt with the problem of infant mortality in a characteristic Separate-General Baptist way: his believers could take Jesus's pronouncements on children simply for what they said, and in addition take comfort in his "devoting" or "dry-christening" rite in which he offered a prayer of blessing over a young child rather than sprinkling it in baptism. Unlike most of his New England brethren, though, Stearns proved himself to be a great believer in the centrally controlled association system of the old General Baptists, and his converts came to accept authority not from systematic creeds but rather from his own patriarchal figure as leader, or "moderator," of his Sandy Creek Association. At the time of George and Rebecca Smith's marriage, Shubal Stearns's Separate Baptist association stretched across the hill country of central and western North Carolina, western South Carolina, and southwestern Virginia alike, with Stearns himself presiding over it as a benevolent, genial, and much-loved old patriarch and autocrat.

But for various reasons, including both North Carolina's Regulators' War and the dramatic Separate Baptist revival brought northward by Samuel Harris and James Read to the caste-bound Virginia Tidewater, the Sandy Creek Association began to fragment about a year before Stearns's death in 1771. In the southern Separates' process of regrouping, which lasted essentially throughout the Revolution and up to the time of the framing of the U.S. Constitution, the majority followed suit with most of their New England brethren and merged with the Regular Baptists on modified, mildly Calvinistic terms and a watered-down, partial acceptance of the Philadelphia Confession. This allowed Regular Baptist doctrine and forms finally to become the norm for American Baptists generally, although in at least one case southern Separates would not even agree to unite with the Regulars unless they received specific promises that they could continue preaching that Christ tasted death for every individual and not only an elect few. Even then, many still refused to be called Regular Baptists, preferring the title of "United Baptist" in honor of their union with the Calvinists, and a sizable group of emigrants to the new state of Kentucky held out as Separate Baptists until after the turning of the new century. And too, though Shubal Stearns was gone, the influence of the benevolent old despot remained strong. The former Separates' union with the Regulars had caused them to frame Regular-style associational constitutions that ostensibly advocated local church autonomy after the Regular form, but many ex-Separates still held fast not only to Stearns's mild Calvinist, nearly Arminian doctrinal mix, his New England Holy Tone, and his worship modes, but his General Baptist associational outlook and his example of leadership as well. They proved entirely willing to let their church associations regulate and control the affairs of their individual congregations, and often regarded the elected moderators of these organizations as miniature replicas of old Stearns himself: a succession, as it were, of rustic backcountry patriarchs who were the preservers, guardians, and enforcers of their Gospel and their traditions.

And so between George and Rebecca Smith's marriage about 1766 and their son John's birth in 1784, whites were slowly but surely conquering the trans-Appalachian region, and a distinct American culture, which was to include among its religious attributes the decline of the Church of England, the competition for souls between Calvinistic and Arminian Protestant groups, the union of the two variants of Virginia Baptists as a denominational entity, and even a brief flourishing of skepticism in some quarters, was taking shape; and only as microcosms within these greater processes can George's, Rebecca's, and their son John's lives be understood. We know nothing of the religious backgrounds of either the Smith or the Bowen families before George and Rebecca's marriage. Guesses could be hazarded that George Smith came of Lutheran stock, his benefactors the Buchanans were Presbyterian, and the Bowen family at the very least knew about the Regular Baptist faith, which had established strong bases both in Wales and Pennsylvania at an early date. The Bowens, living south of the upper James, may even have been exposed to the preaching of Shubal Stearns's disciple William Murphy on the headwaters of the Roanoke in the 1760s, but there is no direct evidence to indicate it. John Augustus Williams says simply that George and Rebecca were members of "the strictest sect of the Virginia Baptists,"[12] that is to say, the Regulars, but he relates no information even as to how they came under Baptist, as opposed to Presbyterian or other sectarian, influence in the first place. Despite Williams's and/or Raccoon John's lack of detail, though, it is almost certain that George and Rebecca were converted, immersed, and admitted to membership in the Regular Baptist church through the ministrations of the sole preacher of that faith living in enormous Botetourt County in the early 1770s: Rev. John Alderson Sr., who moved to the Botetourt governmental seat of Fincastle, a few miles west of the Buchanan settlement, about the year 1773.

Though certainly neither as eccentric nor as charismatic as Shubal Stearns, John Alderson became a colorful frontier character in his own right, and his story, like those of so many other forgotten pioneers in those days and times, deserves to be remembered in realistic rather than legendary terms. Born probably in 1699 or 1700 in Grinton, Yorkshire, he was the son of a clergyman in the Church of England who desired that John should follow his footsteps into the ministry. Like adolescents both then and now, at about the age of eighteen John bucked at the arrangements made for him and expressed a keener interest in marrying a local girl with whom he was infatuated. To prevent the marriage, his remarkably broadminded—and evidently well-to-do—father gave him a horse and a purse of money and advised him to travel for a while, hoping that the experience would make the boy forget the young lady. Like the prodigal son, John soon lost both horse and money, and he arranged with (or, depending on the version of the story, was shanghaied by) a sea captain to be indentured as a bondservant in exchange for his passage to America. He wound up in Hopewell, New Jersey, working for Thomas Curtis, pastor of the Regular Baptist church there. The Curtis family, particularly a daughter named Jane, took a liking to him, and after his term of servitude was over he married Jane and joined his father-in-law's church, where he finally fulfilled his father's dream and became a preacher. When Vicar Alderson, still in England, finally got word from overseas that his son had entered the Baptist ministry, he fondly sent John three of his books on theological subjects, and the volumes survived for many years as heirlooms in the American branch of the Alderson family.

The Aldersons were connected with Hopewell Church until about 1749, when John seems to have taken over the pastoral care of the New Britain Church in Bucks County, Pennsylvania. In the early 1750s, though, he relocated probably to Maryland and began to work with a small congregation of Baptists on a branch of the north fork of the Shenandoah in present Rockingham County, Virginia, known as Smith and Lynville's Creek, where he moved his family and formally gathered the group as a church in 1756. The Smith and Lynville's Creek Church's beginnings were as fraught with danger and hardship as might be expected for that day and place. During the French and Indian War the settlement was subjected to Indian attack numerous times and once was very nearly broken up by a smallpox epidemic, but the Aldersons and their neighbors persevered, Alderson receiving his recognition from the Virginia courts as a dissenting minister in June 1756 and the church finally gaining enough members to join the Philadelphia Regular Baptist Association in 1762. Four years later, Smith and Lynville's Creek Church became one of the charter congregations of the Ketocton Association of northern Virginia.

The Aldersons' move to Botetourt County and the beginnings of their contact with the family of George and Rebecca Smith occurred about 1773. Still active despite his advancing age, John Alderson seems to have formed a business partnership with one Adam Walker to establish a trading post at Miller's Mill near Fincastle, and oddly enough the circumstance coincides with the one period in John Alderson's life in which he stood excluded from the church. We know very little about the causes and how they transpired, the available records indicating only that his exclusion resulted from charges brought against him by two men across the Potomac in Fredericktown, Maryland. But we may wonder if the accusations themselves somehow involved Alderson's one known vice: in a rough, wild day and age and in an isolated region where good books were as scarce as hen's teeth, the preacher was a bibliophile to the point of unreason. In reading his will and his estate settlement one is reminded of Erasmus's quip that when he had a little money, he bought books; if he had anything left over, he bought food and clothing. Alderson boasted a library that included, among other theological and philosophical treasures, volumes of sermons and commentaries by John Flavel and John Owen, W. Keith's sermons and expositions of the Parables, and the works of Andrew Gray; apparently when a volume struck his fancy he would obtain it either on credit from a bookseller or by borrowing money from a friend if he didn't have enough cash on hand, and he was still in debt for books at the time of his death in 1780. His sons and grandsons inherited his books, and his beloved Jane, his book debts. In retrospect from a day in which libraries are available to all, the fault appears rather more amusing and endearing than malicious, but we can easily imagine that a couple of Alderson's book creditors had caught up with him just before his removal to Botetourt County, and in fact very well may have prompted his retreat further into the backwoods. Nonetheless, by 1777, about the same time that his son John Jr., now an ordained minister at Smith and Lynville's Creek in his own right, moved from Rockingham County to the Greenbrier Valley several miles northwest of Fincastle, the old preacher had "made it right" with his church on the Shenandoah and had begun preaching again—if indeed he had ever let the trifling matter of his excommunication at Smith and Lynville's Creek deter him from his calling at Fincastle in the first place.[13]

The young George and Rebecca Smith thus must have heard the Baptist Gospel first in its "Regular" manifestation, perhaps at the trading post at Miller's Mill where John and Jane Alderson and some of their sons made their homes. From what we know of the original American Regular Baptists' usual insistence that their ministers should be schooled at least under the mentorship of more experienced clerics if not formally educated, plus John Alderson's known passion for books, we might expect Alderson's preaching to have been dignified, deliberate, thoughtful, and very probably unemotional, but in this he would have been in keeping with many Presbyterian ministers as well as Regular Baptists and it must have been a style to which most of the Calvinist-reared immigrants were accustomed. Even so, as strict Calvinists, neither John Alderson Sr. nor John Jr. were great evangelists. John Jr. began preaching at about the time the dramatic Separate Baptist revival swept into northern Virginia from the southwest and spurred even some of the fatalistic Regulars to become aggressive soulwinners, and in a region where it was unsafe for a settler even to plow without a rifle or musket swung from his shoulder, John Jr. himself adopted enough of the Separates' evangelical practices to risk his scalp itinerating from Sunday to Sunday between the rude blockhouse forts of the Botetourt County wilderness. Still, he and his father had only made eleven or so known converts by the time of John Sr.'s death, and a good many of these were family members. All belonged, at least technically, to the old congregation based on the Shenandoah in Rockingham County, and in November 1781 John Jr. finally organized them formally into a church of their own, based on the Greenbrier River[14] and which still exists in the border community of Alderson, West Virginia, as the Greenbrier Baptist Church.

It is not known whether George and Rebecca Smith were charter members of this Greenbrier Church. Since the Greenbrier Valley was, after all, a rough and dangerous day's ride from their own home on the upper James, they may not have entered into the new church's constitution, and even if they did they remained in the area less than three years after the congregation was gathered. Nonetheless, John Alderson Sr. was their "near neighbor" until his death in 1780, and until that time he must have provided their frontier community with regular preaching services, including immersion, when required, and communion. It is doubtful that the preacher even knew about Rebecca's first husband or her separation, much less held them against her as bars to church fellowship. Though times and mores would change even before Rebecca's life was over, backwoods communities could be remarkably closemouthed and loyal when they chose to be, especially upon a consensus that life had dealt an innocent young woman an ill hand. For George Smith's part, though barely literate, he must have been enormously impressed not only by John Alderson's fund of knowledge and his store of books but by the fact that Alderson had risen to the station of a clergyman from the lowly place of a bondsman such as he himself had once been. From the tough old Yorkshireman, then, George and Rebecca must have learned to believe "without bigotry"[15] every precept of the Philadelphia Confession, even the most heartlessly fatalistic portions; a copy of the document, alongside a Bible and a hymnal, were the only books they owned. If they couldn't comprehend or explain Calvinism themselves, they knew that their preacher could, and they took their preacher's word because Alderson was probably the only genuinely educated man they had ever known.

In this environment George and Rebecca reared their oldest children. As has been noted, all from Philip, their first, born in September 1767, to William, born in December 1781, were Virginians. The Smiths had thirteen children in all, but their names as listed in many published genealogical tables can be deceptive. Most of the data on these, as well as that of their alleged spouses, appear to have been lifted directly from Louis Cochran's historical novel, and it is genuinely difficult for family researchers to tell at this point how many names Cochran simply made up. John Augustus Williams lists sons Philip, Joseph, George, and William as being older than John, and Jonathan and Henry as being younger, but he names none of the daughters at all, and of course neither of Rebecca's children by Jonathan Whitely. The most dependable of the Smith genealogical listings on the World Wide Web indicates that the sons shown above plus daughters Rebecca (who, as we have noted, could have belonged to Whitely rather than George Smith), Mary, and Elizabeth are the only siblings of Raccoon John Smith whose names are now definitely known.[16] Even so, George and Rebecca apparently never troubled themselves much about their Calvinistic Baptist religion's most horrible proposition, for even in that day of frontier dangers and epidemics they seem to have raised a family of lively offspring, all as healthy as horses and living to adulthood only strengthened by the childhood illnesses they must have endured.

These Virginia years were likewise the time of George Smith's military service, although it probably involved sporadic militia and scout duty rather than regular enlistment since Rebecca seems to have borne children without interruption all through the war. The Revolution ended in the east with Washington's victory at Yorktown, although Daniel Boone and John Todd's defeat at Blue Licks in the Kentucky territory followed it by an entire year. We can safely say, though, that George's own army service was over by the time of the Yorktown surrender, and he turned his attentions fully once again to the care of his family, which by now numbered eight children and/or stepchildren ranging from the age of fifteen years to infancy.

Perhaps armed with a government land warrant given to George as recompense for his military duty, a very common means at that time for state governments to repay soldiers, or maybe simply having been influenced by the persuasive spiels of large grantees such as the Tennessee River Valley's John Sevier, who had gone into the profitable business of land speculation, before long George and Rebecca resolved to move to the southwest. Williams tells us that George had contemplated such a move even before the Revolution,[17] possibly at the urgings of his brothers-in-law Reece and Henry Bowen, Joseph Looney, and William Porter, who had already blazed the trail from Botetourt County to the even more dangerous Clinch and Holston valleys in southwestern Virginia. Certainly modern history texts make much of these early pioneers' intrepid character and readiness to move into the wilds simply from a sense of adventure that we as Americans have now somehow lost. The Bowen brothers and the Looney and Porter families certainly may have possessed something of that adventuresome nature, and most Smith historians and genealogists are content to paint George with the same broad brushstrokes, but actually George's—and for that matter, most of the early settlers'—wants and needs were far more mundane. George Smith had been a bound-boy who, by the help of the Buchanans and his own sweat, had raised himself to the status of an independent small landowner. Williams stresses John Smith's recollections that George was a good farmer with a passion for keeping his land neat and his tools in meticulous order, but that he was of a very simple nature and that his ambitions and dreams never went beyond the boundaries of his own "vine and fig tree." To borrow another old Appalachian expression, according to George's "lights" he felt that he owed it to his sons to bestow upon them the same social status that he himself possessed, and thus his chief concern was to provide them all with sufficient land to make workable farms of their own, as good as, if not better than, his. As an ex-bondsman himself he probably shied away from the notion of letting his sons serve even as tradesmen's apprentices, and this though skilled blacksmiths, coopers, and joiners were valued members of any frontier community. George apparently knew how to read and write a little and he seems to have made sure that all his sons, if not his daughters, did so as well; the oldest boys may even have been taught by John Alderson Sr., since Calvinist clergymen were at that time often the only competent schoolmasters to be found either on or off the frontier. But neither was George concerned that his sons should further their education beyond the ability to read the Bible and the Philadelphia Confession, write well enough to sign their names on legal documents, and do elementary ciphering. George considered the position of a yeoman farmer to be his lot in life, his predestined end as it were, and although he cared little for the finer points of either commerce or education, he was quite willing to risk his life moving further into the wilderness to make sure he could acquire arable land in order that his progeny might inherit his own social status.[18] Historian Altina L. Waller explored this mindset, which remained as something of an Appalachian hallmark for the better part of the nineteenth century, extensively in *Feud,* her study of late nineteenth-century Appalachian social change from the perspective of the famous Hatfield-McCoy conflict.[19] It is noteworthy, though, to find such a frank and explicit confirmation of her conclusions in Raccoon John's recollections to his first biographer.

And so in the early spring of 1784 George and Rebecca (already pregnant with her ninth child) gathered their family, their household plunder, what garden and field seed they could carry, and their livestock, and began their sojourn to the southwest—and as it turned out, to a different kind of strife than they had known in their old home. Comprising what is now eastern Tennessee, originally belonging to the province of North Carolina and much of its earliest population consisting of refugees from the Regulators' War in that colony, the land to be known as the State of Franklin had been ceded that same year to the U.S. Congress by the North Carolina state legislature with no choice whatsoever on the part of "Franklin's" citizens. The new federal government, operating as it was at the time under the weak Articles of Confederation, had no real and enforceable power with which either to receive or to manage this gift, and so it simply ignored the whole matter while still more settlers, egged on by the speculators, moved from both Virginia and North Carolina into what they considered U.S. territory. The older residents, many of whom nursed hot grudges against eastern lowland North Carolina government officials for their highbrow attitudes and actions before and during the Regulators' War, were only further incensed by North Carolina's seeming indifference to them and the subsequent inaction of Congress, and so in August 1784 a large number of them simply took matters into their own hands. They formed a convention, declared their lands as components of an independent American state to be known as Franklin, elected the speculator John Sevier as their governor, and made plans to frame a constitution in December. Shortly after this first convention, North Carolina revoked its cession of the disputed land and claimed it again. The December constitutional convention met anyway, but by this time North Carolina was quite ready to take up arms over the territory, and in fact both "old state" and "new state" parties had already developed within Franklin itself. Congress again chose to distance itself from the entire matter, and so for the next four or five years a nasty little civil war raged as an unwelcome supplement to the settlers' continual worries about sporadic raids from the Cherokee towns to the south. Rival "new-state" and "old-state" courts convened in each of the disputed territory's counties, and both courts levied their own taxes on the harassed landowners. Opposing "old-state" and "new-state" county militias were likewise enrolled to back up the respective claims of their leaders, with the "old-staters" of course being supported more and more from the east as the political strife dragged on and on. By 1789, Governor Sevier's term had expired, and no one was elected in his place; North Carolina once again established its sovereignty over the area, and the proud new state, reduced to anarchy and near-ruin, simply faded from existence.

George and Rebecca Smith settled their family, probably at least by corn-planting time in 1784, on the south fork of the Holston River not far from the border of Virginia, in the area of Franklin that would later be known as Sullivan County, Tennessee. Throughout the four-year civil strife between his "old-state" and "new-state" neighbors, George was said to have remained consistently neutral, his mind and energies occupied entirely with the clearing and cultivation of his new farm,[20] but one can imagine that even mild-mannered George Smith's patience must have been tried at the prospects of appeasing the tax demands of two rival county courts and keeping his older boys out of two separate and sparring militias. We might likewise expect that George and Rebecca relied heavily on their religious faith to sustain them through the ups and downs of the old state–new state war, but as it turned out, here they faced something of a second shock. Baptists there were in plenty around them, true enough, but nearly all were the noisy, undignified, and nearly Arminian children in the faith of Shubal Stearns rather than the Regular type of their Botetourt County background, and they found themselves suddenly in the midst of a Baptist community that must have been almost alien to them. Of the churches in the developing territory, only one, on Sinking Creek in present-day Carter County, Tennessee, between the modern cities of Johnson City and Elizabethton, is thought to have been out-and-out Calvinistic.[21] The others already gathered as well as those to be organized before 1786, Cherokee Creek (also known as Buffalo Ridge), Kendrick's Creek, Bent Creek, Beaver Creek, Greasy Cove, North Fork of Holston, and Lower French Broad River, were all connected with the Separate Baptists' original Sandy Creek Association in North Carolina, and the ministers who served them, Tidings "Tidence" Lane, William Murphy, Jonathan Mulkey, Isaac Barton, James Keel, John Frost, and Alexander Chambers, were every one Separate Baptists from either the Carolinas or Virginia.[22] William Murphy, already mentioned in connection with the Separate Baptist movement in southwestern Virginia and like George and Rebecca Smith a recent immigrant to the Tennessee country, and Tidence Lane were in fact brought up in the ministry under the direct supervision of Shubal Stearns. Isaac Barton was William Murphy's son-in-law, and it may have been at Barton and his wife's behest that Murphy migrated to Tennessee. Lane, brother of the famous Virginia preacher Dutton Lane, had been a member of the Separate Baptists' actual "mother" church on Sandy Creek in Randolph County, North Carolina, had succeeded Stearns as pastor or moderator of that congregation, and had even served as a coexecutor of the childless Stearns's last will and testament when the Regulators' War and its aftermath finally broke the old evangelist's will to live. In this latter office, Lane may have inherited a few books that his old mentor had collected in his pre-Baptist days and had brought south with him from New England as well, as Tidence was known to have

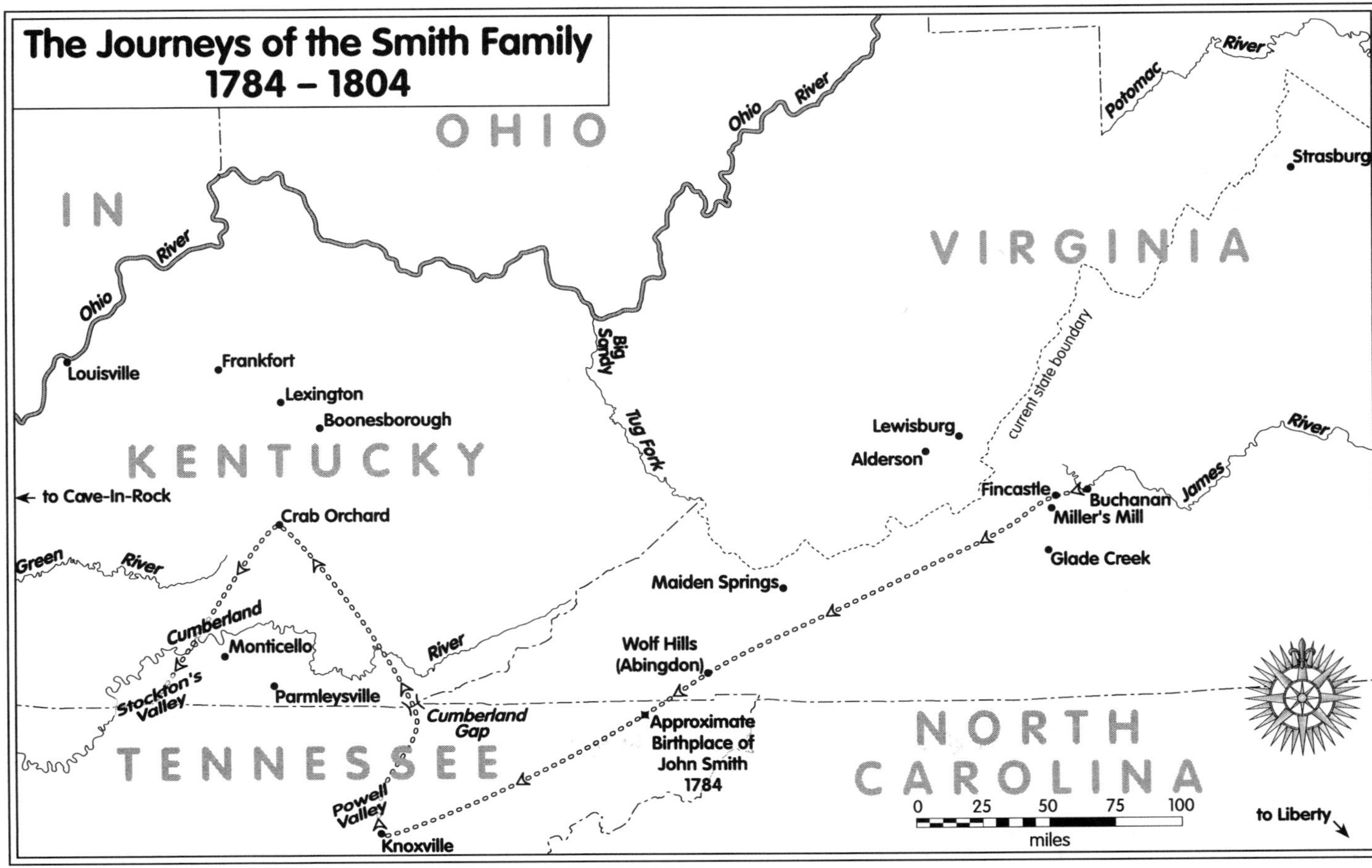
The Journeys of the Smith Family
1784 – 1804
OHIO
IN
VIRGINIA
KENTUCKY
TENNESSEE
NORTH CAROLINA
Ohio River
Potomac River
Strasburg
Louisville
Frankfort
Lexington
Boonesborough
Big Sandy
Tug Fork
current state boundary
Lewisburg
Alderson
James River
Fincastle
Buchanan
Miller's Mill
Glade Creek
to Cave-In-Rock
Crab Orchard
Green River
Maiden Springs
Cumberland River
Monticello
Stockton's Valley
Parmleysville
Cumberland Gap
Wolf Hills (Abingdon)
Approximate Birthplace of John Smith 1784
Powell Valley
Knoxville
0 25 50 75 100
miles
to Liberty

possessed at least three in addition to the Bible that he took literally and a copy of the Philadelphia Confession that he didn't: *Human Nature in Its Fourfold State* by Thomas Boston, *Every Man His Own Lawyer* by Edmund Burke, and "Willson on the Sacraments."[23] One more exhorter, Jonathan Mulkey, was the son of Philip Mulkey, another of Stearns's young Carolina backwoods preachers, who had been an extremely apt imitator of the old man's musical, emotive preaching cadence, and for better or worse, the spiritual ancestor of every brassy, pomaded southern television evangelist ever caught in a scandal.[24] Thus, in moving to their new home, George and Rebecca undoubtedly did encounter a few other immigrants like themselves, familiar with a strict Calvinism, the Philadelphia Confession, and dignified Regular Baptist worship forms, but they found far more Baptists who avowed a belief in "the Bible and it alone" over any "man-made" creed, who set leaders Tidence Lane and William Murphy on the pedestal of patriarchs in the shadow of the lost figure of Shubal Stearns, and who shouted, wept, shook hands, embraced, and washed one another's feet while listening to, in John Augustus Williams's words, "the musical voice of the preacher at meetings, beseeching with melancholy cant for sobbing penitents kneeling at the altar."[25]

The Methodists, though at this time still technically a part of the Anglican or Protestant Episcopal Church, were growing and were likewise active in the early Tennessee territorial settlements, and they had in fact formally established a conference on the Holston River the year before George and Rebecca moved their family to the territory.[26] Perhaps it was a desire on the part of the Separates to identify themselves as possessing a theology distinct from this strong and growing Methodist presence, complemented by the addition of Regulars such as George and Rebecca Smith to their number, as well as the precedent set in 1785 by the similarly constituted Elkhorn and Salem Associations northward in the Kentucky territory, that prompted the Separate Baptists of the Holston Valley to adopt the Philadelphia Confession when they finally "armed off" from the old Sandy Creek Association and organized their own Holston Association in late October 1786. But for whatever reason, adopt it the Holston Baptists did, undoubtedly much to George and Rebecca's satisfaction. Even so, a strict interpretation of the Confession was never a part of Holston Association's essential makeup. Tidence Lane who, given his close relationship with the old patriarch Stearns, was of course elected as the new association's first moderator, remained "not so hard in doctrine as some of his brethren, his doctrinal belief being a modified Calvanism [*sic*]."[27] Although William Murphy, the body's first clerk and second moderator, had been Calvinist enough to oppose an outright Arminian doctrinal stance in the Rapidan Separate Baptist Association to which he had formerly belonged in Virginia,[28] he once explicitly stated that Holston Association had adopted the Confession only as "a general statement of principles" that bound absolutely no one to its strict observance.[29] Moreover, though it is not known whether the members of Holston Association considered themselves truly as "United Baptists" like the

Virginia Separates after they joined forces with the Regular Baptists in 1787, we do know that Holston kept up a cordial relationship and exchanged frequent correspondence with the one remaining Separate body then still standing aloof from the Regulars: the South Kentucky Association of Separate Baptists, which was led by Robert Elkin, himself a preacher from the Virginia/Tennessee border country who had grown up in the church of Tidence Lane's brother Dutton and who had left the area for Kentucky not too many years before George and Rebecca Smith arrived there.[30]

The reader may wonder, and perhaps with good reason, why I have not yet allowed the subject of this biography himself to take the stage. After all, John Augustus Williams begins his tale quite reasonably with Raccoon John's birth, and Louis Cochran introduces him as a teenager garbed in Daniel Boone–style (that of the television series, not the historical figure) buckskins and coonskin cap, already dubbed with the "Raccoon" cognomen and riding that famous steed "Zebulon." On the other hand, Everett Donaldson waits until the third chapter of his first Smith volume to introduce Raccoon John, the first two chapters concentrating on the family's background. Although Donaldson opts to use a slightly different spin on history (especially Baptist history) than has been recounted here, I believe his method to be the better one. For, as I've tried to stress, that background, the context, is crucial. Raccoon John Smith's life, like anyone's, is a story of personal tragedies and triumphs, but he never once engaged in a conflict, social, intellectual, spiritual or otherwise, that he did not take in virtually with his mother's milk—even to the sheer coincidence of his spending his infancy in the time of a petty but troublesome local civil war and his old age in a great and terrible national one.

John Smith was born on October 15, 1784, on the south fork of the Holston River in the portion of Franklin that was to become Sullivan County, Tennessee, the ninth of thirteen children of George and Rebecca Bowen Smith. We cannot know whether he was named for Johannes Schmidt, John Bowen, John Alderson, or even John Calvin, but it is no matter. Their ghosts, along with those of Jacobus Arminius, George Whitefield, and Shubal Stearns, all danced around his parents' hearth. In a sense, they haunted him all his life.

His early childhood was a typical one for the eastern American frontier. The only "anesthetic" that his mother could have had when she bore him was an axe or plow point placed under her bed to "cut the pain." His umbilical cord was tied and he was diapered and powdered with old soft cloths and flour that had been held in a pan over the fire and "scorched"—not because either his mother or the long-forgotten backwoods midwife who delivered him knew that they were sterilizing the articles, but because "scorched things" had a miraculous intrinsic healing power. The word "germ" simply meant the heart of a seed grain. When he was a toddler he may have noticed the scrawny yellow flowers of love apples growing close to his parents' cabin as simple and poor yard decorations, but he would have gotten his hands slapped if he had tried to touch the large, tart berries that developed from them; love apples, or tomatoes as they are now known, were believed by everyone to be poisonous. When he got a cut finger or toe, one of his older brothers or perhaps even his father would have urinated on the wound, the antiseptic quality of the whiskey that both saint and sinner then drank perhaps being not yet widely recognized, and his earaches would have been treated with drops of fresh urine squeezed into his ear from a rag. When he fell prey to other childhood illnesses or infections, he would have heard from his parents that ill humors had taken hold of his body and he was undoubtedly "sweated" or "poulticed," as the case applied, to draw the humors out. When he got old enough to wonder where he had come from, he would have understood (from explanations from his father or older brothers about animal breeding, of course; humans were unmentionable, and boys and girls had to learn the facts of life how and where they could) that a male's highly purified blood, or semen, combined with a female's menstrual blood miraculously to form new life in the womb. And John Smith may have believed these old wives' tales and a host of others just like them all his life, and even taught them to his children, for he lived in a day and place in which hardly anyone knew any better.

In addition to the settlers' troubles over the Franklin issue, it must be remembered that in the late 1780s and early 1790s Indian attacks could still decimate entire neighborhoods as quickly as these epidemics of ill humors. What was afterward referred to by John Sevier's son as "the hottest Indian war" of the period[31] occurred in eastern Tennessee between Cherokees and whites when John Smith was not quite four years old, and even a year after it, and the Franklin controversy, were over, parties of Cherokee stole past the Holston settlements to unite with members of other tribes such as the Shawnee and Delaware to stage raids in southwestern Virginia. The raid that is perhaps now the most notorious (in Kentucky anyway, or at least in the state's eastern mountains, due to the tourism dollars the tragic story generates) resulted in the October 1789 murder of the family of Thomas Wiley on Walker Creek in present Bland County, Virginia, and the six-month captivity of Thomas's wife, Jane, or Jenny. Certainly conditions south of the border in the Tennessee country were little different than those on Walker Creek where the Wiley children perished, and Rebecca Smith and her family easily might have fallen prey to a similar fate but for the vagaries of time and chance. As it was, during this time George and Rebecca's older sons Philip, Joseph, and George Jr. followed the pattern to which their parents had been accustomed all their lives, and participated with their neighbors in campaigns against the Indians whenever it was required to defend their new homes. Williams seems to imply that George Sr.'s advancing age kept him from going on many, if not most, of these expeditions,[32] although reputedly the toughest and fiercest Indian fighter of the settlements upriver in southwestern Virginia, Matthias Harman, was very nearly George's contemporary in age—and Matthias's father, Heinrich, or Henry, himself a German immigrant like George's parents, participated in his last Indian fight when he was past the age of eighty.[33] But with General Anthony Wayne's 1794 campaign into Ohio, culminating in the Battle of Fallen Timbers, the power of the Shawnee, Delaware, and Wyandot tribes against the settlers of the eastern mountains was broken, at least until the next British war. After a young, bold officer by the name of Andrew Jackson took an army and destroyed the Cherokee town of Nickajack in eastern Tennessee in December of that same year in retaliation for Indian attacks on the growing settlement of Nashville, that tribe ceased active hostilities as well,[34] and peace, perhaps the first of its kind they had ever known, came to the lives of the Smith family and their neighbors.

In the meantime, young John had already been introduced to the world of farm work. Though Williams's portrait of this aspect of Smith's upbringing is idealized, in general it is undoubtedly accurate and quite vivid; even in a large family no one had time to be idle when land was to be cleared. George and Rebecca simply had John perform the duties of which a small boy was capable, such as picking up chips and "shelly bark" to start fires, gathering nuts, and carrying water to his father and older brothers, and they gradually augmented those duties as John's size and strength increased. In time John learned to cultivate grain and garden produce, spot and dig ginseng for barter at the trading post, care for livestock, cut wood both for fires and for building cabins, barns, and fences, hunt to supply the table, and read the Bible and write his name at a single four-month "subscription" school taught by an itinerant schoolmaster—in short, all that was expected of a male in his day and age, although Williams lets John admit that he never liked hunting[35] and one wonders how well Smith was truly suited to the rest of his routine. Williams never explored this latter idea in any great detail, the life of "simple and honest toil" being praised generally in nineteenth-century America as a satisfying existence and a great virtue by all classes who were not forced to engage in it, but from the sum total of Smith's recollections to Williams one can hardly keep from the thought that John might have shared Abraham Lincoln's sentiment that his father had taught him to work, but had never taught him to love it.

Of course, it is central to Williams's theme that John Smith did indeed grow up to be smarter than his siblings and most of his parents' neighbors' children, but the writings of his successors to the Smith story too often stress this smartness, as it were, simply as a sort of increased frontier pragmatism and cunning coupled with a gift for storytelling and a rapier sense of humor. John's gifts for spinning a good yarn and telling a joke, the hallmarks of his Bowen kin, are unquestioned, but for most of his life he was anything *but* pragmatic in a worldly or economic sense, and neither was he particularly cunning before hard experience and a few skilled mentors had taught him to be. I argue that Smith's yarn spinning skills and his humor, which was often of a cynical cast even in his youth but never clownish, might have been less a primary personality trait than a mere symptom of a more basic, deep-seated aspect of his character, one which Lincoln shared as well. From what evidence that can be gleaned both in the Williams tale and other sources to be discussed later, that first four-month term of school and the presence of that one long-forgotten teacher affected John Smith indescribably deeply, and from them he developed, over time, a burning desire for both learning and the worldly advancement that learning could bring him. He utilized his story- and joke-telling skills initially as outlets for his frustration at being deprived of better educational opportunities, and later as a means to advance his reputation as a self-made and self-taught man when fate, or Providence perhaps, did send favor his way. I believe that the only discernible difference between the personalities of Smith and Abraham Lincoln in this regard was that Lincoln saw his dreams to fruition strictly in the secular sphere while John, who was of Lincoln's father's generation, found his niche and his notoriety almost by chance in the religious instead. But as we shall see, for a good part of his life, Smith could have been described every bit as accurately as Lincoln in owning an ambition with the characteristics of "a little engine that knew no rest."[36]

We will never know just how many tales of John Alderson in Botetourt, his youthful adventures and misadventures, his rise from lowly bondservant to respected minister, his firm, scholarly Calvinistic preaching, and his eager, nearly comical obsession with obtaining good books, were passed back and forth at the fireside of George and Rebecca's cabin on the banks of the Holston when John was young. References to Tidence Lane's tiny treasury of books could have been mentioned also, perhaps in comparison to Alderson's larger and more zealously collected stock. It is certain, though, that men of the Alderson type, so to speak—possessed of a good schooling, some experience in the wider world, a well-stocked library, and preferably but by no means necessarily religious—attracted John Smith for the greater part of his life as a candle attracts a moth, not only intellectually but sometimes deeply emotionally as well. This does not mean that, two hundred-odd years after the fact, we need to call John's sexual orientation into question. He married twice and sired fifteen children, and evidence will be introduced that he entertained a similar affection for his second wife, who was better educated than many, if not most, women in the rural southeast (sadly) were allowed to be at that time. American mores of the day, dictating the degree of separation of the sexes that was then expected, did produce more than one pair of male intellectuals who could speak of and to one another in the most tender and romantic terms—and in fact, such intellectual relationships between males were hardly considered improper in that day at all. But still, John's later declaration to Albert Allen of the emotions he experienced at his first glimpse of one such male object of his intellectual attraction—"I . . . felt as if I wanted to sit down and *look* at him for *one hour* without hearing a word from any one. I wanted to *scan him,* who had been so much talked of, and who had . . . introduced so many *new* thoughts into my mind" (all emphases in original)—is in fact about as blunt and visceral, though not so elegantly expressed, as anything one sees in the writings of either Oscar Wilde or Carson McCullers. It's certainly nothing that any modern self-conscious fundamentalist or evangelical male would dare let himself say about another male, and even in the late 1860s it was jarring enough for Williams to paraphrase this particular statement and tone it down considerably in his own relation of the incident.[37] But even Williams himself subsequently let another similar, though slightly more subdued, confession slip by him in quoting John's reply to a scholarly, inquiring, and much-appreciated letter from one Thomas Henderson: "I know not when I received a communication which produced the same kind of sensations in my mind."[38] John Smith was indeed an anomaly for the backwoods, a real-life character who actually did seem to fit Søren Kierkegaard's description of his imaginary alter ego Johannes Climacus ("John the Climber") to a startling degree: "In love he was, ardently in love—but with thought or, more accurately, with thinking. No young lover, stirred by that incomprehensible transition whereby love wakens in the breast, by the lightning flash with which reciprocal love bursts forth in the beloved, could be more deeply moved than he was by that comprehensible transition whereby one thought fits with another." But the intellectual resources of Kierkegaard's childhood in genteel Copenhagen were many and readily available, and those of John Smith's in the Holston Valley backwoods were next to nonexistent; given the juxtaposition of John's scholarly inclinations and strong ambitions with his elemental background, it is completely understandable that he should have responded to intellectual stimulation in the most earthy and even sensual of terms.

Conversely, since learning was such a deeply personal and emotional issue for John, he could and often did exhibit a deep and fierce rage, nearly always couched inextricably in that famous sense of humor, toward those whom he sized up as ignoramuses—not individuals such as his father and mother, who had a simple and honest lack either of opportunity or capacity, but rather those he perceived as mere pretenders to scholarship, who professed to own more than they possessed. He thus may have been ambivalent, as he grew up, toward the Baptists among whom his parents had settled in Tennessee. It must be reiterated here that George and Rebecca were followers of the Philadelphia Confession as it had been articulated by old John Alderson; the Holston Association in general, when it had been formed in 1786 from Shubal Stearns's old Sandy Creek Separate Baptist organization, likewise claimed to endorse the document; but the most prominent preachers in the body, including Tidence Lane, William Murphy, and Jonathan Mulkey, at least some of whom appear to have been fairly regular guests at John's parents' dinner table during the course of George and Rebecca's church's "monthly meeting" weekend,[39] could be, like their patriarch Stearns himself, classified at best only as mild Calvinists who honored their newly adopted Regular Baptist creed more in the breach than in the observance, even to the point of "devoting" or "dry-christening" children the way Stearns had taught them.[40] Early on, John may thus have begun to perceive the theological precision of his parents' and old Alderson's Confession as superior to the emotionalism and near-Arminianism of most of his Baptist and all his Methodist neighbors, if for no other reason than the possible low-toned asides he may have heard at home that "they sure don't do it here the way Brother Alderson did back up in the old country." But Calvinism represented the only scholarship and the sole dialectic to which he possibly could have been introduced at this point; thus, almost from the first, he may have regarded the idea of being a Calvinistic preacher like old John Alderson as an intellectual apex, and Arminianism, or even Arminian leanings, as ignorance. Still, most of his neighbors had to have been honest, if inarticulate, in whatever mix of the two schools of thought they held, and so far they were no subjects for John's anger.

His second schoolteacher was a different matter altogether. Setting up another "subscription" school not far from George and Rebecca's farm a few years after John's first four-month educational experience, this man had come to the community claiming to be a competent schoolmaster and an expert in mathematics. Unfortunately, he proved himself to be nothing more than a drunk with a little ability to read, write, and cipher who regarded teaching merely as an easier way than manual labor to keep his belly full of whiskey (or *usquebaugh,* as Williams oddly chose to call it in this instance, an old Celtic word for the beverage that John himself may have picked up from his mother and chosen to use in relating the tale to his biographer). John took the measure of his teacher more quickly than any of the adults in the community did. So far, he had never had a chance to study mathematics, and he was bitterly disappointed to find out that the drunkard actually knew next to nothing about the subject. But he was definitely the first to do something about him. After making a fool of the teacher in front of the whole school by suckering him on the arithmetical problem of "how many grains of corn does it take to make a square foot of mush," for which good old George Smith characteristically gave him only a mild rebuke, John caught the man asleep in his cups at his desk in the schoolhouse, stealthily scooped a shovelful of live embers from the fireplace, and slipped it into the pocket of his coat, which just happened to be made of highly combustible "linsey" or flax—and then let him wake up on his own. As John had hoped, the incident ended both the unfortunate schoolmaster's reputation and his residence in the area[41] as well as causing him to lose his coat and very probably a few calculable square inches of hide near his midsection. It was only the beginning of John's long and successful career of "burning," as it were, those he perceived as dilettantes and hypocrites.

But we're ahead of ourselves. This second educational experience of John Smith would occur not in the Tennessee country but in the mountains of southern Kentucky, where George, Rebecca, and their family would move in the year 1796, where John would spend the rest of his childhood and much of his early adult life, where his older brother George Jr. would have a risky association with America's first known serial killers—and where John would see the world of his adulthood shaped, in the beginnings of the Great Revival of the South.

CHAPTER 2

Training in Christianity

Each age has its own characteristic depravity.

—Søren Kierkegaard

By the spring of John Smith's eleventh year a relative peace had descended on the Holston Valley. More settlers were pouring in from both the northeast and southeast, the Baptist and Methodist religious communities were stable and even prospering in a small way, the older Smith boys were ready to marry off and raise families of their own—and once again George Smith found that arable land with good soil, which he considered his greatest necessity in order to do right by his sons, was getting scarce. As has been noted, he had a total of eight by this time, from twenty-eight-year-old Philip to two-year-old Henry, and though old George was of an age now to settle down, rest, and let at least Philip, young George, and Joseph take the harder labor off his hands, he began to look for new lands again. A preaching associate of William Murphy's in southwestern Virginia, Robert Stockton, had a brother Thomas who only about that time had begun a settlement on a wild, uncleared portion of the upper Cumberland River in southern Kentucky. Whether or not old George got this information from Elder Murphy or from Robert or Thomas Stockton themselves cannot now be known. But it is certain that in 1795 George resolved to forsake his home in the Tennessee territory, take his family northward to Thomas Stockton's valley, and once again break ground on a government land warrant.

Accordingly, in the fall of 1795 George sold his farm on the Holston and took his family westward into the Powell River Valley, probably by following the Holston to its mouth at the frontier Sodom and Gomorrah of its day, the growing trading post known first as Fort White and then as Knoxville,[1] and from thence heading up Powell River as fast as he could in order to keep his sons and daughters away from the boatmen, traders, gamblers, whores, and thieves that haunted the burgeoning frontier town. At the head of the Powell, hard by the border of both Virginia and Kentucky, lay Cumberland Gap and the Wilderness Road to the Bluegrass, and George let most of his family spend the winter here while he, with sons Joseph and John, went on to scout for the location of their new home.

One might wonder why the aging George chose eleven-year-old John to be his and Joseph's partner in this difficult task, rather than his firstborn Philip, young George, or even fourteen-year-old William. He probably had more apprehension about leaving his family back on the upper Powell than concern for his own safety in Kentucky, and he may have felt better in leaving at least four males with the womenfolk, figuring that he and Joseph could look out after young John. At any rate, in the fall or early winter of 1795–1796 Joseph, John, and their father set out from the upper Powell with weapons, pack horses, and farm implements, up through Cumberland Gap and following the Wilderness Road all the way to its fork at Crab Orchard, governmental seat of Lincoln County, near the edge of the central Bluegrass. They then turned southwestward on another rough trace that led to the upper Cumberland River, their destination close to the border of Lincoln and Green counties and very nearly back to the state line. The area is now in the county of Clinton, not too far from its present governmental seat at Albany. Circuitous though their route was, they finally made camp in Stockton's Valley that winter; George claimed a two hundred–acre tract on a small tributary of the Cumberland which is still known as Smith Creek,[2] and that section of the present Clinton County, Kentucky/Pickett County, Tennessee, border country became the home base of George Smith's family for decades to come. Several of George and Rebecca's children ultimately settled and raised their families in present Overton and Fentress counties, Tennessee, a short distance south of Pickett.

Rough and rude though John's upbringing back on the Holston may have been, his sojourn in Stockton's Valley in the winter and early spring of 1796 with his father and brother—and especially the period during which he and Joseph had to fend for themselves while their father returned to Powell Valley to get the rest of the family—was certainly the wildest, most untrammeled, and most danger-ridden time he would ever know. Though he could help Joseph and old George but little in the heavy work of "girdling" trees (that is, stripping rings of bark around their trunks so they would die) and clearing land for spring planting, once at his father's command he took one of the pack horses nearly one hundred miles back to Crab Orchard to purchase corn for seed and meal. Incidentally, on this occasion he first met a young man nine years older than himself, Jeremiah Vardeman, who would prove to be crucial to John in shaping many of his most important life decisions.[3] As it would transpire with Smith, Vardeman had been a young Christian convert as well as a preacher, but at this point in time "Jerry" Vardeman was in a temporarily "backslidden" condition from the fellowship of the Crab Orchard Separate Baptist Church, and John first saw him playing the fiddle for a dance. George Smith would have been aghast had he known that John had sneaked a peek at such a sinful occasion as a dance, and worse yet, met a fiddler. Contrary to the local color frontier romantic conventions Louis Cochran borrowed for his novel, a reel or square dance was considered to be a devil's carnival by both Regular and Separate Baptists as well as Methodists of that day, and fiddlers were regarded by them in about the same light as heavy metal rock groups are by modern fundamentalists.[4] But it must have harmed young John little or none at all, since he arrived back at Smith Creek with his packsaddle of corn having fallen prey neither to the wrath of man nor of the Lord—and as will be shown soon, nebulous as the latter threat was, the former was decidedly real.

Until the Cherokee lost all their Kentucky lands and much of their remaining Tennessee territory to the United States in 1805 due to the dishonest dealings of a subchief named Doublehead, they regarded the Cumberland Plateau near the Smiths' new home as one of their richest hunting grounds.[5] Some Cherokee stayed in the area even after 1805, and a few of these actually managed to remain in southern Kentucky in spite of the tribe's forced removal west some three decades afterward.[6] Dislike hunting though young John might, his mind was a bear trap, springing on whatever knowledge he could pick up, and during this lonely period spent with his father and older brother he often had the chance to go on long walks and explorations through the surrounding forest when he was not needed at their camp. He met some of these Cherokee, and though his older brothers had often engaged in fights against the tribe they were now at peace with the whites and they seem to have welcomed the boy into their midst. John claimed to retain something of their speech from the brief times he shared their company. A tiny smattering of garbled Cherokee became the only "second" language he ever acquired, though the surviving evidence indicates that, if he was able to understand Cherokee, his own pronunciation of the tongue still left much to be desired.[7]

The Cumberland River Cherokee were no threat to the Smiths, but as the territory began to fill up with whites, other sources of peril arose. Of course Thomas Stockton was considered more or less the leader of the embryonic community, and when George Smith brought the rest of his family to their new home in midsummer 1796, Thomas's son Jesse was gratified to learn that his new acquaintances John and Joseph Smith had a pretty sister or half-sister named Rebecca. Jesse Stockton and Rebecca Smith's wedding, which took place later that fall, was perhaps the first ever to be celebrated in Stockton's Valley, and Philip Smith's marriage to Emily "Millie" Atkinson of Tennessee in early 1798 may have been the second or third.[8] Williams tells us that the Smiths had only one other neighboring family at this earliest date, and if this be the case it may have been that of John and Christina Tully and their eight children, who were likewise known to have been among Stockton's Valley's earliest settlers. In 1799 one John Graves is known to have homesteaded a little to the west of Stockton's Valley, and like George Smith, he had left most of the members of his family back in the eastern settlements and brought only one son with him to help him clear his new land. The Graveses were followed soon by others, though, including Jonathan Mulkey's preacher sons John and Philip and their ministerial colleague Isaac Denton, all from the Holston Valley, ready to evangelize and to gather new Kentucky Baptist churches. And in 1797 or early 1798 at the very latest at least one more family of sorts migrated from Tennessee and settled on the headwaters of the Green River some miles northwest of the Smiths, Stocktons, Mulkeys, Dentons, and Tullys. The head of this household was identified by Everett Donaldson as Jesse Roberts and by historian Paul I. Wellman, brother of the noted southern mountain horror story writer Manley Wade Wellman, simply as Old Man Roberts.[9]

There were other whites living to the west of Stockton's Valley, too, but they were not the kind that always made good neighbors. In those days a brisk river traffic had opened up between Kentucky and the French territories, with Kentuckians flatboating commercial products on the Ohio and Mississippi down to New Orleans, and the developing commerce had created a new class of criminals: the river pirates, who gained their livelihood from ambushing flatboats, murdering the crews, and stealing and selling the boats and goods themselves. The Ohio and Mississippi valleys were a long way from the Smiths' new home on the upper Cumberland, but it so happened that the Green, Barren, Salt, and Pond River valleys among others in western Kentucky, where honest settlers were scarce and law enforcement was almost nonexistent except for "regulator" posses led by the few backcountry magistrates, were frequently used by these river pirates and their "fences" as hideouts both for their stolen goods and themselves. This wilderness likewise attracted fugitives from other areas as well as horse thieves and outlaws of almost all other types, and the entire region was therefore given the entirely appropriate nickname of "Rogues' Harbor." Unfortunately, Rogues' Harbor may have come home to the Smiths with Jesse Roberts and John Tully, both of whom were suspected of having criminal contact with some of the outlaws there. It certainly came even closer home to young George Smith, who moved west to the Pond River, a tributary of the Green and right in the bosom of Rogues' Harbor, sometime in 1798 or 1799.[10] And with the introduction of the names of Jesse Roberts and John Tully and young George's relocation, we must make a brief excursus to examine the fifteen minutes' worth of fame earned by one of John's brothers and undoubtedly the most perplexing and disturbing story he ever shared concerning one of his close family members: that of the confrontation between young George Smith and Jesse Roberts's two common-law sons-in-law, Micajah "Big" and Wiley "Little" Harpe, America's first serial killers.

Historians disagree on the details of Micajah and Wiley Harpe's lives before they crossed the Cumberland Gap into Kentucky in the winter of 1798, bringing with them a harem consisting of Jesse Roberts's daughters Betsey and Susan and another young girl named Sally Rice (all were pregnant at the time and either of the two may have been the fathers), but there seems to be a general consensus on at least one aspect of their history: they had already committed two known murders before they ever left the Virginia and Tennessee mountains. The horribly mangled body of their first victim, Moses Doss, had shocked even the toughest old Indian fighters who saw it, and that of their second, a man named Johnson who may have informed against them for horse theft, revealed a modus operandi that they would use again and again after their arrival in Kentucky: the Harpes had eviscerated the body, filled its abdominal cavity with rocks, and sunk it in the Holston River. Only by chance had some of the stones fallen out and the body floated to the surface and lodged in an eddy to be discovered. Whatever may have been the truth about the Harpes, the murders of Doss and Johnson showed that they dearly loved the act of killing, usually with as grisly a technique as possible. They committed no less than four more gratuitous and extremely brutal murders while on a seemingly aimless trek over the Wilderness Road to Crab Orchard and from thence toward Logan's Station (now Stanford) before evidence began to pile up against them and they were captured and arrested in Hardin County, Kentucky, on Christmas Day 1798.[11] Had the Harpes made the same journey three winters earlier, George Smith and his two sons wouldn't have stood a chance against them, much less young John by himself on his journey back to Crab Orchard to purchase corn.

Both the Harpe men and their women were held first at Logan's Station, then transported to the jail at Danville, and their trial date was scheduled for April 15, 1799. While they were awaiting trial the men somehow escaped on March 15 or 16, leaving their women, all of whom had delivered babies in the rude log jail in the meantime, behind. Though historians agree on what happened next, they seem never to have linked its implications. The two Roberts girls and Sally Rice all professed great gladness to be rid of the fearsome Harpes and expressed only a desire to "go back to Tennessee and be reunited with their families," arousing the sympathy of many of the local townsfolk. Accordingly, the charges against them of complicity to murder were dropped, they were released from custody on April 20, and some of the Danville citizens provided them with changes of clothes for themselves and the babies and even an old gentle mare to ride on their long journey back up the Wilderness Road and down Powell Valley. As soon as they had lost sight of the village, though, the women proceeded to the head of Green River and to Jesse Roberts's cabin, where they traded the mare to their father for a canoe and used it to paddle all the way down Green River to Cave-In-Rock on the north bank of the Ohio, a well-known Illinois hideout for river pirates. The two men meanwhile headed for the lower Ohio and Cave-In-Rock overland, murdering at least six more persons who fell into their clutches as they went, and for some reason Colonel Daniel Trabue, father of the youngest victim in this second Kentucky murder spree, accused John Tully in Stockton's Valley of being in cahoots with the Harpes and actually bearing messages to them from their women while they were on their way to Cave-In-Rock.[12] Regardless of the truth of Trabue's allegation, the Harpes and their women were reunited at the river pirate hideout that summer—shortly before being evicted for killing a captive flatboatman in a manner so completely psychotic that it spooked even outlaw leader Samuel Mason and his tough gang of cutthroats there.

Evidence was easy to bury in that day; we will never know the entire story of these two frontier homicidal maniacs, but we actually can make a few very disturbing hypotheses from the few available shreds of data that we have. Even if he had preceded the Harpes and their women into Kentucky, Jesse Roberts could hardly have been unaware of the character of the men with whom his daughters cohabited. Moreover, illiterate newcomers such as the Harpes and their women, entering Kentucky through Cumberland Gap with only the barest knowledge of the state's terrain and watercourses, would have needed considerable help to plan the Cave-In-Rock reunion, to say nothing of how they learned of the existence and accessibility of such an outlaw den in the first place—and both men and women must have obtained the information and agreed upon the plan before the jailbreak ever occurred. If Colonel Trabue's claim hit anywhere near the mark, while the men and their concubines were separated they maintained communication with each other through one of Jesse Roberts's neighbors who for some reason was willing to travel scores of miles into western Kentucky as a messenger. And none of this makes any sense whatsoever unless one assumes that Roberts served as a contact between the Harpes and the leader or leaders of known outlaw gangs operating in Rogues' Harbor, who had heard of the Harpes either before their arrival in Kentucky or very soon afterward and who hoped to channel their destructive mania to killing the leaders of the "regulator" posses that were trying to put them out of business in western Kentucky. For all we know, Roberts may even have encouraged their move to Kentucky for this purpose at someone's request, because if Trabue was correct it could only mean that John Tully was working for Roberts. As will be seen, the old man may have had at least one other paid confederate among his neighbors.

It is known that the Harpes' one single planned, as opposed to random, target in Kentucky was Silas McBee, a "squire" or justice of the peace who lived on Deer Creek in what is now Webster County and who frequently led "regulator" activities against the region's outlaws. It is likewise certain that the Harpes had at least three *known* confederates in southern and western Kentucky besides the aforementioned Roberts and Tully: Moses Stegall, his wife Mary, and John Leiper. The Stegalls lived about four miles from Squire McBee, and Mary Stegall was said to have been cautioned either by her husband or the Harpes themselves never to call them by their real names in the presence of a stranger.[13] But if the above hypothesis be correct, it is certain that the Rogues' Harbor outlaws had gravely underestimated the Harpes; they killed not from passion but *as* a passion they seemed hardly able to control even at the best of times, and when they were at their worst they would murder friend, enemy, or stranger as the opportunity presented. And this was to bring about their undoing, for two of their former allies, one with an extremely good reason, actually served in the posse that finally hunted them down.

But to return to the story: after leaving Cave-In-Rock the Harpes and their women and children appear to have taken a boat down the Mississippi as far as the mouth of the Tennessee River and then poled upstream at least as far as the mouth of Duck River. Their urge to kill seemed to be growing stronger all the time, and after at least four more murders, including that of a helpless little boy, they crossed the mountains back into Kentucky near Stockton's Valley, pursued by a Tennessee posse. They returned to Jesse Roberts's cabin on the head of Green River, but before they got there they killed John Graves and his son as well as possible ally John Tully. Jesse Stockton's brother Nathaniel found Tully's mangled corpse himself, and he persuaded one of the Tennessee possemen, William Wood, who incidentally was a Baptist and who soon afterward moved to Stockton's Valley himself, to ride west with him to notify Colonel Trabue of the Harpes' return to Kentucky. In turn, Trabue notified Governor James Garrard in Frankfort, who initiated a manhunt and offered a bounty for the Harpes' capture. In the meantime the motley Harpe gang, including their women and children, shoved westward again to their quarry on Deer Creek, Squire Silas McBee, but neither McBee nor anybody else yet knew of their intentions, and they kept murdering indiscriminately nearly all the way from Jesse Roberts's back into Rogues' Harbor. The bloody roster of victims in this third Kentucky death spree included an entire family of ten or twelve settlers traveling together, a little slave boy, another small girl, and even one of Big Harpe's own baby daughters because her crying irritated him. And even after this the bereaved mother and the other two women followed Big and Little Harpe like so many dogs.

Soon after this, though, young George Smith suddenly and inexplicably entered the picture. The Harpes and their women and two remaining children arrived at Moses Stegall's about the third week in August 1799 to finalize plans for the McBee murder. They appear to have eaten at least one meal there and perhaps stayed one night, and for reasons now unknown the Stegalls gave Susan Roberts one dollar on the order of John Leiper "for services unspecified."[14] The Harpes then sent their women and children several miles ahead to a prearranged meeting place on Pond River. From the garbled testimony of the Harpe women after their recapture and the actual location where the three were finally taken into custody, Paul I. Wellman believed this location to have been a cave or rock cliff, and this watercourse was the very one to which young George Smith had relocated from Stockton's Valley. The men then made temporary camp on Canoe Creek, not far from Deer Creek, for practice or perhaps just for sport killing another solitary settler and hiding his body underwater in their favorite ghoulish fashion; his body was not found until long afterward. Paradoxically and in a warped sense nearly humorously, they almost simultaneously managed to convince McBee's closest neighbor on Deer Creek, a simple-minded old settler named James Tompkins, that they were itinerant Methodist preachers.

But when they tried finally to carry out the McBee execution on the night of August 21, they botched things completely. The moon was full or very nearly so, and apparently they had the idea they could shoot McBee through a window of his house, but they seem never to have considered that the Squire, like most well-to-do householders on the frontier, kept a pack of big dogs both for use in hunting and as a very efficient alarm system. The pack set to baying as soon as the dogs caught scent of the Harpes. Squire McBee, knowing that any honest men would have "hollered the house" for help when the pack made to set on them, did not call the dogs off, and the Harpes skulked back to the Stegall place in a foul, murderous mood, with Squire McBee now fully aware that something strange was going on in his community.

When Big and Little Harpe got back to the Stegall cabin late that night, they found that Moses Stegall was absent, but his wife was there with her four-month-old baby and a guest, Major William Love, a surveyor from southeastern Kentucky who had business in the area. Probably in rage and frustration at the failure of their previous plan, they stabbed and tomahawked all three, then set fire to the house and hid on a trail near it in the hope that the visible smoke and sparks from the conflagration would awaken Squire McBee, whom they still hoped to kill, and compel him to come and investigate. However, McBee never saw the fire, and when he did learn of it later the next morning he and several other neighbors rode to the scene by another path. After killing two more unwary travelers on the way to a nearby salt lick, whose bodies the men of Deer Creek discovered later that day, the Harpes took the murdered Major Love's mount and one of Stegall's horses and headed back to their women on Pond River.

But this time the Harpes would not walk away from murder scot-free. McBee and his neighbors finally arrived at the burned cabin on the morning of August 22 not long before Stegall returned himself. Moses Stegall was of course wild with grief and fury, and he immediately identified his lodgers of a few nights before as the perpetrators. He put himself into a tight spot with his own mouth in so doing, though, and he knew his position would be even worse if the Harpes were captured and started talking, so he offered to gather a posse to take them dead or alive—for his own sake and that of John Leiper, he certainly would have hoped dead.

Stegall rounded up volunteers, the most willing of whom was Leiper, and after spending the day burying the five Harpe victims and organizing their own ranks, the manhunters set out the next morning led by Squire McBee. They spent one entire day on the trail before they reached Pond River near the present Christian/Muhlenberg County border, and Squire McBee himself was the first to catch sight of the Harpes early on the morning of August 24. The account McBee related personally in his subsequent testimony in relation to the case, and that either he or his family later gave to historians James Hall and Lyman C. Draper, states that he spied Big and Little Harpe on the side of a hill sloping down to Pond River, and they were talking to a third man whom none of the posse recognized at the time. All three were on foot and evidently armed, but Big Harpe held a horse by its bridle. McBee roared out, "There they are!" to the file of hunters behind him. He and the entire posse readied their guns and struck spurs to their horses, but no sooner had they done so than Big Harpe leaped on his horse and tore off in one direction; Little Harpe sped away on foot in another; and the third, still unidentified, man just as quickly ran directly *toward* the posse before "treeing"—that is, barricading himself behind a tree in what every ex–Indian fighter there would have recognized as a defensive combat move, and therefore a hostile act—about seventy yards in front of the mounted hunters.[15]

The unknown man had never called out to the posse thus far, and so McBee made the only logical and safe response to such an apparent threat. He aimed his gun, a "fowling piece" loaded with buckshot and a heavy powder charge, and fired at the one small area of the man's body that he could see at the side of the tree. At least two of the shot hit the man's right extremities and he fell. The other manhunters already had guns drawn and were getting ready to finish off this unknown and potentially dangerous crony of the Harpes when Moses Stegall suddenly exclaimed, "Don't shoot! It's George Smith!"[16]

McBee himself had once met young George, who lived only two or three miles from this very spot, and now he recognized him. The posse lowered their guns and approached him, and though he'd been silent so far he now began to talk, and talk plenty. Smith said he'd been out early that morning looking for strayed horses. He met Little Harpe there "with a kettle in one hand and a rifle in the other," going to the river to fetch water. Little Harpe detained young George at the place where he and the Harpes had been seen talking and, according to Smith's tale, started speaking to him so loudly that Big Harpe had overheard and then ridden up and joined them. Big Harpe had just dismounted, George said, when McBee and the posse rode into sight, and the reason that he himself had fanned out with the Harpes and run toward the posse was that he'd simply been too terrified of both the Harpes and the posse to think clearly; when he jumped behind the tree he didn't even realize how hostile the action must have appeared to the manhunters.[17]

Perhaps because he was so anxious after this near-miss to get his posse on the trail after the Harpes once more, or perhaps because young George was in fact genuinely convincing, McBee accepted the story implicitly. But had McBee taken more time to listen closely to what George told him, he might not have been so quick to let Smith off the hook. It was extremely strange that young George should have believed that he was in danger as soon as Little Harpe had stopped him to talk, unless he already knew who the Harpes were. He never indicated that they had revealed their names. It was well known that the Harpes' preferred methods of murder involved ambush and complete surprise. It was even stranger that young George should be able to pinpoint the exact location of the Harpes' camp, a rock cliff "not more than eighty rods distant" from where they'd been talking,[18] though he said he'd come to the spot from the opposite direction looking for strayed horses. Moreover, young George had known the father and the family of two of the three Harpe women back in Stockton's Valley, and the women and children had had to stay *somewhere* during the two or three days the Harpes had tried to carry out the McBee assassination and the rest of their Deer Creek butchery. This may in fact have been the reason that Moses Stegall already knew Smith as well as he obviously did, and had therefore identified young George to McBee and the posse and thus saved his life. But all the possible inferences were lost in the haste of the moment. The posse split three ways, McBee and a few others rounding up the women and two remaining children, another group led by John Leiper chasing Big Harpe, and the third group chasing Little Harpe. Although Little Harpe was not captured at this time (he escaped down the Ohio to the Mississippi Territory, where he was finally caught and hanged in 1804), Big Harpe was. Some distance from the site of the Pond River confrontation John Leiper shot him through the spine, Moses Stegall finished him off by beheading him with a large hunting knife, and the men mounted the severed head on the sharpened branch of a large tree near a public path that was for years known as Harpe's Head Road. Before riding ahead to link up with Leiper in his pursuit of Big Harpe, though, McBee had returned briefly to the site of the shooting to give his frightened victim some crude first aid and assistance in getting back to his farm, but he found that young George had very quietly—and quickly—hobbled home on his own.

Big Harpe talked much to Squire McBee before Stegall carried out his execution, confessing to at least seventeen or eighteen murders and possibly all of the thirty-nine killings known to have been done by the Harpes. He expressed no remorse whatsoever for any of them except the killing of his own baby daughter. Neither did he implicate Moses Stegall, John Leiper, or young George Smith as his accomplices, although Wellman indicates that Stegall and Leiper both probably hastened his execution for fear that their names would indeed come up if the big outlaw was allowed to talk much longer. Even so, Big Harpe did make one very intriguing statement, and one unusual request, to McBee. He said he had a pair of saddlebags filled with money secreted somewhere *near the head of Pond River,* and although later a considerable amount of coin was said to have been accidentally discovered in the general area of the upper Pond, it is not certain that this money was ever found, or who may have uncovered it.[19] And Harpe asked that a man called "old Baldwin" who lived in present Livingston County, Kentucky, not far across the Ohio from Cave-In-Rock, be brought to him, because it was he, so Harpe said, who had gotten him to commit all his crimes. This "old Baldwin" was indeed a suspicious character, and he was later brought to trial for complicity to murder along with the Harpe women on the basis of this statement, but he was acquitted simply because it was obvious that the Harpes had killed nearly all their victims utterly on the spur of the moment.[20] However, we must still wonder whether "old Baldwin" was in fact an unknown Rogues' Harbor outlaw gang leader with something of the skill if not the flair of the later and infamous John Murrell, and who worked with Jesse Roberts, John Tully, John Leiper, Moses Stegall, and even possibly young George Smith in arranging the Harpes' first bizarre trip to Cave-In-Rock after the Danville jailbreak and then their second journey into Kentucky to assassinate Squire McBee. One thing is certain, though: young

George Smith was implicated by absolutely no one, not Big Harpe, the gang's women, Moses Stegall, John Leiper, "old Baldwin," Squire McBee, or anybody else who knew him, and to my knowledge no Harpe historian has ever reckoned him as being anything more than an "honest settler"[21] and an innocent bystander who came within a hairsbreadth of being Big Harpe's last murder victim.

In fact, young George might not be suspect at all were it not for the pathetic, lame lie he put together for his family when fifteen-year-old John Smith and another brother came to the Pond River country to check on him in the winter of 1799–1800. Somehow, old George and Rebecca back in Stockton's Valley had heard that their son had had some sort of run-in with the Harpes, and they knew from the deaths locally of John Tully and John Graves that this could mean the very worst. The fear they felt can only be imagined, and accordingly they sent John in company with an older brother, not named by Williams, to see if young George were still alive, and if he was, to give him any aid he might need. The following, taken directly from the Williams biography, is presumably the tale that young George told his brothers when they found him:

> The Harpes . . . reached the neighborhood of George Smith, where they halted for a while to rest. Smith had taken his rifle and gone out into the wilds in search of some stock that had wandered. Coming suddenly upon their camp on the roadside, and seeing the women engaged in cooking, he went in carelessly among them, supposing they were immigrants. The men suddenly seized him, and, wresting the gun from his hands, were about to murder him on the spot; but the women begged them to do the foul deed out of their sight. They dragged him into the woods, when the Big Harpe, as the larger one was called, clutched him with a tiger-like grasp, while the other got ready his rifle to shoot him. Smith, though an active and powerful young man, struggled in vain to get loose from the arms of the giant. Finding that escape was impossible, he turned to watch the movements of Little Harpe, who was ready to shoot, and waited only to get a good aim at his victim.
>
> Almost exhausted by his efforts, George struggled in the arms of his foe now only to keep himself screened from the rifle. Again and again he saw the deadly weapon pointed, but grasping his foe closely, and dodging behind him, he managed to keep him in range of the gun. Suddenly the women at the camp shrieked out an alarm; and, at the same moment, a band of armed horsemen dashed into view. The outlaws instantly abandoned their prisoner, and the Big Harpe, leaping on a fleet horse which he had stolen, fled with desperate speed into the wilderness, while the other escaped on foot. On came the avengers of blood. They stopped but a moment at the spot where George was sitting, panting

> and bewildered, on the ground. One of them, supposing him, too, to be a marauder, recklessly raised his rifle and shot him; the ball passed through his arm and leg, inflicting serious and painful wounds. . . .
>
> When they returned to the spot where Smith had been shot, to look after that unfortunate man, they found that he had, in the mean time, crawled from the place, and, calling aloud for help, had been heard by some passer-by, and taken to his home.[22]

Now, of course, Smith history buffs might argue that both these versions of the story of young George's encounter with death are true and can be harmonized somehow. After all, the second version of the tale does explain how young George could have known, without being an accomplice to the Harpes, where their camp was located. However, besides flatly contradicting Silas McBee's unprejudiced testimony both of what he saw and what young George told him, this second Smith version has so many obvious technical flaws even when considered on its own merits that one might wonder how young George's brothers themselves believed it even for one moment. For one thing, if the Harpes had really intended to kill young George in a setting as confined as their camp, their previous record indicates that they would have stabbed or clubbed him from behind before he could realize what was happening; the only reason Big Harpe would have lain hold on him from that direction was to jerk his head upward with a hand or an arm and draw a knife through his throat. For another, the Harpe women were possibly eyewitness to more than half their men's at least thirty-nine known acts of murder, many of them carried out in the most gory manner conceivable and in one unthinkably horrible case the victim having been one of their very own babies. One more murder, even that of a man two of them undoubtedly knew from Stockton's Valley—even if he hadn't been in cahoots with their father—would never have made them beg the Harpes to do the deed out of their sight. No evidence indicates that they'd ever made such a request to their men before, and none whatsoever leads us to believe that the men would have listened to them if they had. But the most telling point is the plain fact that no man trained to survive on the frontier, not even the green and inexperienced teenager John Smith or the blood-mad Big Harpe at his most demented, would have been foolish enough to pinion a victim's arms and hold him so that he could be shot at close range with a heavy .40- to .50-caliber Kentucky long rifle. With flintlocks as with modern firearms, at that nearly point-blank space there was simply too much danger that the bullet or rifle ball would pass completely through the victim's body and injure or kill the man behind, and everyone knew it. And besides all this, the question remains: if the account young George gave to Squire McBee was indeed truthful—and whether it was or not, McBee certainly accepted it as such at the time—why wasn't the same story good enough for young George to tell his own family?

We will never know all the answers, and that may have been just what both

Raccoon John, if not John Augustus Williams in this particular case, intended. I've tried in this volume as much as possible to avoid using straight comparison and contrast between the Williams biography and the Cochran novel with other historical data, preferring to let the objective, in whatever sources it may be found, stand on its own merits. At least some exercise of the technique is unavoidable, though, and this sordid little scrap of history from John Smith's boyhood illustrates the difference between hagiography and biography perhaps better than any other one example in the Smith story as well as aptly demonstrating the necessity of reading *behind,* if at all possible, the writings of any historian, be he or she professional or merely professing, before accepting any historical writing as complete truth or trying to harmonize conflicting accounts simply to maintain preconceived opinions. As genealogy researchers are well aware, the heads of households in the American South one and two centuries ago often listed unmarried daughters who had borne illegitimate children as "widowed" in census records for the sake of their family's and community's concept of honor, even when they, the daughters, the children, and even local census takers all knew that such "widow" classifications were bald-faced lies. Similarly, bad marriages such as Jonathan Whitely's and the young Rebecca Bowen's were never mentioned, as if the studied mental blocking of such events would eventually mean that they never actually happened. I suspect that young George Smith concocted the second version of his encounter with the Harpes, and that his family accepted it and recounted it as the truth, for reasons entirely similar to the two historical situations noted above. A boy raised in a respectable and God-fearing if rude and isolated home, he may have involved himself a little too closely for comfort with the Jesse Roberts family and the underworld of Rogues' Harbor, and he probably realized his folly and the danger in which he had put himself and his family even before he was scared straight by the one-eyed stare of Squire McBee's fowling piece. That's the only way his cock-and-bull account of the gunpoint wrestling match with Big Harpe makes any sense at all; young George may have felt that he had to give his story that much overkill to make his good old father forget about any relationship that the son had maintained with Jesse Roberts's family before he left Stockton's Valley. Full of holes as the tale was, though, it let the family's honor remain intact, and even if any family member suspected its veracity—as I'm sure most did, for the imbecilic detail about the rifle if for no other reason—no one seems to have questioned it openly and they probably all helped promote it because it was what they all so desperately *wanted* to believe about young George, as much in fact as they wanted to lose the memory of Rebecca having been married twice.

At any rate, the most notable dupes of the second story have been Raccoon John Smith history buffs, who have all seemingly accepted it exactly as young George—and maybe Raccoon John himself—hoped that its hearers would. Of course, the possibility does remain that at least some of them checked the other historical records themselves and chose to keep mute, as noted, a selective affliction not uncommon to denominational hagiographers. Louis Cochran even saw fit to make young George a minor but significant character in the first part of his novel, creating for him a sweet wife named "Beulah" and adorable little twin daughters "Rose" and "Sharon," and in keeping with the general level of Smith scholarship, these names, along with George's story, have been transplanted directly from the novel to serious Smith histories and genealogical pedigree charts. Williams himself dropped young George from his book as soon as he could after George's admission to his brothers that he'd had enough of the western life and that he wanted John to return in the summer and help him move back to Stockton's Valley; and since Williams exhibited by far the greater wisdom in taking this course of action, after this chapter so will we.

In the modern fundamentalist view of history, the existential wasteland inhabited by the Harpes and the other outlaws in Rogues' Harbor and at Cave-In-Rock was not supposed to exist in early America—at least in the east, and for the white Protestants to whom God gave the land first as a haven from Old World religious persecution and then as a reward, by way of the American Revolution, for their love of Christian liberty and their general all-around righteousness. People were properly religious back then, to say nothing of being happily and faithfully married to one spouse all their lives, and the Harpes' hellish, desolate landscape belongs only to modern, degenerate times in which Americans have forsaken their uprightness and closeness with the God of their forefathers. But in fact the last years of the eighteenth century were a time in which American Christianity was, again speaking in the same terminology fundamentalists use now, very much on the decline. Among the educated classes, Deism was on a steady rise. This was, basically, the belief that the universe had been created by an unknown and unknowable Higher Power that did not interfere with the regular processes of the cosmos; that this Being was reason embodied, and that the reasoning power it had given its created beings was the sole means by which it could be understood; that the only worship one could give this Being was to serve its creation in a beneficial way; and that any prophet's, priest's, or religion's claims to divine revelation were therefore suspect if not completely ridiculous. Even so, nearly all Deists were great believers in the value of the church as a moral regulator for those not as intelligent, enlightened, and educated as they were. But they wanted to see the churches gradually "enlightened" at least to a degree as well, and Thomas Jefferson once even speculated that the Unitarian Church (which held a belief in one God, in Jesus as a great prophet, and most often a "universalist" belief in the nonexistence of hell and that all mankind would be redeemed in the end, in essence making it the Protestant religion philosophically closest to the principles of Deism) would prove to be the quintessential church of the American South.[23] However, although the uneducated were largely uninterested in the speculations of Deism itself, they too, especially on the southern and western frontiers of the United States, were rapidly losing interest in religious matters, and the various denominations that had formed and grown so dramatically during the previous generation's Great Awakening were by and large in a frantic self-search to try to figure out what had gone wrong for them.[24]

The times were changing again, though, and the spread of Deistic belief would be checked and the religious interest of the general American population would be rekindled. As it happened, ironically, the so-called Great Revival that spread all over the American South and as far east as western Maryland, Pennsylvania, and New York in the first decade or two of the nineteenth century got its start in the very same area of Kentucky where Big and Little Harpe had run wild only a year or so before; and a nearly grown John Smith, having returned to the Pond River country of western Kentucky in the summer of 1800 to help his brother George move back nearer to their parents in Stockton's Valley, was an unknowing witness to its very birth, at Presbyterian minister James McGready's camp meeting in nearby Logan County.

Before we examine the boy's experience at the camp meeting, though, we must pause a moment to look at the boy himself. Considering that he had been entrusted by his good old father with the tasks noted already, we might speculate that John had "gotten his growth" early. We know that, as an adult, he was about five feet, ten inches in height, and that he weighed between 150 and 170 pounds, with a face almost gaunt and angular, a large, sharp Roman nose, and a muscular frame of iron from constant labor. In the fashion of the times he had a thick, bushy shock of hair that he wore long enough to cover his ears partially, but probably never, in keeping with what were then accepted Baptist dress codes as stressed most strongly by the spiritual descendants of Shubal Stearns, below his collar line; it was dark brown or even black in his youth, turning gray fairly early in his middle years, and it was almost pure white in his old age,[25] but in the photographs taken of him at that time we can see that his hair remained thick and heavy to the last. This appearance and especially that of his eyes would suggest, at least to me and perhaps to anyone acquainted with the Bowen family in eastern Kentucky and western West Virginia, that he may have resembled his mother's people more than his father's. The resemblance comes out not so much in the famous engraving that graces the Williams biography or the painted portrait that now hangs in the library of the Lexington, Kentucky, Theological Seminary, but in one of the two known photographs taken of John Smith in his old age. Though cataracts are visible even in the ancient, grainy photograph, one can see that his eyes were pale blue or a very light gray, with heavy lids that somehow combine with the brightness of the irises below to suggest that distinctive pioneer outward persona of imperturbable calm hiding taut nerves, discussed in the first chapter of this work. They were dreamer's eyes, explorer's eyes, and if the long, heavy eyelashes of youth could be added to the photo they would appear, whether by genetics or pure chance, almost exactly identical to the eyes of a good many Bowen men of succeeding generations in central Appalachia.

In addition to John's possible early maturity and wiry physical appearance, though, old George Smith may have entrusted so much responsibility to an unproven youth simply because he saw John as the most dependable of his sons—and young George may have made him see, whether he could ever admit it even to himself or not, just how much difference there was between a dependable son and a wild one. Not that John himself couldn't think and behave like a typical adolescent both then and now, of course. The incident with the teacher noted in the last chapter, which had to have occurred sometime between 1797 and 1799, is proof positive of that, and besides, Williams does list one and perhaps two stories of old George that Raccoon John recounted with fond affection in the last years of his life, but that originally may have come from a teenager's typical perception of his or her parents as just a little dense, anachronistic, ridiculous, and embarrassing. The first involved old George's efficiency, but apparent lack of business sense, as a farmer. A good horticulturist, George often raised fodder to spare from one growing season to another. Thus, by an expression sometimes heard even now in central and southern Appalachia to describe a status of prosperity, he "had old corn to sell," and his neighbors knew, and new settlers were quick to learn, that they could depend on him as a generous source of grain when their own feed sacks were empty. However, the old man never quite caught on to the principles of the free market economy claimed by today's fundamentalist leaders as divinely bestowed upon the United States, and he could not see why the scarcity of a product should justify an increase in its price. To him, a bushel basket held no more when times were bad than it did when times were good, and he stubbornly refused to charge more than two shillings and sixpence for a bushel of corn (in those days, American use of British currency was still common) even when other successful farmers were asking and receiving a much higher price.[26] Raccoon John, who did try at least once to be a successful capitalist and never quite made it, probably shared a smile and perhaps even a laugh with his biographer over this anecdote, and old George comes off as a real-life example of the type of high-principled, old-fashioned mountain farmer favored in local color fiction. However, it can be imagined that an adolescent John's cheeks often burned with chagrin as he saw his father "taken" by buyers who could have resold the corn at a higher price and then laughed behind old George's back for being such a simpleton.

The second story is, admittedly, more open to question, since Raccoon John seems only to have recounted it to Williams during or after the Civil War, and it occurred years before in a completely different context, the too-often romanticized days of the antebellum South. Once, George had an opportunity to purchase some slaves, brought west from North or South Carolina by a trader, at practically a giveaway price. He turned down the deal, but not from any opposition to the "peculiar institution," as Louis Cochran tried to claim for him. Back in Virginia, the ethic of the family's religious mentors, the Aldersons, seems to have been that black Christians should expect to be treated strictly as servants even in cases where they were baptized and joined the church, and it can be imagined that attitudes were little different on the Holston though slaves were scarce there in the early days. George feared rather that the slaves' presence in his household might spoil his children; he wouldn't have a lazy son or an idle daughter, he said, for all the slaves in the Carolinas.[27] In so doing, he may actually have done the unfortunate souls an unconscious disfavor since, as an ex-bondsman himself and a kind and gentle man by nature anyway, he probably would have made a better master than those to whom they were finally sold. But in the days of a victorious Union Army, and Reconstruction beginning in the South, Raccoon John's recollection of this event once more presents a picture of old George as of the stock that made America great—which he actually was. Barbaric as we regard the idea of slaveowning now, though, in John's youth the possession of slaves was a symbol of family class and status; wealthier fathers had blacks perform the chores that poorer parents thrust upon themselves and their children, allowing the well-to-do to send their sons to school, away from home if necessary, to improve their minds and their opportunities. And this too would have been an especially tender point for the adolescent, thoughtful, and increasingly ambitious John. However much he may have reconciled his memories of and attitudes toward his father by the time he recounted them to John Augustus Williams, his stories still carry something of an undertone of perplexity toward a simple, honest, religious, and quietly stubborn old man who seemed to insist on living the life of a poor dirt farmer even though he had the opportunities both in Tennessee and Kentucky to move his family upward at least to "gentleman-farmer" status. And it's a fact that John himself certainly never reared his own sons by his father's example. At different times of his adult life John both owned slaves[28] and hired slave labor from other masters to cultivate his crops and tend his livestock,[29] and although, as events transpired, he did feel compelled to throw at least two and very probably three of his own sons into the adult world of farmwork at a very young age, there is no evidence that he did so to try to influence them to follow in their grandfather's footsteps. Rather, he probably actively discouraged them from the prospect if there was a chance at all that they could do something else. All told, for most of his life John entertained an entirely different attitude toward labor, slavery, and for that matter prosperity in general than either of these two stories would indicate—and humans being the creatures that they are, John would have seen the differences between his own developing attitudes and those of his father just that much more intensely during his teenage years.

But this is not to say that John ever developed the ambivalence, conscious or unconscious, toward his father that Abraham Lincoln did, leaving home never to return as soon as he reached his majority, and refusing to come visit illiterate Thomas Lincoln even on his deathbed. For all his probable impatience with old George's quaintness and gentle, quiet stubbornness, John still loved his father deeply, and nothing reveals this affection quite so cogently as the incident when old George, on reaching a little thicket where he liked to pray alone—the use of such a private prayer spot is another enduring Appalachian religious tradition, by the way—caught John and some of his older brothers in the middle of the thicket playing cards. In that day card playing was regarded with dancing and fiddling as products of the devil's workshop, from its associations not only with gambling but with drunkenness and dueling (which was still legal in Kentucky, and would remain so for many years) as well. Interestingly, in this period it was also a vice associated more with the wealthier slaveowning classes than with yeomen such as the Smiths, and we may therefore wonder about the true causes of the adolescent John's interest in the pastime. But rather than getting angry and yelling at his sons, or taking off his belt and driving them from his prayer thicket as Jesus had cleansed the Temple with his scourge of small cords and like many a Christian father both before and since would have done, old George simply stood there a moment and wept, and then walked off into the forest—and to John, that sight was worse than ten thousand whippings. All the boys were ashamed that they had brought tears to old George's eyes, but John was so smitten with remorse that he could not even sleep that night. His father never introduced the subject to him, but John apologized the very next day for his misdeed and promised never to play cards again. And he kept that promise throughout his long life.[30]

George Smith undoubtedly sensed that the boy respected his counsel even if he didn't always like it, and this may have been the main reason that he entrusted John with so much responsibility early on. But the essential difference in John's personality from those of his older brothers may have made a great impression on George as well. John was harebrained as all adolescents are, and his jokes, directed as they were usually at persons who boasted of "smarts" that they couldn't prove, could definitely be all too rough and rowdy; he had developed the reputation among other local boys of being a good singer of humorous and sometimes perhaps even bawdy songs; and yet, when left to himself, John was painfully shy around girls[31] and almost never went looking for mischief, but actually preferred solitude and time to think. To return to the matter of his distaste for hunting mentioned in the last chapter, John's recollection to Williams of his preferred alternative to the sport makes almost no sense whatsoever unless we read something into it:

> Expert enough with the rifle to bring down a buck or a bear at long shot, [John] nevertheless had but little fondness for a gun. More like Jacob than Esau in his taste, he left it to his brothers to procure the savory venison for the family, while he supplied the kitchen with the daily allowance of hominy and meal. In these times meal was made by beating grain with a pestle in a block of wood hollowed out like a mortar. To this contrivance a sweep was sometimes attached, when the quantity of bread required was very great. The pounded grist was sifted; the coarser part was boiled for hominy, while the finer was made into hoe-cake, or served with milk and butter in the form of mush. To beat corn for a large family was no easy task, and among the

early sounds that were heard at the cabin every morning, was the fall of John's heavy pestle pounding corn for the daily bread.[32]

It seems that John took his pleasure from a task as repetitive and boring as could be found on a mountain farm, one that any of his brothers or sisters would have had to be ordered, perhaps even with a threat from their mother, to do. Certainly it was no more exciting than churning butter, and for all we know John may have volunteered himself for that chore as well. But this begins to make sense only when we remember that while John's arms were employed at such a tedious task, his mind was left free to wander where it would—and at this period of his youth it was probably wandering through what learning he could glean from George Smith's Bible, his hymnal (probably Rippon's Collection, then popular among Baptists), and his copy of the Philadelphia Confession, the only three books to which John yet had access. By this time having attended only one short term of school under a genuine teacher, John was forced to educate himself using what resources he had; and he may have schooled himself in his father's books during his milling, perhaps keeping a volume by him on the rude table, rapidly devouring a page or two in the intervals he rested and then pondering and digesting what he had read as his increasingly muscular arms toiled on to the next rest stop. And if he churned butter for the household as well, which I suspect he may have, he would have had one of the books open across one knee during the whole process. He certainly studied this way later in his life, taking a Bible or another book with him to the field or the woodpile and reading at any time during the day that a break from his labors afforded the pleasure,[33] and he may simply have acquired the habit in childhood and young adulthood as an absolutely vital exercise for his mind while his hands performed repetitive tasks.

Williams tells us that John learned all the family's favorite hymns by heart,[34] and perhaps he memorized every one in the hymnal as well. He undoubtedly would have been familiar with most of the Old World–style minor and modal melodies by which they were sung, too, but to John the hymnal's particular importance may have been as his only source of metrical poems. Better poetry—and indeed, a fair basic education in several other branches of literature, including tales of war and intrigue, tragic, historic, and romantic drama, philosophy, and even some wonderfully salty erotica—he would have found in the Bible itself. For though old George encouraged John to read the Good Book, he never presumed to tell him which passages to apply to himself and which to avoid, or what he should infer from his reading; as far as John's salvation was concerned, old George believed that the Holy Ghost would lead him where it would.[35] And in at least a part of his late teenage years John did indeed read the Bible as literature rather than as dogma, for he openly admitted to James Challen in 1858 that as a youth he had embraced the values of Deistic late-1790s America and had "tried to be" both a skeptic, or agnostic (that latter term hadn't been invented yet), and a universalist (undoubtedly of the type that Thomas Jefferson had hoped would take hold as the church of the South) before he accepted the principles of orthodox Christianity.[36] These two speculations he must have held as strict secrets from his family, though, especially old George, who would have been every bit as heartbroken by the knowledge of his son's flights of thought as he was when he caught John and his brothers playing cards.

But all in all, George Smith knew that John had developed a good deal of intellectual self-discipline despite his occasional and unnerving pranks against ignoramuses, as well as the prospect of a calm head and good sense when he matured a little more; and so, when young George shook hands with the devil and got his fingers burned in western Kentucky, it was perhaps only natural that old George should send John after his reckless brother, to round him up and bring him back home. Thus John found himself at the McGready camp meeting in the summer of 1800,[37] perhaps stopping at the gathering simply to take in the sights or, equally plausibly, in company with a shaken brother who had decided he could do with a few good purgative hell-and-damnation sermons before he faced his parents again.

Whether alone or in company with young George, though, John certainly saw some unusual sights at this gathering. Among the more bizarre phenomena exhibited by the converts at the meeting were the "barks," the "jerks," the "falling," "rolling," "running," and "dancing" exercises, all with self-explanatory nicknames, most of which were regarded as excessive even by those who believed that the Revival in general was a manifestation of the work of God, and the natures of which have been studied and discussed exhaustively by both believing and skeptical historians.[38] (*Glossolalia,* or the speaking of so-called unknown "spiritual" languages, was not a feature of the McGready camp meeting or most other worship gatherings of the Great Revival; it was introduced to the South first by the Shakers and later by the Mormons, who dropped the practice when it became prudent to do so, and it did not reappear until the beginnings of the Pentecostal movement of the late nineteenth and early twentieth centuries.) To be sure, the McGready camp meeting was revivalism in overdrive, and many of its own participants could be unnerved and embarrassed by its more outlandish attributes, but it exemplified a type of emotional worship with which John Smith was not entirely unfamiliar. The proponents of this camp meeting, and indeed all that would spring from it over the next few years, had roots in evangelical denominations or subsects that had broken off from already-established faiths as a result of the Great Awakening of the generation before: the Methodists, who were now independent of the Anglican Communion, the so-called New Side Presbyterians, who had split from and later reunited with the main Presbyterian denomination, and the Separate Baptists, who had grown under Shubal Stearns from combined Methodist, General Baptist, and Separate Congregationalist influences and who had now joined ranks with the Regular Baptists in all the states except

Kentucky. Just as had occurred in the colonial Awakening, mainline Episcopalian, orthodox Presbyterian, and Regular Baptist divines most usually condemned the workings of the Great Revival as mere emotional excess even as their own sects grew by it. Deborah Vansau McCauley, in her *Appalachian Mountain Religion: A History,* argues that James McGready himself, the initiator of the Great Revival in Logan County and by association all over the South, drew on the traditions of his Scottish and Irish forebears and their "sacramental revivals" in the Old Country,[39] but much crossover influence both from American New Side Presbyterianism and from Shubal Stearns's Separate Baptists was apparent as well. After all, McGready had spent part of his youth in the same general area of the North Carolina Piedmont where Shubal Stearns had established his original Separate Baptist community, and the evangelists that had traveled from that base to Virginia for the dramatic Baptist revival of 1765–1775 had conducted camp meetings almost identical to those McGready utilized. Moreover, after McGready obtained his minister's credentials in Pennsylvania, the veritable birthplace of New Side Presbyterianism, he had returned to the Carolina Piedmont and had labored initially with a younger colleague, Barton W. Stone, in newly gathered churches where Separate Baptist influence, spirituality, and revival techniques had been the norm before the Regulators' War and its aftermath had driven so many North Carolinans into the Appalachian mountains.[40] Thus, the Great Revival even at its very beginning can be seen in terms of character and scope as an extension of the previous century's Great Awakening and the forms of evangelicalism that had sprung from it; and whether or not John Smith's parents agreed entirely with this kind of loud, emotional, experience-based worship, he himself had observed it all his life, first under the preaching of Tidence Lane, William Murphy, and Jonathan Mulkey in Holston Association and later with John and Philip Mulkey, Isaac Denton, and others as they preached on the upper Cumberland River and organized the first small Baptist congregations there.

But since John was to live and labor in a world that was virtually molded by the Great Revival that sprang from this camp meeting, a few more words must be said about the concept of religious revival itself, over and apart from the McGready camp meeting's, and for that matter the entire Great Revival's, particular cultural influences. A broad area of the United States wherein the educated minority had increasingly accepted Deism and many others were seemingly losing interest in religion altogether did not metamorphose into "the Bible Belt" by the inhabitants' cool, thoughtful intellectual acceptance of biblical inerrancy or their rational choice to renew their adherence to the orthodox Protestantism of their forefathers. The McGready camp meeting and all the southern revival gatherings that followed in its wake were attended by both believers whose faith was reaffirmed that the great power of God was in their midst, and skeptics, some of whom mocked the antics they saw, but many of whom were persuaded to change their beliefs and be converted themselves. It is not our purpose here to enter into debate over either the literal accuracy of the Bible or the objective legitimacy of any religious revival in particular. An individual's conceptions, or lack thereof, of the being, attributes, and acts of God are strictly subjective even though he or she may base the concepts on evidence he or she believes to be objective, and the possible philosophical basis for the Revival mindset as it applied, and applies, to individuals will be discussed a bit more extensively in the next chapter. But for the time being, to understand John Smith's world it must be accepted that by far most of the Revival's attendees themselves believed that they were caught up in a visible manifestation of the work of God even if many shied away from the weirdest of the "exercises of the Spirit," and it was this belief, based on their own subjective impressions, that *made* the Bible inerrant once again *for* them. It was as if they proved Paul Tillich's contention that mysticism is the mother of rationalism; they formed an entire system of reason on a foundation of insights produced from ecstatic experience.

To put it another and perhaps simpler way, the Deistic intellectual upsurge of the late 1790s had set "belief of the head" over and above "belief of the heart," but the Great Revival reversed the process and actually caused "belief of the heart" to redefine "belief of the head." In this dramatic refashioning of American intellectual mores, the God of Deism slipped quietly into the background, the God of American Protestantism once again took center stage, and belief in biblical inerrancy became not only a doctrinal and intellectual but practically a social necessity.[41] In the process, of course, a good bit of the history of the United States up to this point had to be rewritten either consciously or unconsciously in the minds of American citizens, with some Revolutionary Deists such as Thomas Paine all of a sudden becoming great villains but a great many more (even Thomas Jefferson, in the eyes of some) being beatified as evangelical Christians who let God win the Revolution and create the United States for them. For the same reason or reasons, this was of course also the day of the suppression of individuals' and families' memories of pasts that could be considered checkered according to biblical or at least Gospel and Pauline standards, such as that of John's mother with her wild, unpredictable, and cruel first husband. But for better and worse, the picture of a reality based on an inerrant Bible that was reinforced during the Great Revival has continued, for both great good and great evil, within the culture of rural American, especially southern, Christianity to this day. Only a few readers perhaps would disagree that great good has come from this mindset and this heritage of biblical inerrancy, but if any reader should wonder what I mean by speaking of evil developing within this exact same context, he or she need only read on.

Having set the stage and established the paradigm thereon, so to speak, we need to look at the corollary of this newly reinforced belief of biblical inerrancy: if the phenomena of the Revival made the Bible inerrant in the minds of the Revival's participants, the Bible in turn must legitimize the occurrences of the Revival. Such a corollary did exist, but only up to a certain reference point, after which the sects united in revival began to war with one another even as they labored together. Thus a bit of biblical exegesis is necessary at this point to try to understand the theology embraced by most of the Revival's protagonists, and the points of doctrine over which they ultimately came to quarrel even as the Revival raged on; and we must begin with that portion of Scripture that describes the arrival of the entity to which the work of the Revival was attributed, the Holy Spirit.

In the first chapter of the Acts of the Apostles, we are told that Jesus, just before his ascension into heaven, instructed his disciples to wait at Jerusalem until they were given "power from on high." In the chapter following, the Holy Spirit (or the Holy Ghost, if one prefers the older term) descended upon a group of approximately 120 disciples who were assembled together at the feast of Pentecost, fifty days after the Passover feast at which Jesus had been crucified. They began to speak with other tongues as this Spirit gave them utterance, causing the multitudes who had come to the city for the feast to hear a group of Galileans proclaim the works of the Lord in Parthian, Median, Cretan, Arabian, and at least ten other named languages or dialects. Thus emboldened, Simon Peter began to preach to them the first Holy Spirit–inspired sermon given in the New Testament; to quote verse 38 in chapter 2, he instructed them to "Repent, and be baptized every one of you in the name of Jesus Christ for the remission of sins, and ye shall receive the gift of the Holy Ghost."[42] About three thousand souls hearkened to Peter's words that day and became Christians.

In the eighth chapter of Acts, when the apostles began to spread the Gospel among the Samaritans (among whom it seems to have been news, contrary to the reference in the fourth chapter of the Gospel of John that Jesus preached to them directly during his ministry), we are given an additional detail: that is, that at this time new converts, who were all Jews or of mixed Jewish blood like the Samaritans, received the Holy Spirit after baptism by the imposition, or the laying on of hands, of the apostles themselves. Among their baptized converts in the Samaritan territories was one Simon, who had previously enjoyed a great reputation among the Samaritans in general as a sorcerer and a "great power of God." It is never actually stated explicitly that the apostles laid hands on this Simon for his reception of the Holy Spirit, only that he had been baptized as a believer. But when Simon saw that the Holy Spirit was given by apostolic imposition, he offered Peter and John money to give him their same power to bestow the Spirit on whomever he himself laid hands. Peter immediately returned a curse and a sharp rebuke: "Thy money perish with thee, because thou hast thought that the gift of God may be purchased with money. Thou hast neither part nor lot in this matter, for thy heart is not right in the sight of God." Of a sudden, Peter appears to have found one whose sins were not remitted by the baptismal water; but then again, Scripture never explicitly states that this Simon was ever purged from the church, assuming that it had an organizational structure at this time apart from the apostles themselves, only that he was told to pray that his sin might be forgiven.[43]

But in the account in the tenth chapter of Acts, of the conversion of Cornelius the centurion, according to Scripture the first Gentile Christian, the theological argument used to endorse both the pre-Revolutionary Great Awakening and the early American Great Revival was stated most clearly. Here, Cornelius is described as searching for God, the inference being the God of the Jews, and he was visited by an angel who told him to send to Joppa for Peter, who would tell him how to obey God. Cornelius accordingly sent servants to find Peter, who was staying with another Simon, a tanner, at this time; but as it turned out, Peter was having divine revelations of his own on Simon the tanner's rooftop, and the arrival of Cornelius's men made him put two and two together, so to speak, that the Lord was telling him to take the Gospel to the Gentiles as well as the Jews. When Peter arrived at Cornelius's abode he began to preach, but while he was still speaking, "the Holy Ghost fell on all them which heard the word"; they spoke with tongues like the assembly at Pentecost, and "magnified" God. The Jewish Christians who had come with Peter were amazed that the Spirit had been given to these Gentile hearers, one reason perhaps being that the Gentiles had neither yet been baptized nor imposed by the apostles before exhibiting the manifestations with which they had associated the Spirit; but they took the matter in stride, saying, "Can any man forbid water, that these should not be baptized, who have received the Holy Ghost as well as we?" Accordingly Peter baptized these first Gentile converts, and stayed with them some days.[44]

To make a long story short, George Whitefield, Shubal Stearns, James McGready, and all the firebrands of Great Awakening and Great Revival evangelism based their preaching on the assumption taken from this biblical passage: that God, being no respecter of persons, would do for all Gentile converts what he had done for the very first ones. Not that any modern hearers should specifically expect to be visited by angels telling them to go and hear a particular preacher or preachers (although certainly many arguably impressionable converts did claim such experiences), but that an all-powerful God took the same interest in each individual's conversion that He did in Cornelius's. The direct influence of the same Holy Spirit bestowed upon the 120 at Pentecost, impressed sinners individually and personally with the fact that they needed to entrust themselves—heart, soul, mind, and strength—to the mercies of a Savior, and hence to hearken to the preaching of the Gospel. In turn, the Spirit worked simultaneously upon the minds of Gospel preachers to give them the messages that sinners needed to hear, just as God had given Peter his Pentecost sermon and his allegorical vision on the rooftop at Joppa to carry the Gospel to the Gentiles. Thus the influence that sinners felt at revival meetings during both the Great Awakening and the Great Revival, to fall down, weep, cry out, and sometimes—just possibly—to engage in even more bizarre behavior, was reckoned to be the Spirit of God dealing with them as it had with Cornelius, to convince them that they needed to hear and apply to the Gospel to be saved. At the point they believed and trusted in Jesus totally, with all their being, they were given the same assurance of salvation as was Cornelius and his family, the Holy Ghost as the "seal" of their salvation, and were then fit subjects for baptism and/or the privileges of the church.

As I've indicated, the general impressions of an experience of the New Birth in Christ of course cannot be related objectively, ironically, most particularly for those of us who have undergone it. I believe, though, that I can safely employ one of the terms of William James to assert that it makes one perceive the sacred as firsthand experience rather than mere secondhand belief; were it not so, the biblical inerrantist mindset of the Great Awakening and the Great Revival could never have evolved. I listed examples of born-again conversions both farfetched and more prosaic in my previous work dealing with the ministry of Shubal Stearns,[45] but the best instance to cite as a fairly normative (i.e., middle-of-the-road) Great Revival period case might be that of William Vaughan, mentioned in this work's introduction as one of Raccoon John's close associates in his middle years and ultimately one of his greatest doctrinal adversaries. Vaughan was a year or so younger than Smith, and, like him, was influenced by Deism in his youth; but as he related to J. H. Spencer in his old age, a few years after the Great Revival began he experienced a complete change of attitude:

> [One] Sabbath morning, I was sitting in my door, pensive and disconsolate, when I saw a company of people walking by. On inquiring, I learned that they were going to meeting at an old log Baptist meeting house known as Rocky Spring [later known as Friendship, of the North District Association] about three miles distant. I joined the company, and went with them. As we walked along, a very wicked old man remarked to me that, every six or seven years, a portion of the people went off from the world and became religious. If I ever prayed from my heart, it was as I walked to that meeting. A man by the name of [Joshua] Leathers got up to preach. I had never seen him before. When he rose up I recognized him as [a man whom he had dreamed about a few nights previously], even to the minutia of his dress. George Eve followed him, preaching from the text: "Ye must be born again." All he said was an incomprehensible mystery to me. James Quesenberry followed him from the text: "The great day of his wrath is come; and who shall be able to stand?" He described the various outpourings of God's wrath, frequently repeating the words, "Who shall be able to stand?" Each time I would say mentally, I shall not be able to stand. At the close of his sermon, he invited the mourners to come up and be prayed for. The thought occurred to me, I will not go up there and disgrace myself; I will go to the woods and pray, God can hear me there as well as here. The next thing I knew, I was on my knees at the feet of the preachers, confessing my sins—especially my Deism—and asking them to pray for me. They prayed. One

> woman near me cried out, "Oh, my heart is so hard!" I felt that to be just my case. . . .[46]

Vaughan endured this period of "conviction" for his sins for some weeks, but it had a happy ending:

> It seemed to me that I cried every breath, "Lord, be merciful to me." . . . Suddenly the thought occurred, What a great change has come over me: six weeks ago I could not utter a sentence without an oath; now every breath is a prayer for mercy. Then this text occurred to me: "Now ye have received the spirit of adoption whereby ye cry, Abba, Father." In a moment it seemed to me that the blood of Christ overwhelmed me, and I felt that my burden and distress were gone. I felt such a love for Jesus Christ, that I thought, if he was on earth, and I could get hold of his feet, I would press them to my bosom. Still I did not love him as I wished to. I went out into the fields, and spent the day in prayer, praise, and rejoicing. I felt that God had been merciful to me, but could not tell how. Relief came not as expected. I thought all my exercises should have been more intense [!] I prayed for the return of my burden, and continued to have alternate doubts and hopes, till . . . I went to Friendship Church, related the dealings of God with my soul, and was approved for baptism. Next day . . . I was baptized by James Quesenberry [ellipses added].[47]

For all the drama Vaughan gave his conversion, though, there remains much evidence that great latitude was given to a convert on his or her personal testimony. Raccoon John Smith himself recalled to Albert Allen a different sort of experience related by one of his close friends in 1824, while both he and the friend were still Baptists and John himself considered the born-again experience to be a necessary article of Christian faith. John stated that "After hearing his experience, I would cheerfully have given him the hand of fellowship. *It was one which any Baptist church would have cheerfully received, and was almost substantially such as mine*" (emphasis added).[48] Allen did not list the details either of this particular experience or Raccoon John's own, to which he had thus compared it, although in writing of the same incident some years later, John Augustus Williams did recount John's friend's conversion testimony: "From the time that I could read the Scriptures, I was convinced that Jesus was the Son of God, and was fully persuaded that I was a sinner, and must obtain pardon through the merits of Christ, or be lost forever. This caused me great distress of mind; for I was much exercised under the workings of a guilty conscience. Finally, however, I was able to put my reliance on him, the only Savior of sinners; and from that time on I have had peace of mind."[49] It must be kept in mind that the simple and heartfelt profession of the personal experience was the important thing; the details, such as those noted in both the above testimonies, could and often did vary to either extreme.

After this reference point of unity on the reality of the sacred as proven by individual experiential conversion, though, the snake wriggled into Eden and fellowship and goodwill among the exponents of the Revival began to fall apart along previously established denominational lines. Stricter Presbyterians and Regular Baptists interpreted the influence of the Holy Spirit as coming irresistibly to a predetermined number of elect souls, while Methodists and Separate Baptists were more inclined to preach salvation available to all, giving their hearers dire warnings about the dangers of resisting the Spirit's influence. In this the Separate/Methodist perspective finally triumphed, because to most Americans, whose memories of pre-Revolutionary and Revolutionary days were fading away inexorably and who now believed themselves to be living in a God-created bastion of righteousness, strict Calvinism was no longer needed as a security blanket for uncertain times. Most mainline American Calvinist denominations ultimately more or less "Arminianized" themselves,[50] although their leaders would have been enraged to have their actions categorized by such a term. Still, there remained fringe groups who kept the older school of thought alive in sometimes even more extreme versions than their ancestors had, and who defied the efforts of their more liberal or moderate brethren to establish dialogues with them.[51] Both Regular and Separate Baptists preached that Cornelius and his family were baptized by immersion after being saved as described above, while Methodists and Presbyterians held forth that they were sprinkled or affused—although the Methodists ultimately had to start performing baptisms by immersion *or* sprinkling, according to the individual's preference, just to keep many of their own followers from being drawn away by the vociferous Baptists.[52] And all of them, besides openly criticizing the finer points of each other's doctrines and disparaging the intellectual capabilities and morals of each others' ministers, were prone to accuse one another of accepting converts who related more wild-haired, outlandish, and laughable salvation experiences—visions of angels or devils, sheep on a mountainside with Jesus leading them and holding a shepherd's crook, and whatnot—in order to give themselves the appearance of being more common sense– (in revival context, of course) and Scripture-oriented.[53]

Perhaps the most paradoxical situation within this gyroscope of united sentiment on the reality of the born-again experience and dirty little wars over the interpretation of a set of Scriptures that all those involved believed to be inerrant, though, occurred not between Methodists and Presbyterians or either denomination against Baptists, but between Baptists and Baptists themselves in Kentucky. In North Carolina, Regular and Separate Baptists had begun to merge as early as 1777; the two factions united in Georgia in 1784, in the Tennessee territory in 1786, in Virginia in 1787, and in South Carolina in 1789, and many new immigrant Kentucky Separates joined ranks with their erstwhile Regular rivals in the formation of the Elkhorn and Salem Associations as early as 1785. Still, there remained one large Kentucky Separate clan in the old Shubal Stearns form, known as the South Kentucky Association and led, as noted in the previous chapter, by Elder Robert Elkin. The Virginia United Baptists, now steered by a General Committee that gave its component associations a measure of stability, checks, and balances not unlike the Federal Constitution had given the United States, had had a dialogue going with both Kentucky factions at least since 1788; South Kentucky Association got along harmoniously with east Tennessee's Holston Association as well, exchanging ministers and members who migrated back and forth between Kentucky and Tennessee. Over the years Elkhorn, Salem, and South Kentucky Associations had tried time and again to negotiate a union, and had never been able to bring it off. One early opportunity had been ruined by Separate Baptist minister William Bledsoe, whose father, Joseph, and brother, Moses, were both respected preachers, but who himself had picked the season of negotiations to try and start a "revival" in his church by scrawling apocalyptic messages on a couple of eggs, carrying them with him to meeting one Sunday morning, and claiming to his shocked and frightened congregation that his hens had laid them with the message of judgment already on them. (The Book of Numbers tells us that God gave Balaam a message through the mouth of an ass, so maybe William wanted his hearers to believe—but no, let's just drop that comparison.) The Regular Baptists naturally refused to assume any connection with this incident, and broke off talks; after his exposure and disgrace, William became a fashionable Universalist and then a Deist, and the converts whom he had thus shamefully egged on, as it were, all backslid.[54] Among them, interestingly, had been John Smith's fiddler friend Jeremiah Vardeman.[55]

Another union attempt a few years later was thwarted by an overheated disagreement over particular (Calvinistic) versus general (Arminian) atonement,[56] and in this instance South Kentucky Association was once again embarrassed by a preacher, John Bailey, who had adopted more or less Universalist sentiments himself (he believed hell to be a place something like the Roman Catholic concept of purgatory, although J. H. Spencer states that Bailey may have held "hell redemption" merely as a private belief and only touched on it tangentially when in the pulpit).[57] The union did not materialize, but now South Kentucky Association split over this issue as well as over vague and unrecorded difficulties that existed between South Kentucky moderator Robert Elkin and the respected minister Andrew Tribble. A breakaway South Kentucky faction calling itself Tate's Creek Association elected Tribble as moderator and agreed to adopt Virginia's 1787 partial acceptance of the Philadelphia Confession as the basis for a "correspondence" relationship with Elkhorn and Salem Associations, and in fact Tate's Creek appears to have been the first Kentucky group to style itself as United Baptist after the Virginia form. It must be remembered that, at this period, all Kentucky associations involved in the negotiations were gradually shrinking in numbers due to deaths, exclusions, outmigrations, and the increasing influence of Deism as well as the general cooling of religious interest already discussed. South Kentucky Association's restoration of fellowship and privileges to the suspected Universalist Bailey and his Rush Branch Church in Lincoln County in 1799, effected without comment either on Bailey's personal sentiments or the church's heterodoxy, is an apt indication that the times were a little out of joint. Perhaps Thomas Jefferson was right after all.

But the Great Revival changed all that, or at least so it appeared. As its influence swept into central Kentucky from Logan County, both Regular and Separate Baptists found themselves so busy preaching to worried penitents and baptizing shouting converts that their doctrinal disputes of the past decade and a half were temporarily forgotten. South Kentucky Association itself rapidly grew so large that by 1801 it was forced to divide itself into North and South District Associations simply for the convenience of its ministers and members, and right at this juncture of division, committees of Regular and Separate Baptist ministers once again began to try and negotiate a union. It was finally effected that same year in the heat of Great Revival sentiment, amazingly, completely without consideration of the Regulars' Philadelphia Confession, but on a homemade set of articles that came to be known as the Terms of General Union and which are listed below:

> We, the committees of Elkhorn and South Kentucky Associations, do agree to unite on the following plan:
>
> 1st. That the Scriptures of the Old and New Testament are the infallible word of God, and our only rule of faith and practice.
>
> 2d. That there is only one true God, and in the Godhead or divine essence, there are Father, Son, and Holy Ghost.
>
> 3d. That by nature we are fallen and depraved creatures.
>
> 4th. That salvation, regeneration, sanctification and justification are by the life, death, resurrection and ascension of Jesus Christ.
>
> 5th. That the saints will finally persevere through grace to glory.
>
> 6th. That believer's baptism by immersion is necessary to receiving the Lord's supper.
>
> 7th. That the salvation of the righteous and punishment of the wicked will be eternal.
>
> 8th. That it is our duty to be tender and affectionate with one another, and study the happiness of the children of God in general; to be engaged singly to promote the honor of God.
>
> 9th. And that the preaching Christ tasted death for every man, shall be no bar to communion.
>
> 10th. And that each may keep up their associational and church government as to them may seem best.
>
> 11th. That a free correspondence and communion be kept up between the churches thus united.

Unanimously agreed to by the joint committee:

[Regular Baptists] Ambrose Dudley, John Price, Joseph Redding, David Barrow

[Separate Baptists] Robert Elkin, Thos. J. Chilton, Daniel Ramey, Moses Bledsoe, Samuel Johnson

These Terms of General Union were ratified not only by Elkhorn and the North and South District components of the old South Kentucky Association, but by Salem and Tate's Creek as well as the newly organized Bracken and Green River Associations; in effect, it became the standard abstract of principles for all the Baptists in Kentucky at the time, though most former Regulars still endorsed the Philadelphia Confession along with this new document. Kentucky Baptists also dropped the Regular and Separate designations for the Virginia name and style of United Baptists, but the ecstatic, Great Revival–inspired haste in which the union had been effected made its results disastrous. The framers of the Terms had given a lick and a promise to the main interassociational and diplomatic questions that had thus far set distance between the Kentucky Regulars and Separates with the vaguely worded ninth, tenth, and eleventh articles of the agreement, and not even all the committeemen had agreed specifically on how they should be effected. They never even bothered trying to organize a General Committee like the Virginians had, perhaps in their spiritual intoxication, as it were, not even considering such a group necessary, and the arrangement left the strength of the denomination's unity split up between the moderators of the various associations and based only on their annual exchanges of letters and messengers. Such a union was every bit as weak, and even weaker, than the United States had been under the Articles of Confederation before the Constitution was framed, and not surprisingly, as soon as the revival spirit had cooled down a bit, all the Kentucky Baptists' old problems reappeared and were rendered even worse by the denomination's weak organization. The Regular-based associations, even though they wanted to be as evangelistic as the Separates under whom many of their ministers and members had been introduced to the faith in the first place, started trying once again to "Calvinize" their new correspondents, sometimes using extremely underhanded issues of interassociational diplomacy to do so. The former Separates, who were and would remain accustomed to following their association moderators as quasi-tribal patriarchs and clan chieftains in the mold of good old Shubal Stearns, and who had become increasingly ashamed of being known as Arminians due probably to the term's connection with Methodism, in turn tucked their tails, stayed quiet, and let their leaders defend them as best they could, but they often found their interests "sold out" to keep the union extant.

The end result left the Kentucky Baptists firmly rooted and grounded in a solid maybe. They claimed to be unified even as Regular factions within their ranks made war on Separate factions, the Separate leaders generally quietly and unassumingly parrying Regular offensives and eating crow when it was politically advisable, but once in a while hitting viciously below the belt in return; they claimed to be Calvinists, but only a minority actually wanted strict Calvinist dogma stressed. The publication in America of British Particular Baptist Andrew Fuller's *Gospel Worthy of All Acceptation* was, perhaps quite literally, a godsend to most of them, since its tenets allowed them to maintain the Calvinistic facade they considered respectable and yet still preach with the essentially Arminian zeal they had been using all along anyway.[58] More than once in the General Union's first quarter century of existence, good men on both sides of the Calvinist/Arminian question, to say nothing of moral and ethical as opposed to doctrinal issues, found themselves roundly condemned and stripped of influence for no more than speaking the truth of their consciences, for in this weak political system "giving offense to the brethren" had literally become a sin as heinous as theft or murder. Within the first half of that twenty-five years no less than six acrimonious divisions split the Kentucky Baptist Union, more than one championed by men who had actually served on the joint committee that had framed the Terms in 1801, with those left behind on their sandy middle ground within the Union loudly decrying them as sowers of discord. The political workings of the Kentucky Baptists' General Union must be examined in more detail later, as they related to the life and career of John Smith, but for now we might venture one speculation: the modern Southern Baptist Convention's simultaneous tendencies to hide behind its bureaucratic structure rather than address either doctrinal or social issues in any progressive way, and to exploit that same bureaucracy to carry out the agendas of powerful Southern Baptist politicians, remarked upon in recent scholarly studies made by both insiders and outsiders to the denomination,[59] very well may be a part of its heritage from old Kentucky, its arrogant yet fretful and defensive stance hammered directly out of the Baptist political crises in the wake of the Great Revival.

And to cap off the entire picture of the Great Revival's aftermath, there were the "New Light" denominations—those formed exactly as the Great Awakening had produced the New Side Presbyterians, the Separate Congregationalists, and the Separate Baptists, who at first rapturously believed that they had shaken off the shackles of centuries of error and were now worshiping God in a pure form (or at least a purer one than those of the older denominations from whence they sprung), but who subsequently traveled the same path as their forefathers and established orthodoxies of their own. Perhaps the mildest Great Revival religious order of this sort, the Cumberland Presbyterian Church, came into being right in the territories and among the leaders of the McGready camp meeting. The newly formed Kentucky Presbyterian Synod condemned and disfellowshipped the more enthusiastic of James McGready's preaching partners for having become too Arminian in doctrine and otherwise at odds with the Westminster Presbyterian Confession; the ministers in turn utilized the Cumberland Presbytery to continue practicing the same emotional, experience-based worship brought by McGready to western Kentucky from the Orange Presbytery in North Carolina and its antecedents among the original followers of Shubal Stearns there. J. H. Spencer gave them the droll classification of a Methodist-Presbyterian hybrid, as if his own Baptists had no mongrel genes of their own.[60] Ironically, McGready himself, the man who had in a sense initiated the entire Great Revival, elected to remain with the mainline Kentucky Synod while his former partners carried on the work he had begun, without him.

A better example and another of the new Kentucky Synod's targets was Barton Warren Stone, noted already as McGready's North Carolina associate, who was living in central Kentucky when the Great Revival began. On hearing of his mentor's work and successes in Logan County, he traveled southwest and paid a visit to the McGready camp meeting himself, and he became a zealous supporter of the Great Revival almost from the very first. In fact, Stone himself probably effected the Revival's spread into central Kentucky and from thence to points north and east: when he brought the news from Logan County back to his Bluegrass Presbyterian congregations, the Revival exploded there as well, his own Cane Ridge camp meeting outstripped anything McGready had seen in Logan County for crowds, "barks," "jerks," and dramatic conversions, and when the eastern news media got hold of the story it became literally a national event.

A prophet is not without honor save in his own country, though, and Stone and his closest associates were destined for trouble with their synod. Stone himself had never been a very strong Calvinist, and he had somehow been ordained to the ministry even though he had plainly told his examiners that he accepted the Westminster Confession only insofar as he saw it to be consistent with the word of God.[61] This gave him essentially the same creedal—or noncreedal—stance as that claimed by the Separate Baptists back in North Carolina, and he and his followers in fact did come to embrace immersion as the correct means of baptism, but he also formulated concepts of both the Trinity and the atonement that were at odds with the standard Protestant theology of the times. Though by no means a Unitarian (or an "Arian," as he was slandered for decades by ministers of competing sects, many of whom probably didn't even know who the ancient heretic Arius was or what he believed), he rejected the prevailing idea that Jesus was equal with God the Father,[62] and he believed in the death, burial, and resurrection of Jesus not as a blood sacrifice for the sins of the elect but simply as the means God had chosen to lead men and women to repentance and *at-one-ment* with Him (Stone hyphenated the term in this fashion to convey his point, although of course it wouldn't have worked in the original biblical languages).[63] Perhaps most remarkable of all, though not surprisingly in the context of the times, Stone and his associates were so utterly convinced of the Great Revival's proof of the Bible as an inerrant and completely consistent body of divinity that they preached that the Revival's Divine presence rested not so much in a Trinity-based Holy Spirit leading men and women to repent and seek the teachings of the Scriptures, but rather actually within written Scripture itself. Hence the words of the Gospel themselves carried the power of pardon—and more, the Bible provided its own complete validation of its followers' claims for its inerrancy. In a monumental irony, there is evidence that Stone and his compatriots adopted this viewpoint from a Tennessee parson with whom they worked occasionally, Thomas P. Craighead, who himself used the doctrinal stance to oppose the very same excesses of the Great Revival that Stone and his coworkers embraced.[64]

Stone and his followers separated themselves from the Kentucky Synod just before they were to be disciplined by the body, at first styling themselves as the independent Springfield Presbytery, although the "New Light" nickname clung to them for some years as well. In spite of their doctrinal deviations, though, typical "New Light" or "Stoneite" worship services in this movement's early days were very little different from those of either the Cumberland Presbyterians or the Separate Baptists. The preaching was exhortatory, the churches had "mourner's benches" at which sinners could seek salvation, penitents were urged to pray for the New Birth in Christ, and those who professed conversion were baptized by immersion or sprinkling according to their preference—though, as the movement matured, immersion became virtually the sole mode of administering the ordinance.

Though Stone's stance had considerable appeal for diehard Separate Baptists in Kentucky who were reluctant to accept either the Regular Baptists' Philadelphia Confession or even the Terms of General Union—Benjamin Lynn, who seems to have been the first Separate Baptist preacher ever to settle in southern Kentucky and who may have officiated at the first seven immersions performed in the state, was an early Stone proselyte[65]—the ranks of the Stoneites were augmented and their cause was aided the most by an informal union with a slightly older breakaway Virginia Methodist group known first as the "Republican" Methodists and later, simply as the Christian Church. At its beginning this Virginia faction, led by one James O'Kelley, had separated from the larger Methodist Episcopal body in protest over the autocratic tendencies of its first and most respected American bishop, Francis Asbury. After the break, though, O'Kelley began to evidence theological ideas perceived by conventional Methodists to be heterodox as well. He taught that the Father, Son, and Holy Ghost were not three distinct personages in one divine essence, but rather three mere offices of one Being.[66] This stance, now known as "Jesus Only" or "Oneness" theology, is found nowadays in certain Pentecostal factions as well as a few other sects, among them one extreme exclusivist group known simply as the Church of Jesus Christ, but tracing the possible historical links from the O'Kelley movement to these contemporary sects and modern-day "Jesus Only" Pentecostalism is beyond the scope of this work. At any rate, Rice Haggard, O'Kelley's assistant who was actually the responsible party for the "Christian" name change, emigrated from Virginia to southern Kentucky not long after the Springfield Presbytery separated itself from the Kentucky Synod; he found "New Light" theology compatible if not quite in complete agreement with his and O'Kelley's, joined the Kentucky group, and persuaded them likewise to adopt the Virginians' simple "Christian Church" designation. Haggard has perhaps never been given adequate credit for the stabilizing influence that he gave both these Kentucky and Virginia groups.[67]

For stability was the one thing the Kentucky New Lights needed most of all. Not long after news of the Cane Ridge camp meeting and its dramatic results hit the eastern newspapers and the Great Revival began to spread in that direction as well, the New York leaders of the bizarre, communistic, and celibate United Society of Believers in Christ's Second Appearing, known more commonly as the Shakers, who taught that their founder, "Mother" Ann Lee, was the female reincarnation of Jesus Christ, decided to send missionaries to Kentucky to try their luck among this multitude of frontier converts. Stone's New Lights already harbored a strong concept of the essential sinfulness of all secular governments, even that of the United States, and the communistic Shakers hit them with the impact of a hurricane. They lauded Mother Ann and the Millennium in tongues both intelligible and unknown, danced, sang, and performed other "spiritual" wonders, and they rapidly converted several of Stone's most prominent preaching associates, such as Richard McNemar, John Dunlavy, and Matthew Houston. So successful were they among the New Lights that they were able to purchase land and establish two large Shaker communes in Kentucky within a couple of years, one at South Union in Logan County and the other at Pleasant Hill on Shawnee Run near Harrodsburg, and McNemar, Dunlavy, and Houston all became Shaker leaders. The Shaker schism sent two more of Stone's preaching partners, Robert Marshall and John Thompson, back to the mainline Presbyterian fold in disgust and shame at the direction the New Light movement seemed to be taking; but still, with Haggard's quiet and patient help the Stone movement weathered the storm, survived, and eventually gained a measure of respectability among Kentucky denominations.[68]

This would by no means be the last time that Barton Stone's church would attract the attention of new and ambitious religious elements in the northeast, though—but that, like the more detailed story of early nineteenth-century Kentucky Baptist politics and John Smith's involvement therein, must keep for further discussion later.

Back at the McGready camp meeting in the summer of 1800, these earth-shaking events had barely begun to unfold, and all that young John Smith possibly could have discerned at the time was that he was witnessing an exceptionally vigorous, unusual, and perhaps even frightening series of worship services. Williams records that John was shocked and disgusted at the barking ("Every knee shall bow-wow-wow, and every tongue shall confess"),[69] jerking, dancing, and other antics that he saw, but not, of course, that he was flirting with skepticism, Deism, or universalism at the time.[70] Cochran even has him meet and talk with Barton Stone on the campgrounds, but we may discount that kind of wishful thinking altogether; both Smith and Stone were certainly present at approximately the same time, but Williams records nothing of the sort and if such a meeting and verbal exchange had taken place it would have been too politically advantageous for Smith's biographer *not* to mention it. Willams does allow for John's skeptical tendencies at this time in a qualified sense, sugarcoating them considerably, but mentions nothing of his ever having been a Universalist even though he acknowledges James Challen as one of his own sources.[71] But we must keep in mind that at the time he finally penned the Smith biography, attitudes had changed much, and he had to be careful to present John in a light acceptable to the context of the times. He therefore characterized John as something of a young almost-Christian Socrates, complete with the old Greek philosopher's argumentative skills and sense of humor, searching for truth but not finding it either at the McGready camp meeting or among the Baptists of his home in Stockton's Valley, but who was nonetheless firmly convinced of one unassailable fact: "*that it was his duty to be a Christian*" (emphasis in original).[72] The reemphasis of this social convention more truly was one of the primary products of the Great Revival, but the idea that John was convinced of its inarguable correctness at this stage of his life is very much open to question. Whatever positive or, most probably, negative emotions John actually experienced in Logan County, there is absolutely no evidence that it made any real changes in his beliefs or attitudes. He thus left the grounds with his wayward big brother in tow—for all we know, young George actually could have professed conversion at the meeting, as much in emotional reaction to his experiences with the Harpes and in fear and shame at the prospect of meeting his good old father again as any other impression; if such an event did occur, it would provide one plausible explanation for the extremity of John's shock and disgust—and he returned home to resume his life as before.

Williams goes on to record that John spent much time between his sixteenth and his twentieth year in the company of Isaac Denton, the Baptist minister who lived closest to the Smiths' home in Stockton's Valley. Denton had come up from Tennessee probably at the request of George Smith and the aforementioned Tennessee Harpe posseman William Wood, although there were still not enough Baptists settled in the immediate area to constitute a church.[73] A Caswell County, North Carolina, native of French Huguenot extraction and about the age of John's oldest brother Philip, Denton had come to eastern Tennessee with his parents two years after the Smiths had located there, and had been converted and baptized in Holston Association in 1792. Though not connected with the formation of the new Green River Association, which had been organized in 1799 or 1800 from the small and scattered Holston and South Kentucky Separate churches along the Cumberland and Green Rivers, Denton joined it within approximately a year of its founding, and his colaboring ministers included Robert Stockton, Lewis Ellison, William Grimsley, Martin

Trapp, Levi Rhoden, William Ray, Benjamin Lynn, James Skaggs, and John and Philip Mulkey. Most of these men were, like him, from Holston Association originally, although Ray, Lynn, Skaggs, and probably some others came from the South Kentucky Separate Baptist Association.[74]

In his old age, Raccoon John remembered Isaac Denton as being as strict a Calvinist as his own parents were, and he informed biographer Williams that he often helped the preacher with his farm work and engaged Denton in friendly and respectful Socratic debate, more from a love of argument than from a willingness to learn theology from the older man (from Williams's description of Denton, one comes away with the idea that the preacher was a hoary, hard-bitten old veteran rather than the thirty-one years of age that he actually was when John first met him, and why Louis Cochran saw fit to give the Huguenot-descended Denton a heavy Scots burr is anybody's guess).[75] But we must be very careful of Raccoon John's recollections here. His description of Denton's theology jibes not at all with the information found in Denton's biographical sketch in the second volume of Spencer's *History,*[76] and he never mentions the fact that there were Separates as well as Regular Baptists among Denton's early colleagues or that Holston Association itself was organized originally from mostly Separate churches. John even went so far as to inform Thomas Henderson, in his reply to Henderson's letter noted in the last chapter, that in his youth *all* the Baptists in his immediate neighborhood, not only his parents, were extreme predestinarians.[77] He had his own reasons at the time for so doing, as well as for characterizing Denton as he did to Williams later, but other objective evidence indicates that he was actually never all that close to Denton after his twenty-first year and that Denton actually played only a very minor part in the shaping of John's ministry. Strangely enough, one reason for his early break with Denton may have been that the Baptists in his father's neighborhood, including Denton himself, were actually *not Calvinistic enough* to suit him at that point. This evidence will be introduced and discussed in due course, but to return to John's late teens, one thing is certain: when the Great Revival blew into Stockton's Valley the year following John and young George's return from the west, it left John himself as virtually the sole remaining skeptic in the entire community.

Most of the Separate-descended Baptists of Holston Association, not to mention the South Kentucky group, had always been shouters and weepers, and the Revival simply made a people always intensely emotional about their religion just that much more so. John Smith remembered Isaac Denton stopping in the middle of sermons and dancing uncontrollably (though he never mentioned any of the other Great Revival spiritual exercises in connection with him). The entire community—including those sober Calvinists George and Rebecca Smith, and their sons Philip and William (only two of the born-again converts that Denton made during this period)—was thoroughly convinced that the phenomenon was indeed the great power of God in their midst.[78] It was under these heady circumstances that Denton was finally able to organize the Stockton's Valley (later known as Clear Fork of Spring Creek) Baptist Church a ridge or so away from the Smiths' home on April 1, 1802, with twenty-five members, including John's parents, at least two of his brothers and possibly their wives, and William Wood. The new fellowship was admitted to the Green River Association in July of that same year.[79] Wood also began preaching for the church in the year following, but for reasons known only to himself he did not feel worthy of ordination and would never consent to it.[80] Since he had participated in the Tennessee Harpe posse a few years before, perhaps he felt that, as a man of war like old King David himself, he was unfit to officiate in any fully ordained capacity in the house of God.

John may have appeared hard-hearted to his entire family, and it's probable that his parents, brothers, and sisters were puzzled over why he should not be affected by the Revival as they and the rest of their neighbors were. Particularly William, the brother next oldest to him in age, tried to persuade him to change his attitude toward the Revival. Williams states John's argument as being that "it was unreasonable to suppose that God would send his Holy Spirit from the skies to afflict his people with convulsions—to buffet and mock them, and make them ridiculous,"[81] again trying to show John in Socratic mode. Although in time this selfsame argument would be made by Christian preachers of certain doctrinal stances, in 1801 and 1802 almost the only ones contending for it, especially in rural areas, were in fact the hard-line Deists and skeptics. Stubbornly John stuck to his logic, perhaps with moral support from a new friend: Micah Taul, a young lawyer settled at the governmental seat of the newly formed Wayne County, within which Stockton's Valley was now bounded. Williams mentions Taul only incidentally, possibly because Taul may have been the very first of the close, nearly passionate attachments with intellectuals that John was to make for most of his adult life.

Micah Taul was everything that John Smith was not and had never enjoyed a chance to be. Born in Maryland in 1785 but raised in Fayette County, Kentucky, Taul had been provided with all the educational opportunities that the city of Lexington—known at the time as "The Athens of the West"—had to offer. After his parents moved south to the Cumberland River some fifteen to twenty miles east of Stockton's Valley, Micah, at only fifteen years of age but probably with more schooling than anyone else in the area, was both admitted to the bar as an attorney in the newly organized Wayne County and appointed as the clerk of its court. In fact, it was he who actually named the Wayne County seat Monticello, after the famous Virginia estate of Thomas Jefferson. The admiration he thus evidenced for Jefferson might indicate that young Taul was a Deist, like the president, but we cannot be sure. His father, Arthur, and a brother Samuel were known to have been Baptists in Fayette County, but for some reason they were excluded from the church. Micah's own unpublished memoirs shed no light on his religious convictions, or lack thereof. He was a practical man, on the make one might say, with a very healthy opinion of his own abilities and accomplishments, and he may have pictured himself as some-

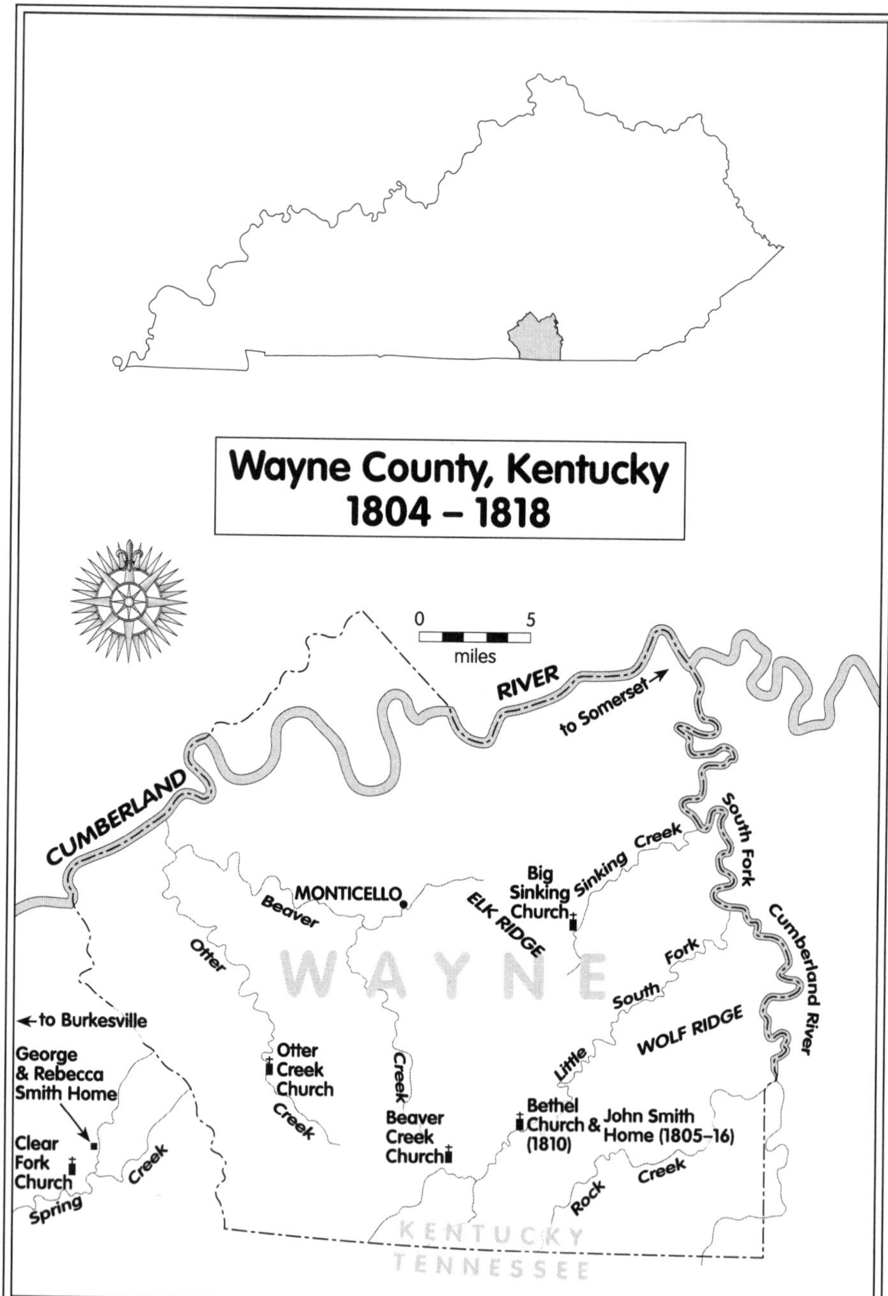
Wayne County, Kentucky
1804 – 1818
0
5
miles
CUMBERLAND
RIVER
to Somerset
South Fork
Cumberland River
Big Sinking Church
Sinking Creek
MONTICELLO
Beaver
ELK RIDGE
Otter
WAYNE
Fork
South
Little
WOLF RIDGE
to Burkesville
George & Rebecca Smith Home
Otter Creek Church
Creek
Creek
Beaver Creek Church
Bethel Church (1810)
& John Smith Home (1805–16)
Clear Fork Church
Creek
Spring
Rock
Creek
KENTUCKY
TENNESSEE

what in the mold of Benjamin Franklin. As to theology, though, he reminds one of Camus's fictional Madame Meursault: while not a professed atheist, he seems never to have given a thought to religion in his life.[82]

It hardly seems credible that the young, rustic John Smith should even have been able to strike up an acquaintance with a youthful frontier aristocrat such as Taul, but both Burkesville to the west of Stockton's Valley and the new Monticello slightly closer to the east were markets for one of the Smith family's most dependable cash crops, ginseng,[83] and it is probable that John met Taul while on a trading excursion in Monticello, or perhaps in accompaniment with his father if the family had any business occurring in the Wayne County court. Once John saw Taul, a boy his own age as a well-educated lawyer and an important court official already, though, he must have been hooked, and even if Taul's patience may have been worn thin by John's continual questions and attempts at conversation, it is certain that he would have been flattered at least a little by the admiration that John undoubtedly showed him. Moreover, Taul's personality was of the civic-minded cast that supported any and all cultural and intellectual improvements in and around Monticello, and for the same reasons he would have encouraged and inspired John to get an education of his own. A few years after this Taul actually did offer to provide John with room and board so he could attend a good school that had been set up in Monticello,[84] although it is doubtful that he ever loaned John any books from his library (on the frontier, these were still too scarce to let out haphazardly). Taul does, however, appear to have ushered John at least to a certain extent into Monticello society, such as it was in those days, and introduced him to a scholarly pursuit that he loved and practiced all his life: formal and social debate.

Williams tells us that John belonged to a debating society at this period of his youth, and there is hardly any possible location that such a group could have existed in rural southern Kentucky in the early 1800s outside a county seat and without the patronage of the few resident professionals and intellectuals such as Taul. Without going into any details about the debating club's location or its membership other than John himself, Williams describes John as quickly having become a champion at the pastime. He learned how to argue both sides of a question logically and persuasively, and on one occasion he won a debate hands down on an affirmative proposition so absurd that no one else would even attempt to argue it. Unwilling to prove such a lame proposition, however, he then offered to argue the issue again, taking the negative side—and he won that debate, too.[85] Micah Taul and those to whom he introduced John in Monticello must have become quickly aware that they were dealing with a razor-sharp if untutored mind, and it is certainly no wonder that Taul should interest himself in John's further education. Though poorly schooled and now in his late teens, John still had the potential to become a lawyer, politician, or some other such professional that would make Stockton's Valley and southern Kentucky proud—if he only seized the day and made the best of his opportunities.

Thus at John's nineteenth birthday in October 1803, his plans appear to have been to wait patiently and work for George Smith until he reached his majority at twenty-one, then strike out on his own with what funds he could muster "to some more favored part of the country, where he might attend a good school and sustain himself by his labor at the same time."[86] Actually, old George may even have known of his intentions and supported them, though he had to have been hurt at John's resistance to the influences of the Great Revival and he undoubtedly never quite understood exactly what made his precocious boy tick. But at this very season old George himself, nearly seventy now if not already past his threescore and ten, was seized with a slow, lingering illness; and what neither James McGready nor Isaac Denton had been able to accomplish with John, the father did without even trying.

All he had to do was to die.

CHAPTER 3

Stages on Life's Way

That [his] father was an extraordinary man was a thing that Johannes at last came to realize. That the father astonished him as no other person did to the same degree, the son knew. But he knew so few people that he had no yardstick by which to measure.

—Søren Kierkegaard

Cercis canadensis, most commonly known as the American redbud, is for most of the year one of the most unprepossessing little trees to be found in the hills of the American southeast. Like its European and western Asian cousin *Cercis siliquastrum,* it is also called the Judas tree, from the old legend that Judas Iscariot hanged himself from the branch of a *Cercis,* a large and imposing tree in ancient times that, since then, in shame and sorrow at one of its number having allowed itself to be so utilized by the arch-traitor, has vowed never again to grow tall enough to support a hanging. Of no use for building and little for fuel, the redbud nonetheless gave Appalachia's pioneers one of their few available food seasonings besides coarse salt and tree sugar (sorghum cane, or "long sweetening," was not introduced to the area until later in the nineteenth century). The earliest settlers learned from their Cherokee predecessors that inserting tender, green Judas tree twigs into cuts of such strong meats as venison, groundhog, and opossum when they were roasted would sweeten the meats' gamy flavors somewhat; and so they called the squat, scrawny tree what the Cherokee did, *no-da-tsi,* or in English, spicewood.[1] Homely, short, plain, and nonutilitarian (except for its twigs' value as seasoning) the tree might be for ten or eleven months of the year, but late March and early April were and are its crowning glory in the southern mountains. At that time, and often accompanied by the last cold snap of a dying winter, the little spicewood tree bursts forth all over the Appalachian hillsides with the very first colors of the new season, small but thick purplish-pink blooms so bright that the trees almost seem to declare that the mourning time for Judas is now past, and to welcome and honor the resurrected Christ at Eastertide with a year's worth of beauty and glory in one short season. A. E. Housman once wrote a poem about the cherry as the loveliest of trees, but had he grown up in Appalachian America rather than England's Worcestershire he might have composed his ode on the brevity and intensity of beauty to the spicewood instead.

A little thicket of spicewoods grew on the hill behind George Smith's cabin, and when the old man died on the first day of spring, March 20, 1804, the small trees must have just begun to bud into their Easter color. Whether or not this was George's prayer thicket, where he was once so grieved to catch his sons playing cards, we cannot say. But this little spicewood copse was the place that John Smith spent a great deal of his free time for nine months after his father's death, praying while the trees passed from their early spring beauty and their summer and fall plainness to their winter barrenness, trying to find his father's God—and to find himself. Did he pick the location because it had been his father's prayer thicket, where his card playing had once brought upon him the shame and humiliation of making his father weep? Did he flee to the most beautiful spot he could find in the Appalachian hills of the early spring of 1804, with the thought that the glory of creation might bring him into closer touch with the Creator? Or did he seek solitude within the little copse of Judas trees because he, having flirted with skepticism, Deism, and universalism, considered himself to be his father's betrayer, and a traitor to all that the old man had held to be good and true? We will never know. But he did emerge from the coppice in December 1804 to relate a conventional Great Awakening– and Great Revival–style conversion experience to Isaac Denton and Clear Fork Church and to be baptized, having metamorphosed from a budding skeptic with ambitions to go somewhere and make something of himself to a Calvinistic Baptist who was determined to remain in the hills as a farmer and, subsequently, as a preacher of the Gospel. If one were superstitious, it was almost as if spicewood had transformative, as well as seasoning, properties. It didn't, of course, but John did, and in a way he may never have considered possible.

Some years later and across the Atlantic in Denmark, another young man named Søren Kierkegaard would suffer through a paradoxical relationship with a father who had advanced himself from serfdom to independence and wealth, and whom he spent his life trying and failing to understand. Kierkegaard's father wanted him to get a theology degree and become a Lutheran pastor and Søren had steadfastly resisted while the father was alive, but after professing a personal conversion experience and no sooner than the father had passed away, the young man performed a complete about-face and began at least to try to carry out his parent's wishes. He himself believed this changeover of his attitudes to be a transformation of his life from the "aesthetic," or in other words, an existence of indifference, without self-actualization, based only on his own desires, reliant on the external world for pleasure, and self-dissipating by the lifestyle's inherent lack of any certainty of meaning, to the "ethical," the beginning of self-actualization that was guided by what self-knowledge he possessed and could further acquire, that compelled him to take hold of his own existence, as it were, and to mold himself inwardly to an ideal based on the useful and purposeful. Kierkegaard himself was the first to admit that neither his "aesthetic" nor his "ethical" lives were objective entities, but rather completely subjective and based on his own inward responses to his experiences, and moreover, that neither he nor anyone else could live a purely and completely ethical life at all times with no reference to the aesthetic aspects of existence. In this view he possessed the choice to live completely as an aesthetic, mundane and without inward meaning, or in despair, torn between the meaninglessness of the aesthetic and the impossibility of the purely ethical. Here, though, Kierkegaard further postulated another mode of existence to which he believed that his two opposing "lives" had carried him: the religious, a synthesis of aesthetic and ethical in which the ethical, by its notion of self-actualization, rational self-creation, and responsible choice, is suspended or negated by an irrational, subjective, and indeed objectively unjustifiable "leap of faith" toward a higher purpose that is itself the essence of the ethical. In short, Kierkegaard reasoned that his father had been the catalyst for his recognition of this dialectic of aesthetic, ethical, and religious, and that the old man had died (at least from his own subjective assessment) "in order that if possible I might turn into something."[2] But he also believed that he had discovered a fundamental truth of human existence: that every individual lived, again and as always subjectively, somewhere in the web of this same dialectic, be it in the aesthetic, the ethical, or the religious sphere.

After that last paragraph, I'm sure that most of my readers will thank me kindly to keep any further such speculations to a minimum. Bear with me for a few moments, though. Kierkegaardian philosophy can be studied on several levels, not all of them related to theology and only a few of which claim any relation to conventional religion, much less the Bible, whatsoever. The above dialectic could be applied to nearly any ideal or aspect of life to which an individual passionately commits. Still, the fact remains that at one of its most basic levels, the dialectic is the very essence of born-again Christianity. The Cornelius story of Acts 10 discussed in the previous chapter carries overtones of it, the centurion's search for the true God representing a change in his life from the aesthetic to the ethical and finally to the religious after obeying a revelation that he should seek the preaching of Peter. One can see hints of it in Augustine's heartbroken, confused prayers to God after becoming totally despondent about his life and his soul, the cathartic outpouring of his private grief followed, like Elijah's still, small voice after the earthquake, the whirlwind, and the fire, by the coo of a small child telling him to "*tolle, lege, tolle, lege*" (take, read, take, read). The "leap of faith" from the despair of conflicting aesthetic and ethical existences is at the core of Martin Luther's declaration that the Apostle Paul's quote from Habakkuk in Romans 1:17 suddenly flung wide the gates of paradise to him, as well as of John Wesley's founding of the Methodist movement after he felt his heart "strangely warmed" at a London church service after hearing Luther's introductory commentary on Romans read. Kierkegaard himself believed that the highest form the ethical existence could take was that of true, heartfelt repentance toward God. The experience of the religious was the fulfillment of true repentance, and by this definition we need only substitute the terms "sinful" for aesthetic, "awakened and repentant" for ethical, and "born again" or "saved" for religious, with of course the Father, Son, and Holy Ghost as both the beginning and the goal of an individual's internal awareness of the dialectic, to make virtually a complete framework for the basic doctrine believed and preached by Wesley, George Whitefield, Shubal Stearns, James McGready, and indeed all the evangelists of both the Great Awakening of the eighteenth century and the Great Revival of the nineteenth. And here perhaps we may begin to look at the more bizarre "spiritual exercises" of both revival periods, especially the latter one, a little more charitably if no less critically. That there was a strong, perhaps dominant, element of hysteria in the revival meetings of the time is unquestioned. But though wild and unsettling the barks, the jerks, and the extreme emotionalism of the McGready camp meeting and all the local and regional manifestations that followed it in the Great Revival may have been when they were observed objectively, on a deeper, subjective level, both the evangelists laboring in the Revival and those responding to the preaching were involved in much more than hysterical applications for fire insurance. If Kierkegaard was right, a fundamental human need too deep and visceral for the then-popular writings of Paine and Voltaire to address caused them to actualize themselves and to try to define their lives under the only terms they could possibly have recognized as aesthetic and ethical, and to seek the ultimate meaning for their existence in the synthesis, the leap in the dark to the religious. Even their later paradoxical disputes and schisms over dogmatic interpretations of a Bible they all believed to be inerrant, and their formations of new denominations claiming to be purer than the old, can be understood at least partially in this context. If Kierkegaard's dialectic be true, nothing indicates that the cycle of aesthetic, ethical, and religious should not manifest itself with differing forms in different cultures, and perhaps especially in cultures experiencing a state of flux. The converts' experiences in the Revival, though undoubtedly similar, were each one utterly personal and subjective, and the disputes occurred simply from their fallacy, and that of humans in general, of trying to objectify that which can never be other than subjective. To borrow Richard Marius's terms in speaking of the heated quarrel between Luther and Erasmus in the early years of the Reformation, after the conversion event that each man believed to be the reference point of his very being, the two worked backward from their deepest concerns about life and faith to declare that they had been led by God's spirit to results that were dictated to each by his own experience.[3] So do we all that hold a religious faith, whether we are willing to admit it even to ourselves or not.

And though John Smith himself scorned the irrational, objectively unjustifiable scenes he witnessed both at the McGready camp meeting and under Isaac Denton's preaching at home in Stockton's Valley during the Great Revival, with the death of his father as his personal catalyst he followed exactly the same path as the Revival's converts did, and in a manner so utterly subjective that Kierkegaard, had he ever heard of John, could have used him as a textbook case for a theological brief. Not that Raccoon John would have been friendly to any such use of his conversion experience, since the account of it that he gave to Williams, or perhaps the editorial spin that Williams put on it, shot it through so fully with interpretations based on what he believed a quarter century after the fact, rather than his beliefs and impressions at the time, that most subsequent historians in the Campbell media tradition have denied that he ever had the experience—and all argue that he didn't need it. But then again, Kierkegaard never regarded the religious life as a static triumph over despair so much as he believed it to be dynamic, a perpetual state of becoming, that, through the tension of the dialectic and its never-ending synthesis, should continue to occur within every individual who hoped to live life meaningfully. In the most common evangelical terms we might likewise describe this process as "Christian growth" or "growth in grace" after conversion, but it was that and more besides. To Kierkegaard, an attitude of complete indifference and one of unreflective, complacent, dogmatic dead certainty in matters of religion were merely two sides of the same aesthetic coin. But the fact is that both he and Raccoon John Smith actually did experience two separate conversions, in each case the latter one taking place years after—and in a more dramatic manner than—the former. In other words, with John's 1804 conversion to the religious life he had not reached an ultimate goal, but had only begun his journey. And since this journey began for him in a little spicewood thicket on a hill not far behind old George Smith's house, we had perhaps best leave the abstract as quickly as we can and return to the hills—and from there examine the first leg of John's pilgrimage, a sojourn roughly a decade long and which might properly be called his spicewood years.

Like most southern mountaineers of his time, old George Smith died intestate, but he bestowed what worldly goods he had to his offspring in what was, or would become, Appalachian mountain tradition. He'd already helped all his sons older than John establish themselves on independent farms like his own, some in Kentucky and others across the line in north central Tennessee, and he'd seen his elder daughters married to men of property or prospects who could likewise provide for them. At his death, he directed that his home farm on Smith Creek be divided equally between his youngest sons Jonathan, who was in his seventeenth year at the time, and Henry, who was almost eleven, with Rebecca and the two remaining unmarried daughters owning the right to make their homes with whichever of the two they chose, should they remain single.[4] That left John in an apparently anomalous position, as the only son in the family not provided with land by the settlement of his father's estate. But here we find the clearest evidence that the old man knew that John intended to leave the hills and get an education—and that, though he may never have understood John's ambitions completely, he freely and affectionately gave him, and them, a father's blessing. For landless though John may have been, at his father's death he did possess some personal estate either in hard cash or barterable articles such as ginseng, grain, and animal pelts roughly equivalent to the value of a small farm,[5] and old George may have endowed him thusly as a "stake" for his travels just like the father of his former pastor Alderson had once done for a headstrong, smart son of his own. George might have reasoned that, after all, Alderson had been as bookish as his own boy John now was, had traveled and survived a few misadventures in his youth, and had nonetheless been blessed with a productive life; and what God had done for a John of a generation before, He could do again for another. Old George's sole request to John was that he should remain at the homeplace a little while longer, as he put it, "at least till Jonathan is old enough to tend to business,"[6] and his only voiced fear was that his brainy son should fall into bad company and dissipation when he struck out on his own. In his final words to John he called on both the Lord and to John's own common sense to deliver and keep him from evil, and shortly thereafter the good old man yielded up his breath.

Even those of us who have had difficult relationships with our parents know that the experience of losing one cuts deeply. Abraham Lincoln coolly refused to visit his dying father, but for reasons known only to himself he still responded to Thomas Lincoln's actual decease by naming his youngest son, born two years following the death, after his father. Such a loss is perhaps especially keen if one has the curious mixture of deep emotional affection and humorous disdain for a parent that teenage John had held for old George. His flights into the realms of the intellectual and his own differences of opinion with his father notwithstanding, John had to have regarded George very much as a spiritual and emotional anchor, and although it could be argued that seventeen-year-old Jonathan, the two teenage girls, and eleven-year-old Henry would have taken the loss as hard or harder than nineteen-year-old John, there can be no doubt whatsoever that John—to borrow another old rural Kentucky expression—had the props knocked out from under him completely by his father's death.

Had he really been the skeptic at heart that he told James Challen he had tried to be while old George was alive, he probably would have shouldered his grief in time, honored his father's last request, and stayed around the homeplace until Jonathan got another year's growth, and then gone on with his original plan of leaving the hills to seek an education. He might have comforted himself with the thoughts that his father had lived a long and good life and that this same end must sooner or later come to all, perhaps with the same hope that George Washington, who usually gave no thought to what lay beyond the grave, had expressed at his mother's death: that his parent had been translated to a happier place. But at nineteen and suddenly without the anchor that he had never fully appreciated until now, John had no such calm resolve; in the absence of his father, his father's God became very real to him in a way that had been heretofore unimaginable. The first change that his mother, siblings, and neighbors probably noticed in him after old George was buried was the departure—temporary, as it turned out—of the sense of humor that he had used so effectively to protect his thoughts from the outside world. He worked morosely and woodenly on the farm and at the house doing chores his father had once supervised and shared with him, with fewer words than usual and never a jest even in the ones he uttered. As the senior male in his household, he was now obliged to serve in Wayne County's militia, the period's local equivalent of the National Guard of our own day, probably in his parents' church brother William Wood's local company under the regimental command of Micah Taul.[7] General militia musters were not only a time for military drill but an opportunity, especially for the younger militiamen, for carousing after the exercises were over, and when John's friends both from Monticello and Stockton's Valley saw him arrive at the drill grounds on muster day they tried to get an advance on their intended festivities with a few of John's humorous songs. But John solemnly refused to sing for them, declaring, "Boys, I've played the fool for you till I have nearly ruined my own soul; I have resolved never to sing for you again while I live."[8]

When at home he spent all the time he could, and no doubt that which he had devoted to reading his three books before, praying in the spicewood thicket. He'd never been a slave to any particular vices, not even the homemade whiskey and brandy that nearly all men and women of that day drank occasionally, and in the case of those regarded as drunkards, more than occasionally. In fact, the only "bad" habits he is known certainly to have maintained were a lifelong fondness for both chewing tobacco and smoking a pipe,[9] although in his culture it was hardly even considered a vice, much less sinful. But he mourned himself as the chief of all sinners, worse than the Harpes even, because he felt that they had been raised like brutes and simply didn't know any better; he, on the other hand, had been reared by God-fearing parents and had rejected the Gospel consciously. In later years John and his biographer scorned this mourning period as irrational and completely unnecessary for a Christian convert, and truthfully, John's own case was drawn out and made more difficult because of his sudden and implicit acceptance, along with his father's concept of God, of old George's Philadelphia Confession and his Calvinistic doctrinal stance as well. He spent a great deal of time worrying whether he was of the eternal elect of God or not, even though he recognized that his fatalistic dogma's own logic rendered his concern over the matter pointless. But at some time in midsummer, after the beautiful spicewood buds had been replaced for the year by small, plain, rounded leaves while he had wrestled with himself over God and his own identity, as an aesthetic who had rejected revelation and was ambitious for a worldly education in clash with the ethical image of his father to which he never felt he measured up, John finally received the religious, the long-sought born-again experience. The reader may wish to compare it to the conversion account of William Vaughan, noted in the previous chapter:

> One morning, while it was yet dark, he arose from his sleepless bed, and went out to his favorite place in the spicewood thicket to pray. The

fragrant bushes were tangled with summer vines, and the dews of the night hung heavy upon them. The startled birds flitted away at his approach, and the solitude was gloomy and chill. He entered the covert, and, bowing himself in prayer, implored rest for his worn and weary soul. He knelt in hope, but arose in despair; his wretchedness and guilt seemed to cleave to him still. He started home through the dusky meadow, the stars still bright above him; but, as he went, a thought, quick and beautiful as a gleam of starlight, glanced into his soul, and dispelled his gloom. It came in the familiar words of [Baptist hymnist Samuel] Stennet, which suddenly occurred to him with a distinctness and power unknown before: ". . . So great, so vast a sacrifice / May well my hope revive / If God's own Son thus bleeds and dies / The sinner sure may live. / Oh, that these cords of love divine / Might draw me, Lord, to Thee! / Thou hast my heart; it shall be Thine / Thine shall it ever be."

Hopeless of mercy as he had so long been, he was nearly overpowered by the sudden discovery of the boundless love of Jesus. He repeated the lines of the hymn with wonder and delight. Every word thrilled him like a voice from the skies. He had long been dwelling on the Lord as a being of infinite justice; he now fixed his gaze on the Crucified One, and saw that he was a being of infinite goodness also; and the cloud of Divine anger seemed to be spanned with the radiance of hope. He thought that this change in the direction of his thoughts could only come from above, and for a while he rejoiced.

His mind was so constituted, however, that he could not experience any sudden transition of feeling without some reflection. He stood there in the dim dawn, and thought on this new phase in his experience. He reasoned that if it was wicked to break the laws of a holy God, as he had done, it was surely ten-fold more heinous to sin against a being of such goodness and love. The Divine love had just been the foundation of a blessed hope; now, it seemed, as he reflected on the subject, to be the ground of a more fearful condemnation. The goodness in which he was about to trust, could not save him; for had he not wantonly sinned against it all?

He fled back in terror to his place of prayer, and cast himself on his face in the dust. He poured out his very soul in tears more bitter, and in supplication more piteous than before. Exhausted at last by his long and painful struggles, he sank into the very extreme of prostrate wretchedness. The human heart could bear no more. His intense feeling and frenzied thought relaxed, and the repose of exhaustion succeeded the conflict. His strong mind then reacted, and he lay for some moments in a state of dreamy peace. His heart instinctively threw off its burden, and he seemed to pass in a moment from "death unto life."

The day had broken, the birds were singing in every bush, the

> dews sparkled in the early light, and the beauty and the freshness of the morning were around him. His heart drank in the influence of the hour, and he was happy.[10]

Though John underwent this travail in the summer months of 1804, no one could persuade him to testify of it in church until near Christmas, mostly because he still let himself be plagued with doubts and fears about whether he was truly of the elect or not. According to Williams, he even became discouraged the first time he attended a worship service for the purpose, on hearing an old and extremely simple neighbor testify that he had seen the Devil, and that the Prince of Darkness was "about the size of a yearlin.'"[11] Finally, though, John did relate his wrestlings of the spirit to the congregation at Clear Fork; all who heard his words pronounced assurance that John had indeed been born again; and he was duly baptized in the branch near the meetinghouse on December 26, 1804, and "laid hands on" as a new church member in the fashion of the old Separate Baptists, by Isaac Denton.[12] Interestingly, after his baptism he never again so much as once doubted the peace of God, or that he had been saved.[13]

One reason for his increased confidence may have been that soon after his baptism he had started preaching—in his sleep. At night, he had such vivid dreams of exhorting that he often yelled out as if he were having nightmares. The first time this occurred it seems to have scared John's nervous, quick-tempered, but good-natured old mother nearly to death, and she stormed to his bed and woke him by shouting in his ear, "John, are you distracted, thus to preach without a call?"[14] One can fairly picture how high he must have jumped off his bed at the sound of that voice, perhaps ending his dream sermon with a fervent "*Oh, Lord!*" as he woke up. But apparently Rebecca, Jonathan, Henry, and the girls had to get used to being disturbed at night, for John preached on in his dreams, according to Williams waiting only for an outward, objective sign from God that he had been called to the ministry—even though to most rural southeasterners both of that day and this, preaching in one's sleep would have been regarded as one sure sign of a "call."

And so John Smith greeted the new year of 1805 as a changed man, or perhaps still just a changed boy. Much, much later he would hold forth that the nonbiblical traditions of men had put him through a lot of unnecessary heartache in obtaining a conversion experience he didn't even need, and he would reinterpret the fact that he had gained confidence in his status of salvation after he had undergone the ceremony of baptism, in a way that he couldn't even have foreseen at this point. But be that as it may, his progression from sinner to saint—or as they say in the hills, his "travel from nature to grace"—is worthy of consideration. He started out as an aesthetic, concerned with his own dreams and ambitions before his father's death shocked him out of the perspective; he wrestled for the better part of a year with the ethical, the image of George Smith, the spiritual anchor of which he may never have been fully aware until the old man was gone; and the religious synthesis at which he arrived, not by his own works but by the leap of faith that transcended both aesthetic and ethical, turned out to be startlingly close to the reincarnation of one of his possible namesakes, a man he had never met except through his parents' reminiscences: John Alderson.

It would, however, be another three years before John was formally ordained to the Baptist ministry, and during that time he established his life even more firmly within the pattern made for him—or by him—in the spicewood thicket. First, he took a portion of the money with which he had intended to leave the hills and used it to purchase a two hundred–acre tract of virtually unimproved land some twenty miles east of Smith Creek, on the Little South Fork of the Cumberland River, about sixteen miles southeast of Monticello and near the present border of Wayne and McCreary counties. His next-oldest brother, William, appears to have settled somewhere in the area beforehand, if not on the Little South Fork itself, perhaps on Beaver Creek or Otter Creek in between the old Smith homestead and John's new holding.[15] In recognition that the area was filling up with settlers, at about the same period the hardworking Isaac Denton organized a small Baptist church on the head of Beaver Creek, serving both it and the Clear Fork congregation as pastor or moderator.[16] In those days and even now among many traditional Separate-descended Baptists in the southeast, churches held worship services only one weekend a month, and ministers often pastored two, three, and even four simultaneously.

Despite the changeover of his ambitions from those of a skeptic scholar to the aspirations of a Baptist farmer-preacher, John did serve another term in school. A wheelwright, Robert F. Ferrill, had just moved to Stockton's Valley from Virginia. He possessed a good education for his time and several books, and he announced his intention to supplement his income from wheelmaking by running occasional subscription schools for the area's children. Though at twenty John might be expected to feel ashamed to sit in a schoolhouse with children half and even a fourth his age, he grasped the opportunity as eagerly as he would have before his father's death, and under Ferrill he received most of the formal education he ever acquired. An increase in his wheelmaking trade forced Ferrill to close his first school after some weeks, but because of his oldest pupil's keen interest in his books he agreed to be John's tutor in exchange for day labor. John thus boarded with Ferrill a few more weeks and learned the rudiments of mathematics, polished his grammar and spelling a bit, and covered a little secular literature, including English translations of ancient Greek and Latin classics.[17] Though Williams of course makes but little note of it, Ferrill may have been the second educated man to which John thus attached himself emotionally as well as practically, but in John's new state of mind the idyll of learning could only last so long. His brother Jonathan was now eighteen and, with their mother's and sisters' and twelve-year-old Henry's help, able to manage without him, and John now had a farm, and a future, of his own. He soon bid farewell to both his family and Ferrill and struck out on his own on the Little South Fork.

When he settled on his new land, two miles or so from the community of Parmleysville up a small branch off Little South Fork known as Horse Hollow, John's new religious persona became more and more evident. The Beaver Creek (later known, apparently, as Mt. Pisgah) Church pastored by Isaac Denton and to which John's brother William may have taken his membership was only a short ride up the Little South Fork three miles or so from Parmleysville, then to the head of a small branch on the west bank and over the hill to the head of Beaver, a total distance at most of six or seven miles and certainly an easier journey than pastor Denton had to make all the way from Stockton's Valley. But this wasn't the church that John sought. Williams states specifically that when John transferred his membership ("lifted his letter") from Clear Fork in 1805, he joined "a congregation whose place of meeting was some fourteen miles distant"[18] from his new home—in other words, hardly any closer to Horse Hollow than Monticello was—but he never mentions this church's name. Louis Cochran actually did mistakenly believe that John took his membership to Mt. Pisgah and so wrote the church into his story, but based on extant Baptist records for Wayne County, there was actually only one congregation that would have fit Williams's description at this point in time and simultaneously lined up with all the other facts he gave and evidence at which he hinted. It was on Big Sinking Creek and was pastored by a man roughly the age of Isaac Denton, one Richard Barrier (or "Byers," as the hill people called him).[19] John thus separated himself from Isaac Denton's pastoral guidance probably less than a year and certainly not two years after Denton had baptized him. Although Stockton's Valley Association, which was organized from the slightly older Green River Association in the fall of 1805 by Denton and his colleagues and was actually Beaver Creek Church's home association,[20] is mentioned time and time again by Williams, Cochran, and Donaldson in connection with John's early career, he was never at any time an ordained minister in the body and very probably never belonged to it at all, even as a layman.

As indicated at the outset of this work, much of the misinformation about this early period of John Smith's life may have arisen simply because he was old and forgetful at the time he dictated his memoirs to John Augustus Williams. If Smith and Williams were knowingly perpetrating a subterfuge, though, their reasons will become clear subsequently. But for now, we may speculate that when John moved to the Little South Fork he knew quite well what he was doing, and it made sense within the religious framework on which he was trying to build his life. Holston Association in Tennessee, from which most of the oldest ministers and members of the churches in Green River and Stockton's Valley Associations had come, had adopted the Philadelphia Confession in 1786 as a general statement of their principles without binding any of their mostly former Separate Baptist members to a strict subscription of the document. As such, the prevailing attitude toward the Confession in both the Green

River and Stockton's Valley Associations was ambivalent at best, and neither of these two groups had so much as mentioned the document in their original constitutions or at their organizational meetings. Of course, this attitude would have been completely out of line with the appreciation of the Confession that George and Rebecca Smith had learned from John Alderson back in Botetourt County, Virginia, and which John, from the circumstances of his conversion to Christianity, now shared.

Richard Barrier's church on Big Sinking was different. Alone of the Baptist congregations in early Wayne County, it belonged not to the Green River or Stockton's Valley Associations, but to Tate's Creek Association,[21] the group that broke off from the old South Kentucky Separate Baptist group in 1794 to adopt a partial endorsement of the Philadelphia Confession and to unite with the Elkhorn and Salem Regular Baptist Associations in the Bluegrass. By now, Tate's Creek had become so decidedly Calvinistic that it had already involved itself in the first of the Kentucky Baptist General Union's previously noted splits, resulting in an acrimonious division of neighboring South District Association. One faction of this split still exists aloof from the mainline Kentucky Southern Baptists as the Separate Baptists in Christ.[22] Rather than staying under Isaac Denton's wing, then, at his earliest opportunity John chose a connection with the only association represented in that isolated area of Kentucky that had a constitution based at least in a qualified sense on his father's beloved old Philadelphia Confession, and this while Rebecca Smith and the rest of her children were seemingly perfectly happy to remain under Isaac Denton's pastoral care at Clear Fork and Beaver Creek.

There may have been another cause, a very personal one, for John's being drawn to Richard Barrier. Barrier came from a German family that had settled in South Carolina.[23] It is conceivable that both he and George Smith Sr. could have spoken with just the trace of a German accent, and if this was the case he simply would have given John one more reminder of his father. Regardless of the excuses John may have given himself for his choice of church membership, though, in light of this circumstance everything that Raccoon John ever told John Augustus Williams about Isaac Denton's and Stockton's Valley Association's doctrinal stance comes open to question, and the "considerate pastor" who presented young John with the very first book that he ever owned personally, a brief defense of Calvinism penned by hymnist Augustus Montague Toplady in refutation of a condemnatory pamphlet written about Toplady by John Wesley,[24] was probably not Denton, as Williams so skillfully implied, but Barrier instead. Indeed, Williams's quote from Denton that he suspected John Smith of "some heresy" even in his early years[25] takes on a new meaning when we consider that Denton may have harbored sentiments more Separate Baptist than Regular.

There was, though, yet one more reason that John was attracted to Richard Barrier and his church on Big Sinking, and it involved neither doctrine nor his personal relationship with the pastor, but opportunity for advancement. Like most early Kentucky Baptist associations outside the settled flatlands of the central Bluegrass, Stockton's Valley Association was and for many years remained a rustic, provincial little body, operating almost as a tiny satellite around the larger Bluegrass General Union power-broker associational cluster of Elkhorn, Salem, North and South District—and, of course, Tate's Creek Associations. In spite of his change of heart about leaving the hills and acquiring an education, John's desire for advancement beyond his mountain roots may have been rekindled a bit by the thought that he might represent Big Sinking Church annually as one of its three or four messengers to the enormous Tate's Creek associational gatherings, in the process coming into contact with the most popular, respected, and influential Baptist preachers in the Kentucky General Union—and with a lot of work and a little luck, conceivably being admitted to their elite clique one day. It is a fact that, eleven or twelve years down the road, with a little help from some influential Baptist politicians and under some extremely intriguing circumstances that will be addressed later, this is exactly what Raccoon John did.

Still, one wonders what might have happened if John actually had done what Williams tries so hard to imply that he did, kept his connection with Isaac Denton and Stockton's Valley Association and established his ministry there at first. For within five or six years after John left Clear Fork Church and Denton's guidance, Stockton's Valley was split literally in half by the Barton Stone Christian movement; and for reasons best known to himself, Williams neglects to mention this circumstance until twenty-odd years after the fact, and even then only incidentally, with no mention of the Baptist association in connection with it.[26] Nonetheless, the fact remains that in 1807 Rice Haggard moved near Burkesville, Raccoon John's other old ginseng market besides Monticello and now the county seat of Cumberland County, Kentucky, to the west of Stockton's Valley, and within three to five years proceeded to convert the preachers John Mulkey, who was the moderator of Stockton's Valley Association at the time, his brother Philip, and a large number of Stockton's Valley Baptists to Stoneite views.[27] Despite their doctrinal differences with the Baptists, the Stoneites of this early day worshiped in almost the same manner as the old Separate Baptists. This may have been a primary consideration to the Mulkey brothers and indeed most who followed them, as well as the increasing politicization of the Kentucky Baptist General Union brought about by the actions of the big downstate associations such as Tate's Creek. Benjamin Lynn, whose transference of membership to the Stoneite group was remarked upon in the last chapter and who was still living, apparently, on Green River to the west of Stockton's Valley and Burkesville, may have entertained similar views. But Stockton's Valley Association managed to survive and even prosper after the split, electing Elder John B. Longan, a former strict Calvinist who had modified his views to preach repentance to all men, as moderator in the place of John Mulkey.[28] Isaac Denton of course stayed on as well, as did another young preacher at Clear Fork who actually did maintain the relationship with Denton claimed for

John Smith by Williams: Jonathan Smith, John's next youngest brother. Jonathan was ordained sometime in or after the year 1815, and for all the mud that Louis Cochran saw fit to sling at his memory, he was never as Calvinistic as John in his youth,[29] nor as devious as John was forced to learn to be in his later years.

Still, we must not assume that John was particularly crafty or calculating at this point in his life. His decision to throw in his lot with Richard Barrier's church was probably based on his belief that the Holy Ghost was leading him in that direction, and he undoubtedly tucked whatever ambitions he may have entertained safely away in his subconscious. We all have the same capability to compartmentalize ourselves mentally, and it gets some of us, particularly preachers, in more trouble than others. But at this time, John did indeed hold the office of ordained minister in a high and fearful respect, and though he could preach in his dreams it was some time before his Little South Fork neighbors and his fellow members at Big Sinking could persuade him to say a few words even at a home prayer meeting. When he did finally make his first effort one night at a neighbor's cabin, he was so overcome by both stage fright and the thoughts of his assumption of the position of God's mouthpiece that he panicked, shouldered his way through the crowd in the cabin, and rushed outside into the dark. Not far from the doorway, though, he tripped over a root and fell flat on his face; this cleared his head and perhaps persuaded him that the accident was a sign from God that he should get up and start doing his job, and he returned sheepishly to the cabin to deliver, as he recalled later, a good discourse for a first-timer.[30]

He improved with prayer, undoubtedly, and probably a good deal of practice as well. For though John was a strict Calvinistic Regular Baptist just as he had perceived his father and John Alderson to be, to succeed at exhorting in the Kentucky backwoods he had to speak in accordance with, as John Augustus Williams put it, "the taste of the times," and that meant the New England Holy Tone of Separate Baptist patriarch Shubal Stearns rather than the calmer and more deliberate and scholarly Regular Baptist preaching mode. To be sure, though, he had a wonderful voice for it. His voice was described by Williams as deep, rich, and heavy even in his youth,[31] and in his mature years by another chronicler as guttural, dry, and husky, with a drawling tone.[32] Moreover, when a natural ability for melody and a rich bass voice are combined with the old mountain pulpit address, it creates a booming effect rather than the "whine" by which the Tone is often described by historians. When John assumed his deep, finely modulated preaching cant, or as the old saying went, "struck the long roll,"[33] according to Williams he could be heard clearly from two miles away.[34]

John undoubtedly considered Richard Barrier as his mentor at this point rather than Isaac Denton, but Barrier was not the only minister with whom he worked regularly. About the time he had moved onto his new lands on the Little South Fork or certainly not long thereafter, an enormous intermarried double family with the surnames of Hurt and Burnett had begun to migrate to

Wayne County from South Carolina via western North Carolina and southwestern Virginia. The head of the Burnett family, Jeremiah, had been married three times, and the Hurt patriarch, Joseph, twice. Joseph's first wife was Eliza Wilson and his second was named Mary, her maiden name unknown. They brought with them to Wayne County a troop of sons and daughters ranging in age from married and marriageable adults to young children, including Joseph Hurt Jr., who was married to Mildred Burnett; Roland Burnett, whose wife was Mary Hurt; James Hurt, a young man about John Smith's age who married Ursula Burnett in Wayne County after the families settled in; William Hurt, his wife Jennie, and his eldest daughter Nancy, who married Jeremiah Burnett's younger son Isaac a few years later in Wayne County; and Joshua Hurt, who had married Sarah or Sally Davis in South Carolina and who seems to have been among the last of the Hurt sons to immigrate to Kentucky.[35] The patriarchs' marital relationships stress a sad fact about frontier living. However short a man's life expectancy could be, a woman's was usually much shorter, and tough pioneer women like Rebecca Bowen Whitely Smith, who had outlived or at least outlasted two husbands (Jonathan Whitely is said to have died in 1801), were the exception rather than the rule. Only the hardiest could live up to bearing a dozen or more children between their seventeenth and forty-sixth birthdays, accomplishing everything that was classified as women's work on a backwoods farm, and surviving diseases ranging from childbed fever to viral epidemics to slow wasting illnesses, for which they had only herbs and superstitions as remedies. On the average, fifty years was considered to be an old age for a woman, and to put it bluntly and even brutally but truthfully, men such as Jeremiah Burnett and Joseph Hurt simply got themselves new wives when the old ones wore out and died, raised new families right along with their married sons and daughters, and the cycle repeated itself again and again because it was the only mode of existence that the frontier knew.

The Hurts and Burnetts were Baptists, and John thus became closely acquainted with the members of the big double family early, undoubtedly including Joseph Hurt's youngest daughter, Nancy, who was a year older than her niece of the same name. But at that time John's most significant contact with the extended family was Isham Burnett, one of the oldest of Jeremiah's sons, who had been ordained to the Baptist ministry at some time during the families' sojourn in South Carolina. Isham and probably the entire churchgoing component of the double family joined Richard Barrier's church on Big Sinking,[36] giving the little backcountry fellowship something of a luxury in the ministrations of two seasoned preachers, Barrier and Burnett, and one young one, Smith. It can be imagined that Barrier and Burnett worked John hard, in a manner of speaking, but probably no harder than they worked themselves in supplying the isolated settlements of eastern Wayne County with preaching on the weekends they were not occupied directly at Big Sinking.

When the Hurts and Burnetts arrived in Wayne County, they had come to stay; as only one example of Jeremiah Burnett's and Joseph Hurt's many children, Isham Burnett remained in the Parmleysville area until his death at age ninety in 1856,[37] the same year in which Richard Barrier died at the age of eighty-eight.[38] There were other settlers of more restless dispositions, though, nomads who came into the southern and eastern Kentucky backwoods only to leave after a few years with hardly a trace, seemingly always seeking a better home just over the next hill. And one of the best examples of these restless, itchy-footed temporary dwellers on the Little South Fork was John Townsend, another South Carolinian and Revolutionary veteran who had been on the move regularly since his discharge from the Continental Army in 1782 and who would remain something of a rover throughout a long life. We do not know his first wife's name, but he probably married her either in the Camden District of South Carolina where he had been raised, or in Wilkes County, Georgia, where he spent his first decade after leaving the military. But sadly, when he arrived on the Little South Fork she had long been left behind, having shared the melancholy fate of Jeremiah Burnett's and Joseph Hurt's first spouses, and she was buried somewhere along the family's circuitous route from Georgia to the Abbeville District of South Carolina, to Knox County in eastern Tennessee, and finally to Wayne County, Kentucky. By this time John Townsend had married again, to another woman whose name is no longer known, and by her had sired a son, John Jr.; of his children by his first wife, he was accompanied by sons James, Hiram, and Henry, and daughters Jane and Anna.[39]

And so it happened that when John finally started coming out of his shell to speak to the opposite sex, sometime in the year 1806, Anna Townsend captured his heart. Williams describes John and Anna's acquaintance as having begun at a "house meeting" somewhere on the Little South Fork where he was the featured speaker of the evening,[40] and in fact we should be glad for Williams's candor even in admitting that John could feel a normal young man's physical attraction to a pretty girl. Most preachers of this same era who composed autobiographies—Barton Stone, Peter Cartwright, and John Taylor come to mind here, and Thomas Vaughan's rendering of his father William's memoirs is hardly any different—almost all seem to try to portray themselves as utterly devoid of concupiscence, deciding to marry simply because the arrangement would aid their ministries and then hardly mentioning their wives ever again, even though after marriage they seemed to be capable of siring children almost every time they hung their trousers on the bedpost. Raccoon John himself, though admitting that he was smitten with Anna Townsend, recounted virtually no details to Williams of their actual courtship, probably because he was equally reserved about speaking of such matters. He probably pursued her as clumsily, confusedly, nervously, and banally as young unmarried preachers have always performed such activities, with musings both euphoric and rueful over Agur's words in the thirtieth chapter of Proverbs about the way of a man with a maid, but he was still successful enough at winning Anna's admiration to "speak to her father about the matter," as the custom of engagement went in those days and occasionally still does in the hills. If John Townsend did not give his blessing to the union, Anna's brother James at least swore that their father did when James "went on" the marriage bond for his sister and prospective brother-in-law, and John and Anna were accordingly wedded on what is claimed by some family genealogists as Anna's twentieth birthday, December 9, 1806. Interestingly, the marriage was not celebrated at either the Townsend or the Smith homes, nor performed by any of the ministers John worked with, Richard Barrier, Isham Burnett, nor even Isaac Denton, but at Monticello by one Elliott Jones, probably a justice of the peace. Though we will never know what really happened, this latter circumstance must make us wonder whether James Townsend's oath was the complete truth, or if old Townsend had proven to be irascible, the young couple had felt compelled to elope, and for John and Anna's sake both James Townsend and Wayne County court clerk Micah Taul may have voluntarily engaged in a little wishful thinking.[41]

It is a great pity that we know so very little about Anna Townsend Smith. Williams does not even provide us with a physical description of John's first wife, and Raccoon John himself may have neglected this detail in what was then simply a matter of course. Though times were changing by the late 1860s, female presences in the lives of prominent male historical figures were still regarded by most historians and biographers as relatively inconsequential and therefore a waste of paper and ink. Louis Cochran depicted Anna as fair haired, small, and rather frail, and for all we know he may have been right in this instance, because her husband was indeed tender, sentimental, and very much attracted to females that he perceived as vulnerable. Once, when John was taken ill suddenly at a church while on a preaching tour, probably with a virus, a beautiful and kind young lady named Elizabeth Mizner gave him water and otherwise tried to see to his comfort until his wave of sickness passed; on learning that the girl had never professed to be a Christian, and pondering that she could be so sweet and caring to him and still be hell-bound, he wept out loud.[42] Stronger evidence for this complex and admittedly possibly male chauvinistic, but nonetheless paradoxically endearing, personality trait will be introduced in the next chapter.

But frail and vulnerably attractive though Anna may have been, the rest of Cochran's characterization delves back into the realm of fancy, particularly in his portrayal of her as having been raised in more genteel circumstances and more accustomed to finery than John was. Williams makes it clear that the young couple were wretchedly poor according to the standards of the 1860s Bluegrass. They had John's acres and a puncheon-floored log cabin chinked with mud, a rude bed and perhaps some chairs that John himself had cobbled together with dogwood and hickory poles and slats, and a fireplace that served as both furnace and stove. Although John himself had no doubt been exposed to conditions slightly better in Monticello among Micah Taul and his intellectual friends, he told Williams that neither he nor Anna really considered how poor they were, since they had never lived with furnishings any more luxurious and neither had any of their close neighbors.[43] In fact, considering John Townsend's restlessness, Anna had perhaps "been raised up by the hair of the head" to a greater degree than John ever had, and she certainly had had to grow more accustomed to packing up, following a wagon or sled to a new home, and breaking new ground than had her new husband. She was probably the oldest surviving daughter in John Townsend's first family, and we do not know how young she was when she had had to bid goodbye forever to her mother. The great tragedy was that she followed in her mother's footsteps, and in exactly the same way in spite of all the tenderness that John possibly could have shown her, before she reached her thirtieth birthday.

For the time being all was well, though, and John and Anna settled in snugly on their little hillside farm in Horse Hollow, in circumstances as happy as a young, freshly in-love frontier couple could expect. Anna was not a Christian when she and John first married, but she expressed a great interest in the religion and in receiving the born-again experience, probably from the time she had first become attracted to her young preacher husband. One of Williams's more poignant stories involves this concern. Anna asked John about the meaning of a certain Scripture text, and he, being fearful that he would impede her path to salvation by the grace of a Calvinistic, predestinarian God, refused to answer her. Nonetheless, according to Williams, Anna did receive the born-again experience subsequently, and even became a renowned singer, "with pathos," of the modal-keyed, mournful old melodies of the Baptist Church of that day; he may actually infer that she had an easier time in obtaining the experience and taking comfort from it than her husband had from his own conversion back in 1804.[44] In spite of these clear statements from Raccoon John's biographer, though, Everett Donaldson claims that Anna probably never experienced conversion and therefore lived and died unbaptized, citing as his reason the fact that Anna's name never appears alongside John's in any early southern Kentucky Baptist church records.[45] Even more strangely, he makes the same claim for John's older brother William,[46] despite the fact that John Augustus Williams pointedly states that William Smith had become a church member some years before old George Smith passed away.[47] But while Anna's and William's names are indeed absent from the records of any congregation with which John was directly involved, the discrepancy can be explained easily. It must be remembered that Isaac Denton's church on the head of Beaver Creek was not as far from the Horse Hollow/Parmleysville community as John's home church on Big Sinking was; as noted earlier, William Smith may simply have "taken his letter" from Stockton's Valley and "laid it in" at Beaver Creek, and if Anna had received her conversion experience at a worship service at this same church, by a tradition that still survives in many eastern Kentucky Old Time Baptist associations, she would have been given the privilege of choosing it, if she wished, for her own home church regardless of where her husband belonged. Donaldson postulates that "these were difficult times for the young couple,"[48] but if this assumption be correct, the true difficulty may have arisen because Anna found Isaac Denton's preaching more positive, loving, hopeful, and simpler than her own husband's was at the time.

During the first year of his marriage to Anna, John molded himself further into the image that had become his ideal since his experience in the spicewood thicket. He cleared land for cultivation by girdling the trees on his hillsides and sparse bottoms, plowing and planting around them, harvesting his crops in the fall, and then cutting and burning the dead timber and pulling up the stumps with oxen or mules. It was backbreaking work, but labor that he had seen his father and brothers perform (and which he himself had assisted in), all his life. Though he still disliked hunting, as a householder he knew that wild game was a necessary supplement to his and Anna's table, so he nerved himself to the task and even acquired a couple of big dogs to track and bring down larger quarry, such as bear.[49] And, of course, he preached on with his mentors Barrier and Burnett, his popularity, his pulpit eloquence, and his skills in debate against the arguments of Methodists and less Calvinistic Baptists increasing all the while.[50]

Not long after John's marriage, talk among the members at Big Sinking Church turned to the question of his ordination as a minister. His former status as an unmarried man very well may have been Richard Barrier's, Isham Burnett's, and the church's sole scruple about "setting him forward" for the office, and as an indication of his general popularity in church and community, there appear to have been at least four new converts to the congregation who refused to be baptized and "take up" membership until John could be ordained and perform the rite for them himself.[51] Still, John was very much the same boy that had put off making his testimony to Clear Fork Church for several months for fear that he was not of the elect, and here again he begged his brethren for more time as he prayed for an objective Divine revelation of his calling to preach. But two events that must have occurred within the first eighteen months of his marriage prompted him to change his mind about resisting ordination. Since each in its own way reveals that, though the esteemed young Calvinist had been largely successful in patterning his life to the George Smith/John Alderson mold, he was still very much John Smith, both will be related below.

The first occurred on an occasion when he went to the field to labor. As a married man he had retained the habits of studying that he had used so effectively as a boy, and now he would often bring his Bible and perhaps his Toplady pamphlet or Philadelphia Confession to the dinner table to pore over while he ate[52] (how much this must have irked Anna, who herself had to work hard to prepare good meals for him with only a fireplace for a kitchen and the most primitive of implements, and who doubtless looked forward to chatting with him over the table and otherwise sharing his company when he came in from the field, can only be imagined). But on this occasion, when he finished hoeing or plowing a long row, he sat down on a rock or stump to rest; he perhaps began to think of a Scripture, Toplady, or Confession passage he had studied that morning, or possibly a book of Robert Ferrill's that he had read while still living in Stockton's Valley, and true to his nature he soon became lost deeply in the abstractions of his mind. So complete was his concentration that, when he came to himself, he found that a large rattlesnake had slithered and coiled right between his feet without his ever having noticed its approach. It must be remembered that, at this day and time and even into the early twentieth century, many hill farmers and their wives went about their house and farm chores barefoot from the first day of May until late fall frosts forced them to resume wearing shoes. It was simply a matter of good economics for them to save their shoes for the times that they really needed them, such as trips to town or to church, and over the summer the soles of their feet became almost as tough as the hooved toes of their livestock. But if John was following the conventions of his neighbors and was barefoot at this time, his fit of abstraction had led him into real danger, and he knew it. He sprang wildly away from the rattler with all the agility that a sudden shot of adrenaline could give him, but the reptile made no move to strike at his feet whatsoever, almost as if it were hypnotized or charmed. On thinking the matter over (perhaps in a nearby clump of bushes in an understandable physiological response to this hairsbreadth escape from a poisonous snakebite) he interpreted the rattler's lack of action as a sign that God really had singled him out for the special protection and status of an ordained minister.

The second event occurred perhaps because of John's inexperience and relative impracticality; to put it bluntly, it would appear that he got cheated royally in a cattle trade, and thereby hangs the tale of his subsequent ordination. He used to like to tell the story of his brother Jonathan's attempt to swap horses with an Irish trader who possessed, undoubtedly among a good many other bargainer's tricks, a keen sense of blarney. At the beginning of negotiations Jonathan set an exorbitant price on his horse, expecting that his opponent would haggle him down to a mutually acceptable fee, but the Irishman replied with mock seriousness, "It would be a great pity, Mr. Smith, to part you and your horse, for you do seem to think so very much of him."[53] But John was never quite willing to put a similarly well-deserved spin of bitter humor on his own trading experience. He bought a large ox from a drover, expecting to fatten and sell it at a profit at Monticello. As hinted above, though, stock traders have always maintained their own special ways of passing off "bum" animals as good ones at least until a bargain is struck, and it so happened that this steer, though an ox anatomically, still possessed very much the spirit and temperament of a bull. It may have been altered too late to make a change in its disposition, and the trader had likely given it some form of herb "dope" that wore off slowly after John had driven it to his farm.

Of course, John was not long in discovering that he was stuck with an animal he could not control, but he was determined to tame the ox somehow and make a profit out of the transaction. He loosed it in a fenced and partially cleared four-acre pasture watered by a little creek or branch running through its middle, and then made ready to put a clog on the animal; that is to say, he fastened one end of a rope or chain to a heavy log with the intention of securing the other end to the ox's horns, so that the added weight and encumbrance would eventually break the steer's spirit and make it docile. The ox was uncooperative from the start, though, and before long John was forced both to call on one of his neighbors for help and to set his dogs on the beast just to try to hold it still long enough to slip the clog on it. The combined efforts of men and dogs were in vain, and the steer eluded them and ran wildly through the pasture. However, in attempting to jump the small watercourse that ran through its middle, the ox became entangled in the limbs of a large beech tree that had fallen across the little creek, and for a moment the tree's whorl of dead branches appeared to hold it fast. By this time John had completely lost his temper—one of the very few instances in his long life in which he admitted so doing, and at this point he was probably angrier at himself than at the ox, for being such a fool as to have been taken in by the spiel of a trader in the first place—and he rushed up to the captive steer, shimmying up and across the tree trunk as he seized the animal's tender nostrils in his work-callused forefingers and gave its snout a hard, painful twist.

He might as well have stood in front of it on open ground and waved a red flag. With a demoniac bellow of pain and rage, the steer freed itself from the beech branches and leaped up and forward, actually clearing the trunk as it made for its new owner, whose own temper had, as might be expected, cooled down just as quickly as the ox had reacted. John turned tail and sped for the split-rail pasture fence as fast as he could sprint, but the steer was just as quick and even more angry. In the best manner of the bull it had once been, it kept pace right behind him, and as John recalled the chase many years later the steer had actually pushed him as he ran.

Williams records that as John was trying his hardest to make that fence and simultaneously avoid getting gored, his thoughts ran something like this: "If the Lord should be with me in this extremity, and deliver me out of this trouble, I will know assuredly that he wants me to preach, and I will no longer scruple to be ordained."[54] That's pretty eloquent prose coming from the mind of a man, even one who valued an education as much as John did, who is scared out of his wits and is running literally for his life; but then again, Williams was, unfortunately, only one of many nineteenth-century biographers who had the annoying habit of cleaning up their subjects' diction to suit the literary taste of the times. Whatever John's thoughts were, though, at just about the time he made this promise either to the Lord, to himself, or both, the ox caught his shirt or trousers on one of its horns and tossed him up in the air with a flick of its massive neck. He fell to the ground stunned but unhurt as the steer thundered madly past him, and by the time the ox had slowed itself and altered its course for another rush he had recovered his feet, raced to the fence, and scrambled over it to safety. When John's unnamed neighbor saw that he was out of danger he probably enjoyed a good laugh at the young preacher's expense, but John himself, believing that the Lord had delivered him from the serpent and the steer, even if not as grandly as he had delivered old King David from the lion and the bear, was now completely convinced of his ministerial calling.[55] He never told Williams the final fate of the ox. Since it was likely off-season for salting or smoking meat, he probably cut his losses, put the steer "across the table," and invited his Little South Fork neighbors and fellow church members to a big barbecue.

And so John was finally ordained to the ministry at Big Sinking Church's monthly "business" meeting on the third weekend in May 1808 by his older partners Richard Barrier and Isham Burnett. By now Barrier had labored with him closely for nearly three years and Burnett perhaps only a year less, if that, and neither man evidently thought it necessary to ask him very many doctrinal or practical questions in the traditional preliminary oral examination conducted before the members of the church. As John recalled it many years later, he was only asked about one subject, and that as a mere formality: whether he was acquainted with the Philadelphia Confession, and if he accepted its precepts. Actually, though he could either have forgotten it or did not choose to remember it, he may have been interrogated about one more matter as well, that being his acceptance of the Kentucky Baptists' Terms of General Union. At this stage in his life and his ministry, John probably didn't like the thought of endorsing a set of articles of faith that advocated tolerance of general-atonement preaching, and Barrier and Burnett may have felt exactly the same way. But during this time in Kentucky Baptist history, it was generally understood that all ministers in the General Union should accept it, although those most strongly Calvinistic often honored it in the breach rather than the observance. But to return to John's account of the events, he answered affirmatively to both questions about the Confession, his two older colleagues knelt with him and placed their hands on his head, Isham Burnett offered up a prayer of blessing for his labors, and at the ceremony's conclusion the church clerk presented him with a written testimonial of his ordained status that was then signed by the two officiating preachers. "Business" then being dismissed, the entire congregation retired to a nearby creek where John baptized the four candidates who had been waiting upon his ordination, and he began his career in the ministry now in earnest.[56]

Though Williams makes no mention of it, among the proudest and happiest of the visitors to Big Sinking Church for the occasion must have been Anna Smith, and for more than one reason. Though she might have preferred that her young husband preach the lighter Arminian-tinctured Calvinism of Isaac Denton, and though he could be abstracted, distant, and more inclined to pore over his little collection of books than to talk to her, she and he were now well on their way to becoming a family rather than just a couple. Anna was about four months pregnant at this time, and their first child, a boy named Eli, would be born that fall—according to one genealogist, on his proud father's twenty-fourth birthday.[57]

Little Eli was followed by three sisters within somewhat less than six years: Jane or Jennie Smith, on April 10, 1810; Elvira, on May 30, 1812; and finally Zerelda Ann, in June 1814. Though one daughter was named for Anna's sister, the names of three of John and Anna's offspring have something of an exotic lilt that is noticeably absent in the names of his children by his second wife. It suggests the possibility that John let Anna choose all her children's names herself, with the exception of the youngest daughter's middle name, which was perhaps bestowed by a doting, if sometimes preoccupied, husband and father. This would have been something of an unusual circumstance in that day when women owned few rights apart from their husband, and we are left to wonder what hopes and dreams harbored by this forgotten mountain girl prompted her to endow three of her four children with the faint whisper of a dim, romantic vision of far-off Palestine and Spain.[58]

During this time, though, John's own dreams were suffering some growing pains all by themselves. Though he must have believed that his conversion in the spicewood thicket would be the peak experience of his life and one that would shape all his future decisions, as he matured he couldn't help but realize that he had opted to remain in a very small and confining place indeed. Even so, perhaps any twenty-five-year-old Christian who has already realized all the hopes that his father has ever envisioned for him and indeed all the ambitions he set for himself at the time of his definitive religious experience would feel the same way as he tried to picture his future. When John was ordained in 1808, Big Sinking Church was still the only Wayne County Baptist congregation in Tate's Creek Association, and it may have been the large downstate body's most remote and isolated outpost. Feeble though the connection was between rustic Big Sinking and the large and increasingly prosperous and refined flatland Baptist churches that made up the nucleus of Tate's Creek Association, it did exist, and we cannot rule out the possibility that John had always harbored at least a subconscious desire ultimately to use it as a springboard to move into this downstate ecclesiastical nucleus and make a name for himself. But the year after John was ordained, a number of equally rustic if not so remote Tate's Creek churches in neighboring Pulaski and Knox counties, to the north and east of Wayne respectively, began to petition the Bluegrass body for the formation of their own regional association, to be called Cumberland River. Not only did Big Sinking opt to join this new group, but so did the Beaver Creek and Otter Creek congregations in southern Wayne County that had heretofore belonged to Stockton's Valley Association. In other words, after this community-wide decision John no longer belonged to a big downstate association but to a little country satellite group no different from the one he had left in 1805, except for the new association's possibly stronger emphasis on Calvinism and the Philadelphia Confession. And although common sense would have dictated the utility of the new group simply for the convenience of the Wayne and Pulaski County churches, one wonders whether John altogether appreciated this action.

Nonetheless, he went along with his brethren in the organization of the new Cumberland River Association, and his name appears along with those of Richard Barrier and Isham Burnett as well as Knox County's Moses Foley and Pulaski County's Stephen and Richard Collier, Wesley Short, Thomas Hansford, Thomas Hill, Thomas Wolverton, Malachi Cooper, Peleg Baker, and Joseph James as the new association's charter ministers at the body's first meeting in October 1809.[59] Having absorbed much Regular Baptist influence while belonging to Tate's Creek Association, the members of the Cumberland River group at first did not follow Separate Baptist custom and elect a patriarchal figure for a virtual lifetime term as associational moderator. Their first such officer, Malachi Cooper, served perhaps no more than a year, and their second, Thomas Hansford, served at most nine years before being replaced by an immigrant from the central part of the state, Elijah Barnes, who actually may have filled some of the more rustic Cumberland River members' expectations for a patriarch. He was loved by all, and for years was known by everyone as Old Daddy Barnes.[60] Thus, if John remained in the Wayne and Pulaski hill country Baptist preaching circuit for the rest of his life, as both his mentors Barrier and Burnett and most of the ministers listed above in fact did, he knew that he must labor unceasingly in the little backwoods churches as he had been doing, and the pinnacle of his accomplishments would have been eventually to win the Cumberland River moderator's office and the patriarch's reputation that Elijah Barnes held. For all his determination to live up to his father's expectations of him, thoughts of being known one day as Old Daddy Smith, decades in the future after he and Anna had grown wrinkled, toothless, and stooped on a hillside farm, rather predictably seem to have soured early on twenty-five-year-old John.

His dissatisfaction, perhaps up to a certain point in time subconscious, was exacerbated at this period by a voice from his past, as it were—Micah Taul. Taul, of course, had remained prominent in Wayne County politics, and as the colonel of the area's militia regiment. Even if he and John had grown somewhat apart and John was now perhaps not quite so enamored of Taul's degree of learning and his position, he probably saw Taul nearly every time he had to go to the county seat on court and tax business and to register the marriages he performed.[61] Though as an ordained minister John was now exempt from militia duty, his yet-unordained brother Jonathan was connected with Taul's local regiment, and in fact Jonathan was Taul's regimental paymaster as well as a sergeant in William Wood's company.[62] We thus see a scrap of evidence that Jonathan shared something of his older brother's intelligence, if not his exact same intellectual bent. But Taul had never quite given up on John himself in terms of encouraging him to continue his education, and just about the time that the new Cumberland River Association was organized—we can date the incident from John's recollection that Eli was a baby at the time, but that as of yet he and Anna had no other children—a teacher of some repute named Rhodes Garth moved to Monticello and opened up an academy. Taul strongly urged John to enroll as a student, even offering him free room and board through the week at his own house in the town. Perhaps not thinking his circumstances all the way though but seeing an opportunity as a Christian adult to acquire the education he had wanted so badly as a skeptical teenager, John readily agreed.

Going back to school while trying to work and raise a family is difficult enough in modern times, and John's case was immeasurably harder. He would have to spend five days a week away from his farm, not counting travel time between Parmleysville and Monticello and his weekend church obligations, while Anna tried to feed the livestock, milk the cows, cultivate the garden and fields, and otherwise manage the place in addition to cooking, sewing, and cleaning, with a baby less than two years old in tow and another one on the way. But John tried it anyway, and Williams reports that Anna did not object, at least not out loud. She may have regarded John as her "head," even as the Apostle Paul held forth and as most women more or less accepted in that day. Or perhaps she could see beyond the hills of Little South Fork in a manner different than her father, and she actively supported her husband in the hope that his schooling would allow them to migrate to a place with more opportunities, with more than just a wilderness farm to clear off and leave behind in a few years.

And so for the last time in his life, John formally enrolled in a school. In keeping with the educational mores of the times, Garth's program of study included the Scriptures, arithmetic, Roman history, orthography (handwriting), and orthoepy (declamation and pronunciation), and John was anxious to soak it all in. Williams notes that he was particularly interested in the last discipline mentioned, for in his travels to Tate's Creek Association as a representative of Big Sinking Church he had already noticed a distinction between his and his neighbors' hill country speech and that of the well-dressed and prosperous flatland preachers. Apparently the New England Holy Tone of Shubal Stearns, and probably the older dialect still spoken in the mountains as well, were already becoming anachronisms in downstate Kentucky; in later life John referred to the latter speech pattern, and perhaps the preaching style, too, as "backwoods brogue,"[63] and he seems to have wanted to lose them as fast as he could. So he set to work, boarding with Micah Taul and perhaps trying, as Louis Cochran suggests, to convert him, and he was happy—until he returned to Horse Hollow after his first week at school and viewed his exhausted wife's valiant but unsuccessful efforts to keep up the farm work without him.

Anna had tried as hard as she could, and although John did not recall that she uttered one word of complaint about her difficulties that week, the job was simply beyond her strength. He spent Saturday trying to catch up on the work, and we may hope that he gave his worn-out spouse a little forbearance and consideration that night; he filled a preaching appointment on Sunday, but walked back to Monticello early Monday morning with worry in his heart. By the time he arrived at the county seat he had already admitted to himself that Anna was simply physically unable to shoulder such a load, and after another uneasy week at the academy he returned home to find his wife even more spent and tired than she had been seven days earlier. Those two weeks at school meant much to him, but at this time Anna's well-being must have meant more, and so he never went back.[64]

This experience could be taken as a testimony to John's character at this juncture, that he should have forsaken something he loved so much for the welfare of his wife and child, not to mention the one on the way, and the story seems all the more poignant because John and Anna's lot—married young, raising a family, wanting to get ahead but unable—has been shared by so many other couples through the years both in the Appalachian Mountains and beyond. But as we shall see, in times to come John would once again see fit to take extended leaves of absence from his home and farm for the sake of his ministerial advancement, and even so, the old wound reopened by Rhodes Garth's school seems to have remained as a constant presence, gnawing at his soul.

It is indeed ironic that one of Langston Hughes's most famous poems can be associated with the outlook of a young man who would one day own slaves, but dreams deferred go through the permutations Hughes described—acquiring a falsely sugary crust, sagging like a heavy load, festering like a sore smelling of rotten meat, even exploding—without respect to skin color. They perhaps never entirely dry up, though, and in the years between the births of Jane and Zerelda Smith, 1810 through 1814, John's deferred dream ran the entire gamut. Though the downstate Kentucky Baptists had fought more or less constantly since the 1801 Regular-Separate union, they nonetheless experienced a renewal of the Great Revival during that same time period, with services only slightly more subdued than they had been at the turn of the century.[65] In the valley of the Little South Fork, Isham Burnett took over the pastoral care of Big Sinking Church while he, Richard Barrier, and John began to "arm off" growing congregations at locations up and down the river as churches in their own right. Barrier joined and was elected pastor of one such church on lower Beaver Creek known as New Hope,[66] and John participated in the constitution of another right down the hollow from his home at Parmleysville, called Bethel, on the third weekend in July 1810; it became his very first pastorate. Though Anna did not transfer her membership to join the new church, John's oldest brother Philip and sister-in-law "Millie" moved near the Little South Fork, became charter members, and served as the congregation's first deacons.[67] Other charter members at Bethel included John and Rebecca (Cross) Parmley, son and daughter-in-law of the settlement's founder; Isham Burnett's brother Roland and his niece by marriage Nancy; Jonathan Blevins (whose wife, the former Katie Troxell, was Cherokee and perhaps part of the same clan that had taught John a smattering of their language when he was a boy); Esther Koger; and

Stephen Vaughn. Despite John's regard for the Philadelphia Confession, though, the document was not mentioned even once in the minutes of the church's constitution. It was gathered on the Kentucky Baptists' Terms of General Union instead.[68]

For most of the Cumberland River ministers, and perhaps in a sense for John as well, it was indeed a happy, and certainly a busy, time. In the year 1812 alone the Cumberland River Association recorded 368 additions by experience of grace and baptism, 107 of them in the church at the head of the river near present Barbourville that was pastored by Moses Foley. Soon afterward the Cumberland River group "armed off" another association under Foley's leadership, known as South Union, and in spite of the eastward spread of the Stoneite Christian movement with Rice Haggard and John's former colleagues the Mulkey brothers—another circumstance that John Smith never mentioned to his biographer, though we can safely assume that he viewed it with distaste at the time—Cumberland River was able to survive and prosper.[69] During all this, John and his colleagues must have been itinerating every weekend through Pulaski and Wayne counties, preaching, praying, and baptizing throughout the bounds of the association as well as at their home churches.

And for all the religious labor that thus might have soothed John's spirit, his dissatisfaction just grew stronger. Not one word does he appear to have mentioned to his biographer about this revival season. Instead, he complained bitterly about the intellectual barrenness of the Little South Fork region, the fact that his own scanty education was the best in the community, and his not altogether ungrounded fear that his children would grow up with no more opportunities than he had had. Though it's a risky analogy, after a comparison of Spencer's and Williams's historical data from the period in question, one cannot help thinking of Raccoon John as an early nineteenth-century clerical version of Chris Offutt. But with that parallel, we might also ask why, if John was so concerned about his community's lack of improving influences, he never thought of sublimating his restlessness at least for a while by trying his own hand as a community schoolmaster. Apparently no such person yet resided on the Little South Fork, and John had to have been acquainted with the fact that not a few Kentucky ministers of all denominations, some of whom had no more education than he had, supplemented their incomes by teaching "subscription" schools, often conducting their classes in community churches loaned for the purpose. If John had wanted to supply both house and master for such a school three or four months out of every year at Parmleysville, all he had to do was to secure his church's permission for the use of the meetinghouse through the weekdays of a fall school term and to invest in a "primer chart," a few cheap pocket New Testaments, and some Dilworth or Webster "blueback" spelling books. He could have recouped his investment easily with the cash, grain, or barterable articles paid to him by his pupils' parents, and all in all it would have been a sounder risk than the one he had taken in buying his troublesome ox. Besides that, he would have given himself some much-needed mental exercise, to say nothing of providing a definite positive service to the young people of the settlement. But if John ever became or even thought of becoming a schoolmaster of this type, he never told his biographer about it, although Williams does mention his trying to tutor young Eli at home.[70] It seems to have been about as appealing a prospect to him as Offutt found in being assigned to teach basic freshman composition. But as the next chapter will show, there's a slight possibility that John could have helped at least one other capable and intelligent Parmleysville teenager learn to read, as well. Someone did, at any rate.

As unlikely as it may seem, John probably had the second moderator of the Cumberland River Association, Thomas Hansford, to thank for the means of altering his ambitions into something more familiar, agreeable, and attainable to him. We could wish to know more about Hansford, but unfortunately his biographical sketch in J. H. Spencer's *History of Kentucky Baptists* is lacking in most of the particulars of his early life.[71] He was no less rustic and illiterate than Richard Barrier and Isham Burnett and perhaps more so than Isaac Denton, and he certainly would have been no inspiration personally to John in terms of culture or educational attainment. Like Denton, though, he probably had some Separate Baptist roots, and how he wound up as a member of the Tate's Creek group, much less the moderator of an association that had sprung from it, is anybody's guess. For unlike John and other Tate's Creek and Cumberland River Calvinists, Thomas Hansford seems to have both believed in and preached the doctrine of apostasy, the idea that an individual might backslide or "fall away" from a converted state by disobedience and stubbornness toward the impressions of the Holy Ghost, and then possibly be reclaimed later by repentance. Though espoused by the Methodists and some, perhaps many, Separate Baptists, the belief was of course a direct contradiction to the dictates of the Philadelphia Confession, and it even violated the fifth article of the Terms of General Union to which the Kentucky Separates had subscribed in order to merge with the Regulars. But Hansford maintained it anyway, and he in fact had one notable success to show for it—namely, Jeremiah Vardeman, the lapsed convert of William Bledsoe mentioned in the last chapter as the fiddler John recalled seeing at Crab Orchard when he was a boy, but by this time one of the most popular young Baptist preachers in downstate Kentucky. Vardeman had farmed briefly in Pulaski County when he was newly married, and Hansford had reclaimed him to Christ from his perilous career as a fiddler by an effective use of the text of 2 Peter 2:22: "But it is happened to them according to the true proverb: the dog is turned to his own vomit again; and the sow that was washed to her wallowing in the mire."[72] Though Vardeman's reputation was to advance miles beyond Hansford's, he was always grateful to Hansford as being the instrument of his redemption, and he seems to have visited the older man as often as he conveniently could. And so to make a rather long story short, Thomas Hansford's big favor to John Smith was to introduce him to Vardeman when his popular protégé dropped in for a visit to the 1810 session of the Cumberland River Association. John remembered Vardeman from his corn-buying trip as a boy, perhaps cracking a joke or two about the incident, and Vardeman in turn was sufficiently impressed with John to take him under his patronage.

The early patronage system of the Kentucky General Union of Baptists must be dealt with extensively in this volume. It shaped Raccoon John Smith's adult life every bit as much as the Great Revival itself shaped his young manhood, and once he became involved in General Union politics he never entirely escaped its mindset. The causes for the development of patronage politics within the General Union can easily be surmised from the previous chapter, but Jeremiah Vardeman's own story might be the best place to introduce the unfamiliar reader to the characteristics of the system. Nine years older, two inches taller, and at least 130 pounds heavier than John, in appearance Vardeman could easily have served as a real-life model for Sinclair Lewis's Elmer Gantry (and in fact, William Faulkner perhaps unknowingly did name one of his Yoknapatawhpa County characters indirectly after the big Kentucky preacher, via an early twentieth-century Mississippi governor who seems to have been a kinsman). Though Vardeman was unquestionably morally superior to Lewis's fictional Gantry, he began preaching to great acclaim in Lincoln County immediately after his rededication and came to love popularity every bit as much as Lewis's character. He had been ordained to the ministry at the Crab Orchard Separate Baptist Church at about the time the Separates and Regulars united in Kentucky, and his church had gone into the half of the old South Kentucky group that had formed the South District Association. Here in South District he came under the mentorship of the older minister John Rice, improving both his preaching and his reputation as he began to attract notice in the North District side of the old South Kentucky Association as well. He may even have turned some heads in the former Regular Baptist Elkhorn Association, the largest, most urbane, and most prestigious such body in Kentucky at the time, but the beginning of Vardeman's real success came neither from his eloquence nor his zeal, but by his demonstration of his political loyalties.

Technically, the Kentucky Regular-Separate union had taken place only between the Elkhorn Regular Association and the two district bodies that had been formed from the old South Kentucky Separate Association. The others that became involved in the merger, such as the Salem and Bracken Regular Associations and the mixed Tate's Creek and Green River Associations, were never mentioned in the Terms of General Union, but they rather simply entered into the group correspondence in the seemingly general spirit of goodwill that had prevailed at the peak of the Great Revival. The Kentucky General Union was thus viewed by most former Separate Baptists as a statewide entity, but the nonspecific language of the Terms, besides neglecting to provide any real cohesive structure for the Kentucky United Baptists, lent itself to varying interpretations of the issues that were supposed to have been resolved. Thus a large majority of South District members, with deep reservations about establishing fellowship with the now-Calvinistic Tate's Creek Association, took an opposing view to the rest of the General Union: to them the union existed only between Elkhorn Association and the two halves of the old South Kentucky group, and they neither needed nor wanted to establish a correspondence relationship with the group that had left South Kentucky in 1794 to adopt a partial version of the Philadelphia Confession.

We can examine what transpired as a representative cross-section of the early Kentucky Baptist politics discussed briefly in the previous chapter. At South District Association's 1802 session, Tate's Creek Association offered a letter of correspondence to South District, causing a fierce floor debate. A motion was made and seconded that the Tate's Creek letter be accepted, a vigorous objection was given, and the issue was brought to a vote. In most modern associations adhering to General Union tradition a unanimous vote would be necessary to establish formal interassociational fellowship in this manner, but at the time and under the constitutions that the various Kentucky groups had framed for themselves, only a simple majority was necessary; and so to ensure that the collection of associations held together in ostensible peace and harmony, a few visitors from Elkhorn, North District, or one or more of the other corresponding groups discreetly—and quite illegally—stood up and cast votes with the delegation. The correspondence between South District and Tate's Creek was thus upheld by the narrowest of margins, and no one quite caught on to what had happened until after the vote had been taken. Unfortunately, polling techniques like this have always been endemic to southern politics, both religious and secular, and if the old maxim is true that politics are always the damnedest in Kentucky, perhaps this was a case of politics being the blessedest.

The South District members opposed to direct fellowship with Tate's Creek let the matter go and bided their time for a year, but they were determined not to let the voting irregularity be repeated. Vardeman, numbered among the minority favoring fellowship with Tate's Creek, knew that his developing acclaim within the neighboring associations would be jeopardized if something went sour with the Tate's Creek correspondence at his home group's 1803 session. Conceivably, all the other General Union associations might even declare nonfellowship with South District, and he would be deprived of most of his opportunities for revival preaching among them and hence his chances at advancement. Other preachers, including John Rice, felt the same way, and when they and Vardeman determined that the former Universalist John Bailey was numbered among the objectors to Tate's Creek, they commenced slinging a lot of mud against their opponent faction for its endorsement of such a heterodox minister as Bailey. It must be remembered that the old South Kentucky Association had apparently unanimously approved Bailey's return to the Separate Baptist fold in 1799, without comment on his private sentiments; no other charge either of heterodoxy or immorality had been preferred against him since that time in South District, and the only possible reason for Vardeman and

Rice's reintroduction of the complaints against him was the fact that he provided a convenient means for them to make their factional opponents look bad, especially in the eyes of the leaders of the other General Union associations.

And so bad matters became worse through that spring and summer, and a repeat of the 1802 South District Association meeting staged itself in September 1803. The delegates from Tate's Creek Association "laid in" their letter of correspondence, the motion to accept it was objected to, and the issue was again brought to a vote. This time, though, the South District delegates monitored the open balloting carefully, and the Tate's Creek correspondence was rejected by a large majority. Vardeman and Rice never even gave the delegates from the other associations a chance to figure out what to do next. They loudly began to object to John Bailey, Elkhorn's visitors joined in the objections, Bailey in turn made some cutting remarks about the tyrannical power that associations seemed to be assuming, and at this heated juncture Vardeman and Rice got up from the assembly and led a minority of churches and delegates away to gather a rump session, which they proclaimed to be the "legitimate" South District Association. Though Vardeman and Rice's actions amounted to a flagrant violation of the tenth and eleventh articles of the Terms of General Union, all the visiting delegates from the other associations, even the former Separates now in North District, followed the Vardeman-Rice minority, taking their letters of correspondence with them. They, including Tate's Creek Association, immediately established correspondence with the minority and left the majority to themselves as, to borrow a more modern expression, a lost ball in high weeds. Included among those left behind in the South District outcast group were Elders Thomas John Chilton, one of the original signers of the Terms of General Union, and Joseph Bledsoe, father of Terms cosigner and North District clerk Moses Bledsoe. And all this happened not quite two years after the document had been framed.[73]

For the next twelve months the South District majority tried hard to reestablish its connections with Elkhorn, Green River, and North District Associations, but at the 1804 round of Kentucky association meetings their overtures of friendship were uniformly rejected in favor of the Vardeman-Rice South District minority. North District Association even passed an "order" forbidding its members to take communion and wash feet at any of the churches numbered in the South District majority, losing at least one of its churches because of the action,[74] and the other associations undoubtedly enacted similar orders as well. Cut off from the rest of the Kentucky Baptists and unfairly maligned by the entire General Union simply because of a problem stemming from the Union's own weak government, the South District majority took back both the doctrine, the practice, and the old name of the South Kentucky Association of Separate Baptists, and from this body the modern denomination known as the Separate Baptists in Christ, the first of the distinctively Appalachian Christian groups having sprung from the work of Shubal Stearns, has come.[75]

But to return to Vardeman's case, in a large sense this split made his fortune. In a moment when the rickety relationship between Regular and Separate Baptists in Kentucky could have collapsed entirely and he stood in danger of losing his budding influence with the General Union as a whole, he and John Rice came up with a solution, albeit Machiavellian, that simultaneously sacrificed the peace in only one association rather than all of them and ensured his own place within the Union's structure. No matter that Moses Bledsoe in North District could now be excluded for the simple act of participating in a footwashing with his father Joseph, still in the cut-off South District group (not that washing his father's feet was high on Bledsoe's list of priorities, as we shall see), and no matter that innumerable other innocent members in both North and South District Associations faced like penalties for similar actions with their friends and relatives; the General Union associational leaders could at least pat themselves on the back in the wistful belief that the Union had maintained its integrity, and in the knowledge that with Vardeman they had a man they could count on both as a popular preacher and an advocate for the Union's interests, whatever they might be.

And so Vardeman's career blossomed. In the wake of an 1810 Elkhorn Association split he moved northward to Fayette County to join the majority faction of that body, and in the process he caught the eye of Jilson Payne and James French, influential newcomers to North District Association from Elkhorn who were trying their best to use their own political influence to "Regularize" the formerly Separate body. Vardeman picked up the pastorates of Lulbegrud and Grassy Lick Churches in North District after associational moderator Robert Elkin and his vassals had run off the two congregations' previous pastor, David Barrow, ostensibly for publicly advocating the emancipation of slaves. He also appears to have given part-time help for a brief while to a third North District church known as Sycamore, destitute of preaching because Payne and French's politicking had driven away Daniel Williams, the minister there, as well; though this subject must be addressed in more detail later, it might be mentioned here that Williams (who may have been a kinsman of Raccoon John's biographer) had been forced out by Payne and French from Lulbegrud, too, before the emancipationist Barrow had ever assumed the pastorate. In Elkhorn, Vardeman held two more lucrative pulpit positions, David's Fork (the site of his membership) and Bryan's Station, and the two Elkhorn and two North District churches under his care gave him one of the earliest forms of a ministerial salary in Kentucky: the trustees of the four churches united and bought him a house and farm on credit in Fayette County, then proceeded to give him regular assistance in paying off the debt.[76] And all the while he remained an eminent revivalist, foregoing his general atonement Separate Baptist roots to style himself as a fashionable "Fullerene" Calvinist once *The Gospel Worthy of All Acceptation* had been introduced in Kentucky,[77] preaching in the choice circuits of the General Union, accepting the monetary gifts that the urbane flatland churches gave him, and dazzling his enormous congregations with a sonorous speaking voice and a diction that was described as "generally accurate, making but few mistakes in his grammar or in his pronunciation," though sometimes allowing himself the use of "provincialisms" or slang for "telling effect."[78]

This, then, was the Jeremiah Vardeman that took the youthful John Smith under his patronage in the fall of 1810. Williams gives us the impression that Vardeman simply gave John his start, so to speak, as a guest preacher in the flatland Bluegrass churches because he was impressed with John's preaching abilities and because he was always generous even if in a sort of blunt and heavy-handed way.[79] Though this was undoubtedly the case, we can easily see that Vardeman had a multitude of reasons for making friends whenever, wherever, and however he could, because the circumstances of his climb up the Kentucky Baptist ladder had already given him so many enemies as well—some of whom were more trustworthy than his friends. And this was the key to the patronage system: at various times Vardeman himself had taken the heat for and supported the projects of John Rice, Jilson Payne, James French, and other key politicos of the General Union associations, rather than remaining loyal to any local group such as his own South District Association during the 1803 split, and these men had granted him valuable favors for so doing. Now to maintain a measure of safety for his own influence within the unstable political environment of the Union, in which anyone's fortunes could take a sudden nose dive, it simply made sense for him to endorse and support young preachers in whom he discovered talent and to try to get them established downstate. He never knew when he'd need a return favor, but if the occasion should ever arise, his own cadre of grateful "boys" in the ministry both to rescue him and, if need be, take the heat for him were the comforting equivalent of an insurance policy.

We cannot be sure exactly what Vardeman's initial intentions for John were. It is known that in the fall of 1810 he was looking for a permanent pulpit supply for the Sycamore Church, which, like his other North District pastorates, was located in Montgomery County. At the time both he and another minister named David Chenault, from Cane Springs Church in Madison County, were giving the church what help they could, but neither man really had the time to do justice to the full duties of the job; besides, it's quite likely that the Sycamore members were bitter about the loss of their home minister Williams to the politicking of Vardeman's and Chenault's own mentors, and that didn't make the task of preaching to them any easier. Thus it's possible that Vardeman considered asking John, as a young outsider with no local political axes to grind, to move north and assume the Sycamore pastorate. But there was one obstacle that seems more than anything else to have precluded the venture: though the Sycamore members were willing to give occasional gifts to their preachers, in true old Separate Baptist fashion they still adamantly refused even to think of supporting a pastor with a salary. And so it turned out that Vardeman got another of his "boys," a young Clark County tailor named William Vaughan—whose conversion experience was listed in the previous chapter, and who has been noted as later becoming one of Raccoon John Smith's closest personal friends and ultimately one of his greatest doctrinal adversaries—to move his membership from James Quesenberry's Friendship Church in Clark County to the destitute congregation at Sycamore. Vaughan served Sycamore as its regular preacher at monthly meetings even before he was ordained to the ministry in 1812 by Vardeman and Chenault, and as pastor for a couple of years afterward until, it seems, the church's lack of a stated ministerial salary ultimately caused him to give up and move his family and his labors to the more generous churches of the Bracken Association.[80] After Vaughan's tenure a Tennessee emigrant minister named Enoch Willoughby joined the church and served it as pastor until his death, and it's probable that the Sycamore members preferred his labors to those of a young Kentucky Baptist political wheelhorse who was continually harping about a salary.[81] But as will be seen, by that time Vaughan had other inducements to put North District behind him as well.

Vardeman thus made do for John between the years of 1811 and 1814 by sponsoring him on at least one itinerant speaking tour through certain outlying sections of the Bluegrass, during which time Anna seems to have had to manage the farm alone for a good many more weeks than she had during John's Rhodes Garth school adventure.[82] He probably let Vardeman arrange additional periodic downstate engagements for him as well. Williams gives us scanty details of these early excursions, although we can safely hypothesize that one of them led him as far west as Campbellsville, Kentucky, where he met another of Vardeman's friends, Isaac Hodgen. Subsequently and perhaps at Vardeman's behest, Hodgen, who was never a strong Calvinist himself, sent John a copy of Andrew Fuller's *The Gospel Worthy of All Acceptation* to try to soften the younger preacher's strict stance on the Philadelphia Confession and acquaint him with the preaching and the theology expected in most of the Bluegrass. Always grateful for the gain of another book, John read it eagerly, but although in time he would repudiate the beliefs he had gotten from his father, he always said that Fuller's more liberal system made less sense than did the Philadelphia Confession itself.[83]

Vardeman's idea still was, of course, someday to break John into a Bluegrass pastoral or evangelistic role where he could provide the greatest service to the Lord, as it were, although service to Vardeman and Vardeman's superiors was by far the more politically important. But just as we may speculate on Vardeman's exact plans to place John, so may we puzzle a bit over John's exact feelings toward Vardeman. Like Isaac Hodgen, the big preacher was never the strict Philadelphia Confession Calvinist that John was in his youth; without really giving the matter very much thought, as a member of Elkhorn Association Vardeman merely welcomed the "Fullerene" version of the doctrine the way most Elkhorn ministers and Kentucky ex-Regulars did, as a means to continue the essentially noncreedal Separate Baptist evangelism through which most had been introduced to the faith in the first place while still remaining fashionably orthodox Baptists. John's and Vardeman's doctrinal systems were thus at odds from the first, although Vardeman's talent for compromise undoubtedly softened the edges of the differences. Moreover, between the two preachers John unquestionably possessed the sharper intellect and the greater ability to utilize logic, and after he began to work with Vardeman he couldn't have been long in discovering that fact on his own. We therefore cannot say for sure that John formed the close and intense, almost passionate attachment to Vardeman that was the case in his relationships with many of the intellectuals he had met and was to meet, but it is certain that he was impressed with Vardeman as a Kentucky Baptist power broker and as his eventual ticket away from the hills. Vardeman was affable, gregarious, and easygoing; in spite of his actions at the 1803 South District Association, he came to detest controversy when there was no projected good to be gotten by it,[84] and he had so charmed the wronged and mistreated Daniel Williams, who had returned on a visit to North District Association in the late summer of 1810, that in the following year Williams had named a son after the man who had supplanted him and David Barrow at Lulbegrud Church.[85] If nothing else, in the process of Vardeman using him and he using Vardeman, John certainly enjoyed the big preacher's company.

Even so, the day would come when John's rage would explode against Vardeman, and for the usual reason that his anger was kindled at anyone: pretensions to wisdom that faded away in the clinch, in Vardeman's own case, to a pale political correctness. Ironically, though, this was the very quality that had up to that point ensured Vardeman's success within the politically volatile General Union, and since John had followed Vardeman as an example, his own as well.

It would be some years yet before John would finally break out of the hills for good and establish a career in the Bluegrass, and he would undergo more than a few adventures and misadventures in the meantime. The development of his labors in the Kentucky Baptist patronage system with Jeremiah Vardeman truly marked the end of his spicewood years, though, and he could never again be satisfied to labor in a place so intellectually, spiritually, and economically confining as he perceived the Little South Fork to be. By the fall of 1814 he'd spent ten years in the tiny thicket he had fashioned from his father's ideals; he knew every twig and bud, and it was just too small for him. Had he really been more at peace within himself, he might have remained content to live out his life as a country preacher like his older mentors Barrier, Burnett, and Denton, and perhaps as a seasonal schoolmaster such as Robert Ferrill; he and Anna possibly would have raised a large family and grown old together, but it simply was not to be.

Ere we depart John's little spicewood thicket to follow his track further, though, we might do well to pause for another moment and give its confines one last good hard look, and to ponder John's exodus from it. In the spicewood thicket behind his father's old cabin back in Stockton's Valley he had been transformed—and at least in part had transformed himself—from a seeker after truth and wisdom, a sometime skeptic and universalist, to a Calvinistic Christian and a preacher after the image of the venerable John Alderson, via his experience of the New Birth in Christ as catalyzed by his father's death. In Kierkegaardian terms, he had passed from the meaningless, accidental aesthetic existence through the deeply self-conscious ethical to the religious, in the subjective manner that is the lot of individual human existence. From his own personal spicewood thicket, as it were, the one he himself had constructed for his life back in 1804 and 1805, he emerged slowly but surely as an increasingly successful, influential, and powerful preacher of the Gospel. But the success required a blood sacrifice, one that he might never even have realized at the first, but which he would discover to be unceasing and increasingly demanding. Like Jeremiah Vardeman, John believed it was his divine calling to preach the Gospel to sinners, to present the glories and joys of salvation through Jesus Christ to his hearers in such a way that they might see and believe his truth for themselves, to share his personal testimony and vision of the New Birth in the hope that others might come to rejoice in their own transcendent experiences of the eternal. He had in fact channeled his entire intellect to focus on this pursuit until he had discovered there was not room enough within his rustic backwoods home to accommodate his vision of it. Now, to make himself more fit and able, in his own mind, to minister to a wider and more cultured audience and thus better provide for his family and his own intellectual peace, he had naively attached himself to a weak, volatile Kentucky Baptist political network with leaders whose primary ethic was the maintenance of their own power and their own status quo at any cost. Even as John believed he was growing in grace and in the knowledge of the truth, and that his advancement in the Baptist Church represented his own personal center of God's will, to maintain his success in this structure he had to accept it, endorse it, labor within its confines and mores, and participate in its group actions willingly. No doubt never even knowing that the early pre-Reformation scholars of the Sorbonne in Paris had held the position that the decisions of ecclesiastical councils were actual reflections of the will of God on earth and were therefore above reproach, he may actually have reconciled the General Union leaders' and associations' blatant politicking with the same thought; this may be seen as an odd belief for Protestants, particularly Baptists, but it still exists in the Appalachian "Old Time" Baptist circles where General Union–style politics are yet maintained, and it could even have been voiced as a defense by Kentucky associational leaders from the very earliest. And so in the dogmatic dead certainty of the correctness of the organized religion which he had espoused, his experience of the religious itself metamorphosed, over time, back to a very tawdry form of the aesthetic existence, the kind that only working evangelical preachers know: certainly a different kind of aesthetic than that which he had known as a poor sinner boy, but an aesthetic no less, and no higher.

CHAPTER 4

Sickness Unto Death

The more a man is able to forget, the greater number of transformations his life can undergo. The more he is able to remember, the more divine his life becomes.

—Søren Kierkegaard

Though picking through the facts of John Smith's early life with a fine-tooth comb has been essential to our purposes thus far, we should be careful of judging him too harshly on the basis of our discoveries. If his modest but increased patronage-based advancement within the General Union structure between the fall of 1810 and the summer of 1814 pointed him directly into a very muddy path, his situation actually made more sense than that of the United States at large. At the midpoint of these same years, the American government had managed to fall headlong into a deep, ripe privy of its own digging—and strangely enough, ultimately climbed out of it with a cocky grin and smelling like a veritable rose.

We speak here of the War of 1812, which, in spite of the hyperbole maintained at the time by American politicians and even in this day to an extent by certain U.S.-based communications media, still remains one of the most foolish military actions in which this nation has ever mired itself. Despite the high-blown arguments voiced at the time by American politicians for the second war between the United States and Great Britain, nothing can change the fact that the main initial aim of a great many prowar congressmen and senators (including Kentucky's Henry Clay and Richard Mentor Johnson, nicknamed "war hawks" in the first use of that term in American history) was to conquer and annex Canadian territory while the British were otherwise occupied in the Napoleonic Wars. Neither can it be denied that, both before and especially after the United Kingdom attended to Napoleon at Waterloo, our old Mother Country gave us the beginnings of what promised to be a very thorough thumping in which a great many young American militiamen, a large percentage of them Kentuckians, were killed. At one point the British Army actually ran both the president and Congress out of Washington, D.C., and burned the White House in retaliation for the American sacking and burning of York, Ontario. But as the crowning absurdity of the whole conflict, the war's most famous battle, that of New Orleans on January 8, 1815, was fought and won by Andrew

Jackson *after* a peace treaty had been negotiated between British and American diplomats and the war had ended at more or less a draw between the two contestants. There were no methods of rapid overseas communications in those days, and so neither Jackson nor the general leading his opponents, Sir Edward Pakenham, had any idea that their two nations were officially at peace when their battle was joined. That didn't stop either Jackson or most other American politicians from exploiting the victory at New Orleans as the crucial factor that caused America to "win" the war, though, and it certainly didn't get in the way of the American people's swallowing the pleasant suggestion whole. Not only did the War of 1812 and the Battle of New Orleans drastically reinforce a rapidly budding American white Anglo-Saxon Protestant nationalism and the notion that the United States was God's Own Country, it created what historians call the Era of Good Feeling, the postwar mood for that entire generation of U.S. citizens, based on completely fallacious assumptions. One wonders if we should hope for future Eras of Good Feeling after ill-conceived and ill-conducted wars, or not. But to return: though John, as an ordained minister, was exempt from military duty,[1] the great and insane conflict gave its own indirect but permanent twist to his life and that of his family.

John's brothers Jonathan and Henry both saw active service in the Canadian campaign led by Kentucky's bellicose old governor Isaac Shelby, and under the regimental command of Micah Taul, while their mother, Rebecca, undoubtedly worried and fretted over them back in Stockton's Valley with vivid memories of her second husband's own Revolutionary War absences from home. As noted, Jonathan served as Taul's regimental paymaster and as a sergeant in Captain William Wood's company. Twenty-year-old Henry was a buck private in the same outfit, as was John's friend and teacher Robert Ferrill and a good many of his former neighbors. Taul's hill country militia was mustered with the thirty-nine other state regiments just across the Ohio River from Cincinnati at Newport, Kentucky, during the last week of August 1813.[2] Included among them was a regiment commanded by Colonel William Dudley, and a James Townsend served in Captain Archibald Morrison's company in this force, although we cannot say with absolute certainty that this was Anna Smith's brother.[3] Shelby's army ferried the river and marched northeastward to Chillicothe, Ohio, linked up with commander William Henry Harrison, and proceeded to the Michigan territory, arriving at the shores of Lake Erie in late September. At Moraviantown, Ontario, not far from Detroit on October 5, they participated in the one significant American land victory in the north, the Battle of the Thames. Luckily, both Jonathan and Henry Smith survived to return home and tell the tale of the great battle, in which Kentucky's Richard M. Johnson was said to have killed Tecumseh, leader of the Iroquois Confederation, which had sided with the British during the war in a futile effort to check U.S. encroachment upon Native American lands. Micah Taul, however, had little to brag about, since he had fallen ill on the morning of the battle and Governor Shelby had ordered him to stay put in his tent.[4] It is not certain that

James Townsend, if indeed this was Anna's brother and John's marriage-bond cosigner, survived to get back to Kentucky. He was discharged from military service for some reason at Port-In-Bay, Ontario, on September 22, 1813, almost two weeks before the great battle, and although he could have come back home, there is some evidence that Anna Smith's oldest brother may have been dead by the fall of 1814.[5]

Back in the hills, especially west of the Little South Fork and Stockton's Valley in Kentucky's cave country, some enterprising landowners with caverns on their properties made a pretty penny mining saltpeter and selling it to the government for making gunpowder. As will be seen in this chapter, in his own poetic way John Smith would later make use of these saltpeter caves to his own profit and advancement as well. At least until the early harvests of the year 1814, though, he remained on his farm on the Little South Fork, perhaps making a little extra money himself selling beef, pork, grain, and produce to local military purchasing agents, pastoring the little Bethel Church at Parmleysville, and going on occasional preaching jaunts to the outlying areas of the Bluegrass under the sponsorship of Jeremiah Vardeman. His response to the war was probably typical of that of the Kentucky Baptist ministry generally: engaging in fervent prayer for his brothers, friends, and neighbors risking their lives on the field of battle, and assuring his listeners that God was on America's side and that their cause was just. For all that, John definitely threw Vardeman and the Kentucky General Union a curveball as the war drew to its close. In the summer of 1814, he, Anna, and their four children abruptly pulled up stakes from Wayne County and migrated south to homestead the northern Alabama lands that Andrew Jackson had wrested from the Creek Nation only a few months before.

Years later, John Augustus Williams translated the Creek Nation's bitter loss of 23 million acres in Alabama into perfect nineteenth-century Americanese by stating that the lands were simply "thrown into market," and he portrayed Raccoon John as having moved to Alabama altruistically for the sake of his and his family's welfare. "Public" lands then under federal control could be patented at $1.15 per acre, with a down payment of only $10 per hundred-acre patent entry and the balance not falling due for four years. Everyone expected that the end of the war would send immigrants flooding southward to the new American territory, inflating the price of real estate, and even a poor man with enough savvy to seize the main chance could patent several thousand acres cheaply, pay off his notes to the government by selling only small portions of it at the expected high prices, and still have enough left over to purchase slaves, grow cotton, and transform himself, his wife, and his children into one of the "first" or socially ranking families in the region.[6] Though the Treaty of Fort Jackson, formalizing U.S. assumption of the Creek lands, was not finalized until August 10, 1814, much of the northern Creek territory—especially around preexisting white settlements such as Huntsville—was "into market" by the spring. So, after a brief fact-finding trip to northern Alabama during which

John seems to have used government terms to buy a small homestead at Hickory Flats in present Madison County as a start,[7] he "lifted" his and Anna's letters from their respective churches and got one of his colleagues (probably either Richard Barrier, Isham Burnett, or Thomas Wolverton, the latter of whom was now serving in Isaac Denton's old pastorate at Beaver Creek) to replace him at Bethel; sold his Horse Hollow farm at the war-inflated price of $1,500; packed up Anna, the children, and Hiram and Jane Townsend (who, apparently, were riding along to help with the young ones); and headed south to patent ten thousand Alabama acres and become a rich man, somehow driving eighty-five hogs and fifty head of cattle along on the trail with only the help of his dogs and the teenage Hiram Townsend to keep his stock together on the long journey.[8]

Anyone who has worked around cattle and hogs knows that the idea of one man and one boy by themselves driving even a modest herd of livestock from the southern Kentucky mountains up hills, down valleys, and across rivers all the way through the state of Tennessee to northern Alabama bespeaks a miracle almost as awesome as the parting of the Red Sea. Besides the facts that John never showed all that much business acumen either before this venture or afterward, and that he had plenty of inducements to remain in Kentucky under Jeremiah Vardeman's patronage and continue to cultivate his prospects in the General Union there, it is perhaps our only clue from Williams that something is not quite right with this picture. In fact John had several stock drovers along on this trip besides Hiram Townsend: namely, his father-in-law John, his other brother-in-law Henry, and perhaps even the youngest in the Townsend family, John Jr., if he was old enough at this time to lend a hand at herding. Smith and his father-in-law very well may have owned both the hogs and the cattle in common, and the Alabama land grant may even have been taken in John Townsend's name. The great mystery is why Raccoon John indicated to his biographer that he, Anna, their children, and one brother- and sister-in-law had journeyed to Alabama and begun their new lives there utterly alone, leaving both of their families back in Kentucky perhaps never to see them again. From the available evidence, John Townsend, his second wife, and the entire surviving Townsend clan made the move at the same time and in company with them.[9] It is as though Raccoon John wanted to leave his first wife's family out of his, and especially Williams's, picture completely. Of course this wasn't the first time, and it certainly wouldn't be the last, that John—or Williams, depending on exactly who was at fault in specific cases—would downplay or altogether neglect to mention individuals whose influences were and are vital to a proper understanding of Smith's life and his later role in the Kentucky religious community, but in most other instances the reasons for the obfuscation of data become eminently clear with a little research. This case is most decidedly murky, and we are left not knowing whether the Alabama migration was actually John Smith's original idea at all. Though he could have gotten caught up in the notion of becoming a wealthy slaveowning planter like those he had seen on his Bluegrass trips with Vardeman, as he claimed, and then persuaded the Townsend family to move with him for Anna's sake, the idea could have come just as easily primarily from John Townsend. The old nomad may have heard of good prospects in Alabama and characteristically decided to pull up stakes and move once more, and Anna, who may have just lost her oldest brother, could have talked her husband into leaving Kentucky because she dreaded the prospect of separation from the rest of her family and was determined to keep her father, her stepmother, and the rest of her siblings as close to her as she could. It's pretty certain that old John Townsend himself had no starry-eyed visions of cotton, slaves, and wealth. A rolling stone who stayed free of moss to the very last, he died in 1843 at the age of eighty-one, since 1814 having homesteaded in no fewer than seven different locations in Alabama's Madison, Limestone, Franklin, Marion, Montgomery, and Coosa counties, not counting the one year he moved north to Hamilton County, Illinois, and then came back.[10] But it's still possible that he, and more likely Anna, used the stories of the prospects for riches that Raccoon John was later to recount to Williams to try to persuade John to make the move in the first place. In any case, John knew he could do probably as well by himself and his children as had the first pioneer Baptist preachers in the Bluegrass, some of whom had left behind yeoman status in Virginia to become very well-to-do landowners in central Kentucky. Though John's reasons for dissembling about this period of his life may always remain something of a mystery, we can uncover a few more clues by an examination of John and Anna's brief and tragic sojourn in their new home.

The family arrived at John's Hickory Flats homestead on November 2, 1814, at first renting a cabin until they could build their own on John's land; it took time to cut logs and more time for them to season, so the project of house-raising may have been put off until spring. Williams admits that John and Anna did have at least one set of neighbors with a house easily visible from their own,[11] but he never indicates that this dwelling probably belonged to the Townsend family. They settled in for the winter, and John began to scout the country for available tracts of land and prospects for advancement. Though his preliminary land deals are not made clear and there are in fact no surviving deeds or other court records whatsoever of his Alabama transactions, that is, unless they were all done in John Townsend's name, he seems to have conducted business of some sort with a few merchants at Huntsville that left them owing him money rather than the other way around.[12] At the Huntsville settlement he would have noted the existence of at least one established church, but it wasn't Baptist: it was a Stoneite Christian congregation gathered by the old Kentucky pioneer Benjamin Lynn, who had moved with his wife, daughter, and son-in-law to the territory as early as 1810, and in fact Lynn was finally gathered to his fathers only about a month after John had first arrived in Alabama.[13] John probably corresponded with Jeremiah Vardeman, Micah Taul, and others of his Kentucky friends, advising them of his progress and perhaps even encouraging some of them to try their own luck in the new land someday. A few years later, Taul in fact did move his family to Alabama, and spent the remainder of his life there.[14] All in all, Smiths and Townsends appear to have been comfortable, hopeful, and ready to celebrate the 1814–1815 holidays happily.

We speak here of the holidays, not Thanksgiving, which was not even recognized back then, or New Year's Day in association with the Christmas season, but rather the Yuletide observances of that time period and of the culture from whence John and Anna and their families had come. There were only two, neither celebrated as lavishly as are modern holidays, but both of which were very likely considered just as important for family togetherness as our own modern perceptions of Christmas: the traditional day of December 25, and Old Christmas eleven days later on January 6. The tradition of Old Christmas had begun in 1752 with the British Parliament's adoption of Catholic Europe's Gregorian Calendar for the nation and its colonies. The Gregorian Calendar made for an abrupt eleven-day shift from the older Julian Calendar that England and its colonies had been using, and initially there had been much superstitious fear and widespread panic among the common people both in the British Isles and America that the government had somehow suddenly brought them eleven days closer to Judgment. All had finally peacefully acquiesced to the use of the new calendar, though, and one of their coping mechanisms had been to celebrate Christmas on the day that the authorities accepted, and then to celebrate it again eleven days later to line up with the old Julian Calendar. Hence the term Old Christmas, and in some parts of southern Appalachia the day's observance continued well into the twentieth century, long after the memory of the old-style Julian Calendar had gone by the board, but with some families' and communities' conviction that Old Christmas was, after all, the true Christmas.[15] As commercial as the twenty-fifth day of December has gotten, perhaps we should take a lesson from the old folks ourselves.

Though John may have been at home on December 25, by the sixth day of January he was out and about again, this time on church-related matters. He related to John Augustus Williams that a few other Baptists had already moved into the new country by that time, and some of these had known his father back on the Holston in Tennessee. He struck up an acquaintance with them, probably at Huntsville or at New Market, the settlement then closest to Hickory Flats, and around Old Christmas they sent for him and asked him to come and hold a preaching service for them, "expressing at the same time the tenderest regard for the memory of his father."[16] The implication is that these east Tennessee emigrants, whom John never actually named, desired preaching as part of their Old Christmas celebrations. Thus at the end of the 1814–1815 holiday season, John was away from Hickory Flats, and it so happened that on the night of January 7 Anna was also called away from home to sing some hymns and otherwise minister to a sick neighbor (probably her stepmother). Hiram and Jane Townsend may have brought the request to Anna, and it is certain that they stayed to take care of Eli, little Jane, and Elvira, but Anna took the baby Zerelda with her and stepped out into the night. The Townsend teenagers and Smith children went to bed, Jane sleeping with her namesake, Eli and Elvira in one small bed together, and Hiram by himself, probably on a pallet on the floor.

About ten o'clock the Smith cabin caught fire. We do not know the cause, only that the blaze started on the roof rather than out of the fireplace or chimney, in itself an unusual circumstance. Perhaps another settler or even John Townsend or John Smith themselves had cleared timber from a patch of land and had somehow contrived to dry it sufficiently to burn, and some embers from the unattended fire had blown to the dry, light poplar shingles on top of the house. But some burning splinters had awakened Hiram Townsend, and after springing up with a painfully blistered face he had contrived to get Jane and her namesake out of the house as the roof dropped bit by bit all around them. Little Eli and Elvira, sleeping separately, were unreachable and helpless, and the burning roof caved in completely, engulfing the house in flames before anything could be done to save them.

Poor Anna, with the baby Zerelda at her breast and giving what comfort she could to the sick neighbor, whoever it may have been, was close enough to hear Hiram's, Jane's, and little Jane's screams, and she saw the blaze light up the woods. She rushed to the spot and, if Williams is to be believed—and he *is* in this instance—came dangerously close to leaping into the crumbling furnace in an effort to save Eli and Elvira or perish trying, but her brother and sister managed to hold her back. Nothing else could be done, and as more distant settlers slowly gathered in, attracted by the blaze, the entire family spent the night around the funeral pyre, sobbing heartbrokenly.

The next morning and many miles down the Mississippi, Andrew Jackson won his great victory over the British, and at Hickory Flats John Smith's cabin slowly finished burning to the ground. Years later, John recalled to Williams that someone had ridden to the home of his father's friends at dawn on that day and had broken the news to him. No one except those who have experienced a similar sudden, hellish loss can even begin to comprehend his state of mind, and he could have been excused for losing his wits altogether. He journeyed home in a daze of grief and horror, tormented by the old bugbear of the Philadelphia Confession that he had insisted upon maintaining: the question of whether his dead children were of God's elect, in which case they were at that very instant basking in the Savior's arms in a land where pain, fear, and death were no more; or if they were not, and that the fire that had burned their little bodies was only a precursor of the torments in which their small voices would wail in agony throughout all eternity, because God's condemnation was always just. To say that this was a vicious, intolerable thought is to make the most pathetic of understatements. John's distracted mind fixed on the idea that Anna had already considered this same perverse possibility, though he must already have known that, despite his teachings, she didn't hold with Calvinism as strongly as he did, and he spurred his horse all the faster in the hope that somehow he might be able to give her a modicum of comfort.

By the time John arrived at the ruins of his cabin, the fire had burned all the way down and the ashes had cooled enough for the men on hand to set about the task of digging out his children's bones from the ruins. John recalled their efforts at this sad chore as his first sight upon his return. Anna sat on a log some distance away, a blanket thrown around her shoulders, Zerelda sleeping innocently and unknowingly in her arms and little Jane at her side still crying bitterly. Anna herself was too grieved even to weep. John picked little Jane up in his arms and took Anna's hand, and the bereaved family walked a short distance into the forest to talk and try to make sense out of what had just befallen them.

They had lost everything in the house save the clothes on their backs and a lump of melted silver that John was later to salvage from the cabin's ashes, and the charred bones of their six-year-old son and two-year-old daughter were being recovered at that very moment by neighbors. But to John's surprise, Anna's thoughts had never gone in the direction that his had taken. Knowing that Eli and Elvira were innocent babies, she had no doubt whatsoever that their tiny souls were at play in the pastures of heaven, but she was nonetheless overcome with guilt for having left them alone with her brother and sister the night before. She despondently begged for John's forgiveness, and he tried to soothe her with the affirmation that she had gone where her duty had called her and that "for some wise and good purpose this blow had fallen upon them."[17] They had nowhere else to go but to the house of John Townsend or that of their only other close neighbor, Anna Miller, and a day or so later they buried their children's bones in what would become the Miller Cemetery at Hickory Flats.[18]

Characteristically, Williams seems not to have considered that Anna probably had a far more rational excuse for leaving the cabin on her mission of mercy that terrible night than John could give for his trip abroad at the Old Christmas season, and John himself never indicated that he let this thought cross his mind. He was a minister, after all, and frequent absences from home was part of the job.[19] But grief that dulls the memory of some sharpens the recollection of others, in neither case necessarily in a rational, unbiased manner. John Townsend, undoubtedly living in plain sight of the ruins of his daughter's cabin, almost certainly did mull over a good many years' accumulation of unpleasant memories. Considering the circumstances of John and Anna's marriage as discussed in the previous chapter, the old man had probably opposed the union from the first. His son-in-law had once spent two weeks in a Monticello school while Anna had worked herself past the point of exhaustion. Afterward, John had been away from home regularly for perhaps even longer periods, gallivanting across downstate Kentucky on preaching tours with Jeremiah Vardeman while he had probably had to send Hiram, Henry, and Jane to Anna for what assistance they could provide her. Then almost as soon as they had all arrived in Alabama and at Old Christmas of all times, the preacher had gone away again, his and Anna's house had burned up in his absence, and now Anna blamed *herself* for Eli's and Elvira's deaths. Though old John might have conceded that his son-in-law was neither malicious nor uncaring toward Anna and the children but only preoccupied with the church and the ministry, and perhaps that his own nomadic lifestyle had not been all that easy on his loved ones either, the cumulative recollections of Anna's hardships as the wife of a traveling preacher easily could have put him, his wife, and his surviving children into silent fury in their sudden, harsh grief.

We speak here of these possibilities because there had to have been *some* reason that the Townsends responded to John as they did in the wake of his and Anna's further sorrows. The bereaved couple raised another cabin with the help of the Townsends and other settlers, and tried to start anew. They were now poorer even than they had been at the beginning of their married life, owning hardly any clothing besides what the Townsends and other neighbors could donate to them, and with Anna forced to halve and scrape dried cymblings (small gourds) to use as cups and bowls.[20] John still had his portion of the livestock, a great deal of land on credit, seventy-six dollars that he had gotten for the melted lump of silver he had salvaged from the ashes of his cabin, and some other cash that represented the Huntsville merchants' debt settlement with him, though, and he made ready with Hiram's help to raise cotton and bury his own grief in the arduous task of making himself at least partially solvent once more. But Anna, understandably, remained in a deep depression, undoubtedly with all the attendant symptoms, including anorexia with its inevitable compromise of her immune system; and in the early spring, when a particularly virulent strain of influenza then known as the cold plague became epidemic throughout the southern states, her tired, careworn body was no match for it. Williams relates that Anna died of pure melancholy, and he has been thus quoted by all his successors to the Smith story, but in 1858 Raccoon John himself indicated to James Challen that the cold plague had been the immediate cause of her death. But the accounts are not mutually exclusive, after all. Had Anna not been forced to endure the horrors of the winter before, she might have been stronger and more able to resist the disease both mentally and physically; and though she must have despaired to leave little Jane and Zerelda, she may even have welcomed her end with the touching hope that now she'd be able to apologize personally to her dead babies for leaving them on that fateful night of January 7. The world was too much with her, late and soon, and Anna Townsend Smith died on April 17, 1815, at only twenty-eight years of age. In a gesture perhaps more poignant than any other he could have made under the circumstances, John used his one remaining article of good clothing, the white cravat that was considered a necessary article of dress for a preacher in those days and that he had worn on his Old Christmas excursion, to adorn her shrouded body in its coffin, and he buried her beside Eli and Elvira.[21]

John didn't even have an opportunity to deal with this fresh grief, to say nothing of worrying about how to feed a nine-month-old baby that hadn't even been weaned yet. Although the cold plague seems to have had a less morbid effect on the young than on the old, the surviving children came down with it too, and then on April 20, which could have been the very day of Anna's burial, John caught the disease himself.[22] Two "Christian women"—John's apparent euphemism for Mrs. Townsend and Jane here—came and took little Jane and Zerelda, and left him alone to care for his own needs. From that time forward the Townsends seem to have abandoned their son-in-law completely. Their other near neighbor, Anna Miller, took him in some days later and procured the services of a Huntsville physician for him. For over a month while he fevered, vomited, smothered, and sweated with the influenza, the doctor gave him the accepted medical treatments of the day, which may even have included bleeding him to release the "humor" of the cold plague within, and he worsened as time dragged on. The doctor's one hard and fast rule was that under no circumstances whatsoever was John to be given any water until the disease ran its course,[23] and as we know now, an influenza patient needs adequate hydration more than any other factor of treatment. If prescriptions of this kind were commonplace, it's no wonder that the cold plague carried off so many victims in the South in 1815. We must wonder if medical (to say nothing of psychiatric) ignorance was thus a factor in Anna's demise as well, and how close to a miracle it was that John survived to tell the tale at all.

As it was, he reached the absolute lowest physical state that he would ever know before the days of his old age, and in the first of two, or rather perhaps three, instances he crept through the valley of the shadow of death spiritually as well. As he recalled it, he didn't even want to live. He completely forgot his Calvinistic speculations on infant damnation as he wept over his two remaining children, themselves recuperating but gone from him now, and he prayed that they could all simply give up the ghost at once and be reunited in a better world than this vale of tears. But still he hung onto life through weeks of fever and suffering.

Sometime in May—Williams seems to date it in July, though there was no way John could have lived without water until then—Anna Miller finally gave up trying to nurse him back to health. Her father, Archibald Woods, who lived about fifteen miles from Hickory Flats, then agreed to take the sufferer in. Woods informed John that he was being taken to his house to die, and John was so low in both body and spirit that he agreed to it, provided only that he would be allowed to drink a little water. Believing that the preacher was moribund anyway, Woods agreed, and after a hot, difficult day spent transporting the bedfast patient in a wagon half filled with cotton, he got him to his farm. He gave John both water and beer to drink, both men believing implicitly that the liquids would be fatal just like the doctor had warned them, but John was too weak and thirsty to care and Woods may even have regarded it as a morally acceptable euthanasia. The refreshment didn't kill John, though; his fever broke, he passed into a strong sweat and a deep slumber that lasted that entire afternoon and night, and by the next morning even he himself knew that he was on the mend.[24]

John completed his convalescence at Archibald Woods's and his strength gradually returned, though for a time his hands and arms shook so badly with palsy that Woods's slaves had to feed him like a child. After a while the palsy disappeared temporarily, but it always returned after he worked hard with his arms, gradually worsening over the years until it finally disabled him from manual labor nearly completely by his late fifties or early sixties.[25] Many days passed before he regained sufficient strength to walk back to Hickory Flats and check on the welfare of his children, and when he did so he found, not surprisingly, that the "friends" who had taken them in were now unwilling to give them back. His hogs and cattle had strayed and were lost as well, that is unless John Townsend himself claimed the entire herd for the benefit of his grandchildren or simply out of pure hurt and bitterness, all except for one cow that John retained and sold to pay off his physician. In short, he was weak, emaciated, and very nearly friendless. Completely destitute except for his wagon, team, a few rude articles of cabin furniture, and the acres he owned on credit from the government, he had become utterly dependent upon the charity of Archibald Woods and Anna Miller. He quite understandably didn't have the heart to try to reestablish himself in a land where he had known so much bitter misery, and he resolved despairingly to cut his Alabama losses completely and return home. He began his journey in late June or early July, having accepted a little cash from Archibald Woods to sustain him along the way.[26]

We all must deal with the slings and arrows of outrageous fortune on our own terms, but John had experienced so much literal horror in Alabama that we may well wonder how he could ever have come to terms with this period of his life with anything approaching honesty. Though he may have been as candid as he dared with John Augustus Williams in the 1860s, as late as 1858 he related to James Challen only that "There are many things connected with this distressing scene that I cannot name."[27] Jackson's victory at New Orleans had already initiated the Era of Good Feeling in America; among its many benefits to white Anglo-Saxon Protestants, men on the make in Alabama were happily realizing the dreams that John claimed he had envisioned, but all his own hopes lay in ashes and sod back at Hickory Flats. Did the nineteenth century in fact produce a stronger breed of men, more able to bounce back from tragedy with a flourish, than those of our own degenerate times? Or did men and women of that era actually cope with their griefs by the various mental dodges that we still utilize today, and that indeed could have been used by all the generations of the human race? The reader may judge. Whether any of us care to admit it or not, the most faithful Christian faced with such a loss as John had suffered cannot keep his or her thoughts from straying to the logic that David Hume and Baron d'Holbach voiced so powerfully a generation before Smith was even born: if God would have prevented an outrage upon innocent children such as Eli and Elvira Smith suffered, and could not, He is not omnipotent; if

He could have prevented it and would not, He is not benevolent. With this view, skeptics of any stamp point out tragic accidents such as this house fire as arguments against the existence either of a benevolent or, at least as far as the created beings of the universe are concerned, an omnipotent and omniscient God.

Still, as a Christian and especially a minister, John would not have been without his own resources even as grieved, bewildered, and thoroughly battered by both his in-laws and his very life as he had to have been. I spoke of the theological discipline of theodicy in this work's introduction; simply put, the entire subject rests upon human efforts to prove propositions such as those of Hume and d'Holbach stated above to be fallacies. But the success of a system of theodicy does not actually depend upon its objective correctness, or for that matter even its objective sense. All that it needs to do to be effective for its own moment and for the individual who seeks comfort by it is to provide just enough positive interpretation for the known facts of a tragedy to make them bearable for the grieving believer to accept as they stand. And so John coped with his losses by formulating a personal theodicy, as all faithful Christians do, perhaps *must* do, in the face of misfortune.

Whatever John Townsend's and Anna's roles actually had been in getting him to undertake the Alabama move, John came to see it at least in retrospect as his own idea, the result of his having become too proud and ambitious in a worldly sense; and to punish this worldly pride, God had therefore taken Anna and the children from him and had then smitten him with illness, putting him through the refiner's fire like a modern-day Job to steer his mind once more to his Divine calling and his duties back in Kentucky. God had scourged him because He loved him, and now, if he continued in obedience to the Divine by reestablishing himself in the Kentucky General Union, all he had lost would be restored, just as in Job's case. The horrible question of infant damnation he now dismissed with the simple intuitive faith to which most believers cling. Jesus had said "Suffer the little children to come unto me, and forbid them not, for of such is the Kingdom of Heaven"; King David and Queen Bathsheba had lost a baby son because of that embarrassing, compromising transgression against Bathsheba's first husband, Uriah, but David had been able to take comfort after the infant's death with the knowledge that one day he could go to the child, though the child could not return to him. Little Eli and Elvira were as innocent as Adam and Eve had been in the Garden before the Fall, and there was therefore no way, despite even John's sacred Philadelphia Confession, that a just God could ever condemn them, and they were now joyfully reunited with their poor mother in the world beyond, where their temporal sufferings were just a dim dream from which they had happily awakened.[28]

So when John related this story to John Augustus Williams many years later, did he in fact consciously and intentionally lie by omitting the details about his in-laws' migration with him and Anna to Alabama, their likely rage at his absence on the night of the fire, and the fact that they abandoned him completely upon Anna's death? It's hard to say. As noted before, Kierkegaard once remarked that his father had died so that he himself, the son, might turn into something. Yet Kierkegaard was well aware that this was not the actual objective reason for his father's demise, but rather only a personal myth by which he could relate to the event on his own. Though perhaps retaining all the elements that mark a lie, John's story to Williams was his *own* truth, the theodicy on which he rebuilt his shattered life, and he clung to it exactly as did the United States as a whole to the Battle of New Orleans as proof of its Divinely endorsed victory in the War of 1812. In John's rebuilt life, his Alabama story had no more room in it for the involvement of the John Townsend family or anything less than his own Job-like heroic role in the entire series of events than American citizens did for the ideas that the United States had actually been the aggressor nation in the War of 1812 or that Tecumseh's confederation, the Creeks, and countless other Native American tribes had fought with whites only to protect their lands against greedy and frantic usurpers. Only after our supposedly Divine Manifest Destiny was realized and "sea to shining sea" became a fait accompli could we as a people finally acknowledge that our nineteenth-century conduct toward Native Americans actually had nothing whatsoever to do with any Divine judgment against them, but we may never be comfortable with taking the thought to its logical conclusion: that our forefathers gained this land simply by a strong, amoral will to power and superior force of arms, and that on this same basis we now hold it against all comers.

But John Smith's truth was not to blame for this larger state of affairs, except as one tiny microcosm, along with a billion others, that together constitute the great macrocosm of human wishful thinking. The absurd simply was not recognized in the Era of Good Feeling by a nation that had just been blessed by God to win a second war against the British, and even if the country hadn't been so favored, our individual human natures are such that we are easily able, quite unconsciously, to mythologize whatever we consider necessary to our purposes anyway. We see the tendency recur, and recur again, chillingly, throughout American history. John had to establish some kind of rationalization for Anna's, Eli's, and Elvira's deaths, especially since the three had been allowed no more say in their fates than had Job's ten children when they were caught up in the great heavenly wager between God and Satan over the soul of that perfect and upright man. But at least it can be said that in the long run John Smith used his truth and his theodicy neither to conquer any new territory nor drive away any prior claimants, but only to decimate a few Kentucky Baptist associations, and to help the future object of his most passionate intellectual attachment establish a new religious movement in the land of the free and the home of the brave.

John's vision of having passed through an ordeal of fire for the greater Divine purpose must have been strong in the late summer of 1815. His actions between July and December of that year were those of a man neither heartbroken nor depressed but purposeful, and given the facts that only eleven months after his children's deaths and merely eight months after Anna's, he had already reestablished his place in the Kentucky General Union, bought another farm on the Little South Fork, and taken a new wife, they seem almost to display an element of the frantic.

He arrived first at his mother's old home back in Stockton's Valley, where Jonathan, who may still have been unmarried at this time, also lived. He spent one or two weeks here resting, but he also seems to have posted a letter to Jeremiah Vardeman, informing his patron of his misfortunes and asking him to address a reply to his brother William's on the Little South Fork. When he left Stockton's Valley and arrived at William's farm, which he evidently wanted to use as his home base until he could buy another tract of land on his own, he found Vardeman's letter waiting for him. Elkhorn Association's annual meeting must have taken place in the interim between Vardeman's reception of the letter and his reply, for in addition to commiserating with him over his losses, Vardeman informed John in his usual blunt but generous way that Elkhorn had taken up a charitable collection for him, amounting to fifty-five dollars and a "bit" (12.5 cents),[29] and that he would be receiving it soon. Since the Elkhorn meeting was already past, John's patron also urged him to try to attend the enormous Tate's Creek Association's annual meeting in Lincoln County that August, perhaps with the suggestion that he'd be bringing the collection and that John could receive it there.

Though still gaunt, weak, and owning only the scruffy cast-off clothing he had gotten from Archibald Woods and Anna Miller in Alabama, John responded with verve and alacrity. The Tate's Creek Association was being hosted that year by Crab Orchard Church, Vardeman's old home congregation, which had by this time left the small but "orthodox" South District remnant for membership in the larger and more affluent body; but when John arrived there on the hot, dusty Saturday of the association's opening service, he was distressed to learn that Vardeman had not come to the meeting as he had promised, and he was engulfed in shame to see that his shabby clothing made him stand out like a sore thumb among the finery of the cultured and genteel downstate members and visitors. Like all Baptist associations with any roots in the Separate tradition at this same time period, the association transacted its business in the host meetinghouse with church messengers and associational correspondents, while larger crowds gathered to sing, pray, and hear preaching at the "stand," some distance apart and usually situated within a grove of trees or brush arbor similar to the setting of a camp meeting. The initial singing, praying, and "introductory sermon" that had opened the meeting at the stand were evidently over by the time of John's arrival on the grounds, and the association's officers, messengers, and correspondent delegates were already crowding the pews in the church house. Initially John just skulked around the meetinghouse doors, seemingly snubbed by everyone as a vagrant, while no less a personage than Luther Rice, the first agent for the American Baptist Board of Foreign Missions in Philadelphia and a former partner of the famous Adoniram Judson in India, solicited the association's support for the new Baptist Board and for Judson's just-established Burmese mission.

For some reason, though, Smith's old friend Thomas Hansford, who was still the moderator of, and for this occasion a visiting delegate from, Cumberland River Association, then left the house for a moment. He spied John sitting on the church steps, and after a handshake, a hug, and a brief conversation he immediately took him out to the stand and arranged for him to take a turn at preaching there. Immediately preceding John in the pulpit was a younger associate of Luther Rice's, undoubtedly Kentucky's own James Ely Welch, who later became a partner of the well-known Missouri missionary John Mason Peck and who was known to have been traveling with Rice at that time.[30] John himself thought that the young man was a seminary student from Philadelphia, and so told Williams; for all his urbane manner, though, Rice's attaché apparently "made a failure" in the stand, sitting down embarrassedly and apologetically with the plea that "if the Lord does not give it to me, brethren, I cannot get it."[31] Disappointed and bored by Welch and unimpressed with John's shabby appearance, the huge stand congregation immediately began to fragment and socialize as soon as Welch took his seat and John got up.

For all his ragged dress, his weakened health, the absence of his patron, and the painful memories of Anna and the children that must have gnawed at his heart in spite of his rationalization of their deaths, John knew that it was now or never. If he left this people with their existing impression of him, the chance to become a "big" downstate preacher would not come again. And so amassing his strength, his deep, melodious, Stearns-inspired voice, and the combined faculties of his studies in the Bible, the Philadelphia Confession, and the books of Robert Ferrill and Rhodes Garth together as best he could, he began to speak. Perhaps we should just let John Augustus Williams take the reins for a moment here:

> He saw that, unless he employed some artifice to detain them, not a hearer would be left. With a noble voice, such as so often had sounded among the hills of Wayne, he called aloud:
>
> "Stay, friends, and hear what the great Augustine said!" and they all stopped to listen.
>
> "Augustine wished to see three things before he died," continued Smith. "Rome in her glory and purity; Paul on Mars' Hill; and Jesus in the flesh." A few now sat down, but many smiled, and started off again.
>
> "Will you not stay," he cried, in a still louder voice, "and hear what the great Cato said?" Many returned and took their seats, and seemed willing to be amused.
>
> "Cato," he continued, "repented of three things before his death: first, that he had ever spent an idle day; second, that he had ever gone on a voyage by water, when he might have made the same journey on

land; and thirdly, that he had ever told the secrets of his bosom to a woman."

The people continued to come back, and began to crowd close to the stand. A few acquaintances, who had not seen him in some time, now recognized him, and passed the word among the crowd—"It is John Smith, of the Little South Fork!" Seeing groups of persons still standing in the distance, he called again with all the strength of his heavy voice: "Come, friends, and hear what the great Thales thanked the gods for!"

"Let us go and hear the fellow," said one; "there may be more in him than we suppose." And they all, at last, sat down nearby to listen.

"Thales thanked the gods for three things: first, that he was endowed with reason, and not a brute; secondly, that he was a Greek, and not a Barbarian; and thirdly, that he was a man, and not a woman. And now, friends, I know you are ready to ask: 'And pray, sir, who are you? What have you to say for yourself?' I am John Smith, from Stockton's Valley. In more recent years, I have lived in Wayne, among the rocks and hills of the Cumberland. Down there, saltpeter caves abound, and raccoons make their homes. On that wild frontier, we never had good schools, nor many books; consequently, I stand before you today a man without an education. [If John were still using the New England Holy Tone, as he probably was at least for this occasion, we can fairly hear him 'striking the long roll' at the beginning of his next statement.] But, my brethren, even in that ill-favored region, the Lord, in good time, found me. He showed me his wondrous grace, and called me to preach the everlasting Gospel of his Son.

"Redemption! Redemption!" he shouted, and his voice sounded through the woods like the tones of a trumpet. He had no Bible, but he quoted, in the same loud voice, his text: "He sent redemption to his people; he hath commanded his covenant forever; holy and reverend is his name."—Psalm 111:9 . . . [T]he morning session of the association was broken up; preachers and people rushed out, and gathered about the platform. Many that could not find seats or places to stand, climbed the trees close by; and the very saplings swayed with people eager to see and to hear. When the speaker reached . . . the last division of his subject, and began to paint the final glory of God's elect, the multitude arose and stood upon their feet; and when he closed his impassionate exhortation, every eye was weeping, and every heart and lip blessed *the man without an education* [emphasis in original].[32]

By a synthesis of his own making—the biblical scholarship of the religious, the quick thinking of one who seizes the moment in the ethical, and the good old early American blarney and showmanship of the aesthetic—John had won the day. No matter that his introductory remarks had all the ludicrous bombast of a southern political stump speech of any era, that the crowd in the church had probably concluded its business and was filing back out to the stand at the time of John's closing comments anyway, or that the atmosphere described at the climax of the sermon was and is the traditional mise-en-scène for the conclusion of an "Old Time" Baptist association's first day of business. The timing couldn't have worked out more perfectly, and with or without Jeremiah Vardeman in tow John's reputation in the Bluegrass was now assured. Some, perhaps many, of the Tate's Creek members could now recall him from a decade before, when he and his fellow rustics Richard Barrier and Isham Burnett may have come to the association grounds shyly and hesitantly, bearing Big Sinking Church's letter of correspondence. The visitors from Elkhorn Association had already opened their purses to him when they had heard Vardeman speak of his tragic losses, and as they recognized him by the rumors buzzing through the crowd, they and the men and women of Tate's Creek Association opened their hearts to him as well. For good measure that day, John even picked up another patron, Jacob Creath, who probably had been entrusted with delivering the Elkhorn collection to him and whose reputation in Kentucky ran a close second to Vardeman's at that time; but more importantly, in the eyes of visitors from Salem, North and South District, and every other Kentucky association as well as Tate's Creek and Elkhorn, John now had a *shtick* that rivaled even the oldest pioneer Kentucky preachers' most lurid tales of fighting redcoats in the Revolutionary War and of being imprisoned in colonial Virginia jails by their cruel British overlords for the crime of preaching the Gospel.[33] After all, ministers had been exempted from Governor Shelby's 1812 draft, so none of the other younger ones present could boast about experiencing any similar trials and tribulations in defense of American Baptist freedom. John Smith, the man raised up without an education, had just outdone the great Luther Rice's own assistant with his good old American common horse sense—and of course, by letting the power of God fill his mouth with words—and no one would ever forget it. The gaunt, ragged young preacher was a self-made American just like the hero of New Orleans, Old Hickory himself, and whether or not these lowlanders had any special regard for John's rustic, uncouth, Holy Tone–chanting brother preachers back in the Cumberland, upper Licking, upper Kentucky, Green, and Big Sandy valleys, they embraced Smith himself, and the image that he stood for, with the exact same adulation that both Andrew Jackson and William Henry Harrison would harness a few years later to propel themselves to the U.S. presidency.

And of course, as the reader has probably already guessed, on this day John gained a name to match his style. The plaintive idea of the young man without the benefits of an education, raised up among the saltpeter caves and raccoons of the Kentucky mountains, came from his own sermon; in the sweetness of his oratorical victory over James Welch, his newest patron Jacob Creath borrowed a bit of his rhetoric by labeling him "a singe-cat from somewhere among the raccoons"; and probably before the Tate's Creek sessions were over,

Creath and John Davis, a minister there at Crab Orchard Church itself, bestowed upon him the nickname that stuck with him until the day of his death, Raccoon John Smith. We have no reason to doubt that he disliked the "ugly name,"[34] as he described it to John Augustus Williams, but he knew better than anyone that it came inescapably with the role he had just assumed. Given subsequent events, he probably hated some aspects of the role itself as well; but it was *his* role now, and he would remain faithful to it, for richer, for poorer, for better, for worse, in sickness and in health—for life.

Raccoon John returned to the Little South Fork in triumph, preaching in the churches of Pulaski County as he traveled southward and enjoying the acclamation of another successful "stand" sermon at Beaver Creek with Thomas Hansford and Isaac Denton, at the Sunday service of Cumberland River Association's 1815 session. Considering that one of Cumberland River's main items of business that year was a discussion about establishing relations with Luther Rice's Baptist Board of Foreign Missions, for all we know, the topic, dear to the hearts of both Jeremiah Vardeman and Jacob Creath, may have been introduced to the body by Raccoon John himself, via a letter written by Rice at Tate's Creek for the officers of the little hill country association.[35]

But still, he had to see to his temporal affairs at least to a small extent. Though he now knew better than ever that he no longer wished to live on the Little South Fork, he had to have a home of his own until a good permanent central Kentucky opportunity turned up, so he took his collection money and, probably with his brother William's help, purchased a little eighty-acre farm (with "appurtenances," likely a cabin and barn) on the northern tributary of the Fork near properties owned by his friends Benjamin Adkins, John and Rebecca (Cross) Parmley, and Joseph Jr. and Mildred (Burnett) Hurt. At this season the patriarch of the Hurt family, Joseph Sr., had taken to his bed in his last illness, being cared for by his son and daughter-in-law James and Ursula and probably to some extent by Joseph Jr. and Mildred as well.[36]

And so at about the same time Raccoon John somehow talked his brother Jonathan into going to Alabama for him and persuading the Townsends to surrender Jane and Zerelda to his care,[37] he also began to pay court to old Joseph Hurt's youngest daughter by his first wife, Nancy. From the vantage point of our own era he appears unbelievably crass and unfeeling to begin seeking a wife so soon after Anna's death, and in fact some of John's neighbors may have felt that way even at the time. Williams admits that the two kept their courtship a secret outside the Hurt family, for the community's speculation seems to have been that John would leave the hills again one day and acquire a rich central Kentucky wife.[38] But we cannot condemn either John or Nancy here. He was lonely and, his Job-like rationalization of his misfortunes notwithstanding, he probably felt that he simply needed companionship to break his despondency over Anna, Eli, and Elvira; Nancy's father was dying and she knew, as an unmarried female caught in the mores of the times, that his demise would probably relegate her to the role of a servant in her stepmother's home or one of her brothers' households, a charity case with no property of her own whatsoever. The Hurts may actually have quietly encouraged the quasi-secret courtship for this latter reason.

But if John and Nancy threw themselves together from a mutual pragmatism in response to forces beyond their control, they were also extremely compatible. Nancy Hurt was a church member already, either at Big Sinking or at Bethel, as well as something of a rarity among young hill women of that time: she could read as well as John himself did, for he told Albert Allen in 1857 that he sometimes examined difficult passages in the Bible and other books and periodicals with her help.[39] Where she had managed to pick up this skill during her family's trek through the Carolinas and Virginia to Kentucky is not known, but as hinted in the previous chapter, it is even possible that John himself had tutored her as a teenager while he and Anna were still living in Horse Hollow. Regardless of the identity of Nancy's teacher or teachers, though, Nancy's erudition let Raccoon John establish not only a physical, emotional, and economic relationship with her as a spouse, but an intellectual one of the type he had craved so desperately all his life, as well. Even a cursory reading of the Williams biography makes it plain that John and Nancy always loved to match wits and trade quips with one another, and on occasion, with only a wink exchanged as a cue, they could very capably "pull a good one over" on condescending visiting preachers and other guests who expected to find the heads of the household illiterate and ignorant.[40] Even if John had been advised, as Williams claims he was, to keep his options open and seek a rich bride downstate, he must have known that if he looked the world over he'd be hard pressed to capture a girl as much "after his own heart" as Nancy Hurt was.

Considering all of Nancy's winsome qualities, then, we may wonder why she had remained single until she was twenty-three years of age and then all of a sudden "started talking to," of all people, a gaunt, dirt-poor, widowed preacher eight years older than she was. Her sole surviving portrait is that of a handsome, dignified matron of middle years with thick, dark, reddish-brown hair partially concealed by a bonnet; though she has a rather despondent expression and is a bit pale, thin, and hollow-eyed, the painting gives apt indication that she had once been a striking beauty. Did the other, younger men of the Little South Fork feel threatened by her intelligence, or perhaps she by their lack of it? Or was there another cause that perhaps either John or his biographer chose not to reveal in *The Life of Elder John Smith*? A few scraps of evidence indicate that there was. In 1852 Raccoon John wrote to a friend that Nancy had "been laboring under a breast complaint, attended with a severe cough," for many years, and that during a recent months-long exacerbation of this affliction he had almost despaired for her recovery. At the date of the letter, though, her health was slowly improving,[41] and in fact she would survive for nine more years after the letter was written. When this information is weighed with the possibility that Nancy's portraitist accurately captured that slight flush on her upper cheeks, not visible in photographic reproductions of the painting but clearly discernible when one views her likeness alongside Raccoon John's on the wall of the Bosworth Library at the Lexington, Kentucky, Theological Seminary, it leads us to suspect that Nancy suffered from tuberculosis, or, as it was known in those days, consumption. Certainly if any modern physician were presented with a patient exhibiting the symptoms described in John's letter, a chronic periodic severe cough with or without the production of blood, plus that gaunt, sad, hollow-eyed look with the telltale flush on the upper cheeks, his or her first attempts at differential diagnosis would include a complete set of chest films and a PPD tuberculin skin test.

Consumption was untreatable and hardly even understood in those days. Bacteria hadn't even been discovered yet, and the common folk wisdom held that a woman somehow made herself susceptible to the disease by getting caught out in the rain or washing her hair during the time of her menstrual period. Actually and ironically, one of the most potentially dangerous places to catch tuberculosis was at a crowded backcountry church meeting, where frontier etiquette still deemed "hawking and spitting" on the dirt or puncheon floor as acceptable behavior and where an entire congregation shared a wooden bucket of spring water on the communion table and a single gourd dipper from which all drank. Depending on the severeness of an initial infection and an individual's own immune resistance, consumption often could be slow-acting, with long remissions in which the bacilli simply grew quietly, forming nodules or tubercles in a sufferer's lungs; but sooner or later the tubercles inevitably ruptured, bringing on a crisis state with its characteristic deep smothering cough and hemoptysis accompanied by nocturnal fevers and sweats, and this vicious cycle of remission and relapse repeated itself over the years until the bacteria finally destroyed the patient's lungs completely from the lower lobes up. The great Andrew Jackson and Henry Clay were both consumptives, though both lived to be old men with much fight in them to the very last, and other, hardier folk such as John Smith himself must have been, could and did develop an effective humoral immunity to the disease after one exposure. Infants, though, were the most dangerously susceptible; mycobacteria have a vicious tendency to go straight to the meninges, the membranes that wrap the brain and spinal cord, in young children, and we shudder to think how many babies must have suffered painful hydrocephalus and death from tuberculous meningitis before the days of antibiotics.

Nancy therefore may have remained single until age twenty-three simply because her periodic exacerbations of "breast complaint" were common knowledge in the little Parmleysville community. There were undoubtedly already enough families that "ran to consumption" on the Little South Fork to warn any prudent young man of the risks involved in establishing such a household for himself. But yet, as Blaise Pascal once phrased it, the heart has its own reasons that reason knows not of, and this lovely young woman's frailty may have made her that much more attractive to Raccoon John. His reaction to the kindnesses shown him by the sweet, young, but unsaved Elizabeth Mizner was noted in the previous chapter, and as also hypothesized, Anna Townsend's own possible physical frailty may have similarly appealed to him. That he still strongly believed himself to be on the rebound from a Job-like ordeal is unquestioned, but his decision to woo and wed Nancy Hurt ensured that he would experience a great many additional sorrows hauntingly similar to those he had undergone in Alabama. As consumptives are often regarded in backcountry folk wisdom even in modern times, Nancy proved to be extremely fertile, bearing eleven children in twenty-one years of marriage until, at forty-four, she was too old to bear any more. Strangely enough, the frequent pregnancies may even have had a beneficial effect on her illness; at least one case, albeit apocryphal, went the rounds of hospital legend several years ago of a pregnant tubercular patient's having the lower lobes of her lungs partially closed off, and consequently temporarily healed, by the pressure of her expanding womb against her viscera and, indirectly, her diaphragm. But of the eight children known to have been born to John and Nancy during the first eleven years of their marriage, three, Eliza Baize, William Pinckney, and Joshua Carroll Smith, died as infants or toddlers of causes never specified; another daughter, Maria, survived childhood, married, and had a family; however, one more daughter, Eliza Ann, likewise died relatively young of causes not recorded, as apparently did all of her children. Of the three older surviving sons, one, John Duke, died in his late twenties of causes likewise unknown, and the other two, Jonathan and James Harvey or Harvey James, were both medically confirmed consumptives. Harvey preceded his parents in death, and Jonathan outlived his father by only a few months. Besides all these, the couple's youngest daughter Mary was reported at the time of her father's death to be in a "very feeble state of health," the implication perhaps being that she had died by the time the Williams biography went to press, though we cannot be sure.[42] No wonder that a writer commented of Raccoon John and his household in 1842 that "this sturdiest of Kentucky's mighty sons has been much afflicted in his family"[43]; it's a fair bet that tuberculosis didn't just run in his children by Nancy, but galloped, sunfished, did depraved handsprings, and terrible as it is to think of little Eli and Elvira perishing of asphyxiation and burning up in the Alabama house fire, it's worse to consider the possibility that Eliza Baize, William, and Joshua just might have died even more slowly, painfully, and miserably with tuberculous meningitis. Though the Williams biography never remarks on Nancy's illness at all, probably because its existence was completely incongruous both with the personal theodicy on which Raccoon John had come to depend as well as the popular perception of the proper family life of an upright Christian minister in the Era of Good Feeling, it was good that John now rejected the doctrine of infant damnation.

So then, if Raccoon John knew or guessed that Nancy was consumptive before he married her, should he have gone through with it or not? How dare we, in this easy age of convenient birth control, rapid diagnostic tests, and powerful antibiotics, presume to answer for him? The question is as pointless as asking either God or man why or how much the quirks of history discussed earlier in this chapter altered our national destiny. To quote another writer regarded with more authority than Pascal, love is stronger than death; many waters cannot quench love, neither can the floods drown it; and if a man were to give all the substance of his house for love, it would utterly be condemned. And though John and Nancy's courtship was probably as hasty and pragmatic as the circumstances indicate, and their marriage full of shared sorrow unavoidable in that age of primitive medical care, there can be no doubt whatsoever that she loved him very deeply and that he returned her affection as much as he was emotionally able to do so. John's theodicy, his interpretation of his Alabama experiences, was a convenient and even necessary mental dodge, and it complemented his new image in downstate Kentucky as a self-made frontier Baptist hero perfectly. Of course he could never publicly admit Nancy's illness, for in an age when nearly everyone presumed that all effects had logical and moral causes, a consumptive family would have made him appear not as a delivered Job, but still under a state of punishment for some unrepented and perhaps even unknown sin. As will be shown subsequently, John may privately have halfway believed this himself, and if he did, it certainly had crucial bearing on his activities after 1827. And yet, if Raccoon John did indeed marry Nancy with his eyes wide open to her condition, it demonstrates that his own love for her was more than just a mere emotion, but an act of will, a choice to be made with a price to be paid, and that he made his choice and paid his price. Nancy certainly paid hers, too. As will be seen, he could have been a great deal more attentive both to her and to his children than he was, especially if her frailty carried some unexplainable appeal to him, but throughout a long, turbulent, and as he once phrased it himself, checkered,[44] existence on God's footstool, Nancy's love and steadfastness for him was one of the few anchors on which he could depend utterly. There is no question that the marriage's logical risks were well worth it to his spirit.

And so it happened that Jonathan came back from Alabama that fall with little Jane and Zerelda, having somehow persuaded the Townsends that the two would be better off in Kentucky near their father. John arranged for him and old Rebecca to take the children in at the old homeplace in Stockton's Valley, while he took another extended, financially profitable and politically successful Bluegrass preaching tour with both Vardeman's and Creath's promotion at the beginning of the holiday season. He then came home to the Little South Fork and married Nancy on Christmas Day 1815. Her stepmother, Mary, formally bestowed permission for the wedding since Joseph Hurt Sr. was too ill to do so, and John's former pastor Richard Barrier performed the ceremony.[45]

Still, circumstances were not altogether harmonious, as they seldom are for any of us, and here we must pause to speak a few more words about little Jane and Zerelda. Sadly, they can henceforth figure hardly any more prominently in this biography of their father than they have in any of the others. It's indeed a great pity, for no other reason than that they were, of all the survivors of Raccoon John's Alabama misfortunes, the least to blame and the most drastically affected. They had lost a brother and a sister together in one night, watched their mother die within only a few weeks, then temporarily lost their father, and after their uncle Jonathan brought them back to Kentucky they probably never saw their Townsend grandparents or any of their mother's people ever again. But for better or worse, children must accept the world as they find it, and so did they. Williams never mentions the girls again after their return to Kentucky, and in fact does not even state their names on a single page of Raccoon John's biography though both were still living when the book first went to press. Cochran works minor references to their childhoods into his novel here and there as completely fictional filler, and Donaldson simply states that "very little" is known about them, although he does take a reference from Williams to suggest that Raccoon John may have sent at least one of them to a downstate girls' boarding school.[46] In the year Donaldson mentions, 1833, though, Jane was already of majority age and Zerelda very near it, and so the Williams passage involving the boarding school probably actually refers to John and Nancy's oldest surviving daughter, Maria, who was in her early teens then. But though Donaldson was quite correct in stating that little is known about the girls, he himself had to have been acquainted with more than he obviously cared to relate.

We have no hard evidence that either Jane or Zerelda ever lived with John and Nancy at any time. Whether this had anything to do with the probability that the little ones had forgotten their father during the months between their mother's death and their return to Kentucky and were consequently afraid of him, or with Rebecca Smith's possible outspoken reservations about letting the girls be cared for by a consumptive stepmother, we cannot say. In fact, it's possible that the only reason that Raccoon John sent for them was that his church required that he "keep his house in order" to maintain his ordination, and therefore he would have felt compelled to assume at least titular responsibility for them once more. But it is most likely that old Rebecca herself raised them in Stockton's Valley, at first with assistance from Jonathan until he moved north, and later with help from Philip and Henry after she broke up housekeeping at the homeplace and she and they moved back across the state line into Tennessee. Raccoon John did write to Jane and Zerelda from time to time, sharing news of himself, their stepmother, and their half brothers and sisters, but as often as not he seems simply to have sent messages to them by his ministerial colleagues who lived in their area. John's surviving papers make it appear that all in all, from the time of their mother's death, his relationships with Jane and Zerelda never became any closer than that of a loving and concerned, but nonetheless somewhat distant, uncle.

For their own part, the girls proved to be closer kin to their fair, forgotten mother and their tough Celtic grandmother than their surviving half sisters, for they remained country women all their lives. Jane Smith married Thomas Jefferson Boles, and they lived and farmed in Caldwell County, Kentucky, not far from where Jane's uncle George had once homesteaded. Their son Henry Jefferson "Jeff" Boles, a Union Army veteran and the only one of Raccoon John's grandsons to "make a preacher," moved eastward and made his home on Flynn's Creek in Cumberland County before migrating to Tennessee, where he joined a branch of the church of his grandfather. He married three times, and one of his sons, Henry Leo Boles, became a renowned minister and college president whom Donaldson perhaps accurately depicts as a chip off Raccoon John's old block.[47]

Zerelda grew up and followed her grandmother and her uncles to the Pickett/Fentress County, Tennessee, area. She married her first cousin, Philip and Millie's son Isaac Denton Smith, and by him bore a large, healthy family, including a namesake for Raccoon John as well as others for Philip and Jonathan.[48] The circumstance of Isaac and Zerelda's marriage is probably the reason that Williams, Cochran, and Donaldson are all so curiously and fretfully quiet about the fates of Anna's daughters, but truthfully, Isaac and Zerelda are no more to be judged or condemned for their union than Raccoon John and Nancy were for theirs. Without endorsing first-cousin marriages, we must admit that they were an infrequent but by no means unknown or unaccepted fact of life in isolated, sparsely settled southern mountain communities before the advent of the modern era. As a matter of fact, one of Jeff Boles's three wives, the mother of H. Leo Boles in fact, was his second cousin, Sarah Smith, who was Philip and Millie's granddaughter. Second-cousin weddings of this sort took place a little more often, and third- and fourth-cousin unions were, and in some locations still are, commonplace. Such marriages existed before the hills were even settled, having been particularly prevalent in backcountry colonial New England, and in fact at least two of the couples who came south from Connecticut with Shubal Stearns in the mid-1750s to establish what would become the distinctive traditional Appalachian mountain expressions of Christianity were themselves first-cousin unions. They even occurred among the gentry from time to time, possibly to retain real and personal estate in the hands of a well-to-do and powerful family. These marriages reflected no particular depravity or even ignorance on the part of any individual or group, but among hill dwellers they were an inevitable byproduct of rural isolation and limited social contact. It could be hoped that the writings of modern Appalachian authors and storytellers concerning this subject might initiate a small change in the public's perception of such so-called scandals and disgraces, but a tolerant or even understanding view of life as it was in the hills still receives no quarter either in sectarian histories and biographies or, for that matter, among prominent contemporary southern country comedians. Raccoon John himself may even have been just a bit ashamed of Zerelda's circumstances, though as events transpired, Zerelda and Isaac's marriage was more fruitful and possibly happier than those of any of his other children.

The nearly two years that Raccoon John and Nancy lived as husband and wife on the Little South Fork were apparently reasonably happy ones, in spite of the fact that the bizarre weather patterns of 1816—remembered in southern and midwestern folklore as the year without a summer, with morning frosts occurring as late as June and July—made that year's growing season one of the very poorest on record in the United States. In these days before the Temperance movement became a widespread religious concern in America, the couple bought their whiskey by the barrel rather than by the bottle, and throughout a long life together they never quite became converted to Temperance principles.[49] Joseph Hurt Sr. died at James and Ursula's house early in the year following the wedding, but probably that fall Nancy gave birth to her first child, Eliza Baize, most likely named after her deceased mother Eliza Wilson and popularized by Louis Cochran with his frontier local color misspelling "Eliza Blaze."[50] Raccoon John farmed and preached, but he seems never to have reassumed the pastorate at Bethel or accepted any other such position with a church in the Cumberland hills. His main field of ministerial labor was now and would remain many miles to the north in the Bluegrass, and by his role as the self-made "singe-cat" raised up without an education somewhere among the raccoons, he was able to supplement his income much more fully than he had in the days of his marriage to Anna. Williams gives little concise information on his travels during these years, but we know that he and Jacob Creath preached at another associational "stand" service at least once in 1816. At North District Association's annual meeting in July that year, hosted by Jeremiah Vardeman's Lulbegrud Church in Montgomery County, associational clerk pro tem Nathan Lipscomb noted that Creath, John Taylor, and "—— Smith" preached at the gathering's Sunday worship service,[51] and this could only have been Raccoon John. Being suddenly thrust into the clerk's job, inexperienced at it, and perhaps a little shaken and nervous to boot, Lipscomb could be excused for leaving out the new Baptist celebrity's first name.

The reason that Lipscomb happened to be serving as clerk pro tem of North District Association that year, though, was a source of great embarrassment to Vardeman, the members of Lulbegrud Church, and very probably most of the association as well. Both the former moderator and clerk of North District, Jilson Payne and James French respectively, were members at Lulbegrud; the reader will recall from the account of Vardeman in the previous chapter that these men were the pro–General Union movers and shakers in North District, and they had been responsible for acquiring Vardeman as the congregation's pastor. Payne in fact owned all the land around Lulbegrud Church, and previously had given the congregation some property on which to build a new meetinghouse. By the year 1816, though, he had provoked a controversy among the members by having his slaves cut an enormous poplar tree on the church grounds, intending to hollow out the trunk and use it as a salt box for preserving meat at his plantation. A portion of the congregation felt that Payne, as the donor of the property in the first place, was within his rights, but as many or more felt that he had overstepped his bounds; and so, in an action Mark Twain would have been proud to invent as a satire, the church had split literally right down the middle over the issue. That didn't mean that they agreed to occupy the building on alternate weekends either, the way most churches at that time handled such divisions. The Payne faction, evidently led by Vardeman and supported by James French, worshiped in the front half of the meetinghouse, and the opposition, seemingly led by another preacher whose identity cannot be determined with absolute certainty, held their own services in the back half, and both sides stridently claimed to be the "legitimate" Lulbegrud Church.[52] It was well that the popular country hymns "Will There Be Any Stars in My Crown" and "No, Not One" had not yet been written. One can fairly imagine the two Lulbegrud congregations singing them to each other across the house at the same time.

Now, it must be remembered that this was not entirely unfamiliar territory to Vardeman. He himself had helped bring about a group-wide split in South District Association in 1803, and it had all worked out in his favor because every other General Union association had accepted his faction's letter of correspondence over the other's. Perhaps he thought that what he had then done for an association he could now accomplish on a small scale for a church, and so at the 1816 North District annual meeting, which Lulbegrud the previous year had agreed to host without knowing that all this trouble would brew up, both factions of the church presented letters to the body, each claiming to represent the "true" membership of the church. Nathan Lipscomb and a Payne ally, Thomas Moseley, were picked perhaps even at Payne and French's own suggestion as clerk and moderator pro tem, respectively, until the controversy could be ironed out. But as it transpired, under Moseley and Lipscomb's leadership the association voted not to recognize either faction as legitimate. Both Lulbegrud letters were "laid on the table indefinitely," the church was declared to be "in disorder," and a small committee was appointed to visit the factions to try and influence them to make peace with one another.[53] Payne and French were thus both knocked out of power completely for as long as the church remained divided. Vardeman got a face full of egg for perhaps the first time in his ministry, and although the visiting Raccoon John undoubtedly sympathized with him and supported him as a loyal vassal should, it can hardly be imagined that he could have resisted a joke or two at Vardeman's expense. After all, in his days in Stockton's Valley, the Little South Fork, and Hickory Flats, he'd split many a log to construct fences, cabins, and barns, but until he visited North District Association in 1816 he'd never seen a log itself split anything—much less a church.

Vardeman never did handle embarrassment, defeat, or even sustained controversy all that well, and so rather than trying to iron the problem out in a constructive way—not that there even could have been any easy solution, as will be seen—he seems immediately to have begun seeking a means by which he could distance himself from North District Association and its difficulties altogether. This included making some tentative overtures to Raccoon John, perhaps even at the 1816 association meeting itself, to move to Montgomery County and take over his two North District pastorates. As part of the preliminary negotiations with both Smith and the churches, Vardeman arranged appointments for John to visit and preach at both Lulbegrud and Grassy Lick the following May.[54] Aware of the Lulbegrud split but perhaps not the complete story behind its causes, John obediently made the trip and did the preaching, but even though he owed liege homage to Vardeman and still very badly wanted to leave the hills permanently for the Bluegrass, he must have entertained grave reservations about stepping into such a copperhead's cradle.

But then an event occurred back on the Little South Fork involving John himself in trouble of a sort similar, on a smaller scale, to that of Jilson Payne at Lulbegrud, and he certainly didn't consider that to be a matter for jokes. It involved the only time that Nancy was ever "brought up on charges" in the church, and sadly, as is all too often the case in such occurrences, she was completely innocent of any wrongdoing. The incident effectively demonstrates the significant change that had occurred over time in Raccoon John's relationships with his hill country neighbors. As noted in the last chapter, he'd become completely disenchanted with the Parmleysville area and frustrated with its lack of intellectual and social prospects as early as 1809, despite the great religious revival there, and after 1810 he'd employed the same outlet for his frustrations that he was yet using: preaching with the bigwigs downstate under the sponsorship of patrons. It's unreasonable to think that he could have kept his growing love/hate sentiment for his rustic neighbors entirely hidden for six or seven long years, but so far as we know, up to this point they had exhibited few, if any, negative reactions against his perceived "airs." After he assumed the role of Raccoon John Smith, the self-made and self-educated frontier hero of the downstate Baptists, though, it can easily be imagined that his fellow farmers and church members on the Little South Fork looked a bit askance at his pretensions, and now, community gossip that Brother John had really "gotten above his raising" must have taken a sharp increase. Not that anyone would have made such an accusation to his face, of course. In little rural communities both then and now that's simply not how things work. The injunctions against gossip and loose talk in Matthew 18, James 3, and other Scriptures are usually more or less disregarded by everyone so inclined and when it can be gotten away with conveniently, and many a sainted old country mother who glorifies God by strictly obeying 1 Corinthians 11 and 1 Timothy 2, never allowing her hair to be cut, also gives the devil his due with a tongue even longer than her hair and sharper than any scissors she could use to trim it. (Begging the reader's pardon here for that particular imagery. It just tends to stick in a country boy's mind. Not all the females are gossipers, and not all the males are closemouthed, either.)

Thus when Raccoon John came back home from that May 1817 visit to Vardeman's Montgomery County churches with a fine set of pure silver teaspoons, custom-made for Nancy by the noted Lexington silversmith and Baptist Samuel Ayers, the stage was set for hurt feelings both in John's household and those of his neighbors. No central Kentucky Baptist family at the time would have considered the use of fine silver tableware as a sin, and neither would most of us today. But from our comfortable vantage point we can barely imagine how happy Nancy, who had been raised on pewter, tin, earthenware, and cymbling gourds like the rest of the country folk on the Little South Fork, must have been to receive such a precious gift from her husband. When neighbor women came to visit and "take the day" with her, as the custom went, she proudly served coffee and tea with the new spoons, explaining that "they were of pure silver, and made expressly for her by her husband's friend, who lived in Lexington." This was a harmless enough boast, of course, made by Nancy more in appreciation of John's thoughtfulness for her than any haughtiness of her own. But on top of Nancy's being able to read, and John's own burgeoning reputation downstate, the silver teaspoons were just too much for her good sisters in Christ, not a few of whom were also her blood relatives, to stomach. Far better had it been that the community had done its duty, obeyed Matthew 18, and spoken to John face to face about whatever reservations they entertained against his perceived pretensions. As it happened, the brethren had kept quiet for years, and the sisters now took it out on Nancy for the spoons instead.

Finally, though, the brethren did speak. As a rule, women had no voice in church business meetings, but the good sisters probably wouldn't give the men any peace at home until they did something about those silver spoons, and so they acted. Raccoon John himself was not charged with any wrongdoing by accepting the spoons from Ayers, but Nancy's possession of them was censured by the church at Parmleysville as an exhibition of worldly pride, a grave, hurtful offense. John had to swallow his temper and assure the congregation in Nancy's behalf that she would "give satisfaction," because if he didn't, he and Nancy would have been disfellowshipped and excluded, and he'd have to give up his preaching credentials. So for the sake of her husband's influence Nancy packed up her spoons and stored them away, never again to bring them out while the couple remained on the Little South Fork, and the Parmleysville brothers and sisters once again rejoiced in the state of peace, love, and fellowship that they prized so highly. Perhaps to assuage Nancy's feelings as well as to ascertain her impressions about moving away from her brothers and sisters—both natural and spiritual—and letting him risk stepping into the Lulbegrud hornet's nest, John took her with him to Montgomery County for another visit in August not long after the North District 1817 annual meeting. They arranged with Eliza Baize's uncle and aunt Joshua and Sally (Davis) Hurt to care for her in their absence.[55]

The spoon incident was the very last straw for Raccoon John as far as the Little South Fork was concerned, and while on that August trip he received the news of the 1817 session of North District Association with some degree of gladness, undoubtedly tempered by sympathy for his patron's further misfortunes. Lulbegrud Church had stayed split, repeating the farce of "laying in" its two contesting letters once more and having its status of disorder reaffirmed; the association's new moderator, David Chenault, had then appointed a committee consisting of one member from each church in North District to "labor with" the two warring factions; the entire business had completely fouled Vardeman's efforts in behalf of Luther Rice to persuade North District to support the Baptist Board of Foreign Missions[56]; and as might be expected, by this time poor Vardeman was so heartily sick of North District that he had openly resigned as pastor not only at Lulbegrud but at Grassy Lick as well and fled back to his Elkhorn Association churches, where his zeal and rare gifts would be more properly appreciated. But Lulbegrud still needed a trustworthy man, an outsider with loyalty both to Vardeman and the congregation's own two overlords but with no obvious axes to grind with either of the two church factions, on which the divided membership could reunite and elect as pastor in his place. Vardeman now being gone from Grassy Lick, too, that church likewise became interested in Raccoon John, and there were two other North District churches, known as Spencer Creek and Bethel, that for some reason also wanted to share a common pastor with Vardeman's former charges.[57]

The four pastoral positions were open and waiting, and Raccoon John's chance to move downstate and hunt with the big dogs had finally come. Ironic it was, though, that he finally realized his golden opportunity in the wake of an occurrence so markedly similar to the one that he and Nancy were letting drive them away from the hills. Raccoon John would come to know the differences as well as the similarities between the two incidents, inside and out, but that's another story.

So as it turned out, Nancy liked the new country, and she and Raccoon John returned to the Little South Fork and quickly sold their little eighty-acre farm to her brother Joseph for $400, the transaction being recorded in the Wayne County courthouse on October 8. They appear to have persuaded Joshua and Sally Hurt and, surprisingly, John's brother Jonathan over in Stockton's Valley to sell their farms and move downstate, too. After asking for and receiving letters of good standing from the church that only a few weeks before had condemned Nancy for her new silver teaspoons, they left the Cumberland hills for good on October 22, 1817.[58] Their second child, Jonathan, was probably born in Montgomery County that winter.

CHAPTER 5

Truth, and a Living

Christianity, which also has, after all, some acquaintance with man and knows what a fine chap he is, how easy it is to get him to engage in and take an oath upon whatsoever cause may be, if only it is a way to a living, a way of making a career. . . . Christianity, therefore, as warily as possible, as warily as the police can act, has erected a barrier with a view to preventing these things from coalescing completely into one: Christianity and a living, Christianity and a career . . . etc.

—Søren Kierkegaard

The site where the historic Lulbegrud United Baptist Church once stood is located near the dividing ridge between Hinkston and Lulbegrud Creeks, approximately two miles off U.S. Highway 60 just west of Mt. Sterling, Kentucky, at the edge of a community now known as Reid's Village and on a small country road called Prewitt Pike. Today, just as it was two hundred years ago, the hamlet has a predominantly Baptist aura about it; there's a Baptist church on the main highway near the Prewitt Pike turnoff, a second on the Pike itself, and a third on Fogg Pike just off Prewitt—and the foundation stones of yet a fourth church, now defunct and with a barn standing in its place, remain where the road crosses the headwaters of Hinkston Creek, before the trail meanders by the former grounds of the old Lulbegrud meetinghouse itself. In addition to the quietly defiant Baptist presence, the area retains a bit of the flavor of both frontier Kentucky and the Old South as well. Lulbegrud Creek is said to have been christened by Daniel Boone after a name he picked from *Gulliver's Travels,* and the portion of the Prewitt Pike road between Fogg Pike and the Lulbegrud Church grounds is believed to have been part of the Warrior's Path, the ancient trace marked on the earliest maps of Kentucky as an Indian road connecting Shawnee settlements in Ohio with those of the Cherokee in Tennessee. But if the ghosts of ancient Native Americans haunt this historic thoroughfare, so do those of Civil War soldiers of a later date; standing proudly but placidly in lush pastures along this section of the road, old and rambling but elegant farmhouses sport romantic antebellum-style names such as The Woods, Belle Aire, and Vergeland, and the parents and grandparents of the Confederate general John Bell Hood are buried in a small cemetery less than a mile away. To one who's suddenly arrived there from the hustle and bustle of Mt. Sterling and U.S. 60, Prewitt Pike is something of a pleasant surprise, sitting peacefully not only at the cusp of the eastern Kentucky hills and the Bluegrass but at the cusp of the new Bluegrass and the old Bluegrass as well.

The historic Lulbegrud Church is long gone, though. A small residential home sits next to the property on which it stood for so many years, and the tombstone of Daniel Boone's nephew Thomas, who succeeded Raccoon John Smith to the pastorate there and who died in 1855, is the only marker to indicate where the churchyard once lay. But if eastern Kentuckians recognized and made pilgrimages to holy places, this secluded location would definitely be the hill country's Canterbury. Old Lulbegrud Church was, in a certain sense, the catalyst for the establishment of two of eastern Kentucky's largest traditional Christian faiths. Raccoon John Smith was, of course, the patriarch of one of these, and its story will occupy the remainder of this volume, but the other evolved from the work of Smith's predecessor in the Lulbegrud pulpit by more than two decades, the church's first pastor, Daniel Williams, and its study must also briefly claim our attention. However, neither man formulated any new precepts; they only strengthened and reinforced those already extant from influences they themselves had received, and Smith actually had a more direct effect on his tradition than Williams, who died in 1820, did on his. But the two faiths are more closely related than perhaps any of their modern adherents know, or would even acknowledge if they did. Strangely, this relationship had its seeds in both men's dealings with the builder of the Prewitt Pike community's one other historic landmark, a picturesque old brick mansion located about half a mile from the Lulbegrud churchyard and known both in Williams's and Smith's day, and our own, as Mt. Pleasant. That builder was Jilson Payne, for some years the moderator of North District Association and the transgressor who ordered the cutting of the log that split the church.

We should be grateful to Everett Donaldson, himself a Montgomery County native, for letting the quaint and perplexing local folktale of the log that split the church hit the printed page after a silence of nearly two centuries. Up to this point no Smith biography but his ever mentioned it. Neither do the minutes of North District Association note its existence, though both the North District records and the writings of John Augustus Williams vaguely detail the multitude of woes that it brought upon Lulbegrud Church. Louis Cochran would have adored the story had he only known about it, and by it he could perhaps have given his arch-villain James French another hapless victim; the very idea that the mere chopping of a tree should engender such controversy sounds just like the beginning of some early American tall tale of the very type on which he patterned his novel, and in essence the story has survived as just that, a tall tale, up and down Prewitt Pike to this day. But the event on which the tale hangs really did happen, and we might think that Raccoon John himself, with his known passion for jokes and witticisms, played a great part in keeping it alive. Everyone involved in the fracas came out looking like utter fools, and this was exactly the type of yarn about the Baptists that Raccoon John most dearly loved to recount in the later years of his ministry.

But Jilson Payne was one subject Raccoon John never talked about in his old age, with the possible exception of one offhand, absentminded comment he made to Albert Allen in 1857, and the story of the log that split the church was a tale he never told to Allen or anybody else. Hence the absence of both Payne's name and Payne's log in the Williams biography, and consequently in Louis Cochran's novel, and the reason why both writers skirt all the way around the fact that four churches in North District Association were "destitute" and needed the pastoral labors of a newcomer like Raccoon John Smith, without ever providing any coherent explanation for the churches' forlorn status. Donaldson's version is more accurate, but like the Williams and Cochran renditions, it bespeaks a lack of knowledge of the context necessary to explain subsequent events. The fact is that Raccoon John's life and ministry after 1817 can never be understood apart from that log, its claimants, and the Kentucky Baptists' earliest political setup that provided the setting for the controversy it sparked. Thus it now becomes our task to backtrack all the way to the days of Jilson Payne's youth and Daniel Williams's early pastorate at Lulbegrud, and fill in the details that Raccoon John so carefully and successfully omitted from his life story. They shape an involved and sordid account and a foundation for his downstate ministry that neither he nor any other preacher would have been proud of, and in fact one that nobody but another preacher working in the same context could even truly appreciate. Thus, if Donaldson had been able to piece together the puzzle of the log that split the church, he might have omitted the story from his writings as well. For like the malt that lay in the house that Jack built, the log that lay in the house that Payne built had a long, convoluted line of characters behind it.

The Paynes were Virginia slaveowning gentry, through and through. In pre-Revolutionary days Jilson's grandfather William had served as sheriff of Fairfax County, Virginia, as well as vestryman and churchwarden of the Anglican Church there, and during the Revolution his father, Edward, had been a commissioned officer in the Continental Army. But though the grandfather had remained a conventional adherent to the state faith, his son had been influenced by the dramatic Virginia social shakeup of 1765–1775 that had given both Regular and Separate Baptists such power over the colony's middle and lower classes. Edward Payne and his wife, the former Ann Holland Conyers, had affiliated themselves with the Ketocton Regular Baptist Association organized in northern Virginia in 1766 by, among other preachers, John Alderson Sr. Edward and Ann thus raised a large family of sons and daughters, Theodosia, Henry, William, Daniel, Sanford, Edward, Jilson, James (Jimmy), and Elizabeth, to believe every bit as strongly in the precepts of the Philadelphia Confession as George and Rebecca Smith, many rungs down the social ladder and living far away in the mountains, taught their own children some years afterward.

For all the differences in the social rankings of the Payne and Smith families, though, Edward Payne was similar in ways to Raccoon John, or at least the man John told Williams he'd hoped to become as a result of his Alabama migration. For after the Revolutionary War ended, Edward and Ann and their older sons, like so many other Virginia Regular and Separate Baptists of the same time period, packed up their belongings, their younger children, and their slaves and migrated west to the Bluegrass, where the family took up sufficient land by legal warrant to make them virtual aristocrats by the time the state of Kentucky was formed in 1792. Edward and Ann settled on the Town Fork of Elkhorn Creek about four miles from the settlement known even then as "the Athens of the West," Lexington, and within a few years Edward had acquired vast holdings both east and west of the city. His properties in what would become Clark and Montgomery counties included 686 acres on Hinkston Creek, two tracts of 400 and 1,000 acres, respectively, on the north fork of Lulbegrud Creek near Hinkston, 3,235 acres on Slate Creek that he owned outright, and 6,427 acres in partnership with others, 3,000 of which were on Slate Creek. If an immigrant family wanted to settle anywhere in northwestern Montgomery County after it was formed from Clark in 1796, there was a good chance that the head of the household would have to buy, rent, or hunt to supplement his table on land Edward Payne or one of his fellow Lexington magnates owned, and the family consequently commanded a great deal of respect from all.[1]

In keeping with their social position, Edward and Ann Payne and their two older sons, William and Henry, became charter members of the premier Lexington Baptist congregation of its day, Town Fork Church, and their pastor was the celebrated John Gano. A native of New Jersey and a longstanding minister of the Philadelphia Association, Gano had enjoyed a long and productive ministry in colonial days, including extended missionary itinerant tours in both the northern and southern colonies, church organization in Virginia and North Carolina (where he actually met and preached for Shubal Stearns once), a stint as a military chaplain in the Revolution, pastorates in both New Jersey and New York City, and at different periods the moderatorship of Philadelphia Association. In his old age he had left the East Coast to try his luck in the "west country" with some of his sons, and Town Fork was his very last pastorate.[2] Most of Edward and Ann's younger offspring were thus probably baptized either by Gano or his earliest preaching associate at the church, Absalom Bainbridge, as they came of age and proved able, under Calvinistic precepts, to relate their experiences of grace. William and Jimmy both became preachers, while Henry and Jilson, like their father, remained either as deacons or as laymen of distinction. Legend has it that Town Fork Church even held worship services for a time in the chapel of Lexington's first institution of higher learning, now known as Transylvania University, and it can be imagined that at least some of the younger Payne sons may have received a portion of their education at Transylvania as well.

The older Payne boys brought wives with them from Virginia. Henry's was Ann Lane, and William's first wife was Mary Grymes, who died rather young. But by the time Jilson married at age twenty-one in early 1789 to sixteen-year-old Dulcinea Harrison, family relations between the large Bluegrass magnate families had begun to grow complex after the southern fashion: everyone in power, so to speak, wound up being related to everyone else, and the pattern would repeat itself to varying extents in succeeding generations. Henry and Ann's daughter Theodosia married Benjamin Taylor, oldest son of premier Kentucky Regular Baptist preacher and chronicler John Taylor. Benjamin Taylor's sister Mary married William French, the son of another prominent early Bluegrass couple, James and Keziah (Calloway) French,[3] who also established a close connection with Jilson and Dulcinea. William Payne's second wife was Mildred Harrison, sister of Dulcinea, and William's daughter by his first wife, named Mary after her mother, married Dulcinea and Mildred's brother Micajah. Most of the Paynes and Taylors remained in the central Bluegrass, but all three of these new families, as well as James and Keziah French, moved east. Jilson and Dulcinea settled on Edward's 1000-acre Lulbegrud tract while their slaves cleared the land and finally finished building Mt. Pleasant for them in 1802, William and Mildred established themselves on a 350-acre tract next to it, and Micajah and Mary moved to the nearby settlement that would become Mt. Sterling, where Micajah became the first circuit and county court clerk when the new county of Montgomery was formed in 1796.[4]

For his part, William Payne helped organize the region's first Calvinistic Regular Baptist churches. Included among them was an arm from the historic Bryan's Station Church in Lexington gathered at the eastern settlement of Grassy Lick in 1793, where Payne worked briefly with Elijah Barnes before the latter moved to Pulaski County[5]; another was located a few miles to the northwest of Grassy Lick and known as Goshen, organized in 1797 and where he served as the first pastor[6]; and a third was at the Mt. Sterling settlement itself, organized in 1798, where he assisted David Barrow, a distinguished Virginia preacher who had just moved to Montgomery County himself.[7] Barrow assumed the pastoral care of Mt. Sterling Church, and Jilson and Dulcinea Payne seem to have been among the charter members there, transferring their letters from Town Fork to enter into the new church's constitution. Other early leaders at this new Mt. Sterling church included John and Elizabeth (Ellis) Coons, son-in-law and daughter of William Ellis, another great Bluegrass land magnate with extensive holdings east of the Payne properties on Spencer and Slate Creeks.[8]

Though Jilson and Dulcinea had no children of their own at this time, it can be imagined that they were almost as close to their nephews and nieces by Micajah and Mary Harrison and William and Mildred Payne as they would have been to their own offspring. Micajah and Mary had a son they named after Jilson, and William and Mildred had a daughter and a son both named for their "double" uncle and aunt. William and Mildred Payne finally left Elkhorn Association and Montgomery County in the year 1802 or a short time thereafter, settling in southern Mason County, joining Bracken Association, and selling their 350-acre Lulbegrud Creek tract to James and Keziah French.[9] At least one of William and Mildred's sons, Buckner Harrison Payne, moved back to Montgomery County with his wife, the former Eliza Ann January, and very probably stayed with his uncle Jilson and aunt Dulcinea as he got himself established in the mercantile business in Mt. Sterling.[10] Others of William and Mildred's children who lived not far from Lulbegrud Creek either in Montgomery or Bath County included John Newton Payne, named for the famous hymnist, and Dulcinea, her aunt's namesake, who married Moses Ryan. For their own part, neighbors James and Keziah French raised a houseful of sons and daughters, including the already-noted William, who married Mary Taylor; Richard, who became an attorney in Mt. Sterling and Winchester; Stephen, who lived in Frankfort; Keziah, named for her mother after a fashion common in that day, and who married James Prewitt; Theodosia, who married the Bath County physician John Hood and who would become the mother of the Confederate general of the same name; and Susanna, who wed Kenaz Farrow, another young attorney who resided in Mt. Sterling.[11]

Thus it would appear that the Paynes and similar families, such as the Frenches and Ellises, had a status in the early Bluegrass somewhat in common with Edgar Lee Masters's fictional character Thomas Rhodes: as far as the Baptists were concerned, they owned the church as well as the store and the bank. But this is perhaps an exaggeration, at least for the period before the Elkhorn Regular and South Kentucky Separate Baptists framed their Terms of Union in 1801. Until that time, Kentucky Regulars could impose no real control over those that wished to remain noncreedal, general-atonement Separates other than trying to persuade the Separates to adopt their Confession and join their ranks, as did the South Kentucky faction that became Tate's Creek Association in the 1790s. And so it happened that, during the time that Jilson Payne's slaves were building Mt. Pleasant for him, a great number of Separate Baptists from south of the Kentucky River also migrated to newly settled Montgomery County, bought or rented land from the great magnates or "laid" small personal land warrants, and built log cabins and meetinghouses with their own hands. Their churches and members were greater in number than those of the Regulars in the same area, and by 1800 they had spread from the heart of South Kentucky Association territory around Boonesborough all the way to the territories of present Powell, Menifee, Bath, Nicholas, Fleming, and Rowan counties. Within a few years, they even managed to plant two small churches across the river in southern Ohio.

Our story here, though, concerns only the Separate churches and preachers in Jilson Payne's own immediate vicinity. These were Lulbegrud Church on the Warrior's Path not far from Mount Pleasant, organized in 1793 and served by Elders Daniel Williams and Elijah Summers[12]; Sycamore, organized at an unknown date a few years later by Williams, probably with the help of yet-unordained minister Ambrose Jones, and located on the creek of the same name at present Jeffersonville some miles to the south of Mt. Sterling[13]; Blue Ash or Bethel, which Summers gathered about 1794 probably with Williams's help, a little to the east near Slate Creek[14]; Spencer Creek, organized in 1795 on the great land grant of John Coons's father-in-law by the South Kentucky moderator Robert Elkin and his younger colleague Moses Bledsoe, son of respected Separate minister Joseph Bledsoe and brother of the infamous William Bledsoe of the egg notoriety mentioned previously[15]; and Bald Eagle on the creek of the same name in present Bath County and which seems to have been formed from at least two groups of settlers, one from Pennsylvania and another from southwestern Virginia's Holston Association, including the families of William Ferguson, Josiah Fugate, and Archibald Prater. Samuel Hanna, a Pennsylvanian who had met the Separate Baptists after his arrival in that section of Bourbon County that later became Nicholas County, may have been the first pastor, but at the time of which we now speak Hanna had moved to southern Ohio temporarily due to difficulties in securing clear land titles and the congregation was now led by one Leonard Turley.[16]

In some cases the great land magnates donated small tracts to congregations for the building of these churches or simply gave the groups informal permission to worship on their properties; but although of the ministers noted Moses Bledsoe was a moderately prosperous man, there seems to have been a real unspoken class and status distinction between Regular and Separate Baptist adherents. This didn't mean that the South Kentucky Association had no effective political structure or voice of its own. It most certainly did, but it must be remembered that the center of Separate Baptist power was several miles to the west of Montgomery County. Back near Boonesborough, Robert Elkin, the closest direct link the Kentucky Separates had to the memory of Shubal Stearns via Elkin's youthful work with Tidence and Dutton Lane, still ran things as the moderator of the South Kentucky Association in the Stearns tradition, and the Montgomery County Separate preachers were in the same kind of spiritual and practical vassalage to Elkin as had been the first southern Separates to Stearns in North Carolina thirty-five to forty years before.

Having lived in perhaps both Virginia and North Carolina in the heyday of the earliest Separate revivals, Daniel Williams had been steeped in Baptist tradition from his youth. His father, Edward, and mother, the former Jemima Anderson, had lived in Stafford and Prince George counties, in Virginia, in the 1760s and had joined the Chappawamsick Regular Baptist Church there in 1767 when he was about four years old. Though we cannot be sure, the family may have moved to the Watauga Settlements of North Carolina/Tennessee border afterward, and Edward was reputed to be a hunting companion of the Boone brothers. Be that as it may, the Williamses were either with the western North Carolina pioneers who settled Boonesborough in the spring of 1775 or among the Virginians Daniel Boone brought to strengthen the fort's population four years later. Thus, before Daniel Williams reached his majority around 1784, he had had to grow up fast. In addition to weathering the Indian attacks against the fort and the farmers trying to raise corn outside its safety, according to family legend both he and his father were present at the bloody Revolutionary War battle at Blue Licks, northeast of the fort, in 1782, where American militiamen lost to a combined force of British and Indians and where Daniel Boone's son Israel was killed.[17]

Though Regular Baptists in Virginia, Edward and Jemima Williams joined Robert Elkin's Howard's Creek congregation in September 1787. Daniel joined the fellowship a month later, being baptized probably by either Elkin himself, Andrew Tribble, or Squire Boone; and his younger sister Winifred joined the church a month after that.[18] Daniel and his wife, the former Violet Crouch, may have first homesteaded in Madison County,[19] where Andrew Tribble cared for another large Separate congregation on Tate's Creek,[20] and it is probable that he got his start in the ministry under Elkin, Tribble, and Boone's direct mentorship. At least at first he seems to have been rather closer to Tribble and Boone than to Elkin. Tribble and probably Boone as well had had a falling-out over some matter or other with the South Kentucky moderator about 1789, and the difficulty had split Elkin's church into "Elkin" and "Tribble" factions that made peace with one another, as it were, but remained as two separate congregations.[21] Thus when the Williams family moved eastward in the 1780s or early 1790s to the territory that was soon to become Montgomery County, they called on Tribble and his colleague Thomas Ammen rather than Elkin and his associates at Howard's Creek to preside at the 1793 organization of Lulbegrud Church, which was probably an "arm" from Tate's Creek that had already been meeting at the Lulbegrud location for some time.[22] For all that, though, when the Elkin-Tribble controversy reached its expected conclusion about 1794 with the creation of Tate's Creek Association under Tribble's leadership from old South Kentucky Association, still under Elkin's, the Williamses and Lulbegrud remained allied to Elkin and the South Kentucky group rather than acquiescing to the partial adoption of the Philadelphia Confession that Tribble and Tate's Creek effected to gain fellowship with the Kentucky Regulars. Tribble's own church even split over the issue at the time, to "Stone" and "Log" Meetinghouses both located on Tate's Creek, the former keeping its alliance with Tribble and the latter going to the Elkin party.[23]

We do not know exactly when Daniel was ordained to the ministry, or the names of the members of his ordaining presbytery. There is a record, though, that he complied with the state laws concerning ministers performing marriages, and had himself bonded and registered as "an ordained minister in communion with the Baptist Society" at the Clark County court on September 22, 1795.[24] During these years before the Great Revival, we may assume that his regular preaching circuit, if such it could be called, included working as partners with Elijah Summers at Lulbegrud and giving him preaching assistance at Blue Ash (Bethel), visiting and preaching for Moses Bledsoe at Spencer Creek and first perhaps Samuel Hanna and later Leonard Turley at Bald Eagle, and accepting repayments in kind from them in his own labors to the south on

Sycamore Creek. Sometime before 1800, though, Elijah Summers departed Montgomery County for the Green River country, and he transferred his membership to the Green River Association not long after it was formed. Moses Bledsoe in turn took his membership from Spencer Creek to Summers's Blue Ash (Bethel) Church.[25] This left Williams, Bledsoe, and Turley among the senior Montgomery County Separate ministers of the day, and all three undoubtedly had to work hard during the lean years of infidelity that preceded the outbreak of the Great Revival.

Montgomery County gained another minister, the distinguished Virginia immigrant David Barrow, in 1798, but although Barrow had been a Separate Baptist in his youth twenty-five years before and in fact was once a protégé of one of the original Virginia Separate preachers, Jeremiah Walker,[26] he was now very much a confirmed Regular and more in the social class of the Paynes and Ellises than that of Daniel Williams, if not Moses Bledsoe, as well. Thus, during these years that Jilson Payne let Williams and Bledsoe hold services at the little Lulbegrud meetinghouse on his property, he and Dulcinea themselves went to church at the new Mt. Sterling Regular Baptist meetinghouse and listened to the distinguished Barrow. As community leaders and as the owners of the property on which Lulbegrud stood, though, they may have dropped in for occasional visits to the Separate congregation, and we may imagine that they were treated with the deferential respect due their class. Besides this, both Payne and his pastor, Barrow, were trustees of the public school on Lulbegrud Creek, which may have met in the church building on weekdays during seasonal school terms, and if this were the case Payne would have had at least a bit of secular interaction with Williams as well.[27]

The office of school trustee was, however, one of Jilson Payne's lesser responsibilities. Even before Montgomery County had been formed he had been a magistrate and tax commissioner in Clark County, and when Montgomery was organized he was appointed one of the new county's three judges of the Quarterly Court, in which his brother-in-law Micajah Harrison served as clerk. Like Micah Taul down in Wayne, he also seems to have commanded the Montgomery County militia for a time, and he represented his county in Kentucky's second Constitutional Convention of 1799. In that same year he was elected to the lower house of the state legislature, where he served until 1803 when he was appointed to the state senate, remaining in office at least until 1808.[28]

During this time Payne lived what we might classify as a typical prosperous Kentucky country squire's existence at Mt. Pleasant. In true patrician (or perhaps political) fashion, he was a "clever" or hospitable man to his neighbors and visitors, and as well as being a pillar in the church he enjoyed hosting home worship services open to all and sundry. William Vaughan recalled an incident of his very earliest ministry in which Payne invited him and one Anson Mills to preach to one of these gatherings at Mt. Pleasant, and after the two ministerial cubs finished their brief, nervous, halting discourses, Payne himself concluded the services and, though he was no ordained minister, outpreached both of them.[29] In a detailed inventory he once made of his real and personal property, Payne noted that, besides his thousand acres on Lulbegrud Creek, his fine brick home, and the usual tools and equipment required to manage a large plantation, he owned five families of slaves plus more that were unattached to families (a total of thirty-four blacks, which made him a small-scale slaveowner when compared to the barons of the Deep South but a very great one for that part of Kentucky); silver plate, tableware, and ivory- and bone-handled cutlery valued at $349, an enormous sum in those days; a great quantity of elegant household "appointments" including "Turkey carpets," "Japan and gilt waiters," ten beds, and a walnut "case of drawers" that he proudly described as "the first piece of furniture made north of the Kentucky [River]," the whole valued at approximately $715; a copper still valued at $100 (of course he supervised the production of his own whiskey and brandy, with none of the stigma that the later Temperance movement brought to the enterprise); a four-wheel carriage valued at $300; and a library that was absolutely immense for its time and place. It consisted of two Bibles and a Scriptural Concordance, twelve volumes of American State Papers, eight bound volumes of issues of the London *Spectator* magazine, twenty-five volumes of various British poets, two volumes of the history of China, three volumes of the complete works of Flavius Josephus, a twelve-volume *Nicholson's Encyclopedia,* a work on meteorology by one Thompson, Dr. Buchan's and Dr. Thompson's separate volumes of *Family Medicine,* Guthery and Cummings's *Geography,* two world Atlases, two dictionaries (one Sheridan's and the other, Walker's), *Doctor Young's Poetical Works,* two *Gazetteers,* six bound volumes of Kentucky laws, a volume on governmental constitutions consisting of the U.S. Constitution and one from each state then extant, Jefferson's *Notes on Virginia,* a biography of Patrick Henry, Murray's *Grammar,* Watts's and Rippon's Hymnals, a volume of the *Clerk's Magazine,* David Ramsay's two-volume 1789 *History of the American Revolution,* a literary work entitled *Dialogues of Devils,* another called *Solitude Sweetened,* McLann's *Essays,* and "a number of pamphlets upon various subjects."[30] Payne must have owned the largest hoard of books in Kentucky east of Lexington and south of Maysville at this period, and although it will be noted that a copy of his own church's Philadelphia Confession of Faith was not listed among his treasures, hopefully we can determine the reason for its absence—as well as the presence of at least some of his numerous pamphlets on various subjects—in the next chapter.

To return to the story, then, beginning in 1800 the Great Revival moved eastward into central Kentucky, and both Regular and Separate Baptists found themselves thrown side by side in revival services and baptisms despite their longstanding differences. Though each of their previous attempts at union had resulted in fiasco, the Revival made the formation of the United Baptists of Kentucky look like a possibility once more, and of course when the Elkhorn and South Kentucky Associations appointed their committees and jointly ratified the Terms of General Union, the possibility became a reality—almost. Jilson Payne was not asked to serve on the joint committee, although David Barrow was a member on the Regular side along with three strong Calvinists, Ambrose Dudley, John Price, and Joseph Redding; on the Separate side, Robert Elkin and Moses Bledsoe served with Thomas John Chilton, Daniel Ramey, and Samuel Johnson.[31] But just as soon as the Revival began to subside a bit and the sentiments of peace and love cooled back down to normal run-of-the-mill human relations, the newly formed Kentucky United Baptists fragmented internally into Regular and Separate factions both striving for power over one another. We examined the generalities of the Kentucky Baptist situation in chapter 2, and dealt with some specifics concerning the involvement of the formerly Separate Tate's Creek and South District Associations, and Jeremiah Vardeman, in chapters 3 and 4. And so in order to begin to understand why, some twelve to fifteen years later, a tall tale would be concocted in the Prewitt Pike community about a log that split a church, we must now examine what was going on at this same uneasy period in the other half of the old South Kentucky Association, North District. For Jilson Payne, as will be seen, was every bit as involved with the brick-by-brick construction of this particular house as his black servants were with breaking their backs to build Mt. Pleasant for him.

Despite the introductions to early Kentucky Baptist politics given in previous chapters, the first interassociational relations between Elkhorn and North District Associations, and for that matter their other correspondent groups that got themselves involved in the Elkhorn-North District fray, may be confusing and difficult for the reader to follow. Even so, a grounding in North District's early world is absolutely necessary in order to understand the situation in which Raccoon John Smith found himself a few years down the road. One must keep in mind that the intrigues to be described herein were all up close, personal, and intense, yet at the same time scrupulously couched beneath a carefully constructed and maintained facade of Christian love, fellowship, and decorum—and also, if it somehow helps explain matters, that each and every one of the participants were professing Christians who were trying their dead-level best to carry out what they considered to be God's will on earth. Actually, this same manner of thinking is necessary to understand the internal struggles of the Southern Baptist Convention over the last twenty-odd years as well. Certainly the actions of the combatants were alike enough, although money and finances were only an indirect part of the older conflict.

When the old South Kentucky Separate Baptist Association held its last meeting in 1801, anticipating the formation of the North and South District United Baptist Associations the following fall, neither Grassy Lick, Goshen, nor Mt. Sterling Churches belonged to it. They were still members of the formerly Regular Elkhorn Association,[32] and after Elijah Barnes's departure some years earlier and then William Payne's migration to Mason County, Barrow took over the Goshen pastorate and Lewis Corban of Bourbon County assumed Grassy Lick's care.[33] But the arrangement still left Barrow with two free weekends, so to speak, and once the union took effect not long after old South Kentucky's final gathering, Daniel Williams, Moses Bledsoe, and Leonard Turley undoubtedly cheerfully invited him to "share their stands" at meetings in the former Montgomery County Separate churches. Williams and the others likewise would have enjoyed the visits of Barrow's congregants, who included Jilson and Dulcinea Payne from Mt. Sterling. So far, so good, but when Elkhorn Association met in its August 1802 session to send letters of correspondence and messengers to the new North and South District Associations, the Payne family's old home church at Town Fork expressed dissatisfaction with the entire process under which the Union had taken place the year before. Evidently John Gano and Absalom Bainbridge didn't like the Terms of General Union, and they thought that the Separates simply should have joined the Regulars in adopting the Philadelphia Confession as both Elkhorn and Salem Associations themselves had done in 1785, Holston Association had done in 1786, and Tate's Creek Association had accomplished partially in 1794. To ease the tension, Elkhorn moderator Augustine Easton appointed a small committee to give Town Fork Church "friendly aid" in accepting the union as it stood. Letters and messengers were sent to both North and South District Association meetings later that fall, David Barrow and Jilson Payne were appointed as Elkhorn's delegates to North District, and Elkhorn brought its session to a close with plans to host the next year's August gathering directly at the aggrieved Town Fork Church itself.[34]

Neither Town Fork Church's nor Elkhorn Association's tensions were relieved when the South District Association held its first annual meeting three weeks after Elkhorn, at Salt River Church in what is now Anderson County, Kentucky,[35] and the difficulty arose concerning the correspondence with Tate's Creek Association. The details of this imbroglio and Jeremiah Vardeman's involvement in it have already been discussed in chapter 3, and we cannot now say whether Elkhorn's delegates to the meeting were among those who stood and voted illegally to uphold Tate's Creek's letter at the session. But this new controversy, added to the one that Town Fork Church had generated in Elkhorn three weeks earlier, must have sent shivers up a good many United Baptist spines. The power of the Great Revival just might not be enough to hold Regulars and Separates together after all. Something had to be done to maintain the circle of correspondence even if ruses had to be employed in the process, because if the Union fragmented so soon after it had been effected, it would only leave Baptists of both types looking like fools and Satan laughing with delight as the victor. And so it happened that, when the first annual meeting of the new North District Association was held at Unity Meetinghouse on Four Mile Creek in Clark County a month after South District's session, on the first weekend of October, both Barrow and Jilson Payne were present as Elkhorn representatives—and it seems that North District moderator Robert Elkin and clerk Moses Bledsoe pretty much let them both commandeer the meeting. Moderator Elkin could have shown so much deference to the Elkhorn visitors simply because he needed their assistance in ironing out the details of the new association's organization. After all, as a longtime Separate Baptist, he'd never before worked in an association that had any formal constitution, rules of decorum, or even written articles of faith save the proclamation of "the Bible and it alone" as a creed. In order to ensure a smooth relationship with Elkhorn, Salem, Bracken, and other newly organized United associations of Regular ancestry, all these things were now necessary. Even so, we can hardly doubt that Town Fork Church's August complaints and the subsequent South District controversy made Barrow, Payne, Elkin, and Bledsoe all edgy over the rapidly weakening links of the new General Union, and we must wonder if the North District officers let Barrow and Payne take such a big hand in North District's business simply for the sake of good defensive politics.

In any case, the articles of faith were easy. Under Elkin's leadership North District simply adopted the Terms of General Union, which both he and Bledsoe along with Barrow had signed as committeemen only the year before, as their abstract of doctrinal principles, and everyone was satisfied with the arrangement. But to frame a constitution and set rules of decorum Elkin had no precedents in his own tradition to work with, and so on the first day of business when he appointed the association's usual working committees, he included Barrow and Payne prominently in the group assigned to draft North District Association's first such instruments. Other members of this committee included Elkin himself, the clerk Bledsoe, Daniel Williams, James Quesenberry, and Isaac Crutcher; on the "committee on the bill of arrangements," the vehicle through which associational moderators in the Shubal Stearns tradition have always enforced legislation upon their followers, Elkin appointed his Terms of General Union cosigner Daniel Ramey along with Edward Trabue, Daniel James, Leonard Turley, and Charles Finnel.

Since we cannot now determine whether or not the Lulbegrud School always operated within Lulbegrud Church's meetinghouse, or if it did, how much Daniel Williams was involved in its day-to-day affairs, the mention of this committee in North District's 1802 minutes is the only documented evidence we have of Williams ever working on any project together with either Jilson Payne or David Barrow. Not that Williams, Barrow, Payne, Elkin, or the others came up with anything novel or even particularly original, though; under Barrow and Payne's leadership, the group seems to have lifted a "sample" constitution and rules of decorum directly from John Asplund's 1794 *Universal Register of the Baptist Denomination,* and presented both for North District's adoption.[36] On the next day of business the new association thus accepted a Regular Baptist governmental policy, expressly declaring itself a council of advice and not an authoritative body, but yet partially or perhaps even totally negating the declaration with the stipulation that it had the power to withdraw from any church which a majority of its members perceived to "act or remain in disorder." For the time being, though, all was well with North District in relation to its sister associations in the General Union, and as a further defensive measure, meetings were scheduled between North District and Tate's Creek Association churches and representatives to forestall any potential South District–style fights between the two bodies. In return for Barrow and Payne's visit, moderator Elkin appointed Daniel Williams and Moses Bledsoe to bear North District's letter of correspondence to Elkhorn's next session the following summer in Lexington.[37]

But the defensive mechanisms Elkin and Bledsoe implemented at the first North District meeting must have seemed insufficient both to Payne and to his new neighbor and fellow Elkhorn member James French. If the two of them could establish some sort of internal political power base friendly to Elkhorn Association and Regular Baptist ideals directly within the former Separate Baptist group itself, they could give Elkhorn just that much more insurance that the Elkhorn–North District correspondence would hold together and that Elkhorn's dominance over it would continue. At least one of the Montgomery County North District preachers, the clerk Moses Bledsoe, seems to have been friendly to this idea as well, even though his own father, Joseph, was an old hard-line Separate Baptist who would ultimately leave the General Union with the South District majority to reorganize the South Kentucky Association. At any rate, the fact that North District and Elkhorn now enjoyed a free exchange of membership transfers made the project's implementation easy. All Payne and French had to do to start the proceedings was to "lift their letters" and bring them to the church of their choice in North District, and of course this turned out to be the closest one to them—Lulbegrud, where Jilson and Dulcinea Payne joined sometime between October 1802 and perhaps June of 1803 and James and Keziah French joined on May 21, 1803. As noted, Jilson and Dulcinea Payne brought their memberships over from Mt. Sterling. James and Keziah French belonged to the Otter Creek Regular Baptist Church in Madison County before this time.[38]

Even if Payne or French had had some charge of immorality preferred against them, their social positions in the Lulbegrud Creek community would have made it difficult for Daniel Williams, or for that matter anyone else, to prevent them from "lettering" to Lulbegrud Church if they desired to do so. The two influential community leaders thus immediately came into positions of power within their new home church at Lulbegrud, and this vantage point undoubtedly enabled them to persuade the church, if not its pastor, to adopt the Regulars' Philadelphia Confession soon after they had joined. Certainly this was the setup at Lulbegrud when Raccoon John Smith first became acquainted with the church.[39] Because of the scanty Lulbegrud data supplied by John Augustus Williams and quoted by Louis Cochran and Everett Donaldson, plus the speculations of native eastern Kentucky history buffs heavily influenced by the later Old Landmark movement, the name of Lulbegrud Church has come down to us in history incorrectly, as originally a Regular rather than a Separate Baptist church.

What *didn't* come down in history besides Lulbegrud's Separate origins, interestingly, was Daniel Williams's irate response to what was occurring in his first Montgomery County congregation. Payne and French were members at Lulbegrud now and he was not, having moved his own membership some years before to the newer Sycamore Church near Jeffersonville, and even if he had kept his name on the Lulbegrud membership roll Payne and French were still more powerful both financially and politically than he could ever hope to be. If the two of them could influence a majority of the Lulbegrud congregation to adopt the Philadelphia Confession, there was little he could do except let the motion pass over his own objections, or rule it out of order as moderator and then lose the ruling on congregational appeal. But Payne and French actually may have contrived to recuse Williams from the whole matter, if indeed Williams did not recuse himself. According to one historical source, the more compliant Moses Bledsoe just happened to stand in as moderator at Lulbegrud in the spring and early summer of 1803,[40] and he most probably helped Payne and French achieve their ends. It must not have mattered really to the two whether Williams agreed with their actions or not, since their next objective was to fill one of David Barrow's unencumbered weekends and elect him as the next pastor of the Lulbegrud congregation.

So Barrow did succeed Williams to the Lulbegrud pastorate,[41] and Williams was left with the responsibility of his church at Sycamore and his usual periodic visits to Spencer Creek, Bethel, and Bald Eagle to give preaching assistance to the ministers and members there. Other, younger preachers likewise probably fairly closely associated with Williams at this point included Bledsoe's assistants Joseph Rice at Spencer Creek and Francis Taylor at Bethel,[42] although the strain that Bledsoe himself had put on Williams may have affected Williams's relationship to these younger exhorters as well. To the east at Bald Eagle, Leonard Turley seems to have found himself suddenly in the same position in which Williams had been put at Lulbegrud. In 1803 he abruptly left the Bald Eagle congregation to join another minister, William Moss, at a church on a tributary of Flat Creek known as Johnson's Fork, and from there he appears to have organized a new fellowship on the East Fork of Flat Creek,[43] both of which were likewise located in present Bath County and at no great distance from his former pastorate. His replacement at Bald Eagle, though, was an extremely curious choice for a former Separate Baptist congregation: Richard Thomas, a minister of Elkhorn Association who would soon prove to be among the most highly and even cruelly Calvinistic preachers ever known in that body.[44] How much that the influence of Payne, French, and Barrow at neighboring Lulbegrud affected Bald Eagle's pastoral selection at this time is anyone's guess.

While affairs were thus getting rearranged in North District Association, Elkhorn began to have the first of its own troubles, due chiefly to moderator Augustine Easton and to the most influential Elkhorn minister of the day: James Garrard, who happened to be the governor of Kentucky at this time. Garrard had for his secretary of state the president of Transylvania University, a British Unitarian minister named Harry Toulmin, and Toulmin succeeded in converting Garrard and Easton, right in the very wake of the Great Revival, to Unitarian beliefs. After Easton published a pamphlet purporting to prove that Jesus Christ was inferior to the Father, a special session of Elkhorn Association was called in the spring of 1803 with David Barrow presiding as moderator. A measure condemning Unitarianism was effected by Elkhorn's delegates, reaffirming their belief in the Trinity as expressed in the Philadelphia Confession, and although Easton bore the brunt of the blame, the governor of Kentucky was kicked out of the Baptist Church as well.[45] For all this, David Barrow's management of the Unitarian controversy has the dubious distinction of being the most relatively fair and least underhanded political action taken by the Elkhorn, South District, or North District Associations during the first years of the General Union's existence. It did have one slight repercussion for North District, too: three of the four churches under Augustine Easton's pastorate at the time remained with Elkhorn, and one of these, Flat Lick in Bourbon County, apparently chose the highly Calvinistic Richard Thomas, who had just picked up the Bald Eagle pastorate in North District, to succeed the deposed Elkhorn leader.[46] Thomas's Baptist political star thus appeared to be rising while Easton's was snuffed out completely, and although Jilson Payne, James French, and David Barrow all undoubtedly endorsed Thomas's advancement at this time, they lived to regret it.

But when Elkhorn met at Town Fork for its regular session on the second weekend of August that same year, 1803, Barrow was not elected to the group's moderatorship on a permanent basis. Instead, the reactionary Calvinist and Terms cosigner Ambrose Dudley, pastor of the Bryan's Station Church, assumed the office, and he maintained it for at least seven years afterward. Daniel Williams and Moses Bledsoe were both present at this gathering with North District's letter of correspondence. Among the crowd of delegates, William Howe; Jilson Payne's brother Henry, and their father, Edward; and the illustrious John Gano were enrolled as representatives from the host church itself, and Gano's son-in-law, John Price, also a Terms co-signer, was elected as Elkhorn Association's clerk. The only serious items of business that the association addressed were to reaffirm the actions taken against the Unitarians at Barrow's special Elkhorn session in the spring, and to allow Town Fork itself to give another gratuitous snub to the former Separate Baptists: "At the request of the Townfork [*sic*] Church the Association voted unanimously that the union with the Baptist[s] South of Kentucky [River] does not in the least remove them from their Constitutional principals [*sic*]." David Barrow was appointed once again to bear Elkhorn's letter of correspondence to North District, this time accompanied by William Wood rather than Jilson Payne since Payne was now a member at Lulbegrud, and after other similar routine actions the association was dismissed.[47]

Thus ended Elkhorn Association's 1803 session, but John Price's minute records could not have told the whole story. Nothing was written down about Price and Henry Payne's being appointed to go with Barrow and Wood to North District in October to address some "difficulty" that had occurred in Daniel Williams's home church at Sycamore, but the two tagalongs were present at the October North District meeting, and this is exactly what happened: Moderator Robert Elkin included himself on the committee he appointed to go to Sycamore and examine this so-called difficulty, and in fact he was the only North District member or minister who served on it. The other committeemen were John Price and Henry Payne themselves, plus three apparently disinterested parties from, of all places, Tate's Creek Association, Peter and Archibald Woods and William Tharp.[48] That an associational moderator should appoint a committee to assist any of the churches under his care with a problem would be no cause for comment or probably even for concern, but this committee's structure was so highly unusual that its creation must have been Elkin's cautious response to some unique and extremely volatile situation.

As a General Union associational moderator, Elkin's aim was unity or at least a passable facsimile thereof. In this case his work was complicated by the facts that, in the interim between the Elkhorn and North District annual gatherings that year, Jeremiah Vardeman and John Rice had already split South District Association in the manner discussed in previous chapters, and North District faced the inevitability of supporting one faction or the other, but not both. The reference point of the image of unity on which Elkin wished to build can be inferred from the ideologies represented on the committee. Henry Payne from Town Fork, host church of the 1803 Elkhorn session, represented the political power of the Lexington church and the Payne family. Elkhorn clerk John Price represented the political power of Elkhorn Association as well as the family of John Gano, and he, Payne, and Gano all stood for strict Calvinism and an absolute commitment to the Philadelphia Confession. The three Tate's Creek Association men likewise held to the Confession, but on the moderate compromise terms by which their association had established its own fellowship with Elkhorn back in 1794. That left Elkin himself, as the sole North District member on the committee, to stand alongside Daniel Williams and his Sycamore flock on the old South Kentucky Separate Baptists' nearly Arminian position. We can thus imagine that Elkin, who had been preaching ever since the year Shubal Stearns died, also sympathized with and supported Williams and his congregation, but Elkin wasn't about to do anything that could possibly spur North District into the same kind of war that Jeremiah Vardeman and John Rice had started over in South District. In short, this committee not only represented the perception of unity entertained by the Kentucky Baptists at this time, but the General Union's coercive force to impose that concept of unity as well.

What could Daniel Williams and his members have done to prompt this covert action on Elkhorn Association's, and consequently on Robert Elkin's, part? We cannot know for sure, but there are only a limited range of possibilities, and the most likely is that Williams himself was extremely upset over Jilson Payne and James French's high-handed maneuvering to influence Lulbegrud Church to adopt the Philadelphia Confession, install David Barrow as the flock's pastor, and make the congregation the nucleus of an Elkhorn political base in North District Association. Since Moses Bledsoe had probably assisted Payne and French in the undertaking only a few months before, Williams couldn't have harbored entirely good feelings toward him either, and very probably Robert Elkin himself deeply resented the Elkhorn intrusion into the affairs of his association although he was not yet in any political position to come down squarely on Williams's side. But regardless, Williams had to go to Lexington with Bledsoe to represent North District at Elkhorn's 1803 session, and the ruling that Town Fork asked the association to adopt—that the union with the Separate Baptists did not "in the least" remove Elkhorn from its constitutional principles—was the last thing that the plebeian farmer, hunter, and preacher Williams needed to hear at this point. He either asked for the floor and made a speech condemning the former Regular body's attitude toward North and South District Associations, perhaps including a pithy and quite true reminder that most of Elkhorn's oldest members and ministers *themselves* had been Separate Baptists when they first came to Kentucky, or he made the same comments a little too loudly in private conversation afterward. In either case, his voice would have fallen on the wrong ears. J. H. Spencer described John Price as "a man of an unpleasant temper, of great asperity of manners, and whose zeal on all occasions [partook] too much of the nature of party spirit,"[49] and it seems entirely within his character to have agitated whatever public or private comments Williams made at the 1803 session into an interassociational crisis on his own. John Gano, who was after all his father-in-law, very well may have encouraged him to do so. Even if Price hadn't personally taken the matter up, Williams had undoubtedly committed the gaffe of making disparaging comments about Jilson Payne right there at Town Fork in front of Payne's father, brothers, and former church colleagues, not to mention the respected Gano, and political incorrectness was no more a forgivable sin two hundred years ago than it is now. And so at the 1803 North District session in October, John Price and Henry Payne must have made Robert Elkin an offer he couldn't refuse: shut Daniel Williams up or run him out of North District Association (they probably really didn't care which), or risk another General Union split of the same type that Jeremiah Vardeman and John Rice had effected over in South District. Thus Elkin put together the committee, using the Tate's Creek men as buffers between the solid Philadelphia Confession stance represented by Payne and Price on one hand and the determined anti-Confession Separate Baptist position of Williams on the other, and it seems to have worked better than anyone could have hoped. The story intended for public consumption was reported in North District's 1804 minutes, that the Sycamore "difficulty" was now "amicably settled."[50] What really happened was that Williams obligingly shut up—*and* eventually left the country, too.

Yes, Baptist associational machinations can, and do, get this complicated, and if plain truth be told the successful Baptist politician borrows more of his skill from the wisdom of the serpent than the harmlessness of the dove. The old saying about the similarity between legislation and sausage is just as true for religious organizations as it is for secular governmental assemblies: if you like either sausage or legislation, be sure never to watch it being made. But here, in the interests of providing a clear background for a series of later events in Raccoon John Smith's ministry, we must dissect the story of Daniel Williams away from the larger maelstrom of early Kentucky Baptist politics and give it just a moment of attention on its own. Although Robert Elkin was in no position to give Williams any overt support in the 1803 difficulty, he probably really would have liked for him to remain in Montgomery County and assist him in his own covert plans for retaliation against Elkhorn and its North District faction—which Leonard Turley, similarly ousted from his position at Bald Eagle by Richard Thomas, in fact did. But Elkin never again entrusted Williams with any responsibility in associational affairs, and from what evidence we have, this was exactly as Williams desired it. As it happened, around this time or certainly within the next two years, Daniel and Violet Williams and several members of both Sycamore and Bald Eagle Churches, including Ambrose and Martha Jones, William and Elizabeth Coffee, William and Catherine Ferguson, John and Margaret Hammond, Archibald and Sarah Prater, and Randal Fugate, migrated to the headwaters of the Licking River in what is now Morgan and Magoffin counties, Kentucky, and resumed their lives far away from the hustle, bustle, and religious intrigue of the Bluegrass. Samuel Hanna returned from Ohio and joined them about the year 1807, becoming Williams's lifelong preaching partner. It is probable that Williams continued as the pastor of Sycamore Church, visiting the flock at Jeffersonville on a monthly basis, at least until the spring or early summer of 1809, when he and Violet transferred their memberships from the church to a new congregation he had organized on the upper Licking the previous fall.[51] As noted earlier, Jeremiah Vardeman and David Chenault seem to have preached to the church afterward until Vardeman's own protégé, William Vaughan, was ready to assume the Sycamore pastorate. Although Williams's new home church in the east, first known as Poplar Meeting-House and later as South Fork of Licking River, and one other under his care, known as Burning Springs and organized by him and Hanna in 1810 at present-day Salyersville, Kentucky, were admitted to membership in North District for a few years before the eastern Kentucky Baptists constituted their own Burning Springs Association in 1813, Williams himself is known to have been present at only three more North District associational sessions in his lifetime. In 1805 he returned to the body to watch the initiation of a bizarre set of actions and intrigues that made his own unfair treatment by the General Union leadership look tame in comparison, and which must also wait to be discussed. For both of his other visits, occurring in 1810 and 1813, respectively, he seems to have attended only because he thought it was absolutely necessary that he be there.[52]

It is interesting to note the modern eastern Kentucky perception of this pioneer Baptist minister. In most local histories he is recognized as the organizer and first pastor of Lulbegrud Church, but his involvement with the church at Sycamore and his relationship to the members at Bald Eagle after Leonard Turley was ousted from the pastorate there have long since been forgotten, even though most of the charter members of the first two churches he and Samuel Hanna organized in eastern Kentucky came directly from the Sycamore and Bald Eagle congregations. But in nearly all cases he is perceived as having migrated to the eastern Kentucky mountains simply because of his close spiritual kinship with Squire and Daniel Boone: that he was a woodsman at heart, and when the Bluegrass began to fill up with settlers he simply took off to the solitude of the wild woods again like a true pioneer.[53] Perhaps this is understandable, since Williams's memories and opinions of Jilson and Henry Payne, James French, Moses Bledsoe, Robert Elkin, and North District Association as a whole were probably subjects he did not much care to discuss even among his friends and family members, let alone pass on to his progeny. Still, though Williams's Burning Springs Association exchanged letters of correspondence with North District for many years, there does appear to have been a degree of antipathy between Burning Springs and North District, with Sycamore Church as the one contact point that the two bodies had between them, that the newcomer Raccoon John Smith clearly recognized, and contrived to exploit, a quarter century after Williams and his friends had packed up and left Montgomery County for good.

But even with Daniel Williams's painful first-hand knowledge of the essential unfairness of the politically volatile Kentucky General Union in its early years, he never came up with a better system for his own eastern Kentucky followers. In fact, his Burning Springs Association (which has turned out to be the "old mother" of nearly every church and denomination now classified as "Appalachian Old Time Baptist" in eastern Kentucky, including the United Baptists, Old Regular Baptists, Primitive Baptists, "Enterprise" Regular Baptists, to a great extent even the region's Free Will Baptists,[54] and one more which will receive its own extensive notice later) managed only to repeat North District's mistakes over the years, the reason being that the General Union system of interassociational correspondence was all that Williams and his followers knew and they could see no constructive way to change it. The Terms of General Union themselves were Burning Springs Association's first articles of faith.[55] Until his death in July 1820, Williams worked happily in his new association with Hanna and several other fairly well-known early local ministers, including his longtime Sycamore associate Ambrose Jones; his protégé at both Sycamore and in Burning Springs Association, William Coffee; Simeon Justice, a jolly, nearsighted, extremely corpulent old exhorter who came to the Big Sandy Valley from Holston Association's Little Ivy Church in

Buncombe County, North Carolina[56]; William Salisbury, a popular exhorter that Williams and Justice may have ordained themselves; and Electious Thompson, a Prince George County, Maryland, native who had lived in both Virginia and North Carolina before moving to the headwaters of the Kentucky River in present Perry County, and from thence to northern Alabama, where he sought his fortune just as Raccoon John Smith had.[57] Ironically, though, out of the entire ministerial company it was Williams, as the first moderator of Burning Springs Association, who enjoyed the patriarchal status created by Shubal Stearns in the North Carolina of his boyhood and exploited by Robert Elkin and other subsequent General Union associational moderators in the central Kentucky of his mature years, and we can only imagine how uncomfortably Williams could wear such laurels.[58]

With Daniel Williams packed up and gone east, North District Association did its part to maintain the titular unity of the Kentucky General Union, and Robert Elkin and Jilson Payne settled down uneasily alongside one another as the not-too-clandestine heads of two distinct and opposing political entities within the former Separate Baptist body. It's usually the case in such associational situations for opposing factions to be counterbalanced by a sizable number of neutral members and churches ready to transfer their allegiance to either, as they can be persuaded or as they believe their own interests require, and the key to either faction's acquisition and maintenance of the upper hand lies in "swinging" those churches and members to its own side. Strangely enough, John Augustus Williams gives us the best and most pithy confirmation of the existence of these opportunistic congregations and members in North District, in speaking of Raccoon John's dealings with them in years to come: "Some wavered, or waited; some watched the signs of the times, intending to trim to the popular gale; others were indifferent, or double minded, and not a few loyally resolved to abide by [whatever] the decision of the association [might be]."[59] To put it in even more blunt but quite accurate eastern Kentucky political terms, Payne and Elkin both had to work for this "trash," or unprincipled, vote in order to stay in power, and their ability to manipulate the "trash vote" determined the course of North District's actions just as certainly as the same process must be factored into successful modern political campaigns.

In keeping with his position, Payne now donated more land to Lulbegrud on which to construct a better house of worship, and when the new Lulbegrud meetinghouse was completed it was an impressive sight. It had three doors to represent the Trinity and twelve corners supposedly representing the twelve apostles, making the structure a modified cruciform shape that had often been similarly used in the construction of Anglican parish churches in colonial Virginia. The pulpit was located at the very center of the house. The so-called Lincoln Marriage Temple at Old Fort Harrod State Park in Harrodsburg, Kentucky, enshrining the cabin in which Thomas and Nancy Hanks Lincoln are reputed to have been married, is said to have been designed using Lulbegrud Church as a model.[60]

Payne's cause was boosted considerably the following year, 1804, when David Barrow succeeded Lewis Corban as the pastor of Grassy Lick Church, and then Barrow took the three Elkhorn churches now under his care and effected the transfer of their membership to North District.[61] Though Richard Thomas never moved his own membership to any North District church, he had likewise taken the helm from Leonard Turley at Bald Eagle with a strong hand. In that same year Elkin either lost or gave up his position of associational moderator to Moses Bledsoe, the latter perhaps running for office on the platform of a middle ground between the Payne and Elkin associational factions and maybe even with Elkin's acquiescence. James French, having been elected as Bledsoe's assistant clerk the year before, was now elevated to the associational clerk's position,[62] and he served in the office almost without interruption over the next thirty years. North District was now able to handle the issue of correspondence with the two warring South District factions by the mild political doublethink and newspeak used only by governmental bodies perceiving themselves to be operating from a position of relative strength and security, thus ensuring the creation of the distinct denomination in west central Kentucky still known as the Separate Baptists in Christ,[63] and for a brief time all looked well between Elkhorn and North District Associations.

Payne and French appear to have planned, over time and with Moses Bledsoe's help, to "Regularize" the former North District Separates to Elkhorn standards, but even though Elkhorn still held technically to the precepts of the Philadelphia Confession, its own strict Calvinism as a whole was steadily softening. His own power and authority within North District now on a sure footing, Payne made his objectives obvious in a genially hypocritical, placatory circular letter that he coauthored with Moses Bledsoe for the association in 1804, and in which he very likely gave Daniel Williams one final, parting rebuke as well:

> Labour [*sic*] to live peaceably with your brethren, either in a church or in associational connections—shun that narrow, bigotted [*sic*] principle which prevents some from either thinking, speaking, or hoping well of those who do not believe and practice just according to their views of what is right and Scriptural in matters of religion. Dare we say that we are right in every thing, that we understand and obey every Scripture exactly according to the design of its Divine Author? Such confidence would not become us—shall we then presume to say, that those brethren who may differ with us on some Scripture, are right in nothing? God forbid. Let us rather exercise more of that charity which hopeth all things, &c. [1 Corinthians 13] and remember that the strong is to bear the infirmity of the weak (*We here beg leave to drop a word to our ministering brethren; be careful not to exhibit, either in private or in public, improper expressions or ideas which will go to wound the*

feelings of your brethren at home or abroad, but to cherish that union which we have lately and happily experienced . . .) [emphasis and ellipsis added].[64]

The whole thing was a matter of hammering thesis and antithesis together over time into synthesis, and although the Regular position was expected as a matter of course to come out on top, Baptist political leaders like Jilson Payne and James French could have given both Kierkegaard and Hegel lessons in the theory of the famous dialectic.

But like party theoreticians both then and now, though, neither man seemed to have caught on to the one fact made clear by the South District controversy and the Williams fracas: the synthesis could not take place in stasis, and the dynamics involved always managed to result in casualties. Now it was Elkhorn Association's turn once again to kick at its own traces, and the results were even uglier than anything Daniel Williams had seen from the committeemen sent in 1803 to straighten out his Sycamore Church. Once during this time, a clerical visitor to the Bluegrass asked Raccoon John Smith's second mentor Jacob Creath how the "brethren" were getting along in Kentucky, and Creath replied, "Badly enough; all the preachers out here want to ride Ball." Many years later, Creath's questioner commented to J. H. Spencer that Creath himself was more anxious to "ride Ball" than any other Kentucky minister he had seen.[65] We lament the fact that the meaning of the quip is now lost to time and obscurity, but the old slang term appears to have implied riding roughshod over one's companions to take the lead in a game or a hunt. At any rate, the story makes a perfect introduction to the next General Union imbroglio, because Creath was involved up to his very eyeballs. Kentuckians seem to have a knack both for "riding Ball" and for never doing anything halfway.

John Gano was finally gathered to his fathers on August 9, 1804, and Creath, the most eloquent and popular preacher in Elkhorn Association at the time (Jeremiah Vardeman had not yet transferred his own membership to the prestigious body), succeeded him as pastor at Town Fork. Though Creath was by no means as Calvinistic or as strict in regards to the Philadelphia Confession as Gano had been, he was embraced by a majority of the Lexington congregation, but the idea that a key Elkhorn pastoral position should be assumed by a moderate Calvinist did not go over well at all with associational officers Ambrose Dudley and Gano's son-in-law John Price, or more highly Calvinistic pastors such as Elijah Craig, Joseph Redding, and Richard Thomas. But rather than staging an open confrontation over the strict versus moderate Calvinist issue with either Creath or Town Fork, which they had no definite assurance that they could win, Elkhorn's leadership elected to bide its time and, in the rapidly developing Kentucky Baptist political fashion, wait for some unrelated event to serve as a catalyst both to condemn Creath and to introduce the Calvinism issue secondarily. Creath soon gave them an opportunity, one whose details were sordid enough even within the forgotten context of that day, but which appear to us now as so bizarre and depraved that we might well wonder if any of the parties involved harbored a single spark of conscience at all.

Creath and another member at Town Fork named Thomas Lewis arranged a swap of two young slave girls appraised at different prices. Creath acquired the more expensive slave, and he gave a promissory note to Lewis for the difference in value between the two. Before the note fell due, Creath's young slave died, and when Lewis demanded payment, Creath used the occasion of the unfortunate girl's death to default. The aggrieved Lewis then brought the matter up before the Town Fork congregation, but a majority of the members sided with their pastor on the grounds that "as Mr. Lewis is rich, and Mr. Creath is poor, the latter should be released from paying the note."[66] This in turn left a minority, which seems to have included both Henry and Jimmy Payne, mightily incensed at Creath, but of course not for the reason that we can see so clearly today: rather than condemning both him and Lewis for callously trading in human lives and hearts as if they were mere chattel, they took the position that Creath's default on the debt proved his business dishonesty. Needless to say, almost every preacher and church in Elkhorn Association eventually wound up taking sides either with Lewis and the Town Fork minority or Creath and the church's majority, but just like Jeremiah Vardeman and John Rice had done to John Bailey a couple of years beforehand, they couched their real reasons for partisanship behind the facade of Creath's swindle of Lewis. A comparison might be useful for clarification. In the South District controversy, Vardeman and Rice had effected their associational split on the position that, since John Bailey held Universalist sentiments, and Bailey was also opposed to South District's correspondence with Tate's Creek, it logically followed that all in South District who opposed correspondence with Tate's Creek were either tainted with Bailey's heresy or too weak in the faith to oppose it, and the General Union would be better off without the entire bunch. In the case now under consideration, Jacob Creath was a moderate Calvinist who had succeeded a strict Calvinist as pastor of a large gentry-class church that had heretofore been a bulwark for Philadelphia Confession conservatism. If Creath could be dishonest in a slave trade, to the strict Calvinists of Elkhorn it followed as a matter of course that anyone who supported his doctrinal stance likewise supported his position in the trade difficulty and was similarly morally and financially untrustworthy. The Creath-Lewis controversy provided the Elkhorn "hardshells" with what seemed to them a perfect reference point from which to attack all instances of Elkhorn's departure from strict predestinarian Calvinism, and the moderates pretty much walked into the trap the strict Calvinists had laid without ever realizing what had happened to them.

Though the moderate Calvinists thus jumped into a defensive position that pretty much required a continuous pretense of appeasement to the reactionaries, they had the advantage of the inertia and apathy of most of Elkhorn's rank and file members, and the moderates consistently maintained the majority and the upper hand in the association without even having to resort to a countercampaign to oust Ambrose Dudley and John Price from their offices. The battle dragged on for six whole years, going from bad to worse the entire time. Before he died about the year 1808, Elijah Craig, once a pioneering young Separate Baptist preacher in Virginia under the mentorship of Samuel Harris, James Read, and Shubal Stearns, but afterward having become a very rich man in central Kentucky, the strongest of Calvinists, and incidentally also the inventor of Kentucky's famous bourbon whiskey, wrote and published a pamphlet entitled "A Portrait of Jacob Creath" that undoubtedly would have gotten him challenged to a duel or at least sued for slander if both he and Creath hadn't been professing Christian ministers and therefore above such demeaning actions. Town Fork responded by convening a council to "pass on" rather than investigate Craig's charges; by the same majority that had upheld Creath in Thomas Lewis's grievance against him, the minister was acquitted once again. Fuming with impotent rage by early 1810, Dudley and Price finally made the desperate move of convening their own minority faction to dissolve the association and reconstitute it according to their own preferences, but that didn't pan out for them either. Their minority group took the name of the Licking Association of Particular Baptists, and a good many ministers, including Joseph Redding, Absalom Bainbridge, and Richard Thomas, and some entire churches went with them. But other individual fellowships divided, with opposing Elkhorn and Licking factions often holding services on alternate weekends in the same meetinghouses. As a matter of fact, both Town Fork Church, of which John Price assumed the pastorate, and Ambrose Dudley's Bryan's Station congregation were numbered among these divided houses, and eventually so was Bald Eagle over in North District because of its connection with Thomas. The Payne family even split over the issue to a certain extent. Jilson in North District Association, William in Bracken, and a good many of their brothers and sisters stuck by the moderate Calvinists, while Henry and Jimmy both came out with the reactionaries and joined Licking. Though many American religious historians regard the Kehukee Association in North Carolina, which rejected national Baptist missionary operations in 1826 or 1827, as the true founder of the so-called hyper-Calvinistic Primitive Baptist movement in the United States, it can be argued that Kentucky's Licking Association, established seventeen years earlier, has a more solid claim to the title.[67] Licking Association has long since disbanded due to lack of membership and support, but at least two churches of its number still survive. One is the Dudley faction of Bryan's Station Church, which now operates as a "Landmark Missionary" Baptist church in Lexington. Another, organized about 1812 by Jimmy Payne in present Rowan County and known as Poplar Grove, is still extant as a member, or as members rather since the church itself split further into factions afterward, of eastern Kentucky's "Old Time Baptist family" as well. A photograph of a baptism performed by elders of one faction of this congregation is on the dust jacket of *The Roots of Appalachian Christianity.*

But though Licking Association had split with the General Union and was now operating on its own authority, the body long remained a formidable influence among Kentucky Baptists simply because the rest of the Regular-based associations in the Union felt like they had to measure up to its standards at least to a degree. Over the years, several newer groups, including Long Run, Franklin, North Bend, and Union Associations, and even Elkhorn itself, attempted to correspond with the body; on one occasion William Payne and Henry Toler from Bracken Association were "invited to seats" at a Licking business assembly,[68] but for one reason or another Licking always managed to find fault with every other association around it and the relationships never lasted long. As late as 1829, at the establishment of the Kentucky Baptists' own first institution of higher learning in the state, Georgetown College, they felt compelled to let two influential Licking Association ministers, Thomas P. Dudley and Ryland T. Dillard, and another prominent layman, Thomas Dudley's brother Jeptha, serve on the college's board of trustees.[69] Elkhorn was probably better off in the long run for the division, and it certainly kept its position of prominence within the General Union, but the uneasy off-and-on relationship between itself and a fair number of its correspondent associations with the "hardshell" Licking body left General Union ministers standing on even shakier ground as to what they actually believed and preached. For as long as the General Union remained as Kentucky's state Baptist organization, no Baptist preacher who wanted to be regarded as politically correct could even give a completely straight public answer about his beliefs of the extent of Christ's atonement. David Barrow's own comments in an 1805 North District circular letter, coauthored with Jilson Payne, best illustrate this newly orthodox United Baptist position:

> We are . . . persuaded, brethren, that you will see your duty and your privilege, to guard against those errors in particular, which prevail amongst persons professing godliness.
>
> The first error we shall mention is that baneful and pernicious principle of Antinomianism [a contemporary and somewhat inaccurate synonym for hyper-Calvinism]; that horrid doctrine, which makes God the author of sin, by charging it on his absolute decrees. Thus the advocates for that doctrine turn the grace of God into licentiousness, and thereby attempt to bring the glorious gospel of Jesus Christ into disesteem. The pernicious influence which this doctrine hath upon the mind, too evidently appears in the lives of its advocates.
>
> *Secondly* [emphasis in original]. The Legalists run to the other extreme, by placing the work of the creature improperly, and thereby expect the pardon of sin, and their justification before God, on their own works; which the Scriptures clearly disapprove of, in point of our justification before our great Creator; but our redemption and salvation is only of our Lord and Saviour Jesus Christ; who "trod the winepress alone, and of the people, there was none with him": but the

> discharge of our duty, which we owe, in point of obedience to God, are good works, when done with proper motives, and go to prove our faith in God, and our love to his word and his declarative glory: and a proof of our own faith to the children of God, and the answer of a good conscience to ourselves.[70]

In short, where complex theological issues were concerned, even strong and successful preachers such as Barrow denounced what they *didn't* believe much more forcefully than they articulated that which they *did.* Though the modern Southern Baptist Church has pretty much laid the questions of election and foreknowledge to rest by "Arminianizing" its atonement doctrine in a modified sense, deemphasizing the Great Awakening– and Great Revival–style emotional aspects of the conversion experience, and accepting the innocence of infants, while still strictly maintaining the Calvinistic tenet of eternal perseverance in grace for all those who have accepted Christ, or "once in grace, always in grace," this early Kentucky "iffiness," overlaid with rather than underpinned by bureaucracy, has remained with it in terms of a host of other issues considered risky to the status quo by Southern Baptist Convention higher-ups.[71] As a sad footnote to the Creath-Licking Association controversy, it is doubtful that the poor young girl who was its unwitting catalyst, living and dying virtually as a head of livestock, even got one flower for her grave, much less a tombstone.

But despite the harshness of the Creath-Licking Association story, it's not an indication that Elkhorn's individual ministers had *no* principles or foresight. Most accepted the status quo of their day simply as the right way to live, as so many of us in our present era do for our own mores, and the politics into which they were drawn were, to them, necessary measures to resist the wiles of the Devil. But there were those associational wheelhorses who, in spite of their respective waffling and sometimes strict insistence on Calvinistic orthodoxy, challenged the world around them and endured the persecution that is the common lot of most visionaries for their efforts. Though the Creath controversy reveals perhaps better than any other historical account the essential collective callousness of whites toward blacks in early central Kentucky and the South as a whole, there was a sizable—and to some, frightening—number of Kentucky Baptist ministers that opposed slavery and advocated emancipation with might and main. Included among them were Joshua Carman, Josiah Dodge, and Thomas Whitman, who very nearly split Salem Association by their strong anti-slavery stance in the 1790s; Cornelius Deweese, John Murphy, John H. Owen, and Elijah Davidson, who openly opposed the South's "peculiar institution" in Green River Association from the constitution of its first churches; Donald Holmes, James Thompson, and Joseph Morris, who kept abolitionist fires alight in northeastern Kentucky's Bracken Association; and even a number of prominent preachers right in Elkhorn Association itself, including William Hickman, John Sutton, William Buckley, Carter Tarrant,

George Smith and his younger brother Stokes—and, of all people, that consummate Regular Baptist statesman David Barrow.[72]

Barrow did hold this one aspect of his life in common with Daniel Williams and a good many of his less well-to-do neighbors in Montgomery County: he owned no slaves, and he and his sons operated their farm by the sweat of their own faces. Barrow actually had been a slaveowner back in Virginia and North Carolina, but once he became convinced of the immorality of the institution, not long after he completed a stint in the Revolutionary Army, he manumitted all his blacks without batting an eye. Spencer records an 1809 opinion from Virginia Baptist historian and leader Robert B. Semple that the action "proved [Barrow's] disinterested zeal to do right," but that "it lessened his resources at home for maintaining a large family, it rendered him suspicious among his acquaintances, and probably in both ways limited his usefulness."[73] But for all this, Barrow was no John Brown zealot. As should be obvious already, he knew how to interact diplomatically and successfully with slaveowning members, such as Jilson Payne and James French, and he advocated not the sudden wholesale manumission of all blacks but rather the more moderate and practical course of gradual emancipation[74]—in essence, a nonslavery stance little different from that urged upon the Baptists' rivals, the Methodists, by the group's own written Discipline.[75]

And so it came to pass that, after the Creath controversy had begun to simmer but before it had heated itself up to a full boil, Elkhorn Association found its August 1805 session flooded with indignant church queries demanding that something be done about the abolitionist preaching that was so injuring the sensibilities of slaveowning members. One wonders if perhaps the essential foulness of the entire Creath-Lewis transaction at Town Fork might have prompted the Elkhorn abolitionist minority to add just that much more fire and vitriol to their pulpit pronouncements. Be that as it may, moderator Dudley and clerk Price knew they'd have to do something to pacify the majority, but at the same time they had no desire to indict any individual minister. Dudley himself had questioned the morality of slaveowning in his younger days,[76] and he knew that any emancipationist would naturally be inclined to distance himself from Creath's actions; and of course, distancing other ministers politically from Creath was exactly what Dudley and Price needed to do to hedge their bets in the coming reactionary versus moderate Calvinist battle. So they and their arrangements committee came up with the following resolution: "This Association judges it improper for ministers, churches, or associations to meddle with emancipation from slavery, or any other political subject; and as such we advise ministers and churches to have nothing to do therewith, in their religious capacities."[77] The associational order—for that's exactly what it was, in the old Separate Baptist style to boot, Regular Baptist associational claims of a mere advisory capability notwithstanding—deeply offended George and Stokes Smith, Carter Tarrant, John Sutton, and William Hickman. Sutton and Tarrant both led emancipationist congregations away from the association, and in fact Hickman became so angry that he withdrew of his own accord from the church for about a year. According to Spencer, though, Hickman returned to the fold after becoming convinced that advocacy of emancipation was a hopeless doctrinal stance that could only injure his own character with influential slaveowners and thus impede the Baptists' glorious progress.[78]

Of course, the offensive Elkhorn order couldn't touch David Barrow directly. He and his three Montgomery County churches had transferred their affiliation over to North District the previous fall. At the same North District meeting at which he, Mt. Sterling, Goshen, and Grassy Lick Churches joined the association, though, Barrow was appointed with two other ministers, Mahalaleel Shackle and Thornton Farrow, to serve as a correspondent delegate to Bracken Association's annual meeting scheduled for early September, about three weeks after the Elkhorn gathering.[79] Despite Barrow's wisdom and the esteem in which he was held generally, this Bracken meeting was his political undoing just as certainly as Daniel Williams's had occurred at Town Fork Church two years earlier. Spurred by the Elkhorn decision of the previous month, Bracken's leaders made the excommunication of the group's own emancipationist ministers, Donald Holmes, James Thompson, and Joseph Morris, and their churches the principal business of the session. We do not know exactly how David Barrow incurred the Bracken leadership's ire. As a prudent man who knew how to work with those who did not hold his own opinions on the slavery issue, he may have stood up only to speak a word in defense of the three Bracken emancipationists. Whatever he said, though, he suddenly found himself caught in a position ironically similar to Daniel Williams's at Town Fork in 1803: Bracken leveled five "charges" against him for "meddling with emancipation," and made plans for their own delegation to present them to North District's meeting in October.[80]

And so the poor beleaguered Elkhorn and North District Baptists made plans to break each other's heads for the glory of God once more. Of course, since Barrow had been the lightning rod that had brought "trouble with the brethren" on North District, the whole thing was touted as having been his fault, but it's almost certain that Jilson Payne and James French came to his defense at least at first. He was, after all, the most prominent preacher in Payne's North District associational faction, and any measures taken against him would inevitably weaken the faction's influence. But it didn't help the faction, either, that for this very same October 1805 association its other prominent minister, Richard Thomas, by now strong also in the Elkhorn faction that would organize Licking Association in a few years, had decided on his own that it was time to shake up North District's Arminian tendencies. Under his guidance, Bald Eagle Church had prepared its own query for the association—namely, "What shall be done with preachers who propagate infant purity?"[81] When church pastors encourage their congregations to send such questions to associations, they generally already know the answers they want to receive, and it's a fair bet that Barrow and Payne composed their circular letter quoted earlier, with its denunciation of "that most baneful and pernicious principle" and "horrid doctrine" of "Antinomianism," as a careful first-line defense against Thomas's Calvinistic extremism, the vocal Elkhorn reactionary minority, and the question. Only now Barrow was on trial, too, and the outcome of such an interassociational confrontation, with battles raged on separate fronts of doctrine, polity, and personality, was anybody's guess.

The aged Robert Elkin, relieved of the North District moderator's office the year before, appears to have remained quiet and bided his time through all the interassociational bickering thus far. Ere long, though, the Baptists of Kentucky would be reminded that the old Virginia and Tennessee Separate, protégé of Dutton and Tidence Lane, and veteran of a great many Indian fights in his young manhood, had learned as much or more of the craft of war from the bloody battles of his youth as he had of Christian leadership from the tradition of Shubal Stearns.

The successful associational officer in the political structure once shared by all Kentucky Baptists, and still extant among the "Old Time" Baptists of the Appalachian Mountains, is of a definite and identifiable character type that has remained unchanged with time.

> He always reminded me of the stereotypic union boss—tough, decisive, and unhesitant in the wielding of power, but stealthily political and closely in touch with the wants and values of the people he led. Furthermore, he was capable—or so his [followers] always said—of remarkable kindness and sensitivity. He was, after all, a religious leader, and that required that he exhibit what his followers would perceive as a moral and ethical character.[82]

> He was a man of great shrewdness; he had a strong, but well-governed, temper; was thoughtful and reticent. . . . Usually he carried a point by strategy; for he seldom stormed an obstacle, or openly quarrelled with an enemy. He would quietly plan, while others would almost unconsciously carry out his designs. Sometimes his purposes seemed to ripen of themselves into execution. [ellipsis added][83]

Neither of the foregoing character portraits were written about Robert Elkin. The former is Howard Dorgan's perceptive firsthand impression of the longtime moderator of the Union Association of Old Regular Baptists of eastern Kentucky and southwestern Virginia, Elder John Layne, who died in 1988, and the latter is John Augustus Williams's description, straight from an aged Raccoon John Smith's recollections, of North District clerk and Jilson Payne's Lulbegrud partner James French, who went to his reward in 1835. In their respective characterizations the two writers portray their subjects' public personae excellently. But John Layne, Jilson Payne, and James French all could have taken lessons in the art of associational management from Robert Elkin, and by the time Raccoon John Smith met French and Payne, Elkin had outfoxed and bested them thoroughly not once, but at least twice. Payne and French could be counted on to be gentlemen, after a sort; as has already been evidenced, Elkin was patient and forbearing even to the point of sacrificing the reputation of an ally, but as soon as he perceived a weakness in an adversary he went straight for the jugular. If Payne and French's actions up to this point represented a clumsy and arrogant but basically well-intentioned effort to impress upon North District Association their concept of a more cosmopolitan outlook, Elkin now showed himself entirely conversant in the role of a rural political demagogue, with all the attendant ability to exploit the suspicious tempers and narrow jealousies of the upcountry farm families who viewed him as a leader and mentor.

Considering Elkin's signing of the Terms of General Union and his long-time leadership role in the old South Kentucky and North District Associations, it is somewhat odd that J. H. Spencer's biographical sketch of the old preacher in his *History of Kentucky Baptists* is among the shortest and most nonspecific in the work, and if Elkin genealogical researchers are to be believed, also one of the most inaccurate.[84] Spencer evidently really didn't want to talk about Elkin, and neither did William Vaughan's son and biographer Thomas, though he admitted that young William had known Elkin well.[85] The two chroniclers may have thought that they had good reason to be so close-mouthed. The weight of evidence indicates that Elkin himself pulled North District out of its combined emancipation crisis with Bracken Association and controversy over infant damnation with Richard Thomas; while his methods were neither pleasant nor even moral unless one counts the code that might makes right, he, like John Layne (and of course Paul Pressler, who himself was fond of the expression "going for the jugular") nearly two centuries afterward, was in close touch with what he perceived to be the wants and needs of the people he led, and by hook or crook he delivered what he thought was best for them.[86]

It would be inaccurate to argue that Elkin's moderatorial skills were a simple reflection of the leadership style of Shubal Stearns back in North Carolina, although Stearns's image was the primary foundation of Elkin's persona. Though despotic after the fashion of a stubborn and bossy but loving older brother to all his followers, Stearns likely didn't have a devious or malicious bone in his body, and he was no politician by any stretch of the imagination. He never managed to achieve the subtlety of leadership he needed to guide his Separate Baptists successfully through the juxtaposition of their lightning growth throughout the settled Southeast and the political upheavals associated with the Regulators' War in North Carolina, and ironic as it may seem, it appears that his genuine Christian simplicity was one of the main reasons that his Sandy Creek Association fragmented during the last two years of his life.[87]

Despite Stearns's hesitant and ambiguous refusal to endorse the North Carolina Regulator movement and his consequent loss of face, though, his patriarchal figure became the idealized, archetypal image of the faithful mountain Baptist leader, and the moderators of later Baptist associations descended from Sandy Creek often had to resort to dirty tricks of the type that poor old Stearns himself didn't even know existed in order to maintain and perpetuate that image.

Elkin, who began to preach in the year that the old Carolina evangelist died, was thus a second-generation mini-Stearns of this type, and his political strength lay in the fact that the younger ministers under his own personal patronage idealized him as the local inheritor of Stearns's mantle from Tidence and Dutton Lane. He could talk his followers into doing almost anything for him simply by his own personal assurance that he knew what was best to keep the faith, as it were, and few if any would even see a reason to question either his plans or his motives. Because he laid low and kept quiet when South District Association split and Moses Bledsoe helped Jilson Payne, James French, and David Barrow oust Daniel Williams and construct their own pro-Elkhorn group in North District, so did his followers, because that was what Elkin wanted them to do in order to keep the peace and maintain the General Union as a viable structure. He may even have gone along with Moses Bledsoe's election as North District associational moderator in 1804 for the same reason. But with the Bracken emancipation controversy the old man saw a perfect opportunity to clip the wings both of the fence-straddler Bledsoe and of Payne's entire pro-Elkhorn movement with no risk of retaliation from any of North District's correspondents, and he deftly played his cards with not so much a rejection of, as a complete disregard for, the moral principle upon which David Barrow stood. The only probable difference Elkin made between the Williams and Barrow controversies was the fact that he had likely attempted to get Daniel Williams to go along with him and play, if not, as Jacob Creath phrased it, "ride," ball; once he perceived that Barrow already had a blood spot on him, so to speak, from the September Bracken meeting, he was flatly and unreservedly out for the new Lulbegrud pastor's hide.

Included among Elkin's most trusted vassals at this time were James Haggard, his preaching associate at the "Old Stone Church" on Howard's Creek as well as the pastor at Boone's Creek; James Quesenberry, who had assumed the care of one of Andrew Tribble's churches, known as Unity, after Elkin's break with Tribble several years before; Edward Kindred, an English immigrant who pastored the Howard's Upper Creek Church, where a number of Elkin's own large family belonged, and another congregation at Red Lick[88]; David Chenault, a son-in-law of Tribble, who had been raised up to the ministry under Quesenberry, Haggard, and Elkin at Unity but who now pastored Cane Springs Church in Madison County[89]; and of course Leonard Turley, who had been ousted by Richard Thomas at Bald Eagle but who was now pastor of the East Fork of Flat Creek Church in present Bath County. These men were the principal actors against Barrow and Payne during the Bracken controversy and afterward, though Elkin personally fought in the fray as well, and anyone familiar with Baptist warfare of this type can discern the beginnings of Elkin's strategy by the identical queries that his church and Haggard's at Boone's Creek drew up to present at the 1805 gathering: "How [should] a church . . . deal with a minister that propagates unsound doctrine, or [is] pernicious to good order?"[90] As noted already, pastors that influence their churches to send such queries to associations generally already know what they want in reply, and it can hardly be doubted that Elkin fully intended to get himself in a position where he could deliver the answers personally.

But ironically, when North District convened its 1805 session at Moses Bledsoe's Bethel meetinghouse, it appeared at first that both the Payne faction and even its related emancipationists firmly held the upper hand. According to J. H. Spencer, Bledsoe and his church had come out openly along with Mt. Sterling in support of Barrow and the emancipationist cause.[91] Either because Bledsoe recused himself from reelection as association moderator for this reason, or the distinct possibility that church politics had now gotten a little too intense for him and he had a case of cold feet, Jilson Payne himself, though not an ordained minister, was elected this year as North District's moderator. After the introductory sermon the church delegates were all registered. The Elkin and Thomas questions and several other queries were read and appointed to be put on the bill of arrangements for the second business day, and the visiting associations laid in their letters of correspondence. Then Bracken's messengers presented their five charges against Barrow, which were likewise put on the bill of arrangements. And just before the close of the first day's business Payne appointed his arrangements committee, just as both he himself and David Barrow had been appointed by Elkin and Bledsoe at previous North District sessions.

Here, Payne made a mistake that would prove politically fatal to Barrow. Courtesy and appearances virtually demanded that he put both Elkin and Bledsoe, as former associational moderators, on the committee with him and clerk James French, and for some unknown reason—one wonders if it might have been a whispered suggestion with all the appearance of honesty and innocence, from Elkin himself—he appointed James Quesenberry as a committeeman as well. If Moses Bledsoe was as pliable in the face of political strength as his later behavior leads us to suspect, this meant that Elkin could now dominate the committee and all the suggestions it could form in its report for answering both Bracken Association and the various queries—even as he had once allowed Payne and Barrow to do, for the sake of the Kentucky Baptist union.

And that appears to be exactly what happened when business was resumed after the Sunday worship service. It took three entire days, not counting Sunday preaching, for the association to settle the Bracken difficulty plus the mountain of queries thrown at it in 1805, a circumstance not seen at a southeastern Baptist association since Shubal Stearns himself lost control of the Sandy Creek

Association in 1770[92] and which has rarely occurred at any similar gathering since. The evidence indicates that the session grew so tiresome that many, perhaps even most, of the church delegates packed up and rode home before the business was totally concluded; one of the last actions the association took that year was to "advise the churches to enjoin it on their messengers to associations in [the] future, to attend the same to the close, unless they obtain leave of absence." As it was, those who stayed around became so tired and cranky that they rudely answered requests from four churches for "yearly" or union meetings to "appoint for themselves, and procure preachers the best way they can." Adding to the general ill feeling was someone's insistence that Barrow and Payne's carefully crafted circular letter be amended to denounce emancipationist preaching right along with "antinomianism" and "legalism." Thus, ironically, Barrow's eloquent indictments against doctrinal extremism were followed by a clearly visible interpolation that declared that Barrow himself was "deluded."

But Elkin got his net laid, and laid well. At the outset of the second day's business, the delegates agreed to the proposal that "all questions should be considered lost unless carried by a majority of affirmative votes, *more than equal to the negative votes and the neutrals, counted together*" (emphasis added). While this might appear to have constituted a firm stance on democracy, it wasn't necessarily so; a great many of the eastern mountain "Old Time" Baptist associations that have descended from North District never take votes on any motion unless an objection is rendered to it, requiring considerable bravery on the part of any individual delegate to introduce such an objection to the words of senior ministers on the arrangements committee. In fact, often the easiest way of keeping a "trash vote" secure is to keep it neutral. Assuming that these mountain associations still follow practices they picked up from North District, this 1805 action actually probably strengthened rather than lessened the executive power of the moderator and his committee, and this, of course, was exactly what Elkin wanted—so long as he was supervising all the crucial legislation himself.

The rest of the time on the second business day was taken up with David Barrow's prosecution, conducted by the Bracken delegates, and then his defense, in which he spoke for himself. At the end of all the bickering, the association came to the conclusion that "Brother David Barrow gave cause of hurt to the Bracken Association by meddling with emancipation, and that his explanations and apologies are satisfactory." Though Payne and French were slaveowners, this was very probably the exact result that both men had hoped to achieve; Bracken was satisfied now, and if their pastor would consent to mind his tongue and his pen for just a bit, the entire crisis just might blow over and go away. Then Elkin dropped his bombshell. The two identical queries from Providence and Boone's Creek regarding appropriate responses to ministers who propagated doctrine either unsound or detrimental to "good order" were taken up and answered thus: "That a church in such a case should withdraw all the power she gave such [a] preacher; and two preachers may suspend or stop such [a] preacher from preaching, until he can be tried by a council of five ministers, whose decision in such [a] case ought to be obeyed, until reversed by the association."[93]

Writing seventy-five to eighty years later under the patronage of the mainline Kentucky and Southern Baptist Conventions, J. H. Spencer could afford to condemn this order as rash, evil, "unbaptistic,"[94] and bordering on "Papal arrogance." While claiming that the Elkhorn and North District Associations were guided by good and wise men who well understood the duties, powers, and privileges of associations and were "jealous" for the rights of the churches, but that they'd all blundered simply because they'd been blinded by the general excitement over the slavery question, he could still censure the emancipationists for provoking the controversy in an America that was simply not yet ready to listen to them.[95] He deals with the 1845 break of the Southern Baptist Convention from American or Northern Baptists, which was effected to maintain the rights of southern missionaries to take their slaves with them on their missionary journeys, essentially with the same complacent philosophy,[96] and his outlook was typical for nineteenth-century Kentucky. Kentuckians collectively remained neither fish nor fowl on the slavery issue; even in the strife-ridden presidential election of 1860, the state was carried neither by Lincoln, Douglas, nor its own John C. Breckenridge, but by John Bell of the Constitutional Union Party, the one candidate who absolutely refused to address the question of slavery in any way whatsoever.[97]

But what Robert Elkin was doing at this volatile 1805 North District session actually had nothing to do with the emancipation controversy in and of itself, except as a means to an end. Spencer either overlooked or chose to ignore the important fact that the committee's 1805 answer on ministerial discipline contained two distinct, conflicting, and possibly mutually exclusive elements. The first part of the decision, that churches should revoke the ordained authority of troublesome ministers, was stock Regular Baptist policy that emphasized the power of the local congregation over the power of the association, and it had to have come from Jilson Payne and James French. The second, implementing the control of a presbytery of elders over and beyond the actions that an individual church might take against a rogue preacher, harked back to the autocratic associational management style of Shubal Stearns, and it was in fact identical to a resolution that the old South Kentucky Association had adopted under Elkin's guidance when it was first organized in 1787.[98] It can hardly be doubted that Elkin and James Quesenberry not only provided this part of the answer, but even insisted on its being presented to the delegates at large. If Moses Bledsoe was caught as firmly between a rock and a hard place at this association as his subsequent behavior indicates, it is doubtful that he would have offered a differing opinion of his own. So the committee's patchwork Regular-Separate recommendation was accepted, Elkin got his old South Kentucky order back on the North District books, and with it he proceeded to hoodwink Richard Thomas, Jilson Payne, James French, and David Barrow all. And neither Elkhorn nor any other Regular-based association in the General Union could do a thing about it.

Richard Thomas's heartless query asking North District what to do about ministers who preached "infant purity" was among the leading items on the final day of business. Though the question might have and very probably did inspire an extremely hot debate that contributed to the delegates' all-around weariness and touchiness by the time they were asked to appoint preachers for union meetings, the arrangements committee's decision carried the day once more: "*If they be preachers in North District Association* [emphasis added], we refer you to the advice given Providence and Boone's Creek Churches, respecting preachers."[99] Of course, Thomas would have been completely satisfied with Payne and French's portion of the answer by itself. No doubt he felt that all churches should revoke authority from ministers who didn't go along with the Regulars' Philadelphia Confession even down to its most cruel implied points, and with such an associational order he could have proceeded happily to cite any North District church that didn't comply with it at any subsequent associational meeting he chose. He may even have thought that, over time and by degrees, he just might be able to persuade North District to adopt strict Calvinist dogma completely. But Elkin and Quesenberry's part of the order hamstrung him. Besides being completely "unbaptistic," as Spencer phrased it, in terms of Regular Baptist usages, the ruling represented a direct challenge from Elkin. To carry out all the measure's provisions successfully and stop one minister from speaking a hopeful word in behalf of the little ones, Thomas would need to find at least four other North District preachers who believed in infant damnation, and among ex–Separate Baptists who were accustomed to "dry-christening" infants just like old Stearns did, such men could be expected to be in very short supply in this one association. In essence, Elkin seemed to be saying, Brother Thomas, we'll word our answer like this for the sake of the peace the General Union; so now, if you can find two North District ministers who are willing to go along with you far enough to silence another for preaching infant purity, and then find three more who are willing to put your victim on trial for it, you're welcome to try your luck. The presbytery system in North District worked only when an old hand like Elkin himself managed it, and there's no evidence that Thomas ever succeeded in his endeavor. Not a single minister in North District was ever censured for upholding the innocence of infants, and in fact most influential members of Payne's faction were probably as opposed to Thomas's stance as was Elkin's group. Disgusted, Thomas finally convinced perhaps half of his Bald Eagle members that North District Association was no fit place for a good Christian, and he pulled this faction away to join Licking Association a couple of years after the hyper-Calvinist body was organized.[100] For all that, a cursory reading of this blunt order as it appears in the 1805 North District minute records is enough to give one an extremely uneasy pause.

But to return to the actions of the association, when Elkin did see fit to implement the provisions of the presbytery system, the results were lethal. Almost a year passed before his true intentions for David Barrow became generally known. But at some point during that twelvemonth, a council of five ministers consisting of James Quesenberry, James Haggard, Leonard Turley, a bewildered Moses Bledsoe (who appears by now completely to have turned his coat on the emancipation issue), and of course Elkin himself began "dealing with Brother David Barrow for preaching the doctrine of emancipation to the hurt and injury of the feelings of the brotherhood." The Elkin-led men then formally presented this report to the 1806 association meeting, arguing that since he "manifest[ed] no disposition to alter his manner of preaching," he should be expelled from his seat in the association and arraigned at his home church at Mt. Sterling. If Payne and French, who had again been elected to their respective offices, had not already recognized the backcountry Separate Baptist political web that Elkin had spun around them, they certainly perceived it now, and there was nothing that Payne could do but allow the committee's demand to come to a vote. Elkin had made sure of all the legalities twelve months beforehand. The motion passed, and Elkin, Bledsoe, Turley, Edward Kindred, an undoubtedly reluctant James French, and Bledsoe's fellow Bethel Church member and supporter Thomas Moseley were appointed to visit Mt. Sterling and bring the church into line. Only two congregations offered so much as a word of protest over what had occurred a year before: Goshen and Strode's Station Churches both asked for an explanation of the Scriptural authority for the actions that the association had taken in 1805, and these were summarily dismissed, in the former case possibly because Barrow was pastor at Goshen and had written that church's query himself.[101] Regardless, though, Scripture couldn't be permitted to get in the way of the politics necessary to keep peace and order among the faithful.

So David Barrow left North District Association never to return, and he took Mt. Sterling Church with him. Mahalaleel Shackle, who had been with Barrow at the fateful Bracken meeting that had initiated the North District emancipation disaster, left as well,[102] and the two joined forces with the ousted Bracken and Elkhorn emancipationists to form their own little group, called the "Baptized Licking-Locust Association, Friends to Humanity."[103] The small emancipationist association had member churches across Kentucky from Mason to Hardin County, and interestingly its membership included Abraham Lincoln's father Thomas. The group fragmented after Barrow's death in 1819, but an offshoot, the Kentucky Abolition Society, of which Barrow served as president for several years, endured in spite of the antipathy of slaveowners.[104] But Barrow's departure from North District didn't mean that all of his members at Mt. Sterling stayed true to his cause; among the more notable defectors back to the bosom of North District from Mt. Sterling were John and Elizabeth Coons, who took their memberships to Moses Bledsoe's Spencer Creek congregation on Elizabeth's father's eastern Montgomery County land grant.[105]

Robert Elkin was once again elected as moderator of North District in 1807, and was now once again in a position of undisputed strength. Bad feelings of the past two years' activities must have lingered on among even his own most devoted followers, though, and perhaps he felt that he could now show a bit of magnanimity and offer a sop to his and everyone else's consciences. At the 1807 session James Quesenberry made a motion that the association "reconsider the whole of the business" surrounding Barrow, and Elkin allowed the resulting lengthy discussion, pro and con, to take place. Then James French moved that the association repeal the entire series of actions it had taken against Barrow in 1805 and 1806, including the "unbaptistic" South Kentucky presbytery method of silencing "disorderly" ministers that Elkin and Quesenberry themselves had implemented. This was an extremely unusual action in that associational clerks rarely attempt, even nowadays, to introduce motions to the floor on their own; but it was seconded and passed, and from all appearances North District completely annulled two years of its work.[106] Moses Bledsoe was even returned to the moderator's office the next year, 1808. But the idea of North District's reconciliation with Barrow proved to be hollow, as the principals in the case against him may have known all along. Barrow, his pride hurt more deeply than anyone could have known except Daniel Williams or anyone else who has ever personally endured such a Baptist associational attack, had already gotten his little emancipation group together, and though North District had never taken Mt. Sterling Church's name off its records, he now refused to "set" communion for any visiting members of North District churches. And so Mt. Sterling's final mention in North District's records until after Barrow's death was a completely ineffective but venomous barb tailored to save the association's and its leadership's face, but fooling no one: "This association withdraws from the church at Mt. Sterling, for denying to the members of the churches which compose this association, the privilege to commemorate with [the] said church, the death of our Lord."[107]

Perhaps fittingly, Moses Bledsoe never quite finished that one year's term of office. He fell ill and died sometime between the last of February and the first of October 1809, and the association's minutes for that year, the last North District session to be held in October before the group changed its annual meeting date to August, carry a brief memorial tribute. It may have been written at the suggestion of Robert Elkin himself, who, as might be expected, had once again been restored to his position of moderator, patriarch, and paragon of North District's and the Kentucky Baptists' noble traditions.[108]

While Jilson Payne and his pro-Elkhorn faction was still an integral part of North District's makeup and indeed still a necessary element to the stability of the fellowship between Elkhorn and North District Associations, his influence had definitely taken a setback. After David Barrow left the association, Bledsoe served as pastor at Lulbegrud in addition to his two other charges at Spencer Creek and Bethel until his death, and during this same time Grassy

Lick appears to have had a succession of interim pastors including Bledsoe and, strangely enough, both Ambrose Dudley and Jacob Creath from Elkhorn.[109] Of course Dudley and the dour Richard Thomas at Bald Eagle were at this same juncture planning their abortive Elkhorn takeover, so it's doubtful that either man was of as much help to Payne as he could wish, and for the time being Goshen appeared lost to the Elkin faction. Despite the church's questioning of the Scriptural authority behind North District's 1805 orders, after Barrow left, its membership elected Elkin's longtime ally Edward Kindred as pastor, and he maintained the office until his old age.[110]

In associational affairs between 1809 and 1810, Elkin called on Payne to serve on the yearly arrangements committee and in other minor appointments, such as the preparation of letters to sister associations, but he always made sure that plenty of his own allies, such as Kindred, Quesenberry, Chenault, and Isaac Crutcher, served on the arrangements committee and in other major functions as well. Leonard Turley, having moved his membership to Long Branch Church from East Fork, seems to have kept his feud with Bald Eagle and Richard Thomas running hot until 1813, most likely with Elkin's support. Knowing full well how difficult it would be for Bald Eagle to drum up support in the association on its own, the old moderator parried complaints against Long Branch from Thomas's congregation with the advice that they should "call on helps from different churches to assist them in their difficulties, so that each church may have an equal number of helps, and not less than six for each church—the helps to be chosen by the churches to whom Bald Eagle and Long Branch Churches may apply." Though not allowing Turley to serve on the arrangements committee, Elkin frequently appointed him as a delegate to visit corresponding associations. Despite the looming loss of Bald Eagle to Licking Association, though, it can be inferred that Payne kept his political strength at least within the former Elkhorn churches that had joined North District after 1802 as well as with Bledsoe's former pastorates at Spencer Creek and Bethel. The Bethel congregation was now led by Francis Taylor and Spencer Creek by Joseph Rice,[111] but Thomas Moseley at Bethel and especially John Coons, after he moved his membership from Mt. Sterling to Spencer Creek, were probably Payne's main contacts within these two congregations. Besides North District and Elkhorn allies, his brother William, still in Bracken Association, could be counted on to represent his interests in terms of relations between Bracken and North District as well.

As later events suggest, it is possible that Robert Elkin even tried to place one of his allies in the Lulbegrud pulpit after Bledsoe's death, but in the wake of the 1810 Elkhorn-Licking schism both Lulbegrud and Grassy Lick succeeded in acquiring Jeremiah Vardeman, who had just moved north to Elkhorn territory, as pastor. Vardeman had transferred his membership from his little pro-Union South District faction to the David's Fork Church in Fayette County, which had been abandoned by Ambrose Dudley when the older minister had split Elkhorn, and also took over the reins of a large faction of Dudley's own home church at Bryan's Station that had elected to remain with the pro-Creath Elkhorn group.[112] These two Elkhorn and two North District churches were able to get together and provide Vardeman with the early Kentucky equivalent of a salaried pastorate, that is, a farm for which they jointly proposed to pay off the debt. It should be remembered that this was the very same season at which Vardeman first cultivated John Smith's clientage when the big preacher stopped by to visit Thomas Hansford at the 1810 session of Cumberland River Association, as well as roughly the same period in which he seems to have established friendship with David Chenault sufficiently to join with him in the temporary pulpit supply of Daniel Williams's old Sycamore Church. Thus with both Chenault and Vardeman's blessings, young William Vaughan, who had been baptized by James Quesenberry and was thus grouped right along with Chenault among the Elkin partisans, got to preach for Payne at a house meeting and then joined Sycamore and was chosen for the pastorate before he was even ordained.[113] Vardeman had become a real General Union factotum by now, with both great and small depending on his favors, and such a star evangelist could only add to Lulbegrud's, Grassy Lick's, and the entire Payne faction's prestige.

This may have been at least part of the reason that, in 1811, Payne recaptured the North District moderator's position for one term along with Thomas Moseley as clerk. Another factor, though, could have been that the association meeting that year was held at Isaac Crutcher's Hopewell Church in Woodford County, a considerable distance west of most of North District's other churches, and the group's minutes that year take note of the fact that several possibly pro-Elkin churches were unable to send delegates. Many of the churches enrolled were represented by only two delegates and a few merely by one,[114] and under the circumstances Payne may have achieved a plurality of votes much more easily than would have been possible if the meeting had been held further east.

But by this time, things had once again begun to look up for both Payne and the Kentucky Baptist cause generally as well. At around this same period North District and the other General Union associations, in spite of all the Spirit-quenching machinations they had undertaken against one another, began to experience a renewal of the Great Revival. If a bit of cynicism is excusable, we may wonder if the Great Earthquake of December 1811, which was so powerful that it actually caused the Mississippi River near New Madrid Bend to flow backward for several hours, created Reelfoot Lake in the western end of Kentucky, and was felt over almost the entire state, had more to do with the season of increased spirituality than the Kentucky Baptists' clean living. Closer home to Payne, his wife Dulcinea finally conceived at the age of thirty-nine and was delivered of a healthy baby girl on February 5, 1812. Jilson proudly named his new daughter Ann Holland Payne after her paternal grandmother,[115] and we might assert with a fair amount of confidence that if he and Dulcinea had ever been disposed to be even halfway tolerant of Richard Thomas's harsh views on infant damnation, their outlook was suddenly and permanently changed. Certainly the Paynes' new pastor Vardeman was outspokenly opposed to the doctrine.[116] Though the United States plunged itself into war with Great Britain when little Ann was only four months old, Jilson, at age forty-five, was now legally exempted from commanding the local militia in the disastrous first Canadian campaigns. Besides his undoubted relief for his wife's and daughter's sake as well as his own, the exemption carried an additional side benefit: though Robert Elkin was elected as North District moderator once again in 1812, along with James French as clerk at Elkin's church on Howard's Creek in Clark County, this election proved to be the old man's last. Payne recaptured the office at the 1813 North District session at Grassy Lick in Montgomery County,[117] and circumstances appear to have allowed him to hold onto it for perhaps three years or so.

The year of Payne's retaking of the North District moderator's chair and the two following it continued to be propitious for Kentucky Baptists in general. Silas Noel of the newly organized Franklin Association began a small Baptist newspaper called *The Gospel Herald,* in which he advocated the formation of an annual "General Meeting of Correspondence" in Kentucky not unlike the old Baptist General Committee in Virginia.[118] Had the Kentucky Baptists established this embryonic form of a state convention at the time of the formation of the General Union in 1801, they might have avoided a great deal of the trouble that had plagued them for nearly a decade and a half, although it's difficult to say just how much support former Separates would have gotten in the checks and balances of such a structure. The local association was still the highest formal organization—and its relationships with its neighboring correspondent groups the only denominational politics—that most American Baptists knew. But times were once again changing, and within a year a great many East Coast associations came together and created the first national Baptist body, called the Triennial Convention, for the purpose of establishing and maintaining foreign missions. Former Congregational missionary Luther Rice, who had been proselytized to the Baptist cause in Serampore, India, along with Adoniram Judson by British Baptist missionary William Carey, was the body's first missions agent, and his initial visit to Kentucky occurred in the year Raccoon John returned to the state from Alabama. According to Rice's own journal, Jeremiah Vardeman and Grassy Lick Church clerk James Mason were among the missionary's most important central Kentucky contacts. Though Rice didn't arrive in the Bluegrass until after North District Association had met in the summer of 1815, Vardeman and Mason alternately lodged him and acquainted him with the best Baptist prospects in the state, including the Tate's Creek meeting where Raccoon John preached. The two even influenced Montgomery County judge David Trimble to dismiss court so Rice could preach and collect missionary money in the courthouse at Mt. Sterling, and Mason loaned the agent a fresh horse so he and James Welch could go visit Daniel Williams and the new Burning Springs Association over in the eastern hinterlands.[119]

All told, Vardeman's and Mason's relationship with Rice indicates that Baptist missions were Jilson Payne's next pet project for North District Association's improvement—not necessarily because he himself, as North District moderator, influenced the two to cultivate the relationship with Rice, but rather because Vardeman encouraged both Payne's and Mason's interest instead. Certainly it was better than trying, as Payne had years earlier, to spread the Regulars' Philadelphia Confession through the churches of the body. And it did indeed appear to be an altruistic cause, although it brought a concern with the relationship of money to salvation and godliness that was completely new, and in many cases extremely repugnant, to Baptists of the Stearns tradition. Shubal Stearns himself had come from New England to North Carolina without either the financial backing of any missionary society or a salary from his congregation; his disciples had brought the movement he initiated into South Carolina, Georgia, Virginia, Tennessee, and Kentucky as they settled these areas, in the exact same manner, neither expecting nor demanding wages for their efforts; and though many had eventually embraced Regular Baptist doctrines and customs in the initial organizations of associations in their respective states, a great number of both ministers and lay members still took Paul's injunction that the love of money is the root of all evil and Peter's warning to ministers not to be greedy after filthy lucre extremely literally. Thus Rice's, the other missionary agents', and the Triennial Convention's bulletins' emphases on subscriptions, budgets, and quotas, coupled with harangues when collections were not large enough and winking hints to pastors that they could find themselves more comfortably supported by stressing missions to their congregations, left a bitter taste in rural Baptist mouths that the altruism of supporting Adoniram Judson's Burmese mission did not wash out for many years. J. H. Spencer was inclined to blame the slow and hesitant growth of the missionary cause in Kentucky on what he called hyper-Calvinism,[120] and it is true that both Licking Association and later Primitive Baptists who insisted on following Calvinistic doctrine out to its logical conclusion did indeed spurn missionary efforts for the reasons Spencer gave. But in early Kentucky, more preachers and laypersons ultimately rejected Triennial Convention appeals simply because of the coldness, impersonality, appearance of facade, concentration on finance, and the specter of a faraway monolithic organization that could assess contributions from participant churches and associations like a tax collector's office that the missionary cause brought to the Baptist ministry. From the Regular Baptist side, John Taylor penned his famous (or infamous) pamphlet *Thoughts on Missions* with these exact fears in mind rather than any Calvinistic fatalism,[121] and for the Separates' part the newly reorganized South Kentucky Association, an Arminian Baptist organization if ever there was one, rejected Triennial Convention missionary appeals on identical grounds.[122] Thus it shouldn't really be surprising that Vardeman, Mason, and essentially moderator Payne's entire pro-Elkhorn faction provided virtually every ounce of support that the Triennial Convention's program ever received within North District Association.

But right at this very juncture occurred the bizarre matter addressed at the end of the previous chapter and the beginning of this one, the log that split the church, and only now can we begin to appreciate it as more than the humorous freak event, supposedly based within a context of frontier high spirits and just a bit of ignorance, on which the legend in the Prewitt Pike community has endured. There's no way that Lulbegrud could have split as it did—over a tree trunk no less, with the two warring halves of the congregation trying to worship on opposite ends of the meetinghouse—in complete independence. The anti-Payne faction couldn't have existed without a pastor or ministerial leader of its own; at that time Lulbegrud had no member preachers, only Vardeman from Elkhorn's David's Fork Church, and even if another minister had belonged directly to Lulbegrud itself he couldn't have challenged Vardeman without a great deal of political backing from some influential outside source. Equally impossible is the idea that Payne had no way of making amends to the church for having the tree cut, either in the form of a spoken or written apology, a monetary settlement, or both, unless it was in the interest of some personage of equal or greater authority to keep the faction opposing him stirred up. Robert Elkin's position of political strength in North District, and his propensity to indulge in politics of this sort, have already been demonstrated. Thus, based on the entire history of both Elkin's and Payne's activities in North District up to the time of the cutting of the tree, the following hypothesis suggests itself as the most plausible analysis of the fracas.

Although David Barrow, Moses Bledsoe, and Jeremiah Vardeman had baptized a great number of new converts at Lulbegrud who would have looked unquestioningly to Payne as their leader and mentor, just as the three ministers themselves did, there was still a sizable contingent of old-line Separates at the church who had been members since Daniel Williams's tenure as pastor. Though they might have remained silent for years, cowed by their Mt. Pleasant neighbor's wealth, education, and position in the secular community, they couldn't have been entirely happy with either the direction Payne had taken the church since he had moved his membership there from Mt. Sterling in 1803, or the methods he used to enforce his wishes. If such a dissatisfied contingent did exist at Lulbegrud, it was only a matter of time before one or more of its members would have complained to Robert Elkin about the matter, perhaps with a bitter observation that the old Separate leader should have given more support to Daniel Williams when he had had the opportunity; and if, or more likely when, this happened, Elkin would have acknowledged the rightness of Williams's cause, professed a bit of repentance, and offered to do something for the dissatisfied faction in recompense. All they'd have to do was "get something" on Jilson Payne, use it as a pretext to withdraw en masse from fellowship with Payne and anyone who opted to stand with him, and Elkin himself could take care of the rest, even to supplying the disgruntled party with a pastor. There is now no way we can know who this minister was, though Edward Kindred and Thomas Boone (who had been ordained at Log Lick

Church in 1815 by Kindred and others, and who had succeeded the aging Kindred as pastor at Goshen at just about this time)[123] were both likely candidates. Boone's relative youth, coupled with his subsequent relationship to Lulbegrud, makes him the most probable of the two. But in any case, Elkin himself had nothing to lose and everything to gain. Neither Payne nor James French would be eligible to serve as associational officers as long as Lulbegrud Church remained in disorder, and no matter who the new association moderator turned out to be, he wouldn't dare accept the Payne faction over the anti-Payne group and risk the Elkin faction's instigating an association-wide split such as had happened in South District in 1803. If Elkin could get himself or at least one of his loyal lieutenants elected as association moderator, he might eventually amass sufficient political strength to favor the anti-Payne faction of the church over Payne's group, and the pro-Elkhorn faction would be out in the cold altogether, again with nothing that any of the correspondent associations could do about it. Elkin was in his early seventies now, though, and it might have seemed good to him to try to get a younger but trustworthy man into the office instead, one through whom he could continue to work without all the direct personal hassles associated with the moderator's position; but regardless, even if neither faction at Lulbegrud were accepted and both their letters were tabled, at least both Payne and French would be completely out of power as long as Elkin himself managed to keep the difficulty alive.

This latter case was, most likely, what happened. As noted, in 1816 Lulbegrud's two letters were tabled at the association, and Payne and French both lost their offices. Payne's ally at Bethel, Thomas Moseley, and Cane Springs Church member Nathan Lipscomb were elected to replace them as moderator and clerk, respectively. The dirty little Lulbegrud war raged on through the twelvemonth, Vardeman finally embarrassedly relinquished his Lulbegrud and Grassy Lick pastorates, and when North District dropped its involvement with the national Baptist missions board in 1817 after only one year, it was the Elkin-led ex-Separates who were responsible for the action. At the 1817 association meeting, David Chenault, noted already as a pro-Elkin preacher of long standing first at Unity and then at Cane Springs, replaced Moseley after the latter's brief, uneasy tenure as moderator of the association, and no less than seven Elkin congregations, Howard's Creek (still pastored by Elkin himself), Howard's Upper Creek (led by Edward Kindred), Unity and Friendship (James Quesenberry), Goshen and Log Lick (Kindred and Thomas Boone working together), and Mt. Tabor (pastored by Thomas White, a former member of the "Log Meetinghouse on Tate's Creek" who had spent some time with the reorganized South Kentucky Separate Baptist Association before reuniting with the General Union and transferring to North District), sent queries objecting to North District's connection with the Triennial Convention. Their stance prevailed in spite of an eloquent pro-missions appeal by temporary associational clerk James Mason in his circular letter for that year.[124]

The association's new moderator, David Chenault, was a tall, heavily built

Madison County farmer a little older than Jeremiah Vardeman, and though having little use either for Jilson Payne's pro-Elkhorn faction or its projects, like Vardeman he was good-natured and affable. His had married Andrew Tribble's daughter Nancy not long before Tribble had split the old South Kentucky Association to form the Tate's Creek group, but instead of joining his father-in-law in Tate's Creek Association he had elected to remain with the Elkin-led body instead. Thus, in the North District mores of the day, his preaching credentials were impeccable. John Augustus Williams was to hint much later that he was a Calvinist,[125] and J. H. Spencer, who actually used Williams as a source of information for him, described him as a hyper-Calvinist,[126] but in fact neither writer portrayed Chenault accurately. His church, Cane Springs, had been organized from the older Unity congregation in August 1803 by Elkin's right-hand men James Haggard and James Quesenberry on exactly three articles of faith: "on believing that the word of God contained in the Old and New Testament[s] is the only infallible rule of faith and practice, on believing in the final preciance [perseverance] of the saints through grace to glory, and on believing in baptism by immersion." In short, it was a typical old-style Separate Baptist church in the Stearns tradition maintained by Elkin, a footwashing church even, and it was led by a typical old-style preacher in the same Separate tradition. Chenault himself was vociferously opposed to any form of salaried ministry, often stating that "a man who preaches for money is a gospel peddler" and that "[the] gospel's as free as the water that runs in the branch." Even so, he often ended this latter statement in a mild jest: "but if you've got any poor calves or colts, run 'em down to my farm."[127] William Vaughan remembered Chenault's propensity to crack jokes and tell humorous stories not unlike Raccoon John's and his own. Once, on meeting Chenault, Vaughan had asked him what had become of another young minister of doubtful competence who had begun trying to preach at about the same time as had Vaughan himself and with whom he had "shared the stand" often in his salad days. Chenault replied that the brother in question had never managed to convince a church to ordain him, and that at last report he had moved somewhere on the Three Forks of the Kentucky River in present Lee County, was living in a little hut, and that he still persisted in his blundering efforts at preaching. Whenever the would-be exhorter could gather a crowd willing to tolerate him, he almost invariably became angry at his hearers' lack of interest and enthusiasm, and he would pause his discourse, stamp his foot, and storm: "Why don't you cry? You are the hardest-hearted sinners I ever saw to sit and listen to such preaching as mine and not cry! Cry, I tell you!"[128]

If Chenault was human enough to appreciate a joke, he was human enough to reveal a few humorous shortcomings of his own as well. Both Spencer and Vaughan comment on the fact that Chenault's ministerial zeal could come and go capriciously, depending mostly on how preoccupied he was at any given time with matters relating to his farm and his little local office of "squire," or community justice of the peace.[129] Too, sometimes he could speak as quickly as he thought, and all too often, quicker. Once, at an association meeting when he had been particularly inspired and excited, he rose from his seat and began to exhort the congregation in classic Stearns style until his face glowed, gesticulating vehemently with muscular arms that, in Vaughan's memory, were "as thick as a man's thigh." Chenault concluded his emotional testimony with the words, "Brethren, I have a feeling on me! Brethren, I have a feeling on me! Lord, help us poor Baptists!" A Methodist preacher in attendance immediately piped up in response, "Amen, for you need it!" Chenault's sermon thus ended with a particularly Spirit-quenching titter not only from the Methodist's friends but the entire congregation, and the embarrassed preacher quickly took his seat and shut up.[130]

But David Chenault proved himself able to treat Payne and his faction with a lot more kindness and forbearance probably than his old mentor Elkin would have liked. Instead of riding hard on Payne, French, and Lulbegrud Church when he assumed the moderatorship of North District Association in 1817, he at least went through the motions of trying to help the church establish peace and harmony once again. As noted at the end of the last chapter, he arranged for a committee consisting of one delegate from each church in the association to meet at Lulbegrud to try to come up with some response that would be satisfactory to both parties, and in spite of his mentor Elkin's probable involvement in the case he seems to have expected that, sooner or later, something would happen to cause the church to reconcile. All in all, it might be said that Chenault was simply a country preacher, knew it, was satisfied with his lot, and had no further ambitions to power: from the record of his administration provided in North District's minutes he seems never to have paid many visits as a correspondent delegate to the larger Regular-connected downstate associations, but rather exhibited a decided preference to visit and assist the smaller hill country satellite groups to the south and east of North District territory. The task of rubbing elbows with the large and genteel Bluegrass bodies he would leave to others, often to North District's Payne-based Regular connections.[131]

However, the ancient Payne-Elkin Regular-Separate tension had done its work all too well through the years, and now not only was Payne completely out of power, he was almost out of ministers as well. He'd lost David Barrow long ago, and then Richard Thomas of that high Calvinist's own accord not long after Moses Bledsoe had died. Jeremiah Vardeman was nursing his bruised ego back in the safety of Elkhorn Association, and William Vaughan had already packed up from Sycamore and gone northeast to Bracken territory, where Payne's brother William still preached. Since there's a good possibility that Vaughan's own relationship with Vardeman made Elkin regard him as a defector, it really wasn't advisable for him to stick around North District even if he couldn't provide the excuse of better financial support in Bracken—not that his taking pay for preaching was something either Chenault or Elkin would have condoned any more than the members at Sycamore had, anyway. During this period Joseph Rice at Spencer Creek and Francis Taylor at Bethel, likewise in a precarious position from their connection with Thomas Moseley, John Coons, and the Payne faction after Moses Bledsoe's death, appear to have done the same thing, either moving to other parts of the state or quitting Kentucky and its so-called United Baptists altogether. All told, Payne was trying to lead at least five pastorless churches in his pro-Elkhorn group: Lulbegrud itself, Grassy Lick, Spencer Creek, Bethel, and the little faction of Bald Eagle still with North District. Elkin had to have been working hard to convince all of them to accept pastors from his own cadre of followers, perhaps even with Chenault's discreet help, and no other preacher in his right mind either in North District or any association neighboring it would have dared come to try to help Payne fill the gap.

There was, however, that young fellow from somewhere up among the coons and 'peter caves on the upper Cumberland, Brother Vardeman's young friend who had cut such a dash at Tate's Creek two summers before and whom Brother Creath had brought to preach at that embarrassing association meeting of a year ago at which Lulbegrud had been declared in disorder. He seemed to be a good orthodox Calvinist, and from his conversation it appeared that he was trying to raise himself out of that same rustic backcountry Baptist mindset that Robert Elkin, and now David Chenault, too, so stubbornly insisted on maintaining in North District. Brother Vardeman had been grooming him for some years now, and evidently Brother Creath thought that the young man was worth the effort as well. If a rank outsider with such intelligence and qualifications as he possessed could be persuaded to move to Montgomery County and pastor Lulbegrud and some of the others, both parties at Lulbegrud might agree to unite under his care, and if they did, Payne's faction still had a fighting chance of reclaiming its ascendancy. Since, in the wake of the ongoing log controversy, Payne's own political weight in the association had been compromised so seriously, the young man might even prove useful as a figurehead leader for the pro-Elkhorn faction, with Payne still pulling the strings behind the scenes. His name, as clerk Nathan Lipscomb had recorded it, was Smith.

Thus stand the real circumstances of Raccoon John Smith's move from the Little South Fork to Montgomery County. He came not as both Williams and Cochran would have us believe, simply a young preacher filling four vacant pulpits as a mere matter of course, and neither as they indicate a man so entirely troubled with questions of the compatibility of the Philadelphia Confession with the pure Gospel Way. He pulled up stakes from the hills to fill a gap in the political structure of North District Association that only a bright and ambitious young man such as he could have done, and as the puppet leader of the group's Jilson Payne pro-Elkhorn faction he did his work well. That he was extremely close to Jilson Payne, even to the point of that oddly passionate intellectual attachment to men of culture and learning that was such a crucial factor in his personality, has not been documented, but it can hardly be doubted;

Payne's library alone would have guaranteed Raccoon John's utter adoration, and we can only imagine how many hours his indulgent new patron allowed him to spend browsing Mt. Pleasant's bookshelves. Under Payne's leadership four of the bereft churches, Lulbegrud, Grassy Lick, Spencer Creek, and Bethel, installed him as pastor and bought him a farm with the agreement to help him pay for it, just like the arrangement in which Lulbegrud and Grassy Lick had participated with David's Fork and Bryan's Station in Elkhorn Association for Vardeman's benefit. Over the course of the next decade Raccoon John restored at least some of Payne's projects successfully. Even before David Barrow died in 1819, John began to cultivate a relationship with the ousted Mt. Sterling Church, and by 1823 he had managed to persuade the congregation to return to the North District fold. While he himself was occupied every weekend with pastoring until 1826, he and Payne got his brother (and now, his own client in the same relationship he had known with Vardeman, Creath, and Payne alike) Jonathan installed as the pastor of the faction at Bald Eagle attempting to maintain its relationship with North District. Both Raccoon John and Jonathan worked hard at persuading the pro-Licking party to dump Richard Thomas altogether and unite with the moderate faction under Jonathan's pastorate as well. Perhaps most importantly, Raccoon John finally brought the entire Payne group back to political prominence by being elected as moderator of North District Association in 1824, and he served in the office capably for two years until politics as usual gave the position back to David Chenault.

Now, all this doesn't mean that Raccoon John carried out his duties with no introspection whatsoever. Williams, Cochran, and Donaldson all agree that Smith experienced a great deal of perplexity and stress in his early years in North District, and there's absolutely no doubt that he did. But the source of his anxiety cannot be blamed entirely either on questions of pure Scripture or a correct set of propositional doctrinal claims, though Williams tries hard to leave that impression and Cochran both echoes and amplifies him. The attainment of not just one, but four important pastoral positions and the chance to expand his career by working in a large downstate association had to have been Raccoon John's dream ever since the first few years of his first marriage.

We can only imagine his disillusionment after he arrived in North District and spent enough time with his new churches and his new patron to gain a real perspective on Payne's, Vardeman's, and the congregations' overtures to acquire him. His new fellow-laborers of both Regular and Separate stock were all supposed to have been *born again,* for Christ's sake, just as he himself had been back in his father's little spicewood thicket in Stockton's Valley. Theoretically that meant that he and they all had, by God's grace and Jesus's blood, spiritually transcended the hates, lusts, fears, and mundane cares of the flesh to enter into the reality of God, and let that reality make a positive, joyous, fruitful, and abundant change in their lives, complete with the promise of heaven when they left this world. All through John's ministry he'd tried to promote Calvinistic orthodoxy as being the best and most accurate expression of this process. The kingdom of God is not meat and drink, but righteousness, and peace, and joy in the Holy Ghost, wrote the Apostle Paul. How on earth could anyone truly reconcile the actions of either the Payne or Elkin parties or the capricious "trash vote" churches in North District Association, all led by born-again men who claimed to take God's Word literally to heart—to say nothing of the born-again politicking carried out by other born-again men all over a Kentucky General Union wherein God seems to have come to be perceived Faulkner-style as not only a gentleman and a sport but as a Kentuckian, too—with the high purpose of the Gospel, the love with which the blood of Christ was supposed to inundate saved souls, and the perfect truth and righteousness to which Jesus promised that the Holy Ghost would lead? Had a wise and all-knowing Lord actually brought two sets of Baptists together in a Great Revival only to have them treat one another as Antichrists to be outfoxed and subdued? Though John had known and parried the arguments of Separate Baptists for years, and would in fact continue to do so for Jilson Payne, what genuine evidence could he see to infer that one side was actually better than the other? And worst of all, if this was truly the way that God's children acted toward one another, how could even he claim that his own personal experience of the New Birth had wrought in him any change for the better at all—was his conversion, after all, just so much malarkey? He'd been a skeptic in his youth, and although he could now never admit to the possibility as much for social as for personal reasons, what if he'd actually been *right* originally and the entire Baptist associational structure was built upon nothing more than some flawed hope?

It got worse. In North District, Raccoon John found himself caught in the middle of, quite literally, everything that was going on. Hurt and angered though he must have been at his old Parmleysville flock's small-minded treatment of poor Nancy over such a trifling matter as those silver teaspoons, he would learn that Nancy's case was mother's milk compared to the complex and refined intrigues he himself had to learn to carry out in order to maintain his and his patron's faction's viability in North District. Had his born-again experience, his ambitions to rise in the world, his Alabama tragedy that he perceived as God calling him back to serve in Kentucky, and his moment of glory at Tate's Creek Association in 1815 truly brought him to no more than this cheap travesty of the Christian life, this whited sepulcher of a church that proclaimed itself to be the keeper of the testimony of God's revelation to man while swarming with corruption and the maggots of hate, jealousy, self-interest, and intrigue within? Should he let his skepticism resurface and perhaps admit that his entire life since 1804 had merely been wishful thinking?

The only mentors that Raccoon John had truly respected as role models thus far, Jeremiah Vardeman and Jacob Creath, were steeped thoroughly in the system, and neither man would ever evidence any positive ideas either of how to rise above it or lead converts out of it. Considering Creath's successful parrying of Ambrose Dudley and John Price's efforts to oust him from Elkhorn

Association over the poor dead slave girl, it's a fair bet that at least he himself actually enjoyed the game. Vardeman had probably likewise gloried in it from the time of his and John Rice's South District scheme, until Robert Elkin had outpoliticked and humiliated him in North District. Raccoon John couldn't have been happy with the thought that, to survive, he'd have to learn to like it as well, but now, what other choice did he have? He'd sold his farm back on the Little South Fork to Nancy's brother, and then brought another brother and sister-in-law as well as his own brother Jonathan north with him, and he now owned no clear title to any real estate whatsoever. He was dependent on four churches controlled by Jilson Payne for his livelihood, and thus his very prosperity hung upon implementing and maintaining Payne's directives. If Payne for some reason found it expedient to drop him—and in Payne's position that was a distinct possibility, since it was and is a simple and amoral fact of political life that a certain substance does indeed roll downhill and subordinates must take blame, whenever expedient, for any failures that might occur in the platforms they carry out for their superiors—all he could do was sharecrop until he could save enough money to buy a little plot of land of his own somewhere else. In years to come, Raccoon John would often tell the story of an experience he had while preaching at Spencer Creek on the fourth Sunday in March 1822. During what he called a "warm exhortation" from the sixteenth chapter of Mark, he was suddenly seized with a sense of inconsistency so deep that he felt compelled to halt his discourse and confess to the congregation, "Brethren, something is wrong—I am in the dark—we are all in the dark—but how to lead you to the light, or to find the way myself, before God, I know not."[132] As usual, the old preacher interpreted the memory in the context of later events, but honest consideration of his actual position at Spencer Creek and the three other churches under his care, and within North District Association, makes the incident all the much more poignant. It also illuminates one of Raccoon John's more pungent quips, which, for reasons best known to himself, John Augustus Williams elected to omit from his biographical study: that exchanging Arminian belief and practice for Calvinism, or vice versa, "would be but to put down one buckeye judge and put up another."[133]

But if Raccoon John felt himself to be in the dark, he wasn't alone. Though still the true power behind the North District pro-Elkhorn faction, Jilson Payne undoubtedly had had a great deal of pride kicked right out of him in the course of his struggles with Robert Elkin, and as a well-read, intelligent, and perceptive man he likely realized both his own shortcomings as a factional leader and the validity of Raccoon John's Spencer Creek admission. Moreover, the Creath war in Elkhorn Association, Richard Thomas's conduct in North District itself, and the birth of his own daughter must have made Payne ponder a great deal on the dangers both of taking the Philadelphia Confession too literally and upholding it too strongly. Both Payne and Raccoon John knew that North District needed some unifying force independent of either Regular or Separate factionalism, not a continual struggle between two parties bent on gaining and maintaining popularity and ascendancy over one another, and it can be imagined that the two spent a good many hours around Mt. Pleasant's hearth, talking in low, guarded tones about both their personal and group leadership difficulties.

And there was the younger generation "coming up" to think about as well. Little Ann Holland Payne was of school age by this time, and though Raccoon John and Nancy's eldest daughter Eliza Baize died in 1819 and Nancy undoubtedly still suffered from periodic spells of "breast complaint," she is known to have borne no less than seven more children before the year 1827. Jilson's brother William and Dulcinea's sister Mildred over in Bracken Association had raised a houseful of sons and daughters now reaching adulthood, and as already noted, some had moved near their uncle and aunt in the Mt. Sterling area. James and Keziah French's younger offspring, such as Keziah, who married James Prewitt, and Susanna, who wed the attorney Kenaz Farrow, were similarly circumstanced. Thus the young people of the region would have been of especial concern both to Jilson and Raccoon John, as well as to William. Little Ann and the preachers' children had seen Baptist fights close-up nearly all their lives, and especially in the case of William and Mildred Payne's offspring we must wonder how much their views of organized religion, if not their very personalities, had already suffered in consequence. Neither the Payne men, James French, nor Raccoon John himself would have wished to leave the sorry North District and Bracken legacies as they stood, for their sons and daughters to inherit. But they had all made their own beds; how could they change anything now without themselves openly rejecting organized religion altogether?

The next chapter of this work, then, will address not only Raccoon John's career as Jilson Payne's figurehead factional leader in North District Association and the consequences that he suffered therefrom, but his and the Payne family's united attempts to find some Divine key to unify North District Association and to free themselves, their church brethren, and their children from the quandary of trying to love one another and yet fighting all the time.

Over the course of my research for this book, I've been privileged several times to take the leisurely drive down Prewitt Pike to the forlorn little knoll on which Lulbegrud Church's twelve-cornered meetinghouse once stood so proudly, and beyond it to quiet and stately Mt. Pleasant. A few of the snapshots I have taken on these excursions adorn the pages of this volume, but among my biggest regrets is that I've never had the chance to see, much less photograph, the ancient salt box crafted so many years ago by the forgotten hand of a Payne bondsman from the log that split the church. Mt. Pleasant's tenant at this writing, who has otherwise been consistently most kind and helpful to my efforts, informs me that the old trough is probably still in the basement, but that the two hundred-plus-year-old cellar is in such bad shape that, to quote her directly, "Not even Freddy Krueger would be willing to go down there now."[134]

My most memorable experience at the historic Payne homestead, though, occurred at the time of my second visit, on an extremely hot summer day in 2001. Mt. Pleasant was deserted that afternoon but for a young Hispanic couple and their baby son, one of many such families who in recent years have migrated to Montgomery County to take over the farm jobs often spurned by local youths nowadays for more profitable and exciting opportunities in Mt. Sterling, Winchester, Lexington, Georgetown, or out of state. The husband was dutifully clearing a high patch of brush with a "bush hog" near the small cemetery where Jilson and Dulcinea Payne are buried, and his wife and child waited patiently in the overheated cab of a pickup truck while he finished the job. They were a proud and handsome but perhaps understandably shy and reserved young pair, but they assured me that the owner of the house wouldn't mind my walking up the driveway to photograph the old mansion and surrounding grounds.

As I made my way up that curving path to the old manse, my mind's eye danced with a thousand images—fields of corn, wheat, hemp, and tobacco harvested many, many generations ago by men and women living in some ramshackle row of tumbledown little cabins away from the main house, bringing the fruit of their labors to the master's enormous barns and earning only a place to sleep, a pittance of food, and the castoff clothes on their backs because they, like the crops they gathered and the livestock they cared for, were considered to be a white man's property. The mistress of the house, Dulcinea, proud and self-conscious of her and her husband's position in Mt. Sterling society, keeping a close eye on the "house girls" with, hopefully but by no means necessarily, a kind disposition and an indulgent heart. The solitary little girl Ann in her ribbons and frills, nursed, brought up, and nurtured right alongside small ones of a darker color, playmates whom she would all too soon be compelled to keep at a distance because Mama, Papa, and the entire weight of tradition and social custom would tell her in no uncertain terms that she was better than they were. And of course the old master, Jilson Payne himself, elegantly dressed and perhaps sitting on the front porch trying to catch a bit of the afternoon's advancing shade, a volume of American state papers and a copy of North District Association's latest minutes spread across his lap, his mind wandering over the possible tactics he might implement to make North District a proper Baptist association and what old Brother Elkin and his "boys" over around Howard's Creek might come up with in retaliation.

But all was quiet, faded, and gone; that generation had come, flourished, and passed away, and now the ancient house, the cemetery, and the undying land itself remain as the only testimonies that it ever existed at all. And then I looked behind me, back down the lane to where that young father was finishing up his day's chore, and remembered another youthful and hope-filled husband who had once brought his wife and family north to Montgomery County and ridden up this very path to try to find a place and a new life for himself in a labor that no one locally was willing to perform anymore—and I pondered on how very little that some of the most basic aspects of life had changed over the years.

The most famous portrait of Raccoon John Smith, an engraving from a portrait painted of him probably sometime in the early 1830s. From *The Life of Elder John Smith* by John Augustus Williams (1870).

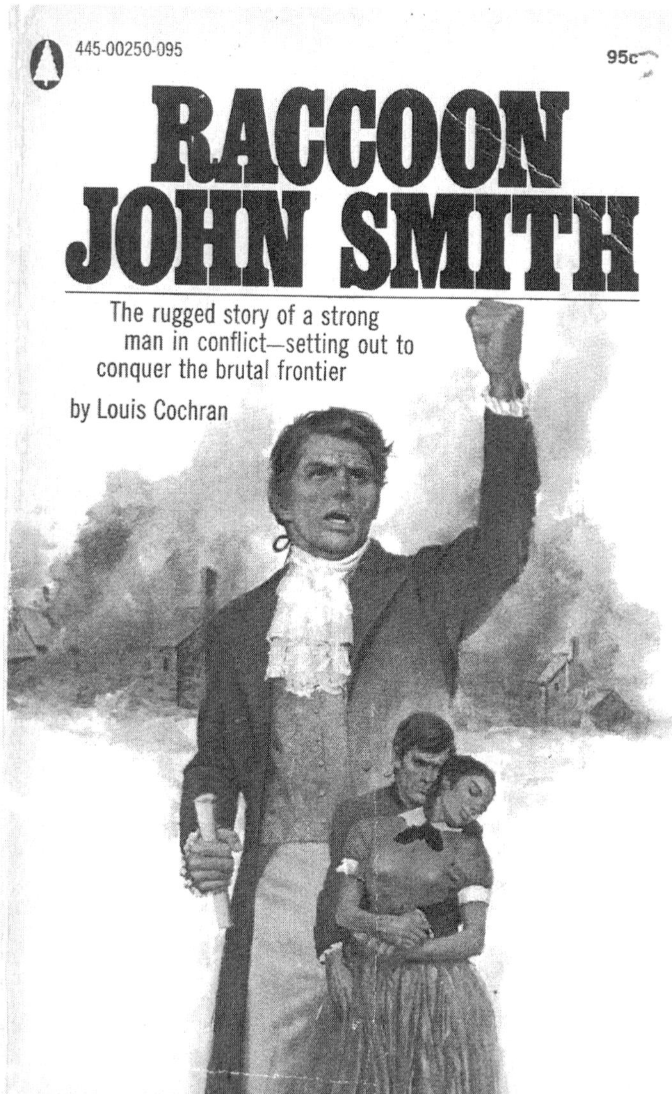

The cover of the paperback Popular Library edition of Louis Cochran's historical novel *Raccoon John Smith.*

Portrait of Raccoon John Smith (1784–1868) at approximately sixty to sixty-five years of age. One can almost see the pain caused by his youngest son's suffering and death in his eyes. Courtesy of the Bosworth Library, Lexington Theological Seminary.

One of the two known photographs of Raccoon John Smith, taken in his extreme old age. Courtesy of the Bosworth Library, Lexington Theological Seminary.

Nancy Hurt Smith (1792–1861), second wife of Raccoon John. Portrait painted probably when she was in her fifties. Courtesy of the Bosworth Library, Lexington Theological Seminary.

Alexander Campbell (1784–1868). Courtesy of the Bosworth Library, Lexington Theological Seminary.

Alexander Campbell in old age. Courtesy of the Bosworth Library, Lexington Theological Seminary.

Thomas Campbell (1763–1854). Courtesy of Scott Harp, www. therestoration movement.com.

This bust of Thomas Campbell is said to have been cast from the old preacher's "death mask." Some say that it is Alexander Campbell's "death mask" bust rather than Thomas's. Courtesy of the Bosworth Library, Lexington Theological Seminary.

Walter Scott (1796–1861). Courtesy of the Bosworth Library, Lexington Theological Seminary.

Nathan Lewis Rice (1807–1877), Alexander Campbell's last opponent in formal public debate.

Richard Hickman Menefee (1812–1841), the brilliant, consumptive young eastern Kentucky statesman who was Raccoon John Smith's last secular political idol. Courtesy of the Menifee County Court House, Frenchburg, Kentucky.

Isaac T. Reneau (1805–1885), one of Raccoon John's southern Kentucky converts and frequent correspondents. Reneau was a Disciple minister as well. Courtesy of the Bosworth Library, Lexington Theological Seminary.

Interior of the restored John and Anna Townsend Smith cabin, now located on the property of the First Christian Church, Monticello, Kentucky. Photo by the author.

The John and Anna Smith house in Horse Hollow near Parmleysville, Wayne County, Kentucky, before the front part of the log structure was disassembled and relocated in Monticello. Courtesy of the Bosworth Library, Lexington Theological Seminary.

The restored John and Anna Smith cabin. Monticello's First Christian Church is in the background. Photo by the author.

A small eastern Kentucky spicewood thicket in early spring. Photo by the author.

The forlorn knoll on which Lulbegrud Church once sat, on Prewitt Pike not far from Mt. Sterling, Kentucky. The gravestone is that of Thomas Boone (1789–1855), who succeeded Raccoon John Smith to the pastorate there. Photo by the author.

Mt. Pleasant, the plantation house built in 1802 by Jilson Payne (1767–1825), Raccoon John's principal political mentor in North District Association. Photo by the author.

The Payne/Prewitt cemetery at Mt. Pleasant, where Jilson and Dulcinea Payne are buried. Photo by the author.

Prewitt Pike, between the old Lulbegrud churchyard and Mt. Pleasant. Photo by the author.

Burning Springs United Baptist Church at Salyersville, Magoffin County, Kentucky, organized in 1810 by Elders Daniel Williams (1763–1820) and Samuel Hanna (1756–1838). Photo by the author.

South Fork Church (first known as "Poplar Meeting-House") at Malone near West Liberty, Morgan County, Kentucky, organized by Daniel Williams in 1808. Photo by the author.

The "Old Stone Church" (later Providence Baptist Church) on Howard's Creek, Clark County, Kentucky, organized and pastored for many years by Elder Robert Elkin (1745–1822). Photo by the author.

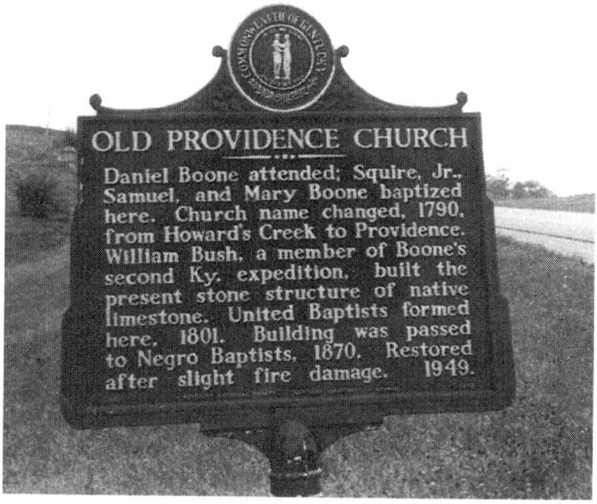

Kentucky Historical Society marker for Robert Elkin's "Old Stone Church." Photo by the author.

White Oak Christian Church in Morgan County, Kentucky, one of eastern Kentucky's earliest Disciples of Christ congregations. It was gathered by Joseph Nickell, according to tradition with help from Raccoon John Smith and under the influence of his preaching, in 1832. Photo by the author.

(Above) The Christian Church at Hazel Green, Kentucky, organized originally by Daniel Williams as a United Baptist congregation in 1813. According to tradition this church, pastored by Joseph Nickell after Daniel Williams's death, was among Raccoon John's earliest targets for Reform evangelism in 1828 and 1829, and is the pioneer Disciple/Christian church of eastern Kentucky. *(Left)* Old Grassy Christian Church, Morgan County, organized by Joseph Nickell in 1833. The presence of this church, as well as that of Hazel Green (Red River) and White Oak, in the territories of Burning Springs Association contributed to the eventual "Old Time" Baptist/Disciple split that occurred in 1834–1836. *(Below)* Goshen Church, Clark County, site of the North District minority council meeting of June 1830 wherein the positions of eastern Kentucky's "Old Time" Baptists were first articulated. Photos by the author.

The graves of John, Nancy, and Harvey (1823–1859) Smith in historic Lexington cemetery, Lexington, Kentucky. Photo by the author.

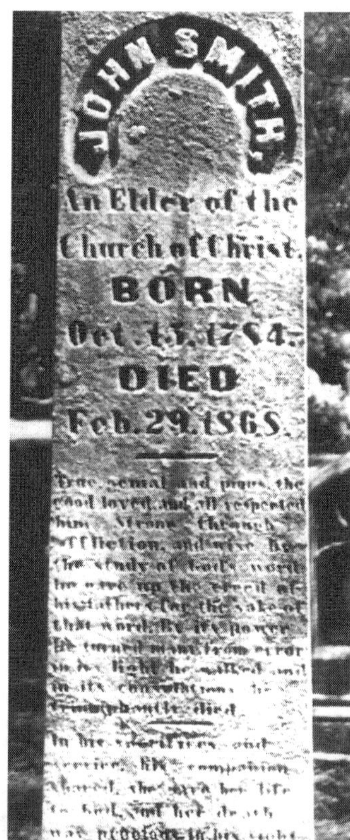

The inscription on Raccoon John Smith's gravestone. Photo by the author.

CHAPTER 6

Why I Make Use of This Newspaper

> I desired to attain an approximation to preaching in the street, or to bring Christianity, the thought of Christianity, into the mind of life's reality and into conflict with its various interests. And to that end I resolved to use this journal.
>
> —Søren Kierkegaard

Charles Dickens once wrote of the best of times and the worst of times, the age of wisdom and the age of foolishness, the epoch of belief and the epoch of incredulity, the season of light and the season of darkness, the spring of hope and the winter of despair. In almost the same vein, John Augustus Williams once romanticized a certain eastern Kentucky community as a place wherein "there was not, at that time, a nobler citizenship in all the land,"[1] and Jilson and Dulcinea Payne's niece Mary Harrison wrote with perfect vitriol of the same hamlet as being "as usual, very dull and gloomy—the meanest place in the world—I keep myself very close. I visit nowhere scarcely for the place has become so notorious for *slander, falsehood,* and *lies* [emphases in original] and I am determined to keep clear if possible. I have a perfect hatred of the place and would rejoice to bid it adieu forever."[2] Charles Dickens was, of course, portraying general conditions in Great Britain and France in 1775 in the prologue of his classic *A Tale of Two Cities*; Williams and Harrison were both specifically describing Mt. Sterling, Kentucky, in the early years of America's Era of Good Feeling. And just as Dickens was correct on all counts about his subject, so were both of the Kentucky writers. Williams portrayed Mt. Sterling as being, if not paradise itself, a rung up the ladder in that direction, which was in fact the exact way Raccoon John Smith regarded the little east-central Kentucky town when he and his family arrived there in late 1817. And yet within and among its most noble citizenship there were tales to make one's hair fairly stand on end: the postmaster seducing a local maiden and being forced to leave town temporarily when she got pregnant, his faithful and evidently extremely long-suffering and tolerant wife in tow; the town elite's two most noted political leaders, "Captain" Henry Daniel and Judge David Trimble (the same one who opened the courthouse to the missionary Luther

Rice in 1815, and himself possibly a member of North District Association at Daniel Williams's old Sycamore Church), putting themselves a step above the rough-and-tumble eye-gouging and nose-biting fisticuffs of the Kentucky pioneers and fighting a duel, with "Captain" Daniel being seriously wounded but with no loss whatsoever of his propensities either for fighting or dueling; and a fatal stabbing at the courthouse door while court was in session, with the assailant's course of action being formally approved because of the general contempt in which the victim was held.[3] Mary Harrison thus regarded herself as a resident of a place nearly the exact opposite of paradise, but somewhere in between her writings and the hagiography of Williams we can get a tiny glimpse of Mt. Sterling as it really existed in those days: neither paradise nor purgatory but actually a warm, homey yet bustling southern town with one foot in the eastern Kentucky mountains and the other in the central Kentucky Bluegrass and likewise a conjunction of godliness and deviltry both shaped by and shaping the course of the continuing Great Revival, possessed of—or perhaps possessed *by*—the characteristics of our modern-day conceptions of Mayberry and Peyton Place, all jumbled together. Anyone's impression either of early nineteenth-century Mt. Sterling, its modern-day legacy crisscrossed by U.S. Routes 60 and 460, or the thousand and one settlements just like it all across the rural Southeast both then and now, depends upon the press such places receive, and from what quarter.

And so when Raccoon John Smith and his family first settled in Montgomery County, Kentucky, near Mt. Sterling, they came looking for a rung up the ladder to paradise, but as we rural dwellers all must, they ultimately settled into their own niche somewhere in between Mayberry and Peyton Place. Joshua and Sally Hurt and their children were a plain farm couple, present only because of the prospect of arable land and their kinship ties with Raccoon John and Nancy and their growing family; Jonathan (though we cannot be sure that Raccoon John's next-youngest brother arrived with them initially) was Raccoon John's own trustworthy client, ready to give his brother what help he could in church and associational work, thereby hopefully making a name of his own even as Raccoon John had done under Jeremiah Vardeman and Jacob Creath; and Raccoon John himself was the fulcrum of the mechanism of the whole family, offering his preaching and his personality to serve as a liaison between Jilson Payne and North District Association, the Regular and the Separate components of the United Baptists, and the Montgomery County gentry with the common people. As anyone in such a position between Mayberry and Peyton Place might expect, he had his work cut out for him.

John and Nancy at first rented a small farm near Grassy Lick Church. Whether they had the advantage of living on property that Jilson Payne or one of his colleagues owned, or merely enjoyed his assistance in obtaining the residence, cannot now be known. They "laid in their letters" and took up church membership at Grassy Lick, which, according to Williams, maintained a somewhat milder and more open-minded Calvinism than did the Payne faction of

Lulbegrud. In any case, though, John couldn't have afforded to join Payne's own church at this time. It was still completely split and deemed in total disorder by North District Association, and he couldn't have afforded to put himself in such a risky political position even with Payne as his patron. But assume the pastorate of the Payne Lulbegrud faction he did, as well as the care of Spencer Creek, Bethel, and his own new home at Grassy Lick, and within a few months he was able to use his own special mixture of earthiness, culture, and humor to reunite the divided church under his—and, of course, Payne's—care. If indeed Thomas Boone did happen to be the pastor of the other half of the divided flock, it's entirely possible that Raccoon John was forced to accept him as an unsalaried (in keeping with early Separate Baptist custom, of course) pastoral associate or assistant. Boone himself may have performed a return act of good faith by transferring his membership from the Separate faction's Log Lick Church to the Regular faction's Goshen Church between 1817 and 1819,[4] although the latter fellowship was still headed by Elkin lieutenant Edward Kindred. Regardless, after more than two solid years of bitter infighting while trying to worship God on opposite ends of the church house, the quarreling members were more weary of the war itself and their consequent loss of influence in North District Association than they were of each other. In terms of the advantages it had brought to the Elkin faction of the association, the division had done its work all too well, and even with Raccoon John's presence and the fact that the Payne family still stood as North District's link to Elkhorn and the other downstate Kentucky associations, the Payne faction would require years to reestablish ascendancy.

A little more than a year after the family had arrived in the county, Grassy Lick and the three other churches now under Raccoon John's care—Spencer Creek with the influence of the Coons family, Bethel under the guidance of Thomas Moseley, and of course Lulbegrud with Payne and James French finally back in power after the terrible breach was healed—made good their promise to buy their new pastor a farm. An available hundred-acre tract assessed at $3,200 was secured not far from Grassy Lick, and the arrangements called for Smith to make the first payment and the four churches to assume the remainder of the debt. No doubt this was the finest farm on which Raccoon John had yet lived, but his and his family's residence there was every bit as tentative and insecure as that of a paid pastor living in a manse. The year following his initial payment, the first example of the "boom-and-bust" cycle of the American economy known as the Panic of 1819 hit Smith and his influential church supporters hard. With the scanty donations of his members and his own small supplemental farm income, he could barely meet the interest on his debt, to say nothing of the principal. Whether his memory were true or clouded, many years later he said that some of his churches had refused to meet their obligations due to their mossbacked stance on the Philadelphia Confession as opposed to his own clear Scripture-oriented preaching. By now it should go without saying that this particular recollection is open to question.

But in any case, rather than lose his new farm due to his members' default, he was forced to secure another loan at the Commonwealth Bank in Mt. Sterling, pay the farm off in a lump sum, and transfer his indebtedness to the bank. A "Colonel" Williams of the county seat, probably Samuel Williams and a friend of Jilson Payne's, offered to be Raccoon John's cosigner without even securing himself by a mortgage.[5] We know nothing of Joshua and Sally Hurt's or Jonathan Smith's possible financial difficulties during this same time.

In fact, we don't know for sure that Jonathan had moved north yet. Though Williams himself admits Jonathan's position at the embattled Bald Eagle Church,[6] Jonathan's name does not appear in any surviving records of the congregation before 1823,[7] although the moderate faction of the church had kept trying resolutely to maintain its relations with North District through ten uneasy years of meeting in the same building as the strict infant-damnation Calvinists. We do know, though, that John and Nancy's firstborn daughter, Eliza Baize, died in the same year as the terrible financial panic, when their firstborn son, Jonathan, was only a babe in arms himself.[8] The baby boy very well may have been born right around the time his uncle had come to Montgomery County, and had therefore been named for him.

And so while Raccoon John struggled to get his tangled finances in order, he preached, tried to be a good pastor and a good neighbor, and in general set out to fulfil his commissioned task. Records for North District Association in 1818 are unavailable, but those for 1819 indicate that in that year he baptized twelve persons at Grassy Lick, sixteen at Spencer Creek, eight at Bethel, and fifty-nine at Lulbegrud,[9] a considerable revival for all four congregations so near the time he and Nancy must have grieved for their daughter Eliza Baize. Another 1819 passing was that of David Barrow (Williams misdated this death to about 1823, and Cochran followed suit), to whom Raccoon John had become very close over the last two years. In what had to have been another of Jilson Payne's strategies to recoup the power and influence of his faction in North District Association and the General Union, Raccoon John invited the aging emancipationist to preach occasionally in Grassy Lick's pulpit, perhaps filling some return midweek appointments at Payne's old home church at Mt. Sterling as well, and in so doing he managed to reestablish an excellent and probably much-sought rapport with Barrow's congregation. Smith visited Barrow at home during the older man's final illness, too, not long before he passed away on November 14, 1819, and Barrow's final words to the younger preacher would prove especially poignant in consideration of Smith's later acquisition of some slaves of his own: "I have no more doubt that God will one day deliver the African from slavery, than that he once rescued Israel, with an outstretched arm, from the bondage of Egypt. Poor Kentucky! Poor Kentucky!"[10]

All things considered, then, Raccoon John must have gotten off to a successful start in spite of his financial woes and the death of his and Nancy's Eliza Baize. At the 1819 North District annual gathering (the group now having changed its meeting time to the fourth weekend in July, a date it would maintain throughout Raccoon John's tenure with the body) he was chosen to deliver the association's formal introductory sermon for the group's 1820 session at Unity Church in Clark County, deep in Elkin/Chenault Separate territory. He seems even to have let his former hill country pastoral colleague Thomas Wolverton know of the honor, because Wolverton traveled downstate for the session in the summer of 1820 to listen to it and, although Cumberland River Association was not in direct correspondence with North District at that time, himself preached at the stand on Sunday. Raccoon John's text for the 1820 introductory sermon, from 1 Peter 3:8, indeed may have been significant: "Finally, be ye all of one mind." While all of Raccoon John's biographers claim, with perhaps a degree of justification, that this is one of the first evidences of Raccoon John's developing rejection of the Philadelphia Confession and his search for Christian unity on the New Testament alone, the fact that he was speaking as a known partisan of one North District faction to both factions in a common assembly makes all the difference in the tone he could have taken. One faith, one mind, and one accord always depends on which side of the fence one assumes in such a situation. And Thomas White of the Elkin faction, the minister who had preached the previous year's session's introductory sermon, had taken a text from Psalm 133:1—"Behold, how good and how pleasant it is for brethren to dwell in unity!"—similarly and probably just as effectively trying to make the other side's point.[11]

Besides the mistimed account of David Barrow's death, Williams only records two other significant stories from Raccoon John's life during these early years, in fact virtually skipping his and Nancy's loss of Eliza Baize almost as if the death were something to be taken in stride and expected—which, even if Nancy's own illness is not taken into consideration, in that day and time, tragically, it would have been. One famous Smith tale, that of his "all in the dark" sermon at Spencer Creek Church in 1822, has already been noted at the end of the previous chapter and, hopefully, has been put into a more accurate context. The other Williams offering is by turns amusing and disturbing, but perhaps all the more significant because it reveals so much about both Raccoon John's personality and his environment in only a few short lines. Besides the North District United Baptists and Licking Association "Particulars" in Montgomery and Bath counties, preachers of other faiths were zealous and active in trying to build up their own churches as well. Methodist circuit riders conducted "class," worship, and even protracted camp meetings at various points in Montgomery County according to their own schedules. The local Presbyterians at Springfield and Mt. Sterling Churches were overseen by the imposing Rev. Joseph Price Howe, colaborer with Barton Stone in the days before the Great Revival and the father-in-law of Jacob Coons, younger brother of Jilson Payne's and Raccoon John's Spencer Creek mainstay John Coons.[12] After 1822, besides these there existed also one established Barton Stone Christian Church, or Church of Christ, on Stepstone Creek near the borders of Montgomery and Bath counties. The church was cared for by Peter Hon, a member of a sizable German-American family in Montgomery County and a former affiliate of the pietistic Church of the Brethren who also pastored small congregations in Fleming and perhaps Nicholas counties. Hon's pietist, separatist heritage adjoined perfectly to the worldview espoused by most of Barton Stone's adherents at the time, and his congregations were slowly growing.[13]

The Shaker commune at Shawnee Run near Harrodsburg even had a toehold of sorts in Montgomery, with the presence of Daniel Dunlavy, who lived not far from Raccoon John. Daniel was not a Shaker, but his brother Benjamin became an elder in the Shawnee Run commune, and Daniel seems to have given the cult some degree of support and a base at his home from which they could proselytize. Like those of any other Baptist preacher, or for that matter a denominational advocate of any stamp in the wake of the Great Revival that had set the region's entire religious context, Raccoon John's responsibilities included making effective attempts at proving why the standards of his own denomination were superior both spiritually and intellectually to those of others. With the combination of his own mental depth, his seemingly innate combativeness, and his sense of humor, he was very proficient at the task.

As luck would have it, two Shaker missionaries, James Congleton and Thomas Rule, began to try to convert Moses Higgins, another neighbor of Raccoon John's and whose wife and daughter belonged to the church at Grassy Lick. Higgins himself had never yet made a profession of his own faith, and Williams gives us the impression that he was slightly dense but well-to-do and hospitable, as the mores of the times demanded that those of his class should be. In other words, as folks of that day and age would have said, though Moses Higgins might not have been of a clever mind he was certainly clever at his dinner table. So after Congleton and Rule had upset Higgins with their exhortations to leave his family and come live as a celibate among the Shakers, and Raccoon John saw Grassy Lick threatened with the loss of a potential member and generous donor, he resolved to do something about it the next time the Shakers came to Higgins's house. He asked Moses to invite him to dinner with the men, that he might use the table conversation to show both Higgins and the missionaries exactly how far the Shakers stood from true biblical doctrine.

The missionaries returned and John got his invitation, and in fireside chat at Higgins's house before the meal was served John handled himself and the doctrines of his denomination with his customary skill. Ere long he had convinced even the not-so-bright Higgins that the Shaker missionaries had simply kept some of their more bizarre dogmas from him, and even before the guests went to the table Higgins was convinced he wanted nothing more to do with the Shakers. But for Raccoon John this wasn't quite enough. The old rage against the pretensions of those who professed a deeper knowledge than they possessed had once again exploded in his breast, and he resolved to add insult to the injury he had already done the Shakers' cause in the Higgins household. One of the more farfetched items the Shakers seem to have preached at that time was that they themselves literally represented the Resurrection and were living as angels above all the temptations of the flesh. Thus they claimed that they were capable of holding their tempers even under the most severe provocations. John wished to put them to the test. In spite of the mores of southern hospitality that made rudeness at the dinner table an almost unheard-of social breach even in the poorest homes, and in fact made such behavior a justified and almost a legal excuse for a duel even among many Kentucky religious folk, he took Higgins aside privately and asked his permission to try to make Congleton and Rule angry. Certainly without thinking the matter all the way through any more than Raccoon John had, Higgins agreed, and the two joined the missionaries at the table.

In keeping with the rules of their sect, Congleton and Rule offered their own table prayer separate from Smith and Higgins's, and here Raccoon John had his chance. He immediately accused the two of praying that his and Higgins's food would become poison to them. Before they quite had time to react, he continued that Rule could neither have confessed nor abandoned all his sins before joining the Shakers, since his misdeeds were undoubtedly so numerous he probably couldn't even remember half of them, and furthermore, if he had confessed to all he had done, the Shakers would have preferred sending him to the penitentiary to letting him live at their commune. That was all it took. Rule sprang up in a fury and for a horrible moment it looked as if he would either challenge Raccoon John to a duel or, perhaps more likely if he had come from the same rough frontier background as Smith, a bloody eye-gouging, nose-biting fight. Smith quickly realized how much danger he had put himself and, more crucially, his reputation into; he was thrown off balance for a moment, but he calmly pressed his advantage. He pointed his finger straight at the seething Rule, looked aside at the flabbergasted Higgins, and taunted, "A mad Shaker, Moses! A mad angel!"[14]

Poor James Congleton, who actually had been angelic enough to preserve his composure during this whole bizarre exchange, now somehow managed to pull his enraged partner back down to his seat and calm him. He asked John to retract his harsh words to Rule, but Smith, now feeling in command of the situation again, arrogantly replied that he never took back what belonged to a man. The two Shakers withdrew from the table and sat apart, now refusing to eat altogether.

After dinner was over, John attempted to be civil and to explain his actions to Congleton and Rule. Whether he succeeded in proving to them that Shaker sanctification doctrine was in fact incorrect, or merely that evangelical Shakers and Baptists were only on par with each other for rudeness and deception when they indulged in polemics, is not known. He urged both men, especially James Congleton, to separate themselves and their families from the Shakers and to rejoin society at large, but by this time Congleton's temper, which he had controlled thus far, had finally reached its own breaking point. Angrily withdrawing his hand from John's cajoling grasp, crossing his arms over his chest, and staring straight ahead, he retorted to Raccoon John the famous words of Jesus to both Lucifer and to Simon Peter: "Get thee behind me, Satan!"[15]

And now to make the evening complete, Raccoon John lost his own tem per. Characteristically, though, he was able to put the diversionary humorous face on his anger that had marked his tenure as a schoolboy and which was to become a trademark of his entire career as a sectarian apologist. Nonplussed again for an instant but quickly grasping the chance for one last heavy-handed jibe at Congleton and Rule, he peremptorily grabbed Rule's arms, wrestled him behind Congleton's back, and barked, "Thomas, didn't you hear him? He says, 'Get thee behind him!'"[16] Before the thoroughly humiliated and astonished Shakers could respond either with words or fists, Raccoon John fled the room, picked up his hat, and left the house.

The sideshow had its desired effect. Shakers never called again at Moses Higgins's farm, and Higgins soon lost interest in the sect altogether. Yet even Williams admits that this was one instance, in a long life embroiled in doctrinal controversy, in which Raccoon John Smith was almost outwitted.[17] Given Williams's treatment of the story, which tries to show Raccoon John in full control throughout, one wonders if perhaps the observation about being nearly outwitted was Raccoon John's own rather than Williams's. But who, or what, outwitted him? The Shakers, or his own ill-concealed bull rage against their pretensions to Scriptural wisdom and holiness, the same inner fury that had once tempted him to dump live coals into a drunk schoolteacher's coat pocket? Caught as he now was between his search for fulfillment and the realities of the consequences of his life choices; between the hills and the town; between Robert Elkin and Jilson Payne; between his pay arrangements with his churches and the looming possibility of the repossession of his farm by the bank; between the Philadelphia Confession and Andrew Fuller's *Gospel Worthy of All Acceptation*; between the deaths of Eli, Elvira, and Eliza Baize, and the 1805 "order" of his new association by which Richard Thomas had tried to forbid preachers to voice a hope for the little ones in the hereafter; between Nancy's continual childbearing and her chronic ill health; and perhaps most significant of all, between the indifference of the aesthetic existence and the attitude of dead certainty of correctness which seemed to make organized religion come back full circle to the aesthetic, he may have perceived, just this once, that he had also allowed himself to be caught likewise between the fourth and fifth verses of the twenty-sixth chapter of Proverbs.[18] He would not make a judgmental error of this magnitude again for several years—or if he did, neither Williams nor any other of his chroniclers saw fit to record it.

But, as the Apostle John observed about the ministry of Jesus in the last verse of his Gospel, there were many other things that Raccoon John said and did during this period that were not formally written down. They may be reckoned by the minutes of North District Association as well as family records of the births and deaths going on around him, and the surviving data is so jumbled and confusing it's extremely difficult at times to place it all in proper order. Sally (Davis) Hurt died not many years after little Eliza Baize, and in

1824 Joshua remarried to a Montgomery Countian, Betsy Pebworth,[19] and started a second family. By the time this occurred, Raccoon John and Nancy themselves had produced five more children: their eldest son Jonathan, as already indicated born probably not long after they settled in Montgomery County; a second son, John Duke, named probably for the Mt. Sterling physician who attended Nancy; a healthy daughter named Maria, born in 1820; a third son named William Pinckney, born about 1822 and perhaps named for John's next-oldest brother who had died in southern Kentucky around this same time; and finally the son James Harvey or Harvey James, born apparently in 1823.[20] The Smith children survived a period of "dangerous sickness" in the family in the fall of the year in which Harvey appears to have been born[21]—almost certainly one of Nancy's periods of "breast complaint," since Raccoon John would not have used the term "dangerous sickness" to describe a routine childbirth—but little William followed his sister Eliza Baize to the grave within a year, possibly from the same affliction that plagued his mother. It is a poignant testimony of Joshua Hurt's closeness to his sister that he named his own first child of his second marriage William Pinckney Hurt, even though he already had a son William Berryman Hurt by his first marriage, and an indication of his respect for his brother-in-law that he named his second son by Betsy as John Smith Hurt. Raccoon John and Nancy showed a reciprocal warmth by naming their fifth son (after Harvey and one more daughter, Eliza Ann) Joshua Carroll Smith.[22] In a day and age in which most parents could expect to see at least one, two, or even more of their offspring taken by death, Raccoon John and Nancy had already reached their quota, as it were, in the first nine years of their marriage. No one knows how difficult a time Raccoon John, coming as he did from a stalwart troop of siblings who had all survived infancy, must have experienced in coping with these losses in terms of the persona he had assumed to ensure his success in North District Association. Neither could it have done much for his peace of mind to know that his brother William, the one with whom he had first shared his conversion experience in the little spicewood thicket so many years before, had now become the first of his siblings to die, leaving behind a wife and a large family to shift for themselves and bringing home to John the awareness that, though he was certainly healthier than Nancy, the same fate conceivably could befall his own children.

Thus stood the family framework around which Raccoon John constructed his public career in North District during these years. But in many ways death marked the milestones of Raccoon John's public life as well. Certainly one of his first "big" funerals at Lulbegrud was that of Dulcinea Payne; some records state that she died in 1821 but others might indicate that she had already passed away by October 1818, when Jilson Payne signed a deed as if he were a single man. Jilson buried her in a small plot at Mt. Pleasant that he had marked off as a cemetery. He remarried soon after this to Ann Michie of Frankfort, who was twenty-two years his junior, and brought her to live with him and his daughter Ann at Mt. Pleasant. He sired no children by his second marriage, but after the death of his younger brother Jimmy he assumed the care of Jimmy's sons, Orlando and George.[23]

Another funeral, in which Raccoon John would not have been called to participate but that nonetheless marked the passing of an era, was that of Robert Elkin in March 1822—interestingly, the very same month in which Smith delivered his "all in the dark" admission to the Spencer Creek congregation. The "log that split the church" at Lulbegrud and North District Association's consequent disavowal of its relationship with Luther Rice's Baptist Board of Foreign Missions had been the old moderator's last major political gambit, and it had worked well. At the time of Elkin's death, his faction—headed now by moderator David Chenault just as Raccoon John served as the figurehead for the Payne faction—had maintained associational ascendancy comfortably for five years. Nonetheless, at the ebb of Elkin's life his callous, cavalier treatment of David Barrow in the settlement of the North District emancipation controversy came back to haunt him, and he was forced to reap in a small measure what he had sown in such a large one. The sad thing is that he may have been too old and senile at the time even to have appreciated the irony in which he found himself caught.

In the early spring of 1821, a black man named Warrick, probably a slave, made a profession of faith and requested baptism and membership in Elkin's Clark County congregation. The church had slave members in plenty, as in fact did almost every Bluegrass Baptist flock, but in this case for some unknown reason Elkin voiced a personal objection against Warrick's being permitted to join the church. Though at this time the word of a white man was generally accepted without question over that of any black in churches and courts alike, and many early Baptist churches made it a rule not to accept any new member without the congregation's unanimous approval, Elkin's congregation overrode their old pastor's objection and accepted Warrick as a member anyway. It's almost impossible to determine their motive with so little information. The most plausible explanation, given all the conditions, is that the church recognized or at least believed that the seventy-six-year-old Elkin was finally slipping into senility, and the members felt that not even a slave such as Warrick should suffer merely because of their longtime shepherd's frailty. On the other hand, they could have used Warrick entirely as an unknowing pawn, to give Elkin a discreet message that he was getting too feeble and that it was time for him to step away from the pastoral helm.

At any rate, decrepit physically or mentally though Elkin may have been, having a black man's word taken over his own was just too much for him. He had been a power in Separate Baptist politics ever since he had brought the original Howard's Creek congregation with him from the Holston Valley to Kentucky in 1780, he was a cosigner of the Terms of General Union, and he had in essence called all the shots for the entire Separate faction of the United Baptists after Jeremiah Vardeman and John Rice had split South District Association. So, with his pride wounded as only a frail, aged, once-powerful man's can be when he recognizes that his influence is slipping away, he personally reintroduced his charges against Warrick at the church's August 1821 business meeting. The accusations were again overruled and dismissed by vote of the congregation, and from that day forward until his death the following March, the old preacher appears never to have darkened the doors of a church again. And so, having separated himself in shame and bitterness from the church and the denomination he had served with such a strong, if not exactly always an altruistic, hand for more than fifty years, Robert Elkin died. North District's 1822 minutes carry a brief memorial tribute to him.[24] His historic church, still active near Fort Boonesborough State Park in Clark County under the name of Providence Baptist Church, joined a few of its kindred congregations the following year in leaving North District and constituting a new General Union body, known as Boone's Creek Association. It might be noted here that, in spite of David Chenault's connection with the Elkin faction, he seems never to have had much to do with the new Boone's Creek body; at the same time that the Elkin churches were dismissed from North District to join it, he and Thomas White helped their colleagues John Gilbert, George Baker, Daniel Duff, and Joseph Ambrose organize a small southeastern Kentucky association known as Red Bird in present Breathitt, Perry, and Clay counties. In keeping with his tastes as noted in the previous chapter, Chenault seems always to have preferred visiting and helping Red Bird and other small rural groups like it to the prospect of ingratiating himself to the more genteel downstate associations.[25]

With Elkin's passing, his and a few other related churches' ostensibly amicable departure from the association, and North District's pro-Separate party now led in fact as well as in name by the younger and more amiable but retiring Chenault, the longstanding Regular-Separate tensions within North District probably eased just a bit, at least temporarily. As such, the association's Payne component now enjoyed an opportunity to do some fence-mending as well as regrouping, and in this Raccoon John was very much involved. Having maintained the relationship with David Barrow's Mt. Sterling Church that he had cultivated during the last two years of the old emancipationist's life, he now gave up the Lulbegrud pastorate to Thomas Boone so he could assume the care of the smaller Mt. Sterling congregation and bring it back into North District. We might note here that Louis Cochran makes a great fuss over Raccoon John's transition from Lulbegrud to Mt. Sterling, creating an entire scenario out of a supposition that the change was prompted by the evil James French's opposition to Raccoon John and his supposed lack of enthusiasm for the Philadelphia Confession. Where he got this idea no one knows, but it certainly didn't come from John Augustus Williams, who states merely that Raccoon John simply resigned the pastorate of one church to assume the care of another.[26] Indeed, Williams even admits that, at this time, French was all for associational reform back to a purer exposition of the Christian religion than either Regular or Separate parties in the association had heretofore practiced collectively; he only opposed such efforts when they became, in his eyes, revolutionary rather than reformist, and in any case Raccoon John did not recall French's ever giving him so much as one cross word.[27] Besides, if Smith had indeed been kicked out of the Lulbegrud pastorate, the church would have defaulted on its contribution to Smith's loan payment, so it is still all the more likely that the Lulbegrud–Mt. Sterling transition, in its financial as well as all other aspects, was amicable and overseen by both Jilson Payne and French. Raccoon John, Payne, and French may have agreed mutually to give up the Lulbegrud pulpit to Boone to mollify the former members of the opposing church faction, and because the number of preachers in the Payne associational coterie was still very small; Payne and French simply didn't have another candidate of their own to install, but with Robert Elkin dead now, perhaps they thought they could handle Boone on their own, with help from Raccoon John and Boone's own fellow members at Goshen as needed. Raccoon John himself was sustained at Mt. Sterling by, among others, William and Mildred Payne's son and Jilson and Dulcinea's nephew, Buckner Harrison Payne, and his wife, Eliza Ann, who were by now well established in the dry goods business in the town and who were regular church attendees but not yet members.[28] We must wonder if the Smith daughter who appears to have been born between Harvey and Joshua in 1825, Eliza Ann,[29] was named by Nancy after her mother as the deceased Eliza Baize had been, or by John himself after Eliza Ann Payne.

But it is certain that James French did not oppose Raccoon John at this point. The North District clerk instead actively supported him. This, as well as the fact that French appears to have been much more at odds with Boone than with Smith at least until the summer of 1824, will become abundantly clear as we examine the minutes of North District Association for the pertinent years. From all appearances, at Robert Elkin's passing and his church's departure to join a new association, the Payne faction began an intense campaign for preeminence once again. This gambit, which was probably structured by Payne, French, and Raccoon John, was not built around a Philadelphia Confession platform, since regard for a strict interpretation of the Confession had been steadily slipping throughout the Regular component of the General Union ever since the split of Elkhorn Association and the formation of Licking Association. It was rather one of unity with an emphasis on the Terms of General Union and a surprising show of respect for the "Scripture only" stance of the Union's Separate Baptist component. Williams does relate that during this period Raccoon John unbound himself from the fetters of strict Philadelphia Confession Calvinism, but he insists that the change was a solo effort on Smith's part.[30] It very well may have been so, at least initially, but he never details Raccoon John's actions in light of the actual contemporary North District politics, allows for the fact that Raccoon John's revised positions at this time met with widespread acceptance both in the Payne faction and in North District as a whole, or admits that Raccoon John was working within the loop of an associational political action committee with a mutually agreed-upon agenda. Besides, this platform of decreased emphasis on the Philadelphia Confession seems to have evolved within roughly the same general time frame all across the denomination's Regular Baptist contingent, and it gradually led to a new, revised mainline Baptist mindset that essentially explains why the Southern Baptist Convention was able to stress for many years that it based its doctrinal stance solely on Scripture without any written creed. The denomination's recent emphasis on its periodically updated Baptist Faith and Message Statements that stress a particular method by which Scripture should be interpreted, and the acceptance of which seems to be increasingly necessary for political survival within the denomination, is a genuine throwback to an older tradition.[31] Still, Raccoon John and the other preachers and writers of the Payne faction of old, like all the Kentucky United Baptists of their day and time, seem to have been a lot more articulate in stating what they were doctrinally *against* than what they were actually for.

Ever since the multiple controversies of 1806–1807, James French, who had consistently retained his office of clerk in North District Association except for the years immediately preceding Raccoon John's arrival, when Jilson Payne's log split Lulbegrud Church, had almost always been chosen by the association to write the circular letters published annually in the group's minutes. He may have been given this honor by both associational factions mutually because of his scholarship (he had attended the College of William and Mary in Virginia)[32] as well as his diplomatic skills as outlined in Raccoon John's description of him quoted in the previous chapter. But unlike the earlier pointed circulars written by Jilson Payne, Moses Bledsoe, and David Barrow in the days of the Payne faction's first rise to prominence in North District, French's compositions usually dealt with abstract topics of Christian piety—meekness, prayer, steadfastness, and whatnot. But beginning in 1822 his yearly circulars assumed the political tone of the earlier North District specimens, this time with a reform bent that quite openly admitted the policy errors of the General Union as a whole over the years. His opening shot, as it were, taken here from North District's 1822 minutes, says it all:

> *Brethren and sisters* [emphasis in original]—Since we have had a name and a place in the churches of North District . . . Are contentions about ministers unknown among the churches, and what is still more to be deplored, are there no dissensions among us about the notions of men whom we have not so much as seen or heard, and for which we have not the poor apology that they are ministers by whom we have believed? [He possibly speaks of John Calvin and Jacobus Arminius here.] And if the first of these is carnal, can the latter be any better? Were Paul out of much affliction and anguish of heart, with many tears, to write to us about these things, would he say, "Are ye not carnal, and walk as men?" Or would it be, "You are turned aside to vain jangling?" O, in what other language he would bewail North Dis-

trict, and exhort, and comfort, and charge the churches, we leave for you to decide.[33]

One followup of this diatribe (obviously justified, though French himself had been just as much an integral cause of the problems he addressed as anyone else) was that Raccoon John was once again selected to preach the association's annual introductory sermon in 1823. Another was that he was now able to bring Mt. Sterling Church back into the North District fold, and a third was that Lulbegrud took the opportunity to send a query to the association that year inviting all churches in the group to send delegates to a special meeting in May 1824 to discuss constitutional reform and to propose new amendments to the association's government. Since in 1823 Raccoon John had been occupied with his transition as pastor of Lulbegrud to that of Mt. Sterling, it's hard to say whether this query was debated, discussed, and earmarked to be sent to the association under his supervision or Thomas Boone's. Regardless, though, Payne and French obviously had to have supported the gambit, and no doubt Raccoon John, as a loyal lieutenant, did so as well. Perhaps the split of another North District church, William Vaughan's original home congregation at Friendship in Clark County, into moderate and strict Calvinistic factions that followed Bald Eagle's pattern in having one party remain in North District while the other left in a huff to join Licking Association, only strengthened the Payne group's call for reform.[34]

French's extremely long circular for the 1823 meeting built upon the one from 1822, and it is in fact a valuable historical document that has long been overlooked and ignored by Kentucky Baptist historians. For the first time on record the importance of the *Separates* rather than the Regulars to the growth of the Kentucky Baptists as a whole was admitted, and even the Separates' insistence on upholding their belief in general, rather than limited, atonement throughout the negotiations of 1789, 1794, and 1801 was praised. The story culminated, however, not so much with any victory of Separate Baptist positions, but rather the glorious *via media* effected by Regulars and Separates with the signing of the Terms of General Union in 1801.[35] But for the letter to admit as much as it did, French, Smith, and the Payne faction had to be running on a compromise platform that may even have taken the Elkin/Chenault faction by surprise, and it almost certainly laid the groundwork for the power bid that Payne and his followers intended to make at Lulbegrud the next May. As indicated before, if Raccoon John had departed from his original Calvinistic sentiments as much as John Augustus Williams claims he had by this time, the letter very probably reflects Smith's hand in the Payne faction's policy formation. But Payne and French's great purpose had to have been consolidating the power that they hoped to recoup at the next July meeting, with Raccoon John as the Payne faction's candidate for the association's next moderator.

In the anticipatory interim, Raccoon John busied himself with North District routine. Since 1818 or at the latest 1819 he had served the association in several ways commensurate with his position as Jilson Payne's lieutenant, including preparing letters of correspondence to sister associations, serving as a North District messenger to other associations' annual meetings, and sitting on North District's arrangements committee with other ministers. In fact, the very last time that Robert Elkin had ever served on this crucial committee, about a month before he finally left his flock over the "insult" they had given him, Raccoon John had served also.[36] For this particular session moderator Chenault, perhaps sensing the Payne faction's resurgence and wanting to appear amicable toward his competitors, had appointed Jilson Payne to serve as a committeeman as well, and in addition Raccoon John had been designated to write the group's letter of correspondence to Franklin Association and had been picked to represent North District at both the Burning Springs and Boone's Creek associational meetings later in the fall. Jonathan Smith was likewise chosen to travel to Burning Springs, which still hosted its yearly session in October, this time at the Low Gap Church on Grape Creek in present Magoffin County, Kentucky, as well as to Bracken Association, which held its meeting a month earlier at Carlisle in Nicholas County.[37] And so perhaps to help introduce his younger brother to this latter northeastern Kentucky body, strengthen his own contacts with his friends in Bracken, or simply provide Jonathan with some companionship, Raccoon John decided to ride along with him to the Bracken gathering.

Raccoon John's relationship to Bracken Association, though perhaps not unusual considering his position in North District, is worthy of some note. Over the years of his tenure as a Payne lieutenant, he seems to have established more friendships among preachers in Bracken Association than among those of his own group. In both Albert Allen's "Reminiscences of Elder John Smith" and Williams's biography, more Bracken ministers are mentioned by name than pastors in North District itself, although two of these Bracken preachers, William Vaughan and William Moss (whom Raccoon John affectionately referred to as "Brother Billy" and "Old Billy," respectively),[38] themselves originally hailed from North District. The Bracken contact most crucial to Raccoon John's career in North District, though, was Jilson Payne's brother William, whose son Buckner was already providing him with financial support at Mt. Sterling Church though he had not yet professed conversion or joined the church. Whether or not Jilson and William Payne and Raccoon John were as closely allied as we suspect from all the historical evidence already noted and discussed, Buckner's largesse alone would have mandated that Raccoon John remain on good terms with his benefactor's father.

Regardless, this September 1823 Bracken Association meeting at Carlisle was, by Raccoon John's own admission, the occasion of one of his more famous quips, and it is important to our story in that it provides a vital reference point for the timetable of all that was to occur over the next year. At some time during or immediately after the series of meetings, a group of the most important Bracken ministers dined together, and they invited Raccoon John, Jonathan, and some of the messengers representing other associations to join them. On this day the main topic of table talk was a young, talented Irish immigrant Baptist preacher named Alexander Campbell, a Presbyterian proselyte who had gotten his start in America with the Baptists in western Pennsylvania's Redstone Association, but who was now connected with northeastern Ohio's Mahoning Association. He had already established a reputation as a skilled Baptist apologist and debater, having trounced noted Seceder Presbyterian dominie John Walker in a formal disputation on the topic of baptism by immersion at Mt. Pleasant, Ohio, in June 1820. Now, in the month following the September Bracken meeting, he proposed to come to northeastern Kentucky to debate the topic once again, this time with Kentucky Presbyterian parson W. L. MacCalla. This was all well and good with the Bracken Association leaders, who were as much in contest with the Presbyterians in that region as Raccoon John himself had been with the Shakers at Moses Higgins's. The problem was that Campbell had started a newspaper, *The Christian Baptist,* earlier that summer and, although he had released only one or two issues so far, had heretofore utilized it to mock and castigate his fellow Baptist clergy right along with their rivals rather than structure the periodical to be a good denominational mouthpiece. Raccoon John's own dry retort to the Bracken preachers' fretful complaints against Campbell's pen was that the Baptist clergy he worked with needed so much of such abuse that he was willing to be whipped almost to death himself in order to see the others killed. For all his indirect defense of Campbell's actions, his own love of reading, and his expressed intention to return to Bracken territory to hear the debate, though, at this time John evidenced not one shred of interest even in leafing through a copy of *The Christian Baptist,* much less subscribing to it. Even so, some unknown diner that day had to have been already sufficiently acquainted personally with Alexander Campbell to pass Raccoon John's quip on to him either by word of mouth or letter, and apparently it gave Campbell a smile.[39]

And so Raccoon John returned to Montgomery County with Jonathan, planning on going back to Bracken territory in October to hear the debate. However, his family's "dangerous sickness" that fall precluded the trip, and probably his excursion to Burning Springs as well. But the platform of his associational party soon caused him to take a renewed interest in *The Christian Baptist.* Sometime near Christmas 1823, Buckner Payne advised Raccoon John to subscribe to the newspaper himself and encourage others in his congregations to do the same.[40] Based on Raccoon John's prior relationship with the Payne family, we are led to suspect that Buckner's father, William, and his uncle Jilson were probably the original catalysts for this action. As an ordained minister and church pastor in Bracken Association, William had to have been familiar already with Campbell's rapidly growing popularity even if *The Christian Baptist* was heretofore merely a succès de scandale among younger Baptists, and he could have passed on the information either to Jilson, Buckner, or both in the hope that Jilson could exploit Campbell's reputation and writings in North District to further his own platform and power bid against the Chenault faction there. Buckner, like Raccoon John himself, at this time was probably nothing more than a mere errand boy for the two older men, but of course, when a Payne family spokesman gave him an order, Raccoon John obeyed as a loyal vassal should.

Ere four months had passed, though, Raccoon John had committed himself both to Campbell and to *The Christian Baptist* in his own intensely personal way. To begin to explain this change of heart, here finally we may tie up a couple of loose ends. The conversion story listed immediately after William Vaughan's narrative of his born-again experience in chapter 2 of this volume, described by Raccoon John to Albert Allen in 1857 as being "one which any Baptist church would have cheerfully received, and was almost substantially such as mine," was Alexander Campbell's own, related by him to Raccoon John in March 1824.[41] But more significantly, the individual with whom Raccoon John became so frankly and blatantly infatuated that he voiced the desire simply to stare at him for an hour without hearing a word from anyone, as we noted in chapter 1, was none other than Campbell as well.[42]

Every Raccoon John Smith chronicler thus far has paused at this point in his story to offer a brief biography of this Alexander Campbell, in all cases heretofore as an apologetic springboard for the doctrinal points their writings advocate. Though perhaps I should reemphasize a nondoctrinal and nondenominational position herein, at this particular milestone we must still make a similar digression. Alexander Campbell was indeed a great Christian leader with many noble and visionary ideas. He was also very much a human being full of the prejudices of his own time as well as manifold contradictions in his thought and outlook, to which he was as blind as the rest of us are to our own inconsistencies, and he never achieved total success in convincing the world at large that he was, as he believed, preaching a unified message. There are a great many biographical studies of Campbell, as well as doctrinal apologies for his thought, already extant; some extremely subjective volumes as well as a few of what I hope are the most objective have already been mentioned in this work's introduction, and more can be found ahead in the bibliography. If the reader desires a more complete picture of Campbell, he or she is cheerfully referred to them. We must concern ourselves here briefly with Alexander Campbell, the man himself, but more importantly with the written and published image of Campbell that, within a brief segment of Raccoon John's topsy-turvy life between Christmas 1823 and March 1824, captured Smith's heart for good.

Like Raccoon John's grandmother Bowen, Alexander Campbell's father, Thomas, was Scots-Irish; though Thomas's father, Archibald, had become a communicant of the Church of England, Thomas himself felt compelled to return to his roots, as it were, and affiliate with the Antiburgher Seceder Presbyterian offshoot of the Church of Scotland. Like Isaac Denton, Alexander's mother, the former Jane Corneigle, was of French Huguenot extraction. Alexander's combined Covenanter/Huguenot heritage thus gave him a great deal in common with Raccoon John's own Calvinistic religious background—to say nothing of his gene pool. Unlike either Smith or Denton, though, Alexander Campbell was a third-generation child of the Great Awakening uninfluenced by the corresponding nineteenth-century American Great Revival. Moreover, he had received an excellent education of the type that Raccoon John lusted after so badly, first in his native County Antrim under his father, who got his start in life as a schoolmaster as well as a Seceder minister, and then at Thomas Campbell's own alma mater, the University of Glasgow in Scotland. The sum total of the mixture proved to be extremely dynamic for Alexander. Thomas Campbell, himself influenced by such Scottish divines as John Glas and Robert Sandeman and the laymen James and Robert Haldane, all of whom left the Church of Scotland and organized movements that they claimed were based solely on precepts expressly spelled out in the New Testament itself and the "restoration" of the primitive, nondenominational Church of the days of the Apostles,[43] was never so much an orthodox Antiburgher Seceder as he was a seeker after a concept of Christianity somehow superseding all the sects and denominations that comprised the Protestant variant of the religion. Embracing this concept as Thomas Campbell did, one might wonder why he even bothered to try to work with the stern and extremely sectarian Seceder Presbyterians in the first place, but whatever the reason, on this noble vision of Christian unity both father and son based their lives.

Thomas preceded his family in their migration to America. Settling in Pennsylvania not far from Pittsburgh, he tried to carry on his Seceder ministry as he had in the Old Country, but found American Seceders to be even more narrow-minded and quarrelsome than their kinsmen in Scotland and northern Ireland. In spite of the opposition of his fellow clerics, he made his ministry ecumenical from the start, and as a result he was quickly censured and disfellowshipped by his synod. His popularity remained high with some mainline Presbyterians as well as lay members from other denominations, though, and in response to his censure by the Seceders he organized the so-called Christian Association, composed of men and women from a variety of denominations who were responsive to his plea for Christian unity. The *Declaration and Address* Thomas Campbell wrote in September 1809 as a sort of charter for this organization has been recognized as one of the great documents of the ecumenical movement, though it was drafted nearly a century and a half before that movement ever gained any real focus and direction among mainline churches.[44]

But being simply a parachurch organization of sorts rather than an entire collection of expatriate churches such as Barton Stone's Springfield Presbytery, the Christian Association never really blossomed. Meanwhile, back in Glasgow at the university, Alexander was suffering some growing pains of his own within the strict, dry confines of the Seceders, so by the time he and the rest of Thomas's family immigrated he was more than ready to join in his father's American work. A little more than a year after Alexander and the Campbell family's arrival in Pennsylvania and in the same spring as Alexander's marriage to Margaret Brown (incidentally, like Raccoon John, Campbell was twice married, the second time to Margaret's best friend Selina Bakewell), Thomas finally let his Christian Association evolve into an independent church under his leadership, known as Brush Run and located near Washington, Pennsylvania. Alexander was ordained as a minister by his father as soon as the church was organized, and the congregation adopted immersion as its sole mode of baptism after Alexander became convinced that the Baptist form of the ordinance was the correct one. Thomas Campbell himself had heretofore never let that particular question become a test of fellowship among his followers, but now Alexander either consciously or unconsciously assumed the reins of his father's work. Father, son, the rest of the professing adults in the family, and the remainder of the congregation were baptized by ministers Matthias Luce and Henry Spears of the Redstone Baptist Association in 1812.

And so, in an ostensible effort to avoid creating another denomination or sect, Brush Run Church sought to affiliate itself to the religious mainstream with the intention of somehow maintaining its own independence and integrity within that framework. The group first applied for membership in a local Presbyterian synod, but was turned down. Then the Campbells sought fellowship with Luce and Spears's Redstone Association, and in spite of some misgivings on the part of both association and church, Brush Run was admitted to the Redstone fellowship in 1815. Having spearheaded the immersion campaign at Brush Run, Alexander was now considered the leader of the group even by his own father.[45] By 1823 he had helped gather two more congregations of like doctrinal and theological outlook, one at Pittsburgh and the other at Wellsburg, in the northern panhandle of what is now West Virginia, and he enjoyed support for his positions among Baptists as far away as Kirtland in eastern Ohio as well. Alexander's earliest nonfamily lieutenants included the Baptist preachers Sidney Rigdon and Adamson Bentley at Kirtland and Walter Scott at Pittsburgh, and Alexander himself subsequently moved his church membership from Brush Run to Wellsburg and his residence to a "panhandle" hamlet known first as Buffalo and later as Bethany. Once settled at Wellsburg and Buffalo/Bethany, respectively, he affiliated himself with the more easygoing Mahoning Baptist Association of Ohio, to which Rigdon and Bentley also belonged and to which Scott soon moved his membership as well.[46]

In spite of the Campbells' newfound friendship with Redstone and Mahoning Associations, evidenced by Alexander's production in 1817 of a circular letter for Redstone in which he argued for the traditional Regular Baptist position on election and predestination,[47] and the Baptists' exploitation of Alexander's debating skills against ministers of "pedobaptist" denominations such as he had demonstrated in the already-mentioned 1820 Walker debate in Ohio, Alexander and his closest followers remained a constant source of irritation to Regular Baptist leaders and a virtual lodestone for younger, disaffected Christians not only among the Baptists but from other faiths. Alexander Campbell, for all intents and purposes, appears truly to have believed that he embraced a pure Christianity that followed Scripture (specifically the New Testament) alone, and one that represented the epitome of true Christian ecumenism. All his closest early colleagues and the majority of those who would follow him in years to come vociferously agreed with him. A great many others, indeed most advocates of all other Protestant denominations, countered that Campbell's Scriptural interpretation was just one among many and they disdained his pretensions to holding the key to the New Testament, as it were; moreover, they perceived Alexander as extremely egotistical, combative, and sarcastic, decidedly prejudiced in his own outlook, and himself as sectarian as anyone else he condemned for the selfsame vice. But basically, Campbell insisted on an interpretation of the New Testament in line with the prevailing secular philosophy of both the Age of Enlightenment and of post–War of 1812 America, a combination of Lockeanism (after writer and philosopher John Locke) and Baconianism (after Francis Bacon), also known as Scottish Common Sense Realism. This philosophical system asserted that human beings, by exercising their innate common sense, could know reality exactly as it exists, with full confidence in their objectivity and accuracy. Campbell argued proof of God's existence through a natural theology with Locke's contention that the human mind was a tabula rasa, or blank tablet, with no ability to create ideas of its own but merely to arrange and rearrange those put within it by outside stimuli; thus being born with no innate idea of God, man had to have been given the idea of God directly by Him, through some primal revelation.[48] That was about as much respect as Campbell had for revelation as it was significant to the Christianity of his day, though. Following through with the postulate that this God of natural theology had given mankind His Son, Jesus, as a Savior as well as the Bible, as he himself called it, as "a book of facts" on which a clear scientific unanimity could be reached by all reasonable men,[49] Alexander Campbell tried to hold forth that the New Testament (after the first chapter of Acts, that is; even the ethical teachings of Jesus in the Gospels, which occurred in the Scriptural time line before the death, burial, and resurrection, were technically a part of the Old Covenant rather than the New)[50] was something of a schematic blueprint from God for mankind's salvation. According to the doctrinal line, this method of interpreting Scripture had a universal and consistent proper application common to all ages of human history; even the Apostles "began with facts and drew from these by induction the proper inferences and rules of action."[51]

Campbell's so-called Ancient Gospel, then, was made up of what he considered to be direct commands, logical deductions, and necessary inferences taken from the Acts of the Apostles and the pastoral letters of the New Testament. We would think that, in the days of the Era of Good Feeling in America, a Protestant biblical literalist could hardly spark any serious disagreement or controversy. The true source of contention and the main fallacy of Campbell's outlook, though, was the supreme subjective paradox of any rationalistic theory: it made its originator dismiss, in Campbell's case more often than not with his trademark harsh sarcasm, any argument that departed from rationality as he himself defined it, even though the evolution and consequent reshaping of his doctrinal positions made the inconsistencies of his own "earlier" and "later" thought glare brighter and brighter over time. We must once again stress that Campbell and his adherents really did believe that their movement maintained an accurate, unadulterated, and completely objective exposition of the absolute quintessential Christian doctrine, and a perfect and charitable ecumenism. Unfortunately, though, for much of his life Campbell was very nearly the nineteenth-century white Anglo-Saxon Protestant evangelical mirror image of modern linguistics expert and political philosopher Noam Chomsky: in his world there could be no genuine disagreement, only truth and error; no differences, only mistakes, or lies.[52] For this reason, among others, he was as adept as Chomsky as well in making ultrazealous converts to his thinking, and then dismissing them, or they him, after he had made some dramatic left turn that they couldn't manage to follow either intellectually or spiritually.

So, then, what was this system of church dogmatics that appeared at first glance to be so biblically orthodox while simultaneously managing to stir up such upset and ill feeling? In his writings, backing up his positions generously with quotations from Acts and the Pauline epistles combined with the ultra-rationalism in which his followers delighted, Campbell argued that the primitive church of the days of the Apostles possessed a pure congregational form of government presided over only by elders and deacons elected by local assemblies individually. Such local assemblies met weekly on the first day for singing (musical instruments were not yet an issue for Campbell, since none of the churches of his experience in Ireland, Scotland, and America had heretofore used them), prayer, the Lord's Supper or communion, worship, a financial contribution to the good work of the fellowship, and preaching or instruction at the hands of the elders.[53] Membership in these local assemblies was based strictly on individual adult profession of repentance to and faith in Jesus Christ as Savior, and baptism by immersion. So far so good, at least from the standpoint of the Baptists with whom Campbell had chosen to make his temporary home; if Episcopalians, Presbyterians, and Methodists disagreed with the idea of congregational government, and if the Campbell method called for the celebration of communion rather more often than did any Protestant denomination except the Episcopalian, the Campbell positions both on church order and admission to membership still remained safely within the bounds of Regular if not Separate Baptist orthodoxy.[54]

The first outward controversies and misunderstandings came from Campbell's technical exclusion of the four Gospels from his exposition of New Testament Church practices, and his initial harsh condemnation of any missionary organization not subject to the control of an individual local church rather than an association, a convention of churches, or any other suprachurch organization. We can best discuss this latter controversy subsequently in relation to historical events as they unfolded, but for now we might illustrate one example of the former contention by noting Campbell's spin on the rite of communion and the Separate Baptist–cherished custom of footwashing as a supplement to the ritual. One could infer a Scriptural commandment to wash feet in connection with the Lord's Supper only from the words of Jesus in the thirteenth chapter of the Gospel of John; nowhere in Acts or any of the epistles is there any clear indication of exactly how, on what occasions, or how frequently the early Church practiced footwashing. Thus in the Campbell economy, footwashing became simply a custom of ancient times, laudable insofar as those who practiced it embraced Christian humility but with no proper place in the ordering of a communion service. It could be argued here with a great deal of justification that Campbell had no appreciation for the rite to start with, the Presbyterians and Regular Baptists of his experience never having practiced it. But Campbell himself never would have admitted, or probably even realized, that his own background could have had any influence whatsoever on his perceptions of the matter. On the other side of the coin, even though the New Testament gave no explicit commands as to exactly how often a congregation should practice the rite of holy communion itself, with his principle of necessary inference Campbell took various passages of Acts and the Pauline letters to rule that the ancient Church took the Lord's Supper weekly and it was therefore now binding on all true New Testament churches untainted with sectarian tradition to do the same. After all, in the essentials of the Ancient Gospel and its corresponding "Ancient Order" there were no true and honest differences but only mistakes or lies, and anyone who disputed Campbell's positions had to have been either unthoughtedly or consciously mixing some of the leavening of the Old Testament into the pureness of the New. This in fact became Campbell's favorite charge against any individual or church that disagreed with the least thing he said, and by it he condemned wholesale any view that happened to clash with his own as "the rubbish of human invention and tradition."[55]

But the main points of controversy Campbell sparked lay not in the practice, or lack thereof, of externals such as footwashing or even weekly communion, but within the rationalistic system of thought that lay behind them. The best, and certainly the most crucial, illustration we can use here is his proclaimed position on the rite of immersion, although he seems to have taken some time to develop it fully and he waffled over the fine points of the issue throughout his career.[56] Proclaiming that the "age of miracles" had ended with the days of the Apostles, Campbell argued that the complete power and demonstration of the Holy Spirit lay directly, and solely as far as modern humankind was concerned, in the written and spoken word of the New Testament itself. Ministers couldn't properly claim to be "called to preach" in the conventional evangelical understanding of the vocation; the Holy Ghost worked exclusively through the words of the New Testament, and although an individual should try to be as persuasive as possible when teaching or preaching, his success depended on his hearers' intellectual acceptance of his message rather than any irrational, subjective "heart impressions" they might experience. Thus God had limited His manifestations of grace to a series of commands that He expected the human race to obey, those being to hear the gospel, to believe in it, to repent, to confess Jesus as the Son of God and Savior, and to be ritually immersed. Obedience to these commands in turn brought God's gracious response: forgiveness of sins, the gift of the Holy Spirit, and eternal life.[57] From an outsider's view these latter principles at least were orthodox enough in terms of evangelical theology, but Campbell's spin implied that the paradigm by which all Protestant churches of either Calvinist or Arminian stamp had interpreted the mechanics of conversion, that of Cornelius in the tenth chapter of Acts and which has already been examined earlier in this work, was completely erroneous. The story of Cornelius's being visited by an angel who instructed him to send for and hearken to the preaching of Peter, by which both Calvinists and Arminians inferred that God gave a special and personal inward spiritual call to each individual in need of salvation, and the detail that Cornelius and his family had been baptized *after* the Holy Ghost had fallen upon them, a joyous personal affirmation from God that they were indeed saved[58]—in essence, the born-again experience—simply had to have been part and parcel of an incident belonging strictly to the apostolic age of miracles, and not relevant to modern times.

The doctrine of justification by faith that had sprung from this belief was absurd in theory and false in fact, Campbell charged; it was unwholesome, full of misery, darkness, and doubt.[59] His own alternative was to postulate that the key to the plan of salvation lay in Peter's speech at Pentecost in the second chapter of Acts: in modern times baptism was not to be bestowed as it had been upon Cornelius's family, as a testimony that those baptized had been redeemed and had received the Holy Ghost, but rather for the express purpose of remitting their sins and conditional upon their obedience to God's commands, as Peter had proclaimed it to the Pentecost crowd in Jerusalem in Acts 2:38.[60] In short, the born-again experience as preached by Baptists, Methodists, Presbyterians, Stoneites, or anyone else who held it as normative for conversion had never been anything more than tradition-tainted hysterical nonsense. Campbell qualified his views on baptism for remission of sins in part with the idea that one is *really* saved when he or she believes in Jesus Christ as Savior and is *formally* saved when he or she is immersed[61] (ironically, this was the same sort of theological speculation that he regularly condemned in others) and he once admitted that he "had never discarded the existence of [born-again] experiences on the part of the sinner, but objected only to the use made of such things as determining the proper prerequisites of baptism."[62] But be that as it may, he managed to convince a great many men, women, and especially young preachers, untrained in such scholarly rhetoric and debate, that the physical water used for the rite of immersion was, literally, the only thing that would wash away their sins. Campbell himself would argue from the standpoint that Martin Luther had been only partially successful in achieving the original Reformation and that he was simply carrying out Luther's valid principles to their legitimate issue.[63] Some of Campbell's later followers would make the bold claim that Luther wasn't even a Christian, not because of his later harsh, merciless anti-Semitism or even his humorously obsessive repetition of the word *scheisse* in his prose and conversation (or *fex,* if he happened to be writing or speaking in Latin), but simply because he hadn't been immersed.[64] The Diet of Worms might as well have been a diet of worms.

Among biblical literalists such as Campbell and the entire gaggle of evangelical Great Revival Protestants with whom he disagreed, this kind of debate could know only one fate: a descent into bitter wrangling over whose view of Scripture was the correct one, with all contestants claiming the Lord as their own partisan. This division of opinion, though, did have its unique psychological, personality-based implications. To many young Americans inured socially both to the Bible as literal cover-to-cover truth and to the religious norms established by the Great Revival, but who had begun to develop, like Campbell himself, the rationalistic philosophy that was fast becoming the conventional nineteenth-century American outlook, who wished to be Christians but were either repulsed by or unable to come to terms mentally with either the abstruseness of Calvinism or the emotionalism of frontier Arminianism, Campbell's views on baptism for the remission of sins brought genuine encouragement and even what was to them a refreshing, dynamic faith. From this vantage point they were entirely glad to echo Campbell's proclamation that he had rediscovered and rescued essential Christianity from nearly two thousand years' worth of sectarianism. As we discussed previously, though, the Great Revival itself had been the one crucial factor in reestablishing belief in the Bible as literal truth throughout much of settled America. That the first-generation immigrant Campbell and his American adherents gained their prominence proclaiming a rationalism based upon, and that evolved from, the very essence of the ecstatic mysticism they condemned is surely one of the great ironies of nineteenth-century American religious history. Moreover, though years were yet to pass before Kierkegaard gave forth his thoughts on the dialectic of the aesthetic, the ethical, and the religious in relation to subjective human existence, and decades longer before his ideas would find an audience outside his native Denmark, the paradigm of salvation given by the Cornelius story in Acts 10 still remained strong in the hearts and minds of most evangelical Christians in spite of the general increase in rationalistic outlook—and evangelicals couldn't even use popular rationalistic terms clearly to articulate *why* it remained so dear to them. Our tour through rural American religious history so far has already amply demonstrated that evangelical leaders of differing theological slants could and did go overboard on hairsplitting doctrinal points, and treat one another like dirt in the name of maintaining and defending what they perceived as truth, but this does not mean that the majority of their lay hearers acted similarly. Thus in another keen paradox, evangelical Baptist, Presbyterian, and Methodist ministers still preached a deeply intuitive faith and a personal, heartfelt Christian experience that echoed not only in the ears of their audiences but also within the very core of their hearers' being, and that's exactly what the laity wanted. To a great many evangelical laymembers as well as clergy, Campbell's position ("Campbellism," they nicknamed it, and his followers, "Campbellites," although in the South the latter title was commonly slurred to "*Cam'elites,*") was nothing but a cold, dry, legalistic parody of the true inner meaning of Christian faith, an empty promise of salvation by water.

Thus stood the key difference of opinion between Alexander Campbell and the "sects," as he called them, but it can be seen clearly that acceptance of one viewpoint over the other did not depend on the essential, objective rightness or wrongness of either so much as it did on an individual's perception of the disputed issue based on his or her own mental outlook, emotional needs, and personality. By and large, those who embraced Christianity on Campbell's terms espoused it just as wholeheartedly as those who believed in and advocated the traditional understanding of the born-again experience. Moreover, we can in fact appreciate the Campbell religious sensibility on the very same terms by which we have attempted to make sense of the traditional born-again experience. Both demanded repentance, and faith not only professed but put to action. Only the mechanics of the externals of each were different. Unfortunately, they were so different that, ultimately, many believers on either side of the question came to view the opposing side as heretical.

In spite of the seeming fresh originality—or ancient orthodoxy, depending on one's opinion—of Campbell's doctrine, his reputation among the Baptists heretofore was merely that of an extremely effective debater for their position on immersion baptism. Thus equipped, he might have proven to be only one more voice crying in the Ohio and Pennsylvania wilderness, were it not for the means he began to employ in 1823, in fact unique in the America of his day, for disseminating his views. Campbell did not acquire his name and fame by itinerant stump speaking, but rather by his founding of *The Christian Baptist,* the periodical Raccoon John Smith had heard condemned so roundly at dinner table discussion during the 1823 session of Bracken Association at Carlisle.

Church newspapers, at least insofar as they served as denominational mouthpieces, were no novelty even in that day and time. Examples sponsored by most American denominations were already numerous on the East Coast, perhaps the pioneer being John Wesley's Methodist *Arminian Magazine,* started in 1778 and publicized in the new United States by Thomas Coke and Francis Asbury.[65] Disorganized though the Kentucky General Union was, a couple of Bluegrass preachers, Stark Dupuy and Silas Noel, had both started Baptist periodicals that were briefly successful.[66] But just as secular newspapers of that day and age were loudmouthed, bombastic tools of the political parties to which their individual editors belonged and which almost never related a news item or story objectively, church periodicals were equally loud and often unfairly written, holding forth the tenets of their own editors and backers at the expense of other evangelical denominations and preachers—and sometimes of truth itself—in the full spirit of the evangelical Protestant culture that had developed in the wake of the Great Revival. As might have been anticipated, *The Christian Baptist* proved to possess a great deal in common with them, but its real distinction from the herd was the fact that Campbell crafted it as a *religious* newspaper as opposed to a *denominational* one. He wasn't trying to back or endorse anyone but himself and those who agreed with him. He and Walter Scott, his main collaborating writer in the early days,[67] skewered Baptists, Methodists, Episcopalians, Lutherans, Presbyterians, and Roman Catholics alike with a hard, combative writing style peppered by much War of 1812– and Era of Good Feeling–blessed military imagery.[68] The fact that Campbell, and Scott, too, propagated their doctrinal stance through a newspaper rather than through the sponsorship of an association, synod, or any other clerical assembly simply blinded a great many people to the fact that any newspaper's editorial slant can itself assume the power of a creed, and that Campbell's editorship of *The Christian Baptist* managed to do just that. His very literary style, independent, combative, and sarcastic as it was, convinced many Americans already imbibing the spirit of nineteenth-century rationalism from so many other cultural quarters that he did indeed back up his claims for heralding the restoration of primitive, apostolic Christianity. Campbell's opponents countered that he and his readers merely substituted the editorial pronouncements of the paper for a more conventional denominational confession, and in later years even some Campbell followers began to realize that the position of newspaper editor actually carried essentially the same weight in their tradition that the office of bishop, association moderator, or convention president did within those of others that Campbell had criticized so roundly.[69] But for good or ill, *The Christian Baptist* initiated the very first mass-media religious movement in American history, blazing the trail for *The Watchtower, The Plain Truth, Good News,* and so many other, newer periodicals likewise claiming to represent pure, unsullied apostolic doctrine—but ultimately representing distinctive religious movements in their own right. Like other such periodicals as well, over time *The Christian Baptist* made its editor and publisher one of the richest Gospel ministers in the America of his day, indeed yet another ironic twist for a man who made his living heaping scorn upon "the Kingdom of the clergy."[70]

Still, being associated with the Pennsylvania and Ohio Baptists gave Campbell an absolutely vital start, since he gained his initial readership for *The Christian Baptist* by utilizing the denomination's available conduits for such projects. In other words, Campbell never could have sparked a religious movement of his own had not Baptists first begun to buy his paper because they expected it to be a conventional Baptist periodical; though some were to throw it down in disgust as he elaborated his principles, others remained attached to it and abandoned it only after much thought, and still others became through-and-through converts to Campbell's doctrinal outlook. But as well as gaining notoriety among the Baptists, the periodical also rapidly became extremely popular among the ministers and members of Barton W. Stone's Christian Church. Both "Stoneite" and "Campbellite" Christianity already had much in common, especially the notion that Christians could and should abandon their quibbling sectarian and denominational differences and unite together to work and worship in pure, apostolic faith, doctrine, and practice. In addition, there seems even to have been some common ground between Stoneites and Campbellites in their beliefs concerning the role of Scripture itself in the conversion of lost souls.[71] But it is certain that Barton Stone and Alexander Campbell approached the idea from different perspectives, Stone's still being much more emotionalistic than Campbell would have considered proper, and thus even though Stoneites embraced the stated ecumenism of *The Christian Baptist,* Campbell's legalistic position on baptism for the remission of sins was at first as controversial to Stone and many of his followers as it was to most other denominations.[72]

The next few years would prove to be interesting. As it was, beginning in the fall of 1823 *The Christian Baptist* became the catalyst for a dramatic state of flux among both the Baptists and the Barton Stone Christians, and it provoked a host of different reactions that would have been impossible to categorize without the benefit of hindsight. Raccoon John Smith observed one such negative reaction at the dinner table at the close of that fateful Bracken Association meeting in September, and it will be remembered that his bitter quip about his fellow ministers caused Alexander Campbell to learn of his existence. But there were positive reactions, too, the primary one as far as Raccoon John was concerned being that the Payne family thought they could utilize *The Christian Baptist* not so much for the reforms that Campbell proposed, but as a possible complement to their own agenda to reassert their factional power in North District Association. Raccoon John's devotion to the Paynes rather than his own doctrinal or even financial independence at this point explains why he did not feel obligated to subscribe to the paper until Buckner Payne advised him that he should do so. Based on the Payne faction's machinations up to and including the July 1823 session of North District Association, it thus follows that William and Jilson Payne were out to utilize Campbell's plea for unity to suit their own already-obvious purposes; hence they would have assigned Buckner, the son of one, nephew of the other, and already a financial patron of Raccoon John at Mt. Sterling Church, the task of spreading the word about *The Christian Baptist* and making sure that their key factional members and church delegates lined up behind Campbell's unity plea in tandem with their own directives. A similar attraction with Campbell may have existed for Jeremiah Vardeman and William Vaughan as well, regardless of what position either man held on the Kentucky Baptist patronage spectrum at this time. At the Campbell-MacCalla debate in Kentucky in October 1823, which Raccoon John didn't get to attend because of the sickness in his family, Vardeman and Vaughan as well as a host of others became seriously interested in Campbell's ideas even though this was the occasion he chose to reveal his position on baptism for the remission of sins[73]—an idea they both ultimately came to despise.

But it's unlikely that the Paynes, at least the patriarchs Jilson and William, ever anticipated Raccoon John's being quite so taken with the writing of Alexander Campbell all on his own. Smith both subscribed to the paper and encouraged his own hearers, including his brother Jonathan, Grassy Lick Church clerk James Mason, Bethel stalwart Thomas Moseley, and the John Coons family at Spencer Creek, to do the same. James Fishback, brother of James Mason's wife, Elizabeth, and himself a reputed Lexington physician and respected minister in Elkhorn Association, likewise became interested in *The Christian Baptist* at about this same time, although we do not know whether Mason's and, indirectly, Raccoon John's and the Paynes', influence was responsible. As Raccoon John recalled in 1857 to Albert Allen, for the one-dollar annual subscription price he got the first seven issues of the periodical—July 1823 through February 1824—together in one package, and a single issue each month following. They at once inspired him and mystified him. He told Allen that he was "much pleased" with many of Campbell's doctrinal analyses, but that others "so plainly ran counter to my former convictions that I could not believe them *true*" (emphasis in original). So intrigued was he that he sat down with the now-convalescent Nancy, a Bible, and his new literary treasures and had Nancy read relevant passages of Scripture as they appeared as references in the articles through which he combed. Though John Augustus Williams tries to sweeten the fact that Raccoon John was perplexed to this degree by his first examination of Campbell's writings,[74] Smith made it clear to Albert Allen that the reading put him into a quandary: "although I did not dare to contradict the statements there made [in *The Christian Baptist*], I could not see their truth."[75]

We could wish that Raccoon John had said more to Allen about specifics—exactly what within those first seven *Christian Baptist* issues pleased him and what didn't. We can be fairly sure that Campbell's attacks against suprachurch missionary boards and societies, so repugnant to modern mainline Baptist historians who have written about the denomination's Campbell period, were only tangential to Raccoon John's own concerns; after all, Robert Elkin's machinations that had foiled Jilson Payne and compelled him to import Raccoon John to Montgomery County had already made North District Association a nonmissionary body anyway, irrespective of either Calvinism or Arminianism. But considering all we know about Raccoon John's life from his early boyhood until his first perusal of the newspaper, we can make a fair guess that he was not only overwhelmingly impressed with Campbell's fund of knowledge and his writing style, but thrilled with the new editor's vituperative slant against "the little popes"[76] among the Baptists and other Protestant denominations. Having given his heart to find intellectual and spiritual fulfillment among Kentucky's United Baptists only to have his aspirations tangled up completely within the folds of General Union patronage politics, forced to score victories for Jeremiah Vardeman and Jilson Payne in order to succeed for the cause of Christ, Raccoon John must have grasped at the ideal of a pure, unfettered apostolic Christianity—even if it was, as of yet, merely a hope-filled abstraction—like a drowning man or woman might have clung to a life preserver. This consideration alone enables us to understand why Raccoon John initially responded with such wild enthusiasm to Alexander Campbell and wanted simply to stare at him, uninterrupted by any other sight or sound, for an hour. If Campbell's plea for unity, unhampered by all the dirty church politics that had become Raccoon John's bread and butter, could be made into reality, the Campbell system would validate the whole of his angst- and grief-fraught life so far as being the simple search for a truth that he had finally discovered in *The Christian Baptist.* Campbell's words resounded not only in Raccoon John's mind but in his soul, and as he and Nancy pored over the pages of those first seven issues of *The Christian Baptist,* he found himself more and more convinced that Campbell very well could be right.

But his years of experience in the General Union had made him as much of a pragmatist as he would ever become. By his own admission to Nancy, he didn't even think a Christian reformation could be accomplished within his lifetime, although he hoped that the next generation might bring it off.[77] Right now, the Paynes wanted to use what they could of Campbell's writing and influence to further the interests of their own Baptist faction, and a major part of that plan called for their managing Raccoon John's campaign to be North District Association's moderator. After all, even Raccoon John himself had to have considered the moderatorial position as the highest clerical honor to which he could aspire in his present circumstances, and in that context he must have long regarded it as the pinnacle of his own hopes and dreams. Very well; even though the Paynes wanted to use him to maintain their own version of the status quo, he still might find himself able, one day, to use the moderator's office independently as a pulpit of true, godly reform instead, and thus play a small part in the religious reformation that he hoped his surviving children would know.

Raccoon John thus happily and hopefully passed the first two months or so of 1824. One could almost venture a speculation that he was primed for his next level, as it were: that Alexander Campbell and *The Christian Baptist* had lifted him out of the tawdry aesthetic existence of church politics into which he had unwittingly "backslidden" from his youthful first experience of the religious, his new birth in Christ after his father's death, and propelled him forward again to yet another subjective but ethical mindset of repentance, reflection, caring, and self-actualization. That is, if one takes seriously the possibility that Kierkegaard might have known what he was talking about.

Northeastern Kentucky at the Beginning of the Campbell Reform 1823 - 1836

1. Lexington; Town Fork Baptist Church; Main Street Christian Church; Mill Street Church of Christ; Lexington Cemetery
2. Georgetown; Great Crossings Church; Georgetown Christian Church; last Kentucky home of John Smith
3. Cane Ridge and North Middletown Christian Churches; Flat Lick Baptist Church
4. Bald Eagle Baptist Church; Sharpsburg Christian Church
5. Boonesborough; the "Old Stone" (Providence) Church of Howard's Creek
6. Howard's Upper Creek Church
7. Goshen Church; birthplace of eastern Kentucky "Old Time" Baptists
8. Lulbegrud Church; Jilson Payne's Mt. Pleasant plantation
9. Grassy Lick Church; Raccoon John Smith's first Montgomery County home
10. Mt. Sterling; Mt. Sterling Church
11. Cane Springs Church; David Chenault farm
12. Tates Creek Church
13. Estill County; Salem, Mt. Tabor, Beaver Pond Churches
14. South Fork Red River Church
15. Slate Liberty Church
16. Carlisle; Carlisle Church
17. Flemingsburg; Flemingsburg Church
18. Owingsville; Owingsville Christian Church; second John Smith residence
19. Maysville (Limestone); Campbell/MacCella debate (1823)
20. Jeffersonville; Sycamore Church
21. Hazel Green/Daysboro; Red River Church
22. West Liberty; South Fork Church ("Poplar Meeting-House")
23. White Oak Christian Church (1832); Low Gap United Baptist Church (1814)
24. Old Grassy Christian Church (1831)
25. Salyersville; Burning Springs Church
26. Caney Creek; last homeplace of Daniel Williams
27. Paint Lick (Paintsville after 1835) and vicinity; Buffalo Shoal (later Old Union) church; Concord Church
28. Open Fork of Paint Creek Church
29. Ohio River Church; Ohio Association territories
30. Louisa; likely eastern boundary of Raccoon John Smith's ministerial field
31. present Morehead; Poplar Grove Church
32. Salt Lick Church

In the beginning *The Christian Baptist* was many things to many people. Its distinctive missionary stance, declaring all such endeavors invalid unless sponsored and controlled strictly by local congregations, very nearly stopped the Kentucky Baptists' support of missionary societies for a time,[78] and the newspaper influenced Baptists in other southern states similarly. A sizable number of these Baptists, though, were willing to accept Alexander Campbell's thoughts on missions while simultaneously rejecting his views on salvation. In late 1826 and the year following, Kehukee Association in North Carolina rebelled against state Baptist conventions, Sunday schools, and the missionary society movement in general and began to style themselves as Reformed Baptists. Campbell gleefully recorded the proceedings in *The Christian Baptist* as if Kehukee Association were endorsing his system,[79] but in fact Kehukee, a Regular-based Baptist association since the late 1760s, was now extremely Calvinistic and the "reform" they initiated echoed Licking Association's actions of more than a decade earlier and merely facilitated the establishment of the hyper-Calvinistic denomination now known as the Primitive Baptists. In another instance the Ohio Association in the extreme southeastern region of that state, another Regular Baptist body descended from the work of John Alderson Jr. and destined to be the ancestor of the Southern Baptists of the Big Sandy and Tug Valleys of eastern Kentucky, took inspiration from Campbell's New Testament emphasis and in 1825 resolved to drop all creeds and confessions of faith for Scripture alone. The group's congregations even voted to style themselves as Baptist Churches of Christ in a compromise between their traditions and the nondenominational appellations that Campbell advocated. The body never did quite accept Campbell's missionary perspective, though, and its 1826 annual session equally enthusiastically endorsed the work of the Ohio Baptist Missionary Society with both correspondence and financial contributions, and invited the Society's general agent, Corbley Martin, to preach at their Sunday assembly with a visitor from eastern Kentucky's Burning Springs Association named Henry Dixon.[80] But with all the combinations and permutations that Campbell had set to stir among the Baptists with his newspaper, possibly the most controversial came from the March 1824 issue of *The Christian Baptist*—the eighth issue and consequently the very first one Raccoon John received after the initial introductory seven-issue mailing. In that issue, Campbell penned a cruel, mocking, merciless satire about the born-again experience, then commonly called "experimental religion," writing as if he had no idea what the term "experimental religion" meant in the first place and then using extremist examples from Baptist, Presbyterian, Stoneite, and Methodist evangelical meetings to castigate their adherents as so many idiots for even deigning to be caught up in such absurdities.[81] To be sure, traditional evangelicals expected to be disparaged like this by Deists and skeptics, but when a professing Baptist preacher mocked his own people in a manner so similar to that which "infidels" affected, they reacted with predictable outrage. The essay cost Buckner Payne and Raccoon John most of the new subscribers they had made for Campbell's periodical, and Smith even told Albert Allen that he didn't know what to make of the controversial article himself.[82] Campbell admitted later that his own father had criticized him for publishing the piece—his defense being that he had "thrown [it] out only to call the attention of the clergy"[83]—and Williams states that Raccoon John was almost ready to concur in the general reactionary opinion that Campbell was a wholly unregenerate, though erudite, man.

Included among those who told Raccoon John that they were discontinuing their subscriptions was his brother Jonathan, and because of this one incident Louis Cochran painted Raccoon John's brother as a whiny, know-it-all, overbearing, spiteful buffoon, a sometimes comic and always obnoxious foil for the great Raccoon John throughout his novel. Raccoon John, whose closeness to his brother is proven by the facts that he named a son for Jonathan and that, about a year after their disagreement over Campbell he gave Jonathan some serious aid with a ticklish bit of church politicking, undoubtedly would have been insulted by Cochran's fanciful portrayal. But historical novels must have their exaggerated heroes and villains, and perhaps the majority of us whose lives will be remembered no more than Jilson Payne's should consider ourselves blessed that our names will never be exploited in the manner that Cochran did Jonathan Smith's. At any rate, though Raccoon John could easily see his brother's point in this matter, he still encouraged Jonathan to keep up his subscription if for no other reason than to benefit himself by learning Campbell's style of writing. It was well worth the dollar, Raccoon John said, "simply to learn, if nothing else, the peculiar manner of the author in expressing *any* idea in few words" (emphasis in original).[84]

Though Campbell had certainly proven himself to be his own worst enemy with the publication of that article, he still enjoyed qualified support in the Bluegrass State, and shortly after the piece's publication he resolved to take another trip to Kentucky. A number of the Bracken Association preachers he had met the previous September at the MacCalla debate now became his hosts for a junket through Mason, Bracken, Fleming, Montgomery, Bourbon, and other downstate counties, and Raccoon John, still extremely eager to meet this fellow servant of Christ that had stimulated his mind so vigorously, proposed to some of his North District colleagues that they should ride over to Flemingsburg to escort Campbell to Mt. Sterling. He later recalled to Albert Allen and John Augustus Williams alike that no one in North District was interested in meeting with or talking to Campbell at this point, so he himself set out alone to get a firsthand impression of the great man. Actually, though, we can't be sure about this latter detail since later in the Allen narrative he makes a casual, perhaps absentminded mention that "old Brother Payne" was present, too.[85] We have no way of knowing whether he was speaking of Jilson or William, but the presence of either or both brothers shows that the Paynes were, like Raccoon John, still willing to give Campbell another chance to prove himself useful to their cause. Thus either John himself, or John accompanied by one of the senior Paynes, set out for Flemingsburg to meet Alexander Campbell, and the encounter only strengthened both the intellectual and emotional hold that Campbell was to exercise on him for the rest of his life.

At Flemingsburg, William Vaughan introduced Smith to Campbell, after a brief parley in which he assured Raccoon John that Campbell was neither a Calvinist, an Arminian, an Arian, nor even a Trinitarian, that he was one of the most pious, godly men that Vaughan had ever met, and that—to quote Vaughan directly—"Lord bless you, he knows everything!"[86] It had rained the night before and the roads were muddy, and the two men came upon Campbell at his hosts' just as he was taking off his riding chaps (known in those days as "sherryvallies"). Here Raccoon John made possibly his most famous observation about Campbell, and insofar as can be determined, the only jest he ever made about the man that included so much as a hint of criticism: "his nose," remarked Smith both to Allen and Williams, "seemed to stand a little to the north." And here too Raccoon John admitted that he wanted to spend an hour looking at his new mentor without anyone saying a word to him, but he never got the chance. Campbell greeted him cordially, remarking that he knew John Smith already though he'd never met him yet—a reference to Smith's pungent quip the previous fall about the ministers he worked with—and shortly afterward excused himself to deliver a sermon at the local Baptist meetinghouse. Smith, Vaughn, and Campbell's traveling companions followed along eagerly.

On reaching the church house, they found that the building was too small to accommodate the immense crowd of curious hearers, and so the members of the church erected a small plank stand at the rear of the structure so that Campbell could preach outdoors. Smith and as many of the other ministers who could conveniently do so parked themselves on the planks, and after singing, prayer, and an introduction, Campbell rose and commenced. Taking merely a conversational tone with his hearers rather than the loud and sometimes musical form of address to which the Flemingsburg hearers were accustomed, he preached on the fourth chapter of Galatians for a period of two and a half hours that Raccoon John later remarked had seemed like only thirty minutes. Campbell was everything that Smith had hoped him to be, because, in Raccoon John's mind, the sermon had transcended Calvinism, Arminianism, and every other *-ism* that existed. That evening he led prayer and devotions for Campbell because none of the other preachers in the company were willing to do so, and on the next morning when they all started out for Mt. Sterling—the mysterious "old Brother Payne" still being in the company—he had the chance to enter into a long conversation with Campbell about "Christian experiences," the details of which have already been noted in this work, that satisfied him completely as to Campbell's character as well as his fund of knowledge. Campbell delivered three discourses at Mt. Sterling, and Raccoon John afterward continued in company with him as far as North Middletown in Bourbon County.[87]

Considering the degree of detail with which Raccoon John remembered his first face-to-face meeting with Alexander Campbell, it must have been one of the peak experiences of his life, and certainly one of his two happiest memories of 1824. Another memorable and presumably happy event occurred at North District Association's annual meeting that July. Although Raccoon John never spoke of this circumstance in later years, we will examine it presently in light of what data we can glean both from Williams and from the association's minute records. But there were dark days for John and Nancy in this twelvemonth, too. It must be remembered that, after the family's "dangerous sickness," William Pinckney Smith died at some unknown date in 1824,[88] and this loss may have occurred between Raccoon John's meeting with Campbell and the events of the summer. Though John and Nancy's grief might have been assuaged a tiny fraction by Joshua and Betsy Hurt's naming of their firstborn son after the little dead boy, John had now lost four of his ten children, and Nancy two of her six. As in the case of Eliza Baize's death some five years earlier, their knowledge of their association's parrying of Richard Thomas's 1805 "infant purity" query couldn't have helped their feelings one bit, and whether or not little William's death had anything to do with it, within a year of the sad occurrence Raccoon John would attack the venerable Thomas with all the considerable political strength he had mustered within North District by that time.

It also was a year of political tumult for America. Andrew Jackson, since the Battle of New Orleans firmly ensconced in the hearts and minds of trans-Allegheny settlers as *the* man of the people, was campaigning hard for election to the U.S. presidency. After a bitterly fought contest against John Quincy Adams and Henry Clay that fall, Jackson's hopes would be dashed when the election was thrown to the House of Representatives and Adams would emerge as the victor when Clay threw his electoral votes to Adams in exchange for the position of secretary of state. Though Jackson might be down, however, he was a long way from out. Almost immediately after his defeat he began to make plans to storm the American electorate again in 1828, with he and his backers even creating their own political organization for the purpose; thus under Jackson's fiery influence was born both the earliest version of the modern presidential campaign and the political organization known ever since as the Democratic Party.

It's hard to say whether secular affairs had any real bearing on the actions of North District Association in this year, but this first Jackson presidential campaign very well could have. Even as Adams and Jackson were competing for the control of the executive branch of the national government, two factions that both claimed to represent the people's best interests were vying for control of the association—even though both North District factions had wielded power before and each had managed to negate most of the good that the other had tried to do. North District history thus repeated itself in this spring and summer. The constitutional conference scheduled by the 1823 association took place in May 1824 at Lulbegrud, although we know virtually no details of the proceedings. Whether association moderator Chenault, church pastor Thomas Boone, Jilson Payne, or even Raccoon John himself presided we cannot say, although later evidence indicates that Thomas Boone harbored considerable antipathy both toward clerk James French and the whole idea of constitutional reform at this time and thus he was not likely to have involved himself in the project any more than he could help. All we know for certain is that the meeting was held and its delegation did come up with some tentative ideas for constitutional amendments to be presented and discussed at North District's regular annual session in July. But then at that second meeting, which was hosted by the Payne stronghold of Grassy Lick, the assembled delegation rejected the Lulbegrud convention's suggested amendments entirely. In a rare move, the association even turned down James French's submission for the year's circular letter, and passed a motion that Thomas Boone write that year's circular instead. Thus, rather than the pointed critique of North District and call for reform that had become French's usual circular offering, the association was treated by Boone to a letter of the older type, an insipid paean to Christian love and fellowship structured so as not to offend anyone and which, consequently, must have accomplished very little in furthering the noble causes Boone claimed to espouse. This, if nothing else, seems to indicate that at this time James French definitely had a better relationship with his previous pastor, Raccoon John, than he did with his new pastor, Boone.

But if the Chenault faction did indeed negate the good of the constitutional conference by these actions, the Payne faction could afford to accept these setbacks with grace and even good sportsmanship. For at this July 1824 session, Raccoon John, who had long cultivated his image among the downstate Kentucky Baptists along the Jacksonian line of self-achieved victory over daunting hardship, finally attained the pinnacle of his career as a Baptist: he was elected as moderator of North District Association. He would serve in the office for two years, and insofar as he could execute his duties within the paradox of North District's Regular Baptist constitution and its Separate Baptist traditions, he did a good job for himself, the Payne faction, and the association as a whole.

By and large, Raccoon John's other biographers have tried to ignore or downplay his tenure as North District moderator, I suspect because they felt their stories had better continuity if they presented Raccoon John as a consistent underdog during these years. For example, John Augustus Williams makes only one reference to Raccoon John's moderatorship, that being an offhand observation that North District's 1825 circular letter was written "with the name of John Smith, as moderator, subscribed."[89] Whether he was actually trying to hint that Raccoon John had written this letter himself we cannot say, but Louis Cochran took it for granted that Smith indeed had written it and so included the detail in his novel's plotline. Actually the missive, which will be examined and discussed shortly, was written by James French,[90] and it may have been a simple resubmission of his rejected 1824 offering, although it's likely that, regardless of what year it was penned, both Raccoon John and Jilson Payne gave French suggestions for its theme and structure. Everett Donaldson notes Raccoon John's reelection as North District moderator in 1825 while saying nothing about his assumption of the position the year before, although he admits that the circumstances "were indicative of the favor he had gained among the messengers representing the various churches composing the association."[91] At least it can be said that Donaldson portrays the Smith time line more accurately than does Williams, who without exception garbles every one of Raccoon John's recollections of his associational administration with events that took place at least one to two years after his tenure as moderator had ended. But the key to understanding this confusing and poorly documented period is remembering that, at this juncture, Raccoon John was not yet a full disciple of Alexander Campbell but was still rather following his political mandate from the Paynes. In other words, he was still trying to carry out Jilson Payne's concept of a reformation rather than Campbell's, and utilizing and advocating the principles of *The Christian Baptist* only insofar as they could conveniently benefit Payne concerns. This is not to say that Raccoon John's enthusiasm for *The Christian Baptist* didn't increase with almost every new issue. It did, and one could argue that even during his associational moderatorship he assumed a pro-Campbell position on many issues that was more outspoken than Jilson and William Payne themselves would have liked. But for all that, Raccoon John still knew quite clearly that he was working for the Paynes, and he tempered his actions accordingly.

He could actually accomplish little at the 1824 session itself. The Payne faction had been out of titular power for eight years now, and as noted above, some graceful and conciliatory gestures toward the Chenault faction, such as a cheerful acknowledgment of the rejection of both the Lulbegrud conference's report and James French's circular letter, were a practical necessity for his appearance as a good sport. Though the appointments he made for letters to be written and delegates to attend corresponding associations were a mixture from both North District factions and involved several of his allies, including Thomas Moseley, James Mason, John Coons, and Jilson Payne himself, for the all-important arrangements committee Raccoon John appointed Enoch Willoughby of Sycamore, Thomas White of Mt. Tabor, Isaac Thornburgh of Cane Springs, and the venerable James Quesenberry of Unity, all known supporters of the Chenault faction. This was another conciliatory, and probably absolutely necessary, gesture. Otherwise, the only associational action Raccoon John supervised was a money appropriation for James French to purchase a new record book.[92] But once North District's 1824 session was finished, Smith began to carry out the real duties of his job with a vengeance, and he probably enjoyed it greatly since it involved dissociating the Paynes with the hyper-Calvinistic Licking Association entirely. The duty was not without some risk, though, since as a mere front man for the Paynes he was still every bit as expendable as David Barrow had once been.

In the previous chapter we noted that Ambrose Dudley and Lewis Corbin, both now affiliated with Licking Association, had each served short pastorates at Grassy Lick Church in the days before Licking had separated from the General Union. As such they had been Payne allies as well, and it appears that, even at this time, they both made occasional visits to Raccoon John's congregations at Grassy Lick and Mt. Sterling to preach. As active ministers in reactionary Licking, though, they were steadily becoming more of a liability than an asset to Jilson Payne, but the general esteem in which they had been held before they broke away from Elkhorn had so far precluded them from much censure among Payne's compatriots. Raccoon John seems to have been the first North District minister to confront them publicly over doctrinal differences, and it is highly unlikely that he would have done so before he was elected moderator of the association. John Augustus Williams notes instances in which each man preached highly Calvinistic sermons, one at Grassy Lick and the other at Mt. Sterling; in his followup sermons as pastor, Raccoon John refuted their strict Calvinism thoroughly. Williams tries to date both stories in or after 1828,[93] and it must be admitted that in Lewis Corbin's case this supposition cannot be ruled out. Corbin lived for years after the incident in question, finally passing away on April 1, 1840. But it is known that Ambrose Dudley died on January 27, 1825,[94] and so Raccoon John's refutation of his preaching had to have occurred at least a few months before that date. In any case, Raccoon John helped to effect the doctrinal shift that Jilson Payne had been trying to establish for his followers since 1823 at least, and Smith also thereby managed to send a further message to the Chenault faction that he could be trusted both to defend the Bible and to tolerate the doctrine of general atonement in his efforts to maintain the Terms of General Union.

Smith's confrontation with Richard Thomas, the author of the terrible "infant purity" query from Bald Eagle Church in 1805, took place either in the spring and early summer of his first term as association moderator or the late summer and fall of his second. Reclaiming Bald Eagle for North District Association had been on Jilson Payne's agenda ever since Thomas had split the church a dozen or so years earlier, and it was as important to his cause as had been his regaining control, through Raccoon John, of the Mt. Sterling congregation a couple of years before. Although Raccoon John must have taken a great deal of personal satisfaction from outwitting Thomas, the action unfortunately accomplished little good either for Bald Eagle or for his brother Jonathan, pastor of the moderate faction still in North District, in the long term. It seems that the two Bald Eagle congregations, for years having shared the meetinghouse on alternate weekends, decided to try to reunite if they could agree on mutual terms. We cannot know how or from what quarter this reunion idea came about, but it's as good a guess as any that Jilson Payne and Raccoon John had come up with it themselves after Raccoon John's 1824 election. Jonathan probably helped them sell the proposal to both sides of the congregation. Anyway, at the meeting both Richard Thomas and Jonathan Smith were present, along with Raccoon John in his role as North District moderator. Thomas presented a written set of very strongly Calvinistic articles of faith for the church to adopt, based on the Philadelphia Confession, and Jonathan responded with a set of much milder articles based probably on the Terms of General Union and the doctrinal positions of the Payne faction at the time. After hearing the two argue back and forth for a while over the relative merits of their confessional statements, Raccoon John finally stood up, took the two creeds from the hands of the disputants, placed them on the communion table with a Bible between them, and intoned—at least according to the stilted prose of Williams who, true to form, mixed this story confusingly with later events—"Since, brethren, neither will accept the creed of the other, let both come together on this Bible, as the only Word of God, and the only bond of union."

"It will never do!" spluttered Thomas hastily and angrily, "It will not do at all! Such a course would let in Arians, Arminians, and every other kind of errorists! It will never do!"

"I cannot agree with my brother," purred Raccoon John in return. "In my judgement, the Word of God excludes all sectarians. But if the Bible, as he says, would admit them, how dare he form a creed to reject them?"[95]

Thomas's response is not recorded, but it can be imagined that Raccoon John had his customary laugh at outfoxing one more opponent who professed to have more knowledge than he possessed. In light of little William's death the year before, he must have enjoyed putting Thomas down for his involvement in the 1805 Bald Eagle query as well. But be that as it may, Raccoon John's ploy on behalf of Jonathan and the Payne faction of North District came to naught. The church united, sure enough, but neither on Thomas nor on Jonathan as pastor of the whole flock; instead they settled on a young preacher named Samuel Jones, who had been raised up from among their own number. Jones seems to have been a Calvinist of more moderate sensibilities than old Thomas though not as liberal as Raccoon John or Jonathan, and he maintained the church in Licking Association.[96] The small Bald Eagle faction adhering to North District simply vanished away within a few years, and Jonathan himself left North District for Bracken Association. He was sent by Bracken as a correspondent delegate to North District's 1828 session,[97] but after this he disappears from the records and essentially from history. Everett Donaldson states that he died shortly thereafter,[98] but this assertion could be open to question; Jonathan might have gone west, as a good many Baptist preachers were doing at this point, or even back to the Kentucky/Tennessee border country. A common name such as Smith is extremely difficult to trace accurately using early census records, and we know only that neither Raccoon John nor Williams ever mentions Jonathan again after the Bald Eagle episode.

Besides the dramatic advantage of presenting Raccoon John as a consistent underdog during this period, Williams's apparent purpose in distorting

Smith's time line as he did was to cast him in as many situations as possible as a through-and-through advocate for Alexander Campbell. Actually, we have very few clues as to exactly how much *The Christian Baptist* had altered Raccoon John's doctrinal outlook thus far. He told Albert Allen that a year passed after his first face-to-face encounter with Campbell before he was "fully convinced of the Scripturality of his views, and commenced the advocacy of the Bible as a sufficient rule of faith and practice."[99] If he told Allen the truth, he assumed this stance in or near March 1825, and his pointed remarks to Richard Thomas and Bald Eagle Church regarding "sectarians" are consistent with it. But it must be remembered that, at the same time, a stance on the Bible as the only true Christian creed was already a time-honored Separate Baptist position, and it was certainly nothing new either to the churches in the Chenault faction of North District or to two of Raccoon John's own churches in the Payne faction, Bethel and Spencer Creek. The Payne faction probably never could have elected Raccoon John as association moderator without recognizing this fact, and thus Smith had not yet been put even in the position of a Campbell controversialist, much less a Baptist underdog. But it is certain that Raccoon John's respect for *The Christian Baptist* and its editor's positions was still growing, regardless of the limits behind which his North District patrons wished to exploit the periodical, and the time was now approaching that John himself could take an even larger hand in shaping both factional and associational policy than he had heretofore enjoyed.

Though he was only fifty-eight years old, Jilson Payne was dying. His health may have been failing gradually all through 1824 and 1825, since he wrote his will in February of the former year and continued to tinker with it until he attached the final codicil on July 12 of the latter. In it he provided for his second wife, his thirteen-year-old daughter, Ann, and his brother Jimmy's orphaned sons, essentially in the Virginia dynastic tradition.[100] Raccoon John is of course nowhere mentioned, not even in the bequest of a single book from Payne's voluminous library, but he did leave Smith a legacy all the same. Though nowhere near as strong as it had been in its early years, the Payne North District faction was now respectable again, and still backed consistently by the Coons family at Spencer Creek, Thomas Moseley at Bethel, James Mason at Grassy Lick, James French at Lulbegrud, and undoubtedly the entire congregation at Mt. Sterling. Buckner Payne had not yet joined there, though perhaps his wife, Eliza Ann, had, and as indicated earlier Raccoon John and Nancy may have named their next daughter Eliza Ann, born in 1825, for Buckner's wife rather than the baby's grandmother Hurt or its own deceased older sister. Smith also enjoyed the patronage of William and Mildred Payne's other sons and daughters, including John Newton, Lucille, and Dulcinea Payne, the latter of whom married Moses Ryan.[101] Though there were as of yet few if any other ordained or recognized preachers or elders included in this number, it comprised the cream of Mt. Sterling society; James French's daughter and son-in-law Susanna and Kenaz Farrow were later enthusiastic Smith supporters as well, and they may have been friendly to Raccoon John by this time also. Kenaz himself was not yet a church member, though Susanna, influenced by her vociferous Baptist parents, may have been.

Thus when Jilson Payne would finally be gathered to his fathers, the leadership of the Payne North District Associational faction would pass, *de facto* if not entirely *de jure,* directly into the hands of Raccoon John Smith himself.

At North District's 1825 annual session, held in July at Daniel Williams's old Sycamore Church near present Jeffersonville, Jilson Payne was absent. His name is mentioned nowhere in the group's minutes for that year. This was the season in which he was making his final alterations on his will, and his health probably simply precluded him from attending. Nonetheless, Raccoon John won reelection as moderator, and he and clerk James French pressed forward with their program. As at the previous year's meeting, little was accomplished in terms of positive legislation, but French's circular letter for 1825—the one Williams tried so hard to suggest, and Cochran insisted, that Raccoon John himself wrote—was the longtime clerk's sternest condemnation of North District's and the entire General Union's shortcomings yet. A portion of it is quoted below, to show not only the development of Raccoon John and the Paynes' unity program but as evidence that the problems regularly experienced by our bold, pious Baptist ancestors were not really worse than, or even all that different from, those common to modern churches:

> We come now to mention some of those things, which have had the most pernicious effect among the Baptists. Not to persecute, cast odium, or wound, not to stigmatize, reproach, or grieve—but solely as a warning, or admonition, to the Baptists of the present day. Some hopeful members have lost their standing, destroyed their usefulness, and given occasion to the enemies of the Lord to speak reproachfully, by illicit commerce between the sexes. Drunkenness has caused much distress. How many strong and useful members have been overcome by ardent spirits [*sic*]. Covetousness has been the source of much disquietude and detriment to society—Conformity to the world has weakened the hands of some, been an occasion of stumbling to others, and of grief to many. Public honors and offices have greatly injured the religious usefulness of some prominent members, and rendered others less conspicuous, more of a burden than a help to the churches. Schisms and divisions have done much to mar the peace and impede the progress of the Baptists. Short as the period is since their first churches were constituted in Kentucky, it is marked with five splits, or divisions, and each of them productive of widely extended distress among the churches. The first of these was Universalism. This took away some preachers and members. Another produced the people now called Separate Baptists. Another terminated in what is called Arianism.

> Another ended in those who style themselves Friends to Humanity. Another has ultimately named themselves Particular Baptists. All these have taken place in Kentucky, besides some other defections of less importance.
>
> Thus the Baptists in this state, who a little upwards of forty years ago consisted of but two sorts, Regulars and Separates, differing nothing in externals, are now become six kinds of Baptists. And all these different sorts (the Universalists and Friends to Humanity excepted) pretty numerous, supplied with preachers, and bidding fair to extend and increase in numbers. And intermixed more or less with the United Baptists, which is the main body, and more numerous than all the others put together, of whom the churches composing this association are part. And the United Baptists are not uniform in their conduct towards those other sorts of Baptists: for some of their associations are in correspondence with some of these other sorts of Baptists, while some other of their associations withhold correspondence from them all, and correspond with the United Baptists only. What is to be the end of these things, will not this contrariety, this inconstancy of the United Baptists in their correspondence, if persisted in, prove a root of bitterness, whereby many, if not all of them, will be defiled?
>
> Beloved brethren and sisters, thus you see the Baptists split into six names, all practicing baptism the same way, and on the same kind of subjects. This state of things is a source of sorrow and anguish of heart to some among us of the United Baptists. And must they be perpetual, are these wounds incurable? Who can tell but that the Baptists of the present day are to be the happy instruments of healing the splits and schisms, of those who have gone before and who should be the first movers in the work of making peace among the poor distressed Baptists? Why [?] let the main body, let the United Baptists have the consolation of making the first advances, and who knows, but He who said when here, "Blessed are the peacemakers," and who has the hearts not only of kings, but of all men in His hands, will crown their efforts with the most ample and joyful success. Amen.

French's language was strong and direct, to be sure, but it remained to be seen how much actual reform he and Raccoon John could accomplish by their mere emphasis on adherence to the Terms of General Union. We must compliment them on addressing all the Union's problems so directly, however, though both French and Jilson Payne themselves had exploited their secular offices and honors in associational politics more than anyone else in North District. But by this period we can be fairly sure that Raccoon John personally believed that the true solution to the political strife, discord, and disunity in both his own association and the Union as a whole somehow lay in following the precepts laid down by Alexander Campbell in *The Christian Baptist.* Jilson Payne and James French must have agreed with him at least insofar as Campbell's idealization of Christian unity, and it is certain that Jilson and his first wife's nieces and nephews in Montgomery County and perhaps even their father and mother, William and Mildred over in Bracken Association, were becoming enthusiastic about at least some of Campbell's ideas as well. But that fall Jilson Payne died, and from this point forward Raccoon John and the younger Paynes shaped the faction's program essentially on their own. Raccoon John still seems to have believed that the reformation for which Campbell called could not be accomplished in his own lifetime, but he was willing to give his best efforts toward laying its initial groundwork.

Payne had penned the last codicil to his will on July 12, 1825, and the will was probated in Montgomery County court on October 3.[102] We do not know his exact death date, but it probably occurred in August or September. He had willed equal shares of Mt. Pleasant to his second wife, Ann Michie Payne, and his daughter, Ann Holland Payne, actually running a boundary line through the house itself, allowing his widow to occupy one side of the structure and his daughter the other. Whether this meant that Ann Holland Payne had been at odds with her stepmother during Jilson's lifetime we cannot say, but the boundary line accomplished little; soon after her father's death young Ann began to receive calls from a Scott County first cousin much older than herself, a widower named William Johnson who was the son of James and Nancy (Payne) Johnson and the grandson of Daniel Williams's old nemesis Henry Payne. She married him at age fourteen on July 26, 1826, and moved to Scott County with him. She and her stepmother subsequently sold the Mt. Pleasant plantation to James Prewitt, who had married James French's daughter Keziah in 1824. In the manner of the time, Jilson Payne's little community of slaves was thus possibly split up in the estate settlement as well, although as we have noted, first-cousin unions among the gentry class often reflected attempts to retain personal estate in the possession of a powerful family. Ann Michie Payne moved to Lexington, and she died in 1849. As for Jilson Payne's only child, we must hope that she enjoyed a happy life, because it was tragically short: though Ann bore children and even named a son and a daughter for her mother and father, she was only the second of William Johnson's four wives.[103] Her son Albert later became the police chief of the city of Louisville; her daughter Dulcinea married Thomas Cooper Coleman, a wealthy Louisville businessman; and her grandson, Albert's son Thomas or Tom Johnson, became one of the richest men in that same city and a pioneer engineer and entrepreneur of America's streetcar industry.

But whether or not Raccoon John had been simply waiting around for Payne's passing in order to implement *The Christian Baptist*'s advice more fully, he remembered doing so within a short time after the older man's death. One weekend of the very same month in which Payne's will was probated, Jacob Coons, younger brother of the John Coons that had been such a pillar for Payne first at Mt. Sterling and then at Spencer Creek, responded to an "invitation" at Spencer Creek and professed conversion. In the manner customary to North District churches of the time, and in fact still common among backcountry Kentucky Baptist congregations especially of the "Old Time" persuasion, Raccoon John told young Jacob to "go on in his own way, and say to the church whatever he pleased." Jacob replied that he had been concerned about the subject of religion for some time, and that although he had seen no strange sights nor heard no strange sounds, he believed with all his heart that Jesus was the Christ, and wished to obey him. Smith jubilantly proclaimed that, "with the Bible in my hand, if I were to die for it, I do not know what other question to ask him!" Jacob Coons was immersed that very same day and became a stalwart member and loyal aide both to John Coons and John Smith.[104] Although Jacob's profession of faith differed little from Alexander Campbell's own, which Raccoon John himself admitted would have been accepted by any Baptist church even before the advent of Campbell's popularity,[105] Smith came to regard this incident as "the very first exemplification of [Campbell's] Ancient Order within the bounds of [North] District, if not of the state [of Kentucky]."[106]

This baptism also afforded Raccoon John the opportunity for one of his characteristic rough jibes at ministers of other faiths, in this case the Presbyterian Joseph Price Howe, Jacob's father-in-law. Though Howe had baptized his daughter Matilda Jane, Jacob's young wife, as a Presbyterian when she was a baby, at her adolescence she seems to have come to what is perhaps a bright teenager's normal reaction to a sternly pious father, becoming something of a hellion. Donaldson hints that Howe was only too glad to marry her off to a "good boy" like Jacob Coons even if he did come from a Baptist family,[107] but Williams indicates that the old dominie clung to the hope that the young couple might both see their respective errors and become good Presbyterians one day. When Jacob was baptized at Spencer Creek, Howe thus became alarmed for the state of Matilda's soul, and immediately began to send her books, pamphlets, and tracts recommending the Presbyterian mode of baptism and church order and urged her to share them with her husband. Disquieted at Matilda's insistence that these tomes were "God's truth" even though she had paid little enough attention to her father's counsel thus far, Jacob appealed to Raccoon John for advice. Smith responded in the manner of Socrates, laying a careful net with a canny series of questions. He first asked Jacob if Matilda professed to be a Christian, and on Jacob's reply that she frankly acknowledged that she was vain, giddy, and a "great sinner," told him to ask her whether she was "in the church" or not. If she claimed to be a church member, Jacob was to pose the question why such a sinner should be a member of the church of God; if she denied that she was a member, he should ask her when the Presbyterians had turned her out.

Young Coons did as he was told, and though Matilda made no claim to be a church member, the question of her exclusion from Presbyterian fellowship completely stumped her. She went to her father for enlightenment, perhaps for the first time since her childhood. Howe told her that he had "initiated" her as an infant, but that, since Jesus once related a parable about tares and wheat in the same field, her worldly-mindedness made him fear that she was merely a tare. Even though that same parable relegated the tares to burning in the fire, apparently Matilda was satisfied with this explanation and so told Jacob. Of course he then went back to Raccoon John—the whole scenario turns almost into a situation comedy here—who then advised him to have her confirm that Howe himself had enrolled her in the church when she was an infant. Upon her positive reply, Jacob was to remind her that, in the Matthean parable to which her father had alluded, tares were sown by the devil; that is, if she was a "tare" as her father feared, and he himself had enrolled her in the church, then old Howe himself must have done the devil's work. This time, when Matilda took her husband's argument back to her father, he said no more, only groaned aloud and paced the floor, and from that time forward Matilda did, in John Augustus Williams's eyes, the right thing: she "listened to her husband's expositions of Scripture, and under his teachings, soon presented herself for immersion."[108] Raccoon John thus enjoyed the double pleasure of gaining another Spencer Creek convert and putting a mossbacked old Presbyterian dominie to shame. But the story does have its dark side. Joseph Price Howe did not live another year,[109] and it is disturbing to think that a fellow evangelical Christian preacher could see fit to humiliate him in his erstwhile-wayward daughter's eyes after this rough fashion, enjoying the process to boot, while even then the old man might have been suffering his final illness.

We wonder whether or not, by this point, the peppery rhetoric of *The Christian Baptist* was making Raccoon John more competitive and bellicose than he was to start with. In terms of a tough, combative style and the nimble use of ridicule and sarcasm juxtaposed with a heartfelt search for truth, peace, and happiness, Smith and Alexander Campbell were kindred spirits even before they met, though perhaps we can understand and appreciate the development of Raccoon John's fighting tendencies better than we can comprehend Campbell's. The fiery young editor was still steadily gaining followers, enemies, and notoriety generally, and Smith's colleagues Jeremiah Vardeman and Dr. James Fishback in Elkhorn Association and William Vaughan, Walter Warder, and William Morton in Bracken remained vocal supporters in spite of the controversial spring 1824 essay on the born-again experience. Williams even makes the claim that Jeremiah Vardeman began to immerse converts according to the Campbell view, that being for the remission of sins, in 1826,[110] although this contention is suspect since most Campbell historians attribute the first zealous implementation of this practice to Walter Scott in 1827.[111] But while Kentucky Baptist pro- and anti-Campbell tensions exacerbated, *The Christian Baptist* also became such an influence among the Stoneite Christian Churches, chiefly through the vigorous efforts of young Stoneite preachers such as John Rogers and B. F. Hall rather than the disposition or approval of Barton Stone himself, that Stone initiated his own periodical, *The Christian*

Messenger, in late 1826. Though *The Christian Messenger* is usually presented by historians as being a complement or a supplement to Campbell's journal, Stone actually may have begun it in competition with Campbell, or at least in an effort to establish a reasoned middle ground between his own perspectives and those of the younger pro-Campbell preachers under his leadership. Stone and Campbell got along reasonably well on a personal basis in later years, but they never entirely agreed on doctrine, and until Stone's death in 1844 the two did a great deal of verbal sparring back and forth, not entirely unlike Campbell with his Baptist critics. Campbell was a steadfast rationalist and aggressive reformer in his *Christian Baptist* days, and Stone was ever the old-fashioned Great Revival evangelist who advocated open communion and who spurned *The Christian Baptist*'s strict doctrinaire stance on immersion baptism though he himself believed in the ordinance with all his heart.[112] As will be shown in the next chapter, *The Christian Messenger* seems to have come to exert an unforeseen and surprising influence on at least one of Campbell's partisans in the General Union early on as well, to the grief and even the anger of those who at the time regarded Campbell as the more orthodox of the two.

But by May 1826 even Campbell had found himself a bit nonplussed by the militant enthusiasm of some of his subscribers. In that year he replied in an editorial to a letter signed by "An Independent Baptist," stating that "This plan of making our own nest, and fluttering over our own brood; of building our own tent, and confining all goodness and grace to our noble selves and the 'elect few' who are like us, is the quintessence of sublimated pharasaism . . . real Protestant monkery, [and] evangelical nunnery."[113] He may have foreseen that, in their rampant campaigns against what he had taught them to perceive as sectarianism, many of his advocates were developing a paradoxical sectarian mindset of their own, one that they couldn't even visualize because they so passionately believed that they had altogether abandoned Protestant sectarianism and denominationalism for pure Christianity and couldn't conceive that they were treating the newspaper itself as if it were a creed. Like Luther of old, though, Campbell in his early years seemed unable to restrain his pen when a personal principle was involved, and like Luther too he could exhibit a markedly greater amount of personal charm than his sermons or polemical writings ever indicated. Early Virginia Baptist historian and leader Robert Baylor Semple was only one of many who found themselves amazed at the difference between Campbell in person and Campbell on paper.[114] And so in 1826, as Joshua Carroll Smith became the latest addition to Raccoon John and Nancy's family after Eliza Ann, militant rhetoric continued to spew forth from *The Christian Baptist*'s pages, tension continued to build between traditionalist and Campbellite Baptists and between old-style Great Revival Stoneites and those of the Rogers-Hall party, and during his second term as North District moderator Raccoon John entered wholeheartedly into a period of ever-increasing controversy.

Sad it was that the matter came to a head for Raccoon John personally over one of Alexander Campbell's best and most honest efforts toward the enlightenment of his readership, a modern translation of the New Testament.

Among Campbell's topics in *The Christian Baptist* in late 1825 and early 1826 had been a series of essays on the history of the English Bible, for the purpose of familiarizing his readers with the pros and cons of each translation, from John Wyclif's in medieval times to the Authorized King James Version. All this was preparatory for his April 1826 release[115] of *The Living Oracles,* a modern translation of the New Testament that was a combination of the work of Scottish Presbyterian scholars James Macknight and George Campbell and Congregationalist scholar Phillip Doddridge. Alexander filled in with other translations as he saw fit, particularly with an American specimen done in 1808 by one Charles Thomson, and he exercised a free hand of his own with the help of his personal knowledge of Greek and the 1805 edition of Griesbach's *Greek New Testament.* He also included over one hundred annotations, somewhat on the order of Martin Luther's book-by-book commentary explaining how his sixteenth-century German translation should be read, William Tyndale's similar notations for the English version that became known as the Geneva Bible, and the editorializing of Cyrus I. Scofield and his colleagues in the "Scofield Reference" King James Version that was first published in 1909 and reissued in a new edition in 1967. Rarely, if ever, has a new Bible translation been issued without someone's inclusion of instructions on how to read and interpret it.

At least with Campbell's annotations and comments the readers of *The Living Oracles* didn't get a wholesale imposition of apocalyptic and dispensational assumptions upon the text of Scripture as did Scofield's myriad readership. Unfortunately, neither did *The Living Oracles* catch on with the Bible-reading public like the Scofield edition did, and it never got the acclaim that it really deserved even among the great majority of Campbell's followers. This is not to say that the new translation didn't have its own problems, for which Campbell was mostly responsible himself. Because of his own beliefs, Campbell insisted on bucking Macknight, Doddridge, George Campbell, and Thomson all and translating the Greek word *baptizien* as "immersion" every time it occurred in the text. Although, strictly speaking, the etymology of the term actually was *to dip* or *to immerse,* it was somewhat unsettling to see John the Baptist suddenly become John the Immerser, and "one faith, one Lord, one baptism" metamorphose into "one faith, one Lord, one immersion." Moreover, Campbell catered to the literary taste of the times a bit and occasionally embellished plain sentences with flowery words of Latin derivation: in the Sermon on the Mount in Matthew, his translation for the King James Version's "a city set on an hill cannot be hid" was "a city situate on a mountain must be conspicuous," and "whosoever shall kill shall be in danger of the judgement" became "whosoever commits murder shall be obnoxious to the judges."[116] And perhaps the most telling mark Campbell laid upon the work, besides his insistence on the word "immersion," was his treatment of the brief italicized phrases interjected by translators in the King James and earlier versions. Since these had been, after all, added in order to put verses or passages into clearer English, he felt free to change them as he personally saw fit. As noted, he did not believe in a special call to the sinner from the Spirit of God outside of the preached word of Scripture itself, and so Paul's comment to the Corinthians that "not many wise men after the flesh, not many mighty, not many noble *are called*" (the italics here indicating the translator's interpolation to clarify the passage) became "not many wise men after the flesh, not many mighty, not many noble *call you.*"[117] It was thus not entirely without reason that one critic contemporary to Campbell condemned him for producing "a New Testament made up of scraps from [Doctors Macknight, George Campbell, and Doddridge], and when neither of them suited, he put in his own rendering."[118]

But in spite of Campbell's personal quirks, which perhaps no individual translator can truly overcome completely, *The Living Oracles* represented a genuine and honest attempt on his part to put the New Testament into modern language for the benefit of the religion he sought to reform. Luther A. Weigle, who headed the translation committee at Yale University in 1952 for the famous (and in the South of a few years ago, infamous) Revised Standard Version of the Bible, praised Campbell for his essential honesty in handling the Greek text and his courage in presenting its meaning, and he acknowledged that Campbell was aware of the basic principles of interpretation and translation. Interestingly, he also noted that *The Living Oracles* actually anticipated the Revised Standard Version's correction of the King James text in many particulars. Campbell scholar Cecil K. Thomas listed a number of these in his own definitive study of *The Living Oracles,* including "be anxious" for "take thought" in Matthew 6:25, "bankers" for "exchangers" in Matthew 25:27, "morsel" for "sop" in John 13:26, "overlooked" for "winked at" in Acts 17:30, and "faint-hearted" for "feeble-minded" in 1 Thessalonians 5:14.[119] However, the great downfall of *The Living Oracles,* at least in the South, was that of the King James Version itself among the Puritans of the seventeenth century and, ironically, the Revised Standard Version among evangelicals and fundamentalists in the twentieth: it was *new,* and that was all that was required to make it religiously suspect. In spite of the seventeenth-century Puritans' dissatisfaction with the King James Version, which, unfortunately in their eyes, omitted the earlier Geneva Bible's own fiery Protestant annotations, by this point in time the King James Version was considered to be *the* Holy Bible by the great majority of American Christians regardless of sect or denomination. Though the attitude has softened a bit nowadays, it is still prevalent, especially in the South among some, perhaps many, conservative and fundamentalist denominations and subdenominations; it is of course visceral rather than logical, but nonetheless as strong within many of these Protestant groups as the stance that enabled Russia's *Raskolniki,* or Old Believers, to withstand state persecution for centuries after their rejection of the seventeenth-century Tsar Alexei

Mikhailovich's mandated reforms of the Russian Orthodox liturgy. One occasionally hears the comment even from some college-trained ministers in the South that they believe that the good old King James is actually a more accurate rendering of God's Word than the original Hebrew and Greek texts from which it was translated.[120]

Thus *The Living Oracles,* though it went through several reprints and revisions during Campbell's lifetime and even afterward, was doomed to only a modest circulation among merely a portion of his Reform advocates, and a handful of Baptists otherwise. Though the translation never suffered the multitude of public bonfires throughout the South that the Revised Standard Version did in the early 1950s, one of the more publicized Kentucky responses to the Campbell translation came from Long Run Association's moderator, George Waller. After burning his copy of *The Living Oracles,*[121] he began his own Baptist anti-Campbell newspaper, *The Baptist Recorder,* along with another prominent minister named Spencer Clack.[122] Between this periodical and Campbell's and Stone's journals, editorial war escalated and continued unabated for at least four years.

But Raccoon John, for one, loved *The Living Oracles* dearly. He may have used it, literally, for the rest of his life both at home and, whenever convenient, in the pulpit. Though his backcountry boyhood had probably made him more familiar with archaic English forms than were the men of his same generation in the Bluegrass, he recalled to Williams that some of the antiquated terms of the King James Version had nonetheless been indecipherable to him until he got hold of Campbell's new version. The only fault he found with the translation—and indeed, the sole circumstance on which he is known to have disagreed openly with Alexander Campbell about anything, after their March 1824 meeting—was Phillip Doddridge's rendering of Acts 16:30, in which the Philippian jailer asks Paul and Silas, "Sirs, what must I do to be safe?" The King James and all earlier English translations had this verse as reading "what must I do to be saved," and John flatly declared that the old version of this passage must have been the truer one. Whether or not his own influence with Campbell had anything to do with the matter, in a later edition of *The Living Oracles* the old rendering of the passage was indeed restored.[123] But all in all, the new translation opened up a new world of thought, reason, and logic to him, and he became one of its most vocal supporters even though it put him at complete loggerheads with fellow General Union associational moderator George Waller.

However, if Raccoon John had wished to keep his high office in North District, he had made a great tactical blunder, and unquestionably he would have realized this if he had not been simply so enraptured with his brand-new modern English New Testament. Oftentimes all it took to sway an association's moderatorial vote one way or another was the skillful planting and spreading of the right rumor and the careful maintenance of just the right scandal. The confirmable truth in such a rumor or scandal might be as small as two grains of wheat mixed in two bushels of chaff, but as is the case with secular power politics, that was all the verity that was needed for an astute politician to get what he wanted. Robert Elkin had known this when North District Association was born, Jilson Payne had learned it quickly after his transfer to the new group from Elkhorn, and it is actually a credit to Raccoon John's character that he was able to sublimate his feelings of risk at this point for the sake of what he was increasingly coming to believe was pure Christian truth. But noble as this attitude was, it didn't do a thing for Raccoon John in terms of Baptist politics. As the spring of 1826 wore on into the summer, rumors about Raccoon John's abandonment of the King James Version must have flown through North District, and the Separate traditionalist David Chenault's chances of regaining the association's moderatorship began to look better and better. Chenault or at least his allies, after all, undoubtedly had to have been agitating the rumors themselves just like the venerated Elkin would have done in the same situation.

Raccoon John didn't make the task of the Chenault rumor mongers any more difficult, however. So liberated did he feel by *The Living Oracles* that he changed his baptismal formulary, the traditional words taken from the twenty-eighth chapter of Matthew that Baptist ministers spoke when officiating at baptisms, from "In obedience to our heavenly command, we baptize this, our brother (or sister) in Christ, in the name of the Father, the Son, and the Holy Ghost," to "By the authority of Jesus Christ, I immerse you into the name of the Father, Son, and Holy Spirit," to reflect the wording of the new translation.[124] And in an action unrelated to *The Living Oracles* but very much aligned with the rhetoric of *The Christian Baptist,* he also changed the manner in which he "ordered" communion services by having his deacons present his communicants with an unbroken cake of unleavened bread and letting each individual break off a small piece for his or her own consumption.[125] Though some of the oldest Baptist pastors in Kentucky had occasionally employed this method or some variant of it in times past,[126] North District custom had long dictated that the preacher or preachers officiating at "the sacraments" should themselves break the bread and pour the wine into cups for the congregation's use.[127]

Another factor that weakened Raccoon John politically in the spring and summer of 1826 was the dissolution of Bethel Church. Though the Bethel congregation had boasted fifty-four members in July 1825, it disbanded at some point in the twelvemonth before July 1826; at least part of the membership seems to have been absorbed by Raccoon John's other congregations at Spencer Creek, Grassy Lick, and Mt. Sterling, who at the 1826 North District annual meeting reported receiving eleven, five, and seven members by letter respectively, and a fraction of the remainder may have gone to Lulbegrud and Goshen, who received respectively six and two additions by letter. Of the specific Bethel members individually, we know only that the longstanding Payne ally Thomas Moseley, and presumably his family as well, joined the Coons clan in worship at Spencer Creek. In a possibly related action occurring in

June of this year also, Spencer Creek Church altered the wording of its old Separate Baptist constitution, with its declaration of the Bible as its creed, to proclaim itself constituted only on the New Testament in accordance with the precepts of Alexander Campbell and *The Christian Baptist.*[128] Raccoon John is never known to have spoken much of his pastoral experience at Bethel to John Augustus Williams or anyone else, and we will never know what exact circumstances surrounded the fellowship's demise. A majority of the congregation could have revolted against Raccoon John's increased use of *The Christian Baptist* and *The Living Oracles* to shape his sermons and modify his conduct of their baptismal and communion rituals, leaving the minority to find homes in Smith's other churches, but we can reach no definitive conclusion with the scanty evidence we have. If such had occurred, David Chenault easily could have "set up" Raccoon John with a split church just as Robert Elkin had probably done Jilson Payne in the days of the Lulbegrud log controversy—and this might even have been sufficient excuse for Raccoon John to agree to the church's dissolution, as a forestalling tactic against the Chenault side. All we can say for sure, though, is that the disbanding of Bethel Church cost Raccoon John three to four votes for moderator in 1826—those that the Bethel delegates would have cast—and in order to maintain his position in spite of the growing Campbell Reform controversy, they were votes he could not afford to lose.

And lose he did, to David Chenault at the 1826 North District Association meeting—even though the session was held at his own pastoral charge of Mt. Sterling. All in all, even Raccoon John's loudest detractors would have been forced to admit that he had had a successful brief tenure as association moderator; in the two years of his care, North District churches had baptized a total of 396 new converts, a sizable number of them at the congregations he himself pastored, although Lulbegrud as well as several fellowships in the Chenault faction had grown respectably as well.[129]

But this one election loss, apart from the rumor-spread controversy over the new translation and related matters, was not the end of the world. Almost since North District's birth the Elkin/Chenault and Payne factions had passed the moderator's office between one another like a hot potato, and in fact Chenault's seven-year first tenure had been an exception, rather than the rule, in length. At this same 1826 session and even though he had lost the moderatorial slot, Raccoon John was still voted as the alternate candidate to preach the introductory sermon for the next year's association meeting at Cane Springs in Madison County. Thomas Boone was voted to preach the introductory sermon itself,[130] but in accordance with longtime Baptist custom, this meant that Raccoon John would be welcoming the crowd and making the opening remarks before Boone's sermon at the preaching stand on the first day of the 1827 session. Besides this honor, either at this time or during the year-long interim between associational sessions he also managed to get an appointment to preach at the Chenault-allied Howard's Upper Creek Church, on the Clark/Madsion County border not far from Cane Springs, for the Friday night before the 1827 association meeting was to begin,[131] another good sign that the members of the association still considered him to be a moderatorial contender. Thus, in spite of the controversies over *The Living Oracles,* Raccoon John conceivably could have hoped to regain his office and his power sooner or later, provided that the churches could be allowed sufficient time to cool off from the *Living Oracles* rumors.

Interestingly, there is a bit of circumstantial evidence that he undertook at least one simple campaign strategy toward this end. Either by letter or direct visit he seems to have called on some of his old mountain contacts back in Wayne and Pulaski counties and arranged for the home association of his youth, Cumberland River, to send delegates north to open a direct correspondence with North District in 1827.[132] Although, as noted earlier, Thomas Wolverton had visited and preached at North District in 1820, before this time Cumberland River had enjoyed only an indirect fellowship with North District via Tate's Creek Association in the Bluegrass and Red Bird Association in the southeastern mountains, and in fact the miles of rough terrain between the Cumberland River and North District territories made direct annual letter correspondence extremely inconvenient for both bodies. The only immediately obvious reason for this attempt at direct relations seems to have been an effort by Raccoon John himself to reinforce the popular image of his backwoods Andrew Jackson–style roots, which, from his long tenure as Jilson Payne's understudy, had no doubt become somewhat tarnished since the days he had first presented it to the Bluegrass associations at Crab Orchard back in 1815.

Even so, now that Raccoon John was out of the moderatorial office, the Campbell controversies continued to inject a very volatile variable into associational politics. While he had served as moderator, no North District church even in the Chenault faction would have dared send a query to the association condemning either Raccoon John or his practices. And even if they had, if he had managed to retain the office, he could easily have appointed his own arrangements committee to dispose of the complaints as he saw fit—and his Chenault opponents knew it, because that was exactly the way Chenault himself would have handled a crisis against his own influence. Now that the election was over, these same churches that had been offended by Raccoon John's increasingly pro-Campbell and pro-*Oracles* stance would feel free to send any queries they might desire against his practices to the next year's association at Cane Springs. Raccoon John must have known that if he could manage to regain the office in 1827 he could deal with the queries on his own terms; if he couldn't, there was a distinct danger that the Chenault crew would either ballyhoo the controversy to the point that the association would eventually expel him as they had done David Barrow in 1806, or at least censure him in order to keep both him and the Payne faction out of power for as long as possible, as Robert Elkin had accomplished with the bizarre log controversy in 1816. Raccoon John had been working hard and determinedly for his own ministerial advancement at least since 1810, and either way he must have looked at it, if he didn't get elected as association moderator once again at Cane Springs in 1827 the repercussions could take him years to overcome.

The next year, 1827, proved to be a time of success for Alexander Campbell's own Mahoning Association and for his Reform movement in the North generally. Walter Scott served as an aggressive evangelist throughout Ohio and the Northeast during this twelvemonth, preaching baptism for the remission of sins, and converts by the hundreds flocked to his message.[133] But though Vardeman, Fishback, and others remained faithful to the cause in Kentucky, with Raccoon John's loss of the North District moderatorial slot the Campbell advance south of the Ohio River seems to have sagged a bit, and it's a shame we don't know more about Smith's actions, to say nothing of his thoughts, meditations, and fears, during the interim between the 1826 and 1827 North District Association meetings. This had to be one of the most emotionally jittery periods that he ever experienced. Gradually but surely, he realized his worst fears about his political prospects. At some time during that tense year, Mt. Tabor and Salem Churches, both in located in Estill County, Kentucky, in North District's southernmost territories and both pastored by Thomas White, voted to send queries to the 1827 North District meeting complaining of the use of *The Living Oracles* in North District pulpits.[134] Lulbegrud, of all places, finally followed suit, but perhaps because of clerk James French's own skillful but ultimately unsuccessful persuasion the church dawdled an exceptionally long time before acting. French finally wrote the necessary documents and presented them for the congregation's adoption at its regular monthly business meeting on the third Saturday in July 1827, only one week before the association was to convene at Cane Springs. Raccoon John later averred that Lulbegrud likewise voted to send complaints to the association against his baptismal and communion deviations at this time, but there is no record of these in North District's minutes.[135] French subsequently confirmed that the communion complaint in question was in fact sent up by Lulbegrud this year just as Raccoon John remembered, but he indicated that Lulbegrud had nothing to do with the grievance about the baptismal formulary; the query condemning it was actually sent by Goshen Church two years afterward.[136] That Thomas Boone was pastor at both Lulbegrud and Goshen during these years, plus the fact that the communion and baptism questions were mere quibbles involving externals and smacked of a distinctly rural Separate, as opposed to an urbane Regular, Baptist outlook, makes Boone more culpable than French for advancing and promoting them; unquestionably the two complaints were not framed in the subtle, careful Lulbegrud and North District clerk's established style, although Raccoon John seems always to have blamed him for them in spite of their previous close working relationship. But in any case, it is impossible now for us to ascertain for certain whether Raccoon John's memories were simply faulty as regarded the baptism query or whether both latter indictments were in fact real.

Besides his longstanding alliance with Raccoon John in the Payne faction, in this particular year French had other reasons to desire some peace and quiet in the association. He had lost two of his own grown children very near this time. One, twenty-three-year-old Stephen of Frankfort, had passed away there from a fever and, to his parents' deep distress, without ever having made a profession of conversion[137]; the other, Keziah, who had married James Prewitt in 1824 and had made her home at the old Payne estate at Mt. Pleasant, had died there while giving birth to her second son, who also perished at that time or shortly thereafter. The grieving French fell out with his son-in-law and soon afterward initiated legal proceedings to gain custody of Keziah's firstborn son, William French Prewitt.[138] We cannot say whether Raccoon John was aware of both these deaths, though he probably knew about Keziah's at least, but he was evidently shocked that Lulbegrud had thrown in its lot with the longtime Chenault ally White in sending a query identical to that of the Estill County churches. However, he knew that James French was a man of many stratagems, and at this time he nonetheless seems to have believed that French would still support him in actual debate at the association meeting itself. As will be demonstrated shortly, were it not for the vagaries of time, chance, and tragedy, French very well might have given him at least a degree of the aid he expected.

By the time Lulbegrud had gotten around to its deliberations and its voting, the unthinkable was happening to Raccoon John and Nancy once again. On July 10, roughly two weeks before Lulbegrud met to vote on the Smith church queries and not quite three weeks before the association was scheduled to convene in Madison County, little Joshua Carroll Smith fell ill to some kind of wasting sickness. Williams of course never identifies the disease, but we have already amply discussed sobering and disturbing possibilities as to what it might have been. John and Nancy kept a dread-crazed watch at the little boy's bedside for sixteen days and nights as he suffered, wracked with torturing pains and his bodily strength slowly ebbing, and finally, on Thursday, July 26, two days before the association was to convene at Cane Springs, the baby breathed his last.[139]

Raccoon John had twenty-four hours to mourn and bury his fifth dead child before reassuming the mask of combined bonhomie, piety, and spirituality that he needed to stand a chance at preventing the Chenault faction's derailment of his moderatorial ambitions at Cane Springs.

The best of times, the worst of times. The Bluegrass, and the hills. A community with the noblest citizenship in all the land, the meanest place on earth. Mt. Sterling and Montgomery County, Kentucky, in the days of America's Era of Good Feeling.

We must wonder how Raccoon John Smith's world looked to him on the gray dawn of Friday, July 27, 1827, at the moment he appeared at his cabin door to gaze at a small pit and mound of earth on the nearby knoll where Eliza Baize and William Pinckney already lay, cradling one more tiny coffin in his arms.

CHAPTER 7

The Attack Upon Christendom, Part I

THE MOMENT

> What counts is to find a truth, which is true for me, to find that idea for which I will live and die. . . . What is truth, but to live for an idea?
>
> —Søren Kierkegaard

American religious historian and scholar Robert Fuller once made some observations that every historian, historical novelist, biographer, and even the casual reader of history should consider. History, he notes, is both descriptive and interpretive. As an academic discipline belonging to the humanities, history is expected to enrich our understanding of all that it means to be human. To do this, he continues, historians frequently need to go beyond what is objectively reported in the historical record and try to reconstruct layers of meaning, motivation, and significance that have perhaps never been fully clear to the participants in a particular historical tradition. For this reason, Fuller correctly asserts, good historical scholarship must be cautious. Ascribing motivations to other persons is a precarious enterprise, fraught with opportunities to impose our own interpretive biases on actions of the past or present. Many contemporary historians are so acutely aware of the potential for interpretive bias that they refrain from judgments of any kind, but the result is often history of the blandest sort. We are left with historical narratives in which every cause is just, every group noble, every belief as sincere and as intellectually credible as any other belief. History of this sort might help us know the past, Fuller concludes, but it does little to help us understand or learn from it.[1]

Though I agree with Fuller on most points, I seriously doubt that the kind of bland, judgment-free historical writing he criticizes can even help us know the past, let alone understand it or learn from it. But the issue of which he speaks is one with which I've wrestled throughout my experience as a historian and biographer. How much, really, does anyone purporting to render an accurate account of past personalities have a right to second-guess the thoughts and moods of his or her subjects? But if such second-guessing is not done, how can we truly view the figures of the past in human, rather than mythological, terms? The best that the biographer can do is to try to ground himself or herself mentally in the closest approximation to the actual environment in which his or her subject lived, and as thoroughly as possible familiarize himself or herself with that environment. If all extant source material is then researched and examined painstakingly before establishing an interpretive bias, at least one can make guesses that are educated and qualified. For all that, however, the danger of misinterpretation is still present.

One extremely pertinent example of the controversies that can arise over the interpretive bias/alleged misinterpretation question is the brief but intense feud that raged a few years ago between two prominent Luther scholars, Richard Marius and the eminent Medieval and Reformation historian and Dutch Reformed clergyman Heiko A. Oberman, over Marius's second Luther work, *The Christian Between God and Death.* Anyone who has ever read much of Marius's other writing in both the fiction and nonfiction genres must concede to the possibility that *The Christian Between God and Death* was marred to an extent, as Oberman so furiously alleged, by Marius's own principal personal obsessions. Nonetheless, Marius presented his thesis in a clear, forceful manner backed up by generous quotations from Luther himself (most if not all of which, countered Oberman, were taken out of context), and the very ferocity of Oberman's attacks on Marius in two blistering reviews in *The New Republic* and *The Historian* could be interpreted as indicative that *The Christian Between God and Death* had nettled Oberman not only because of its title's play on words with Oberman's own Luther biography, *Man Between God and the Devil,* but on a much more personal, gut level than that of a mere academic disputation. Other scholars spoke out in Marius's defense, and his own nine-page reply to the *New Republic* review chided Oberman for "com[ing] to the banquet called Scholarship, and instead of engaging in civilized discussion where all of us can admit the tentative nature of most of our conclusions, you leap onto the table, fling crockery and tableware against the wall, urinate in the faces of the other guests, and berate the host for inviting anyone but you to the feast." He did temper his concluding remarks, though, with the observation that "We are like two old men shouting through a lead door at each other . . . Time will judge us both, will find that both of us have done worthy work, that both of us have made some errors, and I am content with that" (ellipsis appears in source quoted).[2] As if in fulfillment of a prophecy, that old common arbitrator, Time, did emerge as the final victor over both. Marius died of pancreatic cancer in the very year that *The Christian Between God and Death* was published, and Oberman of leukemia and malignant melanoma two years afterward—but not before he had contrived to get in the last word, after Marius's death, with his 2000 review in *The Historian.*[3]

Excuse me for pausing in just a moment of trepidation here. When a biographer or historian receives a harping *à la* Oberman versus Marius, whether the claim of flawed interpretive bias be legitimate or altogether bogus, he or she has two options: either to let the vitriol run off with a shrug or to counterattack as Marius did, opening the possibility that the verbal war thus initiated might escalate with both combatants dropping, or rather perhaps hurling themselves lemming-like, into the crevice between the two verses of Proverbs noted in the previous chapter. To me, neither alternative is satisfactory or even satisfying. Thus far in this study of Raccoon John Smith, as well as in my earlier work on the life and legacy of Shubal Stearns, I've attempted to heed Robert Fuller's counsel and follow my own advice insofar as I have been able. If up to now I have presented a perspective on the life and the environment of John Smith radically different from those related by the denominational hagiographers who wrote before me, at least I've made an honest attempt to base my arguments on a close study of pertinent documents that these same hagiographers appear to have consulted in only a cursory manner, if indeed at all. But my own personal experiences have unavoidably colored my writing as well, and I can only hope that, since the traditionalist General Union–style groups of my homeland and my experience maintain essentially the same variations of doctrine, worship, and business customs that Raccoon John Smith knew nearly two centuries ago, my own interpretation of the mindset that such a religious environment fosters is legitimate as well. For we are now at a turn in Raccoon John's life that, for better or worse, simultaneously defies and demands interpretation. The circumstances are so bizarre that they cannot be related with the blandness so favored, in Fuller's view, by contemporary historians wary of interpretive bias; anyone attempting to discuss them must take some position on them, one way or another.

On July 26, 1827, Raccoon John Smith lost his fifth child, Joshua Carroll, to a wasting illness of at least sixteen days' duration. He buried the little boy the very next day, and immediately made ready to keep a politically important preaching appointment at Howard's Upper Creek Church in Clark County that night and to attend that year's setting of North District Association, at Cane Springs Church in Madison County, the day following. Distraught over associational worries and also the death of his little son, he felt he needed an extra degree of comfort and sustenance on the journey—and so he either asked or demanded that his wife, who had to have been in mourning equal to or deeper than his own, accompany him. Thus, almost as soon as the final spadeful of earth had been thrown on their little boy's grave, the couple left their surviving children, Jonathan, John Duke, Maria, Harvey, and Eliza Ann, in the care of their uncle and aunt Joshua and Betsy Hurt, mounted horses, and set out for the association meeting.[4]

The question that immediately presents itself is, how in the name of decency could Raccoon John have plunged both himself and his bone-weary, grieving wife headlong back into Baptist associational politics in this almost cavalier fashion, not on the morning after their son's burial, but on the very day of his funeral—after having spent sixteen days and sleepless nights at the little boy's bedside as he suffered his terminal illness, to boot? Though in that day and time Kentucky heat and humidity made relatively quick summer burials imperative, one of the most important means of coming to terms with a death was, and still remains, a dependence on custom and ritual in bidding farewell to a loved one. Though Mt. Sterling might have boasted the luxury of an undertaking establishment, even an undertaker would have gone about his tasks at the home of the deceased, and only the more well-to-do residents of the town itself would have depended on such services; in farming communities outside the city limits neighbors pitched in and did virtually all the necessary chores for the bereaved family. These would have included the making of a coffin (wood, with dark cloth tacked inside and out in the case of an adult, white cloth for a child), the bathing of the body in brine, soda, and/or vinegar water for what small preservative capabilities those substances possessed and then dressing it in a newly made shroud and a winding sheet (again, dark colored for adults, white for children), digging the grave, preparation of meals and refreshments for the bereaved family and visiting mourners, and "sitting up" with the body through the night, or nights, until the burial. The more prosperous of the Smiths' neighbors may have brought along a few slaves to perform the menial tasks, while they themselves sat with and tried to comfort the stricken father, mother, and surviving children. For any neighbor to charge a fee for materials used or duties performed at a death and burial would have been considered scandalous, if not outright sinful, but that these customs should be followed with some speed in summertime was a practical necessity that everyone understood. However, one early funeral tradition remained steadfast no matter what the season: except in the case of community emergencies such as epidemics where several wakes and burials had to be held within a short space of time, neither members of a bereaved family nor those of its immediate neighbors performed any of their own house or farm work or engaged in amusements of any kind on the day of a burial. To do so would have been seen as the ultimate disrespect to the memory of the deceased, be it man, woman, or child. An individual who went about his or her affairs at such a time as if nothing had ever happened was simply not a good neighbor, and was accordingly stigmatized by his or her community.[5] For a member of a bereaved family itself to engage in such actions was unheard of, unconscionable, even horrifying. "If any provide not for his own," said the First Epistle to Timothy, "specially those of his own house, he hath already denied the faith, and is worse than an infidel"; and though many rural Kentuckians both then and now have taken this Scriptural precept out of its context to include a great number of familial responsibilities, rare indeed even was the infidel who would transgress community mores when there was a death in the family.

Had Raccoon John himself not followed standard social mores during his residence in Montgomery County, he never could have achieved either acceptance in the community or success in his pastoral charges. What, then, must his neighbors have thought of him when they saw him leave, with Nancy in tow no less, for the preliminaries of an association meeting—in that day and time considered to be a festive community social event, with a "jockey ground" for horse traders and enough whiskey drinking to require the presence of the county sheriff, his deputies, and a "committee on order" appointed by the association itself, as much as a series of worship services and ecclesiastical business meetings—on the day of the burial not of one of his neighbors or parishioners, but of his own little boy? Even a hundred and thirty-odd years after the fact, the devoted Raccoon John advocate Louis Cochran seems to have found the very idea incredible. Evidently believing, or at least wishing to believe, that a printer's typographical error had to have been responsible for the unsettling account in the Williams biography, for his historical novel he dated Joshua's death as having occurred on July 20 rather than July 26; furthermore, the Cochran plotline declared that Raccoon John intended to stay home from the association after the death, but that Nancy—ever in perfect health, and a consistent Patricia Blair to her husband's Fess Parker—insisted that he go and that she accompany him. But Williams's initial account and Donaldson's later one, when examined alongside North District's pertinent minute records and a perpetual calendar of the type that is found in most almanacs, are clear enough: Joshua did die on Thursday, July 26, 1827; North District's annual meeting for that year did begin its proceedings on the fourth Saturday of that month, the 28th; Raccoon John's preaching appointment at Howard's Upper Creek, intended as a preliminary gathering for the association, was scheduled for the evening of Friday, the 27th; and in walking back to their house from Joshua's brief burial service Smith really did ask Nancy to accompany him to Clark and Madison counties for the proceedings on the grounds that many things would be said against him and thus he had to go, yet he could not leave her alone in her bereavement. "Call it not weakness," Williams admonishes us, "if, in that dark hour, John Smith, forsaken by friends, and afflicted of God, turned to his stricken wife for comfort and support."[6]

Though he provides an almost-reasonable excuse for Raccoon John's behavior with the looming associational crisis, as is the case with so much of the early material in *The Life of Elder John Smith,* this is about as far as Williams himself can be depended upon for accuracy. His reluctance to admit Raccoon John's tenure as moderator of North District Association for the years 1824 and 1825 has been noted and discussed in the last chapter, and at this juncture Williams even goes so far as to proclaim the blatant untruth that David Chenault had served in the moderator's office "successively for many years."[7] He seems determined here to try to portray North District Association as a nineteenth-century version of the Diet of Worms and Raccoon John as another Luther, without a friend to stand by him, defending the pure principles of God's Word at the risk of his very life. Though rumors about Smith and *The Living Oracles* undoubtedly were running rampant among the churches and, as Williams does correctly state in a later context, it was (and is) almost impossible to anticipate the exact temper of an association meeting during a time of controversy,[8] such bodies still observed at least the semblance of order and due process. As a longstanding association attendee and officer himself, Raccoon John knew this, too. Even if Chenault and his faction did amass the political strength to expel Smith from the association altogether—in reality, a doubtful point—they'd never do it in his absence, especially in consideration of such an excuse as he had. For this year at least, at the worst they could only make pronouncements against the use of *The Living Oracles* and Raccoon John's new baptismal and/or communion forms as items of new business, and in the most extreme circumstances Smith might expect the group merely to send a committee of preachers and deacons to talk to him about his practices. In such an event, custom still demanded that he be given an opportunity to speak his mind at the 1828 meeting as a matter of "reference," or old business. Both Daniel Williams and David Barrow had been given at least the appearance of that much grace in their own times of controversy, though neither man could do anything to check the political maneuverings forcing them out, and Jilson Payne had been denied his own voice in the association only after his church split over the fateful log.

But even then in John's case, all three of the churches under his care were sending representatives to the 1827 meeting. These included James Mitchell, Walker Chambers, and both John and Jacob Coons from Spencer Creek; Roger Clemens and Joshua Yates from Grassy Lick; and William O'Rear, Benjamin Davis, and John Williams from Mt. Sterling,[9] and at least some of these men and their families must have stopped by or even stayed to help at Raccoon John's home during his bereavement. Though associational battles can and do turn seemingly true and faithful friends into those of the fair-weather variety, of these men Raccoon John could have expected at least the Coonses to stand in the breach in his absence and defend his cause vigorously. If the Williams scenario had been accurate and Raccoon John had in fact never been a North District officeholder, his presence at the meeting would give him an advantage, but still it was by no means absolutely necessary. In sum, then, there were actually only two things that absolutely and unequivocally demanded his attendance at Cane Springs that year. One, of course, was his campaign for reelection as association moderator. The other, incidental to the primary cause, was that the preachers from Cumberland River Association whom he had persuaded the previous year to lay in a letter of correspondence with North District would be there in force as a subtle lobby for his campaign; without Smith's presence the purpose of their journey would be completely negated, and worse, they'd hear talk about his use of *The Living Oracles* at the association grounds and in the business meetings. This of course would cause them to suspect Raccoon John's integrity in persuading them to come in the first place, and they'd take every one of the variations of the gossip they heard back home with them to spread all over the southern Kentucky mountains. And if Raccoon John's Montgomery County neighbors weren't aware of this second reason, they still had to have known about the first.

Grieved as Raccoon John genuinely must have been over Joshua, if he was that worried about what the *Living Oracles* rumors were doing to his ministerial reputation, he should have been just as concerned about community reaction to his behavior on that fateful Friday. The farm families of Montgomery County might be able to snicker indulgently at the pompous rages, pistol packing, and bellicose threats and challenges of "Captain" Henry Daniel, who defeated David Trimble in the local race for congressman that very year because of Trimble's support for John Quincy Adams and Henry Clay in the presidential election of 1824,[10] but they would never have empathized with a preacher's leaving the community on the very day of his son's funeral to seek an office—even a religious one. We cannot imagine what Joshua and Betsy Hurt must have thought as they watched Raccoon John and Nancy ride away on horseback and took the couple's five surviving children[11] home with them, but Williams never mentions Nancy's brother again and it is a fact that not long after this the Hurts, with their own children and most of Joshua's offspring by his first wife, packed up and left Kentucky to start anew in Illinois. The only one of Joshua's children that seems to have remained in Kentucky near Raccoon John and Nancy was the older son William Berryman Hurt, who by that time had married and started a family of his own and who may have continued to give the Smiths part-time assistance with farm labor. Nancy's brother was ten years older than she was, two years older than Raccoon John, and he had lived and farmed in Montgomery County with the Smiths for a decade; we cannot help but wonder if perhaps the apparent contempt shown to the memory of his namesake might have had some bearing on his decision to take his family and leave Raccoon John and Nancy behind. Joshua Hurt died in Illinois in 1831 at the age of forty-nine, and we will never know for sure exactly what prompted his separation from the man who had influenced him to seek his fortune in downstate Kentucky in the first place.[12]

Thus to tell of these events after the manner of Williams and Cochran, Raccoon John becomes Luther at Worms; to give a bare rehearsal of the facts in sequence from a more objective angle makes him appear uncomfortably similar to Camus's Meursault on the weekend of his mother's funeral. But having made such a damning indictment against Raccoon John Smith, I would now speak a few words in his behalf. Though I base this defense on exactly the same kind of risky interpretive bias commented upon by Fuller, I believe that it could be an accurate portrayal of Smith's own mindset, and it actually may serve his cause better than his hagiographers' factual distortions ever could. He had just lost a young son, and no one, then or now, could even begin truly to comprehend the scope of his grief without having undergone a similar devastating loss personally. Even so, there is nothing we can do either for or against a departed loved one, and funeral rites are held not really for the dead, but as a necessary means for survivors to say goodbye and to establish closure emotionally. I suspect that Raccoon John realized these facts through his grief, coldly logical though they were and even though the concepts of emotional closure, or for that matter psychology itself, hadn't even been articulated at this period. But at the same time and regardless of particular cultural variations, in order even to begin to establish such closure we as humans must deal with our dead in a way that proclaims that they and their lives *mattered.* Thus if John did have such a coldly logical realization over the top of a father's grief, it must have been juxtaposed likewise with that same gut feeling well known by anyone who has had to oversee the funeral arrangements of a close family member: that if the customary practices and rites are not carried out with at least a semblance of adherence to community standards, the departed one has, in some way, been personally cheated or wronged. Finally, wrapped around the quandary produced by the grief and these two conflicting ideas in Raccoon John's bosom was another impulse, perhaps one that only evangelical preachers know, in reality completely irrational as well but entirely capable of seeming so utterly reasonable especially in a time of tension or sorrow: that somehow, a decisive battle in the never-ending war between Christ and Satan over the kingdom of God can hang upon one's own individual ministry, and in that context, often upon a Divine test of faith that no other mortal could even presume to understand. The Scriptures tell us that Abraham came within a hairsbreadth of sacrificing Isaac in order that God could test his faith; that the Old Testament judge Jephthah actually did sacrifice his only child due to a hasty vow that he couldn't recant because the Mosaic Law demanded the honoring of an oath once it was made; that David bathed and anointed himself and went right back to business after his infant son's death because he knew that, though the baby could not return to him, one day he would go to the child; that Ezekiel was forewarned of his wife's death but was commanded to go right on prophesying anyway; and that Jesus himself once said, "Let the dead bury their dead, but go thou and preach the Kingdom of God." So in short, Raccoon John very well could have magnified the whole upcoming associational controversy in his own mind into the vision of just such a personal test of faith.

I've seen this particular dynamic at work so often in my own past ministry, as well as within those of many of my preaching colleagues, that I feel that its influence on the mind of a minister should never be underestimated. I once knew an old and much-beloved association moderator who, on two different occasions, got up from his sickbed against the advice of both his physician and his daughters to attend his association so he could be reelected to his customary office. On the first of these occasions he was recuperating from a heart attack, and on the second some other of the numerous maladies of old age; in the latter instance, he was so physically weak that he had to rest his head on the preaching stand while the association clerk called the roll, took ballots, and read off other lengthy items of association business. But in both instances, he was absolutely convinced that his association's maintenance and the perpetuation of its old and sacred traditions depended on his presence at the helm, his conviction no doubt only strengthened by the hospital visits he got from a rival moderatorial candidate who expressed the most tender regards for him and his health as well as repeated exhortations to take it easy and just stay away from the association meeting that year. The famous William Sloane Coffin, whose own extremely busy ministry took severe tolls on his family life, cut short his mourning after his son Alex's accidental death in 1983 because he had somehow convinced himself that his pastoral charge genuinely required his return that badly; though his wife declared that the idea was utterly preposterous and delusional in the kind of blunt and direct language that Martin Luther would have appreciated completely, she supported him because she knew that Coffin had to come to terms with the horrendous loss, among other means, by writing and preaching a sermon about Alex's death.[13] I myself once flouted an injury—and consequently, an extremely worried and proportionately irked spouse as well—to attend a pastors' conference for what I considered at the time to be a matter of the gravest importance for the welfare of my home church.

At least Coffin's grief-spurred actions resulted in some positive good. His poignant sermon/essay "Alex's Death," which he wrote and delivered upon his return to his New York City pulpit, represents possibly the most tender modern articulation of personal Christian theodicy yet framed, and of his considerable written and published output it is perhaps his most famous, and oft-requested, composition. I wish I could say as much for my own efforts at the time of my injury. Ultimately my faithful act of selfless heroism, if that's indeed what it somehow happened to be, didn't amount to a hill of beans in the eyes either of God or of man, and the old moderator's insistence on attending the latter of the aforementioned association meetings might have forestalled a split in the body for two years or so at most. But at the time, both the aged association leader and I really did think that heaven and earth hung on our meeting our respective responsibilities. On the darker side of the coin, I suppose that the most extreme example I ever saw of the kind of thinking an evangelical mindset can conceivably foster under such circumstances involved a mountain Holiness preacher whose tale of woe I encountered not at church but in college as a medical technology student. For some perceived sin he decided that he had to take Jesus's words that "if thy right hand offend thee, cut it off and cast it from thee" literally, and after having done so he nearly bled to death before someone thought to tie a tourniquet around his wrist stump and transport him to the hospital. And his fate was better than that of a first cousin of my grandmother's: in Martin County, Kentucky, in February 1933 her son, a novice exhorter under the influence of a Holiness preacher remembered by the family alternately either as Mary Scalf or Anna Skaggs, strangled his mother with a log chain in order that his flock might demonstrate God's promise of the power of the Holy Ghost to raise the dead in addition to offering snakebite and poison protection. The son spent a good many years in prison for it, while the other preacher or preachers got off without so much as a slap on the wrist, but even long afterward there was a good deal of muttering within that portion of the family that "we'd 'a' got her back from the dead if the law hadn't broke in on us when they did."

In any case, I cannot help but believe that Raccoon John was affected by a mindset very similar, if not the same, to that of most of the examples noted above—at least the ones more closely approaching sanity. Though he appears unbelievably and horribly crass and cold to have insisted on attending that 1827 North District Association meeting, so much so that both John Augustus Williams and Louis Cochran felt compelled to use fiction to find an excuse for his behavior, his motives were probably more altruistic than they appear. After carefully climbing up the house of cards that Jilson Payne had begun with him a decade earlier, he must have felt that the very cause of Christ itself depended on his continued ascendancy or at least his ability to remain in the moderatorial running in his association, and he was willing to go even to this extreme length in order to try to maintain his viability in the association's leadership—all for the sustainment of the Great Commission.

But though Jesus said also that "he that loveth son or daughter more than me, is not worthy of me," even within the evangelical minister's mindset it is much easier to forego concerns about one's own personal health than it is to snub the welfare of one's family members. Abraham no doubt would have much preferred to sacrifice himself rather than Isaac, Jephthah no doubt repented bitterly of his own sacrificial vow, and those of us who are inclined to read tests of faith into our lives and careers are no different. In the fall of 1823, Raccoon John himself had willingly missed the Campbell-MacCalla debate due to the "dangerous sickness" within his family, although the event comprised one of the most significant political gatherings for Kentucky Baptist preachers of that time. And despite the fact that William Sloane Coffin's deepest grief inspired his highest and most touching eloquence, even he must have felt some trepidation at the outset of his actual return to his pastoral obligations. Thus to return to our story, as Raccoon John turned from little Joshua's grave and saddled horses for Nancy and himself to ride to Howard's Upper Creek that night and on to Cane Springs the next morning, we can readily imagine that the quandary into which his conflicting positions as an association leader, church pastor, husband, and father had put him produced a violent rush of similarly conflicting emotions. Even though he must have been convinced personally that he was acting in obedience to the high and unknown purposes of God, not the least of these emotions would have been a sublimated but deep-seated anger and self-loathing at the fact that he had sunk to the level of abandoning his little boy's fresh grave and insisting that the heartbroken Nancy accompany him on what was essentially an ecclesiastical political campaign effort. Of course, her own health status at the time is questionable for other reasons as well, but regardless, she must have desperately needed rest after the sixteen days and nights of Joshua's terminal illness. As it turned out, the entire effort never quite accomplished what Raccoon John had hoped it would. And though his dashed hopes must be discussed in more detail below, I contend that that deep-seated, smoldering anger and keen self-loathing, combined with sorrow over the deaths of his children and a vivid perception of the utter futility of his continued existence as a Kentucky General Union leader, ultimately propelled Raccoon John to yet one more dramatic religious conversion that was to carry him through the rest of his life.

The Smiths arrived at the Howard's Upper Creek meetinghouse at about dusk on the evening of July 27. To his dismay, Raccoon John discovered that the minister who had been instructed to make the preaching appointment for him had thrown in his lot squarely with the Chenault faction, and had advised the congregation to beware of Smith and his doctrine; but nonetheless John appears to have been permitted to preach, and as he recalled it he had a respectful audience. The couple spent the night at the house of one of the members, and proceeded across the Madison County line to Cane Springs early that next morning.[14]

As perhaps should be expected, though, details of the opening of the association on July 28 diverge somewhat between North District's minute records and Raccoon John's recollections to Williams. At least four and possibly five men were present from Cumberland River Association to open the new correspondence with North District: John's Parmleysville pastoral successor Thomas Wolverton; the Cumberland River moderator Stephen Collier; William Haggard; and perhaps both of John's old mentors, Richard Barrier and Elijah Barnes, as well. None of John's Elkhorn friends were present, but John Davis, one of the men who had given him his "Raccoon" cognomen twelve years before, was there as a visiting delegate from Tate's Creek.[15] Though it is not noted, as Thomas Boone's alternate to preach the introductory sermon Raccoon John would have welcomed the crowd and spoken at least a few words after initial congregational singing at the stand, and then called for another hymn, handshaking, and prayer before Boone assumed the pulpit. Though perhaps we can now understand why he desired to project himself as a candidate through this ordeal, considering how fresh and raw as his grief must have been we must still wonder how he managed it. After another song, the delegates and officers retired to the meetinghouse to open the first day's business session while the majority of the congregation stayed at the stand to hear continued preaching and singing. Nancy no doubt would have remained with the stand congregation, since at that time the presence of women in the church house during an association business meeting was frowned upon.

If North District carried on its business in the way deemed customary by most, if not all, of its descendant associations in eastern Kentucky, after the delegates assembled in the house one more minister made additional introductory remarks before another song, another handshake, and another prayer. After this David Chenault, as moderator of the previous year's session, called the meeting to order. In the normal course of things, Chenault then would have appointed or recognized committees to oversee the services at the stand and to keep order on the church grounds, and then clerk James French would have read the associational rules of decorum and the letters from all the churches. This was (and in groups that follow the old traditions, still is) a lengthy, tedious process that took into account not only the congregations' statistics of the previous year and the names of their delegates to be enrolled, but any queries they wished to air as well. If the Williams account is to be believed, it was at this point that order broke down and John made his bid for power. Fresh church queries were never settled on the first day of business; it was customary simply to pass a motion and second that all such questions be put on the bill of arrangements for the second business day's work. But when French read out the three queries from Salem, Mt. Tabor, and Lulbegrud questioning the propriety of using *The Living Oracles* rather than the King James Version, the Lulbegrud query regarding Smith's method of serving communion, and the alleged complaint against his baptismal formulary, Raccoon John knew he'd have to do some quick point-proving and persuasion if he stood a chance of retaking the moderator's position. The only way he could accomplish this was to provoke a debate before ballots were cast for the office, impressing as many church delegates as possible with his qualifications, and then hope for the best in the vote tally. Williams states that none of the queries had mentioned Raccoon John by name, although in a written account made three to four years after this date Smith himself noted that "the name of a certain individual was read out, contrary to the usages of Baptists and the law of Christ."[16] If Williams was right and this was not Raccoon John's own name, Lulbegrud must have cited the translators of *The Living Oracles,* or perhaps even Alexander Campbell himself. But at any rate, when French finished reading all the letters, Smith boldly stood up and asked for the floor. Perhaps expecting Raccoon John to voice the customary motions that the letters all be accepted, that the delegates listed and present be enrolled as the working body of North District Association, and that the queries all be put on the bill of arrangements, David Chenault had to have been taken somewhat aback to hear his rival declare, "My brethren from Lulbegrud need not feel the least concern for evidence to sustain their charges. I plead guilty to them all!"[17]

One wonders why, both then and ever thereafter, Raccoon John cast all blame on Lulbegrud and particularly James French for voicing this query or group of queries, when Thomas Boone had obviously exercised a greater influence on Lulbegrud's actions than French had at this point and Thomas White's Salem and Mt. Tabor Churches were every bit as involved in the controversy as Lulbegrud, and perhaps more so. As will be demonstrated, he had other reasons to oppose both Thomas Boone and James French in times to come, as well as considerable cause to support White. We can say with a fair degree of certainty, though, that he got one of his wishes, since he did indeed provoke the fierce floor debate that he wanted, no doubt to the bemusement of the Cumberland River delegates who were waiting patiently to "lay in" their letter of correspondence. According to Williams, after Raccoon John's rash declaration before the assembly, every speaker that hit the floor attacked him. Though some of their complaints must have addressed the irregularity of the matter's introduction on Saturday rather than Monday, Smith turned the debate into a referendum on his own ministry, answering back with his customary adroitness until he let himself get hamstrung on a technicality. One of the rules of decorum stated that no delegate could speak more than twice on any item of business unless the moderator gave him liberty to do so; custom and usage allowed that if the moderator thus ruled a speaker out of order, the speaker could appeal to the assembly, which would then sustain either the moderator's ruling or the speaker's appeal by a standing vote. Raccoon John inadvertently used up his two free chances to speak before he could make what he considered an effective summation of his positions, the speech that he must have hoped would clinch the moderator's office for him, and when he asked Chenault's permission to address the body further he was turned down. The house rejected his appeal to make a third speech, apparently unanimously; evidently not even the other delegates from his pastoral charges stood up for him in the appeal vote. But by this point on a hot July day in a crowded meetinghouse, it's probable that everyone was so flustered and confused by the unorthodox first-day controversy that they simply wanted to get through the rest of the day's business and go get something to eat and drink. Some things don't change over the years. Raccoon John had seized his chance and blown it, and in the likewise-tedious balloting for moderator that followed, requiring French to call the roll of registered delegates to come up to his table individually to whisper their votes either in his ear or those of two or three "tellers" appointed to make sure the tally was correct, Chenault emerged as victor once more.[18]

So there it was; Raccoon John's mighty act of faith had proven worthless, and he couldn't even boast of producing any valid and beneficial meditations on theodicy to justify either Joshua's death or his own response to it. If he hadn't shown such apparently bald ambition to be moderator once again, the amiable Chenault might even have appointed him as a member of the all-important arrangements committee, which would both schedule the queries for debate and offer advice for their resolution on Monday morning, and he could have defended both *The Living Oracles* and his baptismal and communion practices in that setting. Presiding moderators often gave former holders of the office such appointments as a matter of courtesy anyway, and both Robert Elkin and Jilson Payne had usually followed this convention. But after that fierce and unsettling first-day floor debate Chenault was in no mood to trifle much more with Smith, especially since he must have known exactly what Raccoon John had attempted to do. Instead, after Chenault called for new churches to "lay in" their organizational documents and letters and received no response, he selected his ministerial colleague at Cane Springs Isaac Thornburgh, the Salem and Mt. Tabor pastor Thomas White, John Haggard from Unity, and two delegates from Howard's Upper Creek named Milton and Smith Vivion to serve on the arrangements committee with him and the clerk. None except French had heretofore exhibited any friendly behavior toward either the Payne faction or Alexander Campbell, and both Raccoon John and

French had to have known at that point that Payne/Smith political stock in the association was at the bottom once again. Still, after letters of correspondence were read and delegates from corresponding associations were admitted to "seats in council," Chenault appointed John to write North District's reply letter to Elkhorn Association and to read it for North District's acceptance on Monday, and this was not a chore he would have assigned to Smith if Raccoon John had been entirely out of favor. James French was likewise appointed to write a similar letter for Cumberland River, and finally at the close of a long, hot day's business made only longer and hotter by the floor debate, Thomas Wolverton and Stephen Collier were appointed to preach at the following day's worship service at the stand along with downstate visitors John Taylor and John Allen. The business session adjourned to reconvene at nine o'clock on Monday morning.[19]

Years later, in recalling the events to John Augustus Williams, Raccoon John expressed revulsion at how horribly he had been treated at this Saturday business session by the North District officers and delegates, at least some of whom had to have known about Joshua's death.[20] How much he publicized the tragedy himself is unknown. But in reality, considering his timing and the manner in which he provoked the first day's debate, his very presence, let alone his behavior, undoubtedly would have brought about the same negative reaction from the individual association delegates as he would have received from his neighbors. James French especially, himself recovering from the deaths of a grown son and daughter that very year, couldn't have understood why John was present, much less campaigning for moderator as vigorously, though discreetly, as he was. French's circular letter to the association for this year, which he must have written only a few days before the body convened, took the Jamesian text "Confess your faults to one another, and pray for one another, that ye may be healed," and its thrust was French's own pointed question to the association: "How many conversations do we remember, concerning the improprieties and failings of our brethren, who were absent?"[21] French genuinely seems to have assumed that Raccoon John simply wouldn't be there, and he really does appear to have prepared a subtle defense for an absent Smith in a probable quiet and strategic endeavor to help Raccoon John save at least the Payne, if not the Campbell, cause for another day. This, however, he could of course have accomplished more effectively if Raccoon John had behaved like a normal father and stayed with his family that weekend, and we will never know for sure how much bearing that this conjunction of their children's deaths had on either Raccoon John's or French's later perceptions of one another.

For all this, Raccoon John still fought for his cause and his reputation like a bulldog. Almost all of the Cane Springs church members had opened their homes for the weekend to association visitors, but when John learned that the Cumberland River delegates, some of the "big" downstate political preachers in attendance at the session, and probably the entire committee on arrangements would be spending the weekend at David Chenault's house, he felt that somehow he had to connive an invitation for Chenault's personal hospitality himself and thus sit in with the arrangements committee even though he hadn't been appointed to serve on it. He recalled to Williams that Nancy gave her blessing to the ruse he implemented, although this must be open to question. But regardless, as he and Nancy stood on the steps of the meetinghouse, he called to the departing Chenault in a voice loud enough to be heard by everyone remaining on the grounds: "Brother Chenault, I am going to your house tonight, but my wife says that she is unwilling to go unless you invite her!"

Chenault, probably knowing full well exactly what Raccoon John was about, but unable to give a publicly unmannerly answer, shouted back, "Come along, sister, we have nothing against you!"

And so Raccoon John and Nancy proceeded to Chenault's residence, where, as if nothing whatsoever were wrong, Smith set out to defend his actions of the morning to his old Cumberland River colleagues, the visiting "big" preachers of the Bluegrass, and the arrangements committee as its members deliberated over the Monday morning work schedule.

Chenault received all his houseguests in keeping with the mores of southern hospitality, and after supper his house slaves set chairs out on his lawn where, in the cooling evening, the ministers of the arrangements committee and the association visitors could refresh themselves with drink and conversation while the Monday schedule was drawn up. It had to have been an extremely uncomfortable time for Chenault and everyone else present. Raccoon John seems to have commandeered the conversation, reciting to Stephen Collier, Thomas Wolverton, John Taylor, and the assembled committee exactly why he had changed his baptismal formulary and his pastoral charges' communion order. For some reason he elected to downplay his use of *The Living Oracles,* perhaps because he intended to speak further about the translation at the Monday business assembly no matter what the committee decided. As Smith recalled it to Williams, there were a good many periods of uncomfortable silence, although John Taylor spoke in his defense as regarded his method of breaking the communion loaf and announced his intention to try out the practice in his own churches. Cumberland River moderator Collier gave approval to John's handling of this one question as well, but the rest of his old hill country partners made no answer at all, which, considering the fact that they had come at Smith's own behest, was a very ominous sign politically. But he still put the best face on it that he could. He once again "earnestly entreated" the crowd of ministers around him to point out a single departure he had made thus far from common Baptist usages, "except," as he seems to have put it, "where Baptist usage had departed from the Word of God." On receiving only another stony silence in response, he bravely informed the Cumberland River ministers that they could go home and tell those who knew him there, and whom he still loved, exactly where he stood.[22]

Neither Williams nor North District's minutes tell us the subjects or the character of Stephen Collier's, Thomas Wolverton's, John Taylor's, or John Allen's sermons at the Sunday worship service at the stand, but at some time during that day Raccoon John must have borrowed pen, ink, and paper from Chenault or French to compose the Elkhorn letter of correspondence that he had been assigned on Saturday. One wonders if Chenault and French might not have been very glad, and even grateful, for the chance to supply the articles simply so they and the rest of the members of the arrangements committee could converse in private for a few moments while Smith was occupied with his task. In any case, after Chenault called the second and final business meeting of the session to order at the meetinghouse at nine o'clock on Monday morning and French called the roll of delegates, Raccoon John had to read his letter along with the half dozen or so other men who had been given similar tasks. All of these missives were accepted to be forwarded to the correspondent associations to which they were addressed. But strangely, considering the degree of antipathy that Raccoon John later avowed was manifested to him on Saturday, Smith was now assigned the responsibilities of a North District visiting messenger to no less than three of the association's largest correspondents, Elkhorn, Tate's Creek, and Bracken Associations. Moreover, his Spencer Creek members James Mitchell, Walker Chambers, and John Coons were appointed to accompany him as fellow delegates to the Elkhorn meeting; William O'Rear of Mt. Sterling was selected to go with him to Tate's Creek; and both John and Jacob Coons as well as O'Rear and Roger Clemens and Joshua Yates from Grassy Lick were given similar assignments to Bracken. As if this were not enough, included among the correspondent duties given to his parishioners, Mt. Sterling's Benjamin Davis was appointed to attend Franklin Association, he and his fellow delegate John Williams as well as James Mitchell and Joshua Yates were sent to Boone's Creek Association, and Roger Clemens was assigned to go to Red Bird Association. Again, these were not appointments that would have been given by a Baptist association of North District's type to a minister under the degree of censure that Raccoon John insisted that he was suffering at this point, and neither would so many of his followers have been assigned associational duties of this nature if their churches did not still remain in North District's good graces. Perhaps Smith's own rabid aggressiveness on Saturday had brought him more gain than he could have anticipated after losing the moderator's slot, although we must wonder if he and his church members were given some of these political duties in the hope of keeping him pacified throughout the rest of the business meeting.

But David Chenault's attitudes and tendencies must be figured into the equation as well. Though he had successfully held onto the moderator's office, in keeping with his known tastes he elected not to attend a single one of these big downstate 1827 and 1828 gatherings, but rather chose simply to represent his association at the backcountry Burning Springs, Cumberland River, and Red Bird Associations' yearly meetings.[23] In fact, the only snub he seems to have given Raccoon John in the matter of the correspondence visits was a refusal to appoint him to attend his old home association at Cumberland River, but with all things considered, it's even possible that Wolverton, Collier, and the rest of the Cumberland River visitors now preferred Chenault's presence to Raccoon John's. It's not impossible that Chenault could have considered *The Living Oracles, The Christian Baptist,* and Campbellism in general to have been a downstate urbanites' and flatlanders' problem rather than any concern over Calvinism, Arminianism, or any other *-ism,* and one that he hoped to keep out of North District and rural eastern Kentucky United Baptist business as much as he could. Regardless, it is obvious that Raccoon John had Chenault's full blessing to attend the big Bluegrass Baptist political gatherings and keep his reputation current, if that's what he wanted to do—and considering the fact that he had behaved as he did during the weekend after Joshua's death, that was, apparently, exactly what he wanted to do more than anything else.

Finally, the Williams biography takes up its parable again with the next item of business in the minutes after establishing the details of the correspondence visits: the resolution of the church queries read on Saturday. Here neither the association minutes nor the Williams account says anything about the Lulbegrud complaint on Raccoon John's baptismal formulary, and allowing for the chance that it even existed at all outside an aged Raccoon John's memory we must conclude that it was dropped by the association without further debate. The communion query, the existence of which is verifiable by James French's subsequent testimony, seems to have been dropped similarly, as noted, probably at French's behest rather than Lulbegrud pastor Thomas Boone's. Later Raccoon John even recalled one detail indicating that his harangue to the arrangements committee on Saturday evening had actually produced the desired effect: one of its members, unnamed by Smith but apparently voicing the consensus of the whole committee, spoke up and reproved Lulbegrud for wording its complaints in the manner in which it did.[24]

There was one question, however, that Chenault and the majority of the committeemen were apparently determined to settle, that being the virtually identical queries from Salem, Mt. Tabor, and Lulbegrud condemning the use of *The Living Oracles.* The arrangements committee therefore offered the following resolution for adoption: "Lulbegrud, Salem, and Mt. Tabor express a dissatisfaction against the translation of McKnight [*sic*] and others. This association protests against any translation of the New Testament, except that translation of the New Testament in common use, and advises the churches to do so."[25] It is perhaps significant that the name of Campbell—that of either Alexander or the translator, George—was omitted altogether from the wording, and since James French, as clerk, would have transcribed this resolution at the consensus and dictation of the whole committee, he may have been responsible for the omission out of respect for Raccoon John's regard both for the fiery young editor and for the new translation. But if the reader should suspect that I give undue credit here to French for defending Smith's cause in his own subtle way, two facts must be remembered: first, that the aforementioned circular letter that he wrote and presented on Saturday used the Epistle of James to condemn anyone who openly accused an individual absent and unable to hear, or make a defense against, the accusations; and second, that during the debate and discussion that followed the reading of the arrangements committee's *Living Oracles* resolution, James French was the only individual present that Raccoon John called upon to back up one of his own points. The Monday disputation seems to have been carried on essentially as it would have been among Christians throughout the rural South of both the nineteenth and twentieth centuries. Chenault himself remarked that he had neither seen the translation nor wished to see it but that he thought that George Waller of Long Run Association had done right when he burned it to ashes, and most of the delegates took the position summed up by one old elder who declared that he believed that the King James Version was the only written word of God. This was the man to whom Raccoon John gave his initial answer on Monday, the first of two more free speeches on the subject that the rules of decorum allowed him. Turning to the elder, he asked mildly, "How long, my brother, has it been since the king made his translation?"

"I don't know," replied the elder, characterized (correctly) by John Augustus Williams as "defiantly ignorant."

Smith then turned to the clerk's table in front of the pulpit and inquired of French, "Was it not about two hundred and twenty years ago?"

"I believe it has been about that time," confirmed French.

Raccoon John pressed the advantage that French had given him. "Then is it not a pity," he continued, "that the apostles left the world and the church without any word of God for fifteen hundred years? For, as those intelligent citizens around me know, they wrote in Greek, without the least knowledge of the language into which King James, fifteen hundred years afterward, had their writings translated! But if nothing is the word of God but the King's version, do you not, brethren, pity the Dutch, who have not that version and who could not read one word of it if they had it?"

Here again order broke down. Some saw the logic of Smith's argument and murmured words of assent; others who were still zealous for the King James Version were visibly angered, and as Raccoon John recalled it one of these hit the floor without even waiting for Chenault to recognize him, shook his fist in John's face, and exclaimed, "Brother Moderator, I can not stand it! I would rather die than be run over in this way by a Campbellite!"

The angry delegate should have known that Raccoon John would pounce on both his display of temper and his comment with smooth diplomatic skill, and that's exactly what happened. Here evidently using his second opportunity to speak, Smith turned to Chenault as the moderator stood behind the rostrum in the pulpit and remarked dispassionately, "Brother Moderator, I came here to defend myself against charges of wrongdoing that, I feared, might affect my usefulness if they were not refuted. I have stood for two days before you, alone and, accused of all my brethren, trying, in the very presence of an overwhelming opposition, to vindicate an humble name from the charge of infidelity to the truth I love." He then turned to the assembled delegation. "But, friends," he continued, "if this is the fruit of that Spirit whose influence in conversion I am charged with denying, then do I plead guilty to that charge. For whether such a spirit as this is from God or not, I leave you all to judge."[26]

So says Williams. Raccoon John actually may have remembered his Monday speech accurately, although no charge condemning his beliefs about the operations of the Holy Ghost or the born-again experience had yet been introduced against him, and at this time he was still immersing converts on the profession of their faith in Baptist form.[27] He could have used this opportunity to answer the murmurs of other delegates, rather than any formally presented charge. But as he recalled it, after this a group of about "fifteen or twenty of the more influential brethren" now withdrew to discuss the controversy privately. They requested that Chenault keep the rest of the delegation in session until they returned. These concluded that "John Smith was too good and great a man to be spared from the churches, and too wise to fall into any dangerous heresies; and that time should be allowed him for reflection. They agreed, therefore, to recommend that the whole matter be laid over for one year, feeling assured that by that time the heresy of *Campbellism* [Williams's emphasis] would be forgotten, and Smith would return to the faith of his fathers."[28]

This entire latter scenario is suspect. We must reiterate that Raccoon John had already been appointed as a delegate to represent North District at the big downstate gatherings of Elkhorn, Tate's Creek, and Bracken Associations, and he would not have been given these plum duties if Chenault or the association as a whole intended to put him on the sort of probationary status described here by Williams. Ironically, what appears to have actually happened was that, after the resolution condemning "the translation of McKnight [*sic*] and others" passed by a majority, Raccoon John himself, of all people, was selected to deliver the introductory sermon at the next year's association meeting, and Thomas White was chosen as his alternate.[29] Williams later tries to explain this away with the allegation that Chenault and the association were hamstrung on a tradition: since Smith had been the alternate preacher in 1827, longstanding North District custom demanded that he preach the introductory sermon in 1828.[30] But a glance through the minute records of North District Association shows that this tradition was by no means always strictly followed,[31] and even if it had been observed rigorously an exception definitely would have been made for a preacher under censure for some presumptive heresy. The Williams account would have us believe that Raccoon John escaped the full wrath and condemnation of the association only by the skin of his teeth, but when the minute records and the traditional "old" Baptist business order are figured into the circumstances, it is obvious that Smith actually managed to squeeze a surprising quantity of lemonade out of a very sour political lemon. And so North District appointed its next annual meeting for the fourth weekend of July 1828 at Lulbegrud, and dismissed finally on Monday afternoon[32]—if present "Old

Time" Baptist custom truly reflects eighteenth- and nineteenth-century practice, with a handshake, a timely if ironic hymn such as "My Dearest Friends in Bonds of Love" or "Come Now, My Dear Brethren, I Bid You Farewell," a closing prayer in the meetinghouse, and a final dismissal at the stand.

Raccoon John and Nancy began their journey back home to their surviving children. Williams notes that Smith then began to reflect on his recent experience,[33] and unquestionably this is true. Not the least of his broodings would have been over James French. In spite of his positive assent to Raccoon John's question about the origins of the King James Version and, more significantly, his authorship of that enigmatic yet telling circular letter condemning calumnies and aspersions against an absent brother, Raccoon John now perceived him as nonsupportive if not an actual opponent. Maybe the old man really was affronted by the new Campbell translation. He could even have been genuinely offended by Raccoon John's change in his communion order, though, in the context of the spirit of all the circular letters he had written heretofore, it seems more likely that the Lulbegrud queries that Smith and Williams blamed on him were more the dictation of Thomas Boone rather than the direct composition of the clerk. If French did pen the 1827 circular with Smith in mind, it's almost certain that he was shocked and dismayed to see John and Nancy behave as if their child's death was less important to them than Raccoon John's reelection as moderator. The news of the tragedy may even have reminded French of his own losses that year and made him feel them all the more keenly.

But besides all this, French was thirty years older than Raccoon John, and tired; only a little more than a decade earlier he'd spent two full years out of fellowship with the association in an effort to back Jilson Payne in the log controversy, and perhaps, in consideration of all the circumstances, when Raccoon John baited the delegates into a fracas over *The Living Oracles* on the first day of business with an obviously political agenda French suddenly and simply decided that it was not worth expending his remaining strength to be a vociferous Smith partisan. We cannot know for sure. Eight years after this fateful association meeting, when Raccoon John visited French on his deathbed, he told the old man that, though they had often been thrown in collision, he did not recall one thing that French had ever said to injure or to wound. "You talked but little," Smith observed, "but I used to think that you devised many things. I do not say this now to criminate you in the least; on the contrary, I want you to feel assured that I have not an unfriendly feeling toward you in the world."[34] Undeniably, the relationship between Smith and French was complex from start to finish, and it is hoped that this volume has at least thrown a little more light upon it than has heretofore been given. But for reasons that may have developed only as time went along, one of which must actually wait to be introduced in its proper place and context, Williams consistently portrays French from this period forward as Raccoon John's avowed adversary. Louis Cochran built upon this image to paint the old man as his own frontier local color version of Simon Legree. As we observed earlier, perhaps it is well for most of us that we shall never attract sufficient public notice to be caricatured in such a manner after our deaths.

But Raccoon John's musings on French would have been only one particular in a much larger context of his reflections, hopes, and fears. The Lord had not let his act of faith, if that's what it was, enable him to recapture the North District moderator's seat, and he had felt compelled to fight from the beginning of the session to its end just to try to defend what he now perceived as pure, basic Christianity. He had actually been successful to a surprising degree, and the damage done in 1826 and 1827 did not necessarily preclude him from being elected as moderator again at a later date. But it can hardly be doubted that Raccoon John now had to rethink his whole plan of using the moderator's office as a position of advocacy for a slow, gradual reform so that the next generation might enjoy its fullness. Baptist politics as they existed could ruin the entire enterprise, and with utter caprice. He might have to fight just as hard during the next decade as he had this year simply to retake his office, and this October he would turn forty-three; in a day and age when men and women could call themselves blessed just to reach the age of fifty, and considering the fact that he had already outlived his next-oldest brother William, he may have thought that his prime years were already behind him. And he had spent them all just as Jilson Payne had expended the last quarter century of his life, in a Baptist political battle he could never be certain of winning in any lasting way. It's entirely conceivable that Raccoon John could have despaired at the thought that he was stuck in a rat race, running madly toward a grave which he desperately hoped would bear the fruit of the Apostle Paul's promise to hold no victory over him, since it seemed that he himself could gain no true victory over any aspect of his life, much less his career.

Speaking of graves, Raccoon John and Nancy would of course be coming home to a new one on the knoll near their house, their grief perhaps only sharpened as they rode back to their farm and saw the fresh-turned earth beside two older but equally tiny mounds. Raccoon John had sacrificed even saying a proper goodbye to his son, all for an act of faith that had soured over the weekend into mere, mundane Baptist business as usual, and there was no way that he could ever take his actions back. Hard as his brother-in-law's, his neighbors', and possibly even Nancy's feelings may have been toward him at this point, he may have hated himself more.

And to cap it all off, though Raccoon John probably hadn't even realized it yet, the next year's North District meeting would begin at Lulbegrud on July 26, 1828—the one-year anniversary of Joshua's death.

It is possible that Raccoon John was cheered somewhat by his trips to Elkhorn and Tate's Creek Associations in August and then Bracken in September, but the three gatherings just as easily could have served him merely as painful reminders of that hellish last weekend in July. The August Elkhorn session in particular might have been especially disruptive to his peace of mind. At that occasion the Reform advocate Dr. James Fishback, who was James Mason's brother-in-law, and the small congregation he pastored on Mill Street in Lexington were expelled from the association for having changed their church's name from "Lexington First Baptist" to "The Church of Christ on Mill Street." An opposition faction of the congregation that retained the old name of Lexington First Baptist supplanted them on Elkhorn's roll.[35] Williams states that Fishback had also begun to advocate open communion in his church due to the influence of the writings of English free-communion Baptist Robert Hall,[36] but actually he and his flock had probably adopted a second Reform periodical and a mentor a lot closer to home, who at the time approved both of open communion and the appellation of Church of Christ: *The Christian Messenger* and its editor, Barton W. Stone.[37] In the 1820s Stone still did not accept the idea of requiring immersion as a test of fellowship and communion, and Fishback never did reconcile himself to it though he remained connected with the Campbell movement for the rest of his life, except for a brief hiatus around the year 1836.[38] But at this time also, Stone and Campbell were still sparring with one another in their respective editorials, and despite the fact that Fishback's church very well may have been the first Baptist congregation in Kentucky to boast a dual readership of Campbell's and Stone's papers, most Campbellites still regarded themselves as complete aliens to the Stoneites. Even Jeremiah Vardeman, who, if Williams is correct, was at this very juncture baptizing converts for the remission of sins and who had himself introduced a resolution at this same Elkhorn session declaring that individual churches were the highest ecclesiastical authority known in the word of God and affirming that they should never bring their difficulties to an association for adjustment,[39] had nothing but contempt for Fishback and his church. "Where are now these *Mill Street Christians?*" (Williams's emphasis), Vardeman blustered after the motion expelling them from the association had passed, "Let them seek an asylum wherever they can find it!"[40]

All in all, Dr. Fishback was given a much rougher ride by Elkhorn Association that year than Smith had been given by North District, and we might wonder whether the visiting Raccoon John considered speaking a word in Fishback's defense—and if he did, whether he dared to face down his old mentor Vardeman in so doing. But if the additional clash in Elkhorn wasn't enough for him to contend with, in September he saw the potential for a triumph of the beliefs of his and Jonathan's old enemy Richard Thomas in Bracken Association. At Bracken's session that fall, the members tentatively approved an effort to establish a correspondence with the hyper-Calvinistic Licking Association. After the meeting, word got out that Licking planned to force Bracken to pledge firm support for the Philadelphia Confession in order to effect the correspondence. We do not know what the exact position of William Vaughan, "Old Billy" Moss, William Payne, or Jonathan Smith may have been in this controversy, but pro– and anti–Licking Association parties rapidly formed within the group, and the next year promised to be a time of extreme tension all around.[41] To the north, at Alexander Campbell's home in the Virginia panhandle, grief and sadness reigned: Campbell's first wife, Margaret, died on October 27, and although he remarried to Selina Bakewell within a year, we need not doubt that his sorrow was entirely genuine.

And so in the waning months of 1827 Raccoon John again returned home to his farm and his memories of ten years of hard work both on the land and within North District Association and its correspondents. Though Williams says nothing further about Joshua Hurt, we might safely speculate that Nancy's brother in fact did choose that fall, after crop gathering, to move Betsy and his family to Illinois. Raccoon John's biographer also stresses that Smith was laboring virtually under the censure of North District Association during this season.[42] Though as we have stressed, his fall appointments as messenger to Elkhorn, Tate's Creek, and Bracken give the lie to this assertion, there can hardly be any doubt that Smith was indeed under censure—not by his church brethren as such but, I suspect, rather by his neighbors for leaving Joshua's grave on the day of the little boy's burial to go play ecclesiastical politics at Howard's Upper Creek that same night. Such community censures generally pass after a few weeks, except as they are recounted once in a while when family conversations turn to the past misdeeds of neighbors, but in the fall of 1827 Raccoon John's opprobrium was fresh and probably very strong.

But the quiet looks askance his neighbors must have given him certainly did not constitute all of his worries. He and Nancy had lived on the farm bought for them by his first four pastoral charges for nearly ten years now, but after he had consolidated his debt with the mortgage at the Commonwealth Bank he had still succeeded only in paying the interest on the loan. In other words, the bank owned the farm, and John was no better than a renter paying the interest as rent. In fact, he was in rougher shape than a renter would have been, since he was also responsible for his own property taxes. Raccoon John knew that in order to free himself of the debt he would somehow have to make that farm turn an enormous profit, and with Joshua Hurt leaving for Illinois, Joshua's son William himself having gone to housekeeping, and Jonathan Smith now having moved into Bracken Association territory, John and his three surviving boys—two old enough to hoe corn if they had to, one barely of age even to be set to "thinning" it—were now responsible for most, if not all, of their own farm labor. Williams tells us that Smith seriously considered writing off the entire downstate enterprise as a total loss and moving his family back to the Wayne County hills to make a fresh start, and with all things considered, we have no reason to doubt him on this point. Both Smith's leadership position in Kentucky Baptist politics and the crushing farm debt under which he labored must have been well-nigh unbearable crosses by this time. But Raccoon John realized that such a course would be tantamount to an admission that he had wasted a decade of his life on a foolish dream, and that idea was too much for him to bear as well.[43] So he went out to his fields to work. At the time, it must have seemed to be the only thing left to him.

And then only a few months later Raccoon John was converted—not just that, but perhaps even born again, all anew. Neither Williams, Cochran, Donaldson, nor even Raccoon John himself, as Campbell rationalists, would approve of the terminology I employ here—although, ironically, Williams himself is compelled to resort to near-mysticism in order to recount what happened: "God, who had called and prepared [Raccoon John] to preach the Gospel of His Son, now, by one of those mysterious, but not uncommon, impulses which move like inspiration, took him away from his [mundane labors], and brought him to stand before the people once more." The specific details are thus: apparently Raccoon John had gone out early one morning in January 1828 to split rails for mending a fence. Williams notes that he was working with axe, maul, wedge, and handspike, the common tools for that chore. But right in the middle of his labors he threw down his implements, strode purposefully back into the house with fire in his eyes, marched up to a thoroughly shocked Nancy, untied his coarse work apron (used by farmers in the days before denim overalls to protect their better clothing), tossed it at her feet, and exclaimed, "Nancy, I shall work no more! Get whom you please to carry on the farm, but do not call on me! In all the land, there is not one soul to open his mouth in defense of the best cause under the sun! I am determined, from this time forth, to preach the Gospel, and leave the consequences to God!"[44]

Even in that day when females were regarded virtually as second-class citizens with neither the physical nor mental powers of men, and allowing for the probability that Williams dandified Raccoon John's language a bit in keeping with literary mores of his age, this was indeed a brutal gesture and an abrupt, harsh speech for a husband and father to make—especially a husband in financial difficulties as great as those into which Raccoon John had thrown himself and all his loved ones, and to a wife who had borne eight children in twelve years' time, whose health had been as consistently poor as Nancy's had been, and who might, even at the time, have been carrying the couple's next daughter in her womb. But having exhaustively examined the details of Raccoon John's ministry up to this point, we would be hard put *not* to hark back to these details to come up with a relevant hypothesis as to what had happened to him in the field on that icy January day, and what had prompted his astonishing speech. From the time of his return to Kentucky from Alabama in the summer of 1815 he had ridden the Baptist political steed as long and as hard as he could in an effort to acquire and maintain the career pinnacle of downstate Baptist pastor and association moderator. This was his perception of the destiny to which God had called him—a destiny which he had attempted to thwart, for which the Lord, as John saw things, took his wife and two of his children away from him in retribution for his presumption, but then restored him to health and happiness after his repentance and obedience. Full of fallacy though the propositions of his theodicy may have been, he still must have realized, after his arrival in Montgomery County, that the politics on which he depended for advancement with the downstate Baptists had little if anything of piety or spirituality about them, but were instead completely secular in nature and often frighteningly cynical in character. If, therefore, he was laboring actively (and reasonably successfully) within a system he inwardly despised, it was only natural for him to attach himself to a brand-new theoretical system that proposed to free Christianity from man-made traditions on terms that he could embrace as rational and logical. The peppery editorial slant of *The Christian Baptist* fit this bill perfectly, even though he had first been influenced to subscribe to it by the Payne family in their early efforts to capitalize on it for their own political agenda.

His first face-to-face meeting with Alexander Campbell had confirmed his impression that Campbell and the so-called "Ancient Gospel" might prove to be his deliverance from all that he saw to be wrong with the Baptists. But then when he had tried to use the Payne–North District status quo and his own candidacy for association moderator as a platform for gradual reform, he had found that he must put politics above principle to survive in his leadership role. This in turn had led to the crisis of July 1827, when he had believed that his candidacy and his cause were so badly threatened that he had to forego bidding a proper father's farewell to a dead son in order to attend North District Association and maintain his end of the political fight. Though, as we have seen, he had carried out this mission at least halfway successfully, he had done so not only at the risk of his local reputation but at the expense of his own heart and soul as a parent as well.

Then on top of all that had come the Elkhorn and Bracken fights, and we can easily imagine that, by this point, Raccoon John was thoroughly convinced that ten years' worth of his labors hadn't made a single positive difference within the Kentucky General Union at all. It's a fair bet that, in the fall of 1827 and on into the new year, Raccoon John Smith hated North District Association, hated the Bluegrass and the chain of events that had brought him thereto, hated the roles he felt forced to assume as Baptist church pastor and association moderator, hated the diseases that stole Nancy's and their children's health, hated himself, hated his very life. Though he now suffered from no other physical affliction than the intermittent palsy in his hands and arms that was the remnant of his Alabama bout with the cold plague, despite what chronic ailments Nancy and the children may have had, there is no question that he himself was as demoralized psychologically and spiritually as he had been in Alabama in the spring and early summer of 1815. Everything he touched seemed to turn to ruin, and it must have appeared to him that the only way out of the Baptist rut into which he had so willingly jumped and within which his mentor Jilson Payne had lived and died was the grave. And the entire chain of events that had brought him to this juncture had been initiated by his born-again experience at the ebb of the initial outbreak of the Great Revival, and it had been fueled and maintained by his interaction with other born-again evangelists just like himself in America's Era of Good Feeling, when the circumstances that produced his despondent mindset were not supposed to exist except as accidents that could be remedied quickly by God and common sense.

But if, as we have suggested in previous chapters, Raccoon John's initial commitment to the downstate Kentucky Baptist political system represented an unwitting and naive first step into a second cycle through Kierkegaard's dialectic of aesthetic, ethical, and religious existence, and if his interest in Alexander Campbell and *The Christian Baptist* could be said to indicate the birth and growth of the second step, the ethical with its ultimate highest manifestation of sincere repentance, the political crises and his family tragedy of 1827 had primed him mightily to take that unjustifiable leap of faith in the dark—Kierkegaard's teleological suspension of the ethical—to another, brand-new and renewing religious experience soon thereafter. And from all we can tell, this is exactly what had happened to him out there as he labored at the border of his field on that wintry day. The reader will remember that after Raccoon John regained his health and returned to Kentucky in the wake of his Alabama misfortunes he became well-nigh frantic in his efforts to reestablish both his household and his ministry in the Kentucky General Union. John's delayed but ultimately frenetic response to his griefs and sorrows at the time may simply have been a personal characteristic, a trademark coping mechanism perhaps more than anything else associated with the personal theodicy he had embraced. Here he put himself into a frenzied pace once again, but even through Williams's studied prose we can see a distinct, and intense, difference between the John Smith of 1815 and the Raccoon John of 1828. In 1815 he had still loved the Kentucky Baptists, and had still believed he could find his life's fulfillment in their cause. Now, though he would remain, or at least sometimes claim on an as-needed basis to be, a Baptist for two or three more years, he separated himself entirely from their concerns and his prior ambitions with them to embrace a theoretical concept of pure, unadulterated Christianity whose proofs so far existed only in newsprint—because, literally, there was nothing else he could do to live with himself emotionally and spiritually. He had been a Campbell supporter since he had begun to receive and read *The Christian Baptist,* perhaps even a Campbell partisan since he had first met the editor in 1824, but now he was transformed into a Campbell zealot, pure and simple. Something in his life *had* to make sense, and the precepts of *The Christian Baptist* were all that he felt he had left. Thus, at whatever further financial and health risks he brought upon his family by so doing, he must now preach this so-called Ancient Gospel and, if need be, die in the attempt to prove both to himself and to the world that there could exist a rational, commonsense relationship between God and humankind and a method of salvation that superseded the tawdry experiences that he had known so far.

We must here briefly note that there could have been another aspect of Raccoon John's dramatic gut response to his many sorrows at this critical juncture. He had come to cope with the deaths of his first wife, Anna, and their children Eli and Elvira with the rationalization that God had taken them away from him in order to show him that he should return to his proper field of mission in Kentucky. We might wonder if, now, he viewed Joshua Carroll Smith's death, and perhaps even Eliza Baize's and William Pinckney's as well, in a similar light and with the same theodicy—that they had all been taken from him because he hadn't yet given himself wholeheartedly to the Campbell cause, but had insisted upon working too slowly and remaining within an associational political system wherein the traditions of man took precedence over the commandments of God. A century later another southern Kentucky minister, Burkesville's William Marrion Branham, would use similar reasoning to conclude that God used Branham's infant child's death from meningitis as a means of convincing him of the wrongness of traditional Trinitarian Christian thought and prodding him to embrace and proclaim "Jesus Only" Pentecostalism as the one true Gospel way. In following his perceived vocation Branham literally achieved cult status within parts of that faith community. But in Raccoon John's case, though Williams stresses the significance of Anna's, Eli's, and Elvira's deaths as God's enigmatic but gracious revelation of His plan for John, and there can be no doubt that Smith's own personal theodicy embraced events in exactly this light, Smith's first biographer never examines or even hypothesizes the existence of the latter possibility at all. In fact, by the time he put words to paper, he had good reason not to make such speculations about Raccoon John's second family. But for almost sixteen years after John began his new mission, this idea may have been a powerful, even a central, tenet of his thinking. The great irony is that, if he did believe it, he now felt compelled to let Nancy and his surviving children virtually fend for themselves in order to validate it.

After Raccoon John threw his apron down at Nancy's feet and made his declaration, he left the house and walked two miles or so to his children's schoolhouse, where Absalom Rice, a young man who had joined Spencer Creek Church not long after Jacob and Matilda Jane Coons were immersed and who had likewise exhibited great interest in the Campbell system and *The Christian Baptist,* served as teacher. He asked Rice to have his pupils take the message to their parents that he would preach that night at Thomas Moseley's house.[45] We do not know whether he had made any prior arrangements with Moseley for this engagement, although Moseley had been both his and Jilson Payne's supporter for years and it is possible that he had given Raccoon John permission to hold worship services at his home anytime the preacher chose. But at this meeting, evidently, John gave out further preaching appointments for other locations in Montgomery County and perhaps Bath and Nicholas counties as well, for every afternoon and evening that week. From this point forward his actions seem to exhibit all the characteristics of some *exalté,* neartrancelike fugue state in which he lived for literally nothing but preaching Alexander Campbell's Ancient Gospel. This mindset was to last not for mere days, weeks, or even months, either, but years. From early 1828 until the summer of 1830 he seems hardly even to have been present at his house except during the regular meeting weekends of his three pastoral charges, and until at least 1835 or 1836 he was still, as often as not, away on preaching engagements for the Campbell cause that he himself in large part made a success in eastern Kentucky. And in spite of his extended absences he continued to sire children on Nancy with all the rapid regularity of their marriage heretofore, producing two more daughters, Emily or Emma in 1828 or 1829 and Mary in 1831; hopefully John did find leisure enough at least to attend his wife during the two births.[46]

During this time period, Raccoon John regularly preached two discourses every day besides filling his three weekend pastoral appointments[47]—and these were none of the prepackaged twenty-minute, three-point, alliterative-for-the-biblically-illiterate brain-candy pep talks favored by so many modern pastors, either, but sermons usually two to three hours apiece in length in which he "corrected misconceptions" for about an hour, "exposed popular errors" for a second, and finally "presented the simple Gospel to the people" for the third.[48] He hardly relaxed at all during the day, frequently baptizing converts at night by torchlight since his appointments often required that he return to the road early the next morning,[49] but yet he seldom went to bed before midnight at the home of whatever family offered hospitality to him.[50] Even then, he could know no true repose. So focused was he on his crusade that he slept and woke to read *The Living Oracles* (and perhaps the King James Version as well, at least for comparative purposes) by turns, arising from fitful slumber to light a candle and examine some word or text of Holy Writ that had intruded even into his dreams.[51] His hair grayed rapidly, he found himself laid low by bouts of exhaustion from which he sprang after only the briefest rests only to preach and exhort all the harder,[52] and a Mt. Sterling physician (whether this was Dr. John Duke or one of the town's two other medical men in those early days, Ennis Combs and John Slavens, we do not know) remarked at about this time that Raccoon John was living and laboring for his crusade in a manner that would kill any ordinary man within six months.[53]

His mental status at the time is best illustrated by an anecdote that Williams evidently collected from John and Nancy's oldest surviving daughter, Maria. Once, not too long after spring planting season in 1828 or 1829, after an absence of many days, John made one of his infrequent trips back to his farm. That evening Nancy, who was certainly already either pregnant or with the newborn Emma at her breast, tried to interest him in what was going on with the crops and the livestock and asked his advice for the further management of things that season. But when she attempted to persuade him to go out to the barn, pens, and fields and have a look at the animals, the grain patches, and the garden, he arose from his chair, paced the floor in an agitated manner, and with "a strange enthusiasm" that unnerved her began to sing an old hymn still heard occasionally in "Old Time" Baptist churches in the eastern Kentucky hills: "Oh, tell me no more of this world's vain store, the time for such trifles with me is now o'er!"[54]

Poor, long-suffering Nancy evidently got the message her husband intended to convey, and apparently she did not again presume to distract Raccoon John from his mission with talk about farming. Williams assures us that she committed her support to his endeavors cheerfully and wholeheartedly,[55] but we should perhaps allow ourselves a bit of skepticism toward the claim. In those days both church and society decreed that a husband's order to a wife was law, and Nancy may have felt that she had no other choice. Once, in the middle of an extended evangelistic tour, Raccoon John rode up the path in front of his house and, without even dismounting, tossed her a set of saddlebags full of his dirty clothing and asked her to bring him some clean clothes so he could make a proper appearance at his further stops. She obeyed him, of course, but in reply asked him if it wasn't time that he was getting his washing done somewhere else, though she had attended to it for a long time. Williams, who probably learned this anecdote from Maria also, tries his best to argue that Nancy was merely making a wry joke with a touch of sadness in her voice, but her words themselves show little if any humor. To our modern ears at least, they sound extremely bitter and sarcastic, and considering that Nancy was now responsible for the farm, the taxes, and the interest on the loan as well as all the "women's work" about the place, plus trying all the while to contend with her "breast complaint" and care for at least six young children, she was eminently entitled to indulge herself once in a while in a bit of acerbity. But Raccoon John was undaunted, perhaps not even catching her tone—or if he did, choosing not to acknowledge it. "No, Nancy," he rejoined, "I am much pleased with your way of doing things, and don't wish to change." And off he rode to spread the Word, again.[56]

Over the course of the next decade or so, Nancy sometimes dipped into their meager resources to hire farm hands to perform the most backbreaking labors about their acres. She took her youngest child—not named by Williams, but it had to have been the second-youngest daughter Emma—and hoed corn herself all day long while the little one lay in the shade of elderberry bushes growing along the fencerow. In another instance that occurred at gathering time one year, a group of Raccoon John's zealous young Reform converts who lived nearby came by moonlight while she knelt in the house and prayed for strength, and they cut and foddershocked an entire corn patch for her.[57] Still later, Raccoon John managed to scrape together sixty-five dollars' worth of church contributions and hire out a slave as a field hand from a neighbor, Joseph Hansborough, for a year[58]—money that, with his own presence on the farm, could have been used to make at least a little dent in their debt. Another time John got hold of twelve pistareens (then the equivalent of about $2.40; interestingly, Spanish coin was fairly common currency in eastern Kentucky at this time)[59] from some source or other, but we wonder whether Nancy ever saw or benefited from it; at one point, he offered the money to a rival preacher of Baptist sentiments simply for the chance to debate doctrine with him before a congregation.[60] Somehow Nancy made do, and if she could not manage to sell enough eggs, cream, butter, flax, hemp, and grain to pay off their debt, she at least maintained the interest on the loan and got the taxes paid so that they didn't lose the place.

But there are yet three unsung heroes in Raccoon John's story who must have borne the real brunt of most of the hard labor at the Smith farm, even with the presence of hired men and rented slaves. One old eastern Kentucky saying (which, for some reason, I heard quite frequently at home during my early teenage years) maintains that if one wants a job done halfway, he should send a boy to do it; if one doesn't want the job done at all, he should send two boys. But Jonathan, John Duke, and Harvey Smith, at about ten, nine, and five years of age, respectively, when their father began his great crusade for the establishment of the Campbell Reform (two known to have suffered from tuberculosis and the third possibly afflicted as well) never had the chance to enjoy an adolescent's luxury of doing a job halfway. Neither Williams nor, apparently, Raccoon John himself ever mentioned them much either in praise or in condemnation. From a letter Raccoon John wrote in 1841 we learn that young Jonathan Smith had by then left home and was living in Maysville, on the banks of the Ohio River, and that in that same year John Duke had set out for Illinois. The same letter also indicates that the preacher had sent Harvey away to some school,[61] and Williams notes that John did the same thing for his daughter Maria with Philip Fall's young ladies' seminary in Frankfort.[62] But nowhere can we find evidence that he indulged his two oldest surviving sons with any education past what Absalom Rice could give them locally for four or five months a year. Neither Jonathan nor John Duke seems to have returned home at all once they departed, and both virtually drop out of recorded history for most of their lives. Perhaps due to his slightly younger age, Harvey appears to have enjoyed a few more opportunities and he definitely left behind a clearer historical trail, but for reasons that must keep for later discussion he was, and remains, a complete enigma. The boys' father was absent so much during their formative years that the three may never have felt close to him in the way Raccoon John had so cherished his own relationship with old George Smith, and it's conceivable that the two oldest could even have resented him for setting them out to work at such young ages and then afterward making better provision for Harvey, Maria, and their other siblings. John Duke died in 1846, in his late twenties, and of Jonathan, Williams notes merely that in early 1868 he made his home at St. Louis, where, at the time of Raccoon John's death, he was slowly smothering his own life away in the last stages of consumption.[63] After Jonathan's death, his body was returned to Kentucky and interred near the graves of his parents on June 8, 1868. There is a Mrs. Mary S. Smith who is buried next to him, whose death date is given as December 3 or 4, 1861. This could have been Jonathan's wife, but Harvey Smith is buried on her opposite side; his wife's, or ex-wife's, name was Mary, and thus we are uncertain of this

Mary Smith's exact relationship within the family.[64] We will take a look at Harvey Smith's life in due course, but we cannot yet definitively confirm whether either Jonathan or John Duke ever married and raised families. Even so, there can be no doubt that once their father had thrown down his apron at their mother's feet and told her to get whom she pleased to work the farm, but not to call on him, all three Smith sons had been compelled to grow up quickly. Not because of their father's sickness or untimely death—as was commonly the case for farm boys in those days who found themselves saddled with adult jobs at tender ages—but, ironically, for the sake of their father's life and health.

That Raccoon John Smith willingly and cheerfully gave great personal sacrifice to establish the Campbell Reform in his own little corner of the world is unquestioned. That his closest family members likewise paid a great price toward this end, even if they had little or no choice in the matter themselves, is likewise unquestioned. But regardless, what he did accomplish could almost be described as miraculous, and a great many Christians in his faith tradition would express no qualms about classifying his work exactly in that way.

For the first time in the American South—or at least south of the Ohio River—an evangelist with a rabid zeal that even George Whitefield and Shubal Stearns could have appreciated was successfully proclaiming a Gospel, not based in the conventional Whitefield-Stearns metaphysical context in which the Holy Ghost was asserted to impress a subjective personal testimony of the veracity of the message upon the hearts and minds of individual believers, but grounded in, of all things, a *rationalism* wherein the truth of the New Testament was a given that could be stated without further proof, the preached Word itself was declared to be the only manifestation of the Holy Spirit upon the souls of hearers, and sins were remitted by the blood of Jesus Christ through obedience to the command to repent and be immersed. There have been a great many powerful evangelists in the Campbell religious tradition since the days of John Smith and Walter Scott; Alexander Campbell himself never showed any particular strength as a preacher to the unconverted, but was rather more successful at proselytizing professed Christians to his own mode of thought.[65] But for the most part, later Campbell evangelists labored merely on the foundation that Smith and Scott worked so tirelessly to establish. At this time period no such base existed apart from the strength of these early evangelists' own zeal, and we have already seen what torments of spirit Raccoon John endured to forge his personal mindset. We cannot here address the question of whether Walter Scott operated under similar mental anguish (interestingly, Louis and Bess Cochran's characterization of Scott in *Captives of the Word* indicates that he actually may have; would that Louis had been so objective in his retelling of Raccoon John's story), but we can safely make the claim that what Scott managed to accomplish north of the Ohio River, Raccoon John Smith in large measure personally effected south of it.

This is not to assert that Raccoon John was the sole Campbell evangelist in

Kentucky at this period. He wasn't, any more than Walter Scott could have claimed to be the only Campbell exhorter working the sawdust trail in Ohio. As we have noted already, Barton Stone had his own crop of young firebrands who had become vociferous for the teachings of *The Christian Baptist,* and even before Raccoon John began his personal crusade they were working hard to align the Stone movement with Campbell principles. Besides these (for lack of a better term) "progressive Stoneites" there was James Fishback, now pastor of an independent Lexington church and taking evangelistic tours of his own as a sort of free agent between the Stone and Campbell perspectives. Most other Kentucky Campbell partisans were yet affiliated with the Baptists, and at this date their number still included Jeremiah Vardeman, William Vaughan, Walter Warder, William Morton, George Elley, Josiah Collins, Oliver Steele, and probably even old William Payne. Most or all of these men were at least as friendly to the precepts of *The Christian Baptist* as Raccoon John himself had been before the crisis of 1827. But of them all, Raccoon John was definitely the most thoroughly converted and certainly the hardest-working, and his fiery zeal, based within his own frantic search for peace, meaning, and fulfillment, served as an inspiration both to his hearers and his colleagues. It has been said that a true reformer for any cause is an individual who is able to impress his own personal angst upon the world at large, and Raccoon John undoubtedly fit that bill eminently. He worked tirelessly not only to organize new congregations built solely upon *Christian Baptist* directives, but to try to convert as many established Baptist churches as possible to Campbell views.

Within three months or even less, his results were noticeable. James Mason wrote the following letter to *The Christian Baptist* on April 19 of that year:

> John Smith is certainly a host within himself. The sectarian leaders have found it out, and are barking at him; but the people are following him in crowds, and he is teaching them the Ancient Gospel with astonishing success. You would be amazed to see with what adroitness he handles *the weapons burnished and refitted for him in* The Christian Baptist [emphasis added]. The old, profane swearer and the long professed Deist—many that, to all appearances, were given over to hardness of heart and reprobacy [*sic*] of mind, have bowed to King Jesus. At our last meeting [at Grassy Lick], thirty-six were immersed and added to our church. On last Lord's Day, at Mount Sterling, thirty-seven were immersed, among whom were some of our most respectable citizens—men of the highest position in civil society.
>
> But I cannot deny myself the pleasure of telling you how my soul was filled with joy at seeing a beloved brother according to the flesh, make the confession. Unconscious of it himself till he heard Brother Smith proclaiming the Ancient Gospel, he had been a believer in the Lord Jesus Christ for more than twenty-six years; but because he could not tell what we have always been in the habit of calling a *Christian*

> *experience* [Mason's emphasis], he has been kept out of the fold of God ever since, till a few days ago, when he found out that to believe in the Lord Jesus Christ, and to obey his commands, was all that the Gospel required; he then went down into the water and told Brother Smith he wished him to say *immerse,* instead of *baptize* [again, Mason's emphasis]. Like the eunuch of old, he is now going on his way rejoicing, as happy a man as can be found.[66]

The brother that James Mason spoke of here was John Mason, and from him Mt. Sterling Church soon appears to have purchased a lot on which to construct a new building to accommodate its growing crowds. However, Raccoon John recalled that another Mason—John Thomson Mason, father of Stevens Thomson Mason, the first elected governor of Michigan, and apparently little if any relation to James—was at this time his very first candidate for immersion who insisted on doing things strictly according to the Campbell method Smith was preaching. John Thomson Mason refused to make a personal testimony or "give an experience" in traditional Baptist forms, but rather requested that the ordinance be performed without the added detail. Though Raccoon John had so far indulged his baptismal candidates to some extent, letting them make testimony of their born-again experiences as they wished, after immersing John Thomson Mason he would never again agree to "hear an experience" before baptism. He may have felt that Mason's own prestige in the Montgomery/Clark/Fayette County area was just the little added factor that would enable him to bring his growing flock closer to the Campbell ideal. John T. Mason was every inch the Virginia gentleman and, though living in relative poverty at this time due to some unsuccessful business deals, still owned an interest in one of the very first industries in Montgomery County, an ironworks somewhere to the south of Mt. Sterling on Red River.[67] To return to the James Mason family, though, the above letter to Alexander Campbell was written at what turned out to be some personal cost; during this very year James was running for the Kentucky State Senate from the district which comprised Montgomery and Estill counties, and when his opponent, William P. Fleming, read Mason's enthusiastic missive in *The Christian Baptist* he immediately exploited it for his own campaign, vilifying Mason himself as a sectarian religious extremist who had no place in public office. Mason lost a bitterly contested election to the incumbent Fleming and, by his own admission, between four and five hundred dollars he had sunk into his campaign.[68]

Another contemporary letter, going into some detail as to the identity of a few more of the "men of the highest position in civil society" who had embraced Raccoon John's message, but with the writer's observations couched in the more conventional Great Awakening/Great Revival/Baptist terminology of "hope" or conviction preceding conversion, was written by Micajah Harrison (Dulcinea Payne's brother) to his son Jilson Payne Harrison, who was then studying in Lexington, on April 20: ". . . a meeting in town today by Mr. Smith.

There was 37 baptised [*sic*], including Kenaz Farrow . . . old Jimmy Gatewood has a hope, J. Harvey Gatewood has been baptised. There is a great hope of some of the Harris family, but I am afraid a forlorn one."[69]

We have already made mention of Kenaz Farrow as a Mt. Sterling attorney and, more significantly, the husband of James and Keziah French's daughter Susanna. Thus the success of Raccoon John's message among these "most respectable" citizens also assured that, while his zeal had put his head in the clouds, he had still managed to keep his feet firmly on the ground in terms of the practical aspects of his crusade. Besides the men noted in Mason's and Harrison's letters, Raccoon John's earliest and firmest supporters in the Reform included the Coons family, Thomas Moseley, Absalom Rice, and William and Mildred Payne's sons and daughters Buckner, John Newton, and Dulcinea with their spouses.[70] Perhaps with them should be included their sister Lucille as well, as her suitor and later her husband, Josephus Hewitt,[71] proved to be another one of Raccoon John's most dependable young preaching colleagues.[72] Buckner Payne, immersed only lately himself, likewise began to preach, "neglecting his counting room"[73] to tag along behind Raccoon John in his ever-expanding evangelistic field and his messages apparently meeting with great approval even though Smith frequently had to remind him to toe up to Campbell's *Living Oracles* standards and speak of "the Holy Spirit" rather than "the Holy Ghost."[74] John Newton Payne was a successful young public speaker as well, and was one of the first to be ordained as an elder according to Campbell precepts at Sharpsburg Church, one of Raccoon John's newly gathered Reform congregations.[75] In short, Raccoon John had managed to keep every one of the later principal members of the North District Payne faction solidly behind him, with the one notable exception of James French. Even with the setback of French's disenchantment, we can assume from John's baptism of Kenaz Farrow in 1828 that he had the support of at least some of the French sons and daughters as well. Of course, the stability of this alliance was in large measure due to the fact that the Payne faction as a group had been accustomed to drawing on the influences of *The Christian Baptist* anyway, and James French's defection could have been the only reason that Smith later expressed such negative recollections about him. But the group itself was still as important politically as it had ever been, and with Raccoon John's altered ambitions it was perhaps now even more so.

In addition to Smith's cadre of followers, of the known former Separate churches outside the direct control of the Payne faction he likewise rapidly gained the support of Daniel Williams's old Sycamore congregation at Jeffersonville. We must wonder if the church's own negative experiences of twenty-odd years before with the Payne and Elkin cliques may have prompted its members to throw their support to him, if for no other reason than as a protest against the bureaucracy of North District Association. Though Daniel Williams had left Sycamore for good finally in 1809 and had died in 1820 after organizing the Burning Springs Association and preaching for several years on the upper Licking River in the eastern mountains, at least some of his members still had relatives living in Montgomery County who belonged to Sycamore Church. Among these were Jesse Coffee, younger brother of Burning Springs Association moderator William Coffee, who later moved southeastward himself and transferred his membership to his brother's association.[76] On occasion, rural family grudges can indeed influence church politics in this fashion for decades after a controversy begins. According to family genealogical records, Enoch Willoughby, pastor of the Sycamore flock since William Vaughan had left it in 1815 to move to Bracken Association, had died about 1827.[77] Though from North District Association's minutes we can assume that his place was filled in part by John Fox and Joseph Fanning, both of whom may have been raised up to the ministry under him, two other men, Ezekiel Stewart and Joseph Hon, also represented the church at North District's annual meeting that year.[78] Hon may have been related to Peter Hon, who pastored the Stoneite church on Stepstone Creek near Raccoon John's Bath County field of labor, though it cannot be definitively proven. But Stewart appears to have returned to Sycamore after having homesteaded for some years at the head of Red River in present Wolfe County, transferring his letter back to the Jeffersonville church from another congregation, known simply as Red River, that Daniel Williams himself had organized in that mountainous area.[79] And for whatever reason, both Ezekiel Stewart and Joseph Hon assisted Raccoon John in a singular way in 1828: of all the new churches that Smith gathered that year, five in number and ranging in location from northern Bath County all the way southward into the Montgomery County hills, only one appears to have been gathered in traditional Baptist "arming-off" form, and this was a congregation known as South Fork of Red River, organized from Sycamore and represented at the 1828 association meeting by Stewart and Hon themselves.[80]

Both Fanning and Fox quickly came to espouse and maintain Raccoon John's message as well, and local eastern Kentucky legend has it that Smith's own travels took him to Burning Springs Association's Red River Church, where he personally succeeded in converting it to the Reformation. Though we cannot be sure, it is possible that James Mason's brother John could have effected a positive influence for Raccoon John's message in the settlements near the head of Red River as well. He seems to have remained a bachelor for much of his life, but John Mason did maintain a house for some time in the upper Red/Licking River area and even took a bride, Elizabeth Henry, from Caney Creek a few hollows to the northeast of the head of Red River and the same locality where Daniel Williams had passed the last years of his life and ministry.[81] It is certain, though, that the cause there was taken up early by Joseph Nickell, pastor of the Red River congregation and a frequent Burning Springs representative to North District annual meetings; his assistant, Rancy Maxey; and Nixon Covey, who likewise according to local legend was immersed by Raccoon John himself, began his own ministry the very next day, and became the pioneer Reform preacher in what is now Breathitt County.[82] Raccoon John had to have been well acquainted with Daniel Williams's ancient woes through the recollections of Jilson Payne at Lulbegrud years before, and even though Smith himself had been connected for years with the nemesis of both Elder Williams and the church, his exploitation of Sycamore's longstanding grudge may have seemed to him to be simple common sense. After all, the old Separate preacher Williams had been wronged not by the Gospel that Smith now preached, but by the very entities that Raccoon John now sought to condemn.

Which brings us to another significant question: if Raccoon John was as committed to his crusade as all the evidence indicates, exactly what were his ambitions within North District and the Kentucky United Baptists at this point? Since his January epiphany, Smith had come to believe that neither North District Association nor the United Baptist Church as a whole were legitimate religious entities,[83] and neither John Augustus Williams nor the minutes of the association give any indication that he ever again ran as a candidate for association moderator. If he had, he certainly would have been able to retake the office in 1829, if not in 1828. At the same time, though, he sought to maintain a connection with the association for as long as possible, in the hope of bringing as many of its churches as he could to his own point of view.[84] Since he had now given up Baptist moderatorial ambitions, according to his own "lights," as the saying went, he may even have believed that he had abandoned church and associational politics altogether, and he could have felt that both the Paynes and the elders at Sycamore and the two Red River churches continued to follow his lead simply because they accepted truth.

But if he had convinced himself that he had abandoned politics, both his connection to the Payne family and his success in maintaining an alliance with the Sycamore Church prove that it didn't quite work out exactly that way. We would do well here to reiterate an observation recorded by John Augustus Williams and alluded to in earlier chapters: it was impossible to determine the exact temper of the association before an actual session of the body, especially during a period of strife. Though Raccoon John's fiery preaching since January had been successful in many areas of the association's territory and had at least provoked thought within others, some North District members wavered or waited; some watched for the signs of the times, intending to trim to the popular gale; others were indifferent, or double minded; and not a few loyally resolved to abide by the actions of the association.[85] As shown also, by far the majority of North District churches were noncreedal and nearly Arminian Separate Baptist in origin and consequently prone to lionize those whom they perceived as patriarchs in the style of Shubal Stearns, and the above description fits in perfectly with our picture of a large "trash vote" component that both the Elkin/Chenault and Payne/Smith factions had for years been compelled to court for support. In essence, all this meant that Raccoon John couldn't depend on success merely by giving a straightforward exposition of the principles proclaimed in *The Christian Baptist*; though he might claim to eschew ecclesiastical politics now, he still had to overlay his message with some workable method of campaign. From the overall tone of all the Raccoon John Smith literature of the nineteenth and twentieth centuries, Williams and other writers included, I believe we can deduce at least a rough outline of his platform, and it probably went something like this:

Any Baptist who believed in the special operation of the Holy Ghost and an inward emotional and metaphysical experience of conversion was a Calvinist, and by definition a Regular Baptist (Methodists, who subscribed to this same particular article of faith but were thorough Arminians, didn't figure into this equation, but we shall come to Raccoon John's post-conversion relationships with both Methodists and Presbyterians shortly). Besides insisting that their converts experience weird, nonsensical visions in order to prove the special operation of the Spirit upon their souls, Regular Baptists did not accept the fact that the Bible itself was a sufficient creed, like the good and honest Separate Baptists did, but instead demanded obedience to the vile man-made Philadelphia Confession, which advocated not only the special operation of the Spirit but both predestination and infant damnation as well. When Regular and Separate Baptists had united, the Regular Baptists had essentially forced the Philadelphia Confession and all its beliefs down the Separates' throats, and the Separates had therefore been a persecuted people ever since the Baptist Union had taken place. The Baptist Alexander Campbell, on the other hand, believed and proclaimed that the New Testament alone was the only creed that Christians needed, so to reestablish a stance on the true Scriptural principles that Separate Baptists had historically advocated, the way could be found in the New Testament alone—as expounded, of course, in the pages of *The Christian Baptist.* Raccoon John never emphasized his own prior role with either the Regular Baptist contingent of the General Union or with the Payne faction in this process. He stressed rather that he had once been the strictest of Calvinists, and that both the deaths of his children in Alabama in 1815 and the writings of *The Christian Baptist* since 1823 had shown him that Calvinism was unscriptural. Of course, after he had begun to see the light of truth in the pages of Campbell's paper, the cruel Calvinists David Chenault and James French had tried to destroy him at the 1827 North District annual meeting, even though he had just lost another child. Now in 1828 he stood before the people, determined to declare the Gospel truth to them or die, no matter what Chenault, French, or the very devil himself thought or did.

This was the exact slant in which John Augustus Williams penned *The Life of Elder John Smith,* and although Everett Donaldson at times supplies more accurate historical data, too often he merely echoes the claims of Williams. The rhetoric was amplified, and in a sense brought full circle, by Louis Cochran. But it was no wonder that, in the heyday of Raccoon John's ministry, Silas Noel of Franklin Association could observe to his fellow Baptists that Campbell's followers were always harping about being persecuted because they wouldn't swallow the Philadelphia Confession, and yet he did not know of one single instance in Kentucky in which a Campbell follower had been called into question by a church or an association regarding that point.[86] The rhetoric must have sounded simply too good and too powerful for the Reformers not to use.

Thus stood the presentation of causes in Raccoon John's great Reform campaign; on the implementation of effects, he could be a bit more flexible, as indeed was Alexander Campbell himself. Smith would win a convert in any way he could, be it by stressing the Campbell ideal of Christian unity or the Campbell method of conversion and salvation, although in the early days of the Reform movement he would invariably come down on the side of the method if he was forced to make a choice between the two. But rather than dwelling on the "*really* pardoned" and "*formally* pardoned" distinctions by which his editorial mentor was wont to describe the importance of baptism by immersion, he would often simply quote the text of Acts 22:16—"And now why tarriest thou? Arise, and be baptized [or 'immersed,' if he quoted from *The Living Oracles*] and wash away thy sins, calling on the name of the Lord"—and state that it meant exactly what it said, with no implications of literary allusion or poetic imagery.[87] The more literate and perceptive of his hearers, those who could and consequently did subscribe to and read *The Christian Baptist,* no doubt understood accurately what he was trying to say, but we can be fairly certain that a great many of his rustic hill and backcountry listeners lacked the discernment to do so. Early on, some younger Reform exhorters perhaps of this type and mindset began to add to Campbell's message, lifting one Bible verse, John 9:31, completely out of the context of the Scripture passage surrounding it and publicly and zealously declaring that sinners could not even pray, nor in fact should Christians pray for them; the baptismal water was all in all. A few of these actually refused to pray for Divine assistance when declaring the Gospel to the people.[88] I myself once knew an old matron from a hill country church of the Campbell tradition who avowed with complete personal honesty and integrity up to the day of her death that she had actually *seen* her sins floating away in the creek when she was immersed. Though Campbell-tradition folklore of this sort has perhaps understandably gone under-researched and maybe even unresearched,[89] it does still exist, and very probably not merely in the southern mountains where Smith, Ezekiel Stewart, and Joseph Nickell once labored. Not that Raccoon John would have wished anyone to believe that water could wash away sins in the manner described above, of course, and he seems to have been horrified and disgusted by the idea of anyone's preaching that sinners could not pray.[90] But he could not openly condemn such a mindset with the same vigor that he criticized the doctrines of the Baptists, Methodists, and Presbyterians since, after all, its advocates were on his and Alexander Campbell's own side in the great battle between God and Satan. All in all, there can be little doubt that his own strong, flamboyant personality and those of his colleagues and followers who drew on his strength and reputation and proclaimed the Reform message in his wake, rather than the logical system of their preaching, were a great stimulant both to conversions and to the development of such folklore.

And so rolled the great Campbell Reform through the eastern half of Kentucky in the spring and summer of 1828, whether on the objective truths of its message or simply on the strength of its rhetoric, but in either case definitely and consistently on Raccoon John Smith's fiery zeal. But there existed one more element to Raccoon John's popularity here, one that we must mention in the context of politics before resuming the thread of his life: 1828 was a presidential election year, and sure enough, right in the wake of the Campbell Reform, Andrew Jackson's new Democratic Party was canvassing the nation on his behalf, bent on winning the White House for the Hero of New Orleans that November. All through spring and summer into the fall the campaign song "The Hunters of Kentucky," written by Samuel Woodworth in praise both of Jackson's 1815 victory at New Orleans and of the many Kentucky soldiers who had been in the thick of the fighting there, was sung by liquor-loosened, discordant voices in torchlight processions through the county seats of Kentucky and the rest of the nation, in a campaign based far more on Jackson's colorful personality than any substantive issues and given perhaps its most accurate description by one perceptive historian as a season of smear, cheer, and beer.[91] Old Hickory, the poor Carolina orphan abused by the British and forced to raise himself up veritably by his own bootstraps in the wild southern backwoods, was going to retake the nation in the name of the American common man; and so, just as a gaunt, shabby young preacher back at Crab Orchard Church in 1815 had been able to capitalize upon Jackson's New Orleans image to promote himself as "the man without an education" who could preach with the best of them in downstate flatland Kentucky, so could that very same preacher, still poor but a little better-dressed, older, and arguably wiser, again hitch the wagon of his own popularity to Jackson's star. Raccoon John Smith, poor boy, frontiersman, hunter of Kentucky, common man from the bootheels up, self-taught and brought to Bluegrass Baptist fame by the help of the Lord and his own innate backwoods American common sense, had seen the light, divested himself of all human creeds and philosophies, and was reclaiming Kentucky for plain and simple commonsense Christianity, come hell, high water, or anything else that Satan or the little Federalist popes among the Baptists, Presbyterians, and Methodists might throw at him. In a country that Andrew Jackson was taking by storm at this very same season, how, indeed, could anyone but the most creed-bound sectarians—and, of course, infidels and those secretly in league with Old Scratch himself—resist a positive comparison?

Thus was born the legend of Raccoon John Smith, and as both settlers and evangelists took the Campbell Reform from Kentucky and Ohio to Indiana, Illinois, Missouri, Texas, and all points west, thus it was maintained—and has endured.

Williams and the writers who follow him all claim that Raccoon John expected an enormous backlash from North District's leaders for his actions. Undoubtedly he did, and in fact he found himself in a rather ticklish situation. He had to have realized that, since he planned for the time being to remain with the association, even if he did not intend ever again to campaign for moderator, he must somehow keep himself in at least a semblance of good standing and simultaneously secure a seat on the body's arrangements committee from year to year so he could parry and deflect any potential church queries sent up against the Campbell cause. His experiences of the summer of 1827 had taught him well: the only reason he had come away from the previous year's North District annual meeting with as many small victories as he had gained was his having argued his case so aggressively to Chenault, the downstate visitors, and the arrangements committee on the Saturday evening of the session. There were certain actions he could implement in the interim between annual sessions to provide himself a bit of insurance on this point, and the main advantage he may have employed was his open declaration that he never again intended to seek the moderatorial office. He could easily outmaneuver David Chenault if he managed to acquire an appointment to the crucial arrangements committee, and so he may actually have pledged his own vocal support as well as that of his pastoral charges and newly organized churches to Chenault's moderatorial candidacy.

Though this would seem at first glance to have been an extremely bizarre tactic, it was a workable one. Raccoon John's open advocacy of his old adversary's election as moderator, in and of itself, would have given the not-so-bright Chenault a powerful inducement not only to appoint Raccoon John to the arrangements committee successively, but to encourage the association to admit Smith's new churches as well. Neither Williams nor Smith would have admitted the existence of such a plan and we cannot say for sure that this is what happened, only that it was a tactic that, under the usual political circumstances of a rural Kentucky Baptist association, would have meshed perfectly with what Raccoon John was attempting. But regardless, at some point in the summer of 1828 he got an unexpected opportunity to confirm his own orthodoxy as both a Baptist and a Reformer in the minds of most North District members not already rallying to his side. This series of events must now claim our attention for a few moments.

As we've observed in several instances already, even as a Baptist Raccoon John had long been accustomed to denigrating other faiths publicly and as often as possible with the generous use of his own heavy-handed wit. Since he had seen the light in January, he now included the Baptists among his targets, at least in the manner we have outlined above; but if anything, he was more aggressive against Presbyterians and Methodists than he had ever been. As the Westminster and Philadelphia Confessions were so nearly identical to one another and the Presbyterians were generally much more insistent upon the observation of their formal creed than were by far most of the Regular and

Regularized Separate Baptists, he could tar Presbyterians with the same Calvinistic brush that he used for the Baptists, with the added barbs that the Presbyterians were completely mistaken about the nature and the proper mode of baptism as well as being altogether too obsessed with Greek, Latin, and formal theological training. In a move entirely characteristic of his style, he once replied in what he claimed was Cherokee—albeit fractured beyond understanding even to native Cherokee speakers, so garbled in fact that we might almost accuse him with some justification of speaking in unknown tongues without 1 Corinthians 14's required interpreter[92]—to a Presbyterian minister during a dispute because his opponent dared to hint that a certain Presbyterian principle could be proven more easily if one could read the New Testament in the original Greek.[93] None of his auditors could say who won the point in question, but of course the frontier imagery carried the day for Raccoon John.

He could not accuse Methodists of being bound to Calvinistic creeds, but he could still criticize them both for their written Discipline and for their sprinkling of infants, and in addition he made a great deal of hay out of poking fun at their emotionalistic behavior at their camp meetings. His arguments with them gave occasion for some of his wittiest, and cruelest, barbs. Once he challenged a nearby Methodist leader to a series of debates over the denomination's revival practices, and in the process he brought up several local conversion cases for ridicule; of one fellow who professed the New Birth after he claimed to view the image of Jesus at the top of a tree, he asked where, in the name of all the apostles and prophets, an example could be found in the Bible of anyone who had ever treed his Savior.[94] The debates influenced a good many young Methodists to submit to immersion and join his Reform, much to the distress of older members of the faith. After he immersed one young girl from a Methodist family in the Spencer Creek area, an irate old Wesleyan sister set upon him with the accusation that when he led the girl into the water, he had led her that much further toward hell; he replied blandly to the matron that, if she read her Bible more and her Methodist Discipline less, she would learn that people did not go to that place by water, since there was barely enough on the road to sprinkle a baby. A short time later this same woman again accused him, this time of having a wolf's fondness for Methodist lambs, and he rejoined that he did indeed love them well, but not until they were properly washed.[95]

On another occasion, Raccoon John came to a Methodist meeting and watched a circuit rider christen a child, who was mightily displeased and struggling against the process. A day later at one of his own meetings the same circuit rider was in attendance, so Raccoon John suddenly grabbed the man, began to wrestle and manhandle him toward the creek, and informed him that he was about to be immersed. When the surprised and embarrassed Methodist yelled in protest that he didn't want to be immersed and that it would do him no good without his consent, John shot back that the toddler whom the circuit rider had christened the day before hadn't wanted to submit to that ordinance either, but he'd gotten christened anyway. Both the circuit rider and the audience for whom Raccoon John was performing got the point.[96] Still later, Smith and another circuit rider happened to meet at a small country store or tavern and Raccoon John offered to toss back a glass of wine with the Methodist (remember, this was still the pre-Temperance era, although Methodists were for the most part much more condemnatory of "dram drinking" than were either early Baptists or early Reformers). When the circuit rider insisted on saying grace over his wine, Raccoon John surreptitiously lifted the glass from under the itinerant's upturned nose and knocked it back in one gulp himself, leaving the Methodist staring in surprise at an empty vessel when he opened his eyes. As the crowd of loafers in the store laughed, Raccoon John admonished him that Methodists should do better than follow the Bible only halfway; therein, believers are told not only to pray, but to watch and pray.[97] And perhaps his most famous quip was to yet one more Methodist, a comparison of the ordinance of immersion as practiced by Reformers to the "mourners' bench" provided for the convenience of praying penitents at Methodist, Stoneite, and Separate Baptist services: one was from heaven, the other from the sawmill.[98]

After Raccoon John declared war on the Methodists and they began to fight back, Nancy, having shouldered an enormous burden so that he might be free to roam the countryside and preach, began to remonstrate and perhaps even quarrel with him—when she got the chance, that is, on his brief and sporadic visits home—over the increasing severity of his attacks against denominations among whom he had so long lived in relative peace. But Raccoon John, borne up by the intensity of his January experience, would have none of it, and once again he found utility in speaking of wine, this time for the sake of a parable, to carry his point with her. "Nancy," he said to her one day, holding up a glass of water as he did so, "can I fill this tumbler with wine, until I have emptied it first of water? Neither can I get the truth into the hearts and minds of the people till I have first disabused them of error."[99]

But if Raccoon John was intent on "showing up" the Methodists at every opportunity, this didn't mean that the Methodists themselves were utterly opposed either to the concept of reform, or even Christian unity on at least some of Campbell's terms. They just didn't like the increasingly bellicose, uncompromising style Smith had adopted since his January epiphany, although judging by his interactions with Joseph Price Howe and his encounter with the Shakers at Moses Higgins's, he had been combative enough before. But we must remember that Smith was not the only Reform evangelist itinerating through Kentucky at this point. Among others, James Fishback, who had already been kicked out of Elkhorn Association and who had been mistreated not only by his own Baptists but even by some who were friendly to the Campbell movement as well, sometimes sallied forth from Lexington on evangelistic tours. He preached his own much milder exposition of Reform doctrine which, as we have noted, was very probably already a mixture of Stone and Campbell influences. We would think that Raccoon John might have entertained a degree of sympathy, if not empathy, toward Fishback since he himself had experienced such a rough go at his own association meeting the summer before, but at least by now it wasn't so. *The Christian Baptist*'s stated policy held that churches should "neither invite nor debar" anyone to the communion feast, and this idea has remained more or less intact through the years in all the Reform movement's descendant manifestations to evolve into a practical open-communion policy in each. At this time, though, and at heart, Alexander Campbell himself believed that no one who had not been immersed should be allowed to partake of the Lord's Supper, and his writings of course reflected this mindset.[100] Fishback thus embraced Stone's communion position while dismissing Campbell's, and this was something that Raccoon John was neither constitutionally nor emotionally able to tolerate at this stage. In examining the dispositions and the interactions of these two men, both committed heart and soul to Christian reform, one is almost tempted to compare Smith to Luther and Fishback to Erasmus: at least since his January revelation, Raccoon John had come to despise Fishback for being so lenient on the question of immersion both as a necessity for salvation and as a test of eligibility for communion, but nowhere can we find any evidence that the gentle, open-minded Fishback harbored any resentment toward Smith in return, except perhaps an understandable antipathy toward the flaming bitterness of Raccoon John's zeal. One wonders how James Mason, parishioner of one and brother-in-law to the other, ever managed to steer a neutral course between them. As will be seen, there's a distinct possibility that he didn't. But for their part, Kentucky Methodists found that they could interact quite well with Fishback, being open communionists themselves and appreciative of his broad-minded, almost Erasmian style.

At any rate, included within Fishback's itinerary during the spring and early summer of 1828 was a series of meetings in "the hills of Red River."[101] Exactly where along the river these meetings were held we cannot say with absolute certainty, but the watercourse originated at what was then the extreme southwestern end of Morgan County, near Burning Springs Association's Red River Church. From there it meandered through the southern end of Montgomery to form the boundary between Estill and Clark counties before finally emptying into the Kentucky River at the edge of the Bluegrass. The modern Kentucky counties in the Red River watershed include Wolfe, Menifee, and Powell, as well as Clark and Estill. But at the time nearly all of the area was North District territory, with the exception of the one church at the head of the river that belonged to Burning Springs Association and where, as mentioned already, local legend has it that Raccoon John first converted the congregation and its ministers to the Reformation. If James Mason's brother John lived at this time anywhere near Red River, it is likely that Fishback, as James's brother-in-law and thus by southern standards practically a relative of John Mason himself, would have lodged at John Mason's house as a sort of home base for his excursions.

Of course, there was nothing that Raccoon John could do to prevent Fishback from working in the same territories that he himself was trying to evangelize, although he didn't like it. But when some of Montgomery County's Methodist leaders invited Fishback to speak at Mt. Sterling itself during one of Raccoon John's planned tours away from home, it set Smith's teeth on edge. He literally considered it a pernicious scheme to thwart his own influence and to lead his converts away from true Bible doctrine. He was advised of Fishback's invitation from the Methodists, it seems, probably by James Mason, and though he knew he would be away from home on the date of Fishback's Mt. Sterling appointment, Smith instructed Mason, Absalom Rice, and others among his followers to try to talk his rival into postponing any discourses he might deliver in the town until he returned himself and was able personally to "follow" Fishback in the stand.

Fishback came but would not agree to wait on Raccoon John. He preached a powerful, persuasive sermon from the fourteenth chapter of Romans, the primary thrusts of his argument being that it was wrong to make the mode of one's baptism a condition of communion, since Christians are commanded to receive one another without regard to differences of opinion; that close communionists were inconsistent in debarring believers from the ordinance, while nonetheless being perfectly willing to join them in other acts of worship such as prayer and singing; that close communion engendered a sectarian spirit completely opposite to the spirit of Christ; and most particularly, that Reform evangelists such as Raccoon John were inconsistent to refuse to commune with Methodists and Presbyterians while at the same time urging Reformers to continue participating in communion services at United Baptist churches, since Smith and his colleagues were now declaring openly that the United Baptists had apostatized from the religion of the New Testament. The discourse had its effect, setting many of Raccoon John's listeners to thinking about what they had been taught, and the schoolmaster Absalom Rice even copied down careful notes of Fishback's principal points so that he might show them to his pastor when he got back from his preaching journey.

Raccoon John made it home that night, and though it is a disturbing thought, his timely arrival was possibly prompted more from a desire to meet with and debate Fishback than any impulse to see his own wife and children. But one way or another, probably by a visit from Rice during which he got to examine the notes from the sermon, he learned that Fishback had already spoken and corrupted the minds of his followers. Smith was livid. Though we have noted again and again that he often couched his outbursts of temper within his characteristic sharp humor, this is one instance in which he let fly his anger without any attempt whatsoever to mask it by a joke. He spent a restless, uneasy night at home, and Nancy first caught sight of him the next morning saddling his horse and preparing for a journey to the Red River country, where he assumed Fishback had returned after delivering his Mt. Sterling sermon.

"When will you be at home?" she called out to him. Williams assures us that she asked this question because Raccoon John, when leaving for another preaching tour, always set an hour for his return and usually tried to live up to it faithfully. We cannot say whether these were her exact words or not, but if they were, we might wonder which word in the brief question, the first, second, or last, she emphasized. But whatever her inflection may have been, Raccoon John had only one purpose on his mind. "Nancy," he replied with an unusual earnestness, "Never will I put my foot within this door again to the day of my death till I have found Dr. Fishback; for find him I will, if he is on this side of the ocean!"

Before setting out for Red River, though, he rode to Mt. Sterling to ascertain the damage done to his influence and to his cause by Fishback's allegedly heretical preaching. He found that some of his friends, probably Rice again along with a few others who likewise had learned that he had returned home, had given out a preaching appointment for him at Mt. Sterling Church. But to his surprise, he found that Fishback had stayed overnight with James and Elizabeth Mason and had postponed his journey back to Red River, for the express purpose of hearing Raccoon John preach. The two evangelists met in town and greeted one another courteously, and began to walk together toward the meetinghouse. Williams records their conversation in detail, hopefully accurately:

> "Dr. Fishback," said [Smith], "I was told that you had gone to Red River, but I am truly glad to meet you here."
>
> "I did intend to go," replied [Fishback], "but you have worked such wonders in these parts, that, hearing you would preach in town today, I concluded to stay and learn how it is that you effect such great things."
>
> "Brother Fishback," said [Smith], courteously, "Will you not preach today yourself?"
>
> "No," he replied, "I will not; I stayed to hear you."
>
> As they walked on together to the meetinghouse, which stood on a hill in the western part of the town, Smith, in a kind but frank manner, inquired:
>
> "Brother Fishback, did any of my brethren ask you to postpone your discourse till my return?"
>
> "Yes," replied the doctor, "but my Methodist friends judged it best that I should do as I did."
>
> "You have treated me most unkindly in this matter, Brother Fishback. But Absalom Rice has furnished me with notes of your discourse; and now I say to you in all candor, that if you can argue no better than you seem from these notes to have done, I never will believe but that I can handle you like a baby! Where, Doctor, will you spend the evening?"
>
> "With my brother-in-law, James Mason," he replied.
>
> "Then I am going to Brother Mason's, too," said Smith, "and there I will try the strength of your argument."

"Try it this morning—try it here," said the Doctor, bravely, as they entered the church together.

"No, sir," said Smith, "I have too much generalship for that. I will meet you tonight."[102]

Williams then informs us that, after preaching an able discourse with no caustic references whatsoever to Fishback, and immersing several converts in nearby Hinkston Creek, Smith announced to the congregation that he would be spending the evening—and the night if necessary—at James Mason's, where he would address the matter of Fishback's Mt. Sterling sermon. Raccoon John's choice of the word "generalship" was indicative of his mood at this point; not only did it reflect the military imagery that Alexander Campbell prized so highly, but the fact that Raccoon John took this military imagery, with its implications of battle-style tactics and operations, entirely to heart. He deeply believed that, in preaching the strict message of *The Christian Baptist,* he was a crusader for objective, eternal truth and the peace of God that passed all understanding, and that the souls of his listeners hung in the balance of his words. But in any case, "generalship" he did have over the hearts and minds of his Montgomery County converts, and generalship he employed.

A large crowd came to Mason's that night, and Raccoon John took Fishback's same text from Romans 14 to try to pick his open-communion platform to pieces. He argued that the greater part of the text dealt with "things indifferent," not those "that the King specifically legislates" such as immersion, and that it was wrong to compromise the bond of union itself by "acknowledging as Christians those who, though they profess to believe in Christ as their Savior, refuse to obey him as their Lord." Quoting Romans 14:5 ("Let every one be fully persuaded in his own mind"), Fishback countered that, though he himself personally considered neither pouring nor sprinkling as true baptism, he thought that those who honestly believed in those forms of the ordinance were justified since, to them, the two *were* valid forms of baptism. Challenging the hapless Fishback to "get out of it if you can," Raccoon John retorted that Fishback's logic would eventually lead him similarly to accept anyone who denied that Jesus is the Christ, held a heterodox view of the being and attributes of the Godhead (possibly two stabs here at Fishback's friendliness to Barton Stone), or even doubted the existence of a life after death, simply because they were fully persuaded in their own minds that they were right. And finally, Smith clinched his case by reading an old Elkhorn Association circular letter written by Fishback himself some years before he had come under either Stone or Campbell influence that advocated close communion. Having thus done his best to demolish his fellow evangelist's message in front of James and Elizabeth Mason and a houseful of neighbors, Raccoon John then announced that, on a certain day soon to come, he would preach at Mt. Sterling using the fourteenth chapter of Romans as his text "and that as he would handle the arguments and the name of Dr. Fishback freely, he hoped that gentleman would be present."[103]

We might wonder how many times this particular argument, and a million others over similar subjects, have taken place between Baptists and other evangelicals both before and since 1828, and how much positive good any of them have ever accomplished. We reiterate here, with appropriate irony, that in modern times all the spiritual descendants of Alexander Campbell hold to a communion policy that is, for all practical purposes, open even though many are still as zealously committed to immersion as was Raccoon John himself. But for Smith's Montgomery County Reform followers as well as his orthodox Baptist neighbors, for this one question Raccoon John's personality and his words were enough. On the day of his announced sermon on Romans 14, such an enormous crowd assembled that the members of Mt. Sterling Church were compelled to cobble together an outside preaching stand, just like the ones used in groves and brush arbors at association meetings, simply to accommodate all of his listeners. Perhaps the size of the crowd gave the church just that much more impetus to purchase new property from John Mason and construct a larger meetinghouse. At any rate, Raccoon John again hammered away at Fishback's logic and stressed his and Campbell's personal position on strict communion, and when he was done, "his own brethren were confirmed, and the churches around, on this subject at least, had rest for a season."[104]

Poor Fishback, castigated by Raccoon John and the followers of Alexander Campbell on one hand as being weak in the faith, and ridiculed by his erstwhile brethren the Baptists both then and later as "unstable in all his ways, ever learning, and never able to come to the knowledge of the truth,"[105] on the other, did at least remain true to that of which *he* was fully persuaded. Ironically, though he did not live to see it, his sentiments actually did become normative for at least one branch of the religious movement that Alexander Campbell initiated—all of them, in fact, where the practicalities of the actual conduct of communion services are concerned. And besides that, for all Raccoon John's anger at Fishback, he unknowingly performed an absolutely vital favor for Smith during that tense, wild summer. The Lexington preacher became the perfect scapegoat by which Raccoon John could divert Baptist attention away from himself and his own controversial, flamingly aggressive ministry.

We reiterate that it's impossible to tell for sure if Raccoon John openly disavowed moderatorial ambitions, and pledged the support of his new churches to David Chenault's candidacy for moderator in 1828 in order to secure a position on the association's arrangements committee and to ensure that his new churches would be admitted to membership, although it's possible or even probable. Neither can we say with absolute certainty that, for the rest of the summer leading up to the 1828 North District meeting at Lulbegrud, Smith castigated the name, the beliefs, and the reputation of James Fishback in every North District church in which he could secure a preaching appointment. We do know, however, that Thomas White's Salem Church in Estill County, one of the three that had complained about Raccoon John's use of *The Living Oracles* the year before, again decided to send queries to North District in the summer of 1828. First, the church asked if it was right to correspond with associations whose churches held free communion with "Paido-baptists"; and second, if it was right to correspond with any association whose churches admitted to membership or communed with "Arians."[106] Neither of these questions involved complaints about John Smith, or for that matter, Alexander Campbell, *The Living Oracles,* or *The Christian Baptist* at all. Instead they asked for the association's formal censure of doctrines advocated at this time only by Barton Stone and his followers, and during this period no Baptist or ex-Baptist minister is known to have preached anything resembling Stoneite doctrine on these particulars in North District territories—except James Fishback. Admittedly, White and his church could have come up with their complaints with little or no assistance from Raccoon John. "The hills of Red River" through which Fishback preached that summer may have included the northern territories of Estill County, so perhaps White and his members simply heard Fishback and became offended at him all on their own. Still, it seems unlikely that Salem Church would have taken such actions against a minister who was not even a member of North District Association unless condemnation of Fishback had become a popular topic of conversation in the association, and the only person in the body who could have possibly benefited by agitating it as a cause for concern was Raccoon John. But in any case, James Fishback was a veritable godsend to Raccoon John and his North District Campbell crusade, a wonderfully effective martyr whose alleged errors simultaneously got Raccoon John's own perceived heterodoxy off everyone's minds and made his Baptist orthodoxy relative to Fishback's message all the more clear. Simply put, the tactic of the campaign was that Raccoon John was a "good" Baptist Reformer, James Fishback was a "bad" one—and politically, that one black and white image was all that Raccoon John needed to establish to save his own skin. Thomas White at least was never known to have opposed Raccoon John in any other circumstance, and evidently by 1829 or 1830 at the very latest, Smith could include White, too, as a committed member of his own cadre of followers.[107]

And so for the one-year anniversary of Joshua Smith's death, Raccoon John found his mourning turned into joy, his tears into laughter, and himself vindicated almost in full at the North District meeting at Lulbegrud. If Williams is to be believed, for his appointed task of preaching the session's introductory sermon, Smith actually read from *The Living Oracles* at the preaching stand: a portion of the passage he used, 1 Corinthians 1:25–2:16,[108] is quoted by Williams as having come from the *Oracles* rather than the King James Version.[109] When the delegates retired to the meetinghouse and opened the business session, David Chenault was once again elected moderator, and when new churches were called for, the letters and organizational documents of Raccoon John's five young Reform congregations—Owingsville, Sharpsburg, and Upper White Oak in Bath County, and South Fork of Red River and Slate

Liberty in Montgomery[110]—were accepted by the association without so much as a single objection from the floor.[111] Too, Chenault obligingly placed Raccoon John on the arrangements committee along with himself, clerk James French, Isaac Thornburgh, and others,[112] and after his experiences with Fishback over the summer Smith could cheerfully give the exact answers that Salem Church wanted for its two queries—a curt "No!" to each one. Another church, whose identity is now unknown but was probably Lulbegrud itself, asked that the Terms of General Union, the association's Rules of Decorum, and all the associational "orders" then still in effect be printed in that year's minutes. Raccoon John must have felt safe in agreeing to this, and the documents provided most of the content for James French's circular letter that year. The letter even contained what might have been a brief, oblique, offhand apology for the fact that Richard Thomas had been allowed to introduce the "infant purity" query back in 1805,[113] and in his own way the clerk still may have been trying valiantly to salvage the original North District reform concept that he, Raccoon John, and Jilson Payne had planned years before.

Whether or not this was French's intention, though, as the crowning irony of the meeting Raccoon John wound up staying at French's house and actually sleeping in the same bed with David Chenault. The moderator was lodging at French's for the session, and Williams records that Raccoon John contrived an invitation to the clerk's hospitality as well, just as he had connived to make Chenault invite him home the previous year: "Brother French, you ought to ask me to go along with these brethren, for I will undertake to make them all behave themselves."[114] Ever the southern gentleman, French agreed with a welcome and even a smile, but actually as a member of the arrangements committee Raccoon John would have needed to visit Chenault and the other members over the weekend anyway. At any rate, French's slaves had four or five extra beds prepared in a large room for the weekend visitors, and so long as the guest ministers were willing to sleep two to a bed there was plenty of room for all.

After an evening made convivial both by Raccoon John's wit and the generous quantities of cider that French pressed upon his guests, Chenault, who seems to have remained in a more somber mood than the rest of the crowd perhaps because he had only then begun to realize that his Smith headaches were by no means over, finally went to bed. As the rest of the men were preparing to lie down as well, Raccoon John approached Chenault's cot and remarked, "Brethren, these July nights, I know, are hot, and you do not need that any warm-hearted Christian should crowd with you; yet I must turn in with some of you, anyhow. Brother Davy, make just a little room for me, for I must sleep with you tonight." It was vain to protest against the intrusion, and Chenault knew it.[115]

Thus was brought to application the old and time-honored saying: politics—even among those who have their heads deep within the clouds of an ideal and who swear by all that is holy that they have abandoned the art—makes strange bedfellows.

CHAPTER 8

The Attack Upon Christendom, Part II

THIS HAS TO BE SAID

> O Luther, your responsibility is great indeed, for the closer I look the more clearly I do see that you overthrew the Pope—and set the public on the throne.
>
> —Søren Kierkegaard

Andrew Jackson was elected to the presidency of the United States in the fall of 1828. He took office on March 4, 1829, and after the Great Defender of the American Common Man was safely ensconced in the White House and the Campbell movement became firmly entrenched within North District Association, the labors and accomplishments of North District's own religious version of Old Hickory, Raccoon John Smith, began to snowball. We could wish that space and time allowed us to cover the years between 1828 and 1832 in as much detail as John Augustus Williams did; more than 300 of the work's 578 pages are devoted to detailed accounts of Raccoon John's perspective on both his own activities and the history of the Campbell Reform in general during this brief time span. On February 21, 1829, William Payne over in Bracken Association was finally gathered to his fathers,[1] and so Raccoon John's status as the leader of the General Union political faction that Jilson and William Payne had once headed was now unquestioned. He expanded his circle of labors to include preaching with and sustaining budding Reformers in Bracken, Tate's Creek, Boone's Creek, Elkhorn, and even Green River and Burning Springs Associations—in short, it seemed that wherever in Kentucky that Baptist associations and their Reformer contingents were quarreling and the Reformers stood in danger of losing a battle, Raccoon John was there to appear at the head of their vanguard in defense of the cause.[2] With his help and that of others, Bracken Association was able to crush support for correspondence with the hyper-Calvinistic Licking Association completely, and afterward he staged another successful battle against the Licking Calvinists under the sponsorship of Boone's Creek Association.[3] He and Josiah Collins of Tate's Creek Association paid a visit to David Chenault one wintry day in early 1829, and Raccoon John connived to preach in Chenault's Cane Springs meetinghouse, where he actually succeeded in converting a sizable portion of the membership—including, apparently, even Chenault's ministerial colleague Isaac Thornburgh—at least temporarily to Reform principles.[4] In one of his most memorable evangelistic junkets, he went to the state capital of Frankfort to "storm the sectarian fort of Dr. [Silas] Noel"; he wound up preaching to a congregation that included every member of the state legislature but four congressmen, and they took the name and story of Raccoon John Smith to every corner of the state where it was not already known.[5] All these anecdotes reflect but a drop in the bucket of the sum total of John's exertions in behalf of Alexander Campbell and *The Christian Baptist* after his subtle 1828 coup of the North District arrangements committee, and when Jacob Creath Jr., nephew and namesake of Raccoon John's old Elkhorn mentor and now a rabid young Reformer in his own right, came to Kentucky and succeeded in converting his popular uncle to Reform principles, the partnership of Smith in North District and the Creaths in Elkhorn gave the cause just that much more boost.

In spite of Smith's successes and his zeal, by this time some of his longtime colaborers who had given Campbell his earliest Kentucky support now became disaffected with the great cause and began to oppose Campbell and his newspaper as vigorously as they had once defended him. Jeremiah Vardeman, William Vaughan, and Walter Warder were all included in this group, and now Raccoon John, the Creaths, and Campbell's other followers found themselves making war on erstwhile allies as well. John once publicly humiliated Vaughan by promising him, in front of a church full of people, that he would not expose more than thirteen of "Billy's" blunders because he was confident that the crowd could figure out the rest of his sectarian errors themselves.[6] In turn, Vaughan compared Raccoon John to the legendary New England liar Sam Hyde, who thought that two lies in a story could be canceled out by one truth; to his credit, though, Vaughan made this comparison privately to Raccoon John himself, rather than in front of a congregation.[7] Vaughan could hold his own with Raccoon John, although one wouldn't think it merely from a reading of Williams, but Jeremiah Vardeman was an easier mark. Never the controversialist or the aggressive competitor that his protégé was, Vardeman thrived on popular acclaim even more than Raccoon John did, and he seemed never to be able to come up with a clear, concise explanation for his return to the "old dispensation," as he termed it. The most plausible defense he appears to have given was that he had become chagrined and mortified at the conduct of the Reformers themselves,[8] perhaps exemplified by Raccoon John's own use of James Fishback as both a Baptist and a Reformer scapegoat in 1828. But when pressed for details, Vardeman would more often reply with lame excuses such as the fact that "the preachers" had received but little money before the Campbell Reformation and they would have to get along on still less now, and that he was too old to start "chapter preaching" the way younger

Reform exhorters practiced it. This kind of vacillation played right into the hands of Reformers intent upon publicly condemning any Baptist rhetoric that they heard, and once when Vardeman mouthed the pious platitude that he "intended to die between the Particular Baptists and the Christians, as our Saviour died between two thieves," Jacob Creath Sr. retorted "that if his old enemies, the Particular Baptists, caught him, they would treat him as the old Canaanite king Adonibezek, served his prisoners—cut off his thumbs and great toes, and make him eat bread under their table, all the days of his life; and if he fell into our hands, with whom he had formerly acted, he knew what we ought to do with him."[9] Needless to say, Raccoon John came after his old mentor just as vigorously. Within a year Vardeman, now overshadowed not only by Jacob Creath and Raccoon John but lacking the backbone to be able to give full support either to the Baptist or the Campbell cause as well, quietly tucked his tail between his legs and left Kentucky with his family for Missouri, where, ultimately, he once again gave good service to the Baptist cause until his death in 1842.[10]

But to give credit where credit is due, in reference to Vardeman's apparent avowal that he had become ashamed of the conduct of the Reformers, there can be no doubt that even some of Raccoon John's own followers came to feel exactly the same way. Though Mt. Sterling Church as well as Smith's newly gathered congregations had consistently followed his and Buckner Payne's directives like good soldiers should, minorities at both Spencer Creek and his home church at Grassy Lick had stubbornly remained committed to so-called sectarian principles—that is, the idea that, regardless of whether one was a Calvinist or an Arminian, conversion from the perspective of the Cornelius paradigm of Acts 10 and the born-again experience was still the only valid profession of Christian faith, no matter what Raccoon John Smith, Alexander Campbell, or anybody else said. Those at Spencer Creek seemed not to trouble Raccoon John all that much, either then or afterward,[11] but in the spring of 1829 the sentiments of his Grassy Lick opponents appear to have been exacerbated to the point of no return by the increasingly bellicose stance of the pro-Reform members. Though Williams of course places the blame for the incident entirely on the "Calvinists" of the church (and since Grassy Lick was originally a Regular Baptist church, the Calvinist appellation for once might have been appropriate), actually the Reformers were the guilty party initially in stoking the conflict up to a blaze. As is usually the case in such conflicts, in the end both sets of contestants wound up making themselves look bad.

At the church's monthly business meeting in May 1829 a pro-Smith member by the name of Hokerson requested that clerk James Mason read the church's organizational covenant, a document of fifteen Calvinistic articles of faith. Mason complied, and then Hokerson responded that, as a Christian, he could not live under the precepts of the covenant any longer. A debate ensued, and finally Raccoon John himself, as moderator of the church, stepped into the fray with an expository dissection of the old covenant, explaining article by article how, in his opinion, it plainly contradicted Scripture. He then offered his resignation as pastor, with the stipulation that he be left at liberty to preach wherever the people would wish to hear him. On James Mason's assertion that no one at the church had complained of him and that he should therefore not complain of himself, the church dropped the issue of the resignation; but then another member, David Badger, called for each member present to express his or her views on the covenant—in essence, a referendum on the entire matter. So the vote was taken, a two-thirds' majority prevailed in abolishing the covenant completely, and Raccoon John led the congregation through the rest of its regular order of business, including a motion and second for Mason to prepare Grassy Lick's letter to the forthcoming July North District Association meeting at Unity Meetinghouse in Clark County.

We have no way of knowing whether Raccoon John had arranged for Badger and Hokerson to say what they did in the business meeting to provoke the vote, but evidently Grassy Lick's pro-Baptist minority thought that the action had been staged at least to a certain extent. Such staging has never been uncommon in Baptist business meetings. But in any case, when the church held its next business meeting in June, Raccoon John discovered that the pro-covenant minority had staged a dramatic little performance on its own. Mason got up to read the letter of correspondence he had prepared for the association, and suddenly Reuben McDannold, a leading member who himself had represented Grassy Lick in the association on several occasions, rose from his seat and made an announcement: those who stood together on the old church covenant had already held their own rump-session business meeting, in which they had decided that only those who stood for Baptist principles could be counted as legitimate members of Grassy Lick Church. They had therefore prepared their own letter to the association and appointed their own messengers to bear it.[12] The group appears to have elected as its pastor James Edmonson, a minister of about Raccoon John's age who had been converted and baptized by the venerable Robert Elkin at the Old Stone Church and who was now assisting Thomas Boone at Goshen.[13] As it stood, if Smith, Mason, and the anti-covenant majority of the church sent their own letter to North District, the association would be presented with a repeat of the days of the log that split the church: two letters, both claiming to represent Grassy Lick Church, with the association being forced either to declare in favor of one or the other or to rule both Grassy Lick factions out of order as it had done for the two Lulbegrud factions years before. Thomas Boone and James Edmonson actually may have suggested that the Grassy Lick minority take this action, as it appears to have been a standard associational management technique for the old Separate Baptist warrior who had raised them both up to the ministry. It also may have been one in which Boone himself had participated against Jilson Payne and Jeremiah Vardeman at Lulbegrud. If it worked, Raccoon John would be denied a voice in the association similarly.

But Smith, undoubtedly thoroughly educated by Jilson Payne about the finer points of Elkin's control techniques, was up to the task of parrying the counteroffensive. Instead of calling for a motion from the anti-covenant majority to send Mason's letter and its own delegates to the association, he simply resubmitted his resignation with the additional proposal that he deed his farm back to them. The church could then refund him what he had advanced out of his own pocket toward his farm debt and assume his present indebtedness to the bank. McDannold replied bluntly that this action would not remedy the evil. If Raccoon John left, a "worse" might be called in his and James Edmonson's place, and the pro-covenant minority would far rather have him there than any other preacher of his sort. Moreover, since the congregation had not given him any financial help since he had changed his doctrinal sentiments (as noted in the last chapter, Williams and Smith try to date this withholding of funds long before it probably actually occurred), Raccoon John should rest assured that his farm was now his own as far as Grassy Lick was concerned. Smith asked for his letter of fellowship so that he might join another church that would receive him with his altered views. Nancy, who was present for the meeting as well, likewise asked for hers, David Badger and his wife followed suit, and before the proceedings were done almost every one of Raccoon John's followers had "lettered away" from Grassy Lick and left James Edmonson and the pro-covenant church faction in complete charge of the meetinghouse. Raccoon John soon organized the Grassy Lick defectors as a new and independent congregation on Sommerset Creek, about two miles from Grassy Lick. But to avoid any possibility of a dispute over the new church's status or orthodoxy at the forthcoming North District meeting, the group made no attempt to join the association that year.

Raccoon John himself, though, did not remain with his former Grassy Lick compatriots except as a visiting preacher. He helped to install members Philip Hathaway, Newton Lane, David Cassady, and Samuel Carrington as church elders after the Campbell form, and their labors joined his own and those of John Newton Payne over at Sharpsburg and others in spreading the Reform gospel further. Working at a feverish pace to transact business in the barest semblance of acceptable Baptist order before the July North District meeting at Unity, he went to Mt. Sterling Church and "laid in" his letter of membership. Although the congregation had already written its own letter of correspondence and selected its representatives to the association, he persuaded the church to amend its letter and hold another election for delegates in which he himself would be included.[14] Among Baptists, at least those of today's rural "Old Time" variety who strive to emulate the denomination's practices of days gone by, rigging a messengers' election in this blatant manner is something like the ecclesiastical equivalent of a gerrymander, and such an action is about as odious as presession politicking ever gets. But at this juncture Mt. Sterling Church was still fully behind Raccoon John, and if there was any grumbling from John Mason or any other member or minority about dirty politics it must have been kept effectively suppressed. Thus Raccoon John, the merchant and preacher Buckner Payne, the lawyer Kenaz Farrow, and William O'Rear bore Mt. Sterling's letter to the association at Unity on the last weekend in July.

At this session of the association, which, incidentally, marked a return to the grounds where the first annual meeting of North District Association had been held twenty-seven years before, Raccoon John managed to consolidate Reformer power even further. Only one new church applied for admission, known as Friendship Sweet Spring, but the five new congregations admitted the previous year had all grown respectably, and it is quite possible that others that Raccoon John and the Reformers had gathered had, like the new Sommerset Church, simply chosen not to apply for membership in the association this year. David Chenault was once again elected moderator, almost a sure sign that Raccoon John had advised his followers to vote for Chenault and not himself. By this time, if Smith had indeed been campaigning in his own behalf, he would have won the election hands down. He did contrive, however, to have the association elect an assistant clerk that year, a rare occurrence in North District history, and the delegates'—and Raccoon John's own—choice was Buckner Payne. Whether or not Smith's support had anything to do with Chenault's decision, the moderator likewise picked Raccoon John again to serve on the arrangements committee, this time with the aged James Quesenberry along with Smith's new ally Thomas White and his opponents James French and Chenault himself.

Under Raccoon John's own aggressive, combative influence, the committee parried no less than five queries, from Cane Springs, Goshen, Lulbegrud, Salem, and Sharpsburg Churches. Of these, we may assume that Salem's and Sharpsburg's questions were similar in content and friendly to the precepts of the Campbell movement, as they are noted in the minutes as having been "passed by without debate."[15] Goshen's offering was the complaint against Raccoon John's baptismal formulary change, mentioned in previous chapters; Cane Springs sent a letter indicting certain leading local advocates of the Reform movement, for some reason including James Mason and perhaps even Alexander Campbell as well; and Lulbegrud made the bizarre declaration that, because of all the changes in North District Association over the past couple of years, the church could no longer hold communion services.[16] How Raccoon John managed to blame this last query on James French is anybody's guess, since Baptist tradition leaves the decision on setting a church's communion service in the hands of the pastor or moderator on his assessment that the church is conducting its own affairs in peace. Such is not the prerogative either of a clerk or of deacons. In addition, the sort of intrachurch connectionalism this query implies is entirely Separate Baptist, rather than Regular, in origin, indicating that once again Thomas Boone was behind the complaint rather than French. But regardless of the origin or nature of the complaints, Raccoon John got these three latter queries dismissed without even a comment in the group's minutes, Cane Springs' on the technicality that its grievance involved an individual or individuals who were not even members of the association. He even contrived for James Mason to prepare and submit a written defense of his own conduct.[17]

Perhaps most significantly, though, at this session the body referred James French's annual circular letter to the arrangements committee as well, and at Smith's and the other committeemen's advice the association rejected it entirely and ruled that Buckner Payne should prepare a second circular to be printed in the minutes. Payne really didn't have anything novel to say; his composition is more akin to Thomas Boone's insipid 1824 offering than anything French had written for much of his career as North District's scribe and the Payne faction's party propagandist,[18] but apparently Buckner Payne's brief composition was exactly what Raccoon John wanted. According to Williams, when the last business meeting finally drew to its close, a thoroughly outwitted, mystified, and exasperated David Chenault declared that those who were complained against were now more numerous than those doing the complaining, and that the only course left to those resisting the Campbell movement was to withdraw from those who endorsed it. Though Raccoon John and his cohorts professed to be shocked and mortified at Chenault's words,[19] by this time they might have expected such a response to their actions. They were, obviously, now the victors in the struggle for the hearts and minds of North District Association's membership, and the fact that the body appointed its 1830 annual meeting to be held at Raccoon John's own Spencer Creek Church only reinforced their triumph.[20]

Thus in spite of the secular political and financial losses James Mason had endured the previous year due to William P. Fleming's politicking over his enthusiastic April 1828 *Christian Baptist* letter, as well as his brother-in-law Fishback's humiliation at the hands of Raccoon John Smith, Mason, of all people, should have been overjoyed at this apparent victory of the "Ancient Gospel"—especially since Raccoon John had provided so capably for him when Cane Springs Church had tried to arraign him before the association. But in fact Mason had elected neither to join the crowd of Grassy Lick expatriates at the new Sommerset Church nor to follow the pastor he had supported for so many years in his transference of membership to Mt. Sterling; and his next letter to Campbell, written several months after the hectic 1829 North District meeting, shows nothing of Mason's 1828 enthusiasm. It's a wry, sometimes humorous, sometimes bitter, but always honest and perceptive account of Mason's own take of current events, and it is worthy of notice, if for no other reason, for the number of emasculated, bowdlerized versions of it that have appeared in pro-Campbell and pro-Smith histories. The fact that Reform historians have seemingly felt such a great need to edit it and present only the portions beneficial to their own cause perhaps gives it the ring of truth more than any other factor:

Near Mt. Sterling, Ky., May 15, 1830

Dear Brother Campbell,

You are no doubt much annoyed with scribblers of every description, from every part of these United States, which no doubt takes much of your time in reading them, without taking further notice of their contents. This consideration has prevented me from writing to you as often as I otherwise should have done; but the times having become much more squally than heretofore, I thought I would just give another short history of events as they exist at present among us, not fearing any consequences that may result, for I am not a candidate for office, nor do I intend ever to be again, and therefore I shall not be liable to lose between four and five hundred dollars which the publication of my first letter to you cost me; anything, therefore, that I may hereafter write, which you may think worthy of notice, you may make what use of, you please.

I feel greatly concerned on account of the present state of affairs in the religious world. This concern is increased from seeing those who I believe love the Saviour and love his people, arrayed against each other, as though Christ was divided and Paul was crucified for them. At our last Association, although I had refused to be sent as a messenger from our church on account of the strife that existed in that body, my name was publicly read out as a heretic in a letter from one of the churches, and an extract of the letter I wrote to you given as evidence of the fact. Not being a member of the Association, I deemed it my duty, in self-defense, to reply to the charges in writing, which the Association received and read to the great mortification of my accusers. But that which has destroyed the happiness I once enjoyed in society, is the schism that has taken place in the church where my membership is, on account of an old written creed, as old as the church itself, called the "Church Covenant," which held forth in 11 or 12 articles the old system of John Calvin, and which a majority of the church, with brother John Smith at their head, were determined no longer to put up with; and after voting it out they asked for letters, and constituted, in less than two miles where they meet, to themselves, and have as little to do with those they left as Jews and Samaritans.

I plead [*sic*] with these Campbellite brethren, as they are called, to be patient, and let the old Covenant alone. I disbelieved it as much as any of them, but rather than produce a division of the church I was willing to let it die a more lingering death; for I had no doubt but that brother Smith's preaching the ancient gospel [*sic*], as he was constantly doing, would kill it without any other aid; and I thought it would be better to take the fort by siege rather than to risque [*sic*] the

> lives of our men; but I could not prevail, and things are as above stated. I am yet in the old camp, viewed with a jealous eye by both parties, and not very popular with either; and although my views as respects the gospel of Christ are pretty much in accordance with these reformers of yours, I am afraid to venture myself on board their boat, lest they run afoul of a sawyer.
>
> I spent an evening with brother Smith lately. I told him it was vain to profess and preach reformation unless the world could see it in practice; for if those who have professed to have got out of Babylon do not manifest more of that love and humility, and the spirit of meekness and forbearance which dwelt in the Divine Saviour than those they have left behind, they will make but little progress in doing good; and this temper and this spirit I am afraid are much needed among them. . . .[21]

The remainder of Mason's missive will be quoted in its entirety subsequently. The latter portion of the letter has been cited by Campbell and Smith scholars more often than the first part, but we must reiterate that a comparison of the entire epistle with the scraps of it that appear in the works of John Augustus Williams, Everett Donaldson, and early twentieth-century Kentucky religious historian Alonzo Willard Fortune is, to say the least, enlightening.[22] Perhaps more remarkable, though, is Campbell's personal reply. We hardly need repeat that, when the great Reformer chose to exercise his penchant for it, he was capable of blistering sarcasm toward those who opposed his views on anything. But to Mason he was disarmingly gentle and even apologetic about the conduct of those who followed out his precepts and his own aggressive style to their logical conclusion:

> Brother James Mason's letter deserves much consideration from all the *reforming* brethren [emphasis in original]. Let the reformation have its perfect work upon all its advocates. Let them remember it is not a reformation of sentiments or of systems, but of individual practice and behavior. *What do you more than others?* [Again, emphasis in original.] Aye, that's the question. We have, brethren, much need to take heed of this. Our enemies have good eyes—they can see thorns in our eyes which we cannot see ourselves. We are indebted to our opponents. Let us always thank them for pointing out our defects, provided they do not create any which do not exist. There is no need for this. Among the thousands who now plead for reform, there is no doubt but that many defects may be seen. Let us, then, thankfully receive admonitions however tendered.[23]

Apparently Raccoon John never again spoke about James Mason after recounting this series of events to Williams. We might wonder if he believed that his older friend and supporter had betrayed him in some sense. Regardless, it can hardly be doubted that he was still in the very element of the religious fugue that had held him in thrall for more than a year now, and if he wasn't able to comprehend Mason's disillusionment and newly dispassionate attitude, neither would he have been able to form an objective picture of the reasons for it. Louis Cochran portrays Mason as something of a Nicodemus, well-intentioned but for some reason fearful of committing body and soul to holy truth. That may have been how Raccoon John came to see him as well. But the intensity of John's zeal had by now blinded him to a lesson he could have, and should have, learned from simple pastoral experience: when we mere humans assume the role of soldiers for God in the great war against Satan, sometimes it gets extremely difficult to discern who's fighting for whom.

We now resume the text of the James Mason letter, which concludes with a treatment of events up to and including the spring of 1830:

> . . . The war seems to be waxing very hot, and I think this summer the great battle will be fought, which will drive every one to his proper standard. The North District Association has already had a swarm out of her hive. A foxy old man who has long been clerk to that body, and had possession of her papers and records, has lately took it into his head to call a counsel [*sic*] of such churches as he thought would favor his designs, seven of whom attended by their letters and messengers. These have, according to his designs, advised him to keep possession of the records of North District, and have appointed an association to meet on the fourth Saturday in next month, and have invited all the churches or parts of North District Association that favor their designs, to meet them, and they will consider themselves North District Association. I was instrumental in stopping the church at Grassy Lick from sending [a letter and delegates] to their first meeting, but I am of opinion that I shall not succeed in stopping them again, as a majority that your reformers left behind are of the old Calvinistic stamp, so that no doubt remains when the North District Association meet at the time and place appointed last year, their records and papers with eight or ten churches will be missing.
>
> I was delighted to see yours and old brother Semple's correspondence in the last [issue]. He writes like a Christian, and I love him, though I have never seen him; and whether you had patience to read it or not, if I had room on my paper, I would give you some of *my* [emphasis in original] Christian experience too, which would accord somewhat with brother Semple's, and then I would ask you some hard questions why and how it was that things were thus and

so? But if I am not considered troublesome perhaps I may write about it some other time. Till then believe me to be your affectionate brother,
James Mason

What Mason described in his last two paragraphs was pretty much representative of all that was occurring wherever the Campbell movement had thus far taken hold. As Baptist historian Jesse Fletcher has noted, the 1830 Revolution in France and the death of Pope Pius VIII probably made more news than did Alexander Campbell's quarrel with the Baptist Church. Neither, of course, did the earth shake.[24] But by this time both supporters and opposers of the Campbell Reformation—its advocates already starting to identify themselves merely as "Disciples of Christ" and members simply of "Christian Churches" or "Churches of Christ" in honor of their deep, passionate belief that they were restoring primitive, first-century Christianity to a long-apostate world—were unwilling to compromise, and permanent schism between Baptists and Reformers—or Disciples—was now inevitable. The Baptist ethic of the times, at least as described by John Augustus Williams, was: "Seek first to reclaim these Reformers from their errors. If your efforts should fail, invite them to leave you, and to practice their reformation to themselves. If they will not go at your request, separate them from you in the best way that you can."[25] Contrarily, the Disciples found themselves in the paradoxical position of rejecting everything the Baptists stood for except those elements of worship and doctrine which Campbell approved, and yet stubbornly refusing to separate themselves from a denomination that they all agreed was apostate and error-ridden. It was almost as if they were asking to be kicked out, so they could cry foul against one more instance of persecution. Baptist associations with secure pro-tradition majorities were expelling their pro-Campbell churches and ministers, and associations such as North District wherein the Campbell movement had taken over were losing pro-tradition minorities. This stressful situation existed not only in Kentucky, but in Virginia, Ohio, Pennsylvania, Indiana, and possibly even Illinois as well.

The process started in the late summer of 1829 when Campbell's, Walter Scott's, and Sidney Rigdon's own Mahoning Association in Ohio lost correspondence with all the Baptist associations both in that state and in Pennsylvania after Pennsylvania's small Beaver Association declared nonfellowship with Mahoning. Appomattox Association became the first Baptist body in Virginia to endorse the actions of the Ohio and Pennsylvania Baptists, initiating a chain reaction within all the component groups of the General Association of Virginia Baptists,[26] and the "old brother Semple" to whom James Mason alluded in his letter was Virginia Baptist leader, historian, and author Robert Baylor Semple, with whom Campbell was still arguing hotly. It's doubtful that Campbell shared Mason's assessment that the respected Virginia cleric wrote "like a Christian."

But over the course of that hot, grim summer the war waxed its hottest in

Kentucky, just as Mason implied. Both Thomas and Alexander Campbell even traveled to the Bluegrass to join Raccoon John and his compatriots in the thick of the fray. We might wonder about their purposes in so doing. Neither father nor son ever claimed to want to start an entire new religious organization, and they used both "order" and "logic" as bywords, but even so, they both believed that humankind's acceptance of their interpretation of pure, unadorned, restored Christianity in all its rationalistic simplicity was an integral part of the historical process that would culminate in the dawning of the Messianic Age.[27] They fully expected that the old, hidebound traditionalist denominations that they condemned would ultimately die a natural death in this new age, and that their "restored" Christianity would triumph over all. It is a fact that, in this year, Alexander began publishing a new periodical, *The Millennial Harbinger.* For a brief while it ran concurrently with *The Christian Baptist,* but after about seven concurrent issues Campbell concluded *The Christian Baptist*'s run and let *The Millennial Harbinger* supplant it entirely. The very name of the new journal may be evidence that Alexander and his father simply might have taken their own rhetoric, the wild success that Walter Scott and Raccoon John and their fellow soldiers in Ohio and Kentucky respectively had brought them, and America's Era of Good Feeling itself just a bit too seriously.

In any case, when the Campbells returned to Kentucky they were fully prepared to do battle by Raccoon John's plan of attack. Alexander tried to cajole William Vaughan, who was by now locked into a campaign against Reformer Jesse Holton for the moderatorship of Bracken Association, with compliments that Vaughan was "the clearest-headed man in the state of Kentucky,"[28] promises that he would be better supported financially if he would only commit himself to the Reformation, and pleas that if only he and Walter Warder would declare for the movement that the "whole country" would go into it together.[29] When Vaughan countered the Campbell doctrinal arguments and turned Alexander's sales pitch down,[30] Thomas Campbell found occasion to speak of one of Vaughan's sermons as being "a great philosophical discourse, well conceived and elegantly delivered—a splendid display of Fullerism, and not worth a straw,"[31] and after the moderatorial election in Bracken Association was decided in Vaughan's and the traditionalist Baptists' favor, Alexander, Jacob Creath Jr., and their younger colleague David Staats Burnet all attacked and lampooned "the Bracken Moderator" in the press.[32] Silas Noel of Franklin Association published "The Thirty-Nine Articles," a series of extracts from *The Christian Baptist* and *The Millennial Harbinger* that he employed to call both Alexander Campbell's doctrinal system and his personal integrity into question, and in addition castigated Reformers for disseminating Campbell's "little pamphlets" that claimed to be based on Scripture alone and whining about their persecutions for refusing to submit to the Philadelphia Confession when they well knew they had never been called into question over the document.[33] Campbell retorted in *The Millennial Harbinger* that Noel's composition was "antipodes to any thing I ever taught," but he never subjected "The

Thirty-Nine Articles" to a detailed analysis to prove his charge and disprove all of Noel's.[34] The Creaths, Jacob Sr. and Jr., and Josephus Hewitt contrived to send ten delegates apiece from the churches they pastored to the fall 1830 meeting of Elkhorn Association in order to pack the delegation; Alexander Campbell's father was present at the meeting to witness near-riots both at the preaching stand at the opening of the association and in the meetinghouse while business was transacted.[35] And so on. The enmity that Baptists and Reformers/Disciples generated between one another during 1829 and 1830 alone had a half-life of more than a century, and even in the 1970s it was still warm enough for Harold Sanders to write, as we noted in this work's introduction, that the Kentucky Baptists trained all the guns in their arsenal on Alexander Campbell and blew him out of the saddle. All things considered, though, cowboy metaphor was and is not really any worse than the military imagery that Campbell himself favored. But neither is it any better.

If the reader can excuse an execrable pun, the downstate Kentucky Baptists by and large eventually coped with the Campbell schism by conventional means. That is to say, the majority of them finally followed suit with their Virginia and Ohio brethren and organized a state convention or association for, among other reasons, the establishment and maintenance of denominational doctrinal stability. The Kentucky Baptist Convention was formed in 1832, and although it was disbanded only a few years later, it was reorganized in 1837 and is still in existence. This organization in turn affiliated itself at least in the furtherance of the missionary cause with the Baptists' National Triennial Convention, but when a split within the national body, over the propriety of sending slaveowning missionaries overseas accompanied by their human chattel, erupted a few years later, the proslavery dissidents formed the Southern Baptist Convention in 1845, and the Kentucky Baptist Convention has been a Southern Baptist state auxiliary body ever since. Over time they largely dropped the name of "United Baptist" simply for "Baptist" and, more popularly nowadays, Southern Baptist.

But this didn't mean that all Baptist associations in Kentucky (to give the pun another questionably tasteful exercise) simply accepted the conventions. Whether or not moderator David Chenault's closing statement for North District's 1829 session, as recorded by Williams, had anything to do with it, by the spring of 1830 both Thomas Boone and James French recognized that North District Association as a whole had been taken over completely by Raccoon John and his followers. Had Boone not been raised up to the ministry with such a strong Separate Baptist background, his church at Goshen, which had once belonged to Elkhorn Association, might have returned to it; had not Lulbegrud, to which French still belonged and which Boone also still pastored, once been a Separate Baptist church, French might have been able to persuade Lulbegrud to go to Elkhorn as well. But since it was now obvious that Raccoon John and his followers considered associations to be unscriptural and they intended either to disband North District ultimately or at least reorganize it on their own terms, Boone and French simply announced a meeting at Lulbegrud on the third weekend of April 1830 for all North District churches or parts of churches that were dissatisfied with the Disciple takeover. There, they could organize themselves and establish a platform for their protest by claiming the name and prerogatives of the "old" or "original" North District Association. In that day and age such a plan was considered novel, although since that time it has come to be something of a staple for traditionalist religious subgroups looking for an excuse to secede from larger groups, especially among North District Association's descendants further east in Kentucky.

At this time, it appears that moderator Chenault, still probably trying simply to come to terms personally with the situation and coping with a divided flock at Cane Springs himself, wasn't yet even involved. In fact, the only two North District ministers joining with French in this initial Lulbegrud anti-Reform conference were those of Goshen, Thomas Boone and his assistant James Edmonson.[36] Had James Quesenberry been physically able, he might have joined Boone and Edmonson in their endeavors, but by this time he was seventy-one years of age and feeble, and he died that summer.[37] Another minister, John M. Johnson, is not listed as a direct participant in the conference or its plans, and Isaiah Cornelius, a Goshen preacher who had occasionally served North District as correspondent delegate to other associations, had by this time moved westward in Kentucky to the Sulphur Fork Association, where he embraced the Reform/Disciple movement and also espoused the intriguing belief that the apostles could "remit sins."[38] On the Baptist side of the coin, this John M. Johnson was "turned out" within a year's time as well, for adultery.[39] Evidently, when it rained trouble, it poured, on both sides of the question.

And so French and Boone's proposed Lulbegrud Conference met a few weeks before Mason penned his second letter to Campbell, drawing a grand total of seven churches: Lulbegrud and Goshen themselves, Howard's Upper Creek, Unity, Salem, Mt. Tabor, and New Providence. It will be remembered that both Salem and Mt. Tabor had been under the care of Thomas White, but now White was a firm Raccoon John ally and held his membership at his other pastoral charge, known as Beaver Pond, which remained in Raccoon John's camp.[40] All told, the seven churches now probably represented the combined pastoral charges of Boone, Edmonson, Quesenberry, and John M. Johnson, although it's possible that the absent David Chenault pastored one or two of them as well. Considering that so few North District churches and preachers chose to participate in this meeting, it would seem to have presented about as much danger to Raccoon John's cause as a handful of pesky mosquitoes, but apparently French and Boone's actions made Smith so nervous and uneasy that he chose to attend the Lulbegrud meeting himself as well. Here, in spite of the obvious fact that he was unwelcome, he still managed to "get in his two cents' worth" that he and his followers were still good orthodox Baptists and that the meeting French and Boone had called was completely out of order, until he was shouted down by the delegation.[41]

The group appointed a committee to examine all the old records of the association as well as those of its parent group, the original South Kentucky Separate Baptist Association. After deliberation, the delegates agreed to empower James French "to take charge of the records and papers of North District Association, until he is legally called upon by that Association; which Association can only consist of churches that remain in the former way of practicing the ordinances of baptism and the Lord's Supper, and the old way of administering the constitution of North District Association, and Terms of Union." Rather than attempting to meet with the entire association at Spencer Creek on the first weekend in July, though, they appointed another rump session to be held at Goshen one weekend before the Spencer Creek meeting, the last in June. To it were to be invited, again, "all such churches, or parts of churches, pertaining to North District Association, as are content with the former usage of the churches."[42]

At the June meeting at Goshen—which in all probability Raccoon John didn't attend, due to the cold reception he had received at Lulbegrud two months earlier as well as his involvement in preparations for the scheduled association session at Spencer Creek—three more small congregations, one faction apiece from Cane Springs and Log Lick and, just as James Mason had predicted, Grassy Lick, joined the North District expatriates. David Chenault was now reelected as the group's moderator, with James French still maintaining his longstanding office as clerk, and the ten-church minority body began to frame the first, and possibly the only, articulated manifesto that its descendants, eastern Kentucky's "Old Time" Baptists, have ever had. This minority "old," or "original," North District Association stood, literally, on the established traditions of Elkhorn and South Kentucky Associations when the two bodies first united in 1801, and it accepted as a fundamental bylaw that only doctrine, preaching, and worship forms known among one or both of the two bodies at the time of the union could be recognized and endorsed as orthodox.[43] The group submitted a written position paper to Raccoon John's majority side of the association, meeting on the next weekend at Spencer Creek, where no less a dignitary than Thomas Campbell himself preached with the local stars Jacob Creath Sr. and Jr. and Josephus Hewitt at Sunday worship[44]; but for all practical purposes North District was thoroughly and permanently split.

The Smith side of North District received the Chenault/French side's letter and replied to it with a written diatribe coauthored by Raccoon John and Buckner Payne that was both longer and even more shrill than French's composition.[45] It may have been intended primarily to hold Raccoon John's own Reform/Disciple converts under the wing of his own leadership. If so, it must have served its purpose fairly well, but no Baptist association in the state paid any attention to it whatsoever. Both the Chenault/French and the Smith/Payne factions of North District sent letters of correspondence to all the association's neighboring bodies, and in spite of Raccoon John's own imposing presence and aggressively persuasive arguments at each one of these gatherings, the letters of the "old" North District faction were accepted over his own in each and every case.[46] Thus cast adrift from the Kentucky General Union, Raccoon John's portion of North District only held one more annual meeting, in 1831 at Sommerset, which had finally joined his group at Spencer Creek the previous year after Grassy Lick left to affiliate with Chenault. There Raccoon John encouraged and oversaw the group's formal dissolution,[47] leaving the Chenault/French faction in sole possession of the name of North District Association. We might wonder whether Buckner Payne and the rest of his family appreciated this action entirely, since they had so long been accustomed to exercising political power through the workings of the association.

In that same year, the Chenault/French group took in more church factions, including the small flock from Spencer Creek under the leadership of James Edmonson and, surprisingly, even a minority party from the South Fork of Red River which had been organized originally as a Reform/Disciple church. The reorganized association now solidified the positions of the Goshen Conference with detailed descriptions of "old" South Kentucky Association church practices as its reaffirmed orthodoxy and a reprinting of the Terms of General Union as its articles of faith,[48] and although these remnant North District churches suffered a chronic shortage of preachers, they and their small organization survived. Even so, the group managed to take on the personality of its moderator, David Chenault, in a distinctive way. It will be remembered that he had never shown much interest in maintaining relations with the other big downstate associations that Raccoon John had always been so keen to visit, and after James French's death in 1835 he and the North District group simply let go their connections westward in the Bluegrass. The little association showed no interest whatsoever in joining Elkhorn, Salem, Franklin, Tate's Creek, or other downstate associations in any of their statewide Baptist organizational enterprises. Although Burning Springs Association took at least five years to follow North District's lead completely, by 1842 North District had dropped correspondence with every one of its former "sister" associations except this one eastern Kentucky group.[49] For the rest of his life David Chenault limited his own evangelistic work to the eastern Kentucky mountains,[50] and before his death in 1851 he had the satisfaction of watching his divided Cane Springs Church begin to reunite. Though both John Augustus Williams and Raccoon John probably would rather have died than admit it, the pro-Reform Cane Springs faction led by Isaac Thornburgh since late 1828 or early 1829 had not long remained under Smith's mentorship, but after Raccoon John disbanded his portion of North District in July 1831 it rejoined the Baptists, this time in Tate's Creek Association, that September following.[51] Other rural congregations originally of the Smith party may have followed suit to a greater or lesser extent with the Thornburgh faction of Cane Springs, though we will probably never be able to ascertain how many, or how few.

Though Green River Association and its own satellite bodies in south central Kentucky (including, interestingly, Isaac Denton's Stockton's Valley Association)[52] coped with the Campbell war using means very like North District's, traditionalists in the satellites of North District Association in the eastern mountains, Burning Springs and New Salem Associations, somehow managed to live in peace with the Reformers until about 1835. Burning Springs moderator William Coffee may have insisted on trying to keep his association out of the fray because of the negative experiences his mentor, Daniel Williams, had endured when he was a member of North District. On the other hand, Coffee's associational clerk for several years, Caleb Kash, was a member of Red River Church and a confirmed Reformer, and the fact that he was a "fair scribe" in a region where only a handful of men knew how to read and write may have been just as decisive a factor in holding the association together. North District's Sycamore Church had long been almost the sole contact point between Burning Springs and the larger body, and as we have seen, Sycamore had been pro-Smith almost from the start of Raccoon John's crusade, again perhaps from the rough handling that the church's first pastor had received from both the Payne family and Robert Elkin so many years before. Regardless, though, throughout a long ministry, William Coffee himself continued to exhibit considerable skill in keeping factions of disparate Calvinist and Arminian opinions united in the face of developing theological shifts among his charges, and so perhaps he deserves credit simply for keeping all his flock at peace for as long as he did.

But for whatever reason that the eastern Kentucky associations had remained behind the times, as it were, the peace there couldn't last permanently any more than it had downstate. By 1834, Joseph Nickell of Red River (according to legend at least, with Raccoon John's direct help) had already gathered three independent Disciple churches within Burning Springs territories, on Lick, White Oak, and Grassy creeks in Morgan County, and they refused to have anything to do with such a nonscriptural entity as a Baptist association.[53] Perhaps even before this, Raccoon John himself had taken his crusade further southeastward to the Big Sandy River valley.[54] Either he and the evangelists with whom he was traveling at the time or Nickell, Rancy Maxey, Ezekiel Stewart, and possibly Nixon Covey, working within Burning Springs Association itself, seem to have influenced at least three more United Baptist congregations (Burning Springs's Concord Church at the present Hager Hill in Johnson County, Open Fork of Paint Creek Church in eastern Morgan, and New Salem's Mud Creek Church in southern Floyd County) to adopt Reform principles. The 1834 minute records of Burning Springs Association show Caleb Kash as the body's clerk, list the Red River, Concord, and Open Fork of Paint Creek Churches as members, and carry a circular letter of decided Reformer tone.[55] No minutes for the body are available for 1835, but when the association gathered in 1836 it formally dropped Red River Church for "departing from the order of the United Baptist." Neither this congregation, the two others, nor associational clerk Kash even bothered to show up. Lick Creek actually left the Disciple camp and joined the association, though, and Open Fork of Paint

Creek reappeared in the body one year later with only six members. (Concord did not try to represent itself at a United Baptist association until 1857, and at that time it likewise had only six members.) Mashack Stacy, clerk of William Coffee's home church at Low Gap on Grape Creek in present Magoffin County, was elected clerk for the association in place of Kash, and the group's lengthy 1836 circular letter carries a great many dark apocalyptic references to the depravity of the age as well as condemnations of "Campbellite theory."[56] It would appear that Kash, in his indignation at being censured by his erstwhile brother Baptists, took the association's records away with him and destroyed them; luckily, Burning Springs's first clerk, Alexander Lackey, had made copies of the group's minutes from its 1813 founding until 1824, after which date Lackey served as clerk for New Salem Association. Though over one hundred years were to pass before the loss was rectified, through the courtesy of Lackey's clerical successor in New Salem Association, W. L. Akers, in the mid-twentieth century Burning Springs Association finally received a partial copy of the records of the earliest years of its existence.[57]

The effect of Raccoon John's crusade on easternmost Kentucky was thus, in a certain sense, a microcosm of the Reformation statewide, and it established longstanding and committed local enclaves throughout the area—"Campbellite communities," for lack of a better term, that exist beside and get along, or not, with other native religious groups—for a denomination, or rather nowadays a set of denominations, that has rarely if ever been regarded as a particularly genuine Appalachian mountain faith. Of course, Reform/Disciple evangelists were slower in coming to many central and southern Appalachian areas such as northeastern Georgia, eastern Tennessee, and western North Carolina, and there the movement never did take quite the hold that it did in Raccoon John's old domains. As an example, a popular sourcebook on Appalachian mountain religion claims that at least one manifestation of the Reform did not appear in a certain north Georgia county until 1974, and even then it was looked upon almost as an "outside" denomination.[58] But in the "Campbellite communities" of the Kentucky/West Virginia border country the Reformation/Disciple movement has had a venerable history, and more than once I have heard mild criticism from eastern Kentuckians and western West Virginians who have been raised within this faith tradition about the neglect of Appalachian religious scholars and historians to include Campbell-style worship as a legitimate mountain religious experience. Perhaps Loyal Jones, Howard Dorgan, and Deborah Vansau McCauley, who was herself raised within one branch of the Campbell tradition in southern Ohio, can relate similar anecdotes. Few, however, either of the followers of the movement's later manifestations, or of the native traditionalist Baptists from whom they separated so acrimoniously long ago, realize the true extent of the historical kinship between the two faith traditions, or the impact that each tradition has had upon the other.[59]

Because of the Campbell Reformation, little North District and its "daughter" associations in the eastern Kentucky hills—Burning Springs of Morgan and Magoffin counties (organized 1813), Red Bird of Clay and Perry (1823), Mountain Association of Breathitt, Owsley, and Perry (1856), and Red River of Wolfe (1876, now extinct), as well as the "granddaughter" associations New Salem of Floyd and Pike counties (1825) and Paint Union of Johnson, Lawrence, and Magoffin (1837), and their numerous offspring—never enjoyed the formal fellowship that Baptists statewide had known in the days of the old General Union. They have rather remained a law unto themselves, and their own concepts of Baptist traditionalism. Every one of the known "Old Time" Baptist subdenominations or "families," at least in easternmost Kentucky, be they now called United Baptist, Regular Baptist, Old Regular Baptist, or even Primitive Baptist or "mountain" Free Will Baptist, is descended from North District Association both in terms of history and of temperament. None, literally, realize that they and their Campbellite neighbors were once part of one faith tradition, or that the Campbell schism of the nineteenth century, more than any one other factor, was the primary catalyst for their insistence upon maintaining "the old Baptist ways." Inasmuch as they have been able, they have all upheld their own ideal of "the old traditions" as articulated for them by the disgruntled North District expatriates at Lulbegrud and Goshen Churches so many years ago, and for better or worse they have thus preserved a good deal of the original Separate Baptist (and in the cases of the so-called "Primitive Baptist" associations, even highly Calvinistic Regular Baptist) doctrine and preaching of yesteryear. But if they have thus given their adherents the impetus to maintain and preserve the worship forms first established in the southern uplands by Shubal Stearns in the eighteenth century, those which Raccoon John himself knew so well for much of his early preaching career, they have also made sure that Kentucky General Union–style politics would survive within their fellowship as well. Sadly, individual and group interactions among eastern Kentucky's native Baptists have all too often represented small-time, rural extensions of the same sort of politicking that Robert Elkin, Leonard Turley, David Chenault, Ambrose Dudley, John Price, Jacob Creath, Jilson Payne, and Raccoon John made holy for them nearly two hundred years ago.[60]

It is beyond the scope of this work to deal with the further development either of Kentucky's and Appalachia's "Old Time" Baptists, or of the Southern Baptist denomination at large. However, we should note one more brief speculation from historian Jesse Fletcher: that the so-called Old Landmark movement, claiming an unbroken pedigree for the Baptist Church independent of both Roman Catholicism and Protestantism all the way back to John the Baptist, Jesus Christ, and Jerusalem itself, was, ironically, one of the side effects of Alexander Campbell's editorial pronouncements about his Ancient Gospel. By Landmark Baptist reasoning, if Campbell could allege that he, Walter Scott, and Raccoon John had restored primitive church doctrine and practice to the modern age, the Baptists could do him one better by claiming to be the Ancient Church, which needed none of his so-called restoration because it had never apostatized in the first place. Moreover, the earliest Landmark advocates, the periodical editors and writers James Robinson Graves, James Madison Pendleton, and others, employed a journalistic style every bit as brash as Campbell's own in his early days, and which they very well may have copied from him.[61] Though Old Landmarkism has been condemned at past Southern Baptist Convention meetings and deservedly castigated by influential Southern Baptist writers, including the nineteenth century's Jeremiah Bell Jeter and the twentieth century's James E. Tull, it nonetheless survives as a powerful sacred myth in certain circles of the group's laity, particularly in the South and the Southwest. The belief likewise remains a staple of certain conservative breakoff groups of both northern and southern Baptist ancestry and, of course, in its own special manifestations among rural mountain "Old Time" Baptists.[62]

Whether or not most or all of Kentucky's Southern Baptists ever came to subscribe to the claims of Old Landmarkism, though, one of the beneficial effects that increased bureaucracy brought to the state's mainline Baptist denominational structure was the power to recognize and affirm orthodox Baptist periodicals and to provide a united platform to castigate those perceived as heterodox. Consequently, there have been no more Campbell-style movements within the Southern Baptist group, only conflicts of Baptists against Baptists over various points of the denominational orthodoxy. As has been demonstrated vividly, though, especially within the last twenty-odd years, these intra–Southern Baptist Convention struggles can be harsh and hurtful enough in and of themselves, and it is apparent that they involve personalities not entirely unlike either Kentucky's most venerated pioneer Baptist preachers or the spiritual "Old Time" descendants of these men. In short, if the ghosts of Robert Elkin, James Quesenberry, Leonard Turley, David Chenault, and Daniel Williams are still alive within one segment of the Baptist faith in Kentucky, so are the ghosts of Jilson Payne, Ambrose Dudley, John Price, John Gano, Richard Thomas, Jacob Creath Sr., and Jeremiah Vardeman in another. To say nothing of the ghost of Raccoon John, in both.

A peculiar people all in all, the Baptists, be they of General, Particular, Regular, Separate, United, "Northern," Southern, Free Will, Primitive, or any other persuasion. They were pariahs both in Britain and America at the inception of their denominational identity. Now, in aggregate, they represent the largest Protestant denomination in the United States, with the Southern Baptist Convention leading the pack numerically and the dozens of other Baptist groups extant alongside it laying as equally valid a claim to the Baptist name as can the SBC. They've come a long way in three hundred years in America, and it might be that they now only view one another as pariahs, in terms of differences of opinion over doctrine and practice: fundamentalist versus moderate, Old Landmark versus non-Landmark, "Old Time" versus modernist, and so on, much as former Regulars and Separates once looked askance at each other in Kentucky. But if so, to borrow Saul Bellow's characterization of the members of a particularly contentious Orthodox Jewish synagogue, they are then all pariahs, with the dignity of princes among themselves.

James French and Thomas Boone's reorganized North District Association survived until 1960, having metamorphosed through United Baptist, self-proclaimed "Old" Baptist, and in the years after 1885 even hyper-Calvinistic "Primitive" Baptist identities over the span of its long life.[63] The majority of the group's descendant associations and subdenominations are still alive as spiritual and cultural icons in their native territories, though many of the conservative congregations within their number may be alive today more as simply family and extended family institutions than as genuine community gathering places. But all such North District historical data, as well as that of Burning Springs Association or, for that matter, any other North District descendant group, would have been seen as mere pettifogging by Raccoon John. As far as he was concerned, in the thought and the writing of Alexander Campbell he had found truth—*the* truth for which he could and would live and die—and he had proven himself indeed as a doer of the word, not a hearer only, sharing this truth with the world around him at a nearly inconceivable sacrifice of his own strength, his health, and his family. If anyone was ever a true believer in a cause, Raccoon John was it, and thus in spite of his position as the veritable Campbell scourge of the Kentucky Baptists, none of his denominational opponents ever had much luck in articulating a plausible negative critique of his actions. Though he had shown himself to be a skilled, aggressive, and if need be occasionally unscrupulous ecclesiastical politician, his political aptitude reflected only that he had learned the art and developed the instinct from his Baptist mentors themselves rather than Alexander Campbell, and that he had become an expert in beating the Kentucky Baptists at their own game. His success in converting the majority of churches in North District Association to the Campbell Gospel was based more on his honest and unquestioned zeal for what he perceived as truth than on his political skills, important though they were, and even his most rabid contemporary would-be detractors must have known it.

And so now, having not only embraced the Campbell Reformation as the religious focus of his existence but having largely successfully impressed that religious focus upon his world at large, Raccoon John could afford to allow himself a few moments of reflection on the events of his life. His and Nancy's youngest daughter, Mary Vance Smith, was born in or about 1831,[64] and we might imagine, or hope, that at least in the case of this one pregnancy Raccoon John stayed home to give Nancy a little more assistance than that to which she had had to accustom herself. But as it happened in the spring of the year of Mary's birth, Smith got the urge to go and preach the restored Gospel in his old mountain haunts of Pulaski and Wayne counties, and to see his aged mother and his daughters by Anna once more. By this time Rebecca Smith had broken up housekeeping and was living just across the state line in Overton County, Tennessee, with one of Raccoon John's sisters. Jane and Zerelda may have been staying with Philip or Henry Smith. Jane was of majority age by now, and not too many years afterward Zerelda would wed Philip's son Isaac and Jane would marry Thomas Boles. Cumberland River Association had given off a "daughter" group of its own, South Concord Association, and in keeping with the actions of most of the other Kentucky Baptists it seems to have rejected Raccoon John's faction of North District Association the previous year. The Campbell Reformation had not yet made any great impact either on Cumberland River or Stockton's Valley Associations in spite of the changes that the movement was already effecting among their neighboring Stoneite Christians.[65] But at any rate, Raccoon John went south that spring, determined, as Williams states explicitly, "to go, and tell them how they might be saved."[66]

His reunion with Rebecca Smith was an emotional one for both mother and son. After so many years and the loss of at least one and perhaps two other sons already, Rebecca was overjoyed to see him, and he recalled to Williams that as his mother embraced him and wept upon his shoulder, "all the years of his manhood rolled back in a moment as he felt the pressure of her palsied arms around him. He was a child, a tender-hearted boy again, and he wept his pious tears upon her head." Happy though she was to see him, she was still overwhelmingly grieved at the rumors she had heard of him: that he denied "the good Spirit" that had once given him peace, and that he now preached to poor sinners that water could wash away their sins. She told him brokenly that, for a long time, she had refused even to believe such tales. But now, having had them confirmed, she could only ask plaintively why he couldn't have waited to change his preaching until she was dead and gone. At a complete loss for words to comfort the old woman, John tried to assure her that he never denied the Spirit, only changed his beliefs on the means by which the Spirit was made manifest, and that he had never taught that water could wash away sin. As she wept afresh, he finally offered a jesting proposal to go back to his old doctrinal mindset and mode of preaching for as long as Rebecca should live, if he should survive her, provided that she herself would agree to answer for him at the Day of Judgment. When she observed that she could answer only for herself on that great and notable day, John rejoined that if he, also, must answer for his own conduct, he ought to believe and act for himself in the present. Unable to come up with a reply, she finally agreed with him; and although she was never able to comprehend the nature of John's Reform crusade, to the day of her death she stated that she, at least, had had no hand in it. John ought to be left free, for to his own Master he had to stand or fall.[67]

He had less luck with the preachers he had known in his youth. Richard Barrier, Isham Burnett, Elijah Barnes, Stephen Collier, Thomas Wolverton, and others in the Cumberland River and South Concord Associations had to have been disenchanted with him at least to a degree ever since the political fracas at Cane Springs in the summer of 1827, and now South Concord's moderator, a longtime partner of Isaac Denton's named Matthew Floyd, refused even to call John "Brother."[68] Denton himself forbade Raccoon John to preach in the old Clear Fork meetinghouse where he had first held his church membership, and the circumstance seems to have hurt and angered Smith so badly that he inflated Denton, in his recollections to Williams, into something of a symbol of all that he had supposedly been mistaught in his youth. Naturally, Louis Cochran augmented and embellished this image into the character he gave Denton in his historical novel. Williams tells us that John never saw Denton again after this episode,[69] but his extreme bitterness toward the preacher who had immersed and "imposed" him so many years before is reflected cogently in a letter Raccoon John penned to a younger Disciple colleague, Isaac T. Reneau, in 1842. Apparently Reneau, who lived not far from Stockton's Valley, had informed Smith that Denton was involved in some sort of religious services in conjunction with either the mainline or Cumberland Presbyterians, possibly "union revival" meetings, and Raccoon John acidly observed in reply: "I was amused to hear of old Father Denton working so well for the presbyterians.— Did he think he could get the same spirit to make a few baptists that was making presbyterians? Or did he think that the divine Spirit would effect a divine conversion by means of human appointment? Or will he learn to work in *hive gear* in his old age? I am sure he did not like it when he was young. Well—when men do not understand Gods means of salvation they must have some means of their own" (all spelling, punctuation, and emphases in original).[70]

But certainly one of the most poignant stories Raccoon John ever told Williams, all the more touching because neither Smith nor Williams actually intended it to be poignant, involved a conversation that John had with some of his old friends near Monticello. And here once more we had perhaps best let Williams tell the story on his own:

> [Raccoon John] reached the neighborhood of Monticello on Saturday evening, having made an appointment to preach in that village the following day. That night, in the hospitable cabin of one of his old acquaintances, many that still loved him gathered in to see him, and to hear him talk. They questioned him respecting his new faith, and, in their simple-hearted way, besought him, not without tears, to return to the good old paths from which he had wandered.
>
> They had one test by which they judged whether a man was a Christian or not, and that test they now applied to him.
>
> "Brother John," said one of them—an old man—"we would like to hear your experience again. It has been many a long year since you told it; but we suppose you still remember it," and they all sat down together around him to hear it.
>
> "I will give it to you," replied Smith, "but I shall expect each of you to do the same, for I want to know how the Lord has dealt with you all."
>
> He related, with some minuteness, his experience, to which they listened with pleasure and surprise.
>
> "Why," said one of them, "it is the very same that he used to give us years ago!"

"Certainly," said Smith, "I have never forgotten or denied my experience, for it was real, and just what I tell you. But now I must hear yours."

Each, in his turn, told his experience, varying some little in detail, but presenting substantially the same succession of thoughts and feelings. Each felt that he was the worst of sinners, and that God could not be just and pardon him. When they were all done he inquired, "Do you really believe, brethren, that these discoveries were made to you by the Holy Spirit?"

"Yes, John," said the same fatherly old Calvinist, whose meek face turned solemnly, but tenderly, upon him. "The good Spirit only could have made these things known to us."

"Do you believe, too," asked Smith, "that the Holy Spirit always speaks the truth?"

"Why, John! You *know* that the Spirit can't say anything but what is true!"

"But you say," continued Smith, "that the Spirit assured you, that evening, as you sat disconsolate on the steps by the door, that God could not pardon you, and be just; and yet, on the next day, you got relief, and the same Spirit then assured you that God had pardoned you, and was just! If he really told you these things, did he not contradict himself?"

At this the old man bowed his gray head in thought, and his eyes, still moist from the remembrances of his own conversion, rested musingly on the floor. Lifting up, at length, his honest face, he said, "Brethren, you may be sure that the good Spirit never talks two ways."

"But, my brother," continued Smith, "the Spirit told you that you were the greatest sinner in the world; now, have you ever stolen anything, or murdered anybody?"

"Why, John!" he replied, "I never did such things in my life!"

"But there are men, you know, that do commit these, and even worse crimes. Were you a greater sinner than they? Besides, the same Spirit told the brother sitting by you that *he* was the greatest sinner in the world; and he told the same thing to the *next* brother sitting there; and he told *me,* too, that *I* was the very worst of sinners. Now, how could each one of us be the worst of all?"

"Brethren," said the old man solemnly, "rest assured that the Holy Spirit never contradicts himself!"

"Brother John," said another of them, whose harder features betrayed the greater sternness of his prejudices, "I have often said that if you should ever prove to be no Christian, I would give up religion as a dream. But I see now that you have never known what true religion is. You seem to be utterly in the dark!"

Smith saw that it would be vain to attempt, by any further argu-

> ment, to remove the scales from their eyes. They had been blinded by their early religious education; they were now well advanced in years; and he could not even disturb, much less remove, the prejudice of half a century's growth. [Spelling and emphases in original; again, it should be kept in mind that Williams classifies all non-Methodists who believed in salvation by the born-again experience as related here as Calvinists.][71]

Of course, Raccoon John was not one to give up easily, and over time his persistence paid off. In less than a year he made another journey to the hills, under circumstances more fortuitous for Campbell's Disciples than had existed in early 1831, and among other activities he did manage to gather a small Disciple congregation at Monticello[72] that included, apparently, his and Jeremiah Vardeman's aged preacher friend and mentor Thomas Hansford. Whether Hansford was genuinely converted to Raccoon John's mode of thought or, as J. H. Spencer indicates, the older preacher had simply made an angry Robert Elkin–like response to a perceived lack of respect from his Baptist brethren, we cannot say. Spencer records that Hansford felt himself slighted and neglected by the younger members at the church at Monticello which he pastored; earnest efforts were made by the church to satisfy his grievances, but they were all in vain. He still insisted that he was ill treated, and finally, "as a dernier resort to obtain satisfaction, [he] joined the Campbellites."[73] For whatever reason, though, as Everett Donaldson states, Jeremiah Vardeman had been lost to the cause, but Thomas Hansford, his mentor, had been gained.[74]

Irrespective of gains and losses on either side of the Baptist/Disciple question, however, it's certain that Alexander Campbell's supposed scientific blueprint of Scripture had made the subjective testimonies of Raccoon John's old Wayne County friends well-nigh unintelligible and near-pagan to him. Conversely, his own cold, precise, objective rationalism was, to borrow the time-honored expression, Greek to them. The type of debate that Raccoon John tried so valiantly to maintain at Monticello in the days of yore has been repeated countless times since, throughout the rural South and elsewhere: in barbershops; on courthouse squares between loafers; in sometimes vigorous and angry college dormitory bull sessions among students trying frantically to maintain their static worldviews in the face of an overwhelming number of facts utterly new to them; over radio and television broadcasts; in short, wherever and whenever the religious progeny of the young and fiery Alexander Campbell choose to try to challenge the perspectives of the spiritual heirs of John Wesley, George Whitefield, Shubal Stearns, and all the other pioneer evangelists of America's Great Awakening and Great Revival, and to maintain their own perspectives in the face of the challenges thrown at them. And it is a debate that has never been, nor can be, solved to everyone's complete satisfaction, because believers on both sides of the dispute speak to one another about the exact same things in what amounts to almost completely different theological languages. Both points of view are based on a literalist and inerrantist belief in the accuracy and integrity of the Bible, but invariably, either side of the question perceives the opposite side to be completely in the dark. Raccoon John Smith and his old Monticello Baptist neighbors were, and their heirs in debate still are, so close to one another and at the same time so far away.

At least it can be said that, all in all, Raccoon John had a better year in 1831 than his mentors did. For while John was consolidating Reformer/Disciple power in North District Association's territories and sallying forth to bring the "Ancient Gospel" to his old mountain haunts, even if he was less than successful at first, both Alexander and Thomas Campbell were declaring war against the first major defection that their Reform movement would know. It was significant because it involved the man responsible for opening up Ohio's Mahoning Association originally to Campbell influence: Sidney Rigdon, who had also served as Alexander Campbell's secretary at the 1823 MacCalla debate. By now, Rigdon had become disenchanted with the Campbells because of their unwillingness to implement among their followers the communal lifestyle of the early Christians described in the first few chapters of Acts right alongside their cherished immersion for the remission of sins, and he joined fellow Disciple preacher Parley P. Pratt in embracing the message of one Joseph Smith, a self-proclaimed prophet who had just come to Ohio from New York. Rigdon turned his Kirtland, Ohio, congregation over to Joseph Smith completely, and it was more than likely he who gave Smith's movement, which has come to be known as the Church of Jesus Christ of Latter-day Saints, or the Mormons, the emphasis on baptism by immersion that it has always maintained. Joseph Smith's message—that God had chosen him as a prophet to restore the True Church to earth after centuries of apostasy—was of course just a few steps more extreme than Campbell's own in his early days, and it is certain that Campbell's emphasis on restoring the "Ancient Order" provided a fertile ground within Reformer/Disciple territories for Joseph's claims. Even so, Thomas and Alexander managed to check their losses to a great extent by rushing to Kirtland, carrying on a vigorous anti-Mormon preaching campaign of their own, and excoriating Rigdon in the pages of *The Millennial Harbinger.* Soon, after some questionable business dealings and alleged persecutions, Joseph Smith declared bankruptcy with his feet and fled Ohio, taking Rigdon and his other followers in tow; some years later, after Smith's death, Brigham Young supplanted Rigdon's position in the Mormon hierarchy, and the rest, to borrow a banal cliché, is history.[75] As a rule, Baptist historians have always shown more interest in the early relationship between Disciples and Mormons than have Disciple and Reform historians, many of whom appear to wish to downplay it, but regardless of the stance taken by either side I must give credit where credit is due: had it not been for the efforts of determined genealogists, many of whom were or are Latter-day Saints, contributing to such Internet websites as Ancestry.com and Genealogy.com, this volume would have been much the poorer of information about the Smith, Bowen, Townsend, Hurt, Payne, Mason, and other families that has proven to be crucial to ascertaining the truth of Raccoon John's life story. I imagine, however, that Raccoon John would turn over in his grave to think that his parents, if not he and his own two wives themselves, have, from the appearance of some of the listings on the genealogy websites, been baptized *post mortem* by proxy as Latter-day Saints.

There's no doubt that Alexander and Thomas Campbell felt Rigdon's apostasy from their movement more keenly than they would have liked to show. Still, for now they saw more gains than losses, and back in Kentucky Raccoon John had good reason to be more successful on his second evangelistic trip to the Cumberland hills than he had been on his first. By the time he took his second excursion and convinced his old friend Hansford to join the cause, Barton Stone's Christians, who as we have seen had been a Cumberland Valley presence ever since the days of Rice Haggard and the Mulkey brothers, had formally united with Alexander Campbell's Disciples, and Smith had been able to capitalize upon the new union to the utmost. Amazingly, in spite of his low opinion of certain Stoneite articles of faith as evidenced by his treatment of James Fishback in 1828, Raccoon John himself was one of the principal Disciple advocates for the merger, and a crucial influence in effecting it.

Apologists within the various groups that have descended from this Stone/Campbell union too often portray the merging of the two movements as an easy and convenient meeting of the minds of nearly identical groups, both of whom were committed solely to the abolition of religious sectarianism in the world and to the pure words of the New Testament rather than any man-made religious creed. Kentucky Baptist defenders are likewise keen to proclaim the state's 1801 Regular/Separate Baptist union as something similar, but we have seen already that neither the 1801 Regular/Separate Baptist merger nor the status of the Stone and Campbell groups in the late 1820s was quite this clear-cut. Campbell's erstwhile Reformers, now Disciples, and Stone's Christians were still disparate on several issues, including interpretations of the ordinance of baptism, opinions on an ordained ministry, methods of organization (the only formal chain of communication between the independent Campbell churches at this point was the mailing list of *The Millennial Harbinger,* whereas Stone's people had been wont to employ certain basic organizational structures such as conferences and presbyteries of ministers), and the relative importance of weekly communion.[76] Bad blood over the old "Arian" slur against Stone's Christology remained between the two groups as well, as evidenced particularly within Raccoon John's own Montgomery and Bath County fields of labor.

This is not to say that representatives of both groups had not tried to establish connecting links between individuals wherever they could. The separate congregations of Disciples and Christians at Millersburg, Kentucky, seem already to have united to a certain extent,[77] and Raccoon John's faction of North District Association, meeting for its final session at Sommerset in 1831, had even featured a Sunday sermon by the Disciples' Stoneite neighbor Peter Hon. Raccoon John and John Newton Payne had preached with Hon on the occasion,[78] but given the degree of antipathy that Williams notes existed between Disciples and Stoneites in Montgomery and Bath counties[79] it is probable that Smith and the others made the decision to "use him in the stand" because they had determined that he and his Stepstone Creek Church were among those Stoneites who were orthodox on Campbell principles, rather than because of the preacher's and his congregation's mere connection with Stone. Campbell himself later wrote that Hon "was one of the few individuals with whom I have communed, who, on their own reading of the Acts of the Apostles, and without any teaching other than that of God's Spirit, have been baptized for the remission of sins," and that Hon had been immersed "while yet a Dunkard, with a special reference to Peter's precept on the day of Pentecost."[80] But at any rate, even Campbell himself was careful to identify his support within the Stone movement as coming from "the [D]isciples meeting under the Christian name in connexion [*sic*] with Brother Stone in Georgetown."[81]

Stone and Campbell still sparred editorially as well, and on one occasion, when addressing Campbell's contention that all anti-sectarian reformers who had come before him had merely cleared forests and burned brush to prepare the way for him and his own followers to restore completely the Ancient Gospel, Stone neatly hinted that Campbell was only trying to establish a great name for himself. Campbell was infuriated.[82] While a sizable grassroots movement within both the Stone clergy and laity continued to lobby for union with Campbell's Disciples, others, one of the most vocal an Ohio preacher named Matthew Gardner, condemned Campbell and his influence on the Stone church as resolutely as any of Campbell's Baptist critics had ever vilified him. Campbell's Disciples, Gardner observed, seemed to labor more to reform the churches of other denominations over to their views than they did to reform the wicked from the error of their ways. Though the Stone movement had arisen upon the principle of each individual exercising his or her own private opinion, Campbell had virtually done away with respect for private opinions in his insistence for unity on method. Finally, Campbell had made immersion the one single essential condition of salvation, and anyone who opposed it was stigmatized as being an opposer of the "glorious Reformation."[83] Given that the Disciples themselves harbored reciprocal prejudices against the Stoneites, it was thus no wonder that, as Everett Donaldson notes, bringing such true believers as Raccoon John Smith to the point where they were prepared to enter into fellowship with Barton Stone was no easy task.[84]

How, then, did anyone on either side even *begin* to bring these two opposing viewpoints together? How did Campbell's Disciples so easily gain a union with one group of differing beliefs, only a little more than a year after another denomination, the Baptists, had disfellowshipped them completely? Truth be told, the primary catalyst for the Stone/Campbell union seems to have been from no direct support that Alexander Campbell personally gave the notion, but rather a simple but crucial fluke in the structure, such as it was, of the early Disciples as a denomination. In late 1831, Barton Stone, who lived in Georgetown, Kentucky, and used the community for his, his newspaper's, and his church's base of operations, struck up a close and lasting friendship with one John Telemachus Johnson, an up-and-coming Georgetown Disciple preacher of Jacob Creath Jr.'s Great Crossings Church. As a scion of one of Scott County's "first families" and a veteran of the War of 1812 that his older brother, the congressman and original war hawk Richard M. Johnson, had helped to initiate, John T. Johnson had been elected to his brother's seat in Congress when Richard had gone on to the Senate, but in the fervor generated by the Campbell Reform in 1829 he had given up his secular concerns and become a fiery and effective exhorter for the Campbell cause.[85] A laborer as earnest as Raccoon John Smith himself, Johnson never tried to act the clown or to utilize humor the way Smith did in his own ministry,[86] although the crafty Raccoon John once did contrive to make him laugh at a joke about a French infidel in spite of himself—to Johnson's chagrin, right in church, too.[87] Still, even Raccoon John undoubtedly wished that John T.'s more famous brother Richard, who was to become vice president of the United States in 1837 and have a Kentucky county named after him in 1843, shared something of his sibling's serious turn of mind: while remaining a Baptist at least in name,[88] Richard M. Johnson cuckolded at least four and perhaps as many as seven of his fellow congressmen and senators while he was in Washington, besides indulging almost openly in the most common, least spoken of, and to our modern sensibilities most depraved sexual outlet that was available to wealthy southern planters. At least it can be said of Richard M. Johnson that he was more openly honest than, say, J. Strom Thurmond, and that he tried to treat his children, all of them and regardless of color, decently and bring them up as equals.[89] Like Thurmond and more modern southern politicians, a preacher of any denomination who had been guilty of the same indiscretions as a youth would have been obliged to cover up such matters entirely. Several undoubtedly did.

Anyway, John T. Johnson was, essentially, the link through which Campbellites and Stoneites united. Though it sounds horribly prosaic, the whole thing seems to have fallen into place when Stone asked Johnson to act as his coeditor for *The Christian Messenger,* conditional upon the Stone/Campbell union's actually taking place. We cannot say exactly when Stone first broached Johnson with the offer of coeditorship, only that the proposal was introduced very early in the groups' negotiations[90] and that Johnson did in fact assume the job immediately after the Disciples and Christians united, keeping it for two years or so and then being succeeded at the paper by, among other young Campbell followers, Jacob Creath Jr.[91] But given the fact that the brash, youthful Campbell movement was the first and, at the time, the only example of the brand-new American concept of the mass-media religion, the only paradigm under which an effective merger could truly take place was for the two sides to recognize each other's periodicals, both Stone's *Christian Messenger* and

Campbell's *Millennial Harbinger,* as equally legitimate. The presence of a Campbell Disciple not only on the editorial staff of the *Messenger* but as coeditor right along with Barton Stone was, literally, the sole reason that most committed Disciples would have given such recognition to Stone's newspaper at all. But under these new circumstances, if the Stoneites still had doctrinal and practical irregularities, they could all be fixed—so long as the trustworthy and capable John T. Johnson, and of course later on Jacob Creath Jr. and others, were just given a little time to work with Stone and his followers and to lead them onto the strait and narrow.

Even with "Old Father" Stone's blessing to Johnson's coeditorship, though, not all Stoneites could have been expected to embrace the idea of union on such terms with the Campbell people. A minority refused to countenance any of the union proceedings whatsoever, and of these, most remained aloof, connected with one another on Stone's old principles until they were subsumed in the mid-twentieth century into the United Church of Christ, a diverse and eclectic organization that brought together churches of Congregational and Reformed ancestry all over the United States but which, finally in the twentieth century, did enter into a kind of ecumenical relationship with the most liberal faction of Campbell's modern heirs. Still other Stoneites jumped on the Campbell bandwagon even while retaining pungent and bitter reflections about Alexander Campbell's combative style of setting up his "Ancient Order." For an example of this mindset, the venerable Stoneite minister Samuel Rogers once remarked that "we had mourners' benches in [the old] days, and they were things unauthorized by the Word of God. We [have now] abolished them, and we did right in so doing; but I almost fear that we have done it in such a way as to abolish the mourners too."[92] But for most of the young pro-Campbell Stoneites, the offer of union was an unqualified godsend, and with Johnson's help it became a *fait accompli* in Kentucky even as Alexander Campbell remained poised to continue his arguments against Stoneite belief in *The Millennial Harbinger.*

And here, Raccoon John came into his own. Simple protocol demanded that Barton Stone, as leader of his own movement, treat directly either with Campbell himself or at least one of his most senior representatives. Campbell was far away in the northernmost corner of what was then Virginia, and in Kentucky Smith was the only one whose longstanding commitment to Campbell and whose record of long and hard service entitled him to the reputation of a state leader. Johnson seems to have sprung the union idea on Smith in November 1831 when Raccoon John came to preach a series of evangelistic meetings at Great Crossings Church. Barton Stone and John Rogers both attended the Great Crossings meetings, evidently at Johnson's invitation. Johnson proceeded to get them all to talking with one another, and apparently he persuaded Smith to return to Georgetown in December to negotiate with Stone and Rogers more directly and purposefully.[93]

If Raccoon John didn't favor the union personally, there was little if any hope for its success at this point in time. His words still carried that much weight with the Kentucky Disciples at large. But apparently he was satisfied that Johnson's editorial seasoning would bring *The Christian Messenger* close enough to orthodoxy to make the merger work, and although his actions can be seen as somewhat enigmatic when considered in context with events of later years, for now his diplomacy won the day for the union. The December negotiations were successful, and a final and decisive union meeting between Campbell Disciples and Stone Christians was scheduled to be held at the Stoneite meetinghouse on Hill Street in Lexington on New Year's Day 1832—all before Alexander Campbell, busy with *The Millennial Harbinger* in the northern panhandle of Virginia, even knew what was going on.

That Lexington meeting was Raccoon John's finest hour, and the pinnacle of his career as a minister. His words and actions guaranteed his well-deserved place in the annals of both Stone/Campbell and Kentucky religious history. He and Barton Stone both spoke, and at Stone's request Raccoon John ascended the stand first. In the words of Williams:

> It was now to be seen whether all that had been said, and written, and done, in behalf of the simple Gospel of Christ, and the union of Christians, was really the work of the Lord, or whether the prayers of Stone, and of Johnson, were but idle longings of pious, yet deluded hearts; whether the toils and sacrifices of Smith were but the schismatic efforts of a bold enthusiast; and whether the teachings of Campbell were only the speculations of a graceless and sensuous philosophy. . . .
>
> Smith arose with simple dignity, and stood, prayerful and self-possessed, before the mingling brotherhoods. He felt, as no one else could feel it, the weight of the responsibility that rested on him. A single unscriptural position taken—the least sectarian feeling betrayed—an intemperate word—a proud, unfraternal glance of the eye—might arouse suspicion and prejudice, and blast the hope of union in the very moment when it was budding with so many promises. Every eye turned upon him, and every ear leaned to catch the slightest tones of his voice. [ellipsis added][94]

He proceeded to make an eloquent speech fully addressing both the desirability and practicality of a union between the Stone and Campbell movements. The merger was desirable in that Jesus had prayed for such unity among his children and the apostles likewise had enjoined it, and practical in that, at least in the belief cherished in evangelical circles both then and now, God had but one family upon the earth and that family was to be united upon one Book. Strife and disunity occurred among Christians when hierarchies imposed mere opinions, rather than the series of plain facts, commands, and promises that Alexander Campbell had demonstrated existed in Scripture, as tests of communion upon believers; unity could be achieved only if that which the Bible clearly and distinctly taught could be required of all believers. Though we have already seen the hole through which Raccoon John himself had fallen over this very issue in his debate with James Fishback in 1828, on New Year's Day 1832 in Lexington the workability of the idea seemed so very obvious and clear-cut that no one could or would doubt it. And Raccoon John thus brought his address to a stirring conclusion with the plea, "Let us then, my brethren, be no longer Campbellites or Stoneites, New Lights or Old Lights or any other kind of lights, but let us all come to the Bible, and to the Bible alone, as the only Book in the world that can give us all the Light we need."[95]

The patriarch Stone himself followed Smith in the pulpit, and endorsed Raccoon John's sentiments wholeheartedly. Though confessing that he himself had often been given to speculation in his preaching, he declared his belief in the truth of all that Smith had said with regard to the essentials of faith, and formally gave Raccoon John the right hand of fellowship. As the entire mixed Stone and Campbell congregation sang a hymn, everyone in the packed house followed suit in a group handshake, and the union was suddenly a joyful, established fact.[96] When Campbell learned of it, he simply acted the cheerful good sport and wryly praised the actions of Johnson and Raccoon John "notwithstanding the sparrings of us editors."[97] Even so, not all even of Stone's immediate family were entirely pleased at the new circumstances. Years later, Charles Chilton Moore Jr., a grandson of Barton Stone who was also himself a Disciple preacher for a time as well as a personal acquaintance of Alexander Campbell, gave what was probably his parents' summation of the entire proceeding as follows: "Alexander Campbell . . . accepting the distinguishing religious tenets of my grandfather, added to them the doctrine of 'baptism for the remission of sins,' and urged that doctrine with such special force that it, being quite unpopular, attracted much attention and resulted in the religious body being called 'Campbellites' and in Mr. Campbell taking precedence over my grandfather as the leader in the religious denomination. Stone and Campbell were respectively like Melanchthon and Luther in 'The Reformation,' as the new sect was called; my grandfather being mild, gentle, retiring, and unobtrusive, and Mr. Campbell being very ambitious" (ellipsis added).[98] Interestingly, in his mature years Moore became an atheist, severed all his connections with his grandfather's and Campbell's church, and, in an ironic twist upon the Stone-Campbell movement's mass-media heritage, published an "infidel" periodical in Lexington known as *The Blue Grass Blade.* Nonetheless, jaundiced though Moore's outlook and editorial pronouncements could be, it was remarked of him by perhaps the most prominent Lexington Disciple minister of his own day, John W. McGarvey, that "Charley Moore has said some hard things, but I have never caught him in a lie."[99]

It had been a long, hard road for Raccoon John since that day in early 1828 when he had thrown down his tools at his fencerow and his apron at Nancy's feet and declared that he was determined to preach the Campbell Gospel and leave the consequences to God. And finally now, all his suffering, all his sacrifice and that of his family, all the bone-wearying evangelistic journeys through which he had paced himself, must have seemed worthwhile. As the Psalmist had guaranteed, he had sown in tears and was now reaping in joy; he had gone forth weeping, bearing precious seed, but had returned in triumph, bringing his sheaves with him. At Hill Street Christian Church on New Year's Day 1832, Raccoon John Smith's long search for meaning and fulfillment in the Divine, his tortuous coon hunt through the mountains of southern Kentucky, the flats of northern Alabama, and the pastures of the Bluegrass, finally appeared to have come full circle.

The reader may yet wonder why that I have elected, in this biography of a nineteenth-century frontier Kentucky evangelist, to emphasize so strongly the thought (not to mention the works, as shown in the chapter titles and epigraphs) of a Danish theologian and philosopher who, in his lifetime, knew little of American religion and probably cared less. For one thing, and for whatever a self-taught homeschooled theological opinion is worth, Kierkegaard's postulate of the dialectic of aesthetic, ethical, and religious modes of existence may be one of the few ways—perhaps even the sole way—for pedants of both the faith traditions of Alexander Campbell's *Christian Baptist*/early *Millennial Harbinger* period and evangelical and conservative or fundamentalist Baptists to comprehend one another without condemning each other as heretics, and each other's churches, to borrow the words of the inimitable Peter Cartwright, as trash traps. If Campbell rationalists could accept the dialectic at least as a working hypothesis to try to fathom the reason why so many professed Christians and literalist, inerrantist Bible believers do not see Acts 2:38 exactly in the same way that they do, it might enable them to understand the importance of the born-again experience to evangelicals such as Baptists, and the Cornelius paradigm of Acts chapter 10 around which evangelicals base their beliefs in conversion. Similarly, the very same dialectic could provide a means for non-Campbell evangelicals to understand conservative Reformer/Restorationist thought with a modicum of respect: that, yes, although the doctrine of *The Christian Baptist* was structured around a system of logic with marked differences from traditional evangelical understanding, the commitment of most of the followers of this system as a group provides ample witness that they are indeed in a passionate religious mode of thought and existence, and are as dedicated to spreading the Gospel of Christ, such as they perceive it, as are their evangelical critics. Perhaps such an understanding could even provide a basis by which both Campbell and traditional Protestant evangelical purists might learn to appreciate the presence of honest, heartfelt Christian piety and worship in liturgical and sacramental faith traditions, which have all too often been dismissed by them as practically pagan, as well. In any case, it can't hurt to hope that, by some means, a common ground could be established on which biblical literalist and inerrantist Christians can meet and converse without one group's resorting to anyone's generalship in storming a sectarian fortress that it perceives exists within the other, and with no danger of anyone's opening up the arsenal and blowing an honest and well-intentioned Christian preacher out of the saddle. After all, Alexander Campbell, for all his arrogance, did earnestly wish for the practical unity of God's children more than any other ideal, and though he never completely achieved his aims, some of the trends he initiated have become part and parcel of the doctrines even of the evangelical groups who originally opposed him most vociferously. Had not the nineteenth-century rationalism that was Campbell's driving force been recognized and accepted to at least some extent even by his opponents, such popular modern evangelical concepts as the formulated "sinner's prayer" and the so-called Roman Road, wherein penitents are "led" through a series of Scripture verses found in Paul's Epistle to the Romans to an "acceptance" and oral profession of faith in Christ, might never have developed.

Secondly, and I think significantly, the culmination of Kierkegaard's career as a writer, thinker, philosopher, and theologian was his own call for the reformation of organized Christianity in his native country—an attack on Christendom, as it were, for its manifold faults and failures, in which he employed invective just as vigorous, peppery, and sarcastic as the early Alexander Campbell at his most bellicose. Not that Kierkegaard had the same ideas or even the same goals as Campbell, by any means. As we have seen, Campbell, in his early years, expected to show the human race how to find purpose and meaning through cool, clear common sense, his thesis being that a particular logical system that he had imposed upon the text of Scripture revealed the whole as an objectively verifiable scientific blueprint for both salvation and worship, on which all believers could and should unite. But to Kierkegaard, this was the very antithesis of the essence of Christianity. He once observed that anyone who believed that words could capture God, or that logic could define God's existence, was likely only to confuse erudition with faith and knowledge with truth, and never realize that inward passion which is the mark of faith. The mere acceptance of Christian doctrine did not and could not make a person a Christian; becoming a Christian meant no less than living with Christ and dying with him, spiritually, within the core of one's being. And so in the latter days of his life Kierkegaard lashed out with all the considerable force of his wit and his pen against the corruption, superfluity, and complacency of clergy and laity alike in the Lutheran State Church of Denmark. Though he initiated and maintained this verbal offensive by his own effective use of mass media just like Campbell did, his "corrective," as he called it, had no potential whatsoever to establish any American-style media religion. Kierkegaard was entirely content with the Lutherans' Augsburg Confession, he felt absolutely no need to alter the externals of Lutheran worship, he had no use for what he called "pietistic severity," and he never offered any practical programs of reform. His propositions for the church's spiritual renewal, such as they were, need not be discussed here. Many, if not most, were so outrageous that they could be appreciated only by the perceptive reader as cutting satire or dismissed by the unimaginative as outright insanity. But for all that, they reflect, through and through, his insistence that the purpose of Christianity was not so much to bestow upon the world at large a system of doctrines that could be proven objectively to be correct, but to demand nothing less than a passionate response, from each specific individual within the world, to God. Alexander Campbell preached that the meaning of life could be known as objective truth; Kierkegaard, that it must be *felt* as subjective truth.

In spite of the obvious differences between the Campbell and Kierkegaard pleas, however, they can hardly be called antithetical in all aspects. Both men sought to understand their world and the place of humankind in it. Both based their search from the same vantage point of Christianity, although from markedly different angles and influences, and both had their own very human limitations in so doing. Campbell at least, as a working evangelist and pastor, really did think that he had found the key to understanding the relationship between created and Creator, and that his proclamation of the good news would usher in the beginnings of the Millennial Age even as the sandy foundations of the moldy old man-made, tradition-based order crumbled before the eyes of true believers. Kierkegaard, as a philosopher, had no such confidence in his own conclusions. To him, both indifference and unreflective, dogmatic dead certainty were both to be avoided as aesthetic poison, and so once a "corrective" became the norm, as far as individual believers were concerned it meant only that the new norm would then probably need another corrective. Yet both men gave themselves, heart and soul, to their ideal, the proposition that humankind could find its ultimate fulfillment in relation to its Creator, and thereby know the ultimate, Divinely intended meaning of life.

Though the word loses something in translation, Kierkegaard called this sought-after earthly fulfillment of the religious sphere, this state of complete psychological, spiritual, and philosophical peace, by the title of the *repetition.* Basically, by the repetition he meant one's recovery of the world after renouncing it psychologically, much as evangelical Christians idealize the act of salvation after an individual gives his or her entire soul up to God, the "life, and more abundantly," the "good measure, pressed down, running full" that Jesus promised in the Gospels. But as is obvious, the concept of repetition as Kierkegaard defined it is not only a religious or spiritual proposition to be pondered by believers and theologians, but a literary and dramatic tool to be utilized by storytellers as well: the "happily ever after" in which the hero is ensconced after overcoming whatever conflicts and antagonists that provide meat for the body of a good, stirring tale. And though real life is all too often as far a cry from good drama as is fantasy for meaningful theological ponderings, as long as humans make use of their creative instincts, the concept of repetition, or "happily ever after" if one should prefer to regard it that way, will remain a part of our collective psyche.

And so finally, we return to our own hero, Raccoon John Smith. Unlike either Campbell or Kierkegaard but quite like the great majority of us, he was no original thinker. He first sought, and passionately believed he had found,

God under the paradigms bequeathed to him by his parents, his early environment, and his heritage. After the exercise of his life choices had transformed his perspectives on his religious foundation and his experiences into bitterness, he rejected both by degrees as he sought solace in what was then a bold, novel, and seemingly ultra-clear system of religious thought that proposed to answer all his questions, solve all his problems, and redefine his purpose. He passionately believed that he had found all this, and more besides, in the Campbell system; and though in this volume we have been forced to remark all too frequently on how Williams and other writers have altered Raccoon John's story to suit their own preconceived religious opinions, none of them could have done so entirely successfully unless Raccoon John himself had been in some degree responsible for structuring his own recollections to accommodate the conventions of good, rousing, inspirational storytelling. He was, of course, the protagonist of the conflict; the Baptists were the antagonists, with James French cast in the role of the arch-antagonist and David Chenault and Isaac Denton in subordinate roles; Raccoon John's discovery and application of *The Christian Baptist* was the tale's rising action; the horrors of the 1827 North District Association meeting and his passionate response served as the perfect climax; the victory of Campbell thought in North District was entirely adequate falling action; and the union of Disciples and Stoneite Christians in Lexington on New Year's Day 1832 was, finally and happily, the story's denouement. And the Stone/Campbell union did make for the supposition of a very, very sweet happily-ever-after conclusion, a perfect fulfillment and, using the word in the Kierkegaardian sense, repetition, for the life of a committed servant of Christ and the Holy Scriptures. This was, in fact, exactly where Louis Cochran essentially ended the narrative of his historical novel, although to give credit where credit is due he did have Nancy remind John, who at the conclusion of the story line was rejoicing that he belonged finally to the perfect church, that perfection was hard to come by and that the Stone-Campbell union was only the beginning of the beginning.

Whether Kierkegaard believed that the repetition, as he described it, was merely an abstract ideal to which we should aspire or was actually an attainable reality in life, we can't say with complete confidence. In his works he had the habit of making the characters he created, as well as the pseudonyms he employed, argue contradictory positions—from which he expected his readers to glean their own personal truths. And if ever a writer and thinker loved irony and paradox, Kierkegaard did. With that in mind, as well as the variety of meanings that one single word can own, let us now, in our own conclusion, come to the account of the life of Raccoon John Smith after its joyous 1832 Lexington denouement: his repetition.

CHAPTER 9

The Repetition

My own untruth is something that I can discover only by myself, because it is discovered only when I have discovered it—even if the rest of the world knew it already.

—Søren Kierkegaard

Though we could resume the thread of Raccoon John Smith's life at almost any point after the Stone-Campbell union on New Year's Day 1832, for our purposes Tuesday, November 14, 1843, is as good a date as any and perhaps a better one than most. We know as much or more about that specific day than perhaps any other in Raccoon John's life after his participation in the historic unity meeting in Lexington, and we can in fact use it to put his entire post-union ministry in context. If we employ the logical principles of deduction advocated by Alexander Campbell and so well loved by Raccoon John, we can even make a fair guess what the weather was like in northeastern Kentucky on that fall day more than a century and a half ago: clear or at least no more than partially cloudy, but unseasonably cold and likely to remain so for several days more. We can speak with some confidence here because it is known that, although it was ordinarily still two to six weeks too early for the task, this happened to be the day that Nancy Hurt Smith chose to have her hogs butchered and to "lay in" her family's supply of pork and lard for the coming winter and spring.

Raccoon John wasn't at home to attend to the chore himself. This was of course no new occurrence. Still active as he could make himself despite his fifty-nine years, he'd gone to Lexington a few days before,[1] and it looked as though he'd be there possibly for the rest of the month. Needless to say, Nancy was long used to managing on her own during such periods, and for quite a time after her daughter Mary's birth and the Stone-Campbell union she'd been forced to do so almost as often as she had between 1828 and 1830. First acting as a companion evangelist to the former Stoneite John Rogers to publicize the Stone-Campbell union in local churches throughout Kentucky, and later on as an evangelistic partner to John T. Johnson as well, Raccoon John had spent much of his time from 1832 to perhaps 1835 or early 1836 on the road. According to Williams, during these years "His voice was heard along the valley of the Big Sandy [River] in the east, and upon the banks of the Green River in the west. He proclaimed the unsearchable riches of Christ in the counties upon the Ohio [River], and constituted churches along the borders of Tennessee."[2] He had even taken one or two evangelistic trips back to northern Alabama as if he were striving to plant the "Ancient Gospel" everywhere that he had ever labored as a Baptist, and this though the Stoneite side of the union had been an organized presence in that area since the days of Benjamin Lynn. Alexander Campbell's newspapers and his own seemingly tireless itinerancy had made Raccoon John Smith a legend in his own time among Disciples of Christ from Pennsylvania all the way westward to the new settlements in Texas and Missouri, and for many years his mere presence at any debate or evangelistic function had been regarded as a veritable talisman for Disciple victory, to use Raccoon John's own term, against the beggarly abortions of sectarian spleen.[3] For more than one reason, though, Raccoon John's tours had gotten shorter and less frequent since 1836 and he was, usually, now at home much more often than he had been. Considering that his hands were by now so palsied that they constantly trembled and he practically strained himself even to write a legible letter,[4] it could be argued—and Nancy likely *did* argue, for whatever her pleas were worth—that he had earned the right to lay down his sword once in a while and let younger Disciple firebrands take up the cause.

Nancy very probably did wish that Raccoon John, even with his palsied hands, would come home to supervise the family's butchering personally, perhaps especially since she had to have known that the frosty air would be anything but good for her "breast complaint." Unfortunately, though, it would be well-nigh impossible for anything short of a disaster of biblical proportions to keep him away from Lexington for at least the next two weeks. Alexander Campbell was visiting the state once again, ordinarily at least a once-a-year occurrence but this time for a special occasion: to engage the noted Kentucky Presbyterian minister Nathan Lewis Rice in a formal debate over the questions of baptism, the Holy Spirit, and creeds. Campbell himself is said not really to have desired that the debate take place, but rather assented to it because Kentucky Presbyterians were so eager to have their champion Rice meet Campbell in contest. So finally, Lexington's Presbyterians and Disciples had mutually agreed that the great debate be held in the city's Main Street Christian Church starting Wednesday, November 15, 1843. The contending parties further arranged that John C. Young, the president of Centre College at Danville, along with fellow Presbyterian ministers J. K. Burch, J. F. Price, and J. H. Brown, should stand as formal witnesses to the competition, "seconds" perhaps if we could employ dueling terminology for a comparison, on the part of Rice and the Presbyterian side; that James Shannon, president of the Disciples' own new Bacon College at Harrodsburg, Dr. James Fishback, Aylette Raines, Raccoon John Smith, and, interestingly, another preacher named John Speed Smith should serve in the same capacity for Campbell; and that no less a personage than the great Senator Henry Clay himself, back home on a visit from Washington, should stand as moderator over the entire proceeding.[5] The proposed debate thus assembled many of the most prominent and reputed Kentucky Presbyterians and Disciples, and so Raccoon John had already gone to Lexington for the preliminary arrangements. If Nancy and the children were lucky, they might hope to get one or two Sunday afternoon visits from John while the debate was going on, but he'd be sure to ride right back to the city to stand in the gap for the great cause again so long as the contest happened to last. Nancy knew she might as well go ahead, butcher those hogs, and get the family's pork, lard, and soap put up while this cold snap held on, because as long as the Campbell-Rice debate lasted Raccoon John wouldn't be fit for anything else.

At least farm labor was probably easier for her to obtain nowadays. The Smith family was no longer living in Montgomery County; eight years before, Raccoon John had finally let go of his Grassy Lick property, which had been nothing but a financial headache to him ever since he and Nancy had moved downstate, and had bought another farm on credit, this one in Bath County just outside the county seat of Owingsville. He had a multitude of friends here, having planted Disciple congregations in both Owingsville and Sharpsburg himself back in 1828, and in fact their financial support to him as an evangelist had enabled him to buy, or at least make a sizable down payment on, the new property. Even so, he and Nancy still maintained their church memberships at Mt. Sterling because the congregation had been unwilling to give him up as an elder at the time of their move,[6] and a complicated set of actions which must wait to be discussed had precluded their membership transfers since.

John and Nancy would have settled near friends probably anywhere they had chosen to move in either Montgomery or Bath counties, but here near Owingsville their primary sources for labor were still their relatives more than their neighbors. Although Jonathan and John Duke Smith were both gone from home and far away on their own now, it's possible that twenty-year-old Harvey was still at home at least part of the time, and Nancy's nephew William Berryman Hurt maintained both a family and a sizable farm not far from the Smiths' new property. Too, by this time John and Nancy's oldest daughter, Maria, had finished her schooling at Phillip Fall's Academy in Frankfort, and on March 8, 1839, she had married James Andrew Jackson Lee,[7] Owingsville's most eligible young merchant and banker.[8] Within four years of their marriage the couple had already given Raccoon John and Nancy two granddaughters, and it appears that Maria was expecting again at this time as well.[9] Although Lee, who was known for wearing a cape and a tall silk hat, carrying a silver-headed cane, and disdaining Owingsville's rough board sidewalks to make his way right down the middle of the town's main street as riders and wagoners made room for him,[10] certainly wasn't in the class that dirtied its hands with such menial labor as butchering, he had both slaves and hired men at his beck and call. We might presume that he arranged for them to assist his in-laws, and probably gave them financial help when they needed it as well.

Of the rest of the surviving Smith sons and daughters, on March 23 of this very year eighteen-year-old Eliza Ann had married Edgar A. Freeman, an

Owingsville carpenter[11] and if not as good a match as her older sister Maria had made, a respectable one nonetheless. We noted the 1828 or 1829 and 1831 births of John and Nancy's youngest daughters, Emma and Mary, in the midst of the first blush of Raccoon John's frenetic efforts to establish the religion taught in *The Christian Baptist* and *The Millennial Harbinger*; and although he likewise spent much time between 1830 and 1836 evangelizing across the state with both John Rogers and John T. Johnson, he could take comfort in the way that the Lord had seemingly blessed his family to overcome the difficulties caused by his long absences. Even though a cholera epidemic had wreaked havoc through northern and eastern Kentucky in 1833, Raccoon John's family had remained completely unscathed by the horrible contagion in spite of the fact that Nancy, during another of Raccoon John's extended journeys, had sheltered some panicked travelers who very likely had been exposed to the disease.[12] Considering how many sons and daughters the Smiths had watched perish over the years, the various ways in which they had died, and John's tendency, entirely understandable under the circumstances, to read Divine messages and admonitions into his personal tragedies, if he was looking for any further proof that he was finally on the right track of the strait and narrow and preaching the pure Gospel, he would have accepted this fortunate turn of events as all the assurance that he needed. He and Nancy had not lost a single child since Joshua Carroll, just before John had committed himself body, heart, mind, and soul to the Reformation, and there can be little doubt that his memories of that sordid, rushed funeral had caused him to declare for the Campbell cause as zealously as he had. But there had been no more such horrible events in the past sixteen years, and even if Jonathan, Harvey, and possibly John Duke had inherited the family tendency toward consumption, the Smiths no doubt believed that they had every reason to thank God for their children's current state of health.

Raccoon John and Nancy's pride and joy, though, was their youngest son, the last of their eleven. A "change baby" born in October 1836 a month before Nancy's forty-fourth birthday and right around the time of Raccoon John's fifty-second, Richard Menefee Smith had been named for the successful candidate for Congress from that district at the time, Richard Hickman Menefee, who also represented perhaps one of the last of Raccoon John's close attachments with male intellectuals that seems always to have been such a marked characteristic of his personality. As to the reasons of Raccoon John's peculiar, "almost paternal"[13] fondness for Menefee we cannot be entirely certain. A bright young Bath Countian who had lost his father at age six, Richard H. Menefee had been forced to leave school as a teenager and had worked at a variety of jobs, including both bartender and schoolteacher, to make money to attend Transylvania University and study law. From the legal practice he had established in Mt. Sterling and Owingsville in 1831, he had gone on to politics, first as a victorious candidate for Henry Clay's new Whig Party in the state legislature and then in 1836, before he had even made much of a splash at

Frankfort, on to Washington for Congress. It may have been that the aging Raccoon John unconsciously saw in Menefee something of the boy that he himself once had been, and what he could have accomplished in the secular world if he had not been drawn into the ministry. But Menefee's personal appeal to Raccoon John may have had yet one more factor: the young congressman was also a consumptive (he would die in 1841 after serving only one term in the House of Representatives).[14] With Menefee's record of success in spite of his illness and his harsh childhood, Smith also could have seen within the young politician what he hoped his own tubercular sons could be and could accomplish, especially since he had virtually turned Jonathan, John Duke, and Harvey out on their own to run the farm and fend for themselves and their mother so that he could preach the Gospel. Now that he was older and the great Reform cause was more firmly established in the land, perhaps he could do better at least by Harvey and Richard, and there was still time for Jonathan and John Duke to cope with their difficult pasts, just as Menefee had, and to make something out of their lives. In naming his baby boy after Congressman Menefee, Raccoon John might have intended not only to inspire his youngest son, but his older ones and even himself as well.

But paradoxically, if Raccoon John's naming of his baby had been a gesture of respect and appreciation for a distinguished young Bath Countian, it had also proven to be every bit as much a personal act of defiance to the community wherein Smith worked and ministered, Raccoon John's deliberate thumbing of his nose at the world around him. This was no response to any persecuting Baptists, either, because that denomination no longer had any control or influence over him; now, like the subject of the prophecies of Zechariah in the Old Testament, Raccoon John received his wounds in the house of his friends. To understand why it should have been so, we must look a little more deeply into what had happened and was happening to Alexander Campbell's glorious Reformation movement as it matured. For its adherents it was no longer the corrective, but the norm; and as Kierkegaard so often observed about norms and correctives, as well as the similarity between outright indifference and complacent dogmatism . . .

We noted in this work's introduction that the Campbell movement, after 1832 more properly the Stone-Campbell movement, at present exists in essentially three entities: the Christian Church (Disciples of Christ), the Christian Churches/Churches of Christ (Independent), and the a cappella Churches of Christ, which in turn are further divided into their own subgroups. It is commonly said that the most reactionary faction of the movement, the a cappella Churches of Christ, split from the Disciples in or not long before 1906, and that the division was the culmination of long years of bitter disagreements within the movement over organized suprachurch missionary societies and the use of musical instruments in worship services. The Christian Churches/ Churches of Christ (Independent) evolved gradually, approximately between

1926 and 1950 around an entity known as the North American Christian Convention, as a conservative Disciple split, but for all practical purposes as a middle ground between Disciples and a cappella Churches of Christ and with some characteristics of both. Of course all of these manifestations of the movement claim Barton Stone, Alexander Campbell, and Raccoon John Smith for their own, and as a rule apologists for each Reformation (now more often called Restoration) subgroup present Campbell as having preached a singular, consistent message over the years, based on plain Scripture alone and which their own particular branch of the faith now represents. The one commonality that these apologists often share, regardless of which side they're on, is the contention that the movement was as close to perfection as it ever got during Barton Stone's and Alexander Campbell's lifetimes. Supposedly, evil counselors who appeared on the scene later, or at least late in Campbell's life, were responsible for the movement's divisions rather than either Stone or Campbell themselves. But for all of Stone's and Campbell's integrity, which is unquestioned, many of these conservatives, mostly in the a cappella Churches of Christ and Independent Christian Churches and in a manner greatly similar to that of Old Landmark Baptists, all too often studiously avoid learning much about Campbell or any other important figure of their past and consequently exhibit a marked historical naivete where their faith is concerned. According to Richard Hughes, himself a member of the a cappella faith tradition, they simply fear that to acknowledge dependence on the influences of any human leaders would make them just one more denomination with a human founder like all others, rather than the true, primitive church founded by Christ and the Apostles.[15]

We could wish that space allowed us to examine the religious movement established by Alexander Campbell, augmented by Barton Stone and his followers, and embraced by Raccoon John Smith so wholeheartedly in more detail than what we will be able. Like the Baptists, the Disciples—or Christians, or members of the Church of Christ, or whatever any individuals among their number prefer to be called—were and are a spiritual and earthy, infuriating and endearing set of children of God living in a world full of the children of men, and again we must refer interested readers to the works of Robert Richardson, Leroy Garrett, Richard Hughes, Errett Gates, Louis and Bess Cochran, and others contained in this volume's bibliography for a more comprehensive picture of their history and their faith. Though we must make exceptions from time to time, for the most part we will henceforth refer to them simply as Disciples, since they were still nominally united under that title and around *The Millennial Harbinger* and *The Christian Messenger* during the remainder of Raccoon John's life. Even so, Hughes and, to a lesser extent, Garrett have made a convincing case that the Disciples, even at this occasion of the Campbell-Rice debate, already bore within their structure the seeds for the divisions that would occur in time; later evil counselors or no, Campbell and Stone carried enough responsibility for schism all on their own. Neither were instrumental music nor missionary societies the primary causes for division. As we have seen already, ecclesiastical quarrels usually have both internal and external grounds, and these were mere externals. As scholar David Edwin Harrell is quoted by Hughes, if these people had not disagreed over instrumental music and missionary societies, they would have divided over something else.[16] (Not that I'm not tempted here to put in a good word for a cappella singing. As a child of the "Old Time" Baptists, I prefer it above all other church music, the older the hymns the better.)

Hughes makes a very strong case for the idea that one of the movement's primary potential grounds for division lay in an aspect of theology on which Campbell and Stone, who differed on so many smaller points anyway, stood as far apart as the poles: eschatology, or that branch of theology concerned with death, judgment, and especially the end-times. Though at this early period essentially all Disciples recognized both the *Harbinger* and the *Messenger* as the mouthpieces of the church, neither at this time nor afterward would the two journals synchronize their editorial slants completely in terms of eschatology. John T. Johnson's two-year coeditorship of the *Messenger* did much to align it to a complementary position to the *Harbinger* in terms of emphases on immersion and church order, although Stone never quite gave up trying to urge moderation on readers who were hard-liners for Campbell's method and some of his particular beliefs. But we must remember that, in the days of the great Kentucky Baptist war and for some time afterward, Campbell honestly believed that his interpretation of basic, "scientific," "ancient" Christianity would inevitably spread first over the United States and then over the globe as all other faiths withered away in the advent of the Messianic Age. He was basically an optimist who encouraged Christians to involve themselves in education, politics, and the affairs of the world generally, thereby participating more fully in the dawning of the Millennial paradise he anticipated. Stone's view was radically different. To him, the world could only wax worse and worse until Jesus himself came back to judge the wicked and to gather his children, and as such, the church should keep itself separate from the affairs of the world other than in the barest necessities of paying taxes and obeying civil laws. Though the attitude was to change among Stone's descendants in the faith by the time of World War I, many early Stoneites refused even to join political parties and vote in elections.[17] Thus, though Campbell's viewpoints on many if not most aspects of doctrine had largely triumphed among believers on the Stone side of the movement, Stone's pessimistic view of the world and the end-times still vied with Campbell's optimism in popularity among both readers of the movement's journals and its ministers of the preached word. According to Hughes, though Stone was much milder both in temperament and in doctrine than was Campbell in his early, feisty years, Stone's pessimistic, apocalyptic, separatist worldview was more crucial to the development of the extreme sectarian outlook of the a cappella Churches of Christ, and possibly the Independent Christian Churches/Churches of Christ as well, than was

Campbell's postmillennial optimism.[18] This idea, retorts Leroy Garrett, should be a "hard sell" to most members of Churches of Christ,[19] but nonetheless we can and shall demonstrate herein that this basic difference between the Stone and Campbell views of secular politics was a trouble spot almost from the start of the union.

In truth, though, despite the differences in the *Messenger*'s and *Harbinger*'s editorial slants, Alexander Campbell would hardly have believed that Barton Stone's paper was his movement's greatest potential source of controversy. That distinction, in Campbell's eyes, would have gone rather to one John Thomas, an English physician who immigrated to the United States in 1832 and joined the Disciples a year later. A close brush with shipwreck and drowning on his journey to America had convinced him to think about the affairs of his soul and to pray for guidance to the true biblical faith, and he attached himself to the Disciples and was immersed by Walter Scott in Ohio. Impressed by Thomas's fund of knowledge and his eloquence, Scott arranged for him to meet Alexander Campbell, and both agreed that Thomas should begin preaching forthwith. He seemed to them to possess the culture and the qualities of leadership that the movement badly needed in its fledgling days as an independent religious faith, and when Thomas did follow Campbell's advice and initiate a preaching ministry he was quite successful. But he insisted on publishing his own journal, *The Apostolic Advocate,* as well, and before long Campbell was amazed to learn that his new star preacher was not only proclaiming from its pages that the Disciples represented the only true church, but insisting that immersions performed by Baptists or anyone other than confirmed Disciples were inadequate for admission to the Church of Christ because such immersions had not been made on "intelligent faith." And Thomas practiced what he preached, too: he reimmersed each and every Baptist who came to him to join the Disciples, a practice that Campbell, who himself had been immersed only by a Baptist preacher just as Raccoon John Smith and a great many of the movement's other pioneers had, utterly loathed.

So the *Harbinger* went to war with *The Apostolic Advocate,* and as time dragged on the fight only worsened, broadening out to a variety of Scriptural topics on which Campbell and Thomas disagreed. Although he kept Campbell's emphasis on immersion for the remission of sins along with his own insistence that "alien" immersion would not bring salvation, Thomas also came to embrace a set of doctrinal beliefs very similar to those of the Jehovah's Witnesses of modern times. In addition—no doubt to Raccoon John's own particular disquietude, as the issue had been such a very personal one to him ever since 1815—Thomas rejected the idea that "heathens, idiots, pagans, and very young children" could be saved. Election and foreknowledge had nothing to do with this claim, but rather Thomas's idea that such persons could not form his concept of an intelligent faith.[20] Most of Thomas's distinctive beliefs caught on with only a minority of readers, but his contentions for reimmersion upon the profession of intelligent faith, as well as the complete apostasy of all other

Christian groups besides the Disciples, appealed to a greater number of readers than Campbell evidently anticipated, readers who had once thrilled over rhetoric almost as bellicose in *The Christian Baptist.* Though Campbell never quite admitted it openly, Hughes believes it is possible that he saw in Thomas's extreme rhetoric a not altogether pleasant reflection of his own attacks on Protestantism only a few years before.[21] In other words, if Erasmus had laid the egg that Luther hatched in the days of the original Reformation, Campbell might have admitted at least to himself that he had laid similar eggs for both Sidney Rigdon and John Thomas in this one. And so whether because of Thomas in particular, Campbell's growing weariness with the extreme and bitter sectarianism he himself had once tacitly encouraged among his followers, or, as Hughes also hypothesizes, partly because of Campbell's 1837 debate in Cincinnati with Roman Catholic Bishop John Baptist Purcell in which he emerged as the champion not of his own movement in the West, but of Protestantism as a whole,[22] the once fiery and swashbuckling Alexander Campbell began to mellow out. He came to regard mainline Protestantism, rather than his own exclusive movement, as the expression of true Christianity for the coming Millennial Age, and therefore as his movement's friend rather than its enemy. To be sure, he could still sometimes mouth aggressive platitudes about primitive Christianity, the Ancient Gospel, and the Ancient Order, and only four months before the Rice debate was scheduled to commence he had excoriated a Methodist circuit rider named William Philips for penning a pamphlet entitled "Campbellism Exposed." In what had to have been one of his most shrill diatribes, rivaling anything he had written in his *Christian Baptist* days and so frantic and furious that he hardly even bothered with correct grammar and punctuation, Campbell proclaimed that a sudden, unforeseen, unspecified tragedy that had befallen Philips and his family after the pamphlet's publication was God's direct judgment on the luckless Methodist for his criticism of the Disciples and his ridicule of "the Gospel in the water."[23] All in all, though, after the Thomas affair Campbell would never again criticize other Protestant groups quite as vociferously as he had in *The Christian Baptist.* Like Barton Stone, he now came to recognize that unity on method was simply no longer as important as just plain Christian unity. This liberal, ecumenical, irenic spirit would be adopted by the modern organization still known as Disciples of Christ, as its heritage from both Campbell and Stone.

When a lady from Lunenburg County, Virginia, who had been influenced either by *The Apostolic Advocate* or by Thomas personally, wrote Campbell in the same year as the Purcell debate to ask him if he genuinely believed that "there are any Christians except those who believe, repent, and are buried by baptism," he sent waves of shock throughout the *Harbinger*'s readership by replying publicly, in no uncertain terms: "There is no occasion for making immersion, on a profession of the faith, absolutely essential to a Christian. He that infers that none are Christians but the immersed, as greatly errs as he who affirms that none are alive but those of clear and full vision. . . . I cannot, therefore, make any one duty the standard of Christian state or character, not even immersion into the name of the Father, the Son, and of the Holy Spirit and in my heart regard all that have been sprinkled in infancy without their own knowledge and consent, as aliens from Christ . . . There is no occasion, then, for making immersion on a profession of faith, absolutely essential to a Christian" (ellipses added).[24] Amazed and furious, his readers inundated him with mail protesting that he had now neutralized all that he had ever taught about baptism, and his critics crowed that he had finally surrendered his one vital point, that immersion was essential to being a Christian. Barton Stone and James Fishback both probably suppressed a chuckle. Though Campbell tried to cope with the onslaught of written criticism by having one of his friends, relatives, or *Harbinger* staff members take the pen name of "Christianos" and write a series of ten essays on the new immersion position, the controversy finally got so hot that he had to stop the "Christianos" series with an ambiguous, unrevealing statement of his own, and with a touch of acerbic wit he concluded that there were, after all, very few true "Campbellites" in the country.[25]

Campbell's response to the famous—or infamous, depending on one's point of view—Lunenburg Letter, as it has been called, probably marks the beginnings of the division of the Disciples more than any other single factor, although no one officially recognized the schism until the next century. Thomas and his most devoted followers left the movement altogether not many years after the Lunenburg Letter, and subsequently took the title of Christadelphians. But in all truth, the whole matter might finally have blown over had Alexander Campbell possessed the power to control his followers' use of the press. In a nation whose very Bill of Rights guaranteed this freedom, however, anyone in this pioneer American mass-media religion with something to say and the capital to publish a periodical to say it could do the very same thing as Campbell, Stone, and now Thomas had done. Even at this early date, additional Reform journals were being published and advertised by men of the movement who considered their own intentions to be every bit as noble as Campbell's and Stone's, and who believed that their papers complemented both the two main periodicals, aided the cause of Christ, and even corrected errors just as Thomas believed about his own work. As a matter of courtesy, older journals usually announced and advertised the founding of newer ones, but most of these new periodicals became defunct after only a few issues. A few, though, the earliest being John R. Howard's *Bible Advocate* and Arthur Crihfield's *Heretic Detector,* endured for some years; of later periodicals, two of the most influential and longstanding were and are *The Gospel Advocate* of Tennessee and *The Firm Foundation* of Texas. Problems inevitably occurred, however, when the various Disciple periodicals disagreed with, and all too often condemned, one another over this or that issue, and disputants within the movement formed parties over one or another editor or editorial position. By and large, many of these journals simply revived and maintained the editorial slant of the old *Chris-*

tian Baptist long after Campbell himself had downplayed it; the Thomas emphasis on reimmersion upon an "intelligent faith," without the remainder of Thomas's distinctive doctrines; and, if Hughes is correct, the additional seasoning of the separatist outlook of the original *Christian Messenger.*[26] Others echoed Campbell's more open-minded later teaching that is the foundation of the outlook of the modern Disciples of Christ, and two of these periodicals, *The Christian Standard* and *The Christian Quarterly,* were printed and distributed by the same Cincinnati, Ohio, publishing company that released Williams's original biography of Raccoon John Smith. Still one more, *The Christian Century,* has evolved from a simple Disciple denominational periodical to one of the most popular religious journals among American Protestants in general.

Campbell ultimately came to complain of the "unlicensed press" as the Disciples' greatest enemy. As he put it, "the most fearful omen on my horizon. We have been most reckless in choosing our editors, our scribes, our elders, and our preachers. We have a brood of periodicals the most irresponsible I have ever known. Editors just out of the shell of conversion, a youth converted this year, the next a preacher, the next a scribe, then an editor!" He tried to call for the official limitation of his movement's media efforts to three journals: a weekly for news and announcements, a monthly for general topics, and a quarterly for book reviews and extended studies.[27] His plea was to no avail, though, and in times to come the editors of the movement's periodicals would assume their own clerical and ecclesiastical powers as opportunity to do so fell their way, so much so that it would come to be said commonly that "the Disciples of Christ do not have bishops, they have editors."[28] Though the Disciples of Christ and Christian Churches/Churches of Christ (Independent) have, over time and each after their own preferred form, developed church conventions and/or other basic organizational structures in order to insure their presentation of a unified witness to the world around them,[29] to this day among the a cappella Churches of Christ these religious newspapers provide essentially the same chain of mutual communication between congregations as a traditionalist "Old Time" Baptist association does for its churches. For all practical purposes their editors serve them—or use them, depending on how one looks at it—in the same capacity and political style as association moderators, though the tenets of this faith tradition solemnly declare that it possesses no organizational structure above and beyond the local church.[30] Though the attitude is slowly but, I think, inevitably changing, many members and ministers of the a cappella Churches of Christ[31] and to perhaps a lesser extent the Christian Churches/Churches of Christ (Independent)[32] still insist as well that their respective organizations are in fact *the* church as opposed to merely one denomination, or set of denominations, among many. Alexander Campbell himself began to refer to his movement as "our denomination" as early as 1842,[33] and most if not all of the modern Disciples of Christ cheerfully admit to, though they strictly refuse to emphasize, their denominational status.

To return to our story, then, in the fall of 1843 Campbell and Stone's Disciples were still a unified group at least technically, the *Harbinger* and the *Messenger* still reigned supreme over them, and all of the divisions we have discussed were many years away from being formally recognized. Even so, Campbell had founded his own college in the Virginia panhandle, Bethany, in 1840 as a rival to Kentucky's Bacon College, which had been founded in 1836, and with trustees not only of his own movement (of these, Buckner Payne was one for a time) but from a wide variety of Protestant persuasions. From the very first, chapel services at Bethany were conducted by "respectable ministers of various denominations."[34] Too, in spite of *The Christian Baptist*'s shrill insistence that any missionary efforts except those carried on by a local congregation "in church capacity" were totally unscriptural, in May of that year the *Harbinger* announced a Disciples state convention in Kentucky that was described by historian Alonzo Willard Fortune as "virtually" a state missionary society though it was not called that.[35] The next year Campbell followed up by declaring in the *Harbinger* that "a book is not sufficient to govern the church," and he now formally advocated the establishment not only of state organizations but a national missionary society for Bible distribution and other evangelistic outreach, of the exact same type for which he had blasted Baptists, Presbyterians, and Methodists so ruthlessly less than twenty years before.[36] He was to achieve this goal in 1849 in spite of a great deal of opposition from periodical readers who still clung to the old *Christian Baptist* editorial slant, now rehashed and rejuvenated in newer journals, and he was in fact the president of his own denomination's national missionary society until only a short while before his death.[37]

Laudable though this enterprise may have been, it's certain at least that 1843 wasn't the best of all years for Campbell to accept a challenge to a debate. If, in his younger days, Campbell himself had attacked his "sectarian" opponents with all the skill and grace of a lightly armed and robed Saracen deftly circling a heavily and clumsily equipped Crusader knight, now the ever-growing number of contradictions in the sum total of his editorial pronouncements had put him in the position not of the Saracen, but rather of the Crusader. This was the exact imagery that biographer Robert Richardson employed in speaking of Campbell in the 1843 debate against Nathan L. Rice,[38] and whether for this reason or not, the Rice debate was, in fact, the very last major public disputation in which Campbell was personally involved.[39] Leroy Garrett adds the wry comment that Rice had the advantage of never having written a book, and thus could not be accused of inconsistency.[40]

But all Crusader knights should be allowed the luxury of a loyal squire or two, and if Campbell was indeed a Crusader knight now baking in the hot sun of public scrutiny, encased tightly within the cumbersome, sweaty armor of supremely confident and arrogant but contradictory positions in which he had placed himself over the years, he still had one faithful vassal always at the ready to do squire's service for him. True to form, this vassal, Raccoon John Smith, had departed Owingsville and Bath County days before for the battlefield at Lexington forty-five or so miles away, eager to stand in his place and give his mentor all the support he could, perhaps already thinking of the witty, barbed retorts that he himself could fire off at the hidebound Calvinistic sectarian Rice—not to mention to his fellow squire James Fishback who, whether he chose to exercise his right of comment or not, was, after fifteen years, now in a supremely advantageous position to remark, *I told you so.*

Though John Smith's loyalty to Alexander Campbell was still unquestioned, we might well wonder about his inward response to all the changes having taken place in the glorious Reformation since he had begun to read *The Christian Baptist* in 1824, and had committed himself to it body and soul in 1828. Walter Scott, whom we have noted already as the pioneer promoter of immersion for the remission of sins in Ohio and the man who accomplished north of the Ohio River essentially what John Smith helped to effect south of it, was outspokenly despondent and gloomy about the prospects of the Disciples by 1840. Whether this was because Campbell's promised Millennial Age had thus far failed to appear or because Campbell had now turned his coat and was accusing Scott of "a tendency for a time . . . to exalt beyond measure the importance of the practical restoration of the design of baptism, and to claim that this was in reality the restoration of the gospel" (ellipsis added),[41] when in fact this was the same position that Campbell had taken so often in *The Christian Baptist* and again with the unfortunate Methodist Philips not long before the Rice debate, we cannot say. But in any case, Scott, who himself had moved from Ohio to Kentucky to become the first president of the Disciples' Bacon College and was succeeded by David Staats Burnet and then by James Shannon, noted in an August 1840 letter to Maria Smith's old teacher Philip Fall (now pastoring a Nashville congregation, the brother-in-law of another soon-to-be Disciple editor named Tolbert Fanning, and who appears likewise to have been disconsolate over his dashed hopes for the great cause) that "When you express your doubts of the matters connected with the recent Reformation, I sympathize with you, for the thing has not been what I hoped it would be by a thousand miles. We are indeed 'a sect' differing but little, of anything that is good, from the parties around us. Alas! My soul is grieved every day."[42]

Writing a decade later, after the Disciples' American Christian Missionary Society had become a reality, the doughty Jacob Creath Jr. expressed his disappointment directly to Campbell with a little more indignation: "If you were right in *The Christian Baptist,* you are wrong now. If you are right now, you were wrong then."[43] But in reflecting on Campbell's change many years later, he was disinclined, as Campbell's apologists and defenders in all parties were and often still are, to attach any direct blame for this state of affairs to the great Reformer himself. Though Creath admitted that he could not confirm his story, he had apparently heard somewhere that the change had occurred when "a certain man went to the rich oil men of Pennsylvania, and obtained large subscriptions of money for Bethany College, and by that means obtained influence over the *Harbinger* and Bethany College." The true story about the involvement of "rich oil men" in a Disciple enterprise involved not Campbell or the *Harbinger* either one directly, but rather the 1865 establishment and financial backing of *The Christian Standard* newspaper as a denominational mouthpiece. But this didn't dampen Creath's characteristically American fondness for conspiracy theories. This shadowy malevolent bagman for the oil interests, he contended, accounted "in part for the change that took place in *The Christian Baptist* and the first and best days of the *Harbinger* and its last days." In his eyes, Campbell himself was still wholly free from blame.[44]

We could cite other examples here of the disappointments and perplexities expressed by Campbell's earliest Kentucky followers concerning his change of heart, but for now our point is simply to demonstrate that the topic was one with which Raccoon John must have been familiar, regardless of his own take on the situation. Since Scott and most especially Fall and Creath were well acquainted with Raccoon John as a fellow pioneer Reformer, we can safely assume that any of these men's written and spoken conversations with Smith near this time must have involved deep discussions of this very subject. Everett Donaldson hypothesizes that Raccoon John was opposed to Campbell's American Christian Missionary Society by association, as it were: he did his strongest, most successful evangelistic work preaching the system advocated in *The Christian Baptist,* he was in fact the very first of Campbell's Kentucky followers to preach Reform wholeheartedly, and as such, he therefore must have been "likely among those who, by the close of the decade of the 1850s, had reservations about the direction of the American Christian Missionary Society."[45]

But Donaldson, writing as an apologist for the a cappella Churches of Christ, may be a bit overly eager to present Smith as an advocate of his church's own position. The fact is that we cannot find one single statement that Raccoon John ever made in condemnation of either Campbell's doctrinal shift or his missionary society, and moreover, the weight of evidence indicates that Raccoon John supported Campbell wholeheartedly from first to last, regardless of any of his mentor's own changes. We would perhaps do well to remember once more how fond, even to the point of obsession, that Smith always could become personally with any intellectual who impressed him, and this tendency in and of itself easily could have blinded him to the glaring contradictions and inconsistencies in Campbell's thought and pronouncements that were already obvious to Jacob Creath Jr., Walter Scott, and a host of others. If this did happen to be the case, Raccoon John certainly wouldn't have been the only fire-eating Kentucky Reformer of 1828 and 1829 who settled down easily ten to fifteen years later to accept a respectable role in, as Campbell himself put it, "our denomination," and tried to claim with a straight face and all earnestness that there existed no contradictions whatsoever between *The Christian Baptist* of the 1820s and *The Millennial Harbinger* of the 1840s. His affections for Campbell, no matter how much the man changed his own attitudes, were still such that he once told a younger preaching colleague that he had spoken before all the great preachers of Kentucky, Vardeman, Creath, and others, and that they were no more in his way than so many grasshoppers; but the first time he ever preached before "Aleck" Campbell, he *did* falter—a little.[46]

At any rate, it's certain that Raccoon John attended that first Kentucky Disciples state convention in May 1840. It was held in the Mercer County courthouse in Harrodsburg, and continued for ten days. Messengers from 133 churches in 47 Kentucky counties attended, and it was estimated that these congregations represented about a third of the Disciples in Kentucky. William B. Blackburn of Versailles was chosen as president of the meeting, Philip T. Allen as secretary; John T. Johnson made the opening prayer, and Raccoon John was appointed along with Johnson, B. F. Duvall, Morgan Larue, Samuel Hodgen, Walter Scott, and the venerable Barton Stone as a committee "to receive any communications or propositions for the action of the meeting."[47] In other words, after a decade of independence from the Baptists, Raccoon John once again found himself as a member, and perhaps even the leader, of a Committee on the Bill of Arrangements. But successful though the meeting undoubtedly was, the Disciple movement both in Kentucky and in the nation as a whole was still very much a mass-media religion. It so happened that Walter Scott was running a journal at the time known simply as *The Evangelist,* and as Williams tells us, the state convention certainly wasn't the only thing Raccoon John had on his mind:

> The first of those great gatherings of the churches called *State meetings,* took place in Harrodsburg, Mercer County, at that time the seat of Bacon College; and Smith, though much pressed by business at home, set out for that place.
>
> Some of the brethren were again contending that the name Christian had been imposed by Divine authority—that it was the new name of which the prophet speaks [Revelation 2:17], and that the followers of Christ should always be called by it. Others still believed that it was given by enemies, or assumed by the early disciples themselves; and while they did not object to wearing it, they thought that the name Disciples, or Saints, or Holy Brethren, was just as proper, and that, in fact, these names might be used indiscriminately. Some, in their zeal for the name Christian, had gone so far as to confer it, formally and publicly, with some ceremony, on young converts after their baptism. The controversy on the subject had ceased to be profitable, and, in the opinion of many good brethren, it was doing harm, and ought to be dropped.
>
> When Smith reached Georgetown, on his way to Harrodsburg, he found that [John T.] Johnson himself had prepared an essay on the subject of the Name, which he was about to send to the papers for publication, and he now read it to Smith.

"If Brother Campbell loves you one half as much as I think he does," said Smith, on hearing it, "he will certainly not do you the injury to print it."

"Brother Scott, I know, will print it," said Johnson.

"Yes," said Smith, "Walter, too, is half crazy about this matter of the name, and he will print it; but you ought not to send it to him. Brother Campbell has dropped the controversy himself, and I think you *all* ought to quit. Rest assured, you never will, by all your writing, induce anyone who understands the Book, to adopt one of these names to the exclusion of the others; for we know that, after the name *Christian* was given at Antioch, the sacred writers, speaking of the brethren, still call them disciples; and no matter who gave the other name, they were willing to wear it and to suffer under it."

At Harrodsburg, he found Walter Scott, and he soon expressed a desire to have an interview with him and Johnson . . . [both men as well as several others] gave their attention. [Smith opened the discussion by saying,] "I never did pretend, brethren, to rank myself with great men, but my age and experience, I hope, will give me the privilege of expressing my opinion for the advantage of brethren younger than myself. The controversy about our name is likely to get up a party feeling among the brethren, and therefore it ought to be dropped. Brother Campbell has quit writing about it, and I think you should all do the same."

"Why, Brother Smith," said Scott, with some enthusiasm, "I have an article on hand, which I will publish next month, proving conclusively that God never acknowledges his people, or their works, until they receive their right name."

"If you prove *that,*" replied Smith, "you will kill a thing as dearly as I love my own life."

"What is that, Brother John?"

"The name *Christian,*" replied Smith.

"How will we do that?"

"You learned men have been teaching us that it was some ten or eleven years from Pentecost till the meeting at Antioch. Now, will you indeed prove that God never owned the disciples of Jesus, nor the ten years' preaching of the apostles, nor the thousands of converts they had made, till the time of that meeting? This, surely, you will not attempt to do. But if God cannot acknowledge his children until they have the right name, as you say—and if, however, he *did* acknowledge the apostles and their works before the Antioch meeting—then the name *Disciple,* by which they had previously been called, is the right one, and that of *Christian* is gone forever!"

"But, Brother John," replied Scott, "only one half of the Christian body was formed within that period. The Church was then composed of Jewish Christians, but when the other half was added from the Gentile world, the whole received its right name."

"Now, just think of it, brethren!" Smith rejoined. "The Church of Christ, during all that time, with its thousands of members, and the apostles at their head, was not a body, but a one-legged, one-breasted, one-armed, one-eyed, nameless thing, waiting for its fellow-half to get a name!"

"Really, that won't do, Brother John," said Scott.

"No, Walter; and if you had not been *hypoed* [early nineteenth century slang for hypochondria, then a catch-all word for mental disorders] in some way, you would have seen that it would not do."

"But, Brother Smith," asked Scott, "don't you and your wife give your children names?"

"Walter," replied Smith, "you and other great men have been writing much about the patronymic, or family, name. Now, Nancy and I were so ignorant that we thought our children were all *born* Smiths—that they were entitled to this patronymic name by virtue of their birth. True, we gave them proper names in order to distinguish them from one another; but we never had any idea than that they were all *Smiths* when born. Did you ever quarrel about whether your children should receive, by inheritance, your own family name?"

Scott was silent; the general laugh that followed relieved him from any reply, and Smith let fly another shaft.

"Walter," continued he, "you recently wrote a piece inviting the brethren to send you their written views as to the time when it was proper to confer the name *Christian.* Now, I do wish that some schoolgirl had been at your elbow when you thus wrote, and told you that it was when one was baptized into Christ, and thus put him on—being born into the Kingdom and the Name, when born of water and the spirit; and that you had no more right or authority to confer it by a subsequent ceremony than you had to celebrate the Romish mass.

"Suppose," Smith still persisted, without mercy, "that I had been called on to celebrate the rites of matrimony between you and your sister wife, and that I had duly married you, and pronounced you man and wife; that, in a few days afterward, I had returned, and, calling your friends together, summoned you to the parlor, and informed our sister that I had come to confer on her her new name—that it was now proper that she should take upon herself your name; would she not, with much surprise, have informed me that she had already acquired that name by virtue of the law that had made her your wife, and that she would continue to wear it, too, as long as she lived, without the aid of any of my pow-wowing?" [All emphases in original; ellipses added.][48]

As it turned out, neither Scott nor Johnson ever printed their proposed articles about the Christian name, and this was evidently the result for which Raccoon John was angling. But we have recounted this much of the singular exchange between Smith, Johnson, and Scott at this historic first statewide convention of Kentucky Disciples to demonstrate the difference between Raccoon John's perceptions of his and the great cause's enemies in 1828 and those of twelve to fifteen years later. Needless to say, Raccoon John still debated with and cracked jokes at Baptists, Methodists, Presbyterians, and others whenever the occasion called for it, but if the Smith-Scott exchange is any reliable indicator he now appears to have been much more concerned with those leading members of the Disciple movement who neglected to show a proper respect for the opinions and the wishes of Alexander Campbell himself.

The fact that Raccoon John was such a complete and vociferous Campbell partisan very well may have been the reason that Campbell chose him along with James Fishback, James Shannon, and Aylette Raines, and not Walter Scott, Jacob Creath Sr. or Jr., John T. Johnson, John Rogers, B. F. Hall, or any number of his other eloquent Kentucky supporters, to stand in the gap for him at Lexington in November 1843. If Campbell felt that he was being pecked to death by his own followers for altering his positions, he would have wanted assistance in the Rice debate from men whom he could depend upon utterly for unequivocal support. We have already noted James Fishback's beliefs, which he had never changed in spite of considerable persecution from within the Reform/Disciple movement itself, but which now, finally, happened to be completely in line with the mindset Campbell was trying to foster. Though Raines, himself the editor of a little periodical entitled *The Christian Teacher,* was a bitter opponent of state meetings such as the 1840 Harrodsburg gathering and the complexity of organization which was developing around such assemblies,[49] he also owed his status in the ministry and in the Disciple movement to the direct patronage of both Alexander and Thomas Campbell. Like Scott, Raines had belonged to the Mahoning Association in Ohio before coming to Kentucky in the wake of the Stone-Campbell union; unlike him, Raines had been a member of a Universalist church who, after joining Mahoning, still retained his belief that all humankind will eventually be restored to the fellowship of God. In 1828 the association had threatened to expel Raines, and Thomas Campbell had intervened personally with its leaders, arguing that Raines's private sentiments could not be made a test of fellowship so long as he did not attempt to impose them upon others.[50] Thus, in spite of Raines's present opposition to statewide organization, he was a longtime Campbell acquaintance, and Alexander still probably assessed him as being properly grateful.

And then there was Raccoon John, who, in spite of the fact that he had preached vociferous *Christian Baptist* doctrine with the best of the Reformers for years, had done such an exemplary job in setting Walter Scott and John T. Johnson back on their heels in 1840 when they had threatened to open an editorial can of worms that Campbell very much wanted to keep closed. As a result of his exchange with Smith, the chastened Scott did publish a brief description of Raccoon John's speaking and argumentative styles in his own periodical not long afterward, and in both scope and detail it is worthy of our consideration:

> Quality of voice—guttural, dry, and husky; articulation—measured, slow, perfect; enunciation—full; emphasis—natural and striking; pause—irregular; tone—drawling; action—nervous, indicating *Down with the enemy!*; language—always sifting out the sense; logic—sure, sharp, killing; rhetoric—borrowed from all sources: in nature, from the sun down to the spark of a firefly; in society, from the king to the beggar; in art, from the sublimest to the meanest of human fabrications; and in religion, every thing; eloquence—sparkling, shrewd, and bordering sometimes on the indescribable. But let a man take care how he resigns himself to Smith's wit. It is used as some dangerous animals use their feelers—simply to ascertain where the prey lies: when that is done, the wit is ended, and then woe betide the man that smiled; *he must die the death.* [All spelling, punctuation, and emphases in original.][51]

What makes Scott's analysis of Raccoon John's modus operandi all the more wryly amusing is the fact that he himself, like James Fishback in 1828, had "died the death" at Raccoon John's hands. But if the old saying that actions speak louder than words be true, Scott was perhaps more perceptive than even he himself realized in his characterization of Raccoon John's "nervous, down with the enemy" mannerisms. If an individual has latched passionately onto a system of thought or belief because he or she perceives that the said system might be the only possible means of making sense out of life and its manifold tragedies, and if that system is subsequently revealed not only to be slightly less than perfect but endued with a complete set of unforeseen and distinctively, completely human characteristics all on its own, such knowledge is not likely to promote peace of mind to any great degree. At one time, Raccoon John had perceived and dealt with all whom Alexander Campbell saw fit to label as "sectarians" as his enemies. With his 1840 Harrodsburg performance he apparently bestowed the title of enemy, at least in a qualified sense, on no less a personage than Walter Scott, who had pioneered the preaching of immersion for the remission of sins in Ohio and who had served as Bacon College's first president—but also whom Campbell now sometimes accused of giving the issue of immersion altogether too much emphasis, who could be dissuaded only by Raccoon John's roughest use of cruel wit from writing about a subject that Campbell wanted dropped, and who now openly and gloomily observed that the Disciple movement had not lived up to his anticipations of it "by a thousand miles." As much as Raccoon John had invested in the movement, not only psychologically, emotionally, and spiritually, but physically as well, his observations of current affairs across the Disciple brotherhood would have given him every right to feel threatened. In this decade early Disciple editor John R. Howard of *The Bible Advocate* would be the first to use a line of reasoning still popular with some a cappella Church of Christ conservatives today and claim that the Stone-Campbell movement was not merely *a* church but *the* true church on earth because it bore all the "marks" of *the* true church.[52] Whether Raccoon John was ever able to admit it to himself or not, he was now seeing much unsettling evidence that, however Howard or anyone else defined the "marks" of the true church, Scott's gloomy comment to Philip Fall itself may have been too close to the mark for comfort—the entity to which he had dedicated his life in 1828 as being the "true" church was by now also showing every man-made mark of a plain old sect or denomination.

Raccoon John's experience thus was a repetition indeed, but not an experience he had either wanted or expected to repeat.

Even so, things might have been more bearable for John if he only could have enjoyed some peace of mind in terms of his local Montgomery and Bath County labors. Unfortunately, though, at least in Raccoon John's case, Disciple politics on the local level could be even more tense and baffling than those of the regional and national sort. It's really a shame that Smith's most recent biographer, Donaldson, mentions the name of James Mason's brother John only in the context of modern Church of Christ versus Disciple and evangelical apologetics, and James McVay merely incidentally, if it could be called even that. It is perhaps more of a tragedy for history that John Augustus Williams elected to say nothing of John Mason after his 1828 conversion, or of James McVay in any way whatsoever. But these two men commandeered an enormous chunk of Raccoon John's attention during this period and took away much of his inner peace. All his powers of wit and persuasion, which he had claimed faltered only in the presence of "Aleck" Campbell himself and which had been so decisive against the intellectual pretensions of both John T. Johnson and Walter Scott, seemed to be completely ineffective against both them and their followers.

In truth, Raccoon John had never enjoyed anything close to an idyll in his home field of labor since he had helped forge the Stone-Campbell union. For all the fact that Peter Hon had been allowed to preach at the final North District majority-faction association meeting in 1831, Smith had nonetheless been beset immediately after his return home from the historic 1832 Lexington unity meeting by the elders of the congregations he still pastored for "affiliating with the New Light party." Still knowing little or nothing about the Stoneites and their doctrines, Smith's Montgomery and Bath County followers really believed that their father in the Gospel and the Reformation had committed a grave blunder. One gets the impression that Raccoon John's vociferous young Disciples treated him almost as roughly at this point as he had accused David Chenault and James French of doing some years earlier, and furthermore, that the Payne family may have been behind at least some of the open expressions of dissatisfaction. Though, as we shall see, even Alexander Campbell himself considered the word of the Payne clan to be crucial to his own assessment of Montgomery and Bath County Disciple politics as late as 1842, the family may have felt that Raccoon John had shorn it of its influence and political power by disbanding his, and its, faction of North District Association in 1831. In any case, Smith received some of his most blunt criticism from Buckner and John Newton Payne's sister and Josephus Hewitt's sister-in-law Dulcinea Ryan, who flatly and sorrowfully told him that it pained her to hear that he had united with the "Arians." She could pray, she sighed, with all her heart, for union with such as really honored the Savior, but that she herself loved the truth too well to worship with a people "that denied the Lord who bought them." In her eyes, Raccoon John had injured, if not ruined, the cause, and had wounded beyond expression the brethren that so much loved him. It took a great deal of patient coaxing on Raccoon John's part to change her mind. We might wonder if both Buckner and John Newton Payne shared her sentiments, since, according to Williams, "it required all the weight of his influence, and all the power of the truth" to dissuade his Montgomery and Bath County followers from the notion that he had betrayed both them and the Campbell cause entirely.[53]

In spite of the brouhaha, though, both Raccoon John and the statewide union he had helped to forge survived, and in and of itself this unpleasantness proved to be only a minor interruption to his personal crusade. Over the next four years or so his time was occupied not only with his family's move to Owingsville, but also with evangelistic trips across Kentucky, financed by the cooperative efforts of congregations in the state and taken in company with John Rogers and John T. Johnson. It's probable that, during this period, he entrusted the greater portion of his home pastoral duties to Buckner and John Newton Payne, although he still must have involved himself in the affairs of his congregations as much as he was able.

In *The Legacy of Raccoon John Smith,* Donaldson goes into some detail about Raccoon John's methods of conducting church business. He always called the churches under his care "to order" on one Saturday a month in accordance with their previous Baptist "meeting weekends," and saw to all matters of church discipline at that time. Interestingly, this seems to have been one aspect of Smith's Baptist heritage that he considered to be worth keeping, as Donaldson's description of Raccoon John's technique jibes exactly with the most common format for church business meetings still in use among eastern Kentucky's United Baptists and other Appalachian "Old Time" groups.[54] But whether having gotten its start in Raccoon John's presence or his absence, the trouble with John Mason thus seems to have begun at one of these very business meetings, held at Mt. Sterling. We have noted that the Mt. Sterling congregation purchased some property from Mason not long after he was immersed and joined the church, for the purpose of building a new and larger meetinghouse. According to Donaldson, this tract was located on the present West

Locust Street directly in the town, something of an unusual circumstance at the time since, in those days, church meetinghouses were generally located outside city limits. But in any case, Mason later made the claim that he had been bullied somewhat by the committee of church brethren who had been appointed by the congregation to purchase a site for the building, and that he had consequently not held out for, nor received, a fair price for the tract of land. Somehow this contention turned into a festering sore in Mason's mind, and he seems never to have given the church a minute's peace about it afterward. He refused to give the congregation clear title to the property until it paid him what he declared that the church owed him. Though it seems that Mason maintained residence off and on in Morgan County, his wife's home, as well as Montgomery, internal strife over the question continued within the church for no less than two decades, sometimes with Mason as a member of the church and at other times with him and his followers excommunicated for varying periods. The whole sad affair was documented by bitter litigation.

Donaldson speculates that John Mason became obstinate about the payment for the property because "he was not happy with the direction the church was going in abandoning the Baptist traditional position."[55] However, considering that his own brother James described John in 1828 as "a believer in the Lord Jesus Christ for more than twenty-six years" who had been denied church fellowship because "he could not tell what we have always been in the habit of calling a Christian experience" but who had learned from John Smith that "to believe the Lord Jesus Christ, and to obey his commands, was all that the Gospel required" and had then gone "down into the water and told Brother Smith he wished him to say immerse, instead of baptize,"[56] it's hardly credible that John Mason was any sort of traditionalist Baptist, anxious to espouse the positions of David Chenault and James French. It is more reasonable to speculate that John Mason began to be disenchanted with Raccoon John at the same time that his brother James had: either the summer of 1828 when Smith had given James Fishback such a thorough excoriation throughout North District, or the spring and summer of 1829 when Grassy Lick Church had split over the old church covenant and Raccoon John had transferred his membership to Mt. Sterling, where he and his followers engineered a second messenger election that year to include him as a delegate to North District's 1829 meeting. This was the series of events that had caused James Mason to complain first to Raccoon John, and then to Alexander Campbell himself, about the contentious, obstinate, warlike spirit that was marring the Christian witness of Baptist traditionalists and Reformers alike. In fact, since James's 1830 letter to Alexander Campbell is the last time that his own name appears in print in connection with Raccoon John's, we cannot be sure whether James Mason ultimately remained at Grassy Lick with the Baptists until that congregation finally dissolved, transferred his membership to Sommerset or another local Disciple fellowship and maintained his church connection there, joined another denomination, or simply let his disappointment with Raccoon John get the best of him and dropped churchgoing altogether.

But whatever the cause of John Mason's grudge, there was only one way that conditions at Mt. Sterling Church could progress during its active course: from bad to worse. It didn't even really matter whether Mason had a legitimate gripe or not, because the way he conducted his portion of the affair guaranteed that he would remain unhappy regardless of the outcome. Neither the relative strength of John Mason's Disciple sentiments, his former friendship with Raccoon John, nor even his conceptions of Christian brotherhood and of the peace of God that passeth all understanding were in fact germane to his conduct. Grudge-related affairs of this same type are common in any evangelical denomination with either partial or total congregational rule, be it Baptist, Disciple, or any other, among people who solemnly swear, in the words of the First Epistle of John, that they know that they have passed from death unto life because they love the brethren. Although most similar dirty little congregational wars never advance to the extreme that this particular case reached, the evangelical pastor who has never had to contend with at least one such circumstance is indeed fortunate. Years later, after congregational splits, reconciliations, and ultimatums laid down by Mason in efforts to ban Raccoon John from preaching in the Mt. Sterling meetinghouse altogether, the flock finally simply sought another place of worship and left John Mason with an empty building all to himself.[57] Both John and James Mason died in the year 1855,[58] and we might wonder if Raccoon John ever managed a personal reconciliation with either man. We will probably never know. Still, in 1835 when Raccoon John moved his family to Owingsville, Mt. Sterling Church had nonetheless been unwilling to let him transfer his eldership to another church closer to his new home. We can thus say with a fair degree of certainty that at that point in time his members were still united at least around his personal leadership, even if they were not entirely in perfect union and harmony with one another.

The U.S. congressional and presidential elections of 1836 changed all that, and further complicated the issues. Kenaz Farrow, the Mt. Sterling attorney and son-in-law of James French, had been immersed by Raccoon John and had joined the church at the same time as John Mason, and it so happened that in this year Farrow's brother-in-law Richard French, a lawyer practicing in Winchester, was up for reelection on the Democratic ticket to Congress. We know nothing of Raccoon John's personal political convictions before this time period, although we have made note of the advantages that Andrew Jackson's campaign had presented to his own image in both his 1815 return to the Kentucky General Union and in the tough, hectic initial year of his Reform crusade. By 1836, however, and for all we know at his young, eloquent friend Richard Menefee's urging, Smith had joined the Whig Party that had been organized in 1834 by Henry Clay from the remnants of the old and now defunct National Republican Party in opposition to Jackson's Democrats.

Raccoon John was outspoken in his support for Menefee's congressional candidacy that year, in spite of the fact that a large portion of his hearers at Mt. Sterling and perhaps other churches as well were backing Richard French, not because he was the son of old James French, who had died in 1835, but rather for the sake of his brother-in-law and sister Kenaz and Susanna Farrow and the Democrats. And if this Democrat versus Whig congressional contest did not make for a volatile enough mix for the Montgomery and Bath County Disciples all on its own, it probably didn't help any that John T. Johnson's brother Richard was running for vice president with Martin Van Buren on the Democratic ticket while the Whigs tried to make all the campaign hay they could from Johnson's sexual indiscretions. Raccoon John's unyielding support for Richard Menefee and the Whigs, added to the already-extant John Mason controversy within Mt. Sterling Church, was the perfect recipe for disaster, and in the eyes of many Disciples the resultant escalation of the Mt. Sterling congregational war would have been seen as a complete validation of Barton Stone's and *The Christian Messenger*'s editorial position of politics and voting as being inherently evil. Although hindsight is always clearer than foresight, Raccoon John really should have perceived this potential for trouble and avoided it completely.

In that day, most states held local and congressional elections in mid to late summer and waited, then as now, until early November to open the polls for other national contests. And so sometime probably around the first week of August 1836, Raccoon John stepped over drunks and through crowds of stump orators and "good ol' boys" buying votes to the polls at Owingsville to call out his ballot (voting was done orally and publicly back then, with election officers recording each vote) for Richard H. Menefee. Though that fall Martin Van Buren and Richard M. Johnson held onto the White House for the Democrats for another four years, the summer saw Menefee triumph over Richard French in the congressional race. Then, that October Raccoon John proudly and fondly named his newborn son, the last of his fifteen children by two wives, Richard Menefee Smith. The arrival of their leader's baby boy did nothing to soften Kenaz and Susanna Farrow's feelings of hurt, betrayal, and anger, however, and as Donaldson quotes their son-in-law and fellow Mt. Sterling Church member Belvard January Peters, they would not let the matter go until they had added it to the Mason controversy and let it split up the congregation completely.[59] We can't say with any certainty exactly how Buckner and Eliza Payne and the rest of their clan both at Mt. Sterling and Sharpsburg responded to the situation or what side they took in the division. Donaldson hints that at times during the fracas, the sole consistent support Raccoon John got at Mt. Sterling came from Buckner Payne,[60] although from testimony that Alexander Campbell himself took subsequently from Dulcinea Ryan it would seem that she, her brothers, and the rest of the Payne family reasonably blamed Farrow and Smith in equal measure for the disagreement's escalation.[61] Whatever Buckner Payne's degree of actual support for Raccoon John may have been during this period, he pulled up stakes and left Mt. Sterling a few years afterward, first for Louisiana and then Tennessee, and while in Nashville in the mercantile business he drew on his experiences as North District clerk and Reform propagandist with Raccoon John to establish himself as a writer in the logical and argumentative tradition initiated and inspired by Alexander Campbell. At the risk of sounding crass, for the present we had perhaps better remark simply that the culmination of Buckner Payne's religious career was to hatch one last egg that Campbell had laid. But in any case, we must note here one final conceivable reason for Raccoon John's extremely negative characterization of James French to John Augustus Williams: though even the aging crusader himself may not have been conscious that he was doing so, we cannot rule out the possibility that he vilified French at least in part as a bitter retaliation to the hostility he had endured at the hands of Kenaz and Susanna Farrow and their family.

To return to the escalating controversy in Bath and Montgomery counties, then, Raccoon John, at age fifty-two and having worked tirelessly and selflessly for the Campbell cause for almost a decade, now found himself caught in an extremely humiliating paradox: he'd once dealt with Jilson Payne and James French at Lulbegrud in the matter of the log that split the church, and now the Mt. Sterling heirs of both men seemingly thought of him as the *Whig* that split the church. Even so, as Jeremiah Vardeman had once learned at Lulbegrud, divisions cannot be maintained without some form of leadership on both sides, and for at least two or three years Farrow's faction at Mt. Sterling seems to have had none—that is, unless the church itself had ordained Farrow and John Mason as elders beforehand, and they or another elder siding with them provided Gospel instruction to their partisans during that time. In such a case, though, Raccoon John's longstanding popularity and reputation with the Kentucky Disciples virtually guaranteed that the editors of the major journals (as we have seen, by this time unquestionably the primary Disciple political power brokers) would still recognize him as legitimate. Let Farrow, Mason, and their adherents harp as much as they liked even in letters to the *Harbinger,* the *Messenger,* Scott's *Evangelist,* Raines's *Christian Teacher,* Crihfield's *Heretic Detector,* or any other Disciple periodical; the editorial support that Raccoon John could confidently expect from all these men would still give him and his party all the staying power they needed to survive and press their claim as the "true" Mt. Sterling Church. Under such conditions, it should only be a matter of waiting the other side out.

Thus did Raccoon John occupy his time as Jonathan and John Duke Smith came to maturity and left home, and as Maria was courted and married by James Andrew Jackson Lee; and in May 1840, when he traveled to Harrodsburg to attend the first state convention of Kentucky Disciples and to counsel Brothers Johnson and Scott to quit publishing essays on subjects that Brother Campbell didn't like, this was the situation in which he left his home flock. It would remain neither stable nor with the odds on Raccoon John's side for very much longer, however. That summer a minor but longtime Stoneite evangelist of somewhat dubious reputation, James McVay, moved from Hendricks County, Indiana, to initiate a ministry in the general area of Raccoon John's pastorates. We cannot say exactly what prompted McVay's move to Kentucky. He was born and raised in the state, and he is known to have had a nephew living somewhere between Carlisle in Nicholas County and Sharpsburg in Bath. From subsequent evidence, it appears that he was involved not only with Montgomery and Bath County congregations but with the churches at North Middletown and Cane Ridge in Bourbon County, both historic former Stoneite fellowships of long standing, and he seems to have brought his church membership to North Middletown. But McVay's status as a Stoneite preacher since perhaps 1822 or 1823,[62] who had published reports of his evangelistic tours fairly regularly for several years in *The Christian Messenger*[63] and who had embraced Campbell principles only about 1833, possibly indicating a traditional Stoneite opposition on his part to Christians becoming entangled in secular politics, might suggest that Kenaz Farrow, John Mason, or some other prominent Disciple or Disciples disgruntled with Raccoon John's leadership had arranged and contracted with McVay to come and serve the Mt. Sterling–Owingsville area as an opposition religious leader against Smith. We cannot know for sure. Would Farrow and/or Mason have been hypocritical to act in this fashion, first steeping themselves up to their own chins in secular politics and then hiring a Stoneite opportunist to serve as their mercenary against Raccoon John? Of course, but as a myriad of examples already noted in this volume aptly show, such considerations all too seldom figure into evangelical thought in the first place. The Lord is always on one's own side, Satan inevitably rules the other, and one must battle Satan with any and all means at one's disposal. In any case, to make an effective campaign against Raccoon John's leadership Farrow and Mason needed a qualified, competent, and persuasive preacher on their own side, and whether by pure chance or deliberate arrangement and within six to eight months of McVay's arrival in the area, that's exactly what they got.

It took roughly two years' worth of indignant letters and guarded editorials in the *Harbinger* for the entire story of the Smith-McVay war to become public. Even so, unlike Scott, Johnson, and many others of his pioneer Reform contemporaries, Raccoon John was never a prolific writer, and he seems to have hesitated at first to vilify McVay in the press. However, McVay published a report in *The Christian Messenger* that he had baptized about one hundred persons in northeastern Kentucky between July 1840 and February 1841,[64] and this is an apt indication that he was getting himself established altogether too firmly for Raccoon John to remain comfortable with his presence. In late March and early April 1841 Alexander Campbell paid a brief visit to Kentucky, and Smith used the occasion to complain to Campbell personally about McVay. Campbell commiserated with Smith, recounting some questionable stories he had heard about McVay some years previously when McVay had lived and preached in Maryland and promising Raccoon John that he would cite McVay's misdeeds in the May 1841 issue of the *Harbinger.* He never fulfilled his promise, however, evidently being fearful that his readers would mistake Raccoon John's enemy James McVay for one James T. McVay, an honest minister in Pennsylvania with whom Campbell was on good terms. Exasperated with Campbell in spite of his near-worship of the man, Raccoon John traveled to Indiana that summer on a fact-finding mission against McVay but also managed a bit of incidental evangelizing as well.[65] Finally in September he took matters in hand himself with this letter to the *Harbinger,* in which he bearded Campbell only slightly but let McVay have it with all that he could throw at the man except the real reason he was at variance with him. The epistle in fact exhibits so many curiosities that it will be quoted in its entirety. All emphases are in the original:

> Owingsville, Ky., September 15, 1841
>
> My dear brother Campbell,
> The extracts of letters herewith sent you, will give you an idea of the character of James McVay for 16 or 18 years past. What is added in this letter you may add to the foregoing extracts, and hold me responsible for it. But before I proceed, permit me to say when I saw you in Lexington about the first of April last, you told me of some dishonorable things which you had heard of James McVay in Baltimore some few years past; and I told you of some of his conduct in the part of the country where I live; and if I am not *greatly* mistaken, you then said that you intended to notice said McVay in the May issue of the *Harbinger.* Brother Campbell, am I mistaken in this matter? The cause of my naming this matter at present is this: there was great confusion among some of the brethren here, growing out of what Brother Moss had said to McVay; and hoping it would settle their minds, I told them what you had said at Lexington. Nothing appearing in the *Harbinger,* two or three enemies have (as I have heard) been trying to use it to my prejudice. A word from you on this subject would be gratifying to many, especially to myself.
>
> When James McVay came to this part of the country in the summer of 1840, he told many brethren that the mare he rode had the disease called *the big head.* He borrowed a horse of Brother John Clark to ride about through the country, etc., and at the same time he had put his mare into the hands of his nephew (living between Sharpsburg and Carlisle) to prepare her for the Virginia market, take her there, and sell her for him. His nephew accordingly fattened her, took her to Virginia, and sold her for him; and the brethren and friends bought him another horse. You may call this swindling connected with lying, or call it by what name you please. He was guilty of lying in more than half a dozen other cases, of such a nature that the false-

hoods must have been willful. This I can abundantly prove, and for it you may hold me responsible.

I will here give you a description of James McVay. He was raised in Kentucky. When he first professed religion he united with the people who called themselves Christians (nicknamed New Lights). He soon commenced preaching and left this country; has spent much of his time in the states of Pennsylvania, Maryland, Ohio, and is now living in Hendrix [*sic*] County, Indiana. Perhaps seven or eight years ago he fell into the Current Reformation, but no reformation from his wicked conduct. From all that I can learn of him from 1823 to the present time, he has been the greatest curse to the cause of religion than any man I ever knew. He is about from 42 to 45 years old; about 5 feet from 6 to 8 inches high; well built; dark hair, I think; dark colored eyes; light beard; fair skin; forehead runs high up on each side; but he has two other marks by which he may be known to a certainty. One is a scar on the end of his nose, it having been badly bit [*sic*] in a fight. The other is his *uncommonly sanctified* manner and appearance. Brother L. J. Jameson of Indiana gives a perfect description of this mark in his letter to me, in these words: "I know him [McVay] to be the most complete personification of hypocritical affected sanctimoniousness that I ever saw." His wife has nearly lost her eyesight. He has but one child (a daughter) living with him; and that is not his wife's, but is said to be his own illegitimate offspring. I ought to have said above that he has several letters of recommendation that he carries with him, some of which, at least (you will see from the extracts), were fraudulently obtained.

Now, Brother Campbell, you can publish as much as you think proper of this letter—the extracts I herewith send you—with any additional information which you may have received from other sources. And it is my request that Brethren Stone, Scott, Crihfield, and all the Editors [*sic*] of religious periodicals in these United States, in Canada, and in Texas, may give the same an insertion in their several periodicals. A few pages devoted to this long neglected subject would do more for the cause of Christ than any other matter with which the same number of pages could be filled. It ought to be attended to without delay. This is the decided opinion of your brother indeed,

John Smith[66]

As Campbell himself noted subsequently in relation to the case, in the absence of a complete denominational structure, there was no way of preventing "public imposition" of alleged troublemakers except by "special notices" such as Raccoon John had given to the newspapers. The *Harbinger*'s stated editorial policy was that "in cases of private injury or trespass among brethren, in all questions of morality amongst professors, no man, editor, printer, preacher, or citizen, has any right to publish in word, writing, or in print, any such charges until the church has decided the case"; but "In cases of heresy and unbecoming conduct in public functionaries, when a church, or the eldership of a congregation, or a committee of churches have pronounced their caveat, it is not only proper, but requisite and necessary that such announcements be made for the protection of our brethren and the defense of truth and righteousness."[67] Actually, thus far McVay hadn't been brought to formal trial in a church or anywhere else, but the fact remained that, since the old *Christian Baptist* had so firmly convinced its readers that denominational structures such as associations and extrachurch ministerial committees were unscriptural and therefore wrong, the only organ within the movement with the power to cite churches for their support of an errant minister was the press itself. Campbell affirmed that "the half is not yet told" concerning McVay's misdeeds and apologized to Raccoon John, excusing himself on the grounds of not wishing to make trouble with a possible mixup of Smith's enemy with his good friend James T. McVay.[68] In addition, he sent Raccoon John's letter on to Barton Stone and the editors of the other major journals, and a few months later he even quoted a letter from one of the Indiana contacts Raccoon John had established that summer that proposed to confirm McVay's questionable reputation in that state.[69]

So far, so good, at least as far as Raccoon John's case was concerned. By the spring of 1842 majorities at both Sharpsburg and North Middletown were ready to put McVay on trial, although according to documents published subsequently in the *Harbinger*, Raccoon John's September 1841 letter earned him considerable complaint from McVay's supporters as well.[70] But here Raccoon John ran into a significant snag, one that would recur as an integral problem for the ministers of the Stone-Campbell movement for decades to come. Although Barton Stone, still the editor of the Disciples' other major media mouthpiece, published no more reports of McVay's evangelistic activities, Stone appears to have insisted on maintaining a complete neutrality in the matter and nothing that either Campbell or Smith said or did could persuade him to endorse fully their condemnation of McVay. Whether this was because McVay had originally come from the Stone side of the union and the older man wished to remain aloof from the matter for that reason, or that Stone simply felt like he had been pushed around enough already by Campbell and perhaps by Smith as well, we cannot say. It's possible that he took umbrage at Raccoon John's somewhat high-handed characterization of his side of the movement as "the people who called themselves Christians (nicknamed New Lights)," especially after Smith's apparently genuine overtures of friendship toward him on New Year's Day 1832. If Smith had spoken so haughtily of the group at that time, the union almost certainly wouldn't have been achieved. But we can say with certainty that Stone made only one mention of the controversy in the *Messenger*, in December 1841 at the very bottom of the last page of that month's issue, almost as if it had been tacked on to the galleys of the paper as an afterthought or after considerable debate about whether it should have been included at all: "Brothers John Smith and A. Campbell have advertized [*sic*] James McVay, *not James T. McVay* [emphasis in original], as an unworthy evangelist, and a bad man, and as such should not be countenanced among us. The documents are too lengthy for insertion; nor was it deemed necessary, as the *Harbinger*, in which are the documents, has a wide circulation."[71] At best it was a grudging endorsement of the *Harbinger* article, and Stone's lack of enthusiasm over the issue would have been palpable to anyone reading his terse comments. As with bishops in an episcopal organization, any disagreement between the editors of the movement's major mouthpieces always indicated, sometimes initiated, and often exacerbated, disagreements within the brotherhood itself.

Thus when McVay was finally put to trial for Raccoon John's accusations at North Middletown in April or May 1842, it was under the auspices of somewhat mixed messages from *The Millennial Harbinger* and *The Christian Messenger* and consequent mixed feelings. Smith was present and introduced thirteen separate charges against McVay for lying, including the stories about the horse with the "big head" and McVay's sexual immorality, and all of which he declared himself able to prove although a good many were backed up only by informal affidavits from other preachers in Indiana. Pledging himself "to sustain and prove every allegation, or take it back like a man and Christian," Smith kept the elders, deacons, and witnesses from North Middletown and Cane Ridge occupied for two whole days, "meeting at an early hour and sitting until late." It must have been as alternately entertaining and boring a spectacle as a Baptist association meeting, the North District sessions of 1805 and 1827 through 1829 being cases in point. McVay argued that most of the charges could be investigated properly only in Ohio and Indiana where they had occurred; the church apparently nonetheless believed most of them to be sustainable with Raccoon John's affidavits and letters, although in the end they forgave McVay's "horse with the big head" escapade because they found mitigating evidence that he had not perpetrated an intentional fraud. Though Raccoon John may have felt that he finally had McVay beaten, to his surprise, at the end of the second weary day of the trial, McVay announced some preaching appointments to the congregation, harshly vilified a couple of the committeemen, and left the meetinghouse as if nothing at all was wrong.[72] As it turned out, the proceeding had a positive effect for Raccoon John only at North Middletown and Cane Ridge Churches themselves, and in the eyes of Smith's adversaries at Mt. Sterling McVay might as well not have been brought to trial at all. In spite of all John's careful planning and vigorous notices in the *Harbinger*, he watched impotently as the charges rolled off his opponent like so much water off a duck's back.

Alexander Campbell came to Kentucky that summer for his annual visit, and he made extensive notes of the journey, which he subsequently published in the *Harbinger*. At this time he first learned that the Presbyterian Nathan Lewis Rice was challenging prominent Kentucky Disciples to debate, and he described Rice as "set for the defense of the Westminster theology with, perhaps, so much modification as would suit it to the genius of Kentucky." Thus were first born the plans that would finally bring Campbell back to the state in November 1843 to meet Rice in formal challenge at Lexington. But when he passed through Montgomery and Bath counties on this 1842 trip, he found Disciple affairs essentially in chaos from the ever-worsening conflict at Mt. Sterling, now escalated by James McVay's presence and with Raccoon John seemingly powerless to do anything else about it. After an interview with Dulcinea Ryan, Campbell appears to have decided that perhaps an increase of candor might improve the mood of both sides of the controversy, as he included the following in a *Harbinger* article that November:

> At Mount Sterling we had but a short interview with our veteran brother John Smith, of Raccoon memory. This sturdiest of Kentucky's mighty sons has been much afflicted in his family, and more (as I learned from the excellent Sister Ryan on my way to Sharpsburg) in his own spirit by the unkind behavior of some of his old brethren, instigated by the sly, plausible, and imposing James McVay, of Fairfield, Columbiana fame—of Baltimore and Maryland renown—and lately of Richland, Ohio celebrity—a man, indeed, too well known by both womankind and mankind in all those parts, to be capable of disturbing the mind, or of grieving the spirit of such a giant soul as that which animates the fading tabernacle of Montgomery John Smith. But, alas! Leviathan himself is sometimes annoyed by a sea-snail; and the lion, king of the forest, by a feeble field-mouse! I wonder that the Christian people of Bath and Montgomery could endure it—that a well known, far-famed, and highly esteemed brother of more than a quarter century's residence among them, should be assailed or in any way inculpated by a vagrant preacher unknown to them, and without a clear and full recommendation from any church in the universe.
>
> But John Smith needs a little chastisement, it is alleged, for having been meddling with politics, and for having, in the late revolutionary canvass, or some time before it, in a day of great political warmth, when the pulse of Jacksonism, or Clayism, or some other man-ism was raging above all other febrile heat, presumed to vote—I know not how, nor for whom—but in a way not wholly canonical, as some of his more erudite brethren decided. He is not regarded by those who know him as at all addicted to politics; but if a preacher of the Gospel, when the political thermometer is at 212 degrees, should presume to vote, and only give one of his strongest reasons for it, he is sure to offend some of the flock; and for that reason it is very problematical whether Christian preachers and church elders should warmly espouse any political partizan [*sic*] interest. But no man need preach to Elder John Smith a sermon on such a theme. He is both theoretically and now

experimentally acquainted with the whole subject, in all its bearings; and if the brethren will do him justice, he is disposed to do them and the cause all possible justice.[73]

There's no doubt that Campbell meant well by airing both sides of the question, and deferring to the Stoneite view of secular politics as much as he did. Considering that the Mt. Sterling feud had gone on for more than six years before this particular assessment of it appeared in print, it was long past time for both sides of the conflict to realize that by keeping the matter alive, they were only bringing reproach upon the religious cause that they professed to espouse. And yet, how hot must Raccoon John's cheeks have burned with shame at seeing his very own name appear in *The Millennial Harbinger* in such a way? Though James Mason had used the paper to reproach the aggressive conduct that Smith had exhibited and encouraged among his Montgomery County followers twelve years earlier, with this new article written by Campbell himself Raccoon John finally must have realized exactly how William Vaughan and a multitude of other unfortunates had felt when his mentor had seen fit to excoriate them in public print. Even though Campbell had virtually made breakfast out of James McVay in the preceding paragraph, Raccoon John's own personal dirty laundry was now the public knowledge of the whole brotherhood; his editor, his bishop, for all of Campbell's obvious efforts to be kind, had nonetheless felt behooved to rebuke his conduct openly. It couldn't have been an easy pill to swallow. The situation must have allowed for no positive spin whatsoever, or else John Augustus Williams would have provided it. As it was, Williams remained entirely silent about this dark part of Raccoon John's life.

Even so, the article must have provoked sympathy for Raccoon John's side of the issue in some quarters. Williams mentions that John T. Johnson visited Raccoon John's churches at Sharpsburg and Owingsville in the early part of the year 1843, near the time that Smith's daughter Eliza Ann wed, and he held successful meetings at both places. It's thus apparent that he, at least, did not now hold Raccoon John's Whig politics against his old friend. The revivals must have had at least a bit of salutary effect on Smith's mood, and Raccoon John in turn helped Johnson out in another meeting at Flemingsburg. The two congregations even agreed to support Raccoon John as a paid evangelist once more, and in the month following he and Johnson took a preaching trip to Missouri, taking the small congregation of St. Louis Disciples completely by surprise with their visit. He made no conversions during his eight-day stint of preaching there, but Johnson stayed on two more weeks after Smith left (to take a trip through Illinois, Williams tells us, hopefully to visit John Duke or perhaps Joshua Hurt's widow, Betsy, although his reasons are not specified) and the little St. Louis congregation ultimately gained about thirty-five new members.[74]

But unfortunately, when Raccoon John got back from his travels he found the McVay trouble more alive and well than ever, and with his local opponents now angry not only with him, but with Campbell, too. Two prominent area Disciples whom Campbell identified as "good old friends," possibly Kenaz Farrow and John Mason, although we might suspect James Mason or even one of the Payne brothers as well, had taken umbrage at *The Millennial Harbinger*'s censure of McVay in November 1842. Though Campbell had written plainly enough about Raccoon John's shortcomings as well as McVay's, the two complainants had responded to the *Harbinger* with vituperative letters by which they had also demanded that Campbell cancel their subscriptions. One might suppose that, in the context of a mass-media religious creed, this meant that they were cutting themselves off from the movement as a whole, but it wasn't necessarily so. They still could have read Stone's *Christian Messenger,* Scott's *Evangelist,* Raines's *Christian Teacher,* Crihfield's *Heretic Detector,* or one or more of the newer periodicals that would go on to become mouthpieces of the movement's later factional manifestations. Here was Campbell's great problem with his movement, in a nutshell: for McVay, or any other transgressor of his magnitude and caliber, to be anathematized unanimously and effectively in all the churches, essentially all (or at least a clear majority of) the movement's religious journals had to voice unequivocal and preferably equal condemnation against him. In years to come the movement's most conservative journals would transform such editorial/episcopal machinations into a fine art, but at this point in history and between editors as disparate in personality as Alexander Campbell and Barton Stone always were, it just couldn't happen. Apparently McVay never attempted to write to Campbell himself, although one wonders if Campbell would have consented to publish a letter from him if he had. But at any rate, Campbell took up his editorial pen once more in May even as he readied himself for more scholarly dispute against N. L. Rice in November, now having transformed himself almost accidentally from a more or less objective reporter of local Kentucky news into a furious Smith partisan in his own right:

> Concerning our excellent and useful brother John Smith of Kentucky, we have received sundry documents and attestations relative to the reckless assaults made upon his reputation by the irresponsible James McVay, sometime since noticed on our pages. Some friends of the said McVay, ensnared by his sycophantish [*sic*] hypocrisy have also written certificates of McVay's good standing in their neighborhood at Richland County, Ohio, sometime since. I have learned the history of McVay before he went to Mansfield and since, from various, numerous, and highly respectable sources. . . . And such are my views of the general character of John Smith and James McVay, and such is my faith in the testimony I have of them from ten to twenty years' standing, that nothing that McVay could say or write of Smith could change my views or those of the impartial public, and the multitude of dis-

ciples amongst whom Elder Smith has lived for a quarter of a century . . . I therefore re-affirm my former convictions of James McVay and of our good brother, John Smith, notwithstanding that two of my good old friends discontinued my paper, because, when called upon, I freely declared my views and convictions of this worthy man, whose praise is in more than a hundred churches in Kentucky. These old friends have been rather too politically proscriptive and exclusive in their charities. They have got into bad company when, like Aaron and Hur, they are holding up, not the hands of Moses against Amalek, but the hands of Amalek against Moses. I will still hope that they may repent before they die. The Lord forgive them for their unchristian letter [*sic*] to me! [ellipses added][75]

The Kentucky Presbyterians hammered out the final details for the proposed debate by correspondence with Campbell in July and August 1843,[76] and in the September issue of *The Millennial Harbinger* the final notice about the Smith-McVay feud appeared. It held no news of any settlement between the contending preachers, permanent or otherwise, and in fact was essentially an angry rehashing of points that Campbell had already made in November 1842 and May 1843. Confusion, discord, and hate still reigned supreme, and the only thing that Campbell's last McVay article made clearer was the cause of the controversial preacher's adoption in eastern Kentucky in the first place:

We sometime since announced the shameful conduct of James McVay in Kentucky, and of a little faction of political discontents, who, by this man, as their proper tool for such an undignified work of defamation, sought to crush the influence of one of the greatest and ablest men in Kentucky—I mean Elder John Smith, a brother whose praise is in all the churches of that enlightened commonwealth. Despite of such notice [*sic*], and in prosecution of this project of exterminating the said Smith, the said faction has recalled this broken pitcher from his exile, and sent him out to preach the Gospel of their opposition to this old venerable and efficient minister of the truth, in the humble hope of justifying their opposition. Now, although I may have heard, yet were I to depose in court, I could not now say to what political party Elder Smith or his opponents belong, nor do I wish to know. I condemn the conduct of the party that would weaken the hands of a good man because of political difference. James McVay may preach in the mountains of Kentucky, and baptize hundreds of his converts; but while the mountains stand and are bounded by vallies [*sic*], neither his character nor that of the faction which chose him for their oracle of discord, will commend itself to the approbation and admiration of God, angels, or saints, the Bible being true.[77]

By late 1843, though, James McVay actually had finally shown his colors as something more than a former Stoneite preacher aggrieved by an erstwhile Campbellite preacher's involvement in secular politics: not only was he still "out to get" Raccoon John, but he was now attacking his fellow former Stoneite colleague Peter Hon as well.[78] Unfortunately, it is doubtful that many of McVay's partisans were still reading the *Harbinger.* Nonetheless, the sum total of Campbell's treatment of the Smith-McVay war inevitably leads us to one more speculation as to why the Disciple leader had mellowed so much since the days in which he had polarized Reformers and Baptists in the old *Christian Baptist.* By this time something had to have become glaringly obvious to Campbell which, for all of Raccoon John's own capacity to utilize reason and logic, the entrenched rural American Great Revival mentality may not yet have let Smith accept: no one's interpretation of orthodoxy, not even Campbell's himself, was any guarantor of integrity. It was always easy for a glib-tongued, charismatic leader such as Campbell to hold up scandals occurring within the various denominations he criticized as evidences of their unreliability. Yet when defenders of these faiths pointed out the faults and failings of Campbell's own adherents, it was likewise all too convenient not only to look for ways and loopholes through which to defend such transgressors in their errors, but to counter that the Disciple system allowed not for the perfection of all its followers, but rather for simple doctrinal accuracy. This was the same fallacy into which Martin Luther had fallen three centuries before in his crusade to reform Roman Catholicism, and it was this supreme confidence in doctrinal accuracy that had caused Campbell and so many of his followers to behave as arrogantly as they had—including Raccoon John in his dealings with not only the Baptists, Methodists, and Presbyterians, but James Fishback and the Mason brothers as well. Yet after trying to cope with James McVay and a host of others just like him between 1830 and 1843, and especially in light of the John Thomas controversy and the debate with Bishop Purcell, Campbell had to have realized the fact that good and evil existed side by side in all faiths, and that neither an individual's being confirmed as an adolescent or an adult after being sprinkled as an infant, "shouting the house down" after claiming a born-again experience, nor being immersed in the belief that the execution of the act itself either "formally" or "really" remitted his or her sins could be counted on as an ironclad promise that that same individual could be trusted to behave honorably and treat his or her fellow believers in accordance with the commandments of Christianity's founder. It may have been a hard truth for Campbell to admit, and an even more difficult one for Raccoon John to realize if in fact he ever did, but it was a conviction with greater tolerance implicit in its very acceptance.

This didn't ameliorate Raccoon John's immediate distress, however, because McVay was still active, hostile both to him and to Peter Hon, and supported by a seemingly remarkably large or at least influential number of Smith's former parishioners. Here, again, we might resume our speculations about the reasons that Campbell requested Raccoon John's presence in Lexington as his "second" at the Rice debate along with Fishback, Raines, Shannon, and John Speed Smith: it is possible that, in addition to wishing to acknowledge and commend Smith's personal loyalty to him, Campbell simply wanted to give Raccoon John a place of honor, a more positive bit of recognition in his home state than he had received since the start of his battle with McVay more than three years previously. And although we have no reason to suspect that Campbell actually wished any personal ill to James McVay, neither have we any cause to doubt that, if some obvious misfortune had befallen McVay, his nearly blind wife, or his questionably legitimate daughter, Campbell would have treated the occurrence exactly as he had blusteringly written of the family catastrophe of the hapless Methodist preacher Philips, noted already, in the *Harbinger* only four months before the scheduled commencement of the Rice debate: hard, objective, logical evidence of the direct judgment of God against the transgressor.

And so, having examined the circumstances leading up to the Campbell-Rice debate from every known context and angle relevant to Raccoon John's story, we return once again to the eve of its commencement, the afternoon of November 14, 1843. There is no word in the English language with quite as much promise and potential as "tomorrow," and this Tuesday had to have been a time of boundless hope and eager anticipation for Smith. It held not only the chance for his embattled mentor Campbell to restate and clarify Disciple doctrinal positions, explain away all the inconsistencies that had grown up within the movement over the years, and put the upstart sectarian Rice in his place even as he had done for John Walker in 1820 and W. L. MacCalla in 1823, but a glimmer of hope for Raccoon John himself to begin to break out of the horrible rut in which he had been mired since at least 1836 with the steadily worsening Mt. Sterling–McVay controversies. He had to have looked forward to meeting his own and the beloved Richard H. Menefee's political mentor, Henry Clay, as well. We do not know where Raccoon John lodged in Lexington as he awaited the opening of the great contest on the morrow, but both he and Campbell had a multitude of friends in the city and there's a fair chance that they would have boarded at the same house, dining together, recounting the good old times, and happily planning strategies for the morning's exchanges—even if he and James Fishback still disagreed sharply on what sort of strategies these should be.

And meanwhile, of course, Nancy was stuck at home with supervising the butchering, an arduous, backbreaking, and dirty labor no matter how many helping hands she had managed to acquire for the day, a task as thoroughly and unquestionably mundane as Raccoon John's efforts to assist Campbell in Lexington could ever aspire to be divine. Though slaughtering and butchering are generally begun as early in the morning as is possible, Nancy and her laborers were still hard at it in the afternoon when fourteen-year-old Emma, twelve-year-old Mary, and Richard, who had just turned seven, came home from school; the most likely task with which Nancy herself and any other women present would have been engaged was the "rendering" of lard from the hogs' fat. Twenty-year-old Harvey may have been at home to help with the chore as well, and he may have felt responsible in some measure for the events of the evening. We cannot know. At any rate, one of the necessary component chores of a home butchering, both then and now, is scalding: that is to say, after the hogs are felled and bled, the bodies must be draped with coarse blankets or rough sacking of some sort and boiling water must be poured over them to loosen their tough, bristly body hair. The hair is then scraped from the parboiled skins of the carcasses with dull knives before the bodies of the slaughtered hogs are hung up by the gambrels, or back hoof tendons, and opened and cleaned. On that cold afternoon as a supply for this task, the enormous, low, widemouthed cast iron wash pots that Nancy and the girls used for weekly laundering sat in the barnyard, at least one still full to the brim or nearly so with seething water. Though by this time of day the fire under it had probably begun to burn low, the workers had draped a coarse blanket over the top of the cauldron to keep the water hot. Over this blanket and the rim of the wash pot one of the laborers had lain a hoe lengthwise, most likely to secure the covering from being blown off by a wintry breeze, and it so happened that, as seven-year-old Richard scampered up to watch the proceedings, somebody—one wonders if it might have been Harvey—called for him to lift this hoe from the top of the wash pot and bring it to the work area. Eager to lend a hand and show his mettle as only a little boy in the presence of grown men and possibly a teasing, annoying older brother as well can be, Richard hastened to obey.

In an earlier chapter I mentioned an old hill country proverb about the fallacy of sending a boy, or even two boys, to do a job that measures up to adult specifications. Acerbic though the old maxim is, it's often said with as much affection and love as irritation. Boys simply do not (and if the latest physiological and neurological research is reliable, cannot) think things through the way an adult would before they act, and it's questionable as to whether this tendency improves appreciably through adolescence. And so it was on that fateful afternoon of November 14, 1843: the laborer had no doubt expected young Richard to grasp the hoe by the end of its handle and carefully slide it sideways off the top of the wash pot, but it seems most likely that what the child actually did was lean his torso over the boiling water and attempt to lift the hoe straight up by the midsection of the handle, using his shoulder joint or spine as a fulcrum perhaps in a touching effort to demonstrate to Harvey and the onlooking crowd of laborers how big and strong seven whole years had made him. But whatever the poor little fellow did, the end result is known all too well: he lost his balance and fell forward, taking the blanket with him as he plunged headlong into churning water hot enough to take the bristles off a hog's tough hide.

With howls of horror and anguish, the men grabbed the child by his clothing and lifted him out of the wash pot as fast as they could, no doubt scalding their own hands and arms as they did so, but the damage was already done. Williams tells us that Richard survived for eight hours, and he was charitable to his readers' sensibilities in stating merely that the little boy's sufferings were too heartrending for description.[79] Second-degree water burns with enormous, extremely fragile blisters must have covered the entire surface of the little boy's upper body and face, undoubtedly including his eyes and inside his ears, and it's more than likely he aspirated boiling water in an irrepressible scream reflex and thus scalded his mouth and pharynx as well. Considering that house fire deaths often occur fairly rapidly from smoke inhalation, Richard's fate was unspeakably worse than that of Eli and Elvira nearly thirty years before: no mercifully quick asphyxiation could have taken place here, and moreover, unlike other burns of comparable severity, scalds destroy no nerve endings. Thus to be bluntly and cruelly honest, the long and the short of it is that this seven-year-old child endured the absolute closest possible temporal approximation to the bodily agony that his father believed and preached was the fate of the damned in hell—for two hours longer than Jesus is said to have hung on the cross. The only small mercy that Nancy, herself no doubt frantic almost to the point of insanity with grief and terror, could have effected for him was to summon a doctor from Owingsville to try somehow to get some laudanum down the boy's scorched throat—and since Richard was probably hardly able to swallow even before his traumatized pharynx would have swollen shut in his most likely primary cause of death, it's doubtful that any physician of that day and age could have accomplished even that much. To think on it is, to borrow the words of Melville's Captain Ahab, enough to split the planets and make an infidel of Abraham, yet we do a disservice to the little boy's memory simply to gloss over his sufferings the way Williams did, as too harsh for our sensibilities. For all the resplendence of the poetry of John Keats, he was wrong occasionally: truth is not always beauty nor beauty truth, and sometimes our hearts need to be rent simply to shock us out of out of our pathetic complacency. Of course this was Mel Gibson's rationale for filming *The Passion of the Christ* as he did as well, but not even Gibson would be willing to dramatize such a scene of horror as this—much less consider its implications. William Butler Yeats may have said it better than anyone: "Come away, O human child! . . . with a faery hand in hand; for the world's more full of weeping, than you can understand."

The same afternoon of the accident, some friend of the family or a relative mounted a fast horse and made with all speed for Lexington to break the news to Raccoon John and to bring him back home. No one thought that Richard could live long, but it was hoped at least that father and son might be able to take some comfort in seeing one another one last time. We can no more imagine John's state of mind on hearing the terrible tidings late that night than we can conceive of what it must have been like for him to learn of his cabin fire and Eli's and Elvira's deaths so many years before. For once, concern for Disciple affairs went completely out the window, and the aging preacher set out at a hard gallop, probably by lantern light in pitch darkness since it was so late in the year, with the messenger for the approximately forty-five mile ride back to Owingsville. Though he was sustained on the journey by the bare hope that he could get home in time at least to tell the little boy that he loved him and that he wouldn't have had such a thing happen to him for the entire world and all its glory, it was not to be. Raccoon John's daughter Emily or Emma tells best of his return, in her own words: "I remember well how my father looked that day, when he reached home, weary and worn almost to exhaustion, but with hope beaming in his eye. When told that his boy, the pride of his old age, was no more, he dropped down in the doorway apparently lifeless. The fatigue of his hurried journey and the shock of Richard's death were too much for him; he was unable to get to his room until we applied such restoratives as his case required."[80]

And if, after Raccoon John looked upon the scalded body of his little boy, "such restoratives as his case required" happened to be Emma's euphemism for that which John and Nancy had always kept stored in barrels in their cellar, who among us, in our own comfortable age of grief counseling, psychotherapy, church- and denomination-sponsored ministers' "burnout" retreats, and Prozac, can sit in judgment upon him?

The next five years and eleven months of Raccoon John's life are virtually a blank to us. Williams recounts no data whatsoever about Smith's activities between the latter part of November 1843 and the month of October 1849, and during that same period of time Alexander Campbell, who had been so keen to "take up his part" in Raccoon John's fight with James McVay as late as two months before the Rice debate, mentioned him in the *Harbinger* only once, in April 1847.[81] In fact, the Smith family's terrible tragedy didn't merit a single line in the paper for even so much as a prayer request or an obituary notice, and this though Raccoon John's planned presence at the Rice debate (which, like the War of 1812, actually ended more or less in a draw) had been advertised and both Campbell's fellow writer Robert Richardson as well as Campbell himself in the *Harbinger* subsequently gave detailed, but predictably slanted, accounts of the entire proceeding from first to last.[82]

There were politic, if not purely good, reasons for this nearly six-year period of virtual silence. Of course, it would have taken Raccoon John at least that long to recover even a fraction of the way from Richard's death, not to mention John Duke's subsequent demise in 1846, and it's a testimony to his resilience that he was able afterward to resume a public persona at all—or that he would even wish to. But if Richard's loss itself were not difficult enough to overcome merely on its own, its implications to Raccoon John's life and ministry had to have been utterly staggering. Even Williams and Donaldson admit that Smith was faced, in large part, with a virtual repetition of his tragedy of almost thirty years before.[83] This time he didn't lose his wife or catch a relapse of the cold plague, of course, but the thoughts with which he must have been faced were undoubtedly every bit as insupportable as his broodings of years before, and even more so. In 1815 John had had to construct a theodicy to try to make sense of and assign meaning to the unspeakable horrors which had befallen him in Alabama, and as we have seen, this theodicy had carried him all the way back to Kentucky and his second marriage, and through the ups and downs of his tenure in North District Association as *de facto* and then *de jure* leader of the Payne clan. It had provided an integral element of his courage, dedication, and determination in the first years of his zealot's crusade for the Campbell Reformation; his victories in preaching Campbell's Ancient Gospel had given him enough justification for it ostensibly to satisfy any critic or skeptic, and he had basked in its supreme vindication and fulfillment at Lexington on New Year's Day 1832 with the implementation of the Stone-Campbell union. Whether he had ever allowed himself to admit it or not and regardless of his own personal convictions, he must have been disappointed to observe the warp and woof of all the changes in the movement, in his mentor Campbell, and in the attitudes of his longtime co-laborers through the years of the John Thomas controversy, the debate over the response to the Lunenburg Letter, and *The Millennial Harbinger*'s complete about-face of its position on organized missions. Still, the strength of his faith would have allowed him to view these various strifes as mere temptations along the Christian pilgrim's thorny path through this world, difficulties that could and would be overcome by God's help and the consequent reassertion of the movement's ideals.

If Raccoon John was as keen and as perceptive as his biographers claim and as evidence leads us to believe, his fights with John Mason over the Mt. Sterling Church building, Kenaz and Susanna Farrow over the 1836 congressional election, and their apparent partner James McVay over both difficulties would have been a greater test to his faith. With the involvement of Alexander Campbell in the fracas by Campbell's editorial pronouncements in the *Harbinger,* and Campbell's unsuccessful efforts to mediate the dispute because he couldn't get Barton Stone and the *Messenger* to condemn McVay as soundly as the *Harbinger* did, Raccoon John finally would have been able to see the glaring ribs of a very human nature in a church that claimed to have no man-made structures. Worse yet, it had to have been obvious by now to everyone that his later Montgomery and Bath County fights had taken on an eerie resemblance to the ancient North District battles of his old mentor Jilson Payne against Robert Elkin, and of his own political jousts with David Chenault. And still for all this, with the strength of his faith and his past experiences he could remain patient and even confident, waiting upon the Lord to vindicate him. Campbell himself even seemed to feel that very same way: as we have noted, he had expressed the pious wish in the *Harbinger* that the two old friends who had discontinued their subscriptions and had written him such unchristian letters because of his support for Raccoon John over McVay might have the opportunity to repent before they died, and moreover, at very nearly the same time he had reported the family tragedy of the unfortunate William Philips as a direct result of the circuit rider's having written that scurrilous pamphlet "Campbellism Exposed" and having made fun of "the Gospel in the water."

Thus as Raccoon John had waited on the November debate, he had also waited faithfully on the Lord, and considering all of Campbell's 1842 and 1843 articles both about James McVay and the Kentucky controversy as well as the hapless Methodist Philips, we have little reason to doubt that if some terrible accident had befallen either the persons or the families of John Mason, Kenaz Farrow, or James McVay alike, Campbell would have interpreted and reported the event exactly as he had done against Philips. In other words, if any of these men or one of their sons had gotten himself scalded to death, Campbell would have expressed the most pious and tender sympathies for the bereaved wife or parents while simultaneously exploiting the case as an object lesson on the dangers of fighting against the progress of the Ancient Gospel, and thus battling against God Himself.

And then young Richard, Raccoon John and Nancy's "pet" who had come into the world only after the die had already been cast for most of the matters that so preoccupied his father throughout the little boy's seven short years, had suffered a fate that not even the strictest, most implacable modern court of law would have imposed upon the worst, most hardened adult criminal. Within the system of rationalism which Campbell had convinced his followers that the Creator had ordered the world, the event made no sense whatsoever, but we should be glad that no opportunistic Kentucky Baptist, Methodist, or Presbyterian minister or editor was callous enough to interpret and write about the horrible accident as some kind of poetic Divine justice against Raccoon John for his aggressive stance on the doctrine of baptism for the remission of sins—or worse yet, as a vindication of Richard Thomas's pet doctrine of infant damnation. As it was, though, within the minds of all too many of the simple, God-fearing rural witnesses to Raccoon John's fight with James McVay, all that the tragedy meant was that God Himself had pronounced judgment against Raccoon John and had exonerated McVay, and there wasn't a thing that Alexander Campbell could do about it because he had already made such interpretations legitimate for his readership with his diatribe against the Methodist Philips. We might hope, however, that the brutal nature of this supposed Divine judgment at least gave Mason, Farrow, and McVay pause, and that they owned enough mercy and humanity not to crow about the blessing that the Lord seemed to have bestowed upon them.

Consequently, the most severe trial to Raccoon John, at least in a long-term sense, had to have been the test that this new chapter to his life gave to the entire system of theodicy that had served him well for so many years. If God had taken Eli, Elvira, and Anna from him, he'd turned the experience to his own good by learning and applying the Lord's lessons to him about infant damnation, the Philadelphia Confession, and the necessity of staying where God put him, just as the Lord had apparently intended that he should; if God had taken Joshua from him, he'd once again learned his self-evident lesson, this time about the necessity of total dedication to the Ancient Gospel. And now, long since he felt that he'd passed through the refiner's fire and thought that he knew all there was to know about both the sufferings and the triumphs of Job from the inside out, the tawdry dealings he'd known with Disciple politics between 1836 and 1843 had blighted his life just like Baptist politics had once done, and the entire series of events had culminated in a horror that his own worst nightmares couldn't have matched and which must have left him feeling spiritually right back where he had started in 1815. Rather than the steady progression toward truth, justice, and good that his ministry had seemed to represent since the Alabama house fire and up until the Stone-Campbell union of 1832, the whole thing now must have appeared as a repetition of the very worst sort, a never-ending and vicious circle with death as Alpha, death as Omega, and those shattering thoughts voiced originally by Hume and d'Holbach reverberating mockingly, again and again, around each orbit. And the very fact that neither Alexander Campbell nor any of Raccoon John's biographers ever chose to try to address this terrible period of Smith's life in any meaningful way[84] is apt evidence that they felt they *couldn't* address it without calling the entire worldview that they proclaimed as absolute and universal into question. It didn't inspire faith and thus was best left alone and, ultimately, hopefully please sweet Jesus God, forgotten.

So then, how *did* Raccoon John cope with this latest, crushing sorrow and the apparent victory of the McVay party in his Montgomery and Bath County fields of labor? Since the subject appears to have been such a taboo to him and all his chroniclers both then and up until now, we can't really say for sure. We do know, however, that in the spring of 1847 Alexander Campbell persuaded him to serve as one of eastern Kentucky's scholarship agents for Bethany College.[85] This is the one instance in which Raccoon John is mentioned in the *Harbinger* between late 1843 and 1850, and we might wonder if Campbell wished to involve his old friend in this activity simply as a means to draw him out of the dark hollow of his grief over both Richard and John Duke. Whether or not this be the case, though, it is certain that in the fall of that very year Campbell himself came to appreciate Raccoon John's plight as none other ever could. Campbell and his large family by two wives was no exception to the standards of the day; like Raccoon John, he'd lost sons and daughters as infants and toddlers to illnesses, and others as young adults. But in September 1847 while Campbell was overseas on a tour of Europe and the British Isles, his youngest son by his second wife, Selina, ten years old and named Wickliffe after the first English translator of the Bible, drowned in a swimming accident in Buffalo Creek near his home. Campbell himself did not learn of the accident until he returned to the United States a month later, although he subsequently claimed to have received a vague premonition of sorts on the actual day that the death had occurred. But until her husband came back home that fall, Selina Campbell had been forced to deal with the loss entirely on her own with the help of her neighbors and older children and stepchildren, and in so doing she came up with her own personal theodicy: the boy had already expressed the intention to be baptized when he was a little older, and so with the drowning, the Lord Himself must have baptized Wickliffe at his death.[86] Again we should perhaps be glad that periodical editors of other denominations were not so crass and callous as to portray the accident as a divine judgment against Campbell's and his followers' preaching of baptism for the remission of sins. Though Alexander tried, as a loving father will, to take comfort in the thought that young Wickliffe had been simply too good for this earth and that the Lord had therefore called him to a higher existence, the death affected him so visibly that the reactionary elements of his movement pounced upon it as yet another of their growing number of reasons or excuses as to why their once-swashbuckling editorial leader had mellowed out since the good old days of *The Christian Baptist*.[87] We must then conclude that, even at best, Raccoon John couldn't have come to terms with Richard's death any better than Campbell had with Wickliffe's, and very probably with not even that much peace of mind. At the very least, though, the two battle-scarred Reform warriors were now brothers in grief as well as brethren in the church.

What, then, of Raccoon John's theodicy *after* November 1843? We know no more about it than we do of any recriminations between him and Nancy—or him and Harvey—over the accident that claimed Richard's life. But I suspect that, since both his marriage and his ministry ultimately survived, at least a modified form of his theodicy had to have endured somehow as well. In any case this was another matter on which neither he nor his biographers would have been overly eager to speak. But thinking strictly as a father rather than as an historian, biographer, or minister, I cannot help but wonder how he managed to come up with a reason that he could have lived with for his little boy's horrible suffering and death. Flannery O'Connor's fictional character Ruby Turpin once bellowed in fury to God in the empty sky, "*Who do You think You are?*" She received only the echo of her own voice in reply, but the answer still hit home. Could Raccoon John similarly have shouted heavenward, *Where were You and what were You doing? If You'd been here, Richard wouldn't have died,* in a poignant paraphrase of the lament of Mary and Martha over Lazarus in the eleventh chapter of John's Gospel? And if he had, how appropriately might the reverberation of his own words have answered him, not only for Richard but even for Eli and Elvira almost thirty years, thousands of miles of traveling, and unnumbered sermons before? The agnostic Robert Green Ingersoll once said that when we cry aloud in mourning to God, we are answered only by the echo of our own wailing cry; but to Raccoon John, like O'Connor's Turpin, such an echo just might have been a revelation.

There is yet another sad footnote to Raccoon John's post-1832 Montgomery and Bath County ministry, one that even Williams and Donaldson couldn't manage to downplay entirely. In October 1849, Raccoon John and Nancy broke up housekeeping in Bath County and returned to Montgomery with their two youngest daughters, Emma and Mary. Harvey is nowhere to be found in central Kentucky census records for the period. He may even still have been in school at this time, although we do not know where. But in spite of his father's 1847 field work for Bethany College, he seems never to have enrolled in this institution, and although we cannot know for sure whether or not he ever matriculated at the Kentucky Disciples' own Bacon College, it appears doubtful.[88] By this time James McVay seems to have left the area, though whether he died or simply moved west to greener pastures we cannot say. At any rate, for the first time in their married lives Raccoon John and Nancy became town dwellers, purchasing a handsome two-story residence on North Maysville Street directly in Mt. Sterling and probably with considerable assistance from James and Maria Lee.

Having still maintained his church membership in name at least at Mt. Sterling, Smith tried to reassume a position of responsibility with the congregation there. However, after McVay the church had acquired for its primary pulpit orator one William P. Clark, a young Disciple exhorter who, interestingly, had gotten his start in the southern Kentucky mountains just like Raccoon John had.[89] For all we know, Clark might even have been one of Smith's own converts in that region in 1831 or 1832, because Williams indicates that he was a Baptist proselyte. But whether or not this was the case, it's certain that relations between Smith and Clark soured soon after Smith returned to his old field. We can't say exactly what the initial catalyst was for this latest controversy within contentious Mt. Sterling Church, although it probably had its seeds in the earlier fights with Mason and Farrow. Clark seems to have believed that it had something to do with Raccoon John's unhappiness about having to share pulpit time with him, but evidently it escalated until the younger man accused Raccoon John openly of being "an old drunkard [who] had been so drunk [he] could not hold [his] head up, [and] a disturber of the peace of the churches [who] had kept up an interruption for 20 years." The accusations of drunkenness were probably made in an unfair spirit, but still, it's hard for us to assess exactly how factually accurate they may have been. We've seen already that neither John nor Nancy Smith were children of the Temperance era; with them as with most Kentuckians of their generation, whiskey, wine, and brandy were beverages that carried a definite potential to be abused, but which harbored within them no implicit evil. Moreover, we must remember that whether or not Raccoon John drank much at all during this time, his hands had become so palsied that they nonetheless shook exactly like a longtime alcoholic's. It could have been that Clark, as spokesman for a younger generation more exposed to and influenced by Temperance rhetoric, was guilty of mere hyperbole of the same sort that Raccoon John, as a Reform zealot, himself had employed so effectively against his own opponents in times past. But then again, we must reiterate that Raccoon John was still trying to recuperate from a tragedy that would have shattered the very strongest of parents, in a day when both psychotherapeutic techniques and drugs were unknown; and if, late of an evening when his thoughts returned again and again to his baby boy's last hours upon earth with a throat scalded so badly he probably couldn't even cry aloud, the old man gave his demijohn two or three long, hard pulls too many, the greater sin still would have lain within the heart of the individual who felt qualified to sit in judgment upon him without walking a mile in his shoes. Clark thus could have fit this category easily as well. Even now it remains an attitude to which young evangelicals, still wet enough behind the ears to doubt everything but God, their own concept of biblical inerrancy, their salvation, and themselves, are too easily prone. Of course, the final accusation, of Smith's being a disturber of the peace, was most likely simply borrowed and rejuvenated Mason and Farrow rhetoric.

But if Raccoon John was down, he was still a long way from out. For all we know, his anger at Clark may have even given him a beneficial focus, but in any case he lashed out at the younger man with every bit as much fury as he had bestowed upon James McVay almost a decade before. It is somewhat unsettling, though, to note how similarly packed with hyperbole his words against Clark were in comparison to his complaints against McVay earlier, and this very similitude in addition to the extreme shrillness of his tone weakens rather than strengthens the believability of his arguments. Once upon a time he had claimed that James McVay was a greater curse to the cause of religion than any man he had ever known, and had advised his old friend Campbell that writing about "this long neglected subject would do more for the cause of Christ than any other matter with which the same number of pages could be filled." For this new controversy, he asserted that "if I ever have seen any man, saint or sinner, black or white, who was more perfectly wreckless [*sic*] of the truth than William P. Clark, I do not know it." That "poor, unhappy, unprincipled, and low-flung creature" Clark's allegations were as much "a catalogue of willful, malicious, downright baldfaced, round-plump falsehoods as the father of lies ever told [*sic*]," and whereas James McVay had been an incorrigible and irredeemable swindler and lecher, Clark was an incorrigible, irredeemable liar. Writing about the matter afterward, Raccoon John even called up a spate of churches whose members he avowed would bear witness that he was telling the truth,[90] but of course this is exactly the same thing that he had once done against McVay as well and it hadn't benefited him at all. Thus, as John Mason's war with Raccoon John and Mt. Sterling Church finally subsided for good about the year 1850, the Clark controversy threatened to bloom just as brightly as had the McVay war of ten years before.

But evidently, as Everett Donaldson so aptly phrases it, this time enough was enough. Raccoon John was by now sixty-six years of age, and even he himself must have realized that he was getting too old for this kind of saintly fun and games. In 1851 he simply gave up the fight completely, asked for his and Nancy's church letters, sold his fine new house at a five hundred–dollar loss, and, again probably with considerable discreet assistance from the Lees, moved himself, Nancy, and his remaining family away from Mt. Sterling altogether. It's possible that his steadfast friend John T. Johnson influenced him to do so, as well as perhaps some other younger Disciple leaders concerned about their respected patriarch's reputation. But this time around, Raccoon John entertained no thoughts of returning to the Wayne County hills of his youth, such as he had in late 1827. He relocated to Georgetown, in the heart of the Bluegrass and in Johnson's home territory, and Williams notes specifically that he settled "near the beloved Johnson, where the spirit of Stone still breathed its peaceful influence on the people and the church."[91] We should perhaps be gratified that the old warrior had finally learned to appreciate the meek and retiring nature of Stone, who had died in the year following Richard's fatal accident, even though Stone had tacitly refused to support him during the McVay controversy.

Raccoon John became an elder at the Georgetown church, and in addition picked up once-a-month regular preaching appointments at two rural Scott County Disciple congregations.[92] Besides these labors he was still able to draw on his image as a senior statesman of the Kentucky Disciples and go on short preaching tours both in and out of state, and he was reasonably happy with these excursions, if not entirely so. Williams tells us that in 1857 he presided at a debate between one Rev. T. J. Fisher and Benjamin Franklin, who was the editor of a conservative Disciple journal published in Cincinnati and called *The American Christian Review,* and in 1858 he visited the Missouri Disciples on the occasion of their state meeting.[93] It is possible that Smith liked editor Franklin so well because he may have reflected a very close approximation to Raccoon John's own thought: Franklin was fiercely loyal to the "early" Alexander Campbell of *The Christian Baptist* as being *the* teacher of plain, unadorned Scripture alone, and somehow he simply never recognized the dichotomy in Campbell's teaching that became more and more apparent after the Thomas affair and the Purcell debate. Franklin would thus defend Campbell personally against almost any charge regardless of what Campbell himself thought or wrote after 1837,[94] and this may have been the identical attitude Raccoon John had espoused at the time of his dispute with Johnson and Scott in 1840.

But regardless of where blame could or should have been laid for all that had been said and done over twenty-odd years, Raccoon John's absence from Mt. Sterling seemed to enable the congregation there finally to make peace. The ever-faithful Johnson, along with the Bracken Association Reform pioneer William Morton, visited the congregation and somehow effected a reconciliation between all the parties who had remained at variance for so many years. After Clark left Mt. Sterling and returned to the southern Kentucky mountains, Raccoon John's former missionary partner John Rogers became the church's pulpit orator.[95] Interestingly, Clark rejoined the Baptists once he arrived back in the hills, and informed them when he did so that "his heart had been with them for a year." But so long as Mt. Sterling Church was under

Rogers's leadership, as well as that of those who followed in his wake, including Lewis Pinkerton and Moses Lard, Raccoon John was welcome to come back and visit, and after 1854 he did so from time to time.[96]

The days of the old, hard style as a popular feature of Montgomery County preaching, except in the eyes of those firebrands whose descendants would populate the most reactionary elements of the Stone-Campbell movement, were over. As a tragic, ironic epitaph to Smith's Montgomery County ministry, Raccoon John's old neighbors were now happier with only occasional doses of his preaching, rather than a steady diet of it.

CHAPTER 10

A Concluding Unscientific Postscript

> No; yes, remember me to everyone. I was much attached to them all. And tell them that my life was a great, and to others unknown and unintelligible, suffering. It all looked like pride and vanity, but it was not.
>
> —Søren Kierkegaard on his deathbed,
> when asked if he had any last message for his friends

> Daughter, I want some music to cheer me through this dark valley.
>
> —the last words of Raccoon John Smith

As both America's Era of Good Feeling and Alexander Campbell's sweet dream of a Messianic Age built on the foundations of his Restored Gospel quietly passed away with a whimper in the midst of the northern and southern sectional strifes that would lead finally to the Civil War, Raccoon John spent the autumn years of his life and ministry in genteel Georgetown, ironically, finally in the gracious lifestyle to which he had begun to aspire so many years before in the hills of Wayne County. He was the Grand Old Man of a respected religious denomination (or *the* church, as some of course preferred to think of it) in Kentucky, and his name within it was already, and indeed always would be, legend. He received calls from admiring visitors such as Albert Allen, and recounted to them his recollections of the heroic days in which he first fought to establish the true faith. He and Nancy purchased three slaves (again perhaps with James and Maria Lee's help): a man named Jerry and a woman named Marena in the same year as their move to Georgetown, and after settling there, another woman named Winnie.[1] Thus, finally Nancy's worn hands were relieved of a portion of their drudgery, both the increasingly palsied John and his remaining single son Harvey were spared doing menial chores, and the two youngest Smith girls could receive calls from the local Scott County swains in the atmosphere of southern respectability.

In fact, both Harvey and Emma Smith made what must have been considered extremely good matches, and although very little is known about Mary, she may have done so as well. On December 18, 1852, Raccoon John performed the ceremony for twenty-nine-year-old Harvey to wed Mary C. Stedman, daughter of the well-to-do Georgetown manufacturer and entrepreneur Leander C. Stedman and his wife, Isabella, who herself was a member of the prestigious Kidd family of Fayette County. Almost exactly one year later, Emma Smith married Albertis Ratliff Ringo,[2] scion of a distinguished Fleming and Montgomery County family and one of the wealthiest young men in Georgetown at that time. Like James Lee, A. R. Ringo was a merchant and moneylender, known as "the walking banker" because of his ready propensity to make loans on the spur of the moment directly from his pocket, and he had both a house and business interests in no less an eastern seaboard commercial hub than Philadelphia as well as his home base in the Bluegrass.[3] Along with Lee, too, he may have assumed a portion of his in-laws' debts and expenses, and it's certain that he helped Harvey get a start in business.

Finally, Raccoon John performed the wedding for his youngest daughter, Mary, to W. C. Tomlinson on May 1, 1856,[4] although the joy of the occasion was no doubt subdued by the death that same year of John and Nancy's second-oldest surviving daughter, Eliza Ann, back in Owingsville.[5] According to the 1850 Federal Census of Bath County, Eliza Ann and her husband, Edgar, had one child, William,[6] but it is not certain that either Edgar or William survived her. W. C. and Mary Tomlinson seem to have settled in Audrain County, Missouri, fairly early in their marriage, but Tomlinson appears to have died at some time during or soon after the end of the Civil War; he may have been a soldier and a casualty, but we cannot say for sure. It is likewise uncertain whether they had any offspring or not. Mary remarried to Robert S. Steele in Audrain County on April 3, 1867,[7] and by that time the Ringos had settled in the same county's governmental seat, known as Mexico, as well, and had established a hotel and a bank.[8] Raccoon John was, indeed, a long way from where his plodding, hardworking father had been at the turn of the nineteenth century, anxious to see that all his children were provided not so much with money, because he didn't have any to speak of, but simply with tillable land to perpetuate the ethic that he had taught them.

However, their increased prosperity in and of itself never brought the children of John and Nancy Smith much happiness. Sickliness and both infant and young adult mortality still seemed to be permanent features for the family even in the second generation. We've spoken in this chapter and earlier ones of the deaths of John Duke Smith in 1846 and Eliza Ann Freeman a decade later, and of Williams's comments on Jonathan Smith's consumption and Mary Tomlinson Steele's poor state of health at the time Raccoon John himself lay on his deathbed. While we cannot say with certainty that tuberculosis was the root cause of all these deaths and illnesses besides Jonathan's and Harvey's, considering the family's medical history there's a better than average chance that it was. Though James and Maria Lee's sons and daughters, or at least a majority of them, seemed to thrive, A. R. and Emma Ringo were hit hard by the same griefs Emma's parents had known so well. Despite their prosperity and ostensible ability to procure the best medical care available for the time and place that they lived, of the Ringos' five children only two survived infancy, and of these, one died as a teenager. All the deaths besides that of the teenager occurred during Raccoon John's own lifetime as well.[9]

But of Raccoon John's offspring who survived childhood, Harvey Smith may have been the most uniquely tragic, and for reasons that we cannot now ever hope to learn. Both his marriage into the wealthy Stedman family and his brother-in-law A. R. Ringo's patronage were extremely auspicious for him; when Raccoon John had been at that same age, he would have given his eyeteeth for the opportunities that the young man enjoyed, and even if Harvey did not choose to continue his education at a good orthodox Disciple college like Bethany or Bacon, his future still looked bright. Harvey and his young wife, Mary, moved to Philadelphia, where he either worked for Ringo or in some business of his own with Ringo's assistance, and ere long the couple became the parents of a daughter, named Emma.

Though Harvey and Mary's future may have looked bright, something, some unknown factor or set of factors, must have been wrong with the marriage, and in fact the entire scenario, right from the start. The only historical records we have as to the details of the couple's domestic life were related subsequently by A. R. Ringo and one or two of Harvey's friends, and the sum of the evidence is not pretty. James M. Stevens, who worked for Harvey, described himself as "intimate" with Smith, and said that he had visited him and Mary frequently while they were "boarding" before they bought a house "on Wallace Street, below Twelfth" in Philadelphia, stated that Mary had consistently appeared to be a dutiful and affectionate wife but that Harvey did not treat her kindly and she seemed always to be afraid of him. Nevertheless, Stevens averred that Mary loved her husband devotedly notwithstanding his bad treatment of her. And so in the summer of 1855, evidently after a period of extreme strife with Harvey, Mary took a trip home to visit her parents, traveling west by rail with A. R. and Emma Ringo. Harvey paid for her train ticket and gave her a substantial amount of cash for her and the child. At the time she apparently had every intention of returning, and although she was visibly upset and weeping at her departure, she asked Stevens personally to "take care of Harvey" while she was gone.

For his part, Harvey claimed to have no desire whatsoever that Mary should return to him, and he informed Stevens as well as his other friends and his lawyer, Alfred Fassett, that he intended to divorce her immediately; he could not and would not live with her again. He sold their house and put all their furniture up for auction and apparently let Mary, his parents and sisters, and his in-laws know about this new turn of events entirely after the fact.[10] Perhaps none of us living in this present era, wherein women's rights are viewed in such a different and more beneficial light and mutual-consent divorce and the excuse of "irreconcilable differences" is so readily accepted in society, can comprehend how shocking Harvey's behavior must have appeared, or the multitude of ways in which it could and did hurt his wife more than himself. Of course, Harvey would have been blamed by his in-laws, all their neighbors, and even his own parents for deliberately ending his marriage and breaking up his family. If his father had ever immersed him, which is questionable, there's no doubt that he would have been excluded from the church at this period in its history for such an offense, and in spite of Raccoon John's own parents' checkered backwoods experience with divorce and remarriage, even he and Nancy would have disappointedly concurred that such an action was necessary. But the roles of wife, mother, and mistress of a home were, literally, all that antebellum southern society allowed for girls such as Mary Stedman Smith, and indeed these duties were all that they were trained for. Harvey's insistence on the divorce implied that he believed Mary to have failed grossly and miserably as a wife, and irrespective of the pain she would have felt from her unrequited love for him, the social stigma that Harvey's actions gave her had to have been crushing. The genteel antebellum Bluegrass was a long way from the pre-Revolutionary Virginia mountains, and polite society simply pretended that women such as the fiery young Rebecca Bowen, with the grit, backbone, and resolve not to let life defeat them at any cost, had never existed among their ancestors.

What made Harvey act in this brutal, inexplicable way? Was Mary really so unacceptable as a wife and a housemate that he couldn't even stand the thought of being around her? Not even Harvey's professed "intimate" friend Stevens in Philadelphia was willing to voice approval of his conduct toward her, so that's highly doubtful. Was he resentful because Mary had been raised as a young Bluegrass princess while his own parents had always been poor and he and his mother and siblings had so often been saddled with all the work about the farm because Raccoon John was away preaching and crusading? Did he have some mental problem undiagnosed and undiagnosable in that era, possibly exacerbated either by his perception of his class difference with his wife, or by the trauma of witnessing his little brother Richard's suffering and death? Could he have been one of the laborers at the butchering that fateful day in November 1843 and felt responsible in some way for Richard's fate, or for other reasons did he harbor the suspicion that Raccoon John and Nancy loved him less than they had Richard? Or was his sexual orientation such that his harsh, curt rejection of his wife and child so he could live as a bachelor in a big eastern seaboard city represented a confused, angry, and clumsy attempt to come to terms with it in a day when such things weren't even supposed to be? We cannot know, but neither can we rule any of these possibilities out. All that's certain is that Harvey Smith was a bitter, desperately unhappy young man, and whether through his own fault or that of others he managed alternately to bewilder and to wound literally everyone that ever loved him. From all evidence, on the occasions when he returned to Georgetown to visit his parents he didn't even make any attempt to contact Mary or his child, but under the circumstances it's highly unlikely that the Stedmans would have permitted his visits anyway. They might not even have let Raccoon John and Nancy see their granddaughter either, at least for a considerable time.[11]

Thus all that Raccoon John and Nancy could do was to live with Harvey's decision to break up his family, worry about their son living alone among the fleshpots of Philadelphia, grow grayer, and mourn silently. All their little ones that had died no doubt weighted their hearts with a sadness that never entirely went away, but it's possible that they could have worried and grieved as much or more over their boys that survived. They certainly must have done so for Harvey. But this unhappy situation was not fated to remain static for long. In addition to whatever other chips he carried on his shoulder, Harvey Smith had of course retained the family curse, consumption, and by the summer of 1858 the disease had so weakened him that he chose to give up his Philadelphia residence and come home to spend what little time he had left with his parents.

Raccoon John and Nancy seem to have been visiting Mary Tomlinson in Missouri and John was taking a preaching tour of the Disciple congregations in the northern part of that state when they got the news of Harvey's condition from Emma in Georgetown. In her letter, Emma begged her father to cancel all his speaking engagements and to return home with Nancy forthwith, to meet Harvey when he arrived. With the aging evangelist, though, old habits evidently died hard. In spite of the severity of the news about his youngest surviving son, he chose not to go back to Georgetown immediately, but rather insisted on keeping his Missouri pulpit appointments while Nancy made the arduous journey back to Kentucky alone, traveling by rail continuously for two days and one night. Once again we are left wondering how he managed to do any successful preaching with such unnerving family concerns on his mind, and how on earth he could have sent Nancy back to Kentucky by herself to deal with this fresh calamity. If Richard's death was a repetition of his 1815 Alabama tragedy, his reception of the news of Harvey's terminal sickness harked back to the day of Joshua's burial, when not even his little boy's funeral rites could keep him away from fulfilling what he was so utterly convinced at the time was his duty to the Kingdom of God. Nancy left Missouri on Monday, August 23, 1858, and arrived back in Georgetown two days or so later; Harvey got there about a week afterward, and Raccoon John stayed on the sawdust trail in Missouri until the last of September.[12] With the deaths of Eli, Elvira, Eliza Baize, William, Joshua, Richard, John Duke, and Eliza Ann, the old man may have undergone so much already that his senses were in some measure dulled, or perhaps Harvey really had perplexed and disappointed him so thoroughly—possibly in more than one way, we cannot know—that he simply didn't know what else to do except to go right on preaching.

For all this, though, we cannot say that Raccoon John harbored anything less than a father's love for Harvey, or that he was insensitive to his son's pain and inexorable decline of health. Harvey moved in with his parents and remained at their home; his lungs and throat were so weak that he could hardly speak above a whisper, and local physicians confirmed the judgment of his

Philadelphia doctors that there was no hope for his recovery.[13] On December 27, 1858, a Disciple evangelist named T. M. Allen wrote to *The Millennial Harbinger* about a Gospel meeting that he had initiated on December 11 in Georgetown. In his letter, Allen related that "the venerable Bro. John Smith was with us, but was overwhelmed with sorrow and grief on account of the severe affliction of his son, Harvey; but would occasionally be heard with his well known power and voice."[14]

Harvey Smith hung on for a little less than two months after Allen's letter, dying on or about February 22, 1859, at thirty-six years of age.[15] With the graves of their loved ones scattered through the various places they had lived in Montgomery and Bath counties, Raccoon John and Nancy elected not to try to start another family graveyard in Georgetown, but instead purchased a small plot at the well-known Lexington Cemetery in Fayette County. A great many prominent Kentuckians were buried here, among them Henry Clay, who had died in 1852, and the graveyard seems to have been favored both before and later by Kentucky's Disciple leaders. Raccoon John's old friend and traveling companion John T. Johnson, who died in 1857, was buried here, too, and in years to come so would be such Kentucky Disciple luminaries as Lewis Pinkerton, J. W. McGarvey, Alonzo Willard Fortune, and, temporarily, Moses Lard. And so Harvey was laid to rest at Lexington on February 23,[16] and it may have been at this time that the long-suffering Nancy expressed the wish to be buried beside him.

She had less than three years to wait, passing away herself finally on the fourth day of November 1861 amid the unbridled turmoil raging through the Bluegrass as to Kentucky's position with both the Union and the Confederacy in the Civil War. Earlier that year Raccoon John had attended a meeting of Alexander Campbell's American Christian Missionary Society in Cincinnati, where a resolution supporting the Union had been introduced; though he himself was a Union man, he was of course also now a slaveowner as well, and he had taken part in efforts to quash the motion on the grounds that it was out of order for a religious body even to entertain such a resolution.[17] This may have been the last ecclesiastical business meeting of any sort in which he participated in such a way. But at any rate, when Nancy became sick this last time it is possible that Raccoon John had her transported back to Owingsville to be tended by Maria and the Lees' numerous family servants in her terminal illness. The only surviving anecdote about her death and her wake comes from one of Maria and James Lee's daughters, Mollie Nesbitt, in an interview conducted many years afterward by Disciple historian E. C. Raines. In addition to recalling Raccoon John's habit of smoking a pipe once after dinner each day, Mollie remembered that her grandfather loved flowers, and that when Nancy died he pulled up an entire bush of yellow chrysanthemums and laid them on her body.[18]

Williams eulogizes Nancy Smith as "an exemplary matron of the olden times . . . [who] lived for her husband and her children; to them, under God, she consecrated her life; and in that devotion consisted her happiness and her usefulness" (ellipsis added).[19] For his own purposes Louis Cochran makes her an outspoken, redheaded frontier Boadicea that the toughest backwoodsmen had to respect, a heroine entirely a match for her hard-bitten patriot evangelist hero. But it should not be forgotten that she actually lived somewhere in between, as a woman whose whole life was circumscribed by both the crude medical care and the restrictive social mores of her time, who worked doggedly all her days for very little earthly recompense, who was acquainted more with grief than she was with happiness—and without whom, all through his ministry, Raccoon John Smith absolutely could not have managed. A bunch of yellow chrysanthemums as a decoration for her pall was not much in the way of recognition for the multitude of ways in which she had stood in the gap for him; but then again, as with his donation of his white cravat for Anna's funeral in 1815, there wasn't much else he could have done. Nancy had given her heart to a crusader and he had returned her love as much as he was able. Perhaps that was enough.

After Nancy's death, Raccoon John sold his Georgetown house and spent the remainder of his days alternating between his daughters' homes as a guest, with frequent visits to various Kentucky Disciple leaders, including John Augustus Williams, to whom he was by now dictating his memoirs. He spent most of his time in Owingsville with the Lees and in Mexico, Missouri, with Mary Tomlinson and where A. R. and Emma Ringo relocated in the early 1860s, traveling back and forth between the two towns by rail; however, since his grandson Henry Jefferson Boles later claimed to have accompanied him once in a while on preaching appointments, we cannot rule out the possibility that the old man paid at least one southward visit to his two daughters by Anna as well. A Union veteran, Boles would have been about sixteen at the time his step-grandmother died and the Civil War broke out, and though he grew up in an area of strong Confederate sympathy his grandfather's outspoken Unionist position could have influenced him to join the Union Army over the Confederate.[20]

After Nancy's death and up until 1865, when Raccoon John traveled he took with him a small boy, either his own slave or belonging to one of his daughters, to serve as his valet (the Emancipation Proclamation of 1863 did not end slavery in either Kentucky or Missouri, since they were still loyal Union states). His hands were so palsied by now that he could not feed himself, and the child waited on him hand and foot at table even to the spooning of food into his mouth. Both his granddaughter Mollie in her interview with E. C. Raines and, interestingly, even the minute records of old Spencer Creek Church mention this child as accompanying the aged evangelist. Raccoon John visited and preached at Spencer Creek for the last time in 1865, and at this juncture he took the opportunity as well to visit the old Mt. Pleasant plantation and mansion where he had gotten his start with Jilson Payne so many years before, for one final look upon the historic log that had split the church and thus brought him to Montgomery County.[21] We can only imagine the flood of memories that the old salt trough must have prompted in Raccoon John's mind, and we might wonder as well how many varied regrets were mixed among them.

But in spite of all the temporal commotions of these years, in his old age Raccoon John was remembered not to have lived much in the past, or for that matter, even in the present. After hearing him preach, David T. Wright, editor of *The Christian Pioneer,* wrote of him that "He dwells much in the future, and consequently when he speaks of heaven, the Father, Christ, the angels, and the righteous dead, he speaks with a confidence and a familiarity that deeply impresses you with his strong faith in these glorious realities. His meditations are beyond the confines of flesh, he feels that he's a stranger here, tarrying but for a few days and will then go home to join the redeemed hosts who have gone before."[22] After a lifetime of relative hesitance to put pen to paper that was itself unusual in a Campbell disciple, Raccoon John finally became something of an amateur hymnist, and the verses he wrote concentrate more on heaven and the afterlife than any other subjects. A portion of the most famous surviving specimen attributed to him reads thus:

> There's a region above,
> Free from sin and temptation,
> And a mansion of love,
> For each heir of salvation.
>
> There shall friends no more part,
> Nor shall farewells be spoken,
> There shall be balm for the heart,
> That with anguish was broken.
>
> From afflictions set free,
> And from God ne'er sever,
> We His glory shall see,
> And enjoy him forever.[23]

Unquestionably, Raccoon John was a better preacher than he was a songster. His sentence structure would make one think that he was translating German freehand rather than writing anything original. However, we must take into account the limits that both verse forms and the conventions of the time imposed upon him, as well as the fact that, for all his imperfections, he was still about as good a versifier as anyone presently plying the trade in the modern country- and contemporary Gospel music industries. When left to his own devices, however, the old veteran of the cross could produce more eloquent lines extemporaneously. John Augustus Williams gives this example that he took down one evening at his own hearthside in Lexington as the visiting Raccoon John recounted the story of the Passion of Jesus. When one considers all the sorrow that Raccoon John himself had endured, as well as the degree of legalism that the early followers of *The Christian Baptist* could so often exhibit, the passion that he put into his retelling of the old, old story is itself awe-inspiring:

> I love to think that my life should spring from His death; my healing, from His wounds; my glory, from His shame. If God forsake Him not, I cannot be accepted. If thorns press not His temples, I can never wear a crown of glory. Now in the grave He lies; He must conquer death, or I must sleep forever. If there ever was a time when all the harps of Heaven were still, and not one note of angel music sounded through the skies, 'twas when that lifeless, mangled form was lying in the rich man's tomb! But the voice of God pierces the gloom and silence of the grave; angels attend upon His second birth; with a glorious escort, He passes upward in his chariot of clouds, and enters through the everlasting gates. Those doors were closed when Adam fell; they now receive the Conqueror of sin and death. And, glorious thought! They are still unbarred; and I, and you, and all that follow Him in life, shall one day enter through the gates into the everlasting city of our God.[24]

And so if we consider Raccoon John's Passion Story as his own personal version of kerygma and his last will and testament of sorts upon his ministry, what should we say in sum of this final period of his life, and how must we reconcile it with his earlier years? Could his dramatic 1828 zealot's conversion really have caused him to become so shallow intellectually and emotionally that he did not recognize the terrible parallels between his days as a political wheelhorse in the Kentucky General Union and the ups and downs of his career in Montgomery and Bath counties after the Stone-Campbell union of 1832, even to the griefs that he experienced during both periods? It's doubtful, but again, he would have been neither willing to delve into such thoughts himself nor encouraged to do so by any of his later religious colleagues. As we've seen already, his experiences with John Mason, Kenaz Farrow, and James McVay and the juxtaposition of his dealings with them and his youngest son's death made his life into a tale neither of unqualified victory nor of God's unquestioned leadership, but more the story of his own well-intentioned blundering, in which he had done the absolute best he thought he could with the opportunities he'd been given, but in which neither his own best efforts nor those of Alexander Campbell had proven to be good enough or noble enough to transcend either his own follies and those of the rest of humankind, or the random acts of nature. As I noted in my previous work, essentially he had jumped from the frying pan, not into the fire, but merely into another frying pan. O wild, sweet, festal joys, frenzy without hope.

For whatever reason his previous biographers omitted or downplayed such a significant series of his experiences from their stories, it still speaks poorly of them for having done so. All of them came from a religious culture which, on its thesis of the Bible as a virtual scientific blueprint for humanity's place in the Kingdom of God, insisted that it placed cold hard scientific facts and the ostensibly logical inferences drawn from them on the highest pedestal, and which gleaned most of its rhetoric from its claim to seek, and find, pure truth untainted by superstition, "sectarian" or otherwise. To omit, color, or obfuscate relevant data from a relation of supposed facts on the chance that such data might contribute to the negation of a previously held hypothesis thus became hypocrisy of the worst sort. We are left staring at the possibility which they all seem to have been so terrified to voice: that neither the Baptists of Raccoon John's youthful experience, the Methodists and Presbyterians against whom he competed as a Baptist for souls, nor the Disciples of his maturity could back up their respective claims to Divine guidance over and above each other, with any evidence either of particular inspiration or intercessory assistance from the Source that they all claimed had His eye even on the sparrow and Whose power was supposed to compel them all to love one another. All they had was the Bible as an unquestioned and unquestionable validation of Divine revelation, and in their interpretations of this they disagreed; yet the Bible itself was not the main source of their strife, but rather their own propensities, both individual and collective, to demonize anyone who disagreed with them in what they believed *about* the Bible. Were the facts of Richard Menefee Smith's tragic death and all the circumstances leading up to it therefore more an endorsement of Hamlet's statement that there's a divinity that shapes our ends, rough-hew them how we will, or the eyeless Duke of Gloucester's pained cry in *King Lear,* that as flies to wanton boys are we to the gods: they kill us for their sport? And when we believers wrestle with the issue, could we somehow find ourselves led finally to try to rationalize the conundrum as Peter De Vries's fictional Rev. Andrew Mackerel did, by declaring that the final proof of God's omnipotence is that he need not exist in order to save us? De Vries's own thinking was unavoidably colored by his personal experience, that of the long sickness and eventual death at age ten of an adored daughter from leukemia. But the only one who could have answered this question for Raccoon John personally was he himself, and in his silence, Raccoon John's myth becomes Raccoon John's mystery.

In writing about Martin Luther and the original Reformation, Richard Marius observed that he had once hoped to find an historical precedent in Luther's story relevant to the lives of the young men and women that he taught in the Vietnam era, some example of faith, resolve, courage, or dedication that they could apply to their own increasingly uncertain lives as the shadow of an arbitrary draft and a chaotic, hopeless foreign war loomed larger and larger over their heads. But after Marius researched Luther's role in the Peasants' Rebellion, examined his later writings including his 1540s tracts about the German Jews, and studied the effects of the Wars of Religion that followed his establishment of the Protestant cause, this once-faithful Baptist minister and always-competent scholar came to an extremely unhappy conclusion. The Peasants' Rebellion had occurred primarily because the German peasantry had largely taken literally what Luther had proclaimed in his earlier tracts about the freedoms of a Christian, but Luther had responded to the peasants' pleas for justice as if they were a pack of out-and-out criminals and infidels, fully endorsing their overlords' thorough and cruel suppression of them. Similarly, he had advocated toleration for the Jews, so long as he had believed that they would readily accept his Reformed Christianity; they wouldn't convert, however, and so the same man who wrote the tender lyrics to *Away in a Manger* also penned at least two blistering attacks against the Jews, of which Adolf Hitler himself could have been proud—and for all we know, very well may have been. And finally, as opposed to Roman Catholicism as Luther was after he got the details of his theology worked out completely, he could lash out with just as much fury and condemnation at fellow Protestants such as Zwinglians, Anabaptists, and Schwenkfelders, who had gotten their start at least partially through the influence of his printed tracts but who happened to disagree with him on one or more points. Besides exploiting his power with the Protestant German princes to anathematize the followers of pacifistic, Anabaptist-leaning Kaspar von Schwenkfeld, he actually told von Schwenkfeld himself, literally, to go to hell. This side of Martin Luther has of course often been downplayed by the clergymen and scholars who have written the majority of his biographies, but in fact neither in his dealings with the peasants, the Jews, nor arguably with other, dissenting Protestants did he betray any of the basic principles on which he had founded the Reformation. And so ultimately, Marius gloomily concluded that Luther had no valid word to speak to our time, and for these considerations and others likewise came to reject the Gospel that Luther preached as equally irrelevant and destructive. What Luther and the Reformation achieved and delivered in the third and fourth decades of the sixteenth century and afterward was a long way from both the promise that the movement had seemed to harbor in the second decade, and the quasi-mythical spin that so many of Luther's Protestant biographers gave to his character and to his life. Marius could not come to terms with this kind of dichotomy in a way that would allow his belief in Luther's relevance—or his own personal faith—to survive.[25]

Though the stories both of Alexander Campbell, who in his early years believed with all his heart that he was completing the work that Luther had merely started, and Raccoon John Smith, who from his middle years believed with all his heart that Campbell had restored not only Luther's work but Peter's and Paul's as well, might appear insignificant alongside that of such a world giant as Luther, the parallels between each man's fate at the hands of historians are obvious. And more significantly, so are the parallels between the problems that Luther's life gave Marius and the difficulties inherent in retelling Raccoon John's story as a tale of faith without the careful omissions and obfuscations that all his prior chroniclers have made. And these biographers, or hagiographers rather, had to have been inwardly shaken and unsettled themselves by the facts, if indeed they allowed themselves pause enough to give them serious consideration at all. One wonders how much Barton Stone's own grandson Charles Moore, the Disciple preacher-turned-atheist that we met at the conclusion of the last chapter, might have been influenced by just such events that he himself was able to observe during his own ministry, although it's difficult to ascertain; one cannot discern from Moore's autobiographical writings that he endured any agonies of mind such as Marius underwent, and he appears to have worn both his Christianity and his atheism equally lightly.

But however much I admire both Marius's eloquence and his willingness to address extremely difficult subjects in a painfully honest manner, I cannot share in all his conclusions even though there have been times that I have been sorely tempted to do so. Whether that says more for Marius or more for me, I cannot help but remember that Søren Kierkegaard summed up Luther's career as pithily as did Marius, and much more briefly: to him, Luther confused what it means to be the patient with what it means to be the doctor. He was an extremely important patient for Christianity, with the patient's passion for expressing and describing his suffering and what he felt the need of, as an alleviation. But he just didn't have the breadth of view to be a successful physician of the spirit, and within his own narrow range of tunnel vision he made all of his errors and blunders.

That sort of medical imagery may appeal to me personally in a way that all might not share. Still, it could be one of the few means by which we can view both Campbell and Smith, and even Marius and indeed all Gospel ministers, in complete honesty. We are all better patients than we are doctors. Too, as the grounds for a personal theodicy it's at least no worse than any other and perhaps better than most; any time that patients know more than their physicians, somebody, all too often a multitude of somebodies, is going to suffer. Can a true reformation of Christianity ever be achieved unless would-be reformers can somehow overcome this paradox? Who knows? Arrogant as Luther could be, in his very last letter in German he wrote that we, as Christians, are all still beggars. Whether any of his actions could be taken to imply that he really believed it is another matter. But when all is said, done, and pondered, it may be that the only theodicy that does not ultimately prove itself to be an insult and an obscenity both to the concept of a benevolent God and to the suffering, worshiping humankind that still clings to the concept is the vision of process theology, that to which William Sloane Coffin held so tenaciously in the wake of his grief over his son's death: the idea that God, greater than any mere being or person but rather the Foundation of all being, suffers right along with, and just as intensely as, the humblest individual at the lowest ebb of that individual's despair or the very worst of his or her pain. It's true that the Apostle Paul wrote in Romans 8:22 that "we know that the whole creation groaneth and travaileth in pain together until now," but at the same time we must concede that this proposition will never fit into any rationalistic scheme of doctrine claiming to be verifiable objectively, be it Alexander Campbell's or anyone else's. If it is accepted at all, the acceptance must take place solely on the basis of faith and hope, and nothing else—save, of course and most importantly, charity.

I'm tempted here to continue in this particular vein, and explain further as to how and why I can still have faith in God in the face of such challenges both from Raccoon John's story and my own life that prompted the writing of this volume to begin with, but in truth it may not be the time or the place to do so. Even if it didn't require an excursus as long as sociologist Peter Berger's and Jesus scholars Marcus J. Borg and N. T. Wright's own recent, detailed apologies for their religious convictions in the face of an understandably skeptical world,[26] I have the feeling that, like Kierkegaard, I should be content to present opposing, conflicting viewpoints and let my readers figure out their own personal truths—which, after all, stick to one's ribs a great deal more effectively than any didactic instruction an individual can receive, even if the instructor is as persuasive as Alexander Campbell or Raccoon John. But as it is, and to draw all the varying concepts of theodicy we have outlined in this volume full circle, in Christian belief only one individual has ever stood in the gap between sufferer and healer in the true, full, and complete occupancy of both roles—and that was Jesus of Nazareth, alone. Which brings us back to the aged Raccoon John's personal interpretation of the Passion Story: it is obviously no dry recitation of facts and details, but a heartfelt account of that which he believed deeply, joyfully, and *passionately.* After all these years and through every hurt he had ever undergone, the Gospel, the experience of Christ, the religious over and above that of the heedless aesthetic and as the fulfillment of the despairing ethical, remained his anchor, and he could still speak of the Resurrection in ecstatic tones. Whatever his life story may prove about the efficacy of organized religion or the wisdom of placing too much confidence in any form thereof, his personal experience of transcendence in and of itself, his own individual perception of the reality of God, at rock bottom, must have been what gave him the strength to carry on. If he blundered in misplacing his trust and setting too much store by one particular religious movement or church over another, thereby risking the security and sacrificing the health and happiness of both his wives and his children, and moreover, did this not once but twice, he paid for his mistakes dearly; if he had laid wood, hay, and stubble on a golden foundation, again not only once but twice, he had made an honest error of judgment and was no more guilty of presumption than was any other evangelical minister of his day, and indeed, most in our own as well.

Strangely enough, in a very real way this presumption makes one think of Gilgamesh, the mighty king of old Sumerian legend. Arriving at the gate of Siduri, the winemaker, grieving at the death of his dearest friend Enkidu, sunburned and parched after his quest to find Ut napishtim the ark builder (whom, of course, students of the Bible know as Noah) and the secret of eternal life, Gilgamesh is told by Siduri that he will never really find that for which he is looking; he should bathe himself in water, cherish the little child who holds his hand, and make his wife happy in his embrace, for this, too, is the lot of mortals. The Preacher in the Book of Ecclesiastes says as much himself. But if John Smith had followed such counsel, he would now be remembered no more than the hundreds of his contemporary brother ministers of the Gospel such as Daniel Williams, William Coffee, and Joseph Nickell, in dusty footnotes in dusty pages of local history.

And so who, now, can say whether Raccoon John Smith ever really gained that which his heart truly desired either consciously or unconsciously, or which alternative choices would have been better for him? The cumulative efforts of John Augustus Williams, Louis Cochran, Everett Donaldson, Alexander Campbell, Walter Scott, Albert Allen, James Challen, Leroy Garrett, any number of other brief biographical sketchers, and one lone bothersome country Baptist are but one hundred fifty-odd years and more than two thousand printed pages of feeble attempts to capture the spirit and the essence of the man. And it gives one pause to think that the sum total of our work can be contained within two small words that say it all:

He tried.

Whether or not the leaders of the faction of his great movement that later came to be called Churches of Christ were right in accusing Alexander Campbell of having lost his nerve, his backbone, and perhaps a portion of his reason after his son Wickliffe's death, Campbell maintained the editorship of *The Millennial Harbinger* and the presidency of his new denomination's national missionary society until 1863, and he finally died at his home at Bethany in the new state of West Virginia on March 4, 1866. He outlived his loyal lieutenants Barton Stone, John T. Johnson, and Walter Scott all, and by the time of his death his Reform had grown to encompass more than three hundred thousand members in the United States and beyond. But by this period it had grown irrevocably into at least two distinct doctrinal and practical viewpoints, and the organization was already split so thoroughly by various "Editor Bishops" that the U.S. Church census of forty years after Campbell's death merely recorded the final acknowledgment of two distinct and separate communions, rather than the actual occurrence of any contemporary division. Subsequent "reformations" of Christianity have done little or no better, be they of the later Church of God, Pentecostal, Holiness, or Fundamentalist movements, or modern charismatic television ministries that have claimed to restore original Christianity. It must be said, though, that many of these have acquitted themselves nowhere near as capably as did the fiery young Irish editor that brought the concept of reform to the American South and Midwest with *The Christian Baptist* and *The Millennial Harbinger.*

It so happened on that fateful fourth of March, as Campbell lay bedfast, that his colleague Robert Richardson brought news to him of an attempt then ongoing in Richmond, Virginia, to reunite Baptists and Disciples in that state once more. Campbell expressed deep regret that he and his followers had ever parted company so bitterly with the Baptists in the first place, and observed that the Baptists and his Disciples ought somehow to have remained together for the restoration of the primitive church.[27] We might well wonder how both he and Raccoon John would have fared if indeed they had managed to keep themselves peaceful enough to stick with the Baptists, but by the time Campbell went to his reward, it was forty years and a ton of newsprint too late.

A year or so after Campbell's death, a brand-new religious tract written by an anonymous author calling himself "Ariel" appeared in the bookshops and newsstands of Nashville, Tennessee. Printed by a Cincinnati, Ohio, publishing house that likewise opted to withhold its identity, the little book was entitled *The Negro: What Is His Ethnological Status?* In forty-eight pages of closely printed type, using or at least trying to utilize a fundamental concept of Scottish Common Sense Realism, "Ariel" proposed to refute the infamous old southern myth that blacks were the descendants of Ham and were given their skin color and their lot in life by the curse of Noah in the book of Genesis.[28] If disproving the vile old wives' (and ministers') tale had been Ariel's sole intention, his efforts might have been laudable; but as it was, he offered an alternative theory of black origins, based on his own version of the same so-called Common Sense Realism and a "pure" interpretation of Scripture, that he used to disprove the "Ham" claim, that was even more shocking, and indeed chilling, than any frustrated Confederate war hawk in the embittered South had yet attempted to propagate. Here are Ariel's claims, taken from his own summations on the tract's last four pages (and I admittedly list them with some trepidation here; after all, who knows but that they might be copied onto an Internet website somewhere to buttress the arguments of an Aryan cult, and worse, that a new cult—not only an Aryan cult but an "Ariel" cult—might be born from them?):

1. That Noah and his wife, their sons Shem, Ham, and Japheth and their wives, and consequently the entire human race from Adam to Noah had been white.
2. That (to borrow Ariel's own terminology here) Negroes were created before Adam and Eve and are therefore not human, but beasts, specifi cally the highest order of ape. They are able to learn and imitate human speech and behavior, but like all lower animals, they possess no souls and no hope of an afterlife. As such, Adam and Eve and their progeny are given dominion over blacks, along with the other beasts of the field, by simple and obvious Divine right.
3. That the "serpent" who tempted Eve, and hence Adam, in the Garden of Eden was neither snake nor devil, but a black man, being the only brute

beast developed highly enough to converse with humans. This also explains why the "serpent" was "more subtile" [*sic*] than all the other beasts of the field.

4. That the reason God destroyed the world in a flood was none other than miscegenation; in other words, the Genesis passage that states that the "sons of God" had copulated with "the daughters of men" to produce a race of giants actually meant that white humans had coupled with black "animals" and had produced a race of monsters, neither human nor beast, that God had seen fit to wipe off the face of the earth. (Of course, this meant too that the entire modern Negroid race came from the two blacks that Noah must have stowed on the ark.)
5. That the upheavals and destructions described in the Pentateuch of the Tower of Babel and the cities of Sodom and Gomorrah, and the conquest of the land of Canaan by the Israelites, had been carried out as punishments from God against the heathen for this same sin of miscegenation.
6. That God did not and would not accept any form of religious worship from blacks, since the "plain truth" of the Bible declared unequivocally that none with flat noses could approach God's altar, and besides, blacks were brute animals and had no souls anyway.
7. That the ways of God are "*always consistent, when understood,* and always just and reasonable. It is a curious fact, but a fact nevertheless, and fully sustained by the Bible . . . that God *never conferred,* and never *designed* to *confer,* any great blessing on the human family, but what he *always* selects or selected a white *slaveholder* or one of a white *slaveholding nation,* as the *medium* by or through which that blessing should reach them. Why he has done so, is not material to discuss now; but the fact that he always did so, the Bible abundantly proves" (all emphases in original; ellipsis added). Listed as examples are the patriarch Abraham and the Roman government during the lifetime of Jesus, and more germane to the United States, the Revolutionary patriots Patrick Henry, Peyton Randolph, Charles Thompson, Benjamin Harrison, Thomas Jefferson, George Washington, and James Madison.
8. That the United States had rebelled directly against Divine principles in seeking to abolish slavery and establish black equality through the Civil War, and that therefore the formerly godly but now atheistic America was at that very instant primed for another invocation of God's fierce wrath upon the face of the earth—a wrath that could, quite justly, prove to be as devastating as the Great Flood or the destruction of Sodom and Gomorrah.
9. And finally, that the only thing that the United States could do to avert this just wrath of God was either to send all blacks to Africa or re-enslave them as befitted their true status as beasts. Ariel admitted that the former option was by far the best one, but went on to promise the people of the South that God, in His own due time, would not fail to

destroy the government of the North and reestablish the government of the United States on the Divine principles that the southerners and their ancestors had upheld—if they would only keep the faith. The finger of God was in all this, Ariel advised; southerners must trust Him, because, in the final declaration of the tract, God's word is true.[29]

Ariel's pamphlet thus anticipated many of the arguments of the more notorious Charles Carroll, whose 1900 book, *The Negro,* was so long prized and upheld by white supremacist extremists. Ariel's *The Negro* hit the defeated Confederates of the Tennessee capital, already primed for anything that might help them justify their bitterness, with the impact of a hurricane. Fortunately, not everyone believed it; though all too many hotheads proved entirely willing to swallow it whole, Ariel's idea was so bizarrely extreme that a charitable organization dedicated to supplying artificial limbs for crippled Confederate soldiers, whose leaders and members had to have been pro-South through and through, actually financed a prominent Nashville Southern Methodist minister, Dr. Robert Young, to publish a reply to Ariel and to take a lecture tour for the express purpose of refuting him. Dr. Young, who himself unashamedly admitted to anti-black prejudices normative for white southerners of the time, nonetheless wrote a capable essay, skewering Ariel's thought at every turn and corner. He made what must have been a fatal mistake in the eyes of much of Ariel's most devoted readership, though. He based his arguments not only on Scripture but on the scientific conclusions of prominent eighteenth- and nineteenth-century naturalists, such as Carolus Linnaeus, George Blackie, and Louis Agassiz,[30] and any Christian of Ariel's mindset knew well enough that scientists were more than likely to be atheists and their arguments could never measure up to good old plain Scripture and the consensus of all right-thinking Christians bound to follow Scriptural teaching. Charles Darwin was a naturalist, too, after all.

And so the Gospel According to Ariel endured if it did not actually flourish. Besides the distinct possibility that the author's brand of Common Sense Realism provided the entire theological outlook for the leadership of the Ku Klux Klan, which had been formed in Tennessee only a short time before the evil little book hit the Nashville streets, it was still well known and even propagated privately in some white Nashville churches, particularly Churches of Christ otherwise officially unassociated with the Klan, as late as 1907.[31] Ariel's message seemed to spread insidiously from the city back into hill country Tennessee, and Kentucky, too, where neither the Klan nor the objects of its hatred were as well known as they were in the Deep South. Harry M. Caudill quoted an old eastern Kentuckian who believed that blacks were "skasely human accordin' to the Bible" in his famous *Night Comes to the Cumberlands,*[32] and one of my own mentors in the church, the late Elder J. T. Bailey of Keaton, Kentucky, who was born in 1900, likewise noted having heard the Ariel doctrine in his youth. To his eternal credit, Bailey reacted so strongly against Ariel's claims that he still felt compelled to speak out against them in his old age, long after any of his beloved eastern Kentucky United, Primitive, and "Enterprise" Regular Baptist hearers—hopefully—took such cruel ignorance seriously.[33]

When the tract was new, though, speculation was rife as to Ariel's identity, and that of his unnamed Cincinnati publisher, as well as to the development of his thought. We may never know the complete answer to the two latter questions. There were several publishing companies in Cincinnati at the time, a fair number of them doctrinally and/or denominationally based. Incidentally, one of these, R. W. Carroll and Co., which printed *The Christian Standard* for Isaac Errett, would publish John Augustus Williams's biography of Raccoon John Smith within three years after *The Negro* first hit bookstores. Another, smaller Cincinnati job office was run by the reactionary Disciple editor Benjamin Franklin.[34] But Ariel's choice of a northern publishing house was curious, especially in light of the subject he tried to address; it's no real wonder that the house declined to put its imprint on the tract, and we must wonder if Ariel sought help from some sort of lunatic-fringe element in a northern denomination simply because no southern publisher under Reconstruction government felt safe in touching his manuscript with a ten-foot pole. Neither can we tell if the mysterious writer came up with his twisted and depraved hypothesis entirely on his own, or if he only penned ideas he had heard thrown around perhaps for many years within his own religious and social circles, wherever they might have existed. It should be mentioned, though, that two dates, July 1840 and December 1866, are noted at the end of the tract in the manner that some authors list their times of commencing and finishing literary projects.[35] Although most, if not all, of the latter part of the missive had to have been written during or immediately after the Civil War, we can therefore say with a fair degree of certainty that the bulk of Ariel's convictions about blacks had been festering within his mind for more than a quarter century before he finally published them.

But who on earth was he? Some Tennesseans of the time actually believed that *The Negro* had been written by the great northeastern Congregationalist minister Henry Ward Beecher; that the brother of Harriet Beecher Stowe, the author of *Uncle Tom's Cabin,* could harbor a mindset so diametrically opposed to Stowe's classic makes for an entire other story on its own. Perhaps more believed that Ariel was either an active or a former Methodist exhorter, an idea extremely repugnant to his Nashville adversary Dr. Robert Young. Still, Young admitted it was possible that Ariel could have tried his hand at preaching at least at some point in his life, but that was as far as he would venture his own guesses.[36] No one seemed to notice that Ariel himself had left one clue at the ending of *The Negro*: the bottom of the tract's last page had a note that stated, "Any candid scholar wishing to address the writer is informed that any letter addressed to 'Ariel,' care of Messrs. Payne, James & Co., Nashville, Tennessee, during the summer and fall (1867), will reach him and command his attention."[37] One wonders whether Ariel, stationed right there at Payne,

James & Co. in Nashville all along, was pleased or insulted to hear that Henry Ward Beecher had been credited with his ideas.

Only when the Disciples of Christ Historical Society of Nashville came into the possession of the personal papers of the redoubtable Jacob Creath Jr. after the younger Creath's death in 1886 did the truth finally come out. Included among Creath's papers was a copy of *The Negro* that at long last identified the tract's author. It was Buckner Harrison Payne, and *The Negro* is his only known published writing after his assumption of the North District Association clerk's office and his collaboration with Raccoon John Smith on the association's majority faction's position papers of 1830 and 1831. He survived his most infamous tract's publication by seventeen years, perhaps never having dared to reveal himself openly as its author, and died at the age of eighty-five in 1884, a sick, demented, broken, and twisted old man who had done much to make sure that his own sickness and depravity would endure in the South, like a malevolent ghost, for many years to come.

On the bitterly cold Sunday morning of February 9, 1868, eighty-three-year-old Raccoon John Smith informed his daughter Emma at breakfast that he intended to walk to Sunday school that morning and preach, as usual, at the regular worship service of Mexico, Missouri's Disciple congregation. Why Emma and her husband themselves did not insist on accompanying the increasingly frail old man is not known, but Raccoon John's daughter did attempt to persuade him to stay out of the inclement weather. Her pleas were in vain, though, and refusing even the offer of a carriage, Raccoon John set out on foot.

Since Nancy's death he had often taken an old man's advantage of opportunities to act with a feisty independence, and his actions on this Sunday morning were entirely in keeping with his character. At one point right after the Civil War had ended, he had almost landed himself in the Audrain County jail for refusing to take a loyalty oath then required of Gospel ministers preaching in Missouri. His rationale was that if he swore the oath, he would no longer be preaching by the authority of Jesus Christ, but by that of the Missouri State Legislature, and not even the most reasoned and compelling arguments that A. R. Ringo and the sheriff could muster could shake his resolve. The tough old warhorse had finally been persuaded to leave the state only because a mob of loyal Disciples threatened to storm the jail and free him by force if he were lodged there, and so he returned to the Lees in Kentucky—regretfully—for a couple of years until his legal troubles blew over, only because he didn't want any of his friends to shed their blood for him. As for himself, he'd have been glad to do the jail time out of pure principle and stubbornness; he had informed the hapless sheriff that with the example of the first Christians before him, he'd gladly submit to law and take the penalty, but he'd still preach through the jail windows if any would gather there to hear him.[38]

By the time he'd gotten back to Missouri in the summer of 1867, the state's

Supreme Court had set aside the law requiring the loyalty oath, and so his case was simply dropped. Not too many months afterward, though, he went to war again, this time with a New England teacher of spiritualism who had taken residence temporarily in the city of Mexico and apparently within the local Disciple congregation. Whether or not that this spiritualist had any connection to the famous—or infamous—Nashville Disciple minister with similar inclinations, Jesse B. Ferguson, we cannot say. But when the spiritualist met Smith and asked his opinion of her beliefs, he laid down the gauntlet of challenge as if he were still a young man: he'd prove, he said, any time and to the entire satisfaction of an "intelligent audience," that the "whole thing" was from the devil. Accordingly, a contest of the type that had proven successful for him so many years before against the heresies of James Fishback and the Methodists was arranged for January 1868, and for one last time the aged Raccoon John held forth his part in debate against doctrinal error.

This debate, however, had a twist that the old man had probably never seen before. At the close of Raccoon John's speech, the spiritualist rose from her seat and with closed eyes, presumably in a trance and under the influence of her claimed familiars, began to reply to his argument with the accusation that "it was wicked thus to malign the spirits who had been sent hither to warn those in the form." Most of the men present were virtually struck dumb with embarrassment, but Raccoon John simply took a chew of tobacco and then silenced her with an impatient wave of his hand and the words, "Oh! We don't want to be interrupted now with such stuff as that."

The medium, who had by now sat down again but with her head still thrown back and her eyes still closed, replied that she was not responsible for what she said and did; she had no control over herself, but was completely at the command of her spirits. The doughty Raccoon John retorted that if she had no control over herself, she was in a bad fix, and had better go home. She apparently came to herself then and obliged, but as she departed she told him that she hoped to meet him in another world; to this he replied resolutely that it depended on which world she was going to, whether he wished to meet her or not. Her temper finally nettled, she then stormed out of the meetinghouse, and Raccoon John remarked dryly that he had raised the devil, and had now cast him out.[39]

But finally, on this icy February Sunday, the old man discovered the limits of his physical endurance. Though he had undoubtedly abandoned the New England Holy Tone for a more conversational preaching style at least forty and possibly as many as fifty to fifty-five years before, he nonetheless must have worked up a sweat in the pulpit; according to Williams, those who listened to his discourse that day never forgot the power and zeal with which he spoke, and remarked that it was one of the best sermons that he had ever delivered. But by the end of the service the day had grown even colder, and Raccoon John was taken with a severe chill on his way home. He was pale and shivering by the time he reached his daughter and son-in-law's residence, and as the alarmed Emma hastened to prepare him a cup of hot coffee and help him into some dry clothes, he remarked that he did not remember ever being so cold in all his life. After lunch and a nap he felt better, and would have gone out again to meeting that night were it not for A. R. and Emma Ringo's renewed entreaties against the idea. But the damage was done: the shock of the intense cold to an immune system already weakened by age and weariness, and to a set of lungs scarred from years of the smoke of strong home-grown tobacco, was too much to prevent a heavy case of pneumonia, and the morning found him burning with fever and suffering intensely.

Despite the best medical attentions available, he lay in a delirious stupor for more than a week. Then on the eighteenth day of the month he seemed to rally a bit, and his mind became more active; even his old humor resurfaced from time to time, almost spontaneously. Nonetheless, he was convinced that his race was finally run, and as he received numerous callers—including, interestingly, the local Baptist minister as well as his Disciple friends—he spoke mostly of his impending demise, and how happy he was now to be "nearly home."[40]

Only Emma Ringo seems to have attended him in this last sickness. His daughters by Anna, far away in the hills of south central Kentucky and northern Tennessee, could only have been notified of his condition by mail; Jonathan was 120 miles away in St. Louis, himself too weak with tuberculosis to travel; and Mary, his youngest surviving child, still lived in close proximity to Emma but at this time was in such feeble health herself that she couldn't have been of much help.[41] The Lees of Owingsville seem to have sent William Berryman Hurt's son James to represent them at Raccoon John's deathbed, and perhaps to render A. R. and Emma what assistance he could.[42]

Even so, Raccoon John might have improved further had he only been able to regain his appetite. Word seems already to have gone out among the Disciple brotherhood as to the old pioneer's condition, and on February 25 one W. J. Mason wrote to *Christian Pioneer* editor David Wright that Smith by this time had no appetite whatsoever and ate nothing, but he apparently suffered very little. Though the old man was "not as enthusiastic as some I have seen in his condition," Mason remarked, he was "calm, self-possessed, and entirely satisfied with his prospects."[43] On the evening of that same day, Raccoon John made an oral disposition of his temporal affairs, and asked Emma to write to John Augustus Williams in Kentucky, requesting that Williams, if possible, come to Missouri to attend him in his dying hour and to accompany his body back to Kentucky for the funeral. Sadly, this proved impossible. Williams did not get the message in time to honor Raccoon John's wishes.

Raccoon John lingered for three more days, until Friday the 28th. At the last, knowing his hour was come, his local friends all assembled in his room and he bade them farewell with weak but affectionate handclasps. He then asked to be raised up in his bed, and as Emma attended to him he threw his arms around her neck and spoke his last words, the only indication that he might have felt anything approaching fear at all: "Daughter, I want some music to cheer me through this dark valley." In response, the crowd of grieving Disciples around his bed joined in a trembling rendition of an old Isaac Watts hymn modernized and "corrected" by Alexander Campbell, "*Since* I Can Read My Title Clear." After this, the old man appeared to rest more quietly, and finally at either half past eight or half past ten that night—there are two differing accounts—his long, remarkable life on earth came to a peaceful close.[44]

A wake and possibly a preliminary funeral service as well were held at the Ringos' home over the weekend. On the Monday morning following, an enormous crowd of citizens, including both pupils and teachers of the Disciple Sunday school, accompanied the body, attended by A. R. Ringo and James Hurt, to the train station for the final journey back to Kentucky. The funeral train arrived in Lexington on Wednesday, March 4, and Raccoon John's remains were received by the Disciples of that city, the site of so many historical events significant to their denomination, as those of a fallen father of Israel. After brief services in one of the city's numerous Disciple meetinghouses, conducted by George Elley and a host of others whose lives the old Reform warrior had touched, Raccoon John Smith's casket was borne to the great cemetery on the outskirts of town to lie beside those of Nancy and Harvey.[45] Raccoon John and Nancy's survivors erected a stately obelisk over their graves, inscribed thus:

In Memory of
JOHN SMITH
An Elder of the Church of Christ
Born Oct. 15, 1784. Died Feb. 28, 1868.[46]

True, genial, and pious, the good loved, and all respected him.
Strong through affliction, and wise by the study of the Word—
he gave up the Creed of his fathers for the sake of that Word.
By its power, he turned many from error; in its light he walked,
and in its consolations, he triumphantly died.
In all his sacrifices and service, his companion shared. She gave her life to God, and her death was precious in his sight.

NANCY SMITH
Born Nov. 15, 1792. Died Nov. 4, 1861.

Ere the year was over, Jonathan Smith would be buried nearby as well, in a grave, like those of Harvey's unfortunate daughter Emma and possibly his ex-wife Mary, too, that remains unmarked and virtually forgotten to this day.

In spite of the inaccuracies and exaggerations of John Augustus Williams, and in turn Louis Cochran and Everett Donaldson who were influenced by him, the memory of the man that they all sought to portray was, in its own way, right on target: Raccoon John Smith's life was, in fact, bigger than life. Few of us can expect to achieve a reputation of the sort that he did, but even fewer would be willing to endure the personal griefs and hardships that he suffered in order to attain it.

Yet all of us who perceive God as a reality must, at one time or another, search for the same peace of mind and certainty of meaning that Raccoon John sought so desperately and believed so passionately that he found in Alexander Campbell's rationalistic exposition of Christianity. If, after such a quest, some of us are satisfied, justly or no, simply to try to brighten the corner where we are for what little time remains to us on God's footstool, there are as many or more of our fellow pilgrims relearning Raccoon John's lesson over and over again in their own versions of a repetition. Not too many years after Smith's death, his old fields of labor were re-reformed, as it were, this time by two newer, separate but similar denominations known as the Churches of God now headquartered in Anderson, Indiana, and Cleveland, Tennessee. Drawing on Wesleyan Methodist roots put down in an essentially backcountry Baptist and Methodist soil, the ministers and converts of the Churches of God restored the Cornelius paradigm of salvation and the metaphysical, personal Christian experience of New Birth to compete once again with Campbell-style rationalism in rural areas where the Baptist and Methodist cause had faded due to Raccoon John's and the original Disciples' militant labors and the older, parent denominations' own attempts to enforce an institutional, outside conformity upon country churches. With this, the Churches of God retained the Baptist principle of immersion and renewed an emphasis on sanctificationist and holiness doctrine and practice that was in fact as old as the Methodist movement itself. The Pentecostal Holiness movement of the twentieth century grew, at least in this particular area, from this same seedbed. Thus at present, travelers passing through rural Montgomery and Bath counties as well as those newer governmental districts organized from portions of their original territories—Breathitt, Menifee, Powell, and Wolfe counties from Montgomery, and Morgan, Elliott, and Rowan from Bath—will observe as many or more thriving Churches of God and Pentecostal fellowships nestled placidly along the roadsides as extant Baptist, Christian, Church of Christ, and Methodist congregations. Of course, their own struggles between individuals, churches, and denominational structures are another story—and at the same time, in a large sense, just other variations on some of the very same themes we have examined so exhaustively herein.

We've already had to analyze at least a portion of the feuds that separated the Disciples, Independent Christian Churches/Churches of Christ, and a cappella Churches of Christ in Kentucky as well as throughout the rest of the United States, and for their part, the North District–descended "Old Time" Baptist associations of eastern Kentucky have, in some areas of the mountains, been largely supplanted by, and in others renewed alongside, the Mountain Free Will Baptist movement that grew originally from within their own memberships and which, of course, still draws on the old backcountry Baptist traditions in its own way.[47] In spite of North District Association's demise and all the religious changes merely in the circumscribed area of Montgomery County itself, though, perhaps six to ten old-style United, Old Regular, and Primitive Baptist congregations, many if not most of them connected with the ancient association's descendant groups that remain in the eastern mountains, still eke out a living right in Raccoon John's old stamping ground. If one cares enough to investigate and experience them, rustic worship services such as the fiery young "singe-cat from somewhere up among the raccoons" knew generations ago are still held, replete with the original styles of singing and preaching, at monthly meetings. The religious makeup of the land Raccoon John tried so hard to evangelize thus runs across a broad evangelical spectrum, and throughout each and every denomination or sect noted above, old-fashioned or more contemporary, whether calling itself *the* church or not, the green bay tree of the flesh still thrives, and will continue to thrive, right alongside the cedars of Lebanon.

Hence, if we cared to look merely within the area of Kentucky where Raccoon John preached so many years ago, to say nothing of beyond it, we would uncover a myriad of less compelling but similar stories of conversion from one doctrinal system to another: from Catholic to Protestant; Protestant to Catholic; Baptist to Disciple; Disciple to Church of Christ; Church of Christ back to Baptist, Disciple or Methodist; United or Old Regular to Free Will Baptist, in turn to the Church of God to the Pentecostal Holiness movement to the next Rex (or Gloria) Mundy–style television miracle ministry to beam itself across the airwaves, or conceivably anything else. And all of this because individual seekers have perceived a common, inescapable humanity both within themselves and in their temporal religious affiliation and have gone looking for a higher divinity in another church, only to discover eventually that all the faults and foibles (from both within and without) that they had tried to escape flourished on the other side of the fence as well.

We now leave Raccoon John's story in the earnest hope that he actually did embrace a genuine experience with the transcendent, as opposed to the fictionalizations and sweetenings that his hagiographers seem to have made a permanent part of his memory. For whatever a personal opinion is worth, I feel that he did, in spite of all his mistakes. If anyone deserved peace at the end of his life, Raccoon John Smith did. But still, the best lesson we can learn from both Smith and his hagiographers is the risk inherent in our all too human tendency to mythologize the events we see occurring around us even as America as a whole did during the Era of Good Feeling, as well as those within our own individual lives. Myths may be entertaining, even useful and purposeful, but each and every one of us is headed for a state, regardless of what any of us as individuals believe, where earthly myths will be no more; and on the day we depart this world to travel thereto, the only human biography with which we will be concerned is our own—and how we made it relate to those whom we loved, and who loved us.

Notes

Abbreviations Used in Footnotes and Bibliography

ABHS	American Baptist Historical Society, Rochester, N.Y.
BCML	Bath County Memorial Library, Owingsville, Ky.
DAR	Daughters of the American Revolution, Washington, D.C.
DCHS	Disciples of Christ Historical Society, Nashville, Tenn.
GL	Gelman Library, George Washington University, Washington, D.C.
LTS	Lexington Theological Seminary, Lexington, Ky.
MS–MCL	Mt. Sterling–Montgomery County Library, Mt. Sterling, Ky.
PBL	Primitive Baptist Library, Carthage, Ill.
SBTS	Southern Baptist Theological Seminary, Louisville, Ky.
SCPL	Scott County Public Library, Georgetown, Ky.

Introduction: From the Papers of One Still Living

1. To be fair, it should be noted that one Raccoon John descendant, his great-granddaughter Jouelda "Daisy" Nesbitt Strader, did make the claim in a feature article published in Owingsville, Kentucky's *Bath County Outlook* 92, no. 45 (July 30, 1970): 1 (BCML), that Raccoon John wore a "raccoon hat." However, in the same interview Mrs. Strader also claimed that Raccoon John was a "college man" who left the Presbyterian Church with Barton W. Stone and Alexander Campbell to form the "Campbellite Church." Since Cochran's *Raccoon John Smith* had been published almost a decade before she was interviewed for the article, though, it seems likely that she picked up the detail about the "raccoon hat" from Cochran rather than the other way around. Interestingly, Mrs. Strader herself was an Episcopalian, although at least some members of her family remained with the Disciples of Christ; Mrs. Strader's aunt, Lellie Lee Walden, was for many years the organist for the Owingsville Christian Church.

2. Author unknown, back cover of Louis Cochran's *Raccoon John Smith* (Popular Library reprint).

3. Sanders, 15.

4. Taulman, 207.

5. Spencer, 1:261.

6. Vaughan, 182–83.

7. James 5:14–15, King James Version.

8. Louis Cochran, *Raccoon John Smith,* 365.

9. John Augustus Williams, *The Life of Elder John Smith,* 556.

Chapter 1: The Fatherland

1. John Augustus Williams, 11. We might mention here that Williams preserves one circumstantial hint that George Smith came of "Pennsylvania Dutch" stock: Raccoon John's use of the slang term "pow-wowwing" (p. 545), a saying that early Pennsylvania German settlers picked up from the colony's native Algonquian tribes and which referred to the practices of "charming," remedies, and other forms of "white" folk magic of both German and Native American

origin. It was not a common term among settlers of other ethnicities, and Raccoon John could have picked it up from his father—though modern readers might be horrified to think that such a good Christian as George Smith Sr. could still depend on "charming" and folk remedies. Thanks to Appalachian scholars Gerald Milnes and Tim Konhaus of the *H-Appalachia* listserve for information about the term.

2. Wellman, 6.

3. Ward, 147.

4. Grady, 2:107, 110–15. Several genealogical sources available on the World Wide Web involving both Bowen and Whitley researchers draw similar conclusions from it: for example, see Hall, "My Family Tree," http://awt.ancestry.com/cgi-bin/igm.cgi?op=GET&db=:2909700&id=I9614; and Michaud, "Ancestors (Bowen family genealogy)," http://familytreemaker.genealogy.com/users/m/i/c/Colin-W-Michaud/GENE6-0038.html#CHILD459012.

5. This quirk of Baptist history, known as the Old Landmark movement, will be noted later in this work, but for a more complete discussion see Sparks, 8–9, 232–34, passim.

6. Wolever, 44, quoting the famous Regular Baptist missionary John Gano.

7. Starkey, 81.

8. *Philadelphia Confession of Faith,* 30 (Chapter X, articles 3 and 4).

9. A brief but spirited discussion of this issue can be found in Berger, 149–50.

10. Garrett, 67–69. For detailed discussion, with references, of the material presented in the preceding paragraphs, see Sparks, chapters 1–3.

11. Again, see Sparks, chapters 4–5.

12. John Augustus Williams, 12.

13. Fridley, "The Rev. John Alderson Sr.," http://www.fridley.net/alderson/johnaldersonbio.htm.

14. Benedict, 673–74.

15. John Augustus Williams, 15.

16. Bork, "Elder 'Racoon' [*sic*] John Smith, 1784–1868," http://junebaldwinbork.com/smith/raccoon1.htm. Perhaps needless to say, nothing about any Whitely half-brothers or -sisters is mentioned here. Louis Cochran provides us with the name of one other son, James; some genealogists (who seem to have a very loose grasp on historical connections associated with names) appear to think his name was "Jesse James," but Everett Donaldson (*Raccoon John Smith: Frontiersman and Reformer,* 38) speculates that there was an adopted son Jesse in addition to the eight boys. Donaldson hesitates to quote the Cochran novel without qualifying it as a work of fiction, but others of the sources he quotes directly borrow from it unashamedly. Cochran also indicates that the other two daughters' names were "Fancy Mae" and "Jane." It is genuinely hard to ascertain where he got these names, although he claimed to use genealogical tables provided by some of Philip and John Smith's descendants. If there was a "Fancy Mae," her name probably would have been Frances, and in keeping with the customs of the time she would have been nicknamed "Fanny" or "Frankie" rather than the bucolic frontier local color moniker Cochran chose for her; however, we cannot entirely rule out the possibility that John Smith had a sister named Frances, as he chose that appellation for the middle name of his daughter Emily or Emma (who, by the way, also could have been named for his brother Philip's wife, Emily, or "Millie").

Also worthy of notice here is a letter from Louis Cochran to Roscoe M. Pierson, Librarian of the College of the Bible (now Lexington Theological Seminary), Lexington, Kentucky, dated March 11, 1961, and included in the Raccoon John Smith Historical Papers in that institution's collection of documents. Cochran stated that, although he had accumulated considerable material on Raccoon John through the years, he still lacked any information on the names of Smith's brothers and sisters, the details of his marriages, and the names and birth dates of his children. Pierson replied (March 13, 1961) that John Augustus Williams's papers had been lost by his descendants, and that the Raccoon John Smith Historical Papers only offered scraps of evidence as to the information Cochran was seeking. From my own examination of the papers in question, I can verify that Pierson told Cochran the truth about the matter, and the seminary's collection only strengthens my conviction that most of the details in Cochran's book came from his own imagination and the United States' early 1960s popular perceptions of frontier life.

17. John Augustus Williams, 12.

18. Ibid., 28–29.

19. Waller, 36–39, 58–59, passim.

20. John Augustus Williams, 14.

21. Dorgan, *In the Hands of a Happy God,* 78.

22. Benedict, 791–92; see also Burnett, 318–21.

23. Sparks, 179; Burnett, 556.

24. Sparks, 80–84.

25. John Augustus Williams, 26.

26. McCauley, 115.

27. Burnett, 321–22.

28. Sparks, 189.

29. Ibid., 193.

30. Ibid., 192–94.

31. Wilkins, 16, quoting a son of John Sevier.

32. John Augustus Williams, 15.

33. Connelley, 26–33, n 8.

34. Drake, 55; Wellman, 16.

35. John Augustus Williams, 33.

36. Hofstadter, 118.

37. Allen, 279; compared with John Augustus Williams, 163.

38. John Augustus Williams, 317, quoting Smith's reply to Henderson.

39. Ibid., 25.

40. The earliest known answer to a query regarding this practice by Holston Association reads as follows: "We do not hold it [dry-christening] as a tennant [tenet], but believe that prayer should be made for all men" (Minutes of the Holston Association, 1786–1807).

41. John Augustus Williams, 36–38.

Chapter 2: Training in Christianity

1. Wellman, 19.

2. Donaldson, *Raccoon John Smith,* 36.

3. John Augustus Williams, 31–32.

4. Spencer, 1:233–36. Pioneer Kentucky Baptist preacher John Taylor commented, in his "A History of Ten Baptist Churches" (republished by Mercer University Press and edited by Chester Raymond Young as *Baptists on the American Frontier*) that he thought that a good fiddler was "the devil's right-hand man."

5. Wilkins, 37–38; Donaldson, *Raccoon John Smith,* 35–36.

6. Troxell, "The Wedding Story That Saved the Cherokee People of Wayne County, Kentucky: The Wedding of Rebecca Jane Wood Owl and Joseph Sumpter," http://victorian.fortunecity.com/rothko/420/aniyuntikwalaski/Jane.htm. Though Raccoon John's own involvement in this charming tale is, like so much else written about him, romantic myth, he having moved away from the Cumberland Valley many years before, the principal characters did make their homes in the area and their descendants still live there. The piece's author is one of the couple's descendants. Despite the mythologizing, though, it is of interest to note that one of John Smith's earliest coworkers in the Baptist church in Wayne County, Kentucky, was one Jonathan Blevins, whose wife was Katie Troxell, a Cherokee.

7. John Augustus Williams, 32.

8. Norton, "Descendants of Johann Schmidt," http://familytreemaker.genealogy. com/users/n/o/r/Michele-L-Norton/GENE4-0001.html? Welcome=1008757538.

9. Wellman, 58–61; Donaldson, *Raccoon John Smith,* 40.

10. John Augustus Williams, 41; Wellman, 58–61, 73.

11. The best study I have found of all the older accounts of the lives and grisly careers of the Harpes, comparing and contrasting historians Otto A. Rothert, T. Marshall Smith, Lyman C. Draper, James Hall, J.W.M. Brazeale, the legal testimony of the Harpe women after they were taken into custody, and other documents, is Wellman, chapters 2–6 and 8.

12. Wellman, 58.

13. Ibid., 67–68.

14. Ibid. 68.

15. Ibid., 58–73.

16. Ibid., 73.

17. Ibid., 73–74.

18. Ibid., 74.

19. Ibid., 76; 76 n 5.

20. Ibid., 77; 77 n 6.

21. Ibid., 73.

22. John Augustus Williams, 42–44.

23. Boles, *The Irony of Southern Religion,* 13–14.

24. Boles, *The Great Revival,* 12–24.

25. This description of Raccoon John's physical appearance was taken from a combination of his existing portraits and photographs, and a characterization given by one W. C. Rogers in 1867. Raccoon John Smith Historical Papers.

26. John Augustus Williams, 16.

27. Ibid., 14–15; for the reference to the Aldersons' ethic of black church members, see Lindman, 416 n 46. Thanks to Appalachian scholar Krista M. Loyd of Indiana University Southeast for sharing this material.

28. Donaldson, *The Legacy of Raccoon John Smith,* 47–48.

29. John Augustus Williams, 275.

30. Ibid., 38–40.

31. Ibid., 73–74.

32. Ibid., 33.

33. Ibid., 88.

34. Ibid., 35.

35. Ibid., 24–25.

36. Challen, "Biographical Sketch of Raccoon John Smith," http://www.mun.ca/rels/restmov/texts/jchallen/lcab/smithrj3.htm.

37. We can use the latter part of July 1800 and the month following as a chronological peg here, since the first stirrings of the Great Revival to come were noticed at a sacramental gathering on Red River at the end of June, and the camp meeting itself began in earnest on Gasper River about one month later. Boles, *The Great Revival,* 51–61.

38. For detailed discussions of the McGready camp meeting and the remarkable "spiritual exercises," see Spencer, 1:505–521; and Boles, *The Great Revival,* 61–69.

39. McCauley, 190–95, 221.

40. Johnson, *The Frontier Camp Meeting,* 27–28; Sparks, 120–21, 195–96.

41. Boles, *The Great Revival,* 68.

42. Acts 2:38, King James Version.

43. Acts 8:5–24, King James Version.

44. Acts 10:1–48, King James Version.

45. For the more bizarre examples of the converts of Shubal Stearns, whose pulpit persona was so awe-inspiring that not a few of his hearers actually claimed experiences of seeing the

devil after they had heard him preach, see Sparks, 65–66, 80–82, and 101; for examples of the more conventional born-again experience, which is still the norm in many central and southern Appalachian churches, see ibid., 66, 103.

46. Spencer, 1:221–22, quoting an oral account by William Vaughan that appears to be more accurate than Thomas M. Vaughan's relation of the same incidents in his father's *Memoirs.*

47. Ibid., 1:223–24.

48. Allen, 284.

49. John Augustus Williams, 168.

50. McCauley, 21.

51. The best examples of these are the modern-day "Regular" and "Absoluter" Primitive Baptist organizations, though paradoxically, many of them have more roots in the Separate Baptist, rather than the Regular Baptist, movement.

52. Cartwright, 118.

53. Again, for examples, see Cartwright, 66–68, 119–22; John Augustus Williams, 63–64 (Louis Cochran got much mileage from this one), 71, 159–60; and Vaughan, 80–82.

54. Spencer, 1:231–32; 2:82.

55. Ibid., 1:233–35.

56. Minutes of the North District Association, 1823, quoting a circular letter with detailed historical material collected and arranged by James French.

57. Spencer, 1:80–81; 2:83.

58. John Augustus Williams, 119–20; Spencer, 2:243.

59. Included among the more perceptive modern works noting and/or examining these facets of Southern Baptist life are Ellen Rosenberg's *The Southern Baptists: A Subculture in Transition* (Knoxville: Univ. of Tennessee Press, 1989); David T. Morgan's *The New Crusades, the New Holy Land: Conflict in the Southern Baptist Convention, 1969–1991* (Tuscaloosa: Univ. of Alabama Press, 1996); and David Stricklin's *A Genealogy of Dissent: Southern Baptist Protest in the Twentieth Century* (Lexington: Univ. Press of Kentucky, 2000).

60. Spencer, 1:527–532; see also Boles, *The Great Revival,* 159–62.

61. Boles, *The Great Revival,* 149.

62. Garrett, 85.

63. John Augustus Williams, 435.

64. Boles, *The Great Revival,* 149–50; also D. Newell Williams, 5–8, 6 nn 9–10.

65. Spencer, 1:17–18, 33–34.

66. Boles, 145–46.

67. Ibid., 154–56; see also Garrett, 62–67.

68. Boles, *The Great Revival,* 158.

69. Spencer, 1:519.

70. John Augustus Williams, 47.

71. Ibid., 5.

72. Ibid., 53.

73. Ibid., 35, 48–50; Spencer, 2:221–22.

74. Spencer, 1:17–18, 33–34, 147, 247–50; 2:105–7, 212–14, 221–22; see also Madison, Roundtree, and Cowles, 7–10.

75. John Augustus Williams, 48–50.

76. Spencer, 2:221–22.

77. John Augustus Williams, 317–18.

78. Ibid., 52–53.

79. Spencer, 2:222.

80. Ibid., 2:221.

81. John Augustus Williams, 52–53.

82. Most of the information on Micah Taul in this chapter was taken from letters (November

20 and December 3, 2001) to the author from Dr. Glen Taul, archivist at Georgetown College in Kentucky, a descendant of Micah Taul's brother Samuel and a close student of Micah's unpublished memoirs. See also Rennick, 201.

83. John Augustus Williams, 34–35.

84. Ibid., 94.

85. Ibid., 50.

86. Ibid., 66.

Chapter 3: Stages on Life's Way

1. Thanks to my father-in-law, Carl Bowling, for the explanation of the spicewood's use, and to the memory of my grandmother-in-law, Mrs. Maudie Murphy, who herself regularly used spicewood twigs as seasoning for "wild" meats and who shared the old mountain cooking secret with him.

2. Tillich, 464–72; Kierkegaard, *Journals,* 60.

3. Marius, *Martin Luther,* 458.

4. John Augustus Williams, 54.

5. Ibid., 67.

6. Ibid., 54.

7. The fact that William Wood was the captain of the local Stockton's Valley militia company is evidenced in Hill, 156.

8. John Augustus Williams, 58.

9. For Raccoon John's chewing habit, see ibid., 568. According to a granddaughter, in later life he smoked "only [once] each day. After dinner he took 13-1/2 [?] whiffs, that was all. First long whiffs slowly, then a little puff." (Interview with Mrs. Mollie Lee Nesbitt, by E. C. Raines, November 10, 1932, in the Raccoon John Smith Historical Papers.)

10. John Augustus Williams, 59–61.

11. Ibid., 63.

12. Ibid., 64.

13. Ibid., 71.

14. Ibid., 67.

15. Ibid., 67; Donaldson, *Raccoon John Smith,* 47.

16. Spencer, 1:222.

17. John Augustus Williams, 67–69; 114.

18. Ibid., 70.

19. Spencer, 2:234, 393; Rennick, 15.

20. Spencer, 2:212–13.

21. Ibid., 2:234, 393.

22. Ibid., 1:80–81, 548–49; 2:127–28, 138–40; see also Sparks, 199–210.

23. Spencer, 2:393.

24. John Augustus Williams, 65. For the text of this pamphlet, see Toplady, "Rebuke to Wesley: A Letter to the Rev. Mr. John Wesley, Relative to His Pretended Abridgement of Zanchius on Predestination," http://www.lamblion.net/Articles/toplady_to_ wesley.htm.

25. John Augustus Williams, 145.

26. Ibid., 408.

27. Spencer, 2:214; Donaldson, *Raccoon John Smith,* 96–97.

28. Spencer, 2:222–23.

29. John Augustus Williams, 206.

30. Ibid., 72–73.

31. Ibid., 88.

32. Ibid., 545, quoting Smith's preaching colleague Walter Scott.

33. Cartwright, 134.

34. John Augustus Williams, 88–89.

35. Bork, "Elder 'Racoon' [*sic*] John Smith, 1784–1868," http://junebaldwinbork.com/smith/raccoon1.htm.

36. Unfortunately, very few of the early minutes of the Tate's Creek Association have survived, and the earliest available minute record listing the names of John Smith, Richard Barrier, and Isham Burnett together is that of the Cumberland River Association in 1815 (SBTS Collection). At that time Isham Burnett was pastor at Big Sinking, and Richard Barrier had moved his membership to a new church on lower Beaver Creek called New Hope. John's status in this particular year is addressed in chapter 4.

37. Galloway, *Isham Burnett Family Genealogy,* http://awt.ancestry.com/cgi-bin/igm.cgi?op=GET&db=;1953065&id=I27941.

38. Rennick, 15.

39. Stanford, *John Townsend Family Genealogy,* http://awt.ancestry.com./cgi-bin/igm.cgi?op=GET&db=;1753730&id=I81268875; Treva Jones, "Genealogy Webpage," http://awt.ancestry.com/cgi-bin/igm.cgi?op=GET&db=:2613303&id=I2444; Wayne County Marriage Records, County Clerk's Office, Monticello, Kentucky. See also note 3.41 below.

40. John Augustus Williams, 73–74.

41. Ibid., 74; Bork, "Elder 'Racoon' [*sic*] John Smith, 1784–1868," http://junebaldwinbork.com/smith/raccoon1.htm; Bossong, *Kathy's World Family Tree,* http://awt.ancestry.com/cgi-bin/igm.cgi?op=GET&db=; 1663784&id=I75871580; Wayne County Marriage Records, Clerk's Office, Monticello, Kentucky. Here again we see an example of details made vague by John Augustus Williams and then misunderstood by Louis Cochran, who in turn made historical errors that have passed on into Raccoon John lore. A few words of explanation are necessary. Williams never noted any of the names of Anna Townsend Smith's family except her brother Hiram, and that almost as if by accident. John and Anna's actual marriage record shows that John's bond was signed by James Townsend and that James stated under oath that Anna's parents consented to the marriage. (In keeping with early Kentucky legal forms, the marriage record was not a license in the modern sense, but a $50 cash bond entered into by the groom and a male cosigner of appropriate legal age.) I suspect that Cochran found this information in the same place I did, the Wayne County, Kentucky, clerk's office, during his research for his book, and he assumed that James Townsend was Anna's father. He thus developed James Townsend's character and wrote it into his novel, and most local historians and genealogists who have followed him have taken him as an authority. Interestingly enough, he also took the name of Anna's sister, Jane, and from it created a grandmother for her. He even took the liberty of creating a fictional sister named "Pensy."

After several years of combing through such early marriage bonds in Kentucky county courthouses as an amateur genealogist, though, I have observed that, according to the mores of the times, a father's signing his prospective son-in-law's marriage bond was virtually unknown. After all, if a breach of promise did occur, a father could find himself responsible for a $50 debt to the state with the man who had just jilted his daughter. Usually a brother or close friend of the groom "went on" such bonds, but often an older brother of the bride would perform this service either as a token of friendship and trust to the groom, a commitment to his sister's honor, or perhaps even as a gesture of affection to an in-love, worried, and tearful sister in the case where their parents did not quite approve of the groom. When a father was present at the courthouse and gave his oral consent to a marriage, most county clerks made a direct statement of that fact, and written consents, often drawn up directly by the clerk and then signed or "marked" by the father, were almost always saved as part of the public record; but in this case, since James Townsend was evidently of legal age, clerk Micah Taul was able to accept his oath that John Townsend's consent was legitimate and so noted it. This still leaves us with the question, though, especially in light of the fact that John and Anna were married at Monticello by Elliott Jones rather than by one of the several ministers John worked with in the backcountry, of whether John Townsend actually gave his blessing to the union, or whether the couple eloped to the county seat and James Townsend, siding with young and love smitten Anna and John rather than his possibly recalcitrant father, simply stated that his father approved. See also note 3.39 above.

42. John Augustus Williams, 493–95.

43. Ibid., 75.

44. Ibid., 77; 100.

45. Donaldson, *Raccoon John Smith,* 56.

46. Ibid., 57.

47. John Augustus Williams, 52–53, 61.

48. Donaldson, *Raccoon John Smith,* 56.

49. John Augustus Williams, 81.

50. John Augustus Williams gives one particular example of John's ability at this latter pursuit, which apparently impressed even the more seasoned Barrier and Burnett, on pp. 91–92, but I have elected not to recount it here. John's supposed exposition of Calvinistic doctrine in this instance sounds so suspiciously like the same position advocated by the old Kentucky Separate-turned-Calvinist preacher William Marshall, and ridiculed by John Taylor in his *History of Ten Baptist Churches* and other writings that were popular in early nineteenth-century Kentucky, that I suspect that Smith and/or Williams may have quite honestly mistakenly patched the story together from Smith's garbled memories and Taylor's pen. For a comparison with the above reference, see Spencer, 1:16, and Sparks, 126–27. Taylor does make it clear that the belief in question was by no means widely accepted among Kentucky Baptists, even most Calvinistic ones.

On the other—that is to say, Methodist—side of the coin, we must give credit where credit is due to Louis Cochran for giving a fairly accurate recounting of one story of which John Augustus Williams may have been completely unaware. The famous early Methodist circuit rider Peter Cartwright actually did preach a few times in Stockton's Valley, and once he quite literally stole almost an entire Baptist congregation right out from under the noses of John and Philip Mulkey, using subterfuges such as John Smith would later perfect in his own evangelistic tours to get men and women *away* from the Methodists, as well as the Baptists. See Cartwright, 64–72.

51. John Augustus Williams, 88.

52. Ibid., 88.

53. Ibid., 393.

54. Ibid., 81.

55. Ibid., 80–81.

56. Ibid., 87–88. It must be noted and stressed again here that throughout the Williams biography, for some reason or another, either Williams or Smith stubbornly insists that John's early ministry up to and including this entire transaction took place under the auspices of the Stockton's Valley Association. The reasons for the author's and/or the subject's hesitancy to admit that it took place within the boundaries of the Tate's Creek Association can only be guessed. Some likely hypotheses will be examined subsequently in the text.

57. Bossong, *Kathy's World Family Tree,* http://awt.ancestry.com/cgi-bin/igm.cgi?op=GET&db=; 1663784&id=I75871580.

58. Ibid.; also, Letter from John Smith to Isaac T. Reneau, May 4, 1841, from the Raccoon John Smith Historical Papers. It should be noted that Anna's brother Hiram did have a daughter Zerelda also; it is possible that both siblings named children for their mother, but we cannot say with absolute certainty that this was the case here. See note 3.39 above for references.

59. Spencer, 2:234.

60. John Augustus Williams, 78–80; Spencer, 1:263–64, 2:234–39; 1815 and 1819 Minutes of the Cumberland River Association. Here again, Williams tries to present another of John's early influential contacts as a member of Stockton's Valley Association, when in fact the person in question had nothing to do with the Stockton's Valley body. Elijah Barnes spent his later

years in Cumberland River Association, before that having belonged to Tate's Creek and Elkhorn Associations. Coincidentally but interestingly, Barnes was an early pastor or moderator of a church in Montgomery County, Kentucky, that Smith later belonged to and pastored, and Williams relates a humorous story about Barnes that Spencer picked up and quoted also; it probably came from the lips of Raccoon John Smith. Barnes traveled to his ministerial appointments throughout Lincoln and Pulaski counties in Kentucky on a horse named Old Gray, and once, in a year of drought, he raised insufficient corn to provide adequate feed for the horse. A proposition was made in church to help out "Old Daddy" Barnes with spare grain and, perhaps, money as well, and an objection was made to it on the grounds that the Lord provided His preachers with spiritual blessings on which a minister ought to feed, rather than asking his parishioners for financial aid. Barnes replied, "Yes, but what is Old Gray to do, my brother? He can't live on them sort of feelin's." Both Williams and Spencer used the funny but touching story to illustrate the necessity of paying preachers, but neither they nor Smith included the detail that the controversy occurred at the 1819 session of the Cumberland River Association, while Barnes was moderator of the body. A record of the dispute, couched in the hesitant language generally employed by association clerks in noting such arguments, and a pungent "circular letter" on the subject, are included in that year's associational minutes.

61. A list of these marriages is kept in the Raccoon John Smith Historical Papers.

62. Hill, 153, 156.

63. John Augustus Williams, 94.

64. Ibid., 93–95.

65. Spencer, 1:567.

66. Ibid., 2:234; Minutes of the Cumberland River Baptist Association, 1815.

67. In many if not most early Kentucky Baptist churches, certainly those that had been gathered with any Separate Baptist influence whatsoever, the title of deacon almost always referred to a husband and wife together. At some churches men and women were ordained together to the diaconate, while at others only men were ordained, but in all cases the wife was questioned by the ordaining presbytery of ministers as to her responsibilities, right along with the husband. Many of the old preachers felt that a woman had to prove her qualifications to be a deacon's wife, or deaconess, before the man could even begin to prove his qualifications as a deacon. I can quote no reference to this practice except the many conversations I have enjoyed with older ministers in the United Baptist denomination, but this view of the diaconate and the associated practice continues in many Appalachian traditionalist Baptist churches and associations to this day.

68. Donaldson, *Raccoon John Smith,* 56.

69. Spencer, 2:235.

70. John Augustus Williams, 97.

71. Spencer, 2:419.

72. Ibid., 1:235–36. Interestingly, the famous Virginia Separate Baptist John Leland appears to have been quite outspoken on this very same doctrinal issue. Once, when asked if he believed that all the saints would persevere through grace to glory and get home to heaven at last, Leland shot back, "I can tell you more about that, my brother, when I get there myself. Some seem to make a very bad start of it here!" (John Augustus Williams, 85.)

73. Ibid., 1:80–81, 548–49; 2:87–88, 138–40.

74. Minutes of the North District Association, 1804–1806.

75. See also Sparks, 199–210.

76. Spencer, 1:237–38; Vaughan, 73–74.

77. John Augustus Williams, 131, quoting a letter to James Mason from Jeremiah Vardeman.

78. Vaughan, 72.

79. John Augustus Williams, 96–97, 123.

80. Spencer, 1:224–25; Vaughan, 56–67, 87–89.

81. See also Minutes of the North District Association, 1811–1830.

82. John Augustus Williams, 97.
83. Spencer, 1:243–44; John Augustus Williams, 118–19.
84. Spencer, 1:240.
85. See Sparks, 208.

Chapter 4: Sickness Unto Death

1. Beasley, 5. For the War of 1812, at Governor Shelby's insistence the state revised its militia laws to make all Kentucky males between the ages of eighteen and forty-five eligible for the draft, exempting only ordained ministers. For a brief but interesting look at some of the facts about the War of 1812 discussed herein, see Klein, From 1814, "Tales Keep a'Comin," http://www.nytimes.com/2004/09/11/arts/television/11hist.html.

2. Hill, 153, 156.

3. Ibid., 198.

4. Letter to the author from Dr. Glen Taul, November 20, 2001.

5. Hill, 198; see also excerpts from the Revolutionary pension application of John Townsend from Stanford, *John Townsend Family Genealogy,* http://awt.ancestry.com./cgi-bin/igm.cgi?op=GET&db=;1753730&id=I81268875. When he applied for his pension in Alabama, Townsend mentioned neither James nor Anna as surviving.

6. John Augustus Williams, 97–100.

7. Donaldson, *Raccoon John Smith,* 63–64. Interestingly, one of the earliest settlers in the Hickory Flats, Alabama, area was named George Smith, but this was not John's wayward older brother. George Washington Smith, the pioneer of northern Alabama, was born in Louisa County, Virginia, and came from English stock.

8. John Augustus Williams, 98–99, 105, 108.

9. Stanford, "Townsend Family Genealogy," http://www.ancestry.com/cgi-bin/igm.cgi?op=GET&db=:1753730&id=I81268875.

10. Ibid.

11. John Augustus Williams, 100–101.

12. Ibid., 104. Thanks to Dr. James Stephen Wolfgang of the University of Kentucky for the information regarding the early Alabama court records.

13. Letter from John Chisholm, son-in-law of Benjamin Lynn, to Mr. John Barbee, September 16, 1847, in *The Calendar of the George Rogers Clark Papers* (Utica, Ky.: McDowell Publications, 1985), series J, 37:105–10.

14. Letter to the author from Dr. Glen Taul, December 3, 2001.

15. Jones, 32–35.

16. John Augustus Williams, 99.

17. Ibid., 104.

18. Donaldson, *Raccoon John Smith,* 66–67.

19. We should make note here of a typographical error in the John Smith marriage records in the LTS Collection. A wedding ceremony between James Koger and Aley Majors is noted to have been performed in Wayne County, Kentucky, by John on January 16, 1815, nine days after the house fire. Actually, according to the Wayne County clerk's records the marriage took place on January 16, 1816. Though being away from home was part of the job, there was no way that John could have been so heartless as to journey back to Kentucky right after his children's deaths only to perform a wedding. This little misprint certainly threw me a curve, though, until I got the facts straight.

20. John Augustus Williams, 104.

21. Ibid., 105, 111; Challen, "Biographical Sketch," http://www.mun.ca/rels/restmov/texts/jchallen/lcab/smithrj3.htm.

22. John Augustus Williams, 105, 111; Challen, "Biographical Sketch," http://www.mun.ca/rels/restmov/texts/jchallen/lcab/smithrj3.htm.

23. John Augustus Williams, 105–6.

24. Ibid., 106–8.

25. Ibid.,118, 537.

26. Ibid., 108–9.

27. Challen, "Biographical Sketch," http://www.mun.ca/rels/restmov/texts/jchallen/lcab/smithrj3.htm.

28. John Augustus Williams, 110.

29. Ibid., 117.

30. Rice, Journal, August–October 1815.

31. John Augustus Williams, 113.

32. Ibid., 113–16.

33. I could not resist a little hyperbole of my own here. Like most dramatic tales, these stories of course had another side that was hardly considered in the telling. For what I hope is a balanced account, see Sparks, 116–29, 141–42, 149–55, 159–61, 165–67, 188–92.

34. John Augustus Williams, 277–78; Donaldson, *Raccoon John Smith,* 170–71. Interestingly, this is the only instance in which John Augustus Williams admits, in a nearly six hundred–page work, that Raccoon John's memory could have been faulty. At the time he was dictating his memoirs, Raccoon John blamed Philip S. Fall of Frankfort for inventing and publicizing his nickname in the year 1828; yet Williams had already heard so many other stories by numerous witnesses about how John was nicknamed, including Fall himself, that he felt compelled to add Fall's version in a footnote. As Everett Donaldson reveals, John himself wrote still another story of his nicknaming, which seems to line up with the Fall account and is therefore the most credible variant, to one Samuel McKay in 1835.

35. Minutes of the Cumberland River Association, 1815. Incidentally, the association's statistical table this year shows that Beaver Creek Church had lost one member by death within the previous twelve months, whereas Bethel Church showed no such loss. The death was likely to have been Anna Townsend Smith's.

36. John Augustus Williams, 132, 118; Bork, "Elder 'Racoon' [*sic*] John Smith, 1784–1868," http://junebaldwinbork.com/smith/raccoon2.htm; http://junebaldwinbork.com/smith/raccoon1.htm.

37. John Augustus Williams, 118. Williams states that this trip was made in early September 1815, in which case John could not have made it himself; he is known to have preached at Cumberland River Association on the first weekend in that month.

38. Ibid., 120.

39. Allen, 277–78.

40. John Augustus Williams, 517–20.

41. Letter from John Smith to Isaac T. Reneau, July 5, 1852, Raccoon John Smith Historical Papers.

42. John Augustus Williams, 560, 572. Unfortunately, hardly any Smith genealogists agree with one another completely on the birth order of John and Nancy's family. Williams tells us that Jonathan was the oldest son, Mary the youngest daughter, and Richard the youngest of all the children; in a letter to Isaac T. Reneau dated May 4, 1841 (LTS Collection), John himself said that his oldest son was living in Maysville at that time, his second son had just then departed for Illinois, and that "James" (James Harvey or Harvey James, whose tombstone states that he was born in 1823) was away at school. The second son noted here could only have been John Duke, who Williams tells us died in 1846, and at the time Raccoon John penned the Reneau letter both Jonathan and John Duke must been of majority age in order to be out and about on their own. As a student at some school, the third son, James, still would have been under the supervision of adults. Based on my own examination of all the Smith genealogical tables I could acquire, plus other pertinent records, including Bath and Montgomery County, Kentucky, Federal Census records (as compiled by Alice P. Reynolds, Joanne Peluzzo, and Barbara, Byron, and Samuel Sistler, respectively), the Williams biography, John Smith's letters in the LTS Col-

lection, and cemetery gravestones, I contend that the Smith children were born in the following order, with approximate birth dates: Eliza Baize, late 1816; Jonathan, late 1817; John Duke, 1819; Maria or Mariah M., 1820; William Pinckney, 1822; James Harvey or Harvey James, 1823; Eliza Ann, 1825; Joshua Carroll, 1826; Emily Frances or Emma, August 10, 1828 or 1829; Mary Vance, 1831; and Richard Menefee, October 1836.

We might note here that Maria and Emma's gravestones bear birth dates for both which are impossible to reconcile with recorded events in their lives. Maria's in Bath County claims that she was born in 1829; besides contradicting pertinent Bath County Federal Census records, this would have made her ten years old when she married in 1839. Emma's in Arkansas states that she was born in 1840, which, in addition to similarly contradicting the Montgomery County, Kentucky, 1850 Census, would have made her mother forty-seven or forty-eight years old when she was born, and Emma herself twelve or thirteen when she married. One wonders if both daughters, for the sake of vanity, just might have shaved a few years off their ages in later life. And finally, even with Williams's suggestion of Raccoon John's youngest daughter Mary's frail health, we cannot say definitively that Mary died young. There is a Mary A. Weigand buried in Raccoon John's family plot at the historic Lexington Cemetery; the cemetery records and her tombstone indicate that she was born in 1827 and died on November 11, 1918. Mary Vance Smith, who is listed in the 1850 U.S. Federal Census for Montgomery County, Kentucky, as having been nineteen years old at that time, is known to have married W. A. Tomlinson first and Robert S. Steele second, and with the data we have it is impossible to determine whether this Mary Weigand was John and Nancy's youngest daughter, or a more distant relative, or merely a friend or acquaintance of the surviving family members. According to the Lexington cemetery's records there were to be spaces saved in the Smith plot also for Frank and Lee Clark, and we know neither who these individuals were nor what significance they held with the Smith family.

43. Campbell, "Notes on a Late Tour, No. II," 506.

44. Ibid., 572.

45. Ibid., 118–23; Bork, "Elder 'Racoon' [*sic*] John Smith, 1784–1868," http://junebaldwinbork.com/smith/raccoon1.htm; http://junebaldwinbork.com/smith/raccoon2.htm.

46. Donaldson, *Raccoon John Smith,* 164, quoting John Augustus Williams, 513.

47. Henry Leo Boles, *Biographical Sketches of Gospel Preachers,* 342–46; see also Donaldson, *The Legacy of Raccoon John Smith,* 284–86, and the membership application of Edith Cloud Kirksey, descendant of Thomas and Jane Boles, DAR Collection.

48. Bossong, *Kathy's World Family Tree,* http://awt.ancestry.com/cgi-bin/igm.cgi?op=GET&db=:1663784&id=I75871580.

49. Miscellaneous grocery invoices of John and Nancy Smith, Raccoon John Smith Historical Papers.

50. Bork, "Elder 'Racoon' [*sic*] John Smith, 1784–1868," http://junebaldwinbork.com/smith/raccoon1.htm; John Augustus Williams, 560.

51. Minutes of the North District Association, 1816.

52. Donaldson, *Raccoon John Smith,* 83; John Augustus Williams, 129, 360.

53. Minutes of the North District Association, 1816. Interestingly, in this same year North District also passed an order forbidding its members to be Freemasons. Anti-Masonic sentiment had and would continue to wax and wane throughout the United States during these years and afterward, and the association simply may have been following what seemed expedient for the time; however, we cannot rule out the possibility that Payne, French, and some of their well-to-do colleagues may have been Masons, and that their opponents in the association were attacking them on this front as well. Regardless of the reason, this associational action deeply insulted John Augustus Williams, who was in fact a prominent Kentucky Mason, and some of the ire with which he related the circumstance seeped through to Louis Cochran's prose in *Raccoon John Smith* as well. John Augustus Williams, 130.

54. John Augustus Williams, 131.

55. Ibid., 132–33. The one remaining spoon of this set is in the possession of the Archives

Department, LTS. John Taylor, in his 1820 *Thoughts on Missions* (http://www.geocities.com/baptist_documents/j.taylor.miss.html), notes Samuel Ayers as one of the leading proponents of missionary work in Kentucky at that time.

56. Minutes of the North District Association, 1817.

57. John Augustus Williams, 129–31.

58. Ibid., 133; Bork, "Elder 'Racoon' [*sic*] John Smith, 1784–1868," http://junebaldwinbork.com/smith/raccoon2.htm.

Chapter 5: Truth, and a Living

1. Jilson Payne Family Historical Papers.

2. Spencer, 1:116–27; see also Wolever, 97–107, and Sparks, 19–21, 96–98.

3. Taylor, *Baptists on the American Frontier,* 41–44.

4. Jilson Payne Family Historical Papers; see also Payne, "The Paynes of Virginia," http://www.icon.net/~sdcaller/d0003/g0000220.htm#I1465.

5. Spencer, 1:263–64.

6. Ibid., 1:345.

7. Ibid., 1:368.

8. Minutes of the Elkhorn Association, 1785–1805; Minutes of the North District Association, 1804–1806. Both Jilson Payne and John Coons served as delegates from Mt. Sterling Church to the Elkhorn Association from the date of the church's constitution in 1798 until 1802; John Coons continued in this capacity after Jilson Payne transferred his membership. See also Donaldson, *Raccoon John Smith,* 86, 107–8.

9. Jilson Payne Family Historical Papers.

10. John Augustus Williams, 240–42.

11. Jilson Payne Family Historical Papers; Payne, "The Paynes of Virginia," http://www.icon.net/~sdcaller/d0003/g0000220.htm#I1465.

12. *Minutes of the Burning Springs Association of Baptists,* comp. Dixon and Akers, I, E. See also Spencer, 1:260.

13. Minutes of the South Kentucky Association, 1801; Minutes of the North District Association, 1802.

14. Spencer, 1:308.

15. Donaldson, *The Legacy of Raccoon John Smith,* 19. John Augustus Williams erroneously reported that John Rice rather than Robert Elkin was Bledsoe's partner in the organization, and J. H. Spencer even quoted him.

16. Minutes of the Holston Association, 1786–1807; Minutes of the South Kentucky Association, 1801, and Minutes of the North District Association, 1802. See also John Augustus Williams, 205–7, for a vague history of Bald Eagle Church's pastors. I am much indebted to the genealogical researchers on the Eastern Kentucky Williams message board at Yahoo.com, for invaluable information on the early movements of Samuel Hanna and many of the other figures noted here. Hanna married Mary Cassady in Bourbon County, probably that portion which later became Nicholas, in 1792. He moved to Ohio, where he was apparently associated with North District Association's Ohio River Church until about 1807, when that congregation had John Young ordained as its pastor, and then moved back to Kentucky, further southeast.

17. Unpublished material on Daniel Williams from members of the Memory Hill Foundation (formerly the Daniel Williams Historical Society), West Liberty, Kentucky; Johnson, *Early Morgan County,* 261–65; Stacy, "Daniel Williams," 273; Musselman, "Chappawamsick Baptist Church Records," http://www.rootsweb.com/~vastaffo/cemeteries/chopawamsicbapchurch.htm. At that Prince George County, Virginia, Regular Baptist Church, an Edward Williams and a "Niclo Antherson" joined the church on November 24, 1767, and a "Jemiah Williams" joined on December 2 of that same year. The story of the Williams' involvement in the Battle of Blue Licks is more difficult to prove, with descendants and genealogists disagreeing on its accuracy,

but nonetheless there remains a strong tradition of it in the Williams family. See also note 24 of this chapter. Many thanks to the members of the Eastern Kentucky Williams Message Board at Yahoo.com for their helpful input in this section.

18. Again, thanks to the Eastern Kentucky Williams Message Board, especially church record transcriptionist Pam White.

19. *First "Census" of Kentucky, 1790,* 101. Rather than an actual census, this record is a compilation of the names of heads of households on county tax lists in 1789 and 1790. Daniel and Edward Williams are both listed as taxpayers in Madison County.

20. Spencer, 1:128.

21. Ibid., 1:129.

22. *Minutes of the Burning Springs Association of Baptists,* I, C–F.

23. Minutes of the South Kentucky Association, 1801, and the North District Association, 1802–1806.

24. Scalf, 236. Even though much of Scalf's information about Daniel Williams, and especially his eastern Kentucky partner Samuel Hanna, is inaccurate, this date seems dependable. It is interesting to note that the Tate's Creek Regular Baptist Church of the Elkhorn Association had a messenger named Daniel Williams at Elkhorn's 1800 session, but during this time the subject of our study was known already to have moved to Montgomery County rather than remaining in Madison. SBTS Collection. See also note 17 for this chapter.

25. Spencer, 1:308. Elijah Summers was listed by the Elkhorn Association as a representative from the Green River Association at its 1803 session. SBTS Collection.

26. Spencer, 1:193–94. For more on Walker, see Sparks, 119, 125–27.

27. Jilson Payne Family Historical Papers.

28. Ibid.

29. Vaughan, 47–48.

30. Last Will and Testament of Jilson Payne, probated in Montgomery County Court, October 3, 1825, KHS Collection.

31. Spencer, 1:546.

32. Minutes of the North District Association, 1802–1803; Minutes of the Elkhorn Association, 1794–1804.

33. Spencer, 1:196, 2:25–26; Minutes of the Elkhorn Association, 1798–1804.

34. Minutes of the Elkhorn Association, 1802.

35. Spencer, 1:548–549, 2:127; see also the Minutes of the South Kentucky Association, 1801.

36. Minutes of the North District Association, 1802; compared with the "sample" constitution listed in Asplund. For a discussion of the "abstract of principles" or articles of faith found in the Asplund volume as compared with the Kentuckians' Terms of General Union as well as current articles of faith employed by contemporary Regular, Old Regular, and Primitive Baptist groups, see Sparks, 241–42, 255–56.

37. Minutes of the North District Association, 1802.

38. Jilson Payne and James French first appeared as delegates from Lulbegrud Church at North District Association's 1803 session. Lulbegrud recorded five additions by letter within the previous twelve months. See Minutes of the North District Association, 1803; Donaldson, *Raccoon John Smith,* 84–85; and Cox and Craft, *The Memory Hill Foundation Website,* http://freepages.history.rootsweb.com/~memoryhill/index.html.

39. John Augustus Williams, 135.

40. *Minutes of the Burning Springs Association of Baptists,* I, C–F; see also Cox and Craft, *The Memory Hill Foundation Website,* http://freepages.history.rootsweb.com/~memoryhill/index.html.

41. Ibid.; see also Spencer, 1:196.

42. Minutes of the North District Association, 1803–1807.

43. Ibid.

44. Ibid.; John Augustus Williams, 205–6; Spencer, 2:340, 249. See also Sparks, 206.

45. Minutes of the special called session of Elkhorn Association, April 1803; Spencer, 1:547. See also Sparks, 200–201.

46. Spencer, 1:547–548, 2:240; Minutes of the Elkhorn Association, 1803–1810, and of the Licking Association, 1812 and 1817.

47. Minutes of the Elkhorn Association, 1803.

48. Minutes of the North District Association, 1803.

49. Spencer, 1:138.

50. Minutes of the North District Association, 1804.

51. Records of the South Fork (first known as Poplar Meeting-House) Church, West Liberty, Kentucky, 1808–1809, courtesy of the late Raymond Benton, West Liberty, Kentucky.

52. Minutes of the North District Association, 1805–1813.

53. Johnson, *Early Morgan County,* 261–65.

54. Included among the few exceptions are the Red Bird Association of Primitive Baptists, organized from North District Association in 1823, and its descendant groups in Clay County, Kentucky; the Mountain Association of Old Regular Baptists in Breathitt and Owsley counties, Kentucky, organized from North District in 1856, and the Central and Eastern District Associations of Primitive Baptists, progressive Primitive Baptist bodies that grew out of eastern Tennessee's Holston Association family. Even so, the old-line Separate Baptist kinship between all eastern Kentucky's native Baptist groups is easily recognizable.

55. *Minutes of the Burning Springs Association of Baptists,* I, page 1.

56. Spencer, 2:395–96; Minutes of the Holston Association, 1807.

57. Revolutionary pension record of Electious Thompson, DAR Collection.

58. For further information on Daniel Williams's eastern Kentucky progeny in the faith and the region's "Old Time" Baptists, see chapters 7 and 8 of this work and Sparks, *The Roots of Appalachian Christianity,* chapter 8. Perhaps the supreme irony of the old preacher's life involved his attempt, in his last years, to construct a fine "brick" home for himself on upper Caney Creek in present Morgan County from a pretty, black, easily quarried type of "rock" that he found in abundance there. The "stone" he used turned out to be cannel coal, the most flammable variety of the mineral, and his house burned to the ground, although no one seems to have been lost in the fire. I have often wondered if there wasn't some prophetic message for eastern Kentucky in that series of events, but if there was, nobody, absolutely no one, ever interpreted it correctly. See *Selections from Morgan County History,* 271–72.

59. John Augustus Williams, 250.

60. Spencer, 1:260; see also Isenberg, 26.

61. Minutes of the Elkhorn Association, 1804; Minutes of the North District Association, 1804.

62. Minutes of the North District Association, 1803–1804.

63. The following extract, penned by James French, is taken from the previous reference, and no more perfect example exists of the careful way that early Kentucky (and contemporary "Old Time") Baptists hid their controversies in flowery language: "A letter of correspondence was read from South District Association, and their messenger, Brother Vardeman, invited to take a seat—also a letter from a body of Baptists under the name of South District Association, was presented and read; containing complaints against two of the preachers in the South District Association, and alleging difficulties with some of the churches in the Tate's Creek Association, and urging this association to take up the business; and Brother Thomas J. Chilton, one of the messengers that presented the letter, solicited to be heard in justification of that body of people, which he, with others, represented; but this association being in a habit of correspondence and union with the Tate's Creek and South District Associations, and possessing no control over either of those associations, and neither of them having made a submission of the matter to this association, and without such mutual submission, it could not come within the province of this association to take cognizance of the case; therefore declined to take up the matter, or hear Brother Chilton—whereupon the letter was withdrawn."

64. Ibid., from the circular letter by Jilson Payne and Moses Bledsoe. As was customary, the two had been appointed the previous year to write the missive.

65. Spencer, 1:310.

66. Ibid., 1:310, quoting Thomas P. Dudley, son of Ambrose Dudley.

67. Minutes of the Elkhorn Association, 1801–1810; Minutes of the Licking Association, 1810; Spencer, 1:550–553; 2:240–50; John Augustus Williams, 203–7. It is interesting to note the differences in accounts between the two authors. Spencer tries to maintain the idea that the split absolutely did not occur due to differences in doctrine, rather only because of Creath's character and his difficulty with Thomas Lewis; Williams emphasizes the hyper-Calvinistic angle while never once criticizing Creath. Even so, Spencer uses Williams as a source at some points in his narrative. A careful examination of both authors along with the Elkhorn minutes reveals that both were right, and both were wrong. The difference in reference points lay in the two distinctive doctrines that the authors were trying to hold forth in their respective books.

68. Minutes of the Licking Association, 1817.

69. Spencer, 1:599.

70. Circular letter by David Barrow and Jilson Payne in the Minutes of the North District Association, 1805. Again, in keeping with custom, the two had received the appointment the previous year.

71. See chapter 2, n 59.

72. Spencer, 1:484; 2:97.

73. Ibid., 1:195, quoting Robert B. Semple.

74. John Augustus Williams, 127.

75. Cartwright, 128–29, 195–96.

76. Spencer, 1:184–86.

77. Ibid., 2:17.

78. Ibid., 1:185–86.

79. Minutes of the North District Association, 1804.

80. Spencer, 2:97; Minutes of the North District Association, 1805. Unfortunately (or fortunately, depending on one's perspective) SBTS has no Bracken Association minutes from this period, or any itemized list of the exact charges preferred against Barrow.

81. Minutes of the North District Association, 1805.

82. Dorgan, *The Old Regular Baptists of Central Appalachia,* 160.

83. John Augustus Williams, 309.

84. Spencer, 1:47, compared with *Descendants of Rev. Robert Elkin, 1745–1822,* found in the Clark County, Kentucky, Public Library Collection.

85. Vaughan, 87.

86. Morgan, 56.

87. See Sparks, chapter 6.

88. Spencer, 1:45–47; Minutes of the North District Association, 1802–1806.

89. Spencer, 1:207–8.

90. Minutes of the North District Association, 1805.

91. Spencer, 1:186.

92. Sparks, 162–65.

93. Minutes of the North District Association, 1805.

94. Spencer, 2:119–20.

95. Ibid., 1:196–97.

96. Ibid., 1:687–692.

97. Thanks to Civil War historian Edward R. Hazelett of Paintsville, Kentucky, for this information.

98. Spencer, 2:81–82.

99. Minutes of the North District Association, 1805.

100. Minutes of the North District Association, 1813.

101. Minutes of the North District Association, 1806.

102. Spencer, 2:125.
103. Ibid., 1:186.
104. "Barrow, David," in *The Kentucky Encyclopedia,* 55.
105. John Coons was one of Mt. Sterling Church's regular associational delegates from the church's organization in 1797 through its tenure in Elkhorn Association until 1803; in 1804 and 1805 he represented Mt. Sterling again in North District. His name first appears in North District's minutes as a delegate from Spencer Creek, along with members of the Rice family who were still prominent in Spencer Creek affairs at that time, in 1817, the year that Raccoon John Smith moved to Montgomery County. Minutes of the Elkhorn Association, 1797–1804, and minutes of the North District Association, 1804–1817.
106. Minutes of the North District Association, 1807.
107. Minutes of the North District Association, 1808.
108. Minutes of the North District Association, 1809; see also Montgomery County, Kentucky, Will Book A, 436.
109. John Augustus Williams, 135–36.
110. Spencer, 1:346.
111. Minutes of the North District Association, 1809–1812.
112. Spencer, 1:238.
113. See chapter 3 of this work, as well as Vaughan, 42–56.
114. Minutes of the North District Association, 1811.
115. Jilson Payne Family Historical Papers.
116. Cartwright, 148–52.
117. Minutes of the North District Association, 1812.
118. Spencer, 1, 649.
119. Rice, Journal, August–October 1815.
120. Spencer, 1:571–572.
121. Taylor, *Thoughts on Missions,* http://www.geocities.com/baptist_documents/j.taylor.miss.html; see also Chester Raymond Young's introduction to Taylor's *Baptists on the American Frontier,* 38–39, 50–62.
122. Spencer, 2:140.
123. Ibid., 1:262.
124. Minutes of the North District Association, 1817. Other references to Thomas White and the "Log Meetinghouse on Tate's Creek" found in the Minutes of the North District Association, 1802–1808.
125. John Augustus Williams, 182.
126. Spencer, 1:207–8.
127. Chenault, 173–74 n 51, quoting both Cane Springs Church's old records and recollections from the Chenault family.
128. Vaughan, 50.
129. Ibid., 79–80; Spencer, 1:208.
130. Vaughan, 80.
131. Minutes of the North District Association, 1817–1824 and 1826–1829. J. H. Spencer also briefly remarked on Chenault's preference in this regard: Spencer, 1:207–8.
132. Allen, 277; also John Augustus Williams, 145.
133. Ibid., 278.
134. A photograph of the log that split the church, made some years ago, can be found in Donaldson, *Raccoon John Smith,* 84.

Chapter 6: Why I Make Use of This Newspaper

1. John Augustus Williams, 133.
2. Letter from Mary Harrison to Jilson P. Harrison, June 29, 1830, in Boyd and Boyd, 26.

3. Boyd and Boyd, 24–28, quoting various Harrison family letters.

4. Minutes of the North District Association, 1817 and 1819 (1818 minutes missing). In the former year, Boone was a member and association messenger of Log Lick Church; in the latter, he served in the same capacities for Goshen.

5. John Augustus Williams, 134–36, 142.

6. Ibid., 206–7.

7. Minutes of the North District Association, 1823.

8. John Augustus Williams, 560, 572.

9. Minutes of the North District Association, 1819.

10. Spencer, 1:197; John Augustus Williams, 179–80; Last Will and Testament of David Barrow, written August 1, 1817, probated January 3, 1820, Montgomery County, Kentucky, Will Book B, 314–15.

11. Minutes of the North District Association, 1819–1820.

12. Donaldson, *Raccoon John Smith,* 103–8.

13. Ibid., 145–46.

14. John Augustus Williams, 137–39.

15. Luke 4:8, Matthew 16:23, and Mark 8:33, all in the King James Version.

16. John Augustus Williams, 140–41.

17. Ibid., 141.

18. Quoted verbatim in sequential order from the King James Version: "Answer not a fool according to his folly, lest thou also be like unto him. Answer a fool according to his folly, lest he be wise in his own conceit."

19. Montgomery County, Kentucky Marriage Records, 1796–1860.

20. Here we must reiterate the problems surrounding the determination of the exact birth dates of Raccoon John and Nancy's children noted in chapter 4, n 41. In the 1850 and 1860 Federal Census Records of Bath County, Kentucky (BCML), the daughter Maria indicated that she was born in the year 1820. From Raccoon John's 1841 letter to Isaac T. Reneau (Raccoon John Smith Historical Papers, LTS) we can infer that both the sons Jonathan and John Duke (records of whose namesake can be found in Boyd and Boyd, 20, et al.) were of legal age by that date. Raccoon John's brother William is known to have died in 1822 (Norton, "Descendants of Johann Schmidt," http://familytreemaker.genealogy.com/users/n/o/r/Michele-L-Norton/GENE4-0001.html? Welcome=1008757538); again, considering the uncertain birth dates of most of Raccoon John's children, it is a bit difficult to ascertain whether John's child William was born before or after his brother William's death. See also John Augustus Williams, 560.

21. Allen, 276–82.

22. Everett Donaldson indicates in *Raccoon John Smith: Frontiersman and Reformer,* 109, that Joshua Carroll Smith was three years old in 1827. He cites a questionably trustworthy Clinton County, Kentucky, local historian as his source, but although I cannot refute this claim with any definitive supporting data, I believe circumstantial evidence shows that Joshua could not have been born before 1826. See also chapter 4, n 41; John Augustus Williams, 560; Brown, "Brown Family History," http://awt.ancestry.com/cgi-bin/cgm.cgi?op=GET&db= :2022050&id=I930.

23. Jilson Payne Family Historical Papers; Last Will and Testament of Jilson Payne, Montgomery County Will Book C, 110.

24. *Descendants of Rev. Robert Elkin, 1745–1822*; Minutes of the North District Association, 1822.

25. Minutes of the North District Association, 1823; Spencer, 2:349; John Augustus Williams, 247.

26. John Augustus Williams, 179.

27. Ibid., 309.

28. Ibid., 240–42; Boyd and Boyd, 144–45.

29. In the only Federal Census record in which Raccoon John and Nancy's daughter Eliza Ann can be found, that of Bath County, Kentucky, in 1850, Eliza Ann indicated that she had been born in 1825. Again, see chapter 4, n 41.

30. John Augustus Williams, 145–47.

31. Fletcher, 145–47. Fletcher calls the denomination's current mindset "coercive confessionalism."

32. Donaldson, *Raccoon John Smith,* 84.

33. Minutes of the North District Association, 1822.

34. Minutes of the North District Association, 1823.

35. Ibid. Not even J. H. Spencer goes into quite as much detail about the Kentucky Baptists' union attempts in the late eighteenth century as does James French in this letter. He seems to have kept many of the pertinent historical records that he used for references in his personal collection, and it is a great pity that the originals have not survived.

36. Minutes of the North District Association, 1821.

37. Minutes of the North District Association, 1823.

38. Allen, 278, 280.

39. Ibid.; John Augustus Williams, 165.

40. Allen, 277.

41. Ibid., 281; see also chapter 2 of this work, nn 48–49.

42. Ibid., 279; see also chapter 1 of this work, n 36.

43. Garrett, 37–43.

44. Ibid., 98.

45. Ibid., 124–31.

46. Ibid., 131.

47. Vaughan, 134–43.

48. Garrett, 166.

49. Hughes, *Reviving the Ancient Faith,* 32.

50. Ibid., 275.

51. Ibid., 31, quoting longtime Campbell colleague Robert Richardson.

52. MacFarquhar, 64–66.

53. Hughes, *Reviving the Ancient Faith,* 22.

54. It must be noted here that in its earliest years, Redstone Association went further to preserve congregational autonomy than did a great many Baptist associations of either Regular or Separate ancestry. Once at an association meeting, one church brought charges against another for barring one of its members from taking communion at the accused church; the association refused to hear the charges, declaring that its becoming involved would violate its constitutional principle of church independency. Such an associational response was unknown in southern associations, most especially those of the Shubal Stearns tradition. Minutes of the Redstone Association, 1776–1810.

55. Hughes, *Reviving the Ancient Faith,* 22.

56. Ibid., 7.

57. Ibid., 48–52.

58. See chapter 2, 51–53.

59. Hughes, *Reviving the Ancient Faith,* 28.

60. See chapter 2, 52.

61. Garrett, 135; Tull, 112–13.

62. Allen, 284.

63. Hughes, *Reviving the Ancient Faith,* 172.

64. Ibid., 63, 331.

65. Yrigoen, 1, 36–38.

66. Spencer, 1:567–68.

67. Hughes, *Reviving the Ancient Faith,* 49–50.
68. Ibid., 22–26.
69. Ibid., 334–37; Garrett, 273–74.
70. Garrett, 239; Hughes, *Reviving the Ancient Faith,* 24.
71. See chapter 2, 61; also Boles, *The Great Revival,* 149–50.
72. Hughes, *Reviving the Ancient Faith,* 99–105.
73. Garrett, 135.
74. John Augustus Williams, 153–54.
75. Allen, 277.
76. Hughes, *Reviving the Ancient Faith,* 33, quoting Campbell.
77. John Augustus Williams, 171, 258.
78. Spencer, 1:589–90.
79. Ibid., 1:609.
80. Minutes of the Ohio Association, 1825–1826.
81. Campbell, "An Address to the Readers of *The Christian Baptist, No. IV,*" 4–9.
82. Allen, 278.
83. John Augustus Williams, 166.
84. Ibid., 161–62; Allen, 278.
85. John Augustus Williams, 162; Allen, 280–81.
86. Allen, 278–79; John Augustus Williams, 162–63.
87. Allen, 280–82; John Augustus Williams, 164–69. Robert Richardson, in his *Memoirs of Alexander Campbell,* 2:117, confirms that the Paynes were introduced to Campbell at this time as being a family of influential Kentucky Baptists.
88. John Augustus Williams, 560.
89. Ibid., 205.
90. Minutes of the North District Association, 1824 and 1825.
91. Donaldson, *Raccoon John Smith,* 106.
92. Minutes of the North District Association, 1824.
93. John Augustus Williams, 212–15; the names of the ministers are listed in the chapter heading on 203.
94. Spencer, 1:114; 2:26.
95. John Augustus Williams, 205–7.
96. Spencer, 2:249.
97. Minutes of the North District Association, 1827 and 1828.
98. Donaldson, *Legacy of Raccoon John Smith,* 170.
99. Allen, 282.
100. Last Will and Testament of Jilson Payne, probated in Montgomery County Court, October 3, 1825.
101. Jilson Payne Family Historical Papers.
102. Last Will and Testament of Jilson Payne.
103. Jilson Payne Family Historical Papers; Donaldson, *Raccoon John Smith,* 165.
104. John Augustus Williams, 193–94.
105. See chapter 2, 54 n 48, 405.
106. John Augustus Williams, 194.
107. Donaldson, *Raccoon John Smith,* 103–4.
108. John Augustus Williams, 194–96.
109. Donaldson, *Raccoon John Smith,* 106.
110. John Augustus Williams, 242–43.
111. Garrett, 151–54.
112. For one of the best detailed examinations of the differences between Stone and Campbell, see Hughes, *Reviving the Ancient Faith,* chapter 5.
113. Alexander Campbell, quoted by Hughes, *Reviving the Ancient Faith,* 37; 390 n 45.

114. Fletcher, 144–48.
115. John Augustus Williams, 174.
116. Garrett, 161–63.
117. John Augustus Williams, 253.
118. Garrett, 163.
119. Cecil K. Thomas, quoted in Garrett, 162.
120. Here I must thank a longtime friend from both the church and the academic world, a fellow minister as well as a published author in religious studies and currently a professor of philosophy and religion at a Midwestern college, for a vivid anecdote. I refrain from mentioning his name here due to personal and friendship concerns. Once a college classmate of mine, the gentleman in question was, like me, an eastern Kentucky "preacher boy"; however, unlike me he opted to pursue theological studies at an acclaimed out-of-state seminary before returning home to preach. His denomination at the time (which, unlike most native faiths in Appalachia, has a "national" association, a Bible college of its own, and a fairly sizable and arguably efficient bureaucracy that includes a "Committee on Theological Liberalism") put him through three separate heresy trials simply because of the liberal reputation of the seminary at which he had taken his studies. One of the judges sent from Nashville to try his case made the statement and asked him if he agreed to it; if he had answered positively, he might have spared himself the annoyance of the last two trials. When he returned to the same seminary to pursue doctoral studies, he switched church memberships, and I suppose that the headquarters of the threatened denomination felt safe again.
121. John Augustus Williams, 188.
122. Spencer, 1:449.
123. John Augustus Williams, 175–77.
124. Ibid., 175–76, 183.
125. Ibid., 183.
126. Ibid., 187, 358.
127. Spencer, 2:124.
128. Minutes of the North District Association, 1825 and 1826; Donaldson, *The Legacy of Raccoon John Smith,* 20–21.
129. Ibid.
130. Minutes of the North District Association, 1826.
131. John Augustus Williams, 182.
132. The circumstantial evidence to support this supposition can be found in the Minutes of the North District Association, 1827; and John Augustus Williams, 185–88. No record of direct correspondence between the North District and Cumberland River Associations can be shown to have existed before the time in question.
133. Garrett, 151–54.
134. Minutes of the North District Association, 1827; Spencer, 2:119.
135. Ibid., John Augustus Williams, 180–83.
136. Minutes of the North District Association (Chenault-French faction), 1830.
137. Taylor, *Baptists on the American Frontier,* 363–64.
138. Donaldson, *Raccoon John Smith,* 165.
139. John Augustus Williams, 182.

Chapter 7: The Attack Upon Christendom, Part I

1. Fuller, 191.
2. McDonald, "Having the Last Word" (biographical sketch of Richard Marius published in the online journal *Metro Pulse* of Knoxville, Tennessee), http://www.metropulse.com/dir_zine/dir_2001/1148/t_cover.html.
3. See also Oberman, "Varieties of Protest," http://www.highbeam.com/library/doc0.asp?DOCID

=1G1%3A55361886&rcfid=ip_almanac_hf; and Oberman, "Review—Martin Luther: The Christian Between God and Death," http://www.findarticles.com/p/articles/mi_m2082/is_4_62/ai_64910309.

4. John Augustus Williams, 181–82; Donaldson, *Raccoon John Smith,* 111–12. Williams states that at this time Raccoon John and Nancy had five children, the oldest of whom was ten, which agrees with the data concerning his children's births that we have explored thus far. Neither of his daughters by Anna are mentioned at all, further evidence that their grandmother Smith housed and raised them. We can't entirely rule out the possibility John and Nancy had even had one child after Joshua by this time, but if this were the case, for physiological reasons that are perhaps best not discussed in detail it would have been virtually impossible for Nancy to spend four whole days away from a nursing infant.

5. Ward, 63–67.

6. John Augustus Williams, 181.

7. Ibid., 182.

8. Ibid., 250.

9. Minutes of the North District Association, 1827.

10. Boyd and Boyd, 21, 25.

11. John Augustus Williams, 181–82. He also claims that Joshua Hurt urged Nancy to go, but he errs once more in referring to Joshua as Nancy's "unmarried" brother.

12. U.S. Federal Census, Bath County, Kentucky, 1850; Brown, "Brown Family History." http://awt.ancestry.com/cgi-bin/igm.cgi?op=GET&db=:2022050&id=I930.

13. Cox, 23–24.

14. John Augustus Williams, 182.

15. Minutes of the North District Association, 1827. "Richard Barns" is listed as a delegate from Cumberland River, suggesting a typographical error by James French that may have indicated the presence of both ministers.

16. John Augustus Williams, 182–84, compared with 358, quoting a letter written by John Smith and Buckner H. Payne.

17. John Augustus Williams, 184.

18. John Augustus Williams, 184–85; Minutes of the North District Association, 1827. A correct interpretation of the events in the context of the association's order of business is crucial to understanding what actually happened on this fateful day. In an association such as North District was, and in all its descendant bodies that I have ever been acquainted with in twenty-odd years of attending such meetings, the vote for associational officers is never taken until after all letters from the churches are read and the legislative body of messengers is organized. After the election is decided and officers installed for the coming year, newly constituted churches are invited to apply for membership; then letters from corresponding associations are received and voted upon, and the moderator appoints an arrangements committee to draw up a schedule for the second day's business to be carried out, more often than not with their own advice about how to dispose of any queries. The only time that this particular debate could have occurred was in the interim between the reading of the church letters and the calling of the roll for the moderatorial election.

19. Minutes of the North District Association, 1827.

20. John Augustus Williams, 184–85.

21. Minutes of the North District Association, 1827.

22. John Augustus Williams, 185–88.

23. Minutes of the North District Association, 1827.

24. John Augustus Williams, 358.

25. Minutes of the North District Association, 1827.

26. John Augustus Williams, 188–90.

27. Ibid., 216–19.

28. Ibid., 190.

29. Minutes of the North District Association, 1827.

30. John Augustus Williams, 249–50.

31. This table is taken from the relevant minute records of North District Association showing the group's choices for introductory sermon preacher and alternate from year to year. Asterisks (*) indicate variations from the tradition that Williams claims for North District. Double asterisks (**) indicate times when an arrangements change had been made mandatory by the death of a preacher:

Year	Preacher and Alternate for Next Year	Year	Introductory Sermon Preached By
1802	[not listed]	1803	Robert Elkin
1803	Isaac Crutcher, Moses Bledsoe	1804	Isaac Crutcher
1804	William Morris,* James Quesenberry	1805	James Quesenberry
1805	Robert Elkin, Moses Bledsoe	1806	Robert Elkin
1806	Moses Bledsoe, William Morris	1807	Robert R. Hunt*
1807	Robert Elkin,* Robert R. Hunt	1808	Robert Elkin
1808	Moses Bledsoe,* James Quesenberry	1809	Robert Elkin**
1809	Edward Kindred,* David Chenault	1810	Edward Kindred
1810	David Chenault, Wingate Jackson	1811	David Chenault
1811	Isaac Crutcher*, Edward Kindred	1812	Isaac Crutcher
1812	Edward Kindred, Robert Elkin	1813	Edward Kindred
1813	Robert Elkin, David Chenault	1814	N.A.
1814	N.A.	1815	N.A.
1815	N.A.	1816	David Chenault
1816	Edward Kindred, Robert Brown	1817	Edward Kindred
1817	Thomas Boone,* Thomas White	1818	N.A.
1818	N.A.	1819	Thomas White
1819	John Smith, Samuel Kelly	1820	John Smith
1820	Samuel Kelly, Edward Kindred	1821	Samuel Kelly
1821	Edward Kindred, David Chenault	1822	Edward Kindred
1822	John Smith,* David Chenault	1823	John Smith
1823	David Chenault, Enoch Willoughby	1824	Jeremiah Vardeman*
1824	David Chenault,* Thomas Boone	1825	David Chenault
1825	Enoch Willoughby,* Thomas Boone	1826	Enoch Willoughby
1826	Thomas Boone, John Smith	1827	Thomas Boone
1827	John Smith, Thomas White	1828	John Smith
1828	Thomas White, Thomas Boone	1829	Thomas White
1829	Thomas Boone, John N. Payne	1830	John N. Payne

32. Minutes of the North District Association, 1827.

33. John Augustus Williams, 191.

34. Ibid., 309–10; Donaldson, *Raccoon John Smith,* 164–65.

35. John Augustus Williams, 227–28; Donaldson, *Raccoon John Smith,* 140–41.

36. John Augustus Williams, 227–28.

37. Spencer, 2:29.

38. Garrett, 238–39; Spencer, 2:29–30.

39. John Augustus Williams, 243.

40. Ibid., 228.

41. Ibid., 259–60.

42. Ibid., 193.

43. Ibid., 191.

44. Ibid., 192.

45. Ibid., 193.

46. See chapter 4, n 41. Emily or Emma Smith's gravestone indicates August 10 as her birthday, and in the 1850 U.S. Federal Census of Montgomery County compiled by Barbara,

Byron, and Samuel Sistler, page 338, Raccoon John and Nancy indicated Emma's age as twenty-one and that of the youngest daughter, Mary, as nineteen.

47. John Augustus Williams, 199.

48. Ibid., 225.

49. Ibid., 199–200.

50. Ibid., 226.

51. Ibid., 237.

52. Ibid., 200–202.

53. Ibid., 223.

54. Ibid., 238–39.

55. Ibid., 192.

56. Ibid., 238.

57. Ibid., 239–40.

58. Ibid., 275, 334–35.

59. Trimble, "Recollections of Breathitt," http://www.breathittcounty.com/TrimblesBook.html.

60. John Augustus Williams, 303.

61. Letter of John Smith to Isaac T. Reneau, May 4, 1841, Raccoon John Smith Historical Papers, LTS; see also chapter 4, n 42.

62. John Augustus Williams, 513; see also chapter 4, n 45.

63. John Augustus Williams, 560, 572.

64. Lexington Cemetery Burial Records, Lexington, Kentucky, http://www.lexcem. org. See also chapter 4 n 42 and chapter 9 n 107.

65. Garrett, 154–55.

66. Letter of James Mason to Alexander Campbell, April 19, 1828, quoted in John Augustus Williams, 211.

67. John Augustus Williams, 218–19. For further information on James Mason's brother John, see Donaldson, *The Legacy of Raccoon John Smith,* 26–30.

68. Letter of James Mason to Alexander Campbell, May 15, 1830, in *The Millennial Harbinger,* June 1830, 274; Campbell's reply, 276–77.

69. Letter of Micajah Harrison to Jilson Payne Harrison, April 20, 1828, quoted in Boyd and Boyd, 25. In speaking of the obvious evangelical/Baptist essence of this letter, we might speculate a bit as to exactly how long it took Raccoon John to stem all the Baptist influence in his early Montgomery County Reform congregations. John Augustus Williams's own memoirs (some excerpts of which are in the MS-MCL Collection) reveal some of his own wryly amusing recollections of Reform church services in his youth that, in essence, have "backcountry Baptist" written large all over them. Williams, who was born in Bourbon County in 1824, seems to have been able to take this indulgent, humorous tone when writing about himself and his experiences as opposed to his stance as a Raccoon John propagandist. He recalled that the elder sisters would still weep openly when the "old" songs were lined out in Baptist fashion, and in fact that one or two of the older Reform preachers were very proficient at this method of song leading. The aged sisters' greatest joy, though, was listening to some young, handsome preacher, preferably of frail physical constitution, sing a solo ballad on some graveyard topic (such as "The White Pilgrim," written about the death of Joseph Thomas, a Christian Church minister, and which has since been borrowed and adopted by rural Baptists as well) and cast his eyes heavenward as if he expected to perish at that very moment. Williams's description here likewise depicts a country Baptist staple at least since the days of Elijah Craig, who in his youth was described by John Taylor as appearing as if he had just gotten up from the dead, and the reactions Williams witnessed may have been the good sisters' sensual and emotional equivalent of their frontier mothers' and grandmothers' pleasure in "laying out" young men dead of natural causes for burial, as noted in chapter 1. For another of Williams's wryly humorous anecdotes about the Reformers among whom he lived and worked, one in fact that either William Faulkner

or Flannery O'Connor would have been proud to invent on their own and work into a story, see Donaldson, *The Legacy of Raccoon John Smith,* 78–80.

70. John Augustus Williams, 242, 353.

71. Jilson Payne Family Historical Papers.

72. John Augustus Williams, 353.

73. Ibid., 240.

74. Ibid., 262.

75. Minutes of the North District Association, 1828 and 1829.

76. References taken from the Low Gap United Baptist Church record book, 1814–1860, in the possession of Elder C. C. Murray Jr. of Lexington, Kentucky.

77. Chrystie Myers, "Genealogical Rootsweb Research Homesite," http://awt.ancestry.com/cgi-bin/igm.cgi?op=GET&db=leachmandr&id=I4195.

78. Minutes of the North District Association, 1816–1827. Willoughby's, Fox's, and Fanning's names can also be found as North District representatives in *Minutes of the Burning Springs Association of Baptists,* I, pages 23 and 32.

79. See *Minutes of the Burning Springs Association of Baptists,* I, 29.

80. Minutes of the North District Association, 1828.

81. Mason, "Family History," http://www.tmason1.com/pafg11.htm#148.

82. Trimble, "Recollections of Breathitt," http://www.breathittcounty.com/TrimblesBook.html; see also Minutes of the North District Association, 1816–1829; *Minutes of the Burning Springs Association of Baptists,* I, 1–35; and *Early and Modern History of Wolfe County, Kentucky,* 37–38.

83. John Augustus Williams, 250.

84. Donaldson, *Raccoon John Smith,* 124–25; see also John Augustus Williams, 393.

85. John Augustus Williams, 250.

86. Spencer, 1:625, quoting Silas Noel's Circular Letter to Franklin Association, July 1830. Interestingly, the same reference can be found in John Augustus Williams, 348.

87. E.g., John Augustus Williams, 274–75, 480–81.

88. Ibid., 458, evidently quoting Barton Stone.

89. Once again, thanks to Dr. James Stephen Wolfgang of the University of Kentucky for his input on this question. One of the few references Williams makes to the fact that differing and sometimes bizarre interpretations of the meaning of immersion could be found within the Campbell movement is in *The Life of Elder John Smith,* 470–71. But neither can we say that all of the Campbell Reform's early advocates entirely lost their sense of humor in regard to the new interpretation of the mechanics of salvation. J. Green Trimble, who was born in 1822 and watched the first progress of the Campbell Reform in Kentucky southward from Montgomery County into the mountains when he was a child, relates an anecdote about one Simon Cockrell Sr., whose extended family was much interested in Campbell's Ancient Gospel, but who himself never professed faith or joined a church. Cockrell had the reputation of being kind and generous to a fault to anyone he liked but implacable and unforgiving toward those whom he perceived as dishonest. He was in fact the patriarch of one of the families involved in Breathitt County's most notorious late nineteenth-century feud. So it happened that, at one early season when Joseph Nickell was immersing converts in the North Fork of the Kentucky River near present Jackson after a protracted meeting, Cockrell saw Nickell plunge one man, whom Cockrell disliked intensely, underwater as a new convert. As soon as the brand-new Christian's head popped back above the water's surface, Cockrell roared out, "Souse him again, Joe, for he's a damned dirty dog and it'll take two dips to wash away his sins!" See Trimble, "Recollections of Breathitt," http://www.breathittcounty.com/TrimblesBook.html.

90. John Augustus Williams, 458.

91. Boyd and Boyd, 20.

92. The "Cherokee" sentence Raccoon John spoke in this instance, transcribed directly from John Augustus Williams, 527, reads thus: *"Segilluh unuhsohee unaka howee taw!"* Not

even Durbin Feeling, faculty member and Cherokee linguist at the University of Oklahoma, or any of the native Cherokee speakers I have consulted within one of the Cherokee Nation's major online communities (http://www.cherokee-online.com) can make heads or tails of it. The following are Mr. Feeling's comments, from a letter to the author dated October 21, 2003: "Many times the spelling will hide, whether intentionally or not, the meaning of words. Example: Is the first word sounded as 'see-ghee-luh?' or is it 'seh-gill-oo' or what? It may be someone's name 'see-ghee-lee,' Ezekiel, but the ending of the word '-lee' doesn't come near matching '-luh.' The only word that I can say that I somewhat understand (maybe), is 'unaka.' If 'unaka' is supposed to be the word for 'white' or 'oo-neh-gah,' or linguistically spelled 'uuneeka' then there is inconsistency in pronouncing the 'a' in the word unaka. I would say that these words came from someone who is not a fluent speaker or knows just a few 'words' of Cherokee." Thanks also to Sky Campbell, webmaster at cherokee-online.com, for assistance.

93. John Augustus Williams, 526–27.

94. Ibid., 221–22.

95. Ibid., 224.

96. Ibid., 234–36.

97. Ibid., 498–99.

98. Ibid., 501–2.

99. Ibid., 225. Everett Donaldson, for reasons best known to himself, changed this story to have Raccoon John use milk instead. Donaldson, *The Legacy of Raccoon John Smith,* 36.

100. Garrett, 83. Thanks to Dr. Douglas Foster of Abliene Christian University, Abilene, Texas, for clarification of the movement's communion policies here.

101. John Augustus Williams, 230.

102. Ibid., 228–32.

103. Ibid., 232–34.

104. Ibid., 234.

105. Spencer, 2:30; Taulman, 207.

106. Minutes of the North District Association, 1828.

107. John Augustus Williams, 353.

108. Minutes of the North District Association, 1828.

109. John Augustus Williams, 253.

110. Minutes of the North District Association, 1828.

111. John Augustus Williams, 255.

112. Ibid., 255; Minutes of the North District Association, 1828. Unfortunately, the microfilm image of this year's minutes is slightly marred at the line where the committee members are listed; Isaac Thornburgh's is the only legible name.

113. Minutes of the North District Association, 1828.

114. John Augustus Williams, 255.

115. Ibid., 255–57.

Chapter 8: The Attack Upon Christendom, Part II

1. Payne, "The Paynes of Virginia," http://www.icon.net/~sdcaller/d0003/g0000220.htm#I1465.

2. E.g. John Augustus Williams, 264–69, 276–81, 393–96.

3. Ibid., 258–71.

4. Ibid., 281–85.

5. Ibid., 277–78. Noted here is one of Raccoon John's conflicting tales about the origins of his nickname. See chapter 4 of this work, n 34, and Donaldson, *Raccoon John Smith,* 170–71.

6. Ibid., 303.

7. Vaughan, 183. For the reference to Sam Hyde, see Carl Sifakis, *American Eccentrics,* 7–8.

8. John Augustus Williams, 243.

9. Donaldson, *Raccoon John Smith,* 130–31, quoting Jacob Creath Sr. Chapter 14 of

Donaldson, *Raccoon John Smith,* is a more perceptive analysis of Jeremiah Vardeman's personality than most Baptists will ever admit. The Scriptural reference to Adonibezek is from Judges 1:5–7, King James Version.

10. Spencer, 1:238–39.

11. Ibid., 1:280, notes that this Spencer Creek minority continued to maintain Baptist-style worship independently of the Reformers until 1840, when the members formally dissolved their church constitution. See also Minutes of the North District Association, 1832 and 1840.

12. John Augustus Williams, 286–88.

13. Spencer, 1:280–81; see also Minutes of the North District Association, 1826–1829.

14. John Augustus Williams, 291–92.

15. Minutes of the North District Association, 1829.

16. See John Augustus Williams, 358–59, quoting the lengthy circular written by John Smith and Buckner H. Payne.

17. Ibid.; see also James Mason's letter to Alexander Campbell, May 15, 1830, in *The Millennial Harbinger,* June 1830, 274.

18. Minutes of the North District Association, 1829.

19. John Augustus Williams, 297.

20. Minutes of the North District Association, 1829–1830.

21. Mason's letter to Campbell, May 15, 1830, *Millennial Harbinger,* June 1830, 274–75.

22. See John Augustus Williams, 341–43; Donaldson, *Raccoon John Smith,* 118–19; and Fortune, 88.

23. Alexander Campbell's reply to James Mason's letter, *Millennial Harbinger,* June 1830, 284.

24. Fletcher, 143.

25. John Augustus Williams, 305.

26. Spencer, 1:609–11.

27. Hughes, 29–30, 93–95.

28. Vaughan, 166.

29. Ibid., 268; Spencer, 1:620; see also John Augustus Williams, 387.

30. Vaughan, 165–68, 268.

31. Ibid., 168.

32. Spencer, 1:226.

33. The entire text of Noel's "Thirty-Nine Articles" can be found in Spencer, 1:624–35.

34. John Augustus Williams, 349.

35. Ibid., 365–73.

36. Minutes of the Lulbegrud Conference, April 1830.

37. Spencer, 1:207.

38. Minutes of the North District Association, 1822–1826; *Minutes of the Burning Springs Association of Baptists,* I, page 23; Spencer, 1:412.

39. Spencer, 1:207.

40. Minutes of the North District Association, 1827–1829; Minutes of the Lulbegrud Conference, April 1830.

41. John Augustus Williams, 335–38.

42. Minutes of the Lulbegrud Conference, April 1830.

43. Minutes of the Goshen Conference, June 1830.

44. Minutes of the North District Association (Smith faction), 1830. At this session Smith and his cohorts dropped the name "Baptist" altogether.

45. For the complete text of this document, see John Augustus Williams, 354–61.

46. Ibid., 361–93.

47. Ibid., 415–19.

48. Minutes of the North District Association, 1831.

49. Spencer, 2:122–25.

50. Ibid., 1:207–8.
51. Chenault, 175–77.
52. Spencer, 2:108–13, 215–19; Minutes of the Green River and Stockton's Valley Associations, 2001, courtesy of Mark Hogan of Lindseyville, Kentucky; Madison, Roundtree, and Cowles, 36–50.
53. W. Lynn Nickell, "First Christian Church, West Liberty, Kentucky," and Stacy, "History of Old Grassy Christian Church," 174–79, also, Low Gap United Baptist Church Record Book, 1814–1860, courtesy of Elder Cecil C. Murray Jr., Lexington, Kentucky.
54. John Augustus Williams, 463.
55. Minutes of the Burning Springs Association, 1834.
56. Minutes of the Burning Springs Association, 1836; Minutes of the Burning Springs Association, 1837, courtesy of the late Elder B. C. Ferguson of Paintsville, Kentucky; see also *Early and Modern History of Wolfe County, Kentucky,* 37.
57. For further information on these developments in eastern Kentucky, see Sparks, 226–31, 303–4 n 48.
58. *Foxfire 7,* 110–17.
59. One interesting example of this relationship, and another specimen of Campbell folklore, survives as an anecdote from the infamous Hatfield and McCoy feud. William Dyke Garrett, the Logan County, West Virginia, mountain minister who finally persuaded Devil Anse Hatfield to embrace Christianity, be baptized, and join the church in his old age was not, as has often been claimed, a "Hardshell" Baptist preacher. He was a minister in good standing with Alexander Campbell's Disciples, or Churches, of Christ. And though he undoubtedly believed and preached the doctrines of his church faithfully, he always said that the Lord had shown him the error of his ways and let him know that it was high time he came to the creek to be immersed—not by the Scriptures themselves, but by personally knocking a fiddle out of his hands with a lightning bolt. Raccoon John Smith would have been livid to hear a Disciple preacher tell such a tale, but I suspect that Alexander Campbell, at least in his mature years, would have enjoyed the story immensely. Hatfield and Spence, 97.
60. See Sparks, 228–89.
61. Fletcher, 145–47.
62. See Sparks, 8–9, 232–34.
63. Spencer, 2:125; Minutes of the North District Association, 1960, PBL.
64. U.S. Federal Census for Montgomery County, Kentucky, 1850, 338.
65. Spencer, 2:215, 236.
66. John Augustus Williams, 401.
67. Ibid., 410–12.
68. Ibid., 412; see also Spencer, 2:388–90, 554–56.
69. John Augustus Williams, 405–7.
70. Letter of John Smith to Isaac T. Reneau, May 4, 1841, Raccoon John Smith Historical Papers. Raccoon John's reference to "hive gear" may be a jest in reference to Denton's work with the Presbyterians, that he stood in some danger of "getting stung," as it were.
71. John Augustus Williams, 401–3.
72. Ibid., 472–75.
73. Spencer, 1:419; 2:388–90.
74. Donaldson, *Raccoon John Smith,* 136.
75. Garrett, 258–62.
76. John Augustus Williams, 437; Garrett, 191, 192–94.
77. Hines, *Restoration History Pages,* "Two Major Movements Unite," http://www.christianchronicler.com/History2/movement_unites.html.
78. John Augustus Williams, 415–16.
79. Ibid., 461–62.
80. Campbell, reply to a letter from Peter Hon, March 18, 1843, *The Millennial Harbinger,* May 1843, 234.

81. Donaldson, *Raccoon John Smith,* 151.

82. Hines, *Restoration History Pages,* "Two Major Movements Unite," http://www.christianchronicler.com/History2/movement_unites.html. The debate quoted by Hines here essentially raged through the pages of *The Millennial Harbinger* and *The Christian Messenger* between April and December 1831. Relevant *Harbinger* extracts can be found in the periodical's volume 2, numbers 4–12, and indexed by Ernest Stefanik at http://www.mun.ca/rels/hrollmann/restmov/texts/acampbell/tmh/MHIDXAU.HTM.

83. Hughes, *Reviving the Ancient Faith,* 115, quoting Gardner.

84. Donaldson, *Raccoon John Smith,* 142.

85. Garrett, 174–75.

86. Ibid., 177.

87. John Augustus Williams, 487–89.

88. Spencer, 1:96.

89. Sifakis, 61–63.

90. John Augustus Williams, 449.

91. Garrett, 178.

92. Ibid., 201, quoting Samuel Rogers.

93. Donaldson, *Raccoon John Smith,* 142–43, 154–55.

94. John Augustus Williams, 450–52.

95. Ibid., 454.

96. Ibid., 454–55.

97. Ibid., 449.

98. Moore, *Behind the Bars,* 1.

99. Ibid., 173, quoting minister and college president J. W. McGarvey.

Chapter 9: The Repetition

1. John Augustus Williams, 551.

2. Ibid., 463.

3. Donaldson, *The Legacy of Raccoon John Smith,* 36–37.

4. John Augustus Williams, 537.

5. Ibid., 551; Richardson, 2:501–2.

6. Ibid., 533–36.

7. Bath County, Kentucky, Marriage Book 2, 79.

8. Donaldson, *The Legacy of Raccoon John Smith,* 43.

9. See the transcription of the U.S. Federal Census, Bath County, Kentucky, 1850.

10. Donaldson, *The Legacy of Raccoon John Smith,* 43.

11. Bath County, Kentucky, Marriage Book 2, 79; U.S. Federal Census, Bath County, Kentucky, 1850. In the census, Freeman's first name is listed as Edward; on his marriage record, as Edgar.

12. John Augustus Williams, 514–15. The 1833 cholera epidemic in Montgomery County is further documented by Boyd and Boyd, 28.

13. John Augustus Williams, 539.

14. Frank F. Mathias, "Richard Hickman Menefee," *The Kentucky Encyclopedia,* 624–25. The spelling of Menefee's name here is Mathias's. See also John Augustus Williams, 538–40.

15. Hughes, *Reviving the Ancient Faith,* 2.

16. Ibid., 48, quoting Harrell.

17. Ibid., 106–16. Louis and Bess Cochran also make note of this difference between Stone and Campbell, although they seem to trace its origins to a time after the 1832 union. See Cochran and Cochran, 105–7.

18. Hughes, *Reviving the Ancient Faith,* 3.

19. Garrett, 92.

20. The Birmingham Amended Statement of Faith (Christadelphian), http://www.bereanecclesialnews.com/doctrines/basf.html.

21. Hughes, *Reviving the Ancient Faith,* 38.

22. Ibid., 32–37.

23. Campbell, "News from the Churches," *Millennial Harbinger,* July 1843, 333. In addition, Philips seems to have penned a doggerel song about the Disciple view of baptism. See also Hughes, *Reviving the Ancient Faith,* 7, 387 n 12.

24. Hughes, 39–40; Garrett, 384–85, and Cochran and Cochran, 82, quoting Campbell. See also Gates, *The Disciples of Christ,* 230–32.

25. Garrett, 385–86.

26. Hughes, *Reviving the Ancient Faith,* 46.

27. Cochran and Cochran, 120; Garrett, 274.

28. Garrett, 273.

29. See ibid., 469–521.

30. See Hughes, *Reviving the Ancient Faith,* 141–67, 334–41, 372–73; Garrett, 435–60.

31. Garrett, 433–34.

32. Ibid., 478–79.

33. Campbell, "Notes on a Late Tour, No. II," 506. Here Campbell spoke of "the great subject of the present crisis in our denomination and the world."

34. Hughes, *Reviving the Ancient Faith,* 40.

35. Fortune, 206–7.

36. Garrett, 279.

37. Ibid., 285–91.

38. Richardson, 2:511.

39. Ibid., 2:502.

40. Garrett, 238.

41. Richardson, 2:441.

42. Hughes, *Reviving the Ancient Faith,* 54, quoting Scott's August 4, 1840, letter to Philip Fall, 393 n 25.

43. Ibid., quoting Creath in 1850, 391 n 60.

44. Ibid., quoting Creath in 1877, 391 n 62. See also Cochran and Cochran, 170–71.

45. Donaldson, *The Legacy of Raccoon John Smith,* 45.

46. John Augustus Williams, 482.

47. Fortune, 206.

48. John Augustus Williams, 541–45.

49. Fortune, 209.

50. Garrett, 115, 205.

51. John Augustus Williams, 545, quoting Scott.

52. Hughes, 54–55.

53. John Augustus Williams, 461–63.

54. Donaldson, *The Legacy of Raccoon John Smith,* 22–23.

55. Ibid., 29.

56. See chapter 7 of this work, nn 63–64.

57. Donaldson, *The Legacy of Raccoon John Smith,* 26–30.

58. Mason, "Family History Web Site," http://www.tmason1.com.

59. Donaldson, *The Legacy of Raccoon John Smith,* 28–29, quoting Peters; John Augustus Williams, 538–40.

60. Donaldson, *The Legacy of Raccoon John Smith,* 287.

61. Campbell, "Notes on a Late Tour, No. II," 506.

62. Letter of John Smith to Alexander Campbell, September 15, 1841, *Millennial Harbinger,* November 1841, 536.

63. See *Christian Messenger* 8, no. 5 (May 1834); 8, no. 10 (Oct. 1834); 9, no. 9 (Sept. 1835); 10, no. 7 (July 1836).

64. Ibid., 11, no. 7 (March 1841).

65. Letter of B. K. Smith of Indianapolis, Indiana, to Alexander Campbell, June 16, 1841; *Millennial Harbinger* 12, no. 1 (January 1842): 38–39. An account of this trip, minus, of course, the McVay matter, can be found in John Augustus Williams, 546–47. Raccoon John used the occasion of a poorly publicized and consequently scantily attended night meeting for another of his famous quips: "I hope that none of you will go to sleep, for if you do, the number left awake will be very small indeed."

66. Smith to Campbell, Sept. 15, 1841, *Millennial Harbinger* 11, no. 11 (November 1841), 536, DCHS.

67. Campbell, "News From the Churches," *Millennial Harbinger* 13, no. 9 (September 1843), 429.

68. Campbell, reply to Smith, *Millennial Harbinger* 11, no. 11 (November 1841): 536.

69. B. K. Smith to Alexander Campbell, June 16, 1841, *Millennial Harbinger* 12, no. 1 (January 1842): 38–39.

70. Rash et al., 282.

71. *The Christian Messenger* 12, no. 2 (December 1841): 65.

72. Rash et al., 282–83. Though we cannot say with certainty, this North Middletown visit may have allowed Raccoon John once more to indulge his penchant for cracking jokes. Whether at this occasion or a later one, a Bourbon County magistrate once ribbed Smith for riding into North Middletown on a fine horse, when Jesus had chosen a lowly ass on which to ride into Jerusalem. Raccoon John shot back that asses were hard to find just then, since all the local ones had been voted into office in Bourbon County as magistrates. Donaldson, *The Legacy of Raccoon John Smith,* 38–39.

73. Campbell, "Notes on a Late Tour, No. II," 506–7.

74. John Augustus Williams, 550–51; see also *The Christian Messenger* 13, no. 1 (May 1843): 31–32; *The Millennial Harbinger* 13, no. 4 (April 1843): 190.

75. Campbell, "Elder John Smith and James McVay," 234–35.

76. Richardson, 2:500–501.

77. Campbell, "News From the Churches," *The Millennial Harbinger* 13, no. 9 (September 1843): 429..

78. Peter Hon, letter to Alexander Campbell, March 18, 1843, *The Millennial Harbinger* 13, no. 5 (May 1843): 234.

79. John Augustus Williams, 551; see also Donaldson, *The Legacy of Raccoon John Smith,* 40. According to the Williams account, the boiling water was in a "hogshead" barrel rather than a wash pot, but wash pots were invariably used in the stated capacity for home butchering, and it would have been literally impossible to have transferred the boiling contents of a wash pot over to a hogshead without several of the laborers themselves getting scalded thoroughly. There would have been no reason simply not to leave the water in the wash pots and draw off boiling water directly therefrom with smaller long-handled receptacles for the scalding. Donaldson states that the container in question was a vat, and he must be more correct in this particular.

80. John Augustus Williams, 551–52, quoting a letter from Emma Smith Ringo.

81. Campbell, "Extra," 1. Cochran and Cochran, in *Captives of the Word,* 110, make the allegation that Raccoon John was back in Lexington for the end of the debate because they found the name John Smith on a list of sixty-five ministers who met in the basement of Lexington's Main Street Christian Church around the end of November for an ad hoc discussion about "the organization of the brotherhood." It is doubtful, though, that Louis Cochran took Richard's accident into consideration at all; he certainly didn't for his historical novel. If Raccoon John was present for this meeting, he was tougher, more callous, and shallower than we have heretofore given him credit for being. Actually, it is more likely that the John Smith present for this ad hoc conference was John Speed Smith, not Raccoon John.

82. For more information on the details and the outcome of the Campbell-Rice debate, see Richardson, 2:500–529, and Garrett, 236–39. Someone put out the story that Henry Clay asked for Campbell to immerse him at the completion of the debate, but this is unconfirmed, perhaps being kin to one of the Baptists' favorite apocryphal tales: that John Gano, acting as a military chaplain, had immersed George Washington.

83. John Augustus Williams, 551; Donaldson, *The Legacy of Raccoon John Smith,* 40.

84. As we've noted, Cochran's biography ends essentially with the 1832 union, although he does conclude his novel with a sort of happily-ever-after epilogue. Though Williams touches upon the 1836 congressional election in a tangential way, he never names any of the principals in the fight, nor says one thing about James McVay in any way whatsoever. It is to his credit, though, that he gives a brief account of Richard's death, but given the fact that he had omitted so much data about Raccoon John's North District experiences, especially regarding his tenure as moderator, we might wonder whether he would have included the tragedy in the story if Raccoon John's daughters had not insisted upon it as a memorial to their brother. Donaldson does mention John Mason, but we find out about Kenaz Farrow's involvement only by the writings of his son-in-law, Belvard January Peters, that Donaldson quotes. Neither does he mention James McVay except once as merely having made accusations against Smith, and this though he quotes extensively from at least one of the issues of the *Harbinger* that had a great deal of detail about the progression of the Smith-McVay fight. See Donaldson, *Frontiersman and Reformer,* 149–50, 185, chapter 16 n 10; Donaldson, *The Legacy of Raccoon John Smith,* 11–12, 294, chapter 2 n 2.

85. Campbell, "Extra," 1.

86. Selina Bakewell Campbell, "Biographical Sketch on the Life of Young Wickliffe Campbell," appeared originally in *The Life of A. Campbell, by his Wife,* n.d.; quoted by Scott Harp, http://www.therestorationmovement.com/campbell,_wickliffe.htm. See also Richardson, 2:572–74.

87. Hughes, *Reviving the Ancient Faith,* 44.

88. Letters to the author from Jeanne Cobb, archivist of Bethany College, Bethany, W.Va., December 1–3, 2003; Charles Heaberlin, archivist at Lexington Theological Seminary, Lexington, Kentucky, December 16, 2003; and B. J. Gooch, director of Special Collections, Transylvania University Library, Lexington, Kentucky, January 7, 2004.

89. A report of William P. Clark's evangelism for the Disciples along the Cumberland River in Green, Adair, Russell, and Cumberland counties in Kentucky can be found in "News of the Churches," *The Millennial Harbinger* 13, no. 3 (March 1843): 142.

90. Letter of John Smith to Isaac T. Reneau, July 5, 1852, Raccoon John Smith Historical Papers, LTS. See also Donaldson, *The Legacy of Raccoon John Smith,* 31–32, and John Augustus Williams, 552–54.

91. John Augustus Williams, 554.

92. Ibid., 555; Smith to Reneau, July 5, 1852, LTS.

93. John Augustus Williams, 555–56.

94. Hughes, *Reviving the Ancient Faith,* 77–79.

95. Donaldson, *The Legacy of Raccoon John Smith,* 30–31, quoting Judge B. J. Peters, son-in-law of Kenaz Farrow.

96. John Augustus Williams, 554; Donaldson, *The Legacy of Raccoon John Smith,* 32–33.

Chapter 10: A Concluding Unscientific Postscript

1. Donaldson, *The Legacy of Raccoon John Smith,* 47–48.
2. Scott County, Kentucky, Marriage Records, 1837–1861.
3. Donaldson, *The Legacy of Raccoon John Smith,* 42–44.
4. Scott County, Kentucky, Marriage Records, 1837–1861.
5. John Augustus Williams, 560.

6. U.S. Federal Census, Bath County, Kentucky, 1850.

7. Audrain County, Missouri, Marriage Records, 1836–1879, http://www. ancestry.com.

8. Donaldson, *The Legacy of Raccoon John Smith,* 42–43.

9. Page, "Freeborn Family (Ringo Genealogy)," http://awt.ancestry.com/cgi-bin/igm.cgi?op=GET&db=:1733420&id=I422.

10. Data taken from the depositions of Albertis R. Ringo, Alfred Fassett, William Rouzer(?), and James M. Stevens in the case of *Harvey Smith v. Mary E.* [*sic*] *Smith,* Court of Common Pleas, Philadelphia, Pennsylvania, December term 1859, Raccoon John Smith Historical Papers.

11. Ibid. In spite of the likely bad blood between the Smiths and Stedmans at the time of the divorce, this granddaughter, Emma V. Smith, who seems to have lived and died unmarried, inherited and managed the Smith family plot in the Lexington cemetery until her death at age sixty-eight on April 14, 1922. Poignantly, both she and the Mary Smith buried near Harvey and Jonathan and who very well may have been Emma's mother, lie in completely unmarked graves. So does Jonathan Smith and the unknown Frank and Lee Clark, if in fact the Clarks were ever buried in the plot at all.

12. Letter of John Smith to Zerelda and Isaac Denton Smith, October 26, 1858, quoted in Donaldson, *The Legacy of Raccoon John Smith,* 41–42. In this letter, too, Raccoon John asked Zerelda to give his love to "my old brother and sister Philip and Milly, and tell them that if my health should continue good, that I may at some time pay them another visit before we die."

13. Ibid.

14. Letter of T. M. Allen to *The Millennial Harbinger,* December 27, 1858, Raccoon John Smith Historical Papers.

15. Lexington Cemetery Burial Records, Lexington, Kentucky, http://www.lexcem.org; see also Donaldson, *The Legacy of Raccoon John Smith,* 42. Donaldson claims that Harvey was twenty-eight at his death, but the data on Harvey Smith's tombstone itself appears to be more correct.

16. Lexington Cemetery Burial Records, Lexington, Kentucky, http://www.lexcem.org; see also Donaldson, *The Legacy of Raccoon John Smith,* 42.

17. Donaldson, *The Legacy of Raccoon John Smith,* 45–46; John Augustus Williams, 557.

18. Interview with Mrs. Mollie Lee Nesbitt by E. C. Raines, November 10, 1932, Raccoon John Smith Historical Papers.

19. John Augustus Williams, 559–60.

20. Henry Leo Boles, *Biographical Sketches of Gospel Preachers,* 342–46.

21. Nesbitt interview by Raines, Raccoon John Smith Historical Papers; Donaldson, *The Legacy of Raccoon John Smith,* 47–48.

22. Donaldson, *The Legacy of Raccoon John Smith,* 49, quoting Wright.

23. See Garrett, 192; and Donaldson, *The Legacy of Raccoon John Smith,* 293.

24. John Augustus Williams, 565.

25. In addition to utilizing the late Dr. Richard Marius's two biographies of Martin Luther, I must acknowledge the input of his wife, Dr. Lanier Smythe of Suffolk University, in Boston, Massachusetts, and his former academic colleague, Dr. George Schweitzer of the University of Tennessee at Knoxville, in framing this brief of his thought. In a supreme irony, Marius, who of all Luther scholars probably gave the most careful, honest, and complete exposition of Martin Luther's anti-Semitism, a few years before his death was himself branded as an anti-Semite for political reasons. His fellow Tennessean, Vice President Al Gore, had on occasion employed Marius, who was a professor at Harvard, as a speechwriter; however, in a book review that Marius had written for the Harvard alumni magazine he had made a couple of critical comments on some heavy-handed tactics that the Israeli secret police had been alleged to use, and in the eyes of the editor of the *New Republic* magazine and fellow Gore speechwriter Martin Peretz, this made Marius an anti-Semite. Peretz denounced Marius to Gore and, evidently because of the political damage that the vice president feared Peretz could give him, Gore dropped Marius

like a hot potato without even giving the charge a detailed examination. Sadly, Marius's obituary in the *New York Times* gave more attention to this unsubstantiated allegation than it did to all of his excellent scholarly work. Even Gore's own staff members admitted that Marius had deserved better, and that he had been fired to keep the *New Republic* editor happy. See Wall, "Political Maneuvers," http://www.findarticles.com/cf_dls/m1058/23_117/65014564/p1/article.jhtml.

26. Berger, *Questions of Faith*; Borg and Wright, *The Meaning of Jesus.*

27. Richardson, 2:674.

28. The Scripture in question can be found in Genesis 9:20–27, King James Version. I was first introduced to this theological argument not by my parents or grandparents, but in my fifth year of elementary school by a Christian teacher with a Master's degree from a state-accredited university.

29. Payne (pseud. Ariel), 45–48.

30. Young, 5–14, 38–48.

31. Hughes, *Reviving the Ancient Faith,* 273.

32. Caudill, 41.

33. A tape of Elder Bailey delivering one such sermon, given to me by his daughters after his death, is one of my prized possessions.

34. Cochran and Cochran, 158–60.

35. Payne (pseud. Ariel), 48.

36. Young, 25–26.

37. Payne (pseud. Ariel), 48.

38. John Augustus Williams, 560–64.

39. Ibid., 567–69.

40. Ibid., 570–73.

41. Ibid., 572.

42. James Hurt's presence at this time was noted by the local newspaper, *The Ledger,* as well as the Disciple journal *The Christian Pioneer.* See the Raccoon John Smith Historical Papers.

43. Letter of W. J. Mason to David Wright, February 25, 1868, quoted in Donaldson, *The Legacy of Raccoon John Smith,* 50.

44. John Augustus Williams, 573, notes that the time of John's death was 8:30 P.M.; however, the account of his last hours in *The Christian Pioneer,* in the Raccoon John Smith Historical Papers, states that his death occurred two hours later.

45. John Augustus Williams, 573–74; additional notes on Raccoon John's burial arrangements taken from *The Pioneer,* Raccoon John Smith Historical Papers.

46. The text of the engraving is hard to read, and its date of death may say February 29. The February 28 date of death was taken from the Williams text and the *Christian Pioneer* notice (LTS papers). The *Pioneer* article at least was published before the monument was engraved.

47. For further information on some of these rural southeastern denominations and sects, see McCauley's *Appalachian Mountain Religion: A History,* and Sparks, chapter 8.

Bibliography

Allen, Albert. "Reminiscences of Eld. John Smith, of Kentucky." *The Millennial Harbinger* (May 1857): 276–82. DCHS Collection.

Asplund, John. *Universal Register of the Baptist Denomination in America, 1790–1794.* 1794. Reprint, New York: Arno Press, 1980. ABHS Collection.

Audrain County, Missouri Marriage Records, 1836–1879. http://www.ancestry.com (accessed November 2003).

Baptists in Kentucky, 1776–1976: A Bicentennial Volume. Edited by Leo Taylor Crismon. Middletown, Ky.: Kentucky Baptist Convention, 1975.

Bath County, Kentucky Marriage Book 2. Bath County Court Clerk's Office, Owingsville, Ky.

Beasley, Paul W. "Isaac Shelby." In *Kentucky's Governors, 1792–1985,* edited by Lowell H. Harrison. Lexington: Univ. Press of Kentucky, 1985.

Benedict, David. *A General History of the Baptist Denomination in America and Other Parts of the World.* New York: Lewis Colby, 1848.

Berger, Peter. *Questions of Faith: A Skeptical Affirmation of Christianity.* Malden, Mass.: Blackwell, 2004.

The Birmingham Amended Statement of Faith (Christadelphian). http://www.bereanecclesialnews.com/doctrines/basf.html (accessed September–October 2003).

Boles, Henry Leo. *Biographical Sketches of Gospel Preachers.* Nashville, Tenn.: Gospel Advocate, 1922.

Boles, John B. *The Great Revival: Beginnings of the Bible Belt.* Lexington: Univ. Press of Kentucky, 1972.

———. *The Irony of Southern Religion.* New York: Peter Lang, 1994.

Borg, Marcus J., and N. T. Wright. *The Meaning of Jesus: Two Visions.* San Francisco: HarperCollins, 1999.

Bork, June Baldwin. "Elder 'Racoon' [*sic*] John Smith, 1784–1868," http://junebaldwinbork.com/smith/raccoon1.htm (accessed May 2001); http://junebaldwinbork.com/smith/raccoon2.htm (accessed May 2001).

Bossong, Kathy C. *Kathy's World Family Tree.* http://awt.ancestry.com/cgi-bin/igm.cgi?op=GET&db=; 1663784&id=I75871580 (accessed July–August 2001).

Boyd, Carl, and Hazel Boyd. *A History of Mt. Sterling, Kentucky, 1792–1918.* Mt. Sterling, Ky.: self published, 1984.

Brown, Karen. "Brown Family History." http://awt.ancestry.com/cgi-bin/igm.cgi?op=GET&db=:2022050&id=I930 (accessed July–August 2001).

Burnett, J. J. *Sketches of Tennessee's Pioneer Baptist Preachers.* 1919. Reprint, Johnson City, Tenn.: Overmountain Press, 1985.

The Calendar of the George Rogers Clark Papers. Series J, 37:105–10. Utica, Ky.: McDowell Publications, 1985.

Calvin, John. *Institutes of the Christian Religion.* 1559. Reprint, Grand Rapids, Mich.: Eerdmans, 1989.

Campbell, Alexander. "An Address to the Readers of *The Christian Baptist,* IV." *The Christian Baptist* 1, no. 8 (March 1824):4–9. DCHS.

———. "Elder John Smith and James McVay." *The Millennial Harbinger* (May 1843): 234–35. DCHS.

———. "Extra." *The Millennial Harbinger* (April 1847): unnumbered attached sheet. DCHS.

———. "News from the Churches." *The Millennial Harbinger* (July–September 1843): 240–84. DCHS.

———. "Notes on a Late Tour, No. II." *The Millennial Harbinger* (November 1842): 506–7. DCHS.

Campbell, Selina Bakewell. "Biographical Sketch on the Life of Young Wickliffe Campbell." Appeared originally in *The Life of A. Campbell, by his Wife,* n.d.; quoted by Scott Harp, http://www.therestorationmovement.com/campbell,_wickliffe.htm (accessed November 2003).

Cartwright, Peter. *Autobiography.* 1856. Reprint, Freeport, N.Y.: Books for Libraries Press, 1972.

Caudill, Harry M. *Night Comes to the Cumberlands.* Boston: Little, Brown, 1963.

Challen, James. "Biographical Sketch of Raccoon John Smith." Originally in *Challen's Monthly* (March 1858): 109–11. http://www.mun.ca/rels/restmov/texts/jchallen/lcab/smithrj3.htm (accessed March–August 2001).

Chenault, John Cabell. *Old Cane Springs.* Edited by Jonathan Truman Dickerson. Louisville, Ky.: Standard Printing, 1936.

The Christian Messenger, vols. 8–11 (1835–1841). DCHS.

Cobb, Jeanne, Dr., archivist at Bethany College, Bethany, W.Va. Letters to the author, dated December 1–3, 2003.

Cochran, Louis. *The Fool of God: A Novel Based upon the Life of Alexander Campbell.* New York, Duell, Sloan and Pearce, 1958.

———. *Raccoon John Smith: A Novel Based on the Life of the Famous Pioneer Kentucky Preacher.* New York: Duell, Sloane and Pearce, 1963; reprint, New York, Popular Library, n.d.; reprint, Joplin, Mo.: College Press, 1985.

Cochran, Louis, and Bess White Cochran. *Captives of the Word.* Garden City, N.Y.: Doubleday, 1969.

Connelley, William E. *The Founding of Harman's Station.* New York: Torch Press, 1910.

Cottret, Bernard. *Calvin: A Biography.* Trans. by M. Wallace McDonald. French ed., Paris: J. C. Lattès, 1995; English ed., Grand Rapids, Mich.: Eerdmans, 2000.

Cox, Harvey. "Out in Front: The Radical Witness of Bill Coffin." *The Christian Century,* 121, no. 13 (June 29, 2004): 23–24.

Cox, Sharon, and Hazel B. Craft. *The Memory Hill Foundation Website.* http://freepages.history.rootsweb.com/~memoryhill/index.html (accessed March–April 2002).

Descendants of Rev. Robert Elkin, 1745–1822. Winchester, Ky.: privately printed, n.d. Clark County Public Library, Winchester, Ky.

Donaldson, Everett. *The Legacy of Raccoon John Smith.* Mt. Sterling, Ky.: North Ridge Publishing, 1995.

———. *Raccoon John Smith: Frontiersman and Reformer.* Lexington: Wind Publications, 1993.

Dorgan, Howard. *In the Hands of a Happy God: The "No-Hellers" of Central Appalachia.* Knoxville: Univ. of Tennessee Press, 1997.

———. *The Old Regular Baptists of Central Appalachia: Brothers and Sisters in Hope.* Knoxville: Univ. of Tennessee Press, 1989.

Drake, Richard B. *A History of Appalachia.* Lexington: Univ. Press of Kentucky, 2001.

Early and Modern History of Wolfe County, Kentucky. Compiled by Mrs. Roy B. Cecil. Campton, Ky.: privately published, n.d.

Feeling, Durbin D. Letter to the author, October 21, 2003.

First "Census" of Kentucky, 1790. Comp. by Charles B. Heinemann. Baltimore: Genealogical Publishing, 1971.

Fletcher, Jesse. "The Separation of the Campbells from the Baptists." *Discipliana* 63, no. 3 (fall 2003): 144–48.

Fortune, Alonzo Willard. *The Disciples in Kentucky.* Lexington, Ky.: Convention of the Christian Churches in Kentucky, 1932.

Foster, Robert. "Alexander Campbell's 'Sermon on the Law' in its Historical Context." *Discipliana* 63, no. 4 (winter 2004): 35–45.

Foxfire 7. Edited by Paul F. Gillespie. Garden City, N.Y.: Anchor Books, 1982.

Fridley, David. *The Rev. John Alderson, Sr.* http://www.fridley.net/alderson/johnaldersonbio.htm (accessed February 2001).

Fuller, Robert. *Naming the Antichrist: The History of an American Obsession.* New York: Oxford Univ. Press, 1995.

Galloway, Vicki. *Isham Burnett Family Genealogy.* http://awt.ancestry.com/cgi-bin/igm.cgi?op=GET&db=;1953065&id=I27941 (accessed March–April 2003).

Garrett, Leroy. *The Stone-Campbell Movement.* Joplin, Mo.: College Press, 1983. Reprint, 1995.

Gates, Errett. *The Disciples of Christ.* New York: Baker and Taylor, 1905.

Gates, John A. *The Life and Thought of Kierkegaard for Everyman.* Philadelphia: Westminster, 1960.

Grady, Jamie Ault. *Bowens of Virginia and Tennessee: Descendants of John Bowen and Lily McIlhaney.* 2 vols. Knoxville, Tenn.: self-published, 1969.

Hall, Chastity. "My Family Tree." http://awt.ancestry.com/cgi-bin/igm.cgi?op=GET&db=:2909700&id=I9614 (accessed September–October 2001).

Hatfield, Coleman, and Robert Spence. *The Tale of the Devil.* Chapmanville, W.Va.: Woodland Press, 2003.

Heaberlin, Charles, archivist at Lexington Theological Seminary, Lexington, Ky. Letter to the author, December 16, 2003.

Hill, Sam E. *Report of the Adjutant General of the State of Kentucky: Soldiers of the War of 1812.* Frankfort, Ky.: E. Polk Johnson, 1891. Reprint, Greenville, S.C.: Southern Historical Press, 1991.

Hines, Michael. *Restoration History Pages.* "Two Major Movements Unite." http://www.christianchronicler.com/History2/movement_unites.html (accessed September 2003).

Hofstadter, Richard. *The American Political Tradition and the Men Who Made It.* New York: Knopf, 1948. Reprint, New York: Vintage Books, 1973.

Hon, Peter. Letter to Alexander Campbell, March 18, 1843, with Campbell's reply. In *The Millennial Harbinger* 13, no. 5 (May 1843): 234. DCHS.

Hughes, Richard T. *Myths America Lives By.* Urbana, Ill.: Univ. of Illinois Press, 2003.

———. *Reviving the Ancient Faith: The Story of Churches of Christ in America.* Grand Rapids, Mich.: Eerdmans, 1996.

Isenberg, James L. "The Marriage of President Lincoln's Parents and the Historic Richard Berry Cabin." In *The Lincoln Marriage Temple* (by various authors). Harrodsburg, Ky.: D. M. Hutton, 1931.

Jilson Payne Family Historical Papers. MS-MCL Collection.

Johnson, Arthur C. *Early Morgan County.* Ashland, Ky.: self-published, 1974.

Johnson, Charles A. *The Frontier Camp Meeting: Religion's Harvest Time.* 1955. Reprint, Dallas: Southern Methodist Univ. Press, 1985.

Jones, Loyal. "Christmas and Old Christmas in Appalachia." In *A Kentucky Christmas,* edited by George Ella Lyon. Lexington: Univ. Press of Kentucky, 2003.

Jones, Treva. "Genealogy Webpage." http://awt.ancestry.com/cgi-bin/igm.cgi?op=GET&db=:2613303&id=I2444 (accessed April 2002).

The Kentucky Encyclopedia. Edited by John E. Kleber, Thomas D. Clark, Lowell H. Harrison, and James C. Klotter. Lexington: Univ. Press of Kentucky, 1992.

Kierkegaard, Søren. *Anthology.* Edited by Robert Bretall. New York: Modern Library, 1946.

———. *The "Attack" Upon Christendom.* Translated by Walter Lowrie. Princeton, N.J.: Princeton Univ. Press, 1944.

———. *Johannes Climacus, Or, A Life of Doubt.* Translated by T. H. Croxhall. 1856. Reprint, London: Serpent's Tail, 2001.

———. *Journals, 1834–1854.* Translated by Alexander Dru. London: Collins, 1958.

———. *The Present Age* and *The Difference Between a Genius and an Apostle.* Translated by Alexander Dru. New York: Harper and Row, 1962.

Kirksey, Edith Cloud. Membership application made on the basis of descent through George Smith via John Smith and Jane (Smith) Boles, DAR.

Klein, Jeff Z. "From 1814, Tales Keep a'Comin." *New York Times,* September 12, 2004, http://www.nytimes.com/2004/09/11/arts/television/11hist.html (accessed September 2004).

Last Will and Testament of David Barrow. Montgomery County, Kentucky, Will Book B.

Last Will and Testament of Moses Bledsoe. Montgomery County, Kentucky, Will Book A.

Last Will and Testament of Jilson Payne. Montgomery County, Kentucky, Will Book B. KHS Collection.

Lawyers and Lawmakers of Kentucky. Edited by H. Levin. Chicago: Lewis Publishing Company, 1897.

Lexington Cemetery Burial Records. Lexington, Ky. http://www.lexcem.org (accessed October 2004).

The Lincoln Marriage Temple (by various authors). Harrodsburg, Ky.: D. M. Hutton, 1931.

Lindman, Janet Moore. "Acting the Manly Christian: White Evangelical Masculinity in Revolutionary Virginia." *William and Mary Quarterly,* 3rd ser., vol. 57, no. 2 (April 2000): 416 n 46.

Low Gap United Baptist Church Record Book, 1814–1860. In the possession of Elder Cecil C. Murray Jr. of Lexington, Ky.

MacFarquhar, Larissa. "The Devil's Accountant." *New Yorker,* March 31, 2003, 64–79.

Madison, Anthony, Truman A. Roundtree, and Ruble B. Cowles. *Green River Association of United Baptist.* Elizabethtown, Ky.: privately published, 1976.

Marius, Richard. *Luther: A Biography.* New York: Lippincott, 1974.

———. *Martin Luther: The Christian Between God and Death.* Cambridge, Mass.: Harvard Univ. Press, 1998.

———. *Thomas More: A Biography.* New York: Knopf, 1984.

Mason, James. Letter to Alexander Campbell, May 15, 1830, with Campbell's reply. In *The Millennial Harbinger* 1, no. 6 (June 1830): 274–77. DCHS.

Mason, Terry. "Family History." http://www.tmason1.com/pafg11.htm#148 (accessed February 2003).

Mason County, Kentucky Marriage Records, 1820–1833 and 1834–1844. Comp. by Elizabeth Patton Ellsworth. Maysville, Ky.: privately published. BCML.

McCauley, Deborah Vansau. *Appalachian Mountain Religion: A History.* Urbana, Ill.: Univ. of Illinois Press, 1995.

McDonald, Jeanne, "Having the Last Word." *Metro Pulse* 11, no. 48 (November 29, 2001) http://www.metropulse.com/dir_zine/dir_2001/1148/t_cover.html (accessed October 2003).

Michaud, Ryan C. "Ancestors (Bowen family genealogy)." http://family

treemaker.genealogy.com/users/m/i/c/Colin W Michaud/GENE6 0038.html# CHILD459012 (accessed March 2001).
Minutes of the Burning Springs Association of Baptists, 1813–1824, and of the New Salem Association of Old Regular Baptists, 1825–1983. Compiled by Dexter Dixon and Walter Akers. 2 vols. Pikeville, Ky.: self-published, 1983.
Minutes of the Burning Springs Association (Ky.), 1834, 1836. ABHS.
Minutes of the Burning Springs Association, 1837, from the collection of the late Elder B. C. Ferguson, Paintsville, Ky.
Minutes of the Cumberland River Association (Ky.), 1815, 1819. SBTS.
Minutes of the Elkhorn Association (Ky.), 1785–1810. Microfilm, SBTS.
Minutes of the Goshen Conference. June 1830. SBTS Collection.
Minutes of the Green River Association (Ky.), 2001, courtesy of Mark Hogan, Lindseyville, Ky.; 2003, courtesy of Garry Watkins, Leitchfield, Ky.
Minutes of the Holston Association (Va.-Tenn.), 1786–1807. Microfilm, ABHS.
Minutes of the Licking Association (Ky.). 1812 and 1817. SBTS Collection.
Minutes of the Lulbegrud Conference. April 1830 SBTS Collection.
Minutes of the North District Association (Ky.), 1802–1952. Microfilm, SBTS Collection.
Minutes of the North District Association (Ky.), 1831. ABHS.
Minutes of the North District Association (Ky.), 1831. PBL.
Minutes of the Ohio Association (Oh.-Ky.), 1825–1826. ABHS.
Minutes of the Redstone Association (Pa.), 1776–1810. Microfilm, ABHS.
Minutes of the South Kentucky Association (Separate Baptist, Ky.), 1801. Microfilm, SBTS.
Minutes of the Stockton's Valley Association (Ky.-Tenn.), 2001, courtesy Mark Hogan, Lindseyville, Ky.
Montgomery County, Kentucky Marriage Records, 1796–1860. MS-MCL.
Moore, Charles Chilton. *Behind the Bars: 31498.* Lexington, Ky.: privately printed, 1899. Reprint, Austin, Texas: American Atheist Press, 1983.
———. *The Rational View.* Louisville: Courier-Journal Job Office, 1890. LTS.
Morgan, David T. *The New Crusades, the New Holy Land: Conflict in the Southern Baptist Convention, 1969–1991.* Tuscaloosa: Univ. of Alabama Press, 1996.
"Mrs. Strader Recalls Life in Small Town at Turn of Century." *The Bath County Outlook,* Owingsville, Ky., 92, no. 45 (July 30, 1970). BCML.
Musgrave, Jon. "Frontier Serial Killers: The Harpes." http://www.illinoishistory.com/harpes.html (accessed May 2001).
Musselman, Homer. "Chopawamsick Baptist Church Records." http://www.rootsweb.com/~vastaffo/cemeteries/chopawamsicbapchurch.htm (accessed May 2002).
Myers, Christie. Genealogical Rootsweb Research Homesite. http://awt.ancestry.com/cgi-bin/igm.cgi?op=GET&db=leachmandr&id=I4195 (accessed April 2001).
Nickell, W. Lynn. "First Christian Church, West Liberty, Kentucky." In *Selec-*

tions from Morgan County History. Compiled by Helen Price Stacy and W. Lynn Nickell. West Liberty, Ky.: self-published, 1973.

Norton, Michele. *Descendants of Johann Schmidt.* http://familytreemaker.genealogy.com/users/n/o/r/Michele-L-Norton/GENE4-0001.html?Welcome=1008757538 (accessed March–April 2001).

Oberman, Heiko A. "Review—Martin Luther: The Christian between God and Death." *Historian* (summer 2000). http://www.findarticles.com/p/articles/mi_m2082/is_4_62/ai_64910309 (accessed February 2004).

———. "Varieties of Protest." *New Republic* 221, no. 7, August 16, 1999, http://www.highbeam.com/library/doc0.asp?DOCID=1G1%3A55361886&refid=ip_almanac_hf (accessed February 2004).

Offutt, Chris. *No Heroes: A Memoir of Coming Home.* New York: Simon and Schuster, 2002.

Page, Danielle. *Freeborn Family (Ringo Genealogy).* http://awt.ancestry.com/cgi-bin/igm.cgi?op=GET&db=:1733420&id=I422 (accessed September 2003).

Payne, Buckner Harrison (pseud. Ariel). *The Negro: What Is His Ethnological Status?* Cincinnati: self-published, 1867. DCHS Collection.

Payne, Charles Daniel. "The Paynes of Virginia." http://www.icon.net/~sdcaller/ (accessed May–August 2002).

The Philadelphia Confession of Faith, with Catechism. 1742. Reprint, Sterling, Va.: Grace Abounding Ministries, n.d.

Raccoon John Smith Historical Papers, LTS Collection, Lexington, Ky.

Rash, John, William J. Mason, et al. "Trial of James McVay." *The Millennial Harbinger* 12, no. 6 (June 1842): 282–83. DCHS.

Records of the South Fork (first known as Poplar Meeting-House) Church, West Liberty, Ky., 1808–1838. Courtesy of the late Raymond Benton, West Liberty, Ky.

Remini, Robert V. *Andrew Jackson.* New York: Twayne, 1966. Reprint, New York: Harper and Row, 1969.

Rennick, Robert M. *Kentucky Place Names.* Lexington: Univ. Press of Kentucky, 1984.

Revolutionary Service and Pension Records of George Smith, John Townsend, Electious Thompson, Simeon Justice, and Daniel Williams. DAR Collection.

Rice, Luther. Journal, August–October 1815. Unpublished. Courtesy of Gelman Library, George Washington University, Washington, D.C.

Richardson, Robert. *Memoirs of Alexander Campbell.* 2 vols. Philadelphia: Lippincott, 1870.

Rosenberg, Ellen M. *The Southern Baptists: A Subculture in Transition.* Knoxville: Univ. of Tennessee Press, 1989.

Sanders, Harold G. "The Kentucky Baptist Heritage." In *Baptists in Kentucky, 1776–1976: A Bicentennial Volume,* ed. Leo Taylor Crismon. Middletown, Ky.: Kentucky Baptist Convention, 1975.

Scalf, Henry P. *Kentucky's Last Frontier.* Pikeville, Ky.: Pikeville College Press, 1972.

Scott County, Kentucky Marriage Records, 1837–1861. Microfilm. SCPL.

Selections from Morgan County History. Compiled by Helen Price Stacy and W. Lynn Nickell. West Liberty, Ky.: self-published, 1973.

Sifakis, Carl. *American Eccentrics.* New York: Facts on File, 1984.

Smith, B. K. Letter to Alexander Campbell, June 16, 1841. In *The Millennial Harbinger* 12, no. 8 (January 1842): 38–39. DCHS.

Smith, John "Raccoon." Letter to Alexander Campbell, September 15, 1841. In *The Millennial Harbinger* 11, no. 11 (November 1841): 536. DCHS.

Smythe, Lanier. Letters to the author, January 2003, January 2004.

Sparks, John. *The Roots of Appalachian Christianity: The Life and Legacy of Elder Shubal Stearns.* Lexington: Univ. Press of Kentucky, 2001.

Spencer, John Henderson. *A History of Baptists in Kentucky, 1769–1885.* 2 vols. Cincinnati: self-published, 1886.

Stacy, Helen Price. "Daniel Williams: A Walk Through History." In *Selections from Morgan County History.* Compiled by Helen Price Stacy and W. Lynn Nickell. West Liberty, Ky.: self-published, 1973.

———. "History of Old Grassy Christian Church." In *Selections from Morgan County History.* Compiled by Helen Price Stacy and W. Lynn Nickell. West Liberty, Ky.: self-published, 1973.

Stanford, Robert. *John Townsend Family Genealogy.* http://awt.ancestry.com./cgi-bin/igm.cgi?op=GET&db=;1753730&id=I81268875 (accessed March 2002).

Starkey, Marion L. *The Devil in Massachusetts.* New York: Knopf, 1949. Reprint, Garden City, N.Y.: Doubleday, 1969.

Stefanik, Ernest. "Author Index to *The Millennial Harbinger,* Vols. I–III." http://www.mun.ca/rels/hrollmann/restmov/texts/acampbell/tmh/MHIDXAU.HTM (accessed October 2003).

Stendahl, Brita K. *Kierkegaard.* Boston: G. K. Hall, 1976.

Stricklin, David. *A Genealogy of Dissent: Southern Baptist Protest in the Twentieth Century.* Lexington: Univ. Press of Kentucky, 2000.

Taul, Dr. Glen. Letters to the author, November 20 and December 3, 2001.

Taulman, James E. "Baptists and Disciples of Christ." In *Baptists in Kentucky, 1776–1976: A Bicentennial Volume,* ed. Leo Taylor Crismon. Middletown, Ky.: Kentucky Baptist Convention, 1975.

Taylor, John. *Baptists on the American Frontier: A History of Ten Baptist Churches of Which the Author Has Been Alternately a Member.* Edited by Chester Raymond Young. Originally published as "A History of Ten Baptist Churches, of which the Author has Been Alternately a Member," Frankfort, Ky., self-published (Taylor), 1828. Reprint, Macon, Ga.: Mercer Univ. Press, 1995.

———. *Thoughts on Missions.* Frankfort, Ky.: self-published, 1820. http://www.geocities.com/baptist_documents/j.taylor.miss.html (accessed November 2002).

Tillich, Paul. *A History of Christian Thought.* New York: Simon and Schuster, 1968.

Toplady, Augustus Montague. "Rebuke to Wesley: A Letter to the Rev. Mr. John Wesley, Relative to His Pretended Abridgement of Zanchius on Predestination." http://www.lamblion.net/Articles/toplady_to_wesley.htm (accessed May 2002).

Trimble, J. Green. "Recollections of Breathitt." Initially published in *The Jackson Times,* Jackson, Ky., 1911. http://www.breathittcounty.com/TrimblesBook.html (accessed June 2003).

Troxell, Dan. "The Wedding Story That Saved the Cherokee People of Wayne County, Kentucky: The Wedding of Rebecca Jane Wood Owl and Joseph Sumpter." http://victorian.fortunecity.com/rothko/420/aniyuntikwalaski/Jane.htm (accessed March 2001).

Tull, James E. *Shapers of Baptist Thought.* King of Prussia, Pa.: Judson Press, 1972.

Unpublished material from members of the Memory Hill Foundation, formerly the Daniel Williams Historical Society, West Liberty, Ky. Courtesy of Wardie and Hazel Craft.

U.S. Federal Census, Bath County, Kentucky, 1850. Compiled by Alice P. Reynolds. Owingsville, Ky.: privately published, n.d. BCML.

U.S. Federal Census, Bath County, Kentucky, 1860. Compiled by Joanne Peluzzo. Owingsville, Ky.: privately published, n.d. BCML.

U.S. Federal Census, East Central Kentucky (Clark, Estill, Fayette, Garrard, Jessamine, Madison, Montgomery, and Owsley counties), 1850. Compiled by Barbara, Byron, and Samuel Sistler. Nashville, Tenn.: Byron Sistler and Associates, 1995.

U.S. Federal Census, Scott County, Kentucky, 1850 and 1860. Microfilms. SCPL.

Vaughan, Thomas M. *Memoirs of Rev. William Vaughan.* Louisville, Ky.: Caperton and Cates, 1878.

Wall, James M. "Political Maneuvers." *Christian Century,* August 16, 2000. http://www.findarticles.com/cf_dls/m1058/23_117/65014564/p1/article.jhtml (accessed December 2003).

Waller, Altina L. *Feud: Hatfields, McCoys, and Social Change in Appalachia 1860–1900.* Chapel Hill: Univ. of North Carolina Press, 1988.

Ward, Billie E. *Back Then.* Baltimore: Gateway Press, 1984.

Wayne County Marriage Records, County Clerk's Office, Monticello, Ky.

Weiner, Herb. *Perpetual Calendar.* http://www.wiskit.com/calendar.html (accessed January 2004).

Wellman, Paul I. *Spawn of Evil.* Garden City, N.Y.: Doubleday, 1964.

Wilkins, Thurman. *Cherokee Tragedy.* Norman, Okla.: Univ. of Oklahoma Press, 1986.

Williams, D. Newell. "The Separation of the Springfield Presbytery from the Synod of Kentucky: Predestination or the Revival?" *Discipliana* 63, no. 3 (fall 2003): 5–8.

Williams, John Augustus. *The Life of Elder John Smith.* Cincinnati: R. W. Carroll and Co., 1870. Reprint, Nashville: Gospel Advocate, 1956.

———. Excerpts of journals. MC-MSL.

Wolever, Terry. *The Life and Ministry of John Gano, 1727–1804.* Springfield, Mo.: Particular Baptist Press, 1998.

Young, Robert A. *The Negro: A Reply to Ariel.* Nashville: J. W. M. Ferrin and Co., 1867. DCHS Collection.

Yrigoen, Charles, Jr. "Start the Presses." *Christian History* 20 (winter 2001): 1, 36–38.

Index